D1567346

Shipwrecks, Sea Raiders,
and Maritime Disasters
along the Delmarva Coast,
1632–2004

# Shipwrecks, Sea Raiders, and Maritime Disasters along the Delmarva Coast, 1632–2004

## Donald G. Shomette

THE JOHNS HOPKINS UNIVERSITY PRESS | BALTIMORE

© 2007 The Johns Hopkins University Press
All rights reserved. Published 2007
Printed in the United States of America on acid-free paper

9 8 7 6 5 4 3 2 1

The Johns Hopkins University Press
2715 North Charles Street
Baltimore, Maryland 21218-4363
www.press.jhu.edu

Library of Congress Cataloging-in-Publication Data
Shomette, Donald.
    Shipwrecks, sea raiders, and maritime disasters along the Delmarva
coast, 1632–2004 / Donald G. Shomette.
        p.  cm.
    Includes bibliographical references and index.
    ISBN-13: 978-0-8018-8670-6 (hardcover : alk. paper)
    ISBN-10: 0-8018-8670-8 (hardcover : alk. paper)
    1. Delmarva Peninsula—History.  2. Shipwrecks—Delmarva
Peninsula—History.  3. Pirates—Delmarva Peninsula.  4. Delmarva
Peninsula—Antiquities.  I. Title.
    F187.E2S56 2007
    975.2'1—dc22        2006103121

A catalog record for this book is available from the British Library.

*Title page illustration:* Wallops Island, 1901 (Chesapeake Bay Maritime
Museum, St. Michaels, MD)

*Special discounts are available for bulk purchases of this book.*
*For more information, please contact Special Sales at 410-516-6936*
*or specialsales@press.jhu.edu.*

For Carol

*Happiness is in the taste, and not in the things.*
François la Rochefoucauld

CONTENTS

Many vessel losses on the Atlantic frontier of Delaware, Maryland, and Virginia, known as the Delmarva coast, and in its adjacent shouldering waters, since the first such recorded event in 1632, have played a definitive role in the shaping of both local and national history, maritime lore, and literature. They have influenced national and state laws, the course of the myriad wars of America, and the commerce of nations and empires. Though most losses have ended up as only statistics, the tales of shipwrecks and maritime disasters per se, like those of pirates, buried booty, and sunken treasures, which often overlap them, have long piqued Everyman's interest. They are the stuff of fantasy and adventure, heroism and tragedy, good and evil, greed and charity, but, most of all, of humankind's innate ability to struggle against all odds or perish in the effort. Together they help form much of the fabric that is woven into Delmarva's colorful and unique coastal heritage.

The genesis of this book was in the mid-1970s when I joined the staff of the Library of Congress. Soon after being assigned my tiny office in the subterranean basement of the Thomas Jefferson Building, I began perusing colonial American newspapers on my lunch hours and after hours as part of a personal maritime research project. Though I had no intention of researching or writing about shipwrecks and maritime disasters, great storms, pirates and privateers, Spanish galleons, and the like, I could not long escape them. Like a schoolboy reading Robert Louis Stevenson, I was captivated by the stories in these archival treasures. I began collecting and transcribing every morsel of shipwreck data, every pirate story, every high seas incident I encountered in that vast and wonderful repository and then from many others as well. Thirty years later, I am still at it and have barely scratched the surface.

In setting out to tell a bit of history through the narrow and occasionally subjective anthology of accounts of shipwrecks and maritime-related disasters, I have also tried to present a number of remarkable, and sometime harrowing, events from the perspectives of individuals involved. Conversely, in some cases, I have attempted to present some of the inclusions on a more holistic plane that stresses their regional or global consequences. Some stories tell of individual vessels, such as the USS *Montgomery,* whose tragic loss off Delmarva's shores have come after either an illustrious or an ill-starred career. The account of the disappearance of a small, unidentified Virginia ship of discovery in Delaware Bay in 1632 and the murder of its nameless crew, though marginal in drama, is in many ways as significant historically as the loss of an entire Spanish treasure fleet, including *La Galga,* which is a tale replete with wreckers, pirates, and buried treasure. Others have been included simply because I found the stories moving, inspiring, or touched with irony. Such is the case with the tale of the loss of the Presidential Yacht *Despatch* or the account of the fatal collision between *Washingtonian,* the largest, most modern freighter of her day, and *Elizabeth Palmer,* the last of the great five-masted sailing ships, or the story of the breaking up of *African Queen.*

I have devoted a substantial amount of this work to the maritime aspects of the American Revolution on the Delmarva coast, which claimed an inordinate amount of shipping as victims. The establishment of the British blockade of the Delaware and Chesapeake, blockade-running, privateering, the ugly loyalist waterborne guerrilla warfare that plagued the region, and the world-shaking Battle of the Virginia Capes, which helped guarantee American independence, are narratives that have seldom been addressed from the perspectives of the participants.

Some stories are part and parcel of the famous lore of the Delmarva and simply must be retold, if only to separate fact from the more commonly accepted fiction that adorns most published accounts. Such are the cases with *Faithful Steward, De Braak,* and *Juno,* which are presented without the false patina of mythology that encrusts so many so-called treasure wreck stories. Moreover, as a lover of anecdotal ephemera, I discovered the personal narrative of Congressman Aedamus Burke and the loss of the fast packet *Friendship* too enticing to ignore. No book on shipwrecks would be complete without an address made to the rough-and-tumble industry of wrecking and salvage, both legal and illegal, from the colonial era to the present. Nor could I ignore the Civil War blockaders and privateers that brought the hostilities to the shores of Northampton and Accomack, or the Confederate commerce raider *Florida* that terrorized Delmarva's coastal shipping.

Storms, blizzards, and hurricanes, which have struck the Delmarva with disturbing frequency, often resulted in incredible and dramatic losses. Yet some have also produced substantially positive, if unexpected, benefits. During the horrendous "Blizzard of '88" and the freak combination of hurricane and nor'easter in 1889, literally scores of vessels and lives were lost, particularly at Cape Henlopen. On both occasions uncommon valor exhibited by the men of the U.S. Life Saving Service stirred the admiration of the nation for the only federal service of the day specifically dedicated to saving lives. The tragic impact of both storms would eventually force the federal government to improve one of the largest harbors of refuge on the Eastern Seaboard. In telling the full tale of the terrible hurricane that struck the Delmarva coast in 1933 I have sought to present a weather disaster that, albeit not the most violent in regional history, was certainly among the most destructive and with far-reaching consequences. It is still the model against which all others in the region are measured. Moreover, its opening of a navigable channel into Sinepuxent Bay helped make Ocean City one of the major American summer resort centers on the Middle Atlantic seaboard.

Military losses off the Delmarva were substantial. I could not include them all. That may be for another day. But I could not ignore General Billy Mitchell's famed but controversial sinking of the ex-German navy dreadnought *Ostfriesland* and cruiser *Frankfurt* off the Virginia capes soon after the end of World War I, the first destruction in history of major warships solely by air power. The event would reverberate around the world and influenced forever after the history and conduct of war at sea. Moreover, the later narrative of the German U-boat offensive off the Delmarva in World War II is a microcosm of the opening of the Nazi naval campaign against all of America. At the human level, it is a tale that starkly reveals the skill, cunning, and daring of U-boat skippers and their crews, sometimes against all odds, as well as the incredible bravery of U-boat victims and their will to survive that helped steel America's resolve to obtain the final victory.

In the closing chapters I have tried to address some of the legal, ethical, and cultural problems resulting from the enormous extant shipwreck population on the Delmarva coast. Ship salvage, the advent and effects of the sport diving industry, the conflict between historic preservationists and treasure hunters, and the consequences of each on national and international law have all centered on this incredible coast. They have directly influenced the modern course of historic preservation at the local, national, and international levels.

In writing this book, I have attempted to dip my oars in the waters of time without turning the boat over. I sincerely hope the reader finds the voyage worth the charter.

# From Cape Henlopen to Cape Charles

From Cape Henlopen the coast trends southward for 21 miles to Fenwick Island Lighthouse and then trends south-southwestward for 96 miles to Cape Charles. The coast southward of Cape Henlopen is a chain of low sand beaches, backed by woods, and presents few characteristic features from offshore. There are few towns along the outer beach, and the most prominent marks are the lighthouses and Coast Guard stations, except at the northern end where there are also a few summer resorts with medium sized hotel buildings. There are a few tall water tanks or standpipes. There are no harbors of refuge for deep draft vessels between Cape Henlopen and Cape Charles. Assateague Anchorage can only be used by shallow draft boats as the entrance has only about 10 feet (3.0 m) controlling depth. The inlets are subject to frequent change and their use requires local knowledge . . . The only towns visible from offshore between Cape Henlopen and Cape Charles are the summer resorts of Rehoboth, Bethany Beach, and Ocean City, 5, 16, and 29 miles, respectively, southward of Cape Henlopen. Rehoboth is distinguished by a standpipe, and a large hotel; Bethany Beach by a small group of houses without prominent marks; and Ocean City by two black water tanks and several other prominent objects.

The coast between Cape Henlopen and Cape Charles is fringed with broken ground, on which lumps with depths up to 6 fathoms (11.0 m) are found for distances of 8 to 11 miles from shore . . . There are lightships, or lighted buoys, off the outer edge of the broken ground and deep-draft vessels keep outside of them.

The bays and connecting channels on the coast of Delaware, Maryland, and Virginia form a continuous inland waterway from Lewes Del., southward to Cape Charles. Except for a small inlet which has been cut through the beach from Indian River Bay to the ocean and which has only about 1 foot (0.3 m) in the entrance at low water.

Ocean City Inlet is the only navigable ocean entrance to the inside waters between Cape Henlopen and Chincoteague Inlet and is about half way along this 61-mile stretch.

This inlet, between stone jetties, is marked by a lighted whistle buoy and range lights. It is subject to frequent change. Southward of Chincoteague Inlet there are several inlets through which the inside waters can be reached. All of the inlets have shifting entrances, in some cases marked by buoys.

The inlets and interior waters give access to the villages and summer resorts on the beaches and the adjacent mainland. They are used by a large number of small craft engaged in the oyster and clam industry and inside and outside fishing, and by some pleasure boats. There is some freight business between points inside, and some coasting trade in seafood, wood, and lumber.

There are fish trap areas along the shores and islands of the inland waterway, and these should be guarded against. —*United States Coast Pilot: Atlantic Coast, Section C: Sandy Hook to Cape Henry including Delaware and Chesapeake Bays,* 4th ed. (1937)

---

The party of twenty men that rowed from the eight-hundred-ton French caravel *Dauphine* were undoubtedly nervous that eventful day in 1524 as they approached a shore on which no white man had ever set foot before. Like the handful of explorers, opportunists, and adventurers who had preceded them to the New World, they had come in search of a western route to the fabled lands of the Orient. There is little record, no hint even, of the conflicting senses of wonder, dread, and expectation that any among them except their leader must have felt as they neared an ageless beach, swept and shaped for millennia by wind and tide. From the extent of their long and dangerous exploration of the North American coastline, there can be no doubt that either they or their captain, Giovanni de Verrazzano, had gained some sense of the geographic magnitude of the lands they were skirting on their historic voyage of discovery for King François I of France. They had sailed for days along this low, pristine coastline in a northeast direction from their last landfall, which they had dubbed Annunciation, two hundred miles to the south. Though most of the shoreline they had witnessed had been low and sandy, somehow this one was different.

Verrazzano later informed the king that he had baptized this newfound shore Arcadia, "on account of the beauty of the trees." Ancient Arcadia, in the Greek Peloponnesus, a land once rich in forests of oak and spruce and filled with wild animals, had in classic times come to symbolize an ideal place of contentment. Now the explorers would set ashore on a coast necklaced by a string of islands, sand spits, and shoals nearly 120 miles long, each existing in splendid isolation and naked, natural beauty. Later trailblazers would discover that the strand was shouldered by two great bays, vast estuary systems with innumerable tributaries, watery highways that reached deep into a mysterious continent already occupied by myriad peoples. The islands and islets, often mounted by great sand dunes and hummocks of pine, were backed by salt marshes filled with fish, birds, and countless other forms of wildlife, beyond which lay untold miles of forests teeming with game. Here and there stood shallow estuaries that would have to await future investigators to gauge their true extents.

Verrazzano and the fifty-man crew of *Dauphine* would not stay on the shores of Arcadia for very long, barely three days, having failed to find their long-sought passageway to the Orient. That they were the first Europeans to set foot on the American coastline between what is today Cape Henlopen, Delaware, and Cape Charles, Virginia, probably somewhere between Accomack and Fenwick Island, is almost certain. Not until the passage of nearly another half century would the Spanish be the first to lay claim to Chesapeake Bay, or Bahia de Santa Maria as they called it, and then begrudgingly relinquish it to the English. Explorers such as Henry Hudson, Peter De Vries, and Cornelis Mey would do likewise for the Dutch on the Delaware. The seeds of colonial empire were thus planted on either shoulder of the wild coast Verrazzano had so briefly explored. Only then were the gateways for the westward march of European civilization opened on both great estuary systems. Ironically, the barrier island shores of Arcadia itself would remain a remote, largely unpeopled, and terribly dangerous no man's land for centuries. It was a region hostile to occupation, where great ships crashed against the shore in terrible storms and marooned men died in isolation. It was, because of its remoteness, a place to which pirates, privateers, wreckers, refugees, and hearty, independent-minded individualists retreated. With its shouldering bays and rivers giving rise to several of the great commercial, maritime, and political entrepôts of America, its waters were heavily contested in

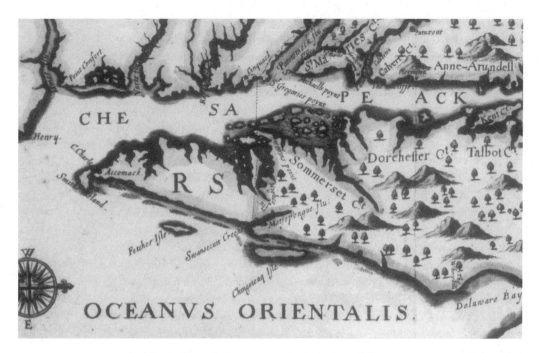

Detail from John Ogilby's 1671 map of Maryland entitled *Nova Terrae-Marie tabula,* copied from a 1635 work by Jerome Hawley and John Lewger, revealing the paucity of information on the geography of the Delmarva coast in the seventeenth century. Note that only three islands—Chingoteag [Chincoteague] Isle, Fetches [Teaches] Isle, and Smiths Island—are indicated. (Library of Congress, Washington, DC)

times of war and welcomed countless unfortunate ships and men to its bosom. It was also a place where professional heroes were made and where lonely watchers helped avert the unwary from pending disaster, where men saved lives instead of taking them. It was, indeed, a unique corner of America where a different kind of history, a forgotten history, was made. Herein I have sought to recount some of that legacy.[1]

The coastline of the Middle Atlantic seaboard between the Delaware and Chesapeake Bays that Verrazzano briefly visited nearly half a millennium ago was not the same that exists today. Though its mainland shores are ancient, its ever-evolving islands are less than five thousand years old, but in many ways they are timeless. One might view the whole as a string of enchanted pearls, sometimes mysteriously connected and at others entirely separated, with each supporting its own mini-ecosystem. They are usually best addressed, however, as a whole that we now call the Delmarva coast, the Atlantic frontier of Delaware, Maryland, and Virginia. These barrier shores make up a veritable archipelago of sand islands that are still, in many areas, largely uninhabited and pristine. Many of the more ecologically fragile areas are currently owned and maintained by federal and state agencies and by private conservation organizations. They form the oceanic perimeter of a vast peninsula that comprises the eastern border of Chesapeake Bay and the southern edge of Delaware Bay. Usually referred to in its entirety as the Eastern Shore, this peninsula includes the easternmost portions of two bifurcated states, Maryland and Virginia, and almost the entirety of Delaware. The eastern side of the peninsula extends from the outlet of the Delaware River into Delaware Bay, along the bay coast to Cape Henlopen, and then southward along the Atlantic frontier for 117 miles to Cape Charles.

The beaches of the Delmarva coast, the most recent exposed boundary of the continental shelf, lie on the very lip of the Atlantic Coastal Plain. It is a dynamic border, this meeting of land and sea, where the waters have been rising as much as six inches or more per century since the last Ice Age and marching ever westward thanks to global warming, glacial melt, crustal subsidence, and other factors.[2]

It is an incredibly vigorous environment where exceptional changes have occurred since the days of early exploration. In many ways it is also the mainland's first line of defense against a perpetually aggressive Atlantic. As such, the sandy terrain of the Delmarva beaches and dunes presents an ever-evolving and changing panorama. The ocean's relentless march westward is most notable when the sea conquers once-distant man-made structures. Some of the most stunning examples are the collapse and inundations of the early lighthouses erected at strategic points along the coast.

As early as 1716, a crude wooden whale-oil lighthouse may have stood on Cape Henlopen. In 1767, however, a more formidable structure constructed of ashlar granite from quarries near Wilmington, Delaware, was erected atop a forty-six-foot sand hill on the cape, 1,552 feet from the shore. At 12:45 P.M., April 13, 1926, it toppled into the sea. Today its remains lie well beyond the surf line. At the entrance to the Chesapeake, on tiny Smith Island at Cape Charles, another lighthouse, a fifty-five-foot tower was raised in 1828 to aid mariners entering and departing the bay. By 1883 encroachment by the sea was claiming thirty feet of the island's shore per year. Today the first Cape Charles Lighthouse, which once stood proud above the highest point of the island, lies beneath the ocean. But if one stares hard enough during an uncommonly low tide, one might just catch a glimpse of the rubble pile that was once the historic light.[3]

And so it is with the whole of the Delmarva coast, oceanfront condominium developments and the U.S. Army Corps of Engineers' vast and expensive beach nourishment programs notwithstanding, with much of its history now resting beneath the waters.

Exposures caused by storm erosion occasionally reveal to even the casual beachcomber natural evidence of the extent of the migration of the Delmarva barrier islands and mainland shores. In 1960, several days of a nor'easter exposed the root structures of a three-hundred-year-old pine forest that had once been inland but could now be seen beginning at the edge of the surf line. Even today, walking along the beaches of Assateague, one encounters ancient roots and turf that were once well inland but now lie exposed at the sea's edge at low tide.[4]

Some sections of the Delmarva coast, most notably Fenwick and Assateague Islands and the archipelagic isles of Accomack and Northampton, Virginia—

Fisherman's, Smith's, Myrtle, Mink, Godwin, Mockhorn, Ship Shoal, Wreck, Little Cobb's, Cobb's, Bone, Hog, Rogue, Revel's, Sandy, Parramore, Cedar, Metompkin, Assawoman, Wallops, and Chincoteague—are in a state of constant flux. Cape Henlopen itself was in 1763 but a gentle protuberant lower lip of Delaware Bay, albeit shouldered by two hidden and enormously dangerous shoals called the Hen and Chickens and the Shears, where scores of ships came to grief. By the late 1880s it had evolved into a very definitive, almost harpoon-shaped, point, and the shoals had migrated and grown, claiming even more victims despite the government construction of a stone Harbor of Refuge.

It is safe to say that varying and conflicting offshore current patterns, littoral drift, accretion, and erosion are constantly in play. Inlets open and close, dunes grow and diminish. Islands move, gradually rotate, enlarge, shrink, disappear, and are eventually reborn in an unending cycle as the shoreline is pushed ever westward. Always the shore is in a state of agitation. And so it is with the offshore bottom where shoals and banks, or "lumps," are constantly in motion, governing the course of navigation and often claiming those who ignore or are ignorant of their ephemeral and deadly characteristics. Offshore shoals such as Fenwick, Isle of Wight, Little Gull and Great Gull, Winter Quarter, Blackfish Bank, and Smith await the unwary at slightly different locales and depths every year. More await the pilotless mariner entering or departing the Chesapeake or Delaware, where ship-killing shoals with such harmless sounding names as Middle Ground, Horseshoe, Overfalls, Brown, and Brandywine still await the unwary. The coastline is liberally littered with submerged, shoally fingers projecting seaward from the shore, especially from the minideltas formed about inlets such as Indian River, Ocean City, Chincoteague, Machipongo, and Ship Shoal. Add fickle weather to the mix of isolation, shoals, and dangerous currents, stir gently with a dash of human frailty, and you have a wicked potion for disaster. These ever-constant variables have molded the course of history on the Delmarva coast. Their most unfortunate byproduct has been, and will continue to be, shipwrecks and maritime disasters on an almost unprecedented scale. It is no small coincidence that such events are so deeply woven into the very fabric of Delmarva coastal culture.

In the early 1970s, where the Maryland-Virginia state line cuts across Assateague Island, there stood a rickety wood-and-wire sand fence running east-west, clearly separating the two jurisdictions. Possibly the only such physical border between two states within the United States, it was a feeble barrier line that belied a contentious history of boundary conflict that has existed since the formation of both Maryland and Virginia. When I first viewed the green slating of the fence, woven together by rusting iron wires, it was largely buried beneath migrating sand dunes, much like the erstwhile divisions between the states themselves. Its actual purpose was anything but contentious. The fence had been erected to separate the famed Virginia wild pony herd, managed by the Chincoteague Volunteer Fire Department, from the Maryland herd, managed by the National Park Service, administrators of Assateague National Seashore. These shaggy, uniquely stunted horses, which walked back and forth across the sand-covered fence line with impunity, seemed to pay little heed to either administration.

On my first visit to this still-isolated and remarkably beautiful stretch of the coast in 1977, less than a four-hour drive from Washington, DC, I viewed the Chincoteague ponies in the wild, at the strategic fence line, for the first time. Like many Americans, as a preteen I had read Marguerite Henry's 1947 children's classic *Misty of Chincoteague* and seen the rather saccharine 1951 movie version. Like many others, I had been intrigued by the captivating legends of the ponies' origins, legends that continue to fascinate thousands of visitors to Chincoteague who come every summer to watch the annual wild pony roundup and penning. Every year since the 1820s, these diminutive and often irascible creatures have been driven down to pens in the town, branded, and some of the foals sold at auction on the last Wednesday and Thursday of July.[5]

The most popular legends emphatically state that the ponies are descended from horses that escaped from a shipwreck in the seventeenth or eighteenth century. One colorful version of the tale relegates the wreck to having been a Spanish galleon. (Perhaps this may be attributed to the fact that the only well-known Spanish vessel loss on the Assateague coast was the great frigate *La Galga*. Wrecked in a terrible mid-August hurricane possibly near old Green Run Inlet, adjacent to the Maryland-Virginia line, the ship was a convoy escort for the 1750 Spanish plate fleet.) A second version has it that the vessel was wrecked on the south end of the island and native Indians rescued the horses. Another suggests the horses were actually put ashore by buccaneers to graze on island grasses, where they could be redeemed at any time. A few skeptics have argued that the little round-bellied ponies were simply descended from domestic animals that had been pastured on the islands by mainland farmers seeking to avoid taxes on them and the cost of erecting fences, and had become stunted by interbreeding, exposure, and a diet of marsh grasses.[6]

There have been many supportive historic references for every argument suggesting what the horses' origins were, and an equal number of rebuttals. Sources indicate that by 1691 free-roaming horses had become so numerous they were destroying crops and were considered a nuisance. The colonial Maryland government was eventually obliged to pass "An Act for the restraining of the unreasonable encrease of Horses in this Province" to rein in the problem. Feral horses were on occasion so abundant on the lower peninsula that they were hunted with dogs.[7] The record is also clear that in the late seventeenth century pirates did stock some of the Virginia islands with game so that they might replenish themselves at some future date, although there has never been a specific mention of horses.

The Spanish wreck story also has some veracity, but not in the case of *La Galga*. Many have tried to specifically link the ponies with that once-great ship, although absolutely no record has ever been found indicating that horses were onboard—and the archival record regarding the loss is substantial. Many other far less famous Spanish vessels, however, were also purportedly lost at various times on the Delmarva coast. One of them was an armed merchantman named *San Lorenzo*. The ship was navigated by Pedro Murphy, a Cuban with Irish roots. As fate would have it, Murphy was destined to become the sole survivor of a tragedy that may well have brought the ponies to Chincoteague.

In 1821 Murphy is reported to have related to a Spanish tribunal his account of *San Lorenzo*'s loss. While en route to Spain, laden with a cargo of gold and silver from the mines of Peru, the ship had run aground on Assateague Island after beginning to break up in a gale. Also aboard were approximately one hundred diminutive draft horses that had been employed for various purposes by the Spanish in the mines of Panama. These animals had been bred to Lilliputian size to allow them to work in the tunnels. Moreover, they had all been blinded to facilitate their handling underground. Owing to native uprisings and instability in the region, the horses were being returned to Spain. Perhaps fortunately for them, given the cruelty of their masters, they would never reach their destination. When *San Lorenzo* was stranded, like many nameless vessels lost without record in these same waters, only Murphy, an unnamed companion, and several of the blinded horses managed to reach shore alive. Though his companion perished soon afterward, the navigator was eventually rescued. He made his way to Philadelphia, and finally to Spain, where he related his tale at an official inquiry. Five years later, an American fishing rights commissioner reported encountering forty-five stunted horses on Assateague. Some of them were blind.[8] The Spanish horses from *San Lorenzo* may well have bred with others already pasturing on the islands, producing the hearty and smaller breed that are now culled and sold at auction every year. Perhaps not surprisingly, the auction has today become the largest tourist draw for the little town of Chincoteague. No record has yet come to light regarding stunted horses on Assateague prior to 1821. Indeed, no mention of these diminutive creatures appears until the annual roundup and penning began about 1825. The famed ponies of Assateague and Chincoteague are, however, just a part of the arcane bounty of shipwrecks on the Delmarva coast.

The Atlantic frontier of Delaware, Maryland, and Virginia, despite its beauty and seductive allure, has until modern times seldom been a destination but always a peril. Its essence is, perhaps, best portrayed by the words of the English poet Algernon Charles Swinburne:

> Here life has death for neighbor,
>   And far from eye or ear
>
> Wan waves and wet winds labour,
>   Weak ships and spirits steer.

As you shall see, the white beaches and green offshore waters of the Delmarva coast, though splendid in their barren magnificence, are littered with the carcasses of many a sturdy ship and perhaps inhabited by the spirits of those unfortunates who took passage in them. The unique history of the coast has been dictated by its isolation, written in its hardships, and read in the ruin of countless lives. Yet it is a component of our history and heritage that is also illustrative of the resilience of Everyman who dared pass by, visit, or settle on these sandy shores, and it needs remembering.

# Indians with English Jackets

Passers-by seldom read the inscription on the monument standing on Pilottown Road in Lewes, Delaware. Dedicated to a man history has largely overlooked, David Pietersz De Vries, founder of the first European settlement in Delaware, the words are plain and simple: "Here was the cradling of a State."

The natives had called this spot, lying within a scimitar-shaped nook of sand hills just inside the mouth of Delaware Bay, Sikoimess or Sikeoyness. The thirty-two men who had set out from the Texel on December 12, 1630, aboard the sloop *De Walvis* to establish a whaling colony on these same shores, however, had another name for it. Arriving in April 1631 under the command of Gillis Hosset, the settlers were stunned and delighted to find the nearby creek filled with beautiful wild swans. They dubbed their new home Zwaanendael, "Valley of the Swans." On a slight elevation just at the mouth of a creek, a place now known as Roosevelt Inlet, they erected a substantial palisaded fort and, from yellow bricks brought with them from the Netherlands, a community dwelling house within. *De Walvis* returned to the Netherlands soon after, leaving the settlers well ensconced in the first Dutch patroonship, destined to one day become part of the State of Delaware.

At Zwaanendael, as elsewhere in New Netherlands, the West India Company delegated the patroonship, the manorial privileges over lands and estates, on Delaware Bay. Partnership had been granted to a party of Dutch adventurers and investors, including David de Vries, Samuel Blommaert, Killian van Rensselaer, and Samuel Godyn, a director of the company. None of these men had sailed on the first *De Walvis* expedition. On May 24 of the following year, however, De Vries, a grizzled forty-eight-year-old veteran mariner, explorer, and world traveler only recently returned from the East Indies, set sail in *De Walvis*, accompanied by a small yacht called *Teencoorntgen,* bound for the Valley of the Swans. His objective was to begin whaling in the great bay it overlooked, then known to the Dutch as the Suydt, or South Bay. Though De Vries was aware that establishing a working settlement amid a howling wilderness, even one blessed with an abundance of beautiful swans, was not for the fainthearted, he could not have envisioned the scene that awaited his arrival.

On that cold December day in 1632 when David Pietersz De Vries first set foot ashore at Zwaanendael, he made a truly horrific discovery. The settlement had been completely destroyed. The bones of its inhabitants and their cattle littered the area in ghastly disarray. From a native informant he learned that an altercation resulting from an Indian theft of a Dutch coat of arms had escalated into an all-out massacre. The first Dutch settlement in Delaware had been annihilated. Though saddened and dismayed, he nevertheless did his best to extract some value from the long voyage from Europe. For several months, he remained in the river simply to feed his men by warily trading for corn, possibly with the same Indians who had wiped out the settlement, while *De Walvis* hunted whales.

Gillis Hosset and his unfortunate band were not, however, the only victims of native hostility. While engaged in negotiations with a band of Lenni Lenape Indians at a tiny Dutch trading station upriver in what is now New Jersey, De Vries observed a number of natives even more hostile than the others, and uniquely attired. "The Indians were from Red Hook," he wrote in his journal, "otherwise called Mantes and had a parcel of English jackets on, which gave me more cause for suspicion, as those were not clothing for them or trading goods."[1]

An old squaw from the nearby Sankikan tribe soon revealed just how the Mantes were able to acquire English jackets: they had seized a vessel filled with Englishmen and killed them. She warned the Dutchman that the Mantes were planning to attack his party the same way. The English boat, described as both a shallop and a sloop, was presumed destroyed as well, becoming the first known European vessel ever lost on the Delmarva coast.[2]

De Vries, who had faced down danger throughout his life, was unmoved, and persisted in his dealing with the natives. Not only did he secure a supply of corn, which was scarce owing to ongoing warfare between several tribes that had devastated croplands, but he was able to acquire a profitable quantity of beaver pelts through trade. Finally, with food again growing scarce, he departed the Delaware and sailed south for the English colony of Virginia in search of provisions.

David Pietersz de Vries, patroon and major investor in the Dutch West Indies Company, was anxious as *De Walvis* entered Chesapeake Bay, sailed up the James River, and made for Jamestown Island, for more than a quarter century seat of a small English colony. Fortunately, after anchoring off the island on March 11, 1633, he was politely received by governor Sir John Harvey. As foreign vessel arrivals were rare, the governor took particular interest in *De Walvis*. After personally greeting De Vries, he inquired where he was from. The Dutchman replied "from the South Bay of New Netherland." The governor asked how far that was from the Chesapeake. "About thirty Dutch miles [leagues]," responded the captain.[3]

The two men walked slowly together toward the governor's house where "a Venice glass of sack" was offered to the visitor. With the mariner and administrator warming up to each other, Harvey proceeded to bring out a chart and revealed to the Dutchman that "the South Bay was called by them My Lord Delaware's Bay." It was strange, the captain must have thought to himself, that there was on the map note of the bay but no indication of the great South River from which he had just sailed. The governor then informed him, incorrectly, that Lord De La Ware, when en route to resupply Jamestown in the summer of

1609, had "encountered foul weather there . . . and finding the place full of shoals thought it was not navigable. They had, therefore, never looked after it since." Nevertheless, he added, with an air of authority that many Virginians had come to resent, "it was their King's land and not New Netherland."[4]

In truth, the first English visitation to the Delaware had been in August 1610, a full year *after* Henry Hudson had entered the bay (giving the Dutch a claim to the region), carried out by Samuel Argall of the Virginia Company. Argall had anchored briefly in a "very great Bay" while en route from New England after searching for a lost provision ship called *Patience* bound for Cape Charles. After departing the embayment he sailed south and fell in among "a great many of shoales, about twelve leagues to the Southward of Cape La Ware." He also noted in his journal: "This Bay lyeth in Westerly thirtie leagues. And the Souther[n] Cape of it lyeth South South-east and North North-west."[5]

Unaware of Hudson's prior visit, the English were excited by Argall's discovery. "We have some hope also by a westerly trade," wrote George Yeardley (later governor of Virginia) in mid-November of the same year, "through a fair and goodly bay lying in the height of 383 [38°20′ N], some 30 leagues from our own [Chesapeake] bay, newly discovered since his lordship's coming hither, from whence we promise ourselves many commodities both of fish from the bay . . . and from the tractable Indians of that place, of whom we have made some trial, both corn, furs, etc."[6]

In a June 1613 letter recounting his experiences and adventures, Argall mentioned for the first time "the De La Ware Bay."[7] These were the first records of English names ascribed to a significant feature of the great bay, most likely Cape Henlopen, and eventually the great embayment itself now known as the Delaware Bay.[8] It was also the earliest mention of the great chain of shoals and barrier islands, the most significant geographic component of the Delmarva coast, that extends as far south as Cape Charles.

De Vries was unquestionably shocked that the governor of Virginia was unaware that the river and the bay it fed had been in the Dutch sphere of interest ever since its verified discovery by Hudson. While sailing on a voyage of exploration in the eighty-ton *Half Moon* on behalf of the Dutch West Indies Company, Hudson had dubbed it South River to differentiate it from the other great waterway he encountered soon afterward and named North River, now known as the Hudson. He was also probably unaware that the original Virginia charter, granted on April 10, 1606, had authorized the English colonization of any lands lying between the 45° and 34°N latitudes, basically any and all territory lying from New England to the northern limits of territory already vigorously claimed or settled by Spain in the south. The charter, however, had subdivided the territory between the Virginia Company and the Plymouth Company, with an overlap area lying between the 38° and 41°N latitudes open for settlement by either. Neither company, however, had been permitted to erect a colony within a hundred miles of one already established by the other, which resulted in an uncolonized and unexplored strip between them.[9]

This intentional creation of a neutral buffer zone, which included northern sectors of Virginia, Delaware Bay, and most of the Delaware River, as well as the

Hudson River, had unwittingly given the Dutch the ammunition they needed to join in the scramble for empire in the New World. Indeed, it was only three years after the original Virginia charter had been granted that Henry Hudson "discovered" the Delaware, a great estuary system the English were entirely unaware of at the time. Other explorers employed by the company, such as Cornelis Hendricksen and Cornelis Mey, followed in Hudson's footsteps. The Netherlands States General quickly and formally recognized the discovery of the explorers in the company employ by acknowledging the establishment of New Netherlands, much of which lay in the buffer zone. Exercising the age-old principle that possession is nine-tenths of the law, the company quickly moved to establish itself on both the South (Delaware) and North (Hudson) Rivers. With settlements erected at Fort Nassau, near present Gloucester, New Jersey, and Zwaanendael, present-day Lewes, Delaware, the hold on the Delaware Valley clear to the capes was no longer simply that of a claimant. Dutch names were given to many prominent features of the region. The bay was dubbed Godyn, after one of the company's leading patroons, or Suydt ("South"), after the river that fed it. The capes at its entrance had been named Cornelis and Mey after the explorer Cornelis Mey (although Cape Cornelis would later be changed to Hindelopen). The names, of course, would later be Anglicized to Capes May and Henlopen. Governor Harvey, it must have seemed to De Vries, was entirely unaware of all of this.

De Vries likely maintained his aplomb in the face of Harvey's assertion of English sovereignty over the Delaware Bay region. He informed the governor, much to the latter's surprise, "that there was a fine river there and that for many years had a fort there called Fort Nassau." The governor responded that it "was strange to him that he should have such neighbors and never heard of them."[10]

Then the governor provided an answer to a mystery that had plagued De Vries ever since he had left Zwaanendael—where the Mantes Indians acquired their English clothing. While trying to convince the Dutchman that English sovereignty technically reigned over the Delaware, he recounted his own efforts to have the region explored. He informed De Vries that he had sent a sloop the previous September, "with seven or eight men, to see whether there was a river there." The sloop never returned, and he was uncertain whether the party had perished or not. Then De Vries related his own story.

"I told him that we had seen Indians in the South River, who had English jackets on, and had also understood from an Indian, who gave us warning, that the Indians had run down an English sloop there, in which were seven or eight Englishmen." Sadly, the governor acknowledged that they must have been none other than his own cockleshell explorers, "otherwise, they who had been sent to discover the South River would have returned long ago."[11]

Thus it was that the English colonists in Virginia learned of their Dutch neighbors on the Delmarva coast. In September 1632 the capture and destruction by Indians of an all-but-forgotten ship of discovery and its nameless crewmen would be the only such massacre of its kind in the region. It would also, unfortunately, be but the first of thousands of maritime disasters to come.

When the Dutch eventually returned to establish a permanent occupancy on the South River, the colony enjoyed less than a convivial relationship with its neighbors. The occasional shipwreck of foreign nationals did little to alleviate the tension. In 1657, when fourteen Englishmen were shipwrecked on Cape Henlopen, the second known loss on the Delmarva coast, they were rescued by friendly Indians rather than massacred. The unexpected visit by Englishmen in Dutch colonial territory had consequences. News of their presence quickly generated rumors along the river and bay coast that one of the neighboring English colonies was planning to assault Dutch strongholds and seize control of the South River. When the shipwreck survivors blurted out that they were actually fugitives from Virginia, all bonded men, indentured servants, who had run away from the colony seeking their freedom, the commander of the Delaware settlements, Jacob Alrichs, was suspicious. Though the men were eventually ransomed off, Alrichs continued to believe them to be an advance party dispatched by either Maryland or Virginia to pave the way for an invasion by infiltrating the general population.[12] Eventually, in 1664, the English would indeed swallow New Netherlands whole, including the settlements on the South River and Godyn Bay, which would henceforth be known as the Delaware. Shipwrecks, however, would continue regardless of who was in control.

Many vessels were lost without record. The inhospitable shores of the Delmarva coast were sparsely populated, and communications were primitive and unreliable at best. Newspapers were nonexistent. Government services and the rule of law were entirely absent on the beaches. If an unfortunate wreck victim survived at all, he may as well have been cast away on the surface of the moon as to become stranded on this beautiful but desolate coast. The words of Henry Norwood, an English barrister marooned with a party of travelers on the coast in January 1650 by the heartless commander of a ship called *Virginia Merchant*, suggest the feeling of hopelessness a castaway would have endured. Finding himself on a frigid, windswept, uninhabited barrier island with no means or hope of escape after three months on a storm-tossed Atlantic was almost more than one could bear.

"In this amazement and confusion of mind no words can express," he wrote, "did our miserable distress'd party condole with each other our being so cruelly abandon'd and left to the despairs of human help, or indeed seeing more the face of man. We entered into a sad consultation what course to take; and having, in the first place, by united prayers, implored the protection of Almighty God, and recommended our miserable state to the same providence which, in so many instances of mercy, had been propitious to us at sea . . . We beheld each other as miserable wretches sentenc'd to a lingering death, no man knowing what to propose for prolonging life any longer than he was able to fast."[13]

Although the record concerning seventeenth-century shipwrecks on the Delmarva coast is scanty, circumstantial evidence exists that suggests by the end of the century they were increasing. On August 19, 1695, Francis Nicholson, captain general and governor of Maryland, appointed that colony's first wreckmaster, Edward Green, of Somerset County, to seize all wrecks on the coast, as well as "all drift Whales or other great ffish" belonging to the king.[14] The appointment suggests that the occurrence of shipwrecks on Maryland's Atlantic seaboard was by then substantial enough to warrant such an office. In fact, the appointment came none too soon, for with the expansion of trade and commerce in the eighteenth century and a seemingly continuous series of European wars spilling over into the Western Hemisphere, shipwrecks on not only the Atlantic coast of Maryland but the shores of Delaware and Virginia as well would increase substantially.

Some early losses were dramatic. Storms and founderings, of course, were among the most common causes of shipwrecks, especially around the shoally entrances to the Delaware and Chesapeake. On November 6, 1706, for instance, a severe gale ravaged the Virginia coast, inflicting major property losses as it pressed northward. An entire fleet of ships was swept up in the storm after departing the Virginia capes. No fewer than fourteen vessels in the fleet foundered on the north coast of Cape Charles after sustaining extensive injuries to their masts and sails.[15]

No less frightening was the tale of another foundering, in the very maw of the Chesapeake, published in the *Maryland Gazette* in February 1729: "A Ship belonging to Mr. Hunt, Merchant in London, Capt. French, Commander arrived about Three Weeks since within the Capes of Virginia; but a strong North-West Wind suddenly rising, drove her back and she had the Misfortune to run aground on Cape Charles, which so much damag'd her, that when she was got off, she sunk in 7 or 8 Fathom of Water, as the Captain was endeavouring to run her over to James River, in order to repair her, and so suddenly, that the Master and Crew could not so much as save their wearing Apparel, except that they had on, the Capt. only saving one Shirt, and 2 Packets of Letters. But the Capt. and all the Men are sav'd."[16]

Another vessel that suffered a similar fate was *Success of Glasgow,* which had just arrived in the Chesapeake in late December 1745 after a six-week voyage from Scotland. After having cast anchor off the mouth of the York River, she was "on the 31st of December last drove with 3 Anchors ahead by a violent North-West Wind, near two Leagues; when she struck upon the Middle Ground [at the entrance to the bay], which beat away her Stern Post: She sank so suddenly, that the Mate and 3 others were drowned; the rest being 16 in Number, got into the Long boat and were drove out of the Capes, without any sort of Provisions; but at length got ashore at Cape Henry; where one of the Men soon expired, through Hardships he had suffered."[17]

Ice was another ship-killer. In early January 1711/12 (OS) an extremely cold winter had inflicted its own peculiar form of disaster on Delmarva shipping. At Philadelphia, the Delaware was frozen solid. Men and horses enjoyed the occasionally amusing experience of walking across the river on the thick ice to the New Jersey shore. Yet ice was anything but amusing for shipping. One of the first known ice casualties was "a fine new Snow laden for Lisbon" and commanded by a certain Captain Cooke. It was later reported that while en route out of the bay, Cooke "lost his foremast a few leagues without the Capes of

Delaware and put back again, and upon Brandywine Shoals was cut to pieces by the Ice, but the men [were] all Saved."[18]

The same weather conditions claimed a second victim soon afterward. On January 22 it was reported in Philadelphia that during the previous week, "several Men from our Lower Counties that belong'd to one Capt. Westdrop in a Ship of 250 Tons, 14 Guns, bound hither from St. Christophers, which was lost in our Bay by the Ice," had been saved, although one had been "cut in pieces by the Ice." The ship, it was learned, had been a French prize taken by a privateer at St. Christopher in the West Indies, and by late accounts Westdrop was doing his best to salvage what he could before the vessel was totally lost.[19]

The most common form of loss, however, was not by ice or storm but by stranding. Strandings were usually caused by weather, poor navigation, ignorance of shifting shoals, being chased ashore by pirates, privateers, or enemy vessels, or simply myriad types of accidents. Usually, every effort was made to save precious cargoes, if not the ship itself. One of the most unique cargoes to be rescued from a shipwreck on the Delmarva coast came at the end of the seventeenth century, when the importation of black slaves from Africa to provide a source of cheap labor in English America had begun to accelerate.

The Spanish had early on established a triangular trade between the Guinea Coast of Africa, the West Indies, and Spain. It was a commerce that dealt not only in slaves but also in sugar, dyes, logwood, precious metals and minerals, and African elephant ivory.[20] Occasionally, French and English interlopers would carry on their own illicit commerce in the same commodities. There is little record, however, that trade in African ivory was undertaken in the Delaware, Maryland, or Virginia colonies. One exception, however, has been found, and it is related to a shipwreck.

On Sunday morning, August 7, 1687, according to a deposition given by one James Lemount in 1691, the ship *Society,* of Bristol, England, was wrecked on the Eastern Shore. One hundred and twenty Negro slaves and a quantity of "Elephant teeth" were landed from the wreck the same day. It is unclear whether the ship was bound for the Eastern Shore or Europe, but one thing is certain. The loss of *Society* provides the only known account of a shipwreck laden with elephant ivory, on the Delmarva coast.[21]

Mentions of shipwrecks, other than in official documents, court cases, and surviving correspondences and journals, were rare until the onset of the eighteenth century and the establishment of newspapers in the Middle Atlantic colonies. One of the first newspaper notices of a standing loss on the Delmarva came in 1712, when it was reported in New York that during the week of October 13 a large, unidentified New England–built sloop appeared to be aground in Delaware Bay and "seem'd to be in danger."[22] On July 29, 1723, another typical stranding was reported twenty miles south of Sinepuxent when Captain Robert Bird's South Carolina sloop *Robert and James* lost her mast during a storm and was driven ashore. Though her crew had been saved, her cargo had been much damaged. Such reports would eventually become all too common in the tabloids printed in New York, Philadelphia, Annapolis, Williamsburg, and Norfolk.[23]

Stories of shipwrecks and salvage, delivered by survivors, local witnesses, wreckers, or by captains of ships just passing by soon became a staple for the journalists of the day, even when there was no loss of life. Often, when a crew made good its escape from a seemingly fatal stranding, there was little left to recover. But as a news story, it immediately became grist for the weeklies. Such was the case of the Bristolman *Richmond,* whose stranding on April 4, 1738, was reported as follows in the pages of the *Virginia Gazette:* "Williamsburg, April 14. About 10 days ago, the Ship *Richmond,* Capt. Smith, from Bristol, bound for Rappahannock [River], with a very considerable Quantity of Goods on board, run on the Middle-Ground, near the Capes, and receiv'd so much Damage that she had in a small time, 6 or 7 Feet of water in her Hold, upon which the Captain, Passengers, and the whole Ships Crew left her, with the Sails standing, and went for Help to save what Goods they cou'd; but on their Return, cou'd not find the least Appearance of her; so that they know not whether she is beat to Pieces, and was wash'd away; or got off by the Help of her Sails, and is drove elsewhere."[24]

With navigational aids on the coast nonexistent until the erection of a single crude wooden lighthouse on Cape Henlopen about 1716, pilot error was a common cause of loss. When Henry Hudson "strooke ground" with his rudder while exploring the Delaware, he pointedly recommended that anyone exploring "this great Bay . . . have a small Pinnasse that must draw but four or five foote water . . . to sound before him." With countless ship-killing shoals such as the Middle Ground at the mouth of the Chesapeake, and the Shears and Overfalls at the entrance to the Delaware awaiting to snare the unwary, a knowledgeable pilot was an absolute necessity for entering and departing vessels. Yet pilots were fallible.[25]

The first known reported event of a fatal pilot error resulting in ship loss on the Delmarva occurred on October 27, 1713, when the twenty-six-gun frigate *Carleton,* of London, a ship of four hundred tons, was arriving from London via Madeira with a thousand bushels of salt and thirty-six pipes of wine. The vessel, it was later stated in the press, "unfortunately [was] lost in the [Delaware] Bay by the unskillfullness of the Pilot who ran her a Ground, where she split." Although the wine was saved, the ship and her cargo of salt became a total loss. Pilot errors would continue to account for many losses.[26]

Not to be ignored as shipping hazards during periods of both peace and war was the ever-present danger of pirates and privateers. As early as 1683, sea rovers had begun to employ the sparsely inhabited islands of Accomack County, Virginia, as ideal sanctuaries where they could seek respite, careen their ships, forage for wild game, and occasionally trade some of their ill-gotten gains with the locals. In 1690 and again in 1698, pirates had come into Horekill Roads, just inside of Cape Henlopen, and raided the town of Lewes. Such events did little to discourage those inclined to barter with freebooters bearing foreign commodities that colonists were otherwise forbidden to trade in by various Navigation Acts. Residents of Lewes were said to have even bartered with the notorious buccaneer William Kidd in 1699, only a year after pirates had raided the town. Also in 1699, when Captain John James, commander of the pirate ship *Providence Frigate,* arrived at the entrance of Chesapeake Bay, it was not to trade but with the specific intention of capturing the Royal Navy guardship *Essex Prize.*

He very nearly accomplished his objective. In 1700 a pirate fleet under the direction of the French freebooter Lewis Guittar, in the twenty-gun ship *Le Paix,* came to off the Virginia capes and captured and sank the sloop *George,* the ship *Pennsylvania Merchant,* and an unidentified vessel near Cape Henry before being defeated in bloody battle by HMS *Shoreham,* Captain John Passenger commanding.[27]

Such episodes became frustratingly common on the Delmarva coast. In 1710 and again in 1720 French privateers conducted raids into Lynnhaven Bay, Virginia, just inside Cape Henry. Noted pirates such as Benjamin Horningold, Edward "Blackbeard" Teach, and "Black" Sam Bellamy had found hunting off the Virginia capes as much to their liking as in any waters of the West Indies.[28]

The destruction wrought by sea rovers along the Delmarva coast seemed unending, and the perpetrators were of all nationalities. Their depredations and sinking of ships provided almost weekly fodder for the colonial press. The *American Weekly Mercury,* a Philadelphia newspaper, reported in 1724 on one such piratical endeavor and the resultant loss of the victim on the Delmarva's shores. On Friday, June 5, an unidentified Charleston, Massachusetts, brigantine, commanded by Captain Thomas Mouswel and bound from Boston for Virginia, was captured somewhere between Capes Henlopen and Charles by a Spanish pirate ship of fourteen guns and a multinational crew of eighty brigands. Mouswel and three of his hands were ordered to board the pirate. The freebooters retained the brigantine's master and one of the crewmen as hostages and "sent two Spaniards, one Savayard, one Frenchman, and a mulatto onboard the brigantine as a prize crew." As soon as the pirate crew had boarded their prize, the Frenchman, who had apparently been forced into signing on with the corsairs after his own ship had been captured earlier, attempted to "join the Englishmen aboard." When the prize crew tried to force the mate and the remaining Englishmen to steer their ship for Havana, owing to "the English mans Dexterity in altering the Compass (with a Load Stone) they lost the Ship the first Night, and afterwards unanimously set upon the Pyrates, overcame them on Tuesday the 9th instant [and] run the Brigantine a Shore on Cape Henlopen." The ship was a total loss, with only some cider aboard being saved.[29]

During wartime, privateers (privately owned ships bearing "letters of marque and reprisal" or commissions from their governments to capture or destroy enemy vessels for profit), frequently infested American and West Indian waters. The consequences for merchantmen plying their trade out of the Delaware and Chesapeake were often fatal. Not a few would meet their ends wrecked in the breakers of the Delmarva coast. One such case was the Philadelphia brigantine *Delaware,* Captain Taylor commanding.

On September 15, 1748, a small convoy of English merchantmen departed Port Royal, Jamaica, bound for London under the protection of a thirty-gun man-of-war. Included among the convoy vessels were *Delaware;* a Philadelphia brigantine called *Dolphin,* Captain Seivers commanding; a Boston sloop commanded by a Captain Foresight; and an unidentified ship commanded by a Captain Forbes. From the beginning the voyagers suffered through one catastrophe after another. The first misfortune was prescient, for while rounding the west end of Cuba, *Dolphin* was wrecked on a sunken reef called the Colleradoes. Forbes rescued Captain Seivers and his men, but bad luck dogged the convoy's wake. On October 2, soon after the rescue, *Delaware* fell in with several French and Spanish privateers and was subdued with ease by one from Cape François, Hispaniola. Three days later Forbes's ship was also attacked and taken by the same privateers, who then demanded a ransom of $2,500 for its release. Whether the ransom was paid or not may never be known. What is certain, however, is that the privateers were unable to keep *Delaware*.[30]

On October 11 a heavily armed Rhode Island privateer called *Defence* appeared on the scene. The polyglot French and Spanish prize crew aboard *Delaware*, outgunned and outmanned, immediately abandoned their captive and rowed ashore to the Cuban mainland. The Rhode Islanders took *Delaware* without a fight, making her their own legal prize. A new prize crew—this time English—and provisions were placed aboard, and all sails set for Rhode Island. Although the sturdy merchantman made excellent time, owing to heavy weather it was impossible for the prizemaster to take a midday observation of the sun to plot his position. Then came the final tragedy. On October 14, "it blowing hard, and having had no Observations for some time, she struck upon the Hen and Chicken [Shoal], a little to the Southward of Cape Henlopen, and ran ashore on the Cape." Though it was expected that most of the cargo would be saved, it was felt the ill-fated *Delaware* would probably not be so fortunate.[31]

Sadly, for the next 250 years thousands more would follow in her wake.

# 2

## A Good Many Chests of Money

The bloody four-year conflict known in Europe as the War of Austrian Succession and in the Americas as King George's War had been a grim struggle. It had finally been concluded with the signing of the Treaty of Aix-la-Chapelle in 1748 by the wearied principal combatants, England, France, and Spain. Like many such contests between great empires throughout history, this war had ended in little more than a draw that merely promulgated the continuation of the status quo, namely the restitution of colonial conquests in the Americas and the Far East, and confirmed certain monarchies to power. Indeed, little had been resolved by force of arms except to insure that the cosmopolitan paranoia infecting the mightiest kingdoms of Europe would continue unabated. No nation, however, was more xenophobic about its incredibly rich empire in the Western Hemisphere than Spain.

Within a few decades of Columbus's discovery of the New World, Spain had enslaved the great Aztec, Mayan, and Inca empires and established hegemony throughout most of Florida, in Central and South America, and in much of the West Indies. The efforts to explore, appropriate, and colonize these vast and rich new territories, and to carry home the incredible wealth gained by conquest, had quickly led to the establishment of a complex maritime system linking the Old World with the New. Over time, a sophisticated convoy operation was instituted and refined. By 1566, two heavily armed fleets were being fielded annually. The first, called the Flota, embarked for Mexico in the spring, usually in April or May, for calls at Mexico, the Mosquito Coast of Central America, Cuba, and Hispaniola. After provisioning and watering at Puerto Rico, the Flota passed Hispaniola, Jamaica, and Cuba before landing at Vera Cruz, Mexico, to take on the treasures of New Spain. The second fleet, called the Galleones, embarked for Panama about August to take on the treasures brought up from Peru and Chile and carried across the isthmus. It was then on to Cartagena and the Spanish Main to take on emeralds and other precious stones, and pearls from the fisheries of Isla Margareta. Both the Flota and Galleones then sailed to rendezvous at Havana for the return voyage to Spain. The usual homeward course from Cuba was through the Florida Straits, riding the Gulf Stream northeastward up the Atlantic coast of North America. After passing the latitude of Bermuda, the fleet turned due east to the Azores and then toward home. It was a tried and true course that would vary little for more than two hundred years, a pipeline of treasure that insured Spanish supremacy in both the Old and New Worlds. By the end of the War of Austrian Succession, that supremacy, which had been sorely tested, had been all but exhausted.

Havana harbor was a hotbed of activity as the 1750 Spanish treasure fleet readied itself for the long and perilous voyage to Spain. It was August and the hurricane season was already upon them. Yet this convoy was a far cry from the enormous hundred-ship armadas that had sailed during the heyday of the great plate fleets of the sixteenth and seventeenth centuries. Indeed, the vessels that were assembling beneath the mighty guns of Morro Castle numbered just seven. They had been placed under the overall command of Captain-General Don Juan Manuel de Bonilla, a brave and courageous man but one occasionally prone to indecision.[1]

The most important ship was the *Almirante,* or "admiral" of the fleet, Bonilla's five-hundred-ton, four-year-old, Dutch-built *Nuestra Señora de Guadeloupe,* alias *Nympha.* She was owned by Don Jose de Renturo de Respaldizar, commanded by Don Manuel Molviedo, and piloted by Don Felipe Garcia. *Guadeloupe* was a big ship, and had been allotted a substantial cargo of sugar, Campeche dyewoods, Purge of Jalapa (a laxative restorative plant found in Mexico), cotton, vanilla, cocoa, plant seedlings, copper, a great quantity of hides, valuable cochineal and indigo for dyes, and most importantly, as many as three hundred chests of silver containing 400,000 pieces-of-eight valued at 613,000 pesos. Among her passengers was the president of Santo Domingo, Hispaniola, as well as a company of prisoners.[2]

The thirty-gun galleon *Nuestra Señora de los Godos,* commanded by Captain Don Pedro de Pumarejo, with Don Francisco de Ortiz sailing as supercargo (a representative of the cargo's owner) and silvermaster, was manned by a hundred men. She carried perhaps the most illustrious passenger list in the fleet, which included the viceroy of Mexico and his consort, the governor of Havana and his family, and the intendant (quartermaster general) of Chile and his family.[3] Nor was her cargo anything to scoff at, for it included 150,000 pieces-of-eight in 350 chests, cochineal, and other objects valued at over $600,000, as well as general goods similar to *Guadeloupe*'s. One passenger carried an unregistered personal fortune of 200,000 Spanish milled dollars as well as a great quantity of diamonds.[4]

Three "register" ships, two Spanish and the other Portuguese, also readied themselves in the harbor. The Portuguese register *San Pedro,* belonging to Lisbon, was largely owned by English interests and was one of only two annual ships from Portugal permitted to sail with the Spanish fleet. Described variously as a frigate and as a snow, she had most recently sailed in May 1749 from Lisbon for Cartagena, on the Spanish Main, laden with bale goods. Having reached South America without incident, she had then taken on a cargo of cocoa, Brazil dyewoods, cochineal, logwood, and "a great quantity of money estimated at

$600,000," and then embarked for Havana to join the annual homeward-bound fleet. Her commander was an Irishman named John Kelley who, like many of his Catholic countrymen ever since the conquest of his homeland by Protestant England, had found comfortable employment in His Most Catholic Majesty the King of Spain's navy. His ship's master and supercargo was Don Manuel Martinez de Aquair.[5]

The second register ship, *Nuestra Señora de Soledad,* was referred to as both a Spanish brigantine and a small frigate captained by Don Manuel de Molbudro. Don Jose Renturo de Respaldizar, her supercargo (and owner of *Guadeloupe*), was also embarked aboard. Like other vessels of the fleet, the ship was laden with cochineal, hides, sugar, and at least fourteen chests containing $40,000 in silver.[6]

The Cartagena packet ship *El Salvador,* nicknamed *El Glonorico,* like *San Pedro,* was referred to as a snow in some reports. She was also owned by Don Jose Respaldizar who, although already embarked aboard *Soledad,* was to serve as her supercargo. Laden with 240,000 pesos register treasure besides private money, $140,000 in gold and silver, cocoa, logwood, Brazil dyewood, cochineal, and balsam, the ship was commanded by Captain Don Juan Cruanas with Don Francisco Arizon serving as master.[7]

A small zumaca, or schooner-rigged advance boat, one of the king's ships, called the *Nuestra Señora de la Merced,* had also joined the gathering fleet. Like the rest, she was laden with a cargo of mahogany, cochineal, hides, snuff, and "a good many Chests of Money." Manned by eight men, *La Merced* had last sailed from the Mosquito Coast on the Gulf of Campeche to Porto Bello and from there to Havana under her commander, Captain Don Antonio Barroso.[8]

The guardian and most heavily armed ship of the fleet was *La Galga,* "the greyhound." This big fifty-gun frigate had sailed once before from Cadiz, in March 1748, as one of three convoy escorts for a fleet of merchantmen bound for New Spain. She was thus no stranger to the American coastline, or the dangers posed along the route by either nature or the enemies of Spain alike.[9] Command of *La Galga* had fallen to Don Daniel Huoni, (variously referred to as Don Daniel Huony, Woni, Mahoney, and even Onness). Like John Kelly, Huoni was "an Irish Gentleman," an ex-patriot who had long been in the service of the king of Spain. The ship's master, like most of its crew, was a Spaniard; his name was Don Thomas Velando.[10]

Because she was well armed and manned, and designated as the only convoy escort ship of the fleet, *La Galga* was also laden with a most valuable cargo. Most of her lading had been shipped by the king's own Royal Company and included more than six hundred sacks of snuff, bundles of tobacco wrapped in fine linen, thirty cedar chests containing more than a million cigars, hundreds of mahogany planks deemed "the best which could be got" and destined for use in the construction of the interior of a new royal palace in Madrid, and four chests of official papers relating to the Spanish empire in the Americas. Not surprisingly, there was also a substantial quantity of gold and silver plate, numerous chests of doubloons, and treasures and other property belonging to the Catholic Church.

As aboard *Guadeloupe,* securely chained below decks were more than fifty English, Dutch, and French prisoners, mostly mariners being sent home to Spain for purportedly violating Spanish colonial territorial waters for the purpose of smuggling.[11]

Huoni was well aware that Spanish gold had more than once tempted the English to attack both the Spanish Main and homeward-bound plate fleets. As recently as October 1748, a British squadron had assaulted seven war galleons off the north coast of Cuba in a bold effort to capture an entire treasure fleet that had been delayed in sailing. Although the effort had been defeated after seven hours of combat, it had cost Spain two of its finest warships. Spanish privateering raids against English settlements on the Cape Fear River in North Carolina and on the Delaware coast did little to compensate for the loss. Now Huoni would have to pass perilously close to one of those same shores that had so recently been assailed.[12]

Nevertheless, the Spanish were anxious to get under way. Even though Spain was temporarily enjoying a brief state of amity with her traditional rivals, they knew that the longer the fleet remained in port, the more danger there was for enemies, even pirates, to prepare an ambush. But it was the weather that proved the most worrisome. Through bitter experience gained over two hundred years, the Spanish were well aware that the hurricane season was already upon them. Yet they were willing to crowd that season, gambling that fear of the weather had driven potential attackers from the sea lanes. Finally, on August 18, after all preparations had been completed, Captain General Juan Manuel de Bonilla ordered the flag raised aboard the Almirante to signal departure.

Although the weather was less than favorable, the Spanish fleet managed to depart Havana harbor and cross the Florida Straits to the coast of Florida without mishap. With experienced pilots aboard, they proceeded to enter the hazardous Bahama Channel. At the head of the fleet, *La Galga* plowed through the turquoise waters followed by *La Merced, Los Godos, San Pedro, Guadeloupe,* and *El Salvador,* with *La Soledad* bringing up the rear.[13] Carefully at first, they proceeded past the Florida Keys, always keeping within sight of land but a safe distance from the deadly coral reefs that had claimed the lives of so many of their predecessors. Their speed increased as they picked up the powerful Gulf Stream. There was little hint, however, that the early tranquility of the voyage enjoyed by many of those embarked would soon be tragically shattered.

On August 25, as the fleet entered latitude 29°N off the deadly shores of Cape Canaveral, Don Pedro de Pumarejo, commander of *Nuestra Señora de Los Godos,* eyed the skies with increasing concern. In the early afternoon great Cimmerian clouds began to blacken the horizon to the northwest, offering a clear presentiment of impending danger. Suddenly, "at three in the afternoon the wind hit us with great force from the north." Within a few hours, the blow had achieved gale force, hurling now out of the north-northeast with a terrifying intensity that increased with every passing minute. By evening, the tempest had shifted dramatically, now attacking from the south-southeast. By 8:00 P.M. the wind was so strong and loud that even voice communication on the quarterdeck of *Los Godos* was impossible. The storm was soon deemed a full-blown hurricane, with horrendous winds now varying from every point of the compass.[14]

At the head of the fleet, *La Galga* began taking on water but plowed resolutely on, seemingly impervious to the increasingly vicious assaults of nature. Others, however, found themselves in more desperate straits. *Los Godos* was forced to sail with only fore and mizzenmasts unfurled. She soon found herself drifting to windward of *La Galga* and *Guadeloupe* and was obliged to furl her mizzens to bring her back to the fleet. By nightfall, she had safely rejoined her sister ships, but her difficulties were immediately renewed as she was forced to sail before the wind. In an instant, her tiller was carried away, and her foretopmast sheets were ripped asunder. Control of the ship and contact with the fleet were entirely lost. Her launch and boat had been severely damaged. Desperately, Pumarejo struggled to regain control of the ship. He ordered the mizzen cut away to bring her around to the wind, even as the lower deck was awash under several feet of water but still seemed manageable. On the evening of August 26, the hold began to fill. "Then," Pumarejo later reported, "our work started." Unable to reduce the flooding even with two pumps working constantly, the captain ordered the great guns, the oven, and the injured boats thrown overboard. The larger livestock onboard, many of which had already been killed "by the pounding seas," were also tossed over, but to seemingly little avail. Hour after hour, day after day, the mountainous black ocean waves repeatedly washed over the ship. After each onslaught, *Los Godos* emerged intact, but always a little weaker than before. The timbers at her head were soon pounded so badly that the sea gushed freely through opened seams, filling her with nine feet of water below decks.[15]

*San Pedro* was in an equally dire situation. The stern of the Portuguese register had been stove in, and all of her boats had been carried away. With six feet of water in the hold and one mast already blown away, she began wallowing ever deeper in the heavy, dark troughs of the ocean. Captain Kelly also ordered as much of the cargo as could be spared tossed overboard to prevent foundering.[16]

Briefly *Los Godos* sighted *Guadeloupe* on the twenty-eighth and observed that her mizzenmast was gone. Signals were exchanged. Both captains, by dead reckoning, acknowledged that their ships were by now probably "dangerously close to the Carolina coast" and should seek to avoid it at all cost. Then contact, the last there would be between them, was lost. By dusk, the wind had subsided somewhat, but the heavy seas continued to pound away. The water level in the hold of *Los Godos* was still increasing. "Our two pumps," Pumarejo later reported, "only made us lose our breath. Even the chaplain and myself worked the pumps, swimming in the water that always reached above the waist." A new tiller, installed to replace the old one just washed away, was soon split in half. Pumarejo ordered yet another one rigged, but the seas simply stripped the bolts from the locks. Then the majestic lion figurehead that had graced the bow was ripped off by a giant wave. With each sickening roll, the forecastle dipped deeper and deeper beneath the troughs yet somehow managed to resurface. By now there was eleven and a half feet of sea in the hold. "We kept taking water," recalled the captain, "and now realized there was no remedy to our plight other than the Virgin Mary . . . Thus we hoped for the dawn of the 29th, and as we waited, the top foremast fell, which was our only control of the ship."[17]

Pumarejo refused to surrender and ordered his men to reinforce the body of the ship so that its seams would not open worse than they already had. Everyone, including the captain, officers, priests, crew, and prisoners, worked without respite, struggling for their lives to keep *Los Godos* afloat. Holes were chopped through the between-decks floors to let the waters pass more readily to the pumps below. By the morning of the twenty-ninth, depression was universal. "Finding ourselves in a miserable condition," Pumarejo reported, "we started dumping things overboard: chests, mattresses of officers and passengers, and cargo between decks, such as hides, dyewoods, meat, boxes—and always manning the pumps as our only hope of survival. At 8 we were hit by a great sea, and then another at 9½ [A.M.], so that all the oakum of the first deck were wiped out, water running all the way down, flooding our victuals, sails, gunpowder, etc."[18]

By now, every man and woman in the fleet despaired for his or her survival. As the distended gaggle of ships reached 33°N latitude, all pretensions of maintaining convoy formation were abandoned.[19] For seven days and nights, sea and sky had merged as one vast gray entity, visibly bifurcated only by the white-tipped frothing of gigantic wave crests. Now, as the hapless fleet, dispersed over many miles, was pushed relentlessly toward the coast of the Carolinas, each ship's crew assessed the grim prospects awaiting them. Many prayed for salvation, others for redemption.

The Outer Banks of North Carolina, toward which most were being driven, like much of the Delmarva coast to the north, is a narrow strip of low, sandy coastal barrier islands, occasional perforated by shoally inlets. Each was isolated and separated from the mainland by vast, shallow sounds, occasionally thirty or more miles broad. The most prominent and easternmost feature of these remote isles is a hook of land known as Cape Hatteras, which juts into the Gulf Stream like the fin of a giant shark. It is here that the warm northbound current collides head on with the frigid waters of the Labrador Current. At this juncture a submerged, shallow, treacherous bar stretches many miles seaward. Known as Diamond Shoal, it causes the waters to remain in a constant, dangerous state of turbulence even in the calmest weather. Southwest of Hatteras, projecting from the underbelly of the Outer Banks, lies a second but no less hazardous projection called Cape Lookout, from which another perilous, submerged sandbar quietly awaits the unfortunate.[20]

The crewmen of the Cartagena register packet boat *El Salvador* were the first of the Spanish fleet to encounter the ship-killing shoals of the Outer Banks, and certainly among the most unfortunate. On the night of the twenty-ninth, when they first discerned the sound of breakers on the shore near Topsail Inlet, not far from Cape Lookout, somewhere between fifteen and eighteen leagues south of Ocracoke Inlet, it was already too late. Whatever *El Salvador*'s precise location may have been, the historic record is quiet about her last moments as she was driven ashore, stove by the waves, and split asunder on the beach. Only three crewmen and a ship's boy managed to escape from the shattered wreckage, albeit after saving eleven big boxes of the king's silver. Even as the bodies of the dead were dashing against the beach, human scavengers arrived to pick the bones of the late transport.[21]

*El Salvador* had not initially been alone in her final struggle for survival near Topsail Inlet, for near the site of her tragic loss, a Bermuda sloop had also become briefly stranded. Commanded and owned by a pair of Englishmen named Ephraim and Robert Gilvert, the sloop had been fortunate enough to escape destruction and had been quickly refloated. Then, incredibly, as the four bruised and half-drowned survivors of *El Salvador* watched in utter disgust, the Bermudan came to anchor by the sandbank where the packet boat had split open. Despite the turbulent seas, the Gilverts commenced salvaging whatever could be removed, including sails and rigging, and then several chests of registered treasure. Not long after the Bermudan had departed, the wreck was again savaged by a renewed assault of wind and waves, and rapidly disappeared forever beneath seven to eight feet of sand.[22]

The crewmen of *Nuestra Señora de la Soledad* were far more fortunate than their compatriots aboard *El Salvador*. Captain Molbudro and his men had fought bravely to manage their charge to the very last, although everyone aboard knew their probable fate. Somewhere between ten and twelve leagues south of Ocracoke, near old Drum Inlet, the little frigate was also lost, together with most of her cargo of cochineal, hides, and sugar. Miraculously, her officers and crew not only survived but also managed to haul ashore all fourteen boxes of silver, later reckoned by North Carolina authorities to contain 32,000 pieces-of-eight, as well as some other lading.[23]

The majestic *Nuestra Señora de Guadeloupe*, the Almirante of the fleet, with "its Masts broke Short," somehow rode with the storm until August 30. Having been unable to take a reading because the sun had not appeared in days, Bonilla suddenly found his ship being helplessly blown toward a low, sandy coastline he correctly assumed was Hatteras. When "the weather became [a] little less boisterous and the wind shifted to S.W.," he brought the ship to anchor with two cables on end approximately five to six leagues south of the cape. Throughout the night, his ship rode out the storm, her cables straining and stretching, and her crew "expecting every moment to be driven ashore." But the anchors held.[24]

The next morning, Bonilla took stock of his ship's shattered condition. She had lost her rudder, mizzenmast, main and foretop mastheads, and all of her sails. Her hold was full of water, and there were few provisions aboard (most having been ruined or thrown overboard). It was, he knew, imperative to seek a safe anchorage inside Ocracoke Bar to make whatever repairs possible. To maneuver the great ship in such a damaged condition across the notoriously dangerous bar in dirty weather would require not only a superb act of seamanship but also a considerable dose of good luck. Fortunately, the winds had subsided somewhat, although the seas remained dangerously high. He thus ordered a jury rig, a new sail fixed to the yard, and "after a great deal of trouble, care and charge," the ship was again able to maneuver a bit under her own sail—but just barely.[25]

Bonilla was aware that he was now in a former enemy's territory, where hostility toward the Spanish for depredations conducted less than two years earlier were still fresh in everyone's memory. Moreover, many of his crewmen, led by a charismatic boatswain's mate named Pedro Rodriguez, wanted to simply run the ship ashore and save themselves. Some panicked crewmen, ignoring orders, even went into the hold and began throwing overboard everything they could lay their hands on. Apprised of their wishes and actions, Bonilla was furious. "I opposed it," he later reported, "considering that the lading would be lost, and spoke to the officers and sailors in such strong terms as I could, to induce them to take care of His Majesty's interest. I promised them in the name of the principals, double wages as soon as we were in safety." His appeal fell on deaf ears, and a state of outright mutiny threatened. When he ordered one of the ship's boats to be lowered to explore the coast for a safe haven, the insurgents senselessly hacked it to pieces. Unable to trust his own men, Bonilla quietly managed to dispatch several passengers ashore in a tiny pinnace to reconnoiter the country. On their return, they informed him that they had seen cattle tracks going inland indicating the presence of inhabitants. He immediately determined to see for himself. Accompanied by an Englishman (possibly one of the prisoners) who had once lived in the Carolinas and had been entered on the muster roll of the ship at Havana, he set off to reconnoiter. From a few isolated inhabitants on the coast he discovered he was indeed on a most wild and desolate shore. The closest safe anchorage was inside Ocracoke Inlet, five leagues away. They were the same killing grounds where the infamous pirate Blackbeard had been defeated and beheaded in bloody battle more than thirty years before.[26]

Bonilla and the Englishman did not return to *Guadeloupe* empty-handed, for while ashore they managed to hire an experienced local pilot to determine if it was even feasible to get the Almirante over Ocracoke Bar. The ship, it was soon evident, would have to be substantially lightened to get her in. Bonilla promptly purchased a small packet boat fortuitously found lying at Ocracoke to tow his ship over the bar. To protect the king's interests, in the event the effort failed and the ship was lost, he took the precaution of ordering the chests of treasure brought up from the hold and carried ashore in the pinnace and several canoes that had also been purchased at Ocracoke. He nevertheless fretted that once ashore the treasure would be liable to capture by any strong force that might be in the vicinity.[27]

After two days of backbreaking labor, more than fifty chests of silver had been hauled onto Ocracoke Island. Yet, even as the unloading was under way, a near mutiny once again interceded. Again led by Rodriguez, a large party of sailors seized all of the arms they could find. The sailors, fearing the loss of their ship might be used as an excuse to deny them payment of their salaries, since she had not completed her voyage, threatened to abandon ship unless immediately paid. Bonilla gave in. "I will give you your wages, and a gratuity," he promised, "if you will carry all of the silver and cochineal ashore." The sailors demanded their wages on the spot. Bonilla noted caustically that there was certainly enough money onboard for everyone to be paid off but that he had no authority to dip into the king's treasure to do so. As far as the mutineers were concerned, however, they had already ended their voyage and demanded their pay without delay, $100 a man. If the admiral refused they would simply abandon the pumps and let the ship sink where she lay outside the bar.[28]

Somehow, Bonilla convinced the mutineers to return to work, but his troubles continued. While in the middle of breaking bulk, several sailors began to indiscriminately smash open passengers' trunks, robbing them of jewelry and private property and committing other "outrages." Neither the captain nor Rodriguez, hitherto the acknowledged leader of the disgruntled crewmen, could persuade the thieves to return the stolen goods. The mate, having lost control of some of his own followers and worried of charges that likely would be leveled against him, now "looked upon himself as a man lost for ever."[29]

Despite the spate of lawlessness, Bonilla eventually regained control and the unloading was finally resumed. Preparations to bring *Guadeloupe* across the bar proceeded, albeit not quite as planned. The pilot, who had returned from the shore with Bonilla, had brought with him a makeshift rudder to replace the one lost by the Almirante, but it did not fit the ship and proved useless. Nevertheless, the packet boat began the slow process of towing the galleon toward the inlet. Finally, after a three-day effort, the great ship lay securely ensconced in the anchorage behind Ocracoke, the same road in which the greatest pirate in history had fought his famous battle to the death.[30] Sadly for Bonilla, *Nuestra Señora de Guadeloupe* was not going anywhere soon. And pirates still abounded at Ocracoke.

Even as Bonilla and a small, loyal cadre of seamen struggled to rescue as much treasure and cargo as possible from their imperiled ship, the remaining vessels of the fleet, which had swept even further northward, had continued their individual life-and-death struggles with the sea. For seven days Captain Pumarejo and his crew had fought valiantly to save *Los Godos*. They tossed everything overboard, retaining only the king's treasures and some small cargo. There was little more that could be done except pray for a miracle and plug up holes. "The wind and sea," wrote the demoralized commander, "are so strong we are persuaded to die."[31]

On August 30, a half hour after noon, as Pumarejo's men completed more work reinforcing the hull, a sudden calm fell over the sea, "but the sky looked horrible." The eye of the storm was passing over, and the captain seized the moment to put on some canvas to regain a modicum of control, but in vain. Within ninety minutes, the hurricane resumed, this time with a ferocious wind blowing in from the southeast. *Los Godos* ran on under bare poles, pressed first in a north-northwest direction, then on a north-northeasterly course, and finally back to the west, her stern always to the sea. Collision with the land seemed inevitable, yet all aboard hoped "to prolong our drift and to hit the shore with the least possible force."[32]

The weary men of *Los Godos* continued to work the pumps throughout the night and into the morning of August 31. About eight o'clock the winds began to subside and conditions improved dramatically. The storm had finally passed.

Pumarejo ordered some sails raised on the naked masts and began to search for a landing spot. At nine, land was sighted. Three hours later the sun appeared, and the captain took his first sighting in a week. He estimated his position at 36°4' N and knew that the beach lay due west. With his ship in sinking condition, there was now little choice but to steer for it and hope for the best.[33]

"By noon," Pumarejo later reported, "we were two leagues from shore, in latitude 36 degrees, 38 minutes. Noticing a creek which seemed like a port entrance, we sailed for it. About one league from shore, in 6 braces of water, I decided to drop anchor, persuading everyone that we were already safe, and that we [had] worked too hard to abandon the ship now. A Spanish flag was hoisted, and we fired our cannon repeatedly. We were approached by a pirate [wrecker's] canoe that was there to pick up the spoils of two English ships that had sunk on Saturday the 29th, with no survivors except a boy. The canoe approached us around five in the afternoon. We brought a man aboard, who informed us this was the end of the coast of Carolina to the north, that there were no port facilities, that the two lost ships were about half a league away, and that 15 miles to the north was the Virginia River [Chesapeake Bay]. He said he would guide us there, where we would be able to find a local pilot. Accepting his offer, we awaited a divine favor. The water [in the hold] stayed 7 feet through the night."[34]

With weather improving, *Los Godos* pressed on for the Chesapeake at 2:30 the next morning, "hoping to save the remaining cargo that had not been damaged by the sea." Soon after noon, as the ship approached Cape Henry, Pumarejo espied two vessels limping toward his own. One was *San Pedro,* almost mastless, and the other was a stranger, a Spanish sloop later identified as *Mariana,* Captain Don Antonio Ianasio de Anaya commanding, blown well off course while bound from Campeche for Santo Domingo with a cargo of logwood, hides, and snuff. Pumarejo later reported, "When defeated by the hurricane, she [*Mariana*] met the aforesaid Portuguese [*San Pedro*] in whose company she arrived at this inlet of Cape Henry." Several hours later, a pilot boat from Hampton appeared on the scene to shepherd the "terribly shattered" trio into the harbor. The miracle Pumarejo and his men had prayed for had been granted. It was not so for *La Galga* and the little zumaca *Merced.*[35]

Six leagues above Cape Charles, Don Antonio Barroso and his seven men had struggled to keep their charge, *La Merced,* a safe distance from the coast without losing their lives or the "good many Chests of Money" and other cargo aboard. The Machipongo Shoal proved their undoing, as the king's schooner was driven ashore. Barroso and the crew, however, managed to reach the beach soon after their ship was stranded on the shoals. Then they watched as its back was broken and then savagely beaten to pieces.[36]

But what of the great and majestic shepherd of the fleet, *La Galga,* the greyhound? Captain Huoni's command, like all of the ships under his care, had indeed been pushed helplessly before the winds, albeit far to the north of the rest. He had, in fact, parted company with the Flota about the latitude of Bermuda, and passed by the Outer Banks and Virginia capes without sighting them. Like all of the ships in the convoy, however, *La Galga* had been driven relentlessly westward, as her mainmast, foretop, and mizzen masts snapped, and more than seven feet of water filled her hold. At Huoni's order, seven guns had been pushed overboard as the lumbering giant wallowed deeper and deeper between each crest of the sea. Later, another fifteen would follow.[37]

When the first chilling sound of waves dashing against a shoreline was heard above the storm, Huoni and all aboard knew their ship's inevitable fate. Then, with a sickening bump that jarred all aboard, *La Galga* struck a shoal, tearing off her rudder in the process. Within seconds she was driven into a shallow trough between the mainland and the bar. The captain immediately ordered an anchor dropped. The big warship's forward motion came to a sudden halt in five fathoms of water, albeit straining every fiber of her cable to hold firm.[38]

Even as the great anchor clawed its flukes into the sandy bottom, pandemonium ruled on deck. The ship had already "received so much damage, that they could scarce keep her from sinking," and the crew were well aware that she might soon bilge and break up beneath their feet. In a near panic, several men hoisted out the small boats, but to no use as all were immediately stove to pieces as they were lowered.[39]

Captain Huoni retained his composure throughout the crisis, even if many of his men did not. With the ship certain to break up at any time, he ordered the release of the prisoners confined below decks. Many crewmen and prisoners alike chose to take their chances by swimming ashore through the pounding surf. Three unfortunates drowned, including two Spaniards who had "tied so much Money round their Waists, that they sunk with it," and a Mr. Edgar of New York, who had succumbed while swimming toward his freedom.[40]

Never losing sight of his mission, Huoni struggled to save both his crew and as much of the king's property as possible, particularly the treasure. With enormous waves smashing against the side of his ship, the captain set his weary men to lashing together a raft, probably from the deck cargo of mahogany, upon which they might transport both the treasure and themselves to safety. The official Spanish account later stated that the endeavor was a success. Only one soldier was lost and "a good deal of Money" and "other Things of Value" were brought ashore and "mostly saved." The effort was probably more costly than the formal government reports indicated, however. Reports in the colonial American press, undoubtedly related by liberated prisoners who had been there, stated that "two Men, and two Chests of Money, were wash'd off and lost."[41]

After considerable effort, *La Galga*'s haggard survivors, Spanish, English, French, Irish, and Dutch alike—now leveled to equality through misfortune— finally gained the shore.[42] Don Daniel Huoni may have pondered his good fortune at surviving, but the struggle that lay ahead, to bring his men and the king's treasure home safely to Spain, was undoubtedly foremost in his thoughts. For as far as the eye could see lay nothing but an uninhabited strip of sand backed by shallow dunes and hummocks covered by sparse vegetation. A hasty reconnaissance revealed that behind the dunes lay a wide, shallow sound. They were, the captain suspected, on one of the coastal barrier islands of either Virginia or Maryland, entirely cut off from the mainland. Yet, the Spanish were anything but alone, for English eyes had watched them from the dunes, even as they had hauled their weary bodies onto the beach—along with the king's treasure. The wreckers had arrived. As night fell, no one noticed the prisoners as they slipped off into the darkness and freedom.

It was not long after the stranding of *La Galga* that the Spaniards and the local inhabitants made contact. The initial encounters proved entirely peaceful. Huoni was first informed that his ship had come to grief on Assateague Island, in Virginia territorial waters. The locals of these destitute shores were no strangers to shipwrecks and had for years eked out profits from scavenging materials and cargoes from many unfortunate strandings. "The Commodore who is an Irishman and Speaks very Good English," the Sheriff of Worcester County, Maryland, later wrote, was asked by the inhabitants "for the Vessell to give it [to] them but he told [them that] the Owner of the Land owned the Ship and he could not give her." The captain was, however, delighted to learn that at the little river port of Snow Hill, in Worcester County, Maryland, he could procure a vessel to carry his men and the salvaged treasure to Hampton Roads where they might regroup with other survivors of the fleet. Thus, with renewed hope and a final look at the sad wreck of *La Galga,* the Irish sea captain and his Spanish stalwarts set off. "The Commodore and his crew of Soldiers," it was reported soon after in Annapolis, "got of the Neighbours Small Crafts and Came a Cross our Sound to the Main, and got his Riches Over and Carted them to Snowhill, which Consisted Chiefly in Silver Several very heavy Chests, and got two Sloops at Snowhill" to carry them to Elizabeth River, Virginia.[43] With the Spanish finally gone, the wreckers of Assateague immediately set about their work.

It was probably while at Snow Hill that Huoni first learned that almost as soon as he had departed from the beach, the "Country People" began to turn out in numbers to plunder the wreck, which remained ensconced on the bar just as the Spaniards had left her. Indeed, it was soon being reported as far away as Annapolis that "People at and about Worcester County, are every Day, in good Weather, fishing what they can out of her, and have found a considerable Booty." Huoni was further informed that there were four Virginians, Ralph Justice, William Gore, Thomas Crippen, and Thomas Bonnewall, apparently managing the organized looting of the Spanish king's property "to the value of some Hundred Pounds." Still believing that the wreck lay in Virginia territory, the captain wrote to the president of the Executive Council of Virginia requesting an opinion as to what might be done.[44]

In the meantime, as word of the disaster spread, Sheriff John Scarborough of Worcester County arrived on the scene to investigate and found that the wreckers and their slaves were indeed already hard at work. Their scene of industry was formidable. The ship still lay on a shoal of sand. "She has," the sheriff reported, "many large Pieces of Cannon on board two fine Anchores at her bowes abundance of all Sorts of Rigging and Sails in her hold and amount Supra." The salvors had already removed two hundred small arms, together with belts and slings, swords and bayonets, some very large copper pots of several sizes and smaller ones in abundance, all of the ship's standing and running rigging, iron crowbars and a variety of tools, as well as many thousands of pounds of tobacco "made Strong in Wrappers." The salvors had "hove the Tobacco out for the Sake of Linnen Wrappers and the Tobacco now on board is [in] good Order." Moreover, there was still onboard a substantial quantity of very valuable mahogany. "There is many thousands of pounds worth," the sheriff noted, "if it could be got before the Ship bursts with the Sea and Sinks into the Land."[45]

The initial reportage on the location of La Galga's fatal contact with the coast of America was muddied at best and totally inaccurate at worst. The first official Spanish account, which was replicated by a report presented to President Thomas Lee of the Virginia Council, acting governor of Virginia, stated the loss occurred fifteen leagues north of Cape Charles. The first account reaching a major port, the city of Philadelphia, was carried by former prisoner Captain James Maloney, of the ship Shepherdess, which had earlier been seized at Havana. Maloney stated that La Galga struck Chincoteague Shoal and two days later was driven onto Chincoteague Island. It was also reported the ship was cast away fourteen leagues south of the Delaware capes. Another prisoner account, that of Captain Walter Wrench, master of a Virginia ship also seized at Havana, was published at Annapolis in the Maryland Gazette but possibly confused the wreck with that of La Merced stranded on Machipongo Shoal.[46]

Although Scarborough had conversed with some of the wreckers, he was uncertain as to whether or not the wreck lay in Virginia or Maryland waters and recommended that the salvors "be easey" until he had secured the opinion of Governor Samuel Ogle and the Council of Maryland. As they had told Huoni, the wreckers informed the sheriff in no uncertain terms that "the Vessel was in Virginia as there were several Gentlemen with their Slaves all at work from Virginia" and they simply were not about to pay heed to anything anyone said to them, least of all some official from Maryland.[47] The sheriff, however, got a different version from the actual inhabitants of the area, who had already asked permission from Huoni to salvage the ship. The "People living on the Beach," Scarborough informed the governor, "tell me that she lies two miles within Maryland lines," and therefore right of salvage belonged to Lord Baltimore, the proprietor of Maryland.[48]

Taking the opportunity of informing Ogle and the Council of Maryland of the disaster, via one Thomas Harris, who was traveling to Annapolis, Scarborough reiterated from what he had learned that the Spanish warship had, in fact, "Stranded on our Beach." On September 13 the governor took action, noting that La Galga "hath been deserted by the Commander Officers & Mariners thereof after they had Saved all they could of the Rigging Equipment & Cargoe of the said Ship" and that "Several Evil Minded Persons have contrary to all Law and Justice" taken possession of the ship's guns, tackle, apparel and equipment, and other goods and cargo, as well as "several Parcells of Money" for their own use. He instructed Sheriff Scarborough to retrieve all of the materials salvaged by the locals "untill the Right thereto shall be Lawfully determined," and empowered him to call into service as many persons as deemed necessary to execute the directive. Moreover, he was instructed to find out who the culprits were and what had originally been left behind in the ship's inventory when the Spanish departed. Ogle also wrote President Lee of Virginia requesting that he find out where the materials were that had already been stolen from the wreck "taken into the Possession of some Persons within your Govern[men]t" but "lost within the Limits of this Province."[49]

It may have been when Sheriff Scarborough met with Captain Huoni, presumably while the latter was securing transports at Snow Hill, to learn what had been left behind when *La Galga* was abandoned, that Scarborough informed him "that her Decks were cut up by the Country People of both Provinces and Carried away." The captain may also have informed him that not only the Virginians already mentioned but also a "Gang" of Marylanders, including Thomas Robins, Daniel Miflin, and one Mr. Dalason, had "carried away Effects and Stores to the Value of a Considerable Sum." These had already been seized by the sheriff.[50]

The trip from Snow Hill to Hampton Roads for Huoni and his men had proceeded without incident. On reaching Norfolk the captain penned a letter to Ogle to request that the king of Spain's rights and interest in the wreck be preserved. In the interest of amity and the recent treaty of peace agreed by England and Spain, the king must be allowed to recover what rightfully belonged to him "after deducting the Customary Salvage" or "what the Law allows to the Possessors in such Cases." The captain concluded with a sad note that he had learned "that a late Storm having broke the Hull to Pieces, 200 Stock or Planks of Mahogony that were Cast on Shore on [the] Virginia Side [of the border] were Purchased (as reported) at a very low Price by a Merchant of Snow Hill."[51]

Upon reception of Huoni's letter on November 3, Ogle responded favorably. He assured the captain that he would do everything he could to recover the plundered goods and had already issued orders to that effect. He recommended that the captain authorize some person to receive the mahogany and the other effects previously recovered.[52]

As the affair at Assateague was playing out, that at Ocracoke was entering a new phase. As soon as Bonilla managed to subdue his rebellious crewmen with promises and bring his ship to a questionably safe haven behind Ocracoke Island, it had been necessary to temporarily depopulate *Guadeloupe* of most of her manpower to offload the rest of the treasure. Unfortunately, during the ship's first night behind Ocracoke, while Bonilla and part of his crew were still ashore, a Bahamian snow named *Carolina* appeared on the scene and quietly made fast to the ship. Bonilla had worried about such unexpected arrivals. "I was afraid," he later wrote, "of the insults from Englishmen who resorted to the coast." Deeming the Almirante fair game, the snow's crew boarded her, apparently without opposition from the handful of Spaniards left aboard, stormed the guard room in an effort to seize firearms locked therein, and then tried to steal some silver that had been stored in the pilot's house ashore. The guards Bonilla had placed at both places had remained loyal and soon repulsed the invaders. Nevertheless, before the raiders left they proceeded to plunder part of the ship's lading and break open a chest containing a packet of letters.[53]

Detail from Joshua Fry and Peter Jefferson's 1775 *Map of the most Inhabited part of Virginia containing the whole Province of Maryland,* showing the barrier islands of Virginia's section of the Delmarva coast. Note that "Chingoteaq" (Chincoteague) Island is indicated above the oft-disputed Maryland-Virginia boundary line. *La Galga* was believed stranded above the line, while *La Merced* was lost on Machipongo Shoal, well to the south and clearly in Virginia territorial waters. (Library of Congress, Washington, DC)

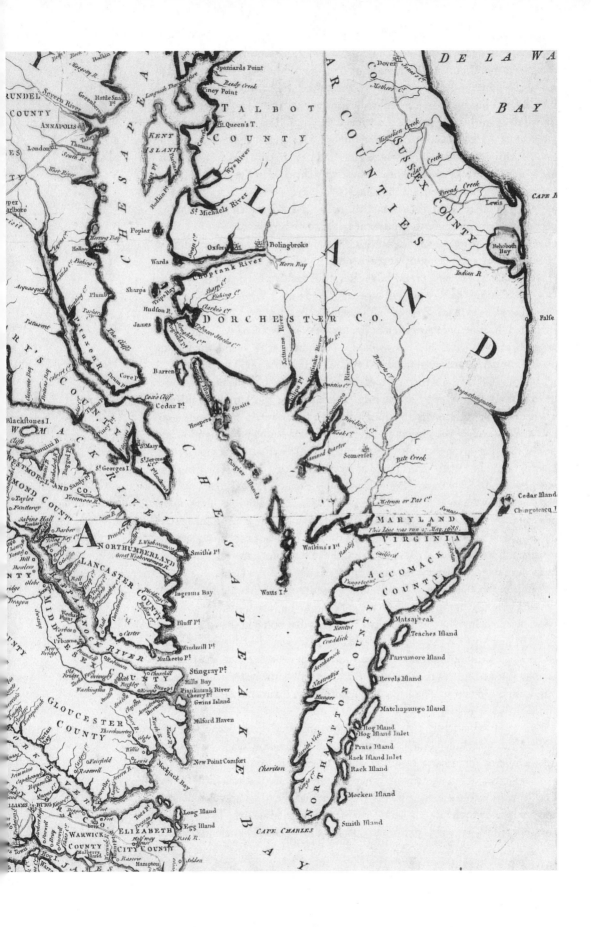

The prevailing lawlessness seemed only to revive the mutiny. The crew again demanded more money. The captain offered them nine dollars a month, but they wanted twelve. Again he promised them their wages, and again most were subdued, but not for long. Undoubtedly fearing retribution later when they returned to Spanish authority, and convinced they would receive little more than promises, some found and chartered an English snow and then departed, leaving Bonilla with but a handful of loyal seamen and passengers to protect the treasure. Ironically, Rodriguez was among those who chose to stay.[54]

Beleaguered at every turn, Bonilla had little choice now but to seek the assistance of his country's erstwhile enemy, the provincial government of North Carolina. The Ocracoke pilot was thus sent by sea to obtain the support of Governor Gabriel Johnston to provide adequate vessels to take *Guadeloupe*'s lading to Hampton Roads or to some other secure port. Bonilla was unaware that the governor was already well apprised of the tragedy that had befallen the Spanish. Don Jose Renturo de Respaldizar, supercargo aboard *La Soledad,* who had survived the calamity that had befallen his own ship and then made his way to New Bern, had informed the governor of the loss of possibly as many as five of the seven ships in the fleet. He had also lodged a complaint regarding the looting of *El Salvador.* Johnston immediately issued orders for the apprehension of the piratical Gilverts and their crew and the confiscation of their sloop. Indeed, he may have even helped the survivors secure passage to New England from whence they planned to take ship for Cadiz. Bonilla, however, was entirely ignorant of the events to the south and stayed focused on his own preservation and that of the king's property in his charge. He also dispatched a letter to Captain Huoni, whom he learned had arrived at Norfolk, seeking his assistance in moving the far more important treasure from Ocracoke to safety. The captain-general was well aware that the treasure was no longer safe in a simple pilot's home, no matter how strong the guard might be. He had had to split up his few remaining loyalists, with one party guarding the ship and the other protecting the treasure ashore. He thus decided to reconsolidate his forces, treasure, and cargo by moving them all back to the ship.[55]

Returning to *Guadeloupe,* Bonilla again found himself in a most precarious position. Though lying behind Ocracoke Island, the low shoreline provided poor shelter against the foul fall Atlantic weather that buffeted the coast. Moreover, the anchorage he was in was so shallow that even at high water, *Guadeloupe*'s keel was bumping against the bottom. When the tide ebbed, the hull was literally battered against the shoal by the rise and fall of the water, and the sternpost was now in danger of collapse. He tried shifting his anchorage, but to little effect.[56]

At this critical juncture, two bilander sloops appeared on the scene. One was a New Englander called *Seaflower,* commanded by Zebulon Wade, of Scituate, Massachusetts, the other a New Jerseyman from Perth Amboy named *Mary,* Samuel FitzRandolph master and owner. Despite the piratical actions of the last English visitors to the scene, and his own fears that the newcomers might play another "scurvy trick," Bonilla guardedly viewed the arrival of the two sloops as an opportunity. The winds remained high and the water quite shoal in the shelterless cove, and his ship might be bilged at any worsening of the weather. With "the Intrigues and Artifices of Pedro Rodriguez Boatswain of the said ship His Men very mutinous and ungovernable, [and] the said Boatswain having got most of the Men on His side and under Pretence of going to Virginia," there seemed little choice. Calling his remaining loyalists together for a conference, the admiral proposed employing the two shallow-draft sloops "to keep his money and other effects on board, 'till he could either hire or buy another ship." It was so agreed. For some reason, perhaps to curry his favor, Rodriguez was sent aboard *Mary* to negotiate an arrangement to carry the cargo to Norfolk. One of FitzRandolph's crew, William Waller, of Woodbridge, New Jersey, served as interpreter. Within a short time, *Mary*'s master had agreed to transport the lading to Virginia for a fee of 570 pieces-of-eight. A similar agreement was made with the master of *Seaflower*. Soon afterward the Spaniard returned with fifteen hands in a launch to haul the two sloops alongside *Guadeloupe*.[57]

On or about October 5, as the transfer of treasure was under way, a certain Colonel Innes arrived bearing a letter from Governor Johnston, summoning Bonilla to New Bern to answer charges of illegally breaking bulk in the colony without permission. Bonilla, who had been expecting assistance, not a summons, was stunned. Fortunately, having also been sent to specifically inquire into *Guadeloupe*'s situation, the colonel was not unsympathetic to the Spaniard's plight. He had become immediately suspicious of the intentions of *Mary* and *Seaflower* and expressed his fears to Bonilla that the sloops would attempt to run away with the treasure. He even volunteered to take possession of them. In the meantime, a sloop-of-war might be provided for the purpose of carrying the money to safety. But to do so, it would be necessary for Bonilla to accompany him to meet with the governor. The Spaniard readily accepted. Rodriguez, however, now backed by many of the remaining crew and fearing that if the English got their hands on the treasure neither he or his men would ever be paid, vehemently protested and "would not suffer the Money to be moved." Nevertheless, Bonilla set off immediately with the colonel.

To prevent any larceny while he was away, although fifty-five chests of treasure along with a substantial cargo of cocoa, cochineal, and sugar had already been transferred to *Seaflower* and upward of fifty-four to *Mary*, Bonilla ordered the loading operation halted. He issued written instructions to the mate, signed by both himself and Captain Molviedo, to have the two vessels' sails carried ashore where they would be guarded until his return, for without sails the two sloops could not possibly leave. Then he ordered ten loyal armed men placed aboard each vessel to prevent any underhanded actions. The holds of both vessels in which the treasure chests had been stowed were to be barred, locked, and kept under constant guard.

Such precautions, it turned out, mattered little. Seven crewmen aboard *Mary*, at first without the knowledge of their captain, had already conspired to rob the kitty locked up aboard their own vessel. Two of the conspirators, Thomas Edwards and Kinsey FitzRandolph, slipped into the water and cut a hole at the foot of the larboard cabin, through the bulkhead and into the hold in which the treasure had been stored. With the guards standing outside the cabin entirely unaware, the bank was successfully raided twice without detection right under their noses. In one robbery alone, FitzRandolph retrieved 748 pieces-of-eight, 708 of which he gave to his father while retaining the rest for himself. The raids continued, and the piratical crewmen were so successful that they twice divided the spoils. Some among them, however, were for calling it quits before their thievery was discovered. William Waller took the opportunity of a visit to another sloop that was then riding innocently at anchor in Ocracoke to book passage back to his home at Middletown, New Jersey, and escaped clean with his share of ill-gotten gains. Yet the seamen's escapades palled by comparison to a cabal hatched between Captain Wade, Captain FitzRandolph, and one Owne Lloyd, who "had armed themselves for that purpose, to run away with what was put on board their vessels."[58]

True to form, Pedro Rodriguez proved as untrustworthy as ever and may have even been a partner to the larcenous conspiracy that ensued. Whatever his later excuses may have been, he had neglected to remove the sails of at least one, and possibly both, of the bilanders and had posted no guard onboard *Guadeloupe*. On October 9, with Bonilla far away, and a fresh, fair wind blowing, the English pirates, led by Owne Lloyd, put their plan into action. About noon and without warning, the two vessels cut their cables and put out to sea. The astonished Spaniards immediately took up pursuit in a longboat, firing their guns as they scuttled along like an elongated waterbug. *Seaflower*, commanded in the action by one William Blackstock, alias William Davidson, and navigated by Lloyd, nevertheless successfully carried off "55 chests of money, some trunks of gold and silver wrought plate, and 155 bales of cochineal and other things." Though described as a "dull Sailer" and carrying no more than ten men aboard, and soon also pursued by the *Guadeloupe*'s pinnace, the pirate sloop made a clean escape over the bar and sailed away for the West Indies. FitzRandolph's sloop, however, had the misfortune of missing stays and, perhaps slowed in the escape effort by the plugged hole in her side cut by the crew, ran aground in the roads. She was quickly boarded and captured by a launch from *Guadeloupe*. On learning of the piracy, Bonilla was devastated. "I fell very ill of shock," he morosely informed the Marquis de la Ensenada, "and nearly died. I am very weak and in ill health now." He placed the blame for the affair squarely on Rodriguez, who with fifty men under his command had failed to stop the slow-sailing *Seaflower* and had succeeded in taking *Mary* only because she had run aground.[59]

Bonilla once again requested aid from Governor Johnston. The governor immediately ordered His Majesty's sloop-of-war *Scorpion* to sail for Ocracoke Bar and take onboard "fifty Chests of Dollars, and thirteen Bags of Cochineal, and a few small other matters," as well as some wrought silver, one small chest of precious jewels, twelve silver plates with spoons and forks, and 134 bales of cochineal, all that remained of the cargo. He also dispatched expresses to the West Indies and all parts of North America "to give Notice of the Robbery, and likewise Two Schooners well Man'd and Arm'd, to Search the Coast least they [the pirates] should be lurking [in] some Creek there." Boatswain's mate Rodriguez, with the help of the English, was placed in irons for his refusal to move the silver, an act of mutiny punishable by death.[60]

...

The fateful hurricane of August 1750 had been a dreadful disaster to shipping on the coast. Besides the Spanish casualties, no fewer than nine English ships had been lost on the mid-Atlantic seaboard alone, three of which had succumbed at Currituck Inlet, leaving but a single survivor. Two ships and a schooner from Barbados had been lost at Ocracoke, and two sloops and a schooner had stranded at Hampton, Virginia. Yet for days, weeks, and months after the loss of the Flota, the two ships that had managed to make Hampton Roads, *Los Godos* and *San Pedro,* and their officers and crews lived in a netherworld of colonial English bureaucracy. Hoping to refit and sail for home with what treasure remained, they soon learned that both their ships' repairs and departure would be seriously delayed.[61]

President Lee ordered an inspection of their papers and the inventory of their cargo "and so take care that no civility due to the subject of a Province in amity with His Majesty be wanting, and they be not on any Pretence whatsoever suffered to carry on any illicit Trade as this is a Thing that is new, never having happened here before."[62]

By early October, Don Felipe Garcia, *Guadeloupe*'s pilot, who was unaware of the latest events at Ocracoke, had finally arrived at Norfolk to charter a vessel to begin the salvage of his ship and what cargo remained in her. He brought news of the loss of *El Salvador* and *Soledad* and informed his comrades in the city that Governor Johnston had already begun investigating the illegal salvage of the former by the Gilverts and the impounding of their sloop and imprisonment of its captain. Captains Huoni of *La Galga* and Barroso of *La Merced* had by this time also arrived safely at Norfolk. Huoni quickly petitioned President Lee, albeit not without some trepidation, for permission to hire ships to transport the cargoes salvaged from the fleet back to Spain. His fellow officer, Captain Pumarejo, was not sanguine about their chances. "Because greed is inseparable from these neighbors," he had already concluded about his nation's former blood enemy, "because of their limited reasoning, and the great disobedience of our own seamen, added to the rebellious character of the inhabitants of this coast who know no Justice and Government other than their interest, I live in constant fear of being insulted [assaulted] with no defence [other] than Providence."[63]

Pumarejo's fears were not to be realized, for the Council of Virginia readily gave its permission to land and warehouse all cargoes and to dispose of at public auction whatever goods were damaged. If the ships were found unseaworthy and had to be condemned, all passengers aboard were to "have Free Liberty to go home with all their Goods and Effects in the Ship *Jubilee* or any other Vessel they shall think proper."[64]

Soon after permission was granted to unload the ships, a survey of *Los Godos* was conducted and reported to the president of the council. The inspectors discovered "that by the violence of the weather the ships bow is started from the butts end and the stern post loose from the transum two beams and several knees broke the ends of several other beams worked off the stamps and upon the whole find the floor and futtock timbers quite rotten and decayed and of consequence incapable of being repaired and in our opinion ought to be condemned." A survey was also carried out on *San Pedro,* which was determined to be "too rotten to be repaired" and without "being wholly rebuilt anew which will amount to the value of a new ship she cannot proceed nor be repaired."[65]

On November 6, Lee gave Pumarejo and his associates permission to carry their cargoes to Europe and expressed the desire, for their own safety, that "they will leave this colony before Winter sets in too hard." Undoubtedly with an eye to the issue of territorial sovereignty in the Spanish American colonies and cordial reciprocity for future treatment of English mariners, he insured that they be furnished with everything that was necessary as friends and trusted "that the good image they have had here will occasion those Nations to use his Majestys Subjects well that may at any time fall into their hands." Not until the end of March 1751 would Bonilla, ailing and humiliated, petition the Council of Virginia, into whose colony he had moved after saving what was left of the treasure and abandoning *Guadeloupe* to an uncertain fate. A broken and dispirited man whose career was unquestionably at an end, he sought only permission to hire a ship to transport himself, his officers, and his passengers to old Spain.[66]

In the meantime, Captain Huoni, having also vigorously sought a passport to Spain, did his best to address the issue of the illegal salvage of *La Galga* by the wreckers on Assateague. He wrote the Council of Virginia complaining that valuable properties had been stolen from the wreck by Virginians "and desir'd the Opinion of the Board what Measures were proper to be taken." The Council promptly ordered the individuals mentioned to appear before it on Friday, November 2 to answer the complaint. No one appeared—or ever would—but Captain Huoni and his men were granted their passport and were soon homeward bound, carrying what was left of the king's treasure with them.[67] By then, the bones of their great ship, guardian of one of the last great treasure fleets to sail from the Americas, had already begun subsiding beneath the moving sands and shoals of Assateague Island.


The treasures of the ill-fated 1750 Spanish fleet, purloined by the likes of Zebulon Wade, the Gilverts, and the wreckers of Assateague Island, were not easily forgotten by either the Spanish or the colonial administrations of Maryland, Virginia, and North Carolina. Indeed, the capture of *Mary* had given the Spanish some cause to crow. While recognizing the lawlessness of the acts of some of their countrymen, however, many Englishmen in the colonies feared the consequences of potential Spanish reprisals against mariners of their own nation.

"It is much feared," wrote the editor of the *New York Gazette,* "the Master and Mariners [of *Mary*] will meet with condign Punishment besides bringing a lasting Infamy on the British Nation, for their Treachery to People in Distress;— and give the Spaniards a Plea for using poor Englishmen ill, that may have the Misfortune to fall into their Hands. They will doubtless think they ought to have Justice done them; notwithstanding if any of our Vessels from the Bay [of Campeche] happen to be lost on their Coast, or put into their Ports in Distress, they not only seize the Vessels and Cargo, but make the Men Prisoners; altho' they have in Nature no more Right to the Wood in the Bay, than the English have to the Mines in Mexico. Their Depredations and Captures on the High Seas by the Guarda Coastas, is a Piece of Villany little inferior to this robbery; tho' tamely suffered by us, who are near becoming the dupes of all nations."[68]

In mid-November, it was reported in Boston that a mysterious, unnamed "Spanish gentleman belonging to a large and rich ship of his nation" lately cast away on the Carolina coast, possibly Respaldizar, was in town attempting to locate and retrieve $150,000 in silver coin and other effects, including $100,000 worth of cochineal, purloined from the wreck of the *Guadeloupe* by Zebulon Wade's sloop *Seaflower,* which was believed to be in New England. Bostonians were anything but positive about the Spaniard's chances. "But we dare not promise," wrote one newspaper editor, "upon the skill in Astrology as to predict that all the money, &c. will be recovered, and that the master and his accomplices will be apprehended. For a man with such a number of dollars about him, may be said to have powerful hands."[69]

There was, however, to be some justice. On November 5, William Waller, who had participated in the *Mary*'s piracy before that ship's capture and then returned home with more than two hundred pieces-of-eight, was interrogated about his role in the act. He quickly implicated everyone who had a hand in it before and after, and he was immediately arrested for the crimes of piracy and robbery on the high seas. Ever the weasel, Waller managed to escape before his trial, but by July 1751 he had been recaptured, tried, and presumably punished. Then it was learned by an express from the island of St. Thomas, in the West Indies, that his former associates, Owne Lloyd and his men, had also been captured on St. Eustatia, but not before having buried much of the money on a small key known as Norman's Island. A treasure hunt of substantial proportions soon ensued on the islet, where as many as ninety thousand pieces-of-eight were dug up by a horde of residents from nearby Tortola before authorities could step in.[70]

The whole tragic affair was not without its repercussions. The unheralded arrival of the once formidable and heavily armed Spanish fleet on the Virginia coast had served to point up glaring weaknesses in the colony's defensive posture even while at peace. "This accidental coming of the Spaniards," wrote President Lee to the Commissioner of Trade and Plantations, "has shown the necessity of one or more forts to the seaward for it was not in the power of this government to have prevented their coming as they did without leave into the harbour of our most considerable town of trade."[71]

But it was the conduct and lawless acts of the wreckers of Assateague that stimulated the most response by the Council of Virginia. Irate over the failure of their first summons to the wreckers to account for the actions, they again issued a directive on July 21, 1751, that they appear at Williamsburg.[72] Again no one came—or ever would.


On February 7, 1751, an advertisement appeared in the *Virginia Gazette* announcing the sale at public vendue of the hulk of *Guadeloupe,* alias *Nympha,* said to be "not Five Years old, as she now lies lately moored in a Harbour near

Core Banks, not far from Occocck [*sic*] Inlet . . . with her Rigging, Guns, Sails, Stores, &c." The sale was to be held at Edenton, North Carolina, on Tuesday, March 5, 1751. An inventory was to be seen at the time of sale at the house of Messrs. Watson and Carries, merchants, in Suffolk, and Andrew Sprowles, merchant in Norfolk. The ship was purchased and refitted by one Charles Elliott and entered back into commercial service. On October 27, 1752, Elliott advertised for seamen "willing to enter themselves on board the ship *Nympha,* bound for Cadiz."[73]

# 3

## The *Roebuck*'s Horns

The genesis of the American War for Independence has long been the subject of academic investigation, as have the political, military, and naval tactics practiced by the combatants. Yet one of the principal means Great Britain employed in its efforts to crush the rebellion, namely the strangulation of rebel trade and commerce through naval blockades, has been little explored. The Delaware and Chesapeake Bays, whose waters supported such key American commercial entrepôts and maritime centers as Philadelphia, Norfolk, Portsmouth, Annapolis, and Baltimore, were early on destined to become the focal points of vigorous blockading efforts and frequently the scenes of naval combat.

The blockade was not a tactic new to warfare. The investment of a port, harbor, waterway, or coastal area by ships of war to strangle an enemy's trade and military capabilities has been practiced at least since Hellenistic times. Not surprisingly, it was one of the first modes of action adopted by the mightiest sea power on the planet, the British Royal Navy, to close off the important Delaware estuary little more than two months after the first shots of rebellion had been fired on Lexington Green. It was a natural course of action adopted by British strategists that was destined to send countless ships to the bottom.

Soon after the siege of Boston had begun, Vice Admiral Samuel Graves, commander in chief of the American Station, fearing the spread of insurrection throughout all of the colonies, requested that several strong warships be immediately commissioned and sent to reinforce the extant naval forces already in America.[1] As the fires of revolt spread throughout New England, the Lords of the Admiralty were forced to respond. On July 6, 1775, they issued strict instructions to Graves to suppress the rebellion of the four New England colonies in conjunction with His Majesty's land forces, "and to seize & detain . . . all Ships & Vessels belonging to the Inhabitants of those Colonies, such excepted as you shall find, upon good Evidence & Information, to be bona fide the sole property of Persons who have been in no shape concerned in the Rebellious proceedings within those Colonies." The admiral was to send to New York, Delaware Bay, Chesapeake Bay, and Charles Town, South Carolina, each "a small detached Squadron, under the

Command of an Able & discreet Officer." These officers were to "to do all that in them lies to prevent any Commerce between the Colonies of New York, New Jersey, Pennsylvania, Virginia, Maryland & the Carolinas, and any other Places than Great Britain, Ireland, or His Majesty's Islands in the West Indies, including Bermuda & Bahama Islands." At any place where rebellion was evident, the squadrons were authorized "to proceed by the most vigorous efforts" against all such foes and facilities. They were empowered to search any vessels and seize and detain those carrying contraband, arms, munitions, or military stores. They were also to take onboard "any governors or officers compelled to seek asylum and [to] protect His Majestys subjects." To institute the blockade, Graves was to be given, in addition to the fleet already in American waters, the immediate services of HMS *Experiment,* 50; *Roebuck,* 44; *Phoenix,* 44; *Acteon,* 28; *Lizard,* 28; *Milford,* 28; and *Solebay,* 28. Over time, many more men-of-war, both great and small, would be sent to join them to wreak unrelenting hell and havoc on the rebel marine, commerce, and ports alike.[2]

Ordering ships to North America was one thing; actually fielding them was something else. Typical of the difficulties in dispatching warships across the Atlantic were those encountered by the Admiralty in sending off HMS *Roebuck,* a spanking new fifth-rate man-of-war built at Chatham Dockyard in 1774.[3] This majestic 886-ton fighter had been laid up at Portsmouth awaiting final refitting for more than a year. The delay was officially attributed to labor problems that had plagued the Admiralty when Lord Sandwich, in a fit of pique, fired all the shipwrights and was then obliged to negotiate with them to finish the job under less than ideal conditions.[4] Thus, it was not until August 25 that *Roebuck* was deemed ready to take aboard a full complement of 130 seamen and 120 Royal Marines.[5]

On September 9, under the direction of a tough, resourceful, and well-connected commander, Captain Andrew Snape Hamond, *Roebuck* finally upped anchor at Portsmouth and set sail for America and the besieged city of Boston, fully armed with eighteen- and nine-pounder batteries. Her first destination was Fayal, in the Azores, to take on supplies for the ship's company, after which it was on to Halifax to disembark her most important passenger, Vice Admiral Marion Arbuthnot, the new commander of the Halifax Station. And then to Boston.[6]

Arriving at Halifax about November 3, Hamond was surprised to find that he was to place himself under Arbuthnot's command to defend the city against an expected rebel attack rather than proceed to Boston as planned. Arbuthnot formally issued him the same orders sent to Graves regarding the suppression of the rebellion, with the added directives: "to Seize and Send to Boston, all Ships and Vessels belonging to any of the other Colonies in North America, Laden with Provisions, Rum, Live Cattle, Hay, Salt, Lumber, Melasses, Fuel or any Sort of Naval Stores wither they are in Breach of any Act or not." He was also to take and destroy "rebel pirates wherever they can be found" and all insurrectionists in the harbors and coasts of the New England colonies. If the opportunity arose, he was "to seize delegates to Congress, rebel officers or principal raiders and abettors to rebellion, as well as all vessels carrying emigrants from Great Britain and send them to Boston or Rhode Island," where the Royal Navy had bases. It was a tall order indeed.[7]

Owing to the dissipation of the threat against Halifax and the eruption of rebellion throughout all of the colonies, however, Captain Hamond's attention would soon be directed elsewhere. Far to the south, in the colony of Virginia, the royal governor, the Earl Lord Dunmore, had been forced to retire to a small flotilla of ships in Norfolk harbor after suffering a military defeat at the Battle of Great Bridge. On Christmas Day, Hamond was instructed "to use all convenient dispatch in Compleating your Provisions to Six Months of all Species and your Stores to the allowed Proportion for Twelve Months" and "proceed without loss of time to Virginia and take command of HM ships on that station and Employ them as you shall find best for His Majesty's Service" until the arrival of a senior officer. After "leaving sufficient force in the Chesapeak[e] Bay," he was then to proceed to the rebel-infested Delaware accompanied by a twenty-gun ship or sloop-of-war "to Guard the Entrance of the River Delaware by Cruizers until the Navigation is Open, and His Majesty's Ships can Anchor in the River." He was also to use his utmost endeavors "to prevent any Supplies getting to the Rebels, to annoy them by all means in your Power, and to protect and defend the persons and property of His Majesty's Loyal and Obedient Subjects. You can also procure as many good Pilots as you can for the River and Coast of the twelve United Colonies, and bear them as a Supernumerary List for Victuals only to be supplied occasionally to the Kings Ships."[8]

Thus was set in motion one of the first of many destructive chapters in the campaign of coastal blockading during the American Revolution, not just of the Delaware but of the Chesapeake as well.

The campaign and travails of the captain and men of HMS *Roebuck* in Virginia were closely linked to the twilight days of royal control in that colony. Neither skipper, crew, nor ship would be able to attend to the Delaware assignment for nearly six months. Not until the early spring of 1776, accompanied by the tender *Maria,* would *Roebuck* sail out of the Chesapeake to establish a formal blockade on the Delaware. When Hamond finally arrived on Monday, March 25, 1776, in Old Hoar Kill Road, a mile off Cape Henlopen Lighthouse, a system of rebel coast-watchers under the direction of a Delaware Bay pilot named Henry Fisher, an agent for the Pennsylvania Committee of Safety, was already in place. The big warship's arrival was immediately observed. Signals were raised to warn all vessels in the vicinity. One of these was a pilot boat schooner owned by Fisher, which had just departed from Lewes bound for Philadelphia. Owing to the approach of evening, however, the boat failed to see the signals.[9] By eight the next morning, "the wind being light and Northerly and Ebb Tide," the schooner was well aware of the enemy warship and frantically stood up the Delaware in an effort to escape. *Roebuck* spotted it. Armed boats were sent off in pursuit and soon overtook the hapless pilot boat. Thanks to an incoming fog, the schooner's crew managed to escape in a skiff into Broad Kill Creek, and their boat was easily taken.[10]

In the afternoon Hamond observed two small sloops heading down the bay, and immediately outfitted the pilot boat with small arms and muskets and manned her with several seamen commanded by Lieutenant George Ball. The schooner and *Roebuck*'s tender *Maria* were sent off in hot pursuit, and the two sloops were soon taken.[11] One of the prizes proved to be the *Polly*, commanded and owned by William Bowen, bound from Philadelphia to North Carolina "with Nine pound Shot, iron and Groceries." She was determined by Hamond to be "of some consequence, as she was laden with Shot & Stores for a Battery Erecting in North Carolina; and had on board several articles of merchandize very useful to the Ships Comp[an]y."[12] That afternoon, Hamond ordered the groceries from *Polly* distributed among *Roebuck*'s company. The following day, at noon, both sloops were hauled alongside of the warship and scuttled, the first fatalities of the Delaware blockade.[13]

The regimen that would be established by the blockaders over the coming weeks and months was neither effortless nor without danger. The shoals and coastline of the Delaware capes were forever changing and could be fatal. Moreover, rebels infested the shores, making any foraging for water or provisions a risky proposition. On the third day of the blockade, the hazards of such duty were underscored while *Roebuck* was lying at anchor between the Delaware capes. When the warship's lookout spied several vessels standing in from the sea, Hamond immediately ordered *Roebuck* to take up the chase. *Maria* soon joined in the frolic. At 6:00 P.M. the warship came up and spoke with the sloop *Dove*, an unfortunate Yankee vessel sailing in ballast that had just been taken prize farther up the bay by Lieutenant Ball in the pilot boat. The "large New England sloop," commanded by Captain T. Atkinson and owned by M. Denie, was captured while en route from Plymouth for Philadelphia to take on a cargo of corn. Having little use for the empty prize and not enough manpower to take her to Halifax, Hamond had her disposed of. "I rather chose to destroy them," he later wrote regarding the fates of *Dove* and other vessels that would soon fall into his clutches, "than weaken my Ships company by Sending men on board to Navigate them."[14]

In the meantime, *Maria* had come in to report on another adventure that same morning. And she had quite a tale to tell.[15] One of the vessels she had chased had at first been mistakenly identified as *Lord Howe*, a tender supposed to have been ordered up to the Delaware from the Chesapeake ahead of *Roebuck* in early March.[16] The vessel, however, proved to have been an American warship, a sloop of ten guns and about seventy men, which had narrowly escaped capture. Unbeknown to the British, they had just missed bagging the Continental Navy sloop *Hornet*, Captain William Stone commanding. The appearance of the first armed American warship in the area evoked an immediate response. Without delay, Hamond made sail in quest of the enemy but soon lost her in the darkness and returned to patrol off Cape Henlopen Lighthouse.[17] In the meantime, *Maria* and the ship's cutter, commanded by a Lieutenant Leak, had managed to capture yet another sloop, this one called *Dolphin*, which had been anchored inside the protective Hen and Chickens Shoal. Commanded by a Captain T. Burgess and owned by J. Simpson, of Dartmouth, the prize had been bound for

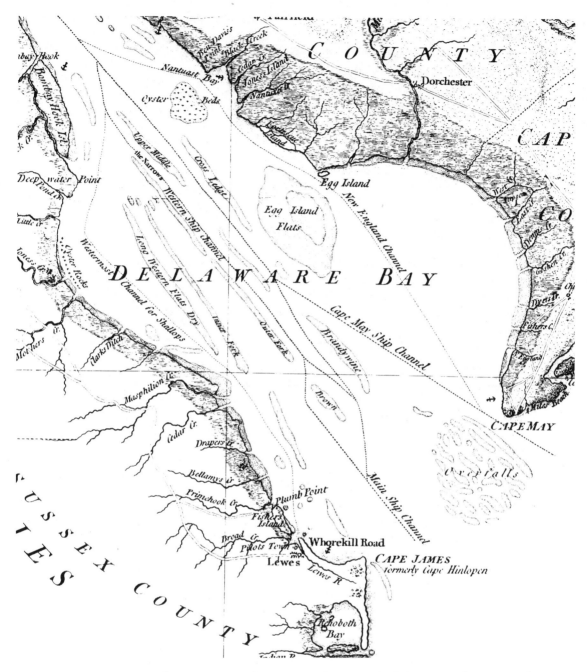

Detail from William Faden's *The province of New Jersey Divided into East and West, commonly called The Jerseys,* 1777, showing the myriad channels and shoals that complicated the mission of Royal Navy blockaders during the early days of the American Revolution (U.S. Naval History Division, *The American Revolution, 1775–1783: An Atlas of the 18th Century Maps and Charts; Theaters of Operation*)

Philadelphia in ballast when taken. Like *Dove* before her, she had no valuable cargo aboard and was of no use to Hamond; she was scuttled soon afterward.[18]

Not all of the losses incurred during the opening days of the blockade were American. While *Roebuck* was chasing the rebel warship, Lieutenant Ball was having his own problems. In the dark of morning on March 29, his steersman fell asleep at the helm and the schooner ran upon a shoal near Cape Henlopen. Ball, the pilot, and two sailors managed to escape and make it safely ashore. All were taken prisoner by American military forces, which then descended on the wreck and stripped it of all items of value, including ten muskets and five pistols thrown overboard by the crew.[19]

With the Royal Navy's blockade (if not control) of the bay now a hard fact, the potential danger of a British offensive operation against Lewes, or more likely Philadelphia, was uppermost in everyone's mind. Nearly every American militia unit within a twenty-five-mile radius of Cape Henlopen was summoned to the little port of Lewes. By April 1 nearly a thousand men had come in, with every one of them wondering what the enemy's next move might be.[20]

The cruiser and her little consorts continued their aggressive depredations unimpeded. A sloop named *Betsey,* from Chincoteague for Philadelphia with oats and tobacco, was the next to fall victim. Taken by *Maria,* she was hauled alongside *Roebuck* and sunk.[21]

Though many chases proved fruitless, sightings of American warships continued to increase. On Sunday, March 31, *Roebuck* chased the Continental brig *Lexington,* commanded by Captain John Barry, but was given the slip when the American boldly ran across the Overfalls Shoal to escape.[22] On April 5, the schooner *Sally* (Seymour Hood, master; E. Batcheler, owner, from Ocracoke, North Carolina, to Philadelphia with pitch tar and turpentine) was taken and relieved of her cargo as rebel warships watched from across the bay. The prize was promptly scuttled off Cape Henlopen. Her master and a passenger were set ashore in their own boat the next day.[23]

News of the blockade spread quickly. Undeterred, many outward-bound vessels took precautions to avoid capture by hanging in close to the dangerous shoals where the deep-draft *Roebuck* dare not go. As spring arrived at Philadelphia, now the political hub of the rebellion and the focal point of enormous maritime and naval activity, four strong privateers or warships were reported under construction "and will in a few days sail on a cruize to intercept the transports expected to arrive in America from England." From time to time, blockade-runners that had eluded *Roebuck* and her tenders would arrive in port bearing powder and other military stores. Their accounts of close calls and near captures thrilled newspaper readers. When two blockade-runners from Curaçao arrived with military stores on April 5, their tales of a hair-raising escape raced about the city. "They were chaced on their passage," it was reported, "by an English frigate which was once so near one of them, that she fired a bow-chace gun at her, and killed a negroe man who was at the helm, but the wind dying away, and dark coming on, the sloops altered their course, when the King's ship lost sight of them."[24]

Another narrow getaway occurred when a schooner was observed trying to slip by the blockaders by hugging the Henlopen shore. The vessel was called *Farmer,* and she had been dispatched several weeks earlier by the Council of Safety of Sussex County, Delaware, to procure a supply of gunpowder in the West Indies.

The outbound voyage of *Farmer* was apparently undertaken without incident. Her commander, Captain Nehemiah Field, had successfully managed to obtain a substantial stock of gunpowder at Dutch-owned St. Eustatia and promptly sailed for the Delaware to complete his mission. The day of *Farmer's* return, Saturday, April 6, had been blessed with moderate weather perforated by occasional small showers. HMS *Roebuck* and *Maria* had, as usual, been maintaining a vigilant lookout for blockade-runners off Delaware Bay.[25]

About midday, Hamond dispatched *Maria* on a routine pursuit of a vessel discovered within the Hen and Chickens Shoal. The chase proved to be *Farmer,* which somehow managed to elude her pursuers by doubling back out to sea. At daybreak on Sunday, Captain Field once more tried approaching Delaware Bay, again from the south. As before, *Roebuck* spotted his ship off Cape Henlopen Lighthouse. On being discovered, the "small schooner," as she was described, quickly attempted to run ashore to prevent capture and to save her cargo.[26]

Captain Charles Pope of the Delaware Continental Battalion, commander of American forces stationed at Lewes, soon afterward provided the following report on the battle to save *Farmer* and her all-important cargo: "On Sunday the seventh of April," he wrote, "an express came from the light-house guard to Lewes, with intelligence that Captain Field, who commanded a schooner sent by the Council of that county to St. Eustatia for powder, had just arrived, and demanded assistance to unload her. I gave orders for the troops to march as soon as boats could be had to ferry them across the [Lewestown] creek, which the inhabitants procured with amazing despatch. We then marched with the utmost expedition to reinforce our guard, which had taken post by the schooner to assist in discharging her cargo, mostly coarse linens; she then lay seven or eight miles to the southward of our Cape; at the time of our arrival, the tender [*Maria*], making sail, bore down upon the schooner, on observing this the men immediately ran her on shore."[27]

Though Pope's troopers had been marching double time at the rate of seven miles per hour to reach the schooner before the enemy's tender arrived, the effort proved to be in vain. Just before their arrival, the tender had taken up a position off the shore to welcome them with a barrage of swivel gun and musket fire, which was returned with interest. The firefight continued without letup by either side until the Americans perceived the enemy to be lying too far away for either side to do any damage. The American firing subsided though the British continued for several hundred more rounds, albeit without effect. In the meantime, some of Pope's men proceeded to unload the schooner while others amused themselves by picking up the enemy's cannonballs as they struck and rolled across the beach.[28]

Not amused by the rebel braggadocio, *Maria's* skipper dispatched a barge to secure assistance from *Roebuck,* then lying to the north of the cape. Soon, the great ship was under way, but was obliged to come to anchor outside of the Hen and Chickens, too far from the action to be of any help. "About the time the ship [*Roebuck*] turned the cape," Pope later reported, "the tender anchored within musket shot of the schooner [*Farmer*], and kept up a continual fire with her swivels. We had by this time got two swivels in the schooner loaded with grape shot, and a constant fire for two hours was kept up on both sides. We undoubtedly wounded their men, for we perceived some to fall, and others ran to their assistance; they made several efforts to purchase their anchor, which we prevented by our fire, but at last they succeeded; fortunately however one of our swivel shot cut their halyards, and down came their mainsail, which obliged them to anchor once more. At last the wind shifting, they had a boat to tow them off; we then turned our fire on the boat, when two men were seen to fall; the barge returning from the ship joined to tow them out. Our men escaped unhurt. The militia officers, at Lewes, acted with a spirit which does honor to their county."[29]

Soon after the fight to salvage the stranded blockade-runner *Roebuck* gave chase to another strange sail that proved to be the *Lord Howe* tender from Virginia. The new arrival bore only the grim news of a successful American naval raid on New Providence in the Bahamas. The attack had been conducted by a fleet fitted out at Philadelphia (which had sailed well before *Roebuck*'s arrival on the Delaware), and was expected to be returning to that port at any time. Coming close on the heels of the costly effort to seize *Farmer*, the new intelligence cannot have been well received. Nevertheless, Hamond immediately took care to place his ship in the best manner he could to intercept the American squadron "by cruizing all day within sight of the Light House, and lying close to it in the Night."[30]

Having lost at least four men to the rebels, and anticipating additional losses, Hamond took the opportunity of *Lord Howe*'s entrance upon the scene to strengthen his own ship's company by stripping the newly arrived tender of men. Then, "thinking it unsafe to trust my people and ammunition any longer in a vessel that can neither Sail, or is properly equiped for War," he ordered her dismantled and sent back in the company of *Maria* to join Lord Dunmore on the Chesapeake.[31]

As *Roebuck* single-handedly maintained the blockade of the Delaware capes, Vice Admiral Molyneux Shuldham had taken over at Halifax as senior commander on the station. On April 11 the admiral drafted explicit instructions to Hamond regarding a recent Act of Parliament ponderously entitled "To Prohibit all Trade and intercourse with the several Colonies in North America therein named during the continuance of the present rebellion within the said Colonies," which basically reiterated previous directives while adding some missions. The captain was therein instructed to seize all vessels belonging to or trading with the colonies, especially those containing military cargoes, and send them to Halifax. As the rebels were endeavoring to arm and provision both an army and a fleet, the captain was again directed "to do your utmost to Take, Sink, Burn or destroy these Pirates wherever they can be found." Moreover, he was ordered to stop all vessels and inspect them for correspondence or other communications aiding, abetting, or otherwise furthering the rebellion. The act even went so far as to order that any ships found ballasted with flint stones, which might be used to produce musket flints, were to have the ballast thrown into the sea.[32]

Hamond was buoyed to learn that Shuldham was sending him a reinforcement and specific instructions on his mission but dismayed to find the former would be minimal, owing to the need to provide convoy escorts and ships for campaigns elsewhere.[33] It was evident that the day-to-day activity of the blockader was now going to be constantly tested by rebels willing to try every trick in the book to elude capture.

On April 11 a merchantman called *Chance* was observed coming down the Delaware from Philadelphia. "She did all she could to avoid me," Hamond later reported, "by going out at the Cape May Channel where I could not follow her, but as soon as I saw she was fairly out, I gave chace to her and come up with her." The master, Thomas Rose, immediately produced an English register and declared that his ship, bearing a cargo of flax and staves, belonged to a merchant in London. The cargo, he claimed, was a remittance for payment of debts and was legally shipped agreeable to an Act of Parliament of the previous December. Hamond at first believed the story, but upon examining the papers of a passenger named Graham, he discovered proof that the ship and cargo were the property of Mr. Joseph Carson of Philadelphia, "an Active Man in the Rebellion" and one destined to become one of the leading privateering speculators in all of Pennsylvania. The ship, which was bound for Cork, Hamond then learned, had recently imported a considerable cargo of powder and arms from Holland. He manned her with a prize crew of seven and sent her to Halifax to be tried and condemned in Admiralty Court.[34]

Two days and several unsuccessful pursuits after the *Chance* capture, Hamond spotted the Continental schooner *Wasp* escorting a sloop and three other vessels through Cape May Channel. He ordered up a chase, but to no avail. Had the hunt been successful, the captain would have had a prize indeed, for onboard the sloop was Congress's own Silas Deane, bound for Europe as one of America's first ministers to the Court of France, with requests for military stores.[35] Though *Wasp* escaped, patriot forces knew that the pressure was on. There were, the American press reported, "so many tenders cruising upon the coast, and the caitiffs on board so very vigilant since the proclamation came over directing the distribution of prizes, that it is almost impossible for any vessel to escape them."[36]

If the blockade was causing duress on American shipping, the patriot forces of Delaware were determined to make blockade duty for the enemy as difficult as possible. By the middle of April, at any given time, between fifty and one hundred·men were on duty day and night between the lighthouse and at the mouth of Lewestown Creek. When the British sought permission to be allowed to fish off the local shore, presumably within range of American guns, the rebels refused them and suggested that they could go to Newfoundland for their fish.[37] Nevertheless, Hamond persisted in his stringent command of egress into and out of the bay. The cat-and-mouse game between blockader and blockade-runner continued unabated.

On April 22 two sloops and two schooners, guided by a pilot boat, were observed coming down the bay steering for Cape May Channel. With *Roebuck* lying in Lewes Roads and knowing he could do little even if he could reach the shallow water passage in time, Hamond decided to allow the rebels to pass out of the channel. He might then give chase in the open Atlantic where there was a fair prospect of success. The Americans pressed on into the open ocean with a westerly wind at their backs. After a spirited chase of twelve leagues and an hour-long bombardment, *Roebuck* first overtook the schooner *Dolphin* (William Knox, master; John Pringle, owner; bound for St. Eustatia with hams and bread) and sent her to Virginia. He then took the pilot boat belonging to one John Baldwin. With night coming on, however, he was obliged to give up pursuit of the other three vessels. Much to his dismay he learned from prisoners that the two sloops had been the Philadelphia privateers *Congress* and *Chance,* armed with four-pounders and thirty men each. Although he could not have known it, they were the first two American privateers to receive commissions and instructions under congressional resolutions passed on March 23 and April 3, 1776. They would cause enormous havoc to British shipping during their short but meteoric careers.[38]

The following night *Roebuck* intercepted a Danish brig from St. Croix bound for Philadelphia allegedly to pick up children and families belonging to several Englishmen who had settled upon the island. Hamond, being suspicious that it was little more than a trick to carry on a correspondence with the rebels, ordered the admittedly neutral vessel seized. Finding the brig "not of the least value," he released her and sent her back to St. Croix "to inform the Governor, that no regard would be payed to any of his papers, let the pretence be what it would; and if he persisted in sending any more Vessels to the continent under the authority of his Government, it would be looked upon as a breach of neutrality." Tiny Denmark, neutral or not, posed little military or naval threat to Great Britain, yet such threats to convention by the Royal Navy would soon become the order of the day. After all, by the last week in April, there were no fewer than forty-six British men-of-war, not including armed tenders, operating on the American Station.[39]

Being but a single vessel assigned to patrol such a large area, *Roebuck* soon found herself being challenged time and again by the smaller, faster, and lighter-draft American sloops and schooners. Most had learned to hug the inside of Cape May Channel, which was proving too shoal for the hulking blockader to swim in. Time and again Hamond was frustrated by his lack of a small sloop or two to block such avenues. Moreover, he had received recent intelligence concerning a possible attack by American warships, indeed a whole fleet, being fitted out by Pennsylvania inside the capes. The rebels hoped either to assail him or, even more disconcerting, to escape into the Atlantic to capture British or loyalist shipping.[40]

Some help was on the way. On April 27 Vice Admiral Shuldham, as promised, ordered HMS *Orpheus,* 32, Captain Charles Hudson commanding, to cruise between the west end of Long Island and Cape Henlopen to relieve some of the pressure on Hamond.[41] In the meantime, *Roebuck* was still on her own, albeit with a small tender that had been taken into service to aid her.

The same day Shuldham was writing out his orders to Hudson, *Roebuck* was dragging for an anchor she had lost two miles northeast of the lighthouse. About 2:00 P.M., all efforts were abandoned when a small schooner was observed standing up the bay. Hamond ordered two boats manned and armed and sent after her; he then made sail after them to provide support. An hour later another schooner appeared, and Hamond promptly took up pursuit, leaving the small boats to fend for themselves. The vessel proved to be none other than the elusive Continental schooner *Wasp*. The chase was on. Two hours later, while still in hot pursuit east of Brandywine Shoal, *Roebuck*'s leadsman reported the water shoaling up fast. Suddenly the big warship missed stays and found herself hard aground on the lower end of the shoals. At that moment, the small boats returned with their prize, a pilot boat schooner called *Ranger*, Captain John Hunt master, from St. Eustatia for Philadelphia laden with coarse linens and arms for the rebels. Her crew, who made their escape in a skiff during "a stark calm," had totally abandoned her. Impressed with the speed and maneuverability of the Delaware pilot boat, Hamond adopted the new prize as a tender but retained the name *Ranger*.[42]

*Roebuck*'s commander was deeply concerned about his precarious position, stranded and alone on a shoal in the heart of enemy-infested waters. He immediately dispatched his tenders to Virginia to secure assistance "in case I could not get the Ship off." At four o'clock the next morning, however, the tide lifted her without any apparent damage, and she sailed for Old Hoar Kill Roads. Then she stuck fast once more, but aided by an east wind and by temporarily lightening the ship of cannons, she was again able to get off.[43]

Rebel shipping, awaiting a chance to escape from the Delaware, capitalized on *Roebuck*'s brief absence. On the morning of April 28, reported Henry Fisher, "there is to be seen a Brig[an]tine, two Schooners, two Sloops, the French Tartan & one Pilot Boat, all going down under Cape May, out of Reach of the *Roe-Bucks* horns."[44]

News of *Roebuck*'s first grounding—but not her escape—reached Philadelphia on April 29, and the Pennsylvania Committee of Safety, believing her to be helplessly stranded, moved instantly to seize the opportunity to destroy her once and for all. At 11:00 A.M. an order was issued to Captain Thomas Read, commander of the infant Pennsylvania State Navy's armed warship *Montgomery*, to proceed down the river and bay and join eight row galleys belonging to the state navy under Commodore Andrew Caldwell and the Continental Navy warship *Reprisal*. The commodore, however, had already reconnoitered the Brandywine Shoal and discovered *Roebuck*'s escape, and the expedition was promptly called off.[45]

*Roebuck* continued her role as the hungry, stalking wolf, diligent and dangerous. At daybreak on April 30, accompanied by John Baldwin's recently captured pilot boat, she breakfasted on an unidentified schooner. The prey was chased and driven ashore near the False Capes. With high surf running, the schooner, later identified as belonging to the firm of King and Harper of Philadelphia and bound in from Hispaniola, was completely beaten to pieces in but a short time. The cargo, with the exception of some molasses, was saved.[46]

Later in the morning, near the Hen and Chickens, *Roebuck* pursued yet another vessel, an inward-bound sloop, but was stymied by the onset of a sudden fog. Hamond nevertheless armed *Ranger* and sent her off in pursuit. The sloop was run ashore by her crew to escape capture. Then, discovering yet another ship to leeward, the British took up a third pursuit. This time, the chase proved to be the king's ship *Fowey,* a sixth-rate vessel of twenty-four guns, Captain George Montagu commanding, bearing dispatches and orders from Admiral Shuldham. In the meantime, as the fog dissipated, the sloop that had run ashore had gotten off and, seeing the two warships and tenders together, erroneously—and fatally—concluded that they were part of Commodore Esek Hopkins's Continental squadron, which had recently sacked New Providence in the Bahamas. She made a signal to speak with *Ranger.* Immediately discerning the American's actions to be nurtured by mistaken identity, Hamond hoisted false colors and bore away to anchor in Henlopen Roads to decoy the sloop in. The ruse worked. The victim, named *Little John* (J. Darrel master, Davenport & Co. owners) was taken without further adieu. The new prize had recently sailed from Bermuda for Philadelphia laden with salt, limes, molasses, and rum. The master informed Hamond that "as he had heard that Admiral Hopkins [ship] had lower Deck Ports," he had assumed *Roebuck* to be him.[47]

Finding *Little John* to be well fitted and promising to be a fast-sailing vessel, Hamond renamed her *Pembroke* and placed a midshipman and fifteen seamen aboard. After arming the new addition to his little squadron with four three-pounders and an equal number of swivels, he sent her off on a cruise in company with *Ranger* "for the more effectual annoying the Enemy."[48] The captain's blockade seemed to be growing in strength by the hour, with *Roebuck, Fowey,* two sloops, and a pilot boat working hard to seal off the Delaware. Yet even more power was en route, for on April 30, having received Hamond's request sent to Virginia for assistance, HMS *Liverpool,* Captain Henry Bellew commanding, set sail from Hampton Roads bound for Cape Henlopen.[49]

On the morning of May 2, *Ranger* and *Pembroke* returned with yet another new prize, the schooner *Dolphin* (T. Woodhouse, master; Henry Cowper, owner; bound from Philadelphia for St. Croix with flour, bread, and staves). That same afternoon, *Liverpool* arrived from Virginia and *Fowey,* in desperate need of refitting, was ordered to take her place on the Chesapeake and make repairs. Two days later, Hamond was further reinforced by the armed brig *Betsey* from Norfolk, Thomas Slater master, which had been sent up by Dunmore at the captain's request.[50]

Despite the increased number of British cruisers off the Delaware, rebel blockade-runners continued to slip through the net. A schooner from St. Eustatia easily sidestepped into Indian River Inlet, and another laden with gunpowder from the same place sent ashore for a pilot to do the same.[51]

Hamond continued to fret over his inability to cover all critical points. On May 4 he wrote to Major General Henry Clinton in New York, informing him of his difficult position. He was unhappy with the news that he was only getting one permanent warship to assist him on the Delaware. As for clearing a passage up the Delaware to Philadelphia, without a body of troops at his disposal, such a move was out of the question, and he saw no benefit to it except for a chance to bombard the city. It was his belief that maintaining a blockade of the Delaware to cut off navigation was more useful, but the navy was already spread far too thin, owing to the imminent peril to Virginia and Lord Dunmore's forces. The departure of *Fowey* from the Delaware would hurt, especially as it had been learned, much to everyone's dismay, that the rebels in Pennsylvania were at that minute fitting out more privateers and regular warships. Not only would they be able to contest the Royal Navy for control of the river, many more ships were likely to escape into the open Atlantic. He warned that "unless we get more Small Vessels [they] will do mischief among our Scattered Transports &c." expected to be arriving with troops from Europe.[52]

Drinking water aboard *Roebuck* began to fall short, her casks having been lightened to reduce her draft. On May 5 Hamond decided to hazard a foraging expedition up the river to replenish his empty casks and reconnoiter enemy strong points and naval defenses. With *Liverpool* and three tenders in company, he conducted the first aggressive British foray of the war into the Delaware. It would not be the last.[53]

With the east-southeast wind blowing fresh, and the three tenders taking soundings in advance of the two great warships, the procession was instantly observed at Lewes by coast-watcher Henry Fisher. The alarm soon spread. By 11:00 P.M. the British, already in sight off Reedy Island, had come to anchor for the night a little below Bombay Hook. The citizens of nearby Port Penn, expecting an immediate attack, were terrified and prayed for assistance from upriver. The city of Philadelphia, however, was already mobilizing defenses while the now-substantial Pennsylvania State Navy river fleet was being hurriedly manned and armed.[54]

With celerity the Pennsylvania Committee of Safety ordered Captain Thomas Read, now acting commander of the state navy in the flagship *Montgomery,* to take thirteen armed row galleys, a fire ship, and some small boats down the river "to attack, take, sink, destroy, or drive off" the oncoming British. The next morning Hamond's squadron, unaware of the forces gathering to oppose it, pressed slowly and cautiously up the river. Late in the afternoon, *Liverpool* dispatched her cutter to bring off a sloop sighted near the shore but, finding it "impracticable" to do so, set her afire. Then, at 8:00 P.M., they came to anchor off Morris Listons. Everyone knew that the next day's advance would probably result in some form of action, although neither Hamond nor his officers much feared the American galley fleet.[55]

The cloudy morning of May 7 introduced itself to the Delaware with spring rains and a fresh gale blowing. As the British squadron approached New Castle, *Roebuck* again sighted and gave chase to several rebel ships, including the elusive Continental schooner *Wasp,* now with Captain Charles Alexander commanding, but in vain. About 1:00 P.M., off Christiana River, Hamond fired at a schooner that promptly ran aground trying to escape into the little waterway and was then abandoned by her crew. Two hours later, in company with the squadron, he ordered his ship to anchor off the creek and sent boats, manned and armed, to get the schooner off. Unable to do so, they proceeded to unload her cargo of bread and flour. Off New Castle, Hamond considered foraging in the town, but he observed through a spyglass many carts carrying off goods and all of the windows and doors closed and shuttered. Not a wisp of smoke issued from a single chimney. With the town being abandoned, the pickings would be minimal. At that very moment, the Pennsylvania State Navy and several ships of the Continental Navy were setting sail from Marcus Hook to do battle the next day.[56] Hamond came to anchor off the mouth of the Christiana that evening to await them.

The following morning was ushered in with fair breezes and a fine haze that later turned to a dead calm and fog that would not clear before midday. Shortly after noon, Hamond sighted the American galley fleet, commanded by Captain Henry Dougherty, descending the Delaware. "It was a fine day," recorded one of thousands of eyewitnesses, "and the banks of the river, out of reach of the shot, were lined with spectators, and every house near the shore filled."[57]

The battle commenced. "We met them under Sail (as the Tide ran too rapid to lie with a Spring upon the Cable)," Hamond later reported, "and being obliged to engage them at a distance they chose to fix on, which was scarcely within point blank shot." The galleys, which were dispersed in the shallows where the British could not venture, were careful not to approach any closer than a mile and, "being such low objects on the water," proved difficult targets. Moreover, they were intentionally stationed in such a manner that the flotilla was never fully engaged at any given time. This was done to prevent a well-directed British broadside from destroying many of them at once. For the next two hours the two squadrons exchanged a heavy fire. Finally the American fleet, having expended much of its precious ammunition, was forced to retire into shoal water, though with only one galley having been struck and one man killed. The British, however, suffered the loss of the brig *Betsey,* which was captured by *Wasp* in a bold foray while *Roebuck* was otherwise engaged.[58]

Unfortunately for Hamond, just as the Americans were retiring, *Roebuck* ran aground on a soft mud bank in shallow water near Carney's Point, a little above Deep Water Point, and once again found herself immobile and helpless. Observing her distress, *Liverpool* and the tenders came up to provide a screen of protective fire if the Americans returned and to render assistance in getting the flagship off the shoal. Having soon heeled over so far that her gunports had to be closed to prevent flooding, *Roebuck* was again in a most desperate situation. Hamond grew dispirited for the first time in many days. He resolved that if the enemy reappeared, he would have little choice but to transfer his flag to *Liverpool* and abandon and burn his ship to prevent her capture. But that proved unnecessary.[59] The crews of the two great warships struggled desperately well beyond midnight to heave *Roebuck* from the shoal. An anchor and two stream cables were laboriously carried out in small boats in an endeavor to get her off, and three picket boats were kept rowing back and forth throughout the night to prevent surprise attack. In the process the warship's stream anchor and two hawsers were lost, but by 4:00 A.M., May 9, hidden by a thick fog, she was again in her own element, floating free and undamaged.[60]

By 8:00 A.M. the fog had cleared, and Hamond could finally discern the American fleet lying two miles above him. With his resolution revived, he ordered all sails piled on to pursue the enemy gunboats, but the Americans retreated under sails and oars toward the western shore. With the tide ebbing and less than six inches of water between *Roebuck*'s keel and the bottom "in the best ship channel . . . which was not a quarter of a mile wide," Hamond had little choice but to call off the chase and come to anchor. As the Americans seemed unwilling to be drawn into combat, and with the British having an insufficient force to pass the rebel gunboats, heavy shore batteries, and submerged obstructions discovered in the waterway ahead, the two British commanders decided to retire farther downriver. Hamond later suggested that he had reasoned from that vantage point they might lure the Americans down to destroy them in waters where the big warships could more readily maneuver.[61]

At 2:00 A.M. the British commander again observed the enemy fleet, now increased to twenty-two sail, descending like a swarm of angry bees. The Americans, though inexperienced and somewhat deficient in ammunition, with barely a forty-five-round allowance remaining per vessel, seemed rejuvenated and eager to reengage. Between 4:30 and 5:00, Hamond and Bellew again weighed anchor and turned south "under an easey sail" in hopes, they later claimed, of drawing the rebels farther down into open waters where the British would have the sailing advantage. As hoped, the American flotilla, led by the galley *Warren,* Captain Thomas Houston commanding, immediately followed, albeit remaining at a safe distance and always keeping to shoally waters.[62]

At a range of three-quarters of a mile, the galleys again opened "a smart fire." This time the American shooting was well directed and continued for the next four hours with great effect. *Liverpool* immediately suffered several shots through her sails and hull, and one in the bowsprit, while *Roebuck* was struck repeatedly between wind and water. Hamond later claimed that he was forced to return fire not only against the rebel fleet but also against forces ashore, and he ordered several of his guns to respond with round and grapeshot. Again and again *Roebuck* was struck. Several cannonballs passed clearly through the ship, some in her quarter. On several occasions she was raked fore and aft. One shot caromed lengthwise along the deck, destroying everything in its path. Another eighteen-pound ball lodged in her side barely three strakes above the water's edge, with yet another on the opposite side nearly as low. Still another passed through an upper port, destroyed a gun carriage, and dismounted a nine-pounder, wounding two men and killing another by ripping his arm off. Then six men were injured by a powder cartridge explosion, two quite seriously and others by splinters. The rigging, sails, and spars, particularly several mizzen and foretopmast shrouds, were struck frequently and cut to pieces or injured. The longboat, which had been damaged in the first fight, was now entirely out of commission. Attesting to the rebels' accuracy, the carpenters later reported, after nearly a week's worth of repairs and plugging holes, that no fewer than forty enemy cannonballs would have to be removed from *Roebuck*'s hull, and there were some that could not be removed at all.[63]

At 10:00 P.M., as neither side had visibly gained an advantage, the firing finally ceased, and the American fleet turned in to New Castle. Despite his ship's injuries, Hamond then ordered the squadron to drop down to the vicinity of Reedy Island "in hopes to draw them [the Americans] down the River." In truth, however, the British had had enough. Though Hamond spotted eleven enemy sail lingering in the vicinity the next morning, the galley fleet, now quite short of ammunition after having expended seven tons of powder, could not be brought to action. It seemed doubtful that either side was eager to reengage.[64]

For the next three days, Hamond and Bellew would occupy their crews in making repairs to their ship and refilling water casks. The Americans, who in the two engagements had suffered only two or three wounded but considerable damage to their vessels, continued to maintain their stations. On May 11 the rebel fleet commanders convened a council of war and determined that until ammunition was brought down they would initiate no further aggressive action but remain where they were.[65]

Not surprisingly, the Americans took great heart in the retreat of the British squadron that had been devastating trade. The blockaders, in the eyes of such leading Americans as John Adams, had clearly come off second best and had "diminished, in the minds of the People, on both sides of the River, the Terror of Men of War." The Americans had held the field, and the British had retired. Hamond, of course, provided a different view for the record, stating his satisfaction that the enemy had expended so much precious powder and shot, obtained with so much difficulty "to so little purpose." Neither he nor Bellew saw much value in pressing on upriver. They had tested the Americans' resolution and defenses and found them substantial. On May 15 they arrived in the roads off Lewes the worse for wear and a bit wiser.[66]

The American defense effort most certainly had some effect. Soon after returning to the anchorage, Hamond made a significant decision. "Being now confirmed in my opinion that nothing could be done in the River Delaware without more Ships, a Bomb vessel, and a body of Troops to act with them, I im[m]ediately turned my thoughts toward the expedition going on to the Southw[ar]d and accordingly took resolution of leaving the *Liverpool* to cruize off the Capes to intercept the Trade of Philadelphia, and to proceed with *Roebuck* to join Sir Peter Parker [off Charleston]." The following day, *Roebuck* sailed, leaving Bellew with orders to join him in Hampton Roads when he needed provisions and water but to maintain the blockade until then.[67]

Thus ended HMS *Roebuck*'s first devastating blockade of the Delaware during the American Revolution, a largely solo performance that had resulted in innumerable chases, captures, firefights, several large engagements, and no fewer than a dozen American vessels sent to the bottom. The British would continue the blockade off and on throughout the war. In January 1777, *Roebuck* herself would again return to her old hunting grounds off the Delaware, the first of several visits, to resume her vigil. In the spring of that year she would participate in one of the most dramatic pursuits and destruction of an American vessel in the war, and then in the bitterly contested battle for control of the Delaware itself.

# 4

## A Column of Liquid Fire

It was a blustery, freezing night in December 1775 when Captain William Rhodes, master of the merchant sloop *Victory,* arrived at Providence, Rhode Island, accompanied by two mysterious French gentlemen who had taken passage with him from the West Indies. At the time, the attentions of all New England, in fact all of America, were keenly focused on the drama unfolding around the nearby Port of Boston. Ever since March 19, when Massachusetts's citizen soldiers had openly engaged in armed insurrection against the Crown at Lexington and Concord, a rag-tag rebel force that some said would never hold together had been besieging a British army. The revolt had electrified America and Europe even as the Western world slowly began choosing sides. On August 23, King George III had declared all of his American colonies except Canada to be in a state of rebellion and sedition, and New England had seen nothing but blood and fire ever since. British ships had ruthlessly bombarded Stonington, Connecticut, and Bristol, Rhode Island. Employing Newport, Rhode Island, as a base, they had recently begun marauding attacks all around the islets and shores of Narragansett Bay. The raids, ironically, had the reverse effect of reducing loyalist support in the area to the point of near extinction.

Miraculously, a formal siege of Boston had somehow been maintained under the steadfast direction of a tall Virginian named George Washington, but only with the greatest of difficulty. Washington's army of volunteers, barely five thousand men strong, was lacking in every necessary—food, clothing, blankets, guns, munitions, money, but most of all in discipline. His troops were a mélange of independent-minded and untrained men who were prone to leave at a moment's notice at the slightest provocation or implied insult. On the night of Captain Rhodes's arrival at Providence, December 10, the entire Connecticut contingent of the army, whose short-term enlistments had just expired, was already preparing to depart for home. The siege, and possibly the entire rebellion itself, was in jeopardy of collapse. But Captain Rhodes's two mysterious passengers were about to help change all of that.

The day after *Victory*'s arrival, Rhodes introduced the pair of foreigners to Nicholas Brown, one of the province's leading merchants and an ardent supporter of the insurrection. The two Frenchmen, neither of whom spoke a word of English but conversed in only their native tongue or Latin, presented them-selves as Messrs. Emanuel Michael Pliarne, the king of France's armorer at Cape St. François, and Pierre Penet of Paris. Neither offered credentials, but Rhodes, who had learned of their intentions while carrying their secret cargo from the West Indies, vouched for each.[1]

The two strangers had heard of Brown's trading firm, Nicholas & John Brown Co., and were well apprised of its reputation and prominent connections with the rebel cause. They had come, they said, to establish a link between their own company and a solid American trading partner such as his. The unexpected ar-rival of foreign merchants wanting to form business ties, in itself, was not un-usual. What seduced Brown was the commodities in which they wanted to trade. Their objective, he quickly discerned, was to sell military supplies, in par-ticular gunpowder, twenty tons of which they had brought with them as an en-trée for ready distribution to the American insurrectionists. Moreover, they brazenly stated that they could and would supply the entire continent, if re-quired, with whatever was wanted, be it arms, powder, saltpeter, clothing, or any other goods required to promulgate the war of rebellion. Brown must have also been pleasantly surprised when his guests informed him that they would like to meet with General Washington to secure his personal recommendation for them to the Continental Congress. Brown, who might also profit from such an unexpected relationship, admired their panache and readily agreed to serve as matchmaker.[2]

Being a man of caution, however, Brown quickly consulted that same night with several learned and trusted colleagues, who declared that the two strangers "seem sensible." He then eagerly reengaged his two guests in a discussion regard-ing the proposed business at hand and precisely how he might serve as a middle-man in future trading arrangements. Though cash in the colonies was, and always had been, in short supply, he was able, he said, to send spermaceti candles, whale oil, tobacco, and a variety of provisions and products that would serve as com-modities for trade to either the French West Indies or directly to France and re-ceive in return gunpowder and other war materiel from France or Spain. He would even provide the vessels. The risks, of course, would be enormous, but the benefits to the cause and, of course, the potential for huge profits were worth it.[3]

That such trade with neutral countries would be deemed as contraband and illegal by Great Britain, which considered the revolt by its colonies as an internal affair, and perhaps might even be viewed by the British as a casus belli against France and Spain, was not even mentioned. The two Frenchmen informed Brown that once a contract had been agreed upon, Penet would be taking up res-idence in America to open a trading establishment while Pliarne would sail to Nantes, France, to manage the European arm of operations. All they needed was an audience with the general and a letter of introduction from him to Congress to get the ball rolling. Brown was eager to provide the push.[4]

The following day, thanks to the merchant's personal intercession, Penet and Pliarne were granted an audience with Governor Nicholas Cooke of Rhode Is-land. The governor was impressed enough to provide them with a letter of intro-duction to General Washington. Three days later, on December 14, they arrived at the American encampment at Cambridge "leading a large convoy" of vehicles laden with the much-needed gunpowder. The conspicuous display produced the desired effect on both Washington and his troops. Though in great need of every necessary of war to conduct his siege, especially gunpowder, the general characteristically demurred from entering any form of contract on his own but accepted the gunpowder anyway. Claiming ignorance regarding the Continental assembly's plans for securing additional war supplies for his dwindling forces, he suggested—as they hoped he would—that the two Frenchmen visit Congress in person. He then personally prevailed on Governors Cooke of Rhode Island and Trumbull of Connecticut to provide them carriage to Philadelphia at the public expense. The general quickly penned a letter of introduction to John Hancock, president of Congress, informing him of their objectives. In their behalf Cooke also dispatched an express to alert the Rhode Island delegates to Congress, noting: "They [Penet and Pliarne] appear to be Persons of some Consequence, and I hope may be useful in beginning a Negociation with the Court of France for Assistance, which I look upon as a most important Object." He also wrote to Hancock: "I hope their Visit to North America will be an Introduction to such Measures as may be attended with happy Consequences to the United Colonies." It was everything the two Frenchmen, who had appeared on the scene entirely without warning or credentials other than the actual gunpowder they brought with them, had hoped for—and more.[5]

On December 29, Penet and Pliarne arrived in Philadelphia and formally presented themselves the following evening to Congress. The assembly was taken entirely by surprise, for here unexpectedly at its very door were two agents of a foreign firm, possibly even of the French government itself as some suspected, bearing letters of introduction from Washington and eager to establish a commercial relationship that would provide all the arms, munitions, and supplies needed for the war effort. It seemed too good to be true, for their arrival could not have come at a better time. Only a month earlier, Congress had formed the Secret Committee of Correspondence to establish foreign ties and support. Now, uncharacteristically, the assembly acted immediately. A resolution was passed "That the same [letters of introduction] be referred to the Secret Committee, who are directed to confer with the bearers, and pursue such measures as they may think proper for the interest of the United Colonies." The following afternoon the two Frenchmen met behind closed doors with two members of the committee, Silas Deane and Samuel Ward.[6]

Thus began one of the most covert operations of the American Revolution, one filled with spies, intrigue, and danger. It was also one destined to end in perhaps one of the worst wartime marine disasters in the early history of the Delmarva coast.

The fires of rebellion had burned brightly in English North America during the summer of 1775, but procuring and paying for the necessary hardware for Americans to fight one of the mightiest military powers on the planet had been a contentious issue from the beginning. Like Congress itself, the Revolution was a work in progress. On September 18, Congress began to firmly, but deliberately, systematize the procurement of military supplies. Among its first initiatives, the Secret Committee had moved to contract for the importation and delivery of five hundred tons of gunpowder, cannons, and musket locks, and ten thousand stand of arms. To do so, however, required Congress to grant the committee wide discretionary authority and permission to draw on large funds that it would need to advance to select reliable contractors.[7] As the war intensified, the powers and authority of the committee, whose meetings were always conducted in secret, had grown exponentially. It was soon exporting produce to the West Indies and in return importing supplies of every sort necessary for the promulgation of the revolt. By April 1776 the committee was even authorized to arm and man vessels of war on friendly foreign shores. Soon, its web of commercial ties had begun to penetrate many neutral or friendly European and West Indian ports to the distinct advantage of the common cause.[8]

The cloak of secrecy under which actual field operations were conducted, and the specifics regarding ships and men that carried them out was exceptionally thick. With America lacking every industry necessary to provide war materiel, the task of keeping Washington's army and the infant Continental Navy armed, provisioned, and healthy with goods imported from Europe and the West Indies was enormous. Moreover, for many ships and the men that manned them, running the British blockade of American ports to keep the Revolution going was often as dangerous as any battlefield.

The difficulties often began with the British network of informers and spies in both America and Europe, often supported by the many loyalists who had not succumbed to the invocations of the rebellion. Almost from the beginning, the operations of Penet and Pliarne were known to the Royal Navy. Within a week after their secret presentation to Congress, Captain Hyde Parker, commander of HMS *Phoenix,* then lying at New York, informed Lord Sandwich: "It is certain that the Rebels get at present supplied with Gun powder from the French. A few days since I am well informed two French Men passed through this City in their way to the Continental Congress with passes from Mr Washington the Rebel General at Cambridge, these Men had landed a Cargo of Gun powder to the Eastward, and are supposed to be gone in order to settle for the furnishing of further supplies."[9]

Another Philadelphia informant, Gilbert Barkly, reported on the specifics of the Frenchmen's meeting with Washington and Congress and noted that one of the men would be returning to France, via Holland, to organize the shipments of arms and supplies to the rebels. The other "is to Continue at this place, to negotiate the affairs of that Perfidious Kingdom [France], who great Britain may be assured, watches every opportunity to involve and distress, though at the same time they are Sensible, they are plunging thousands into death and destruction, but this they matter not Provided they carry their diabolical ends."[10]

The two men concluded their clandestine business with the Secret Committee by the first week of February. On the eighth, Penet sailed for Europe while Pliarne commenced setting up shop in Philadelphia, just as Gilbert Barkly had predicted. Within a month of Penet's departure, British agents had learned, much to the Crown's dismay, that the firm's first contract with the United Colonies was "to furnish the Congress with £80,000 Value of military stores of all kinds." Unhappily for the king, the success of their operations was phenomenal. Within a year, the firm would have offices or agents in Baltimore, Alexandria, Charleston, Nantes and Bordeaux, Cape François, St. Domingo, and St. Peter, Martinique, and intimate ties with several congressional agents who also served as integral components of their company's operations.[11]

It mattered little to the Americans that Penet and Pliarne were neither actually agents of the French government as they had implied nor bona fide merchants with a proven record. What mattered most to the Secret Committee was that they could produce the goods, which they did. One of the first orders placed with the firm, of course through the convenient auspices of Nicholas & John Brown, was for "6000 good striped blankets for soldiers, 6000 yards of brown and blue broad cloths for officers uniforms, 800 yards of different colors to face them, 6 tons of lead, 200 stand of arms such as used by French Infantry, 500 good double bridle locks, 50 barrels of 100 lbs of gunpowder." And that was just a start![12]

Before all was said and done, Penet and Pliarne would help supply the American Revolution with the very grist of war, despite the neutrality of their country. Many ships, American vessels chartered by the Secret Committee as well as the firm's own, would arrive at Nantes and depart in utmost secrecy bound for America, laden with guns, powder, and clothing to keep the Revolution alive. Many of the westward-bound ships, owing to their incendiary cargoes, sailed as veritable floating bombs.

The origins and history of one such ship that tempted the fates, a vessel first known as *Success,* is largely cloaked in mystery. The only thing certain about her first employment in the service of Congress was that in the fall of 1776 William Lux, the Continental agent in Baltimore, had chartered her. Her first known mission, under the command of a Captain Hill, was to import 29 barrels, 378 half barrels, and 48 quarter barrels of powder, on the public account of Thomas Mumford.[13]

About the end of October 1776, soon after successfully delivering her initial cargo of powder, *Success* quietly sailed again, this time for France, under the command of Captain James Anderson, an officer as brave as he was resourceful. The voyage, conducted in utmost secrecy, was to be of enormous importance to the cause of independence. With a cargo of tobacco consigned to the Secret Committee's agent at Nantes, Thomas Morris "on Acct. of the Continent," her lading was to be sold to the Nantes branch of Penet and Pliarne & Co.[14] At Nantes she was to take onboard a top-secret cargo of war materials desperately needed by the Continental Army. On October 27, the Secret Committee signed a charter party to *Success*. The subsequent covert voyage to France was carried out without record or apparent incident.[15]

The first intimation of the safe passage of *Success* came on December 13 when Captain Lambert Wickes, who had arrived at Quiberon Bay, France, in command of the Continental warship *Reprisal* (bringing with him Benjamin Franklin and his entourage), reported that the merchantman had recently arrived at

Nantes.[16] After being renamed *Morris,* undoubtedly to confuse British agents, the ex-*Success* prepared to sail for Philadelphia about January 24, 1777, laden with salt and arms for the Continental government.[17] Departure, however, was apparently delayed, as Lord Stormont, the British ambassador to Paris, who was in constant contact with British spies in the countryside and on the coast, reported on February 19, 1777, that the ship was only then on the point of sailing for America. The ambassador also reported in a dispatch to Lord Weymouth that Pierre Penet and Nathan Rumsey, both described as American agents in Nantes, had been employed in fitting out the ship, and another named *Elizabeth and Mary,* at Corrine, nine miles from the city. The British, however, had no idea of just how much or what type of military cargo *Morris* (née *Success*) was to carry or how pivotal to the success of the Continental Army it might prove.[18]

When *Morris* finally sailed for America, her cargo included a number of cannons, 2,500 muskets, gunlocks, 2,100 barrels (35 to 40 tons) of gunpowder, and woolen clothing for the army of General Washington, valued at 250,000 livres (or £50,000), as well as 500 muskets for Maryland and a quantity of private cargo. She also carried top-secret documents from the Continental Commissioners in Paris intended for the Secret Committee of Correspondence.[19]

For obvious reasons, *Morris*'s departure from France and voyage to America were conducted in total secrecy and have left little record. Her arrival on the North American coast in mid-April was something else. During her absence, the British had reestablished a robust blockade, under the direction of Captain Andrew Snape Hamond, commander of HMS *Roebuck,* off the mouth of the Delaware. Its purpose was to cut off the delivery of arms and supplies destined for the revolutionaries. Hamond had returned to the Delaware about April 10 for his third tour of blockade duty there and to relieve an earlier blockade force commanded by Commodore William Hotham. Unlike during the opening days of the Delaware blockade, the new squadron was a strong one and included HMS *Roebuck, Pearl, Camilla,* and other fast and powerful ships that patrolled in several parallel corridors from as far out as twenty-five and fifty leagues and as close in as the shoal lines of the Delaware capes.[20]

On April 11, the day after Hamond had taken command of the blockade, *Morris* arrived beneath the mantle of a morning fog. She was later described by the commander of *Roebuck* only as "a large Merch[an]t Ship" for the details of her appearance, like her history, were entirely unknown. The channel approaches to the bay were heavily guarded and the probability of discovery was high once the fog lifted. To slip through in the mist was imperative. Yet it was not to be. As soon as the first blockader spotted the incoming merchantman, it jumped into action. HMS *Camilla,* Captain John Linzee commanding, was patrolling five or six miles southeast of Cape Henlopen Lighthouse when the fog began to dissipate about 8:00 A.M. Through the mist, Linzee observed a large ship that had anchored to the northward of the lighthouse and fired a gun to bring her to. The mystery ship, seeking escape, ignored the warning and immediately fled. Linzee took up the chase. His quarry, of course, proved to be *Morris.* Her master, determined not to surrender his important cargo, promptly "hoisted rebel Colours," tacked, and about 10:00 A.M. stood directly in for the lighthouse. It was a calculated move by the Americans that was well anticipated by the British, who had become experts in such matters during their long months of blockade duty here and elsewhere. Moreover, they had adapted their deployment to a format not unlike the "wolf pack" tactics employed by German U-boats nearly a century and a half later. *Camilla* first occupied the rebel's attentions, firing several more guns directed at the runner as she sped for the shore.[21]

Captain Anderson managed to briefly escape *Camilla* only to run squarely into *Roebuck*. Captain Hamond had skillfully maneuvered his ship to cut off the fleeing American from gaining the entrance to the bay and was moving in for the kill. Still determined to deny the enemy his ship as a prize, Anderson boldly turned *Morris*'s prow directly toward the shore although by now the chances of escape of any kind must have seemed remote. *Roebuck* was relentless in her pursuit and maintained a constant firing of her broadside in a vain effort to force the merchantman to come to. She soon found herself stymied by the sandy banks of the Hen and Chickens.[22] Despite being heavily outgunned, outmanned, and outsailed, but temporarily protected by the shoals, Anderson returned the fire of his assailants for nearly three hours "in a most brave & gallant manner" while maneuvering his vessel where the big warships dare not go. Not to be denied, *Roebuck* launched three boatloads of men to conduct an all-out boarding operation with sword and pistol. Faced by such overwhelming odds, the end for *Morris* now seemed an almost preordained certainty.[23]

Within a short time, however, Anderson had achieved his goal, and run *Morris* hard ashore at the bow about a mile east-southeast of the Cape Henlopen Lighthouse, on the inside of the Hen and Chickens. Almost as soon as their ship struck, many of her men "run out to the Bowsprit and jumped over Board."[24] Those who made it ashore included the mate and fourteen of the crew. There were also two unidentified Frenchmen who were landed along with a packet of important letters for the Continental Congress.[25] It was now 10:30 A.M., and though *Roebuck* had been unable to close, albeit keeping up a smart fire all the while, *Camilla* finally managed to come up. Captain Linzee had soon dropped his best bower anchor in three fathoms of water and quickly rigged a spring on the cable. Then, the helmsman adeptly veered his ship to within two cable lengths of the stranded merchantman, and Linzee prepared to open a point-blank fire.[26]

Even as *Camilla* was busily occupied positioning herself, Anderson, who had remained aboard *Morris* with a half dozen stalwart seamen, worked feverishly to lay a train of powder to a barrel of explosives. If he could not bring the ship in, he was determined to destroy her and deny the enemy the satisfaction of a rich prize. At that precise moment, *Camilla* opened up with her big guns. On the second broadside, *Morris* suddenly erupted in a horrendous explosion, undoubtedly before her captain had intended, for he and six of his men were instantly atomized with their ship. The precise cause of the premature blast was never fully explained although it was later claimed at Philadelphia that "by the Match burning too fast" the explosion had taken place well before expected. Perhaps a lucky shot hit the powder train, or some other accident had occurred. Whatever the cause, the destruction was tremendous. The log of *Camilla* recorded that "the Explotion gave the Ship [*Camilla*] so great a Shock that every Pain of Glass in the Windows were Broke. The Ship Tending In Shore struck the Ground abaft was Obliged to cut the Cable & Spring & runoff."[27]

Hamond's later description of the disaster was equally telling: "When she blew up with a most terrible explosion, forming a column of liquid Fire to a great height, and then spread into a head of black smoke, showering down burnt pieces of wood &c which cover[e]d a space round about for near ½ a Mile on the Water that included our ship & the [three] Boats (which were endeavoring to prevent her running ashore) but no Person [onboard *Roebuck*] was hurt by the fall . . . The Explosion was not only heard at Philadelphia (60 Miles off) but many windows were broke in the City by the shock. All the *Roebucks* windows were compleatly smashed, not being much more than the length of a Cable from the explosion. [When the smoke cleared away] not the smallest vestige of her remained to be seen Except on the surface of the water."[28]

Although the disaster had seemingly been total, a great deal of cargo, including guns, gunlocks, and clothing, had been blown intact onto the shore by the blast. The following day, Henry Fisher, the Delaware pilot and ever-observant agent for the Pennsylvania Navy Board, organized a roundup effort to salvage whatever he could from the beach. Efforts were also launched to fish among the wreckage for cannon that had been lost with the ship.[29]

On April 15, in a letter to Daniel St. Thomas Jenifer of Maryland, Robert Morris wrote, "There was onb[oar]d 2500 Muskets for the Continent and the Mate writes me a good many will be saved unless the Tories plunder or Seize them, I am now sending down orders & assistance & whatever is saved of our share shall be delivered to your order, I expect they will be brought up to Dover & suppose they may easily be Conveyed from thence into Your State." On the same day, Morris wrote to Caesar Rodney at Dover requesting him to hire wagons and send them under militia guard to carry off the salvaged goods.[30]

The recovery effort was undertaken with considerable success. On April 25 the Secret Committee of Congress noted in a letter to Rodney that "from Mr Purdy at Lewis Town we learn that he has been pretty Successfull in collecting the goods that were Saved from the Ship *Success* lately blown up at the Capes; and that he was waiting for the Waggons which you were so obliging as to promise to Send down for the purpose of bringing up those goods. We doubt not these waggons are gone forward and must beg leave to trouble you further with this business. We request you will inform yourself of the Situation of the Enemys Ships of war in the Bay, and Should you find that those goods can be Safely transported by water from your Place or from Rheedy [*sic*] Island; that you will have them put onboard some Craft at either of the places, and sent up here as expeditiously as possible. Should this mode be dangerous, you will please to order the waggons to proceed up to this city."[31]

On May 1, Robert Morris informed Governor Thomas Johnson of Maryland: "The Arms that came in the Ship blown up at our Capes I am told [were] generally damaged in the explosion, the Continent had 2500, onboard & for your State 500, but the Packages are all blown to pieces and the Muskets mixed therefore of what is saved we must receive in proportion & I am now Sending for the whole to this City to have them put in order & divided, that done I will inform Your Excellency or the Council of Safety & deliver what I receive as my proportion to their order."[32]

The loss of much of *Morris*'s valuable military cargo to the cause of American independence had been substantial despite the salvage effort. The ramifications of the ship's destruction will never be known. But as one leader of the Revolution, William Whipple, observed, "the greatest loss is the life of the Captain whose bravery on this occasion is without example."[33]

As the Revolution continued, the list of men, their ships, and cargoes lost in action would grow to monumental proportions. Many of them would fall victim to the very same warships that had claimed *Morris* and her heroic commander, Captain James Anderson. Yet the indomitable struggle for American independence would go on, and the waters of the Delmarva coast would be carpeted with the bones of ships and men who paid the ultimate price for liberty.

# Le Serpent

The recent British depredations on the Delaware, in particular those perpetrated by HMS *Roebuck,* had been disastrous. Some in the Pennsylvania Assembly believed the Pennsylvania State Navy should have acted more aggressively in May 1776 and in later traumatic events such as the *Morris* affair. Some accused the Pennsylvania naval commanders of timidity. The criticisms triggered a significant upheaval among the officers of the infant fleet. The first and worst dissension had been exhibited by the commanders of the thirteen row galleys that bore the brunt of early fighting on the Delaware. Despite claims that the fleet lacked adequate ammunition, the Committee of Safety ordered a series of senior command changes. Not surprisingly, a near revolt by the officer corps and several resignations of key commanders ensued.[1]

Among the first to resign had been Captains John Hamilton and James Montgomery, commanders of the galleys *Congress* and *Chatham.* "We wou'd not have it believ'd from this resignation," they informed the Committee of Safety on August 1, 1776, "that we mean to abandon the cause of the Independent States of America. No, it partly proceeds from a desire of Serving in a larger Sphere of Action, whereby we may Have an opportunity of rendering our Country some More essential Service, than we have any prospect of doing here."[2]

Both Hamilton and Montgomery would have ample opportunity to serve their country—and their own interests as many other mariners were choosing to do—by engaging in the time-tested expediency of warfare at sea called privateering. As early as March 23, 1776, the Continental Congress had passed several resolutions, one of the most notable being "That the inhabitants of these colonies be permitted to fit out armed vessels to cruize on the enemies of these United Colonies."[3] The fielding of privately owned vessels to make war on the foe, primarily to capture enemy merchantmen and their cargoes that could be sold for profit, soon became one of the most hotly pursued endeavors for investors and mariners alike during the long years of warfare that would ensue. Privateering was a long-recognized and legitimate mode of conducting warfare in the Western world, employed from the reign of Edward I on down, and particularly useful for a country with virtually no navy. Though some accused the institution of privateering of diverting men, money, and resources from various states and the Continental Navy, the benefits were substantial. The issuance of commissions, called letters of marque and reprisal, to privately owned vessels to harass the enemy, especially its commerce, was cost-effective for a country that lacked a national treasury. Moreover, it offered the potential for enormous profits for individuals and syndicates who invested in it and mariners who conducted it.

Though thousands of men rushed to the call of privateering, some prominent military leaders were opposed to it. John Paul Jones despised the practice. "The common class of mankind," he wrote, "are actuated by no nobler principle than that of self-interest. This, and this only determines all adventures in privateers, the owners as well as those they employ."[4]

Neither Hamilton nor Montgomery suffered from a moral opposition to engaging in privateering or securing a new command of ships that offered a chance for both adventure and wealth. Soon after resigning his Pennsylvania navy command, Hamilton was engaged by a syndicate headed by John Cox and John Chaloner, merchants from Batsto, New Jersey, and Philadelphia, to command the twelve-gun brigantine *General Mifflin* on a privateering cruise. On August 27 the Pennsylvania Council of Safety, "Agreeable to a Resolve of the Honorable Congress," granted a formal commission to Hamilton. Three days later, Montgomery was also granted a commission for the twelve-gun privateer *General Montgomery*.[5] The fortunes of the two ships, however, would be vastly different, with the latter producing a substantial profit for its investors and crew and the former a terrible tragedy and financial disaster.

Little is known about the first and only cruise of *General Mifflin* other than that she operated for a while in the West Indies in company with another well-known and soon-to-be famous Pennsylvania privateer called *Rattlesnake,* Captain David McCulloch commanding. Sometime in mid-February 1777, within sight of Barbados, the two vessels fell in with and captured the English merchantman *Elizabeth,* Captain Thorpe commanding, bound from London for the Leeward Islands. From then on, Hamilton's luck would spiral downward, though more than £3,000 worth of "prize effects" had been transferred aboard. Soon after the capture, finding pickings poor, Hamilton and McCulloch parted ways, with Hamilton turning his ship's prow homeward toward the Delaware. Within days, *Elizabeth* would be retaken and sent into Jamaica.[6] But *General Mifflin* and many of her crewmen would never make it to Philadelphia.

On March 6, as the privateer approached the Delmarva coast, Captain Hamilton kept a watchful eye for British cruisers, at least two of which were known to be patrolling off the Chesapeake.[7] The weather was exceedingly cold and snowy. Hamilton was undoubtedly concerned. Getting out of the Delaware was one thing, but getting in during a bone-chilling winter snowstorm was another. That the captain was uncertain of his location is without question. That his pilot, because of weather, may have believed himself to be off the entrance of the Delaware is probable. Whatever the cause, however, the results were disastrous.

With a terrifying series of bumps, privateer brigantine *General Mifflin,* "by the ignorance of the pilot," ran hard ashore on the bar off Sinepuxent, Maryland. Within a short time, the buffeting of the sea and wind caused the ship's seams to split. The hull was bilged and the hold quickly filled with water. More than ninety crewmen and officers crowded onto the quarterdeck, the only sanctuary remaining. Though they could hear the surf breaking nearby, no one moved.[8]

Throughout the night, nearly five score wet and frightened seamen huddled together on the quarterdeck, suffering terribly from the stormy winter cold. The following morning, all that could be seen from their precarious vantage point was a pristine snow-covered shoreline, barren and desolate for as far as the eye could see. Somehow—the record does not elaborate—the entire crew made it ashore, but for many frostbitten sailors it was already too late. Seventeen men would die on the frozen white beach before local inhabitants or wreckers could render "timely assistance." *General Mifflin* and her prize cargo were entirely lost, thus earning the distinction of being the first warship to become a casualty on the Delmarva coast in the Revolution. She would by no means be the last.[9]

The outbreak of the war had found many ships of the Royal Navy in dry dock—out of commission, in need of considerable repairs, or literally sinking at anchor. Many of them were antiquated, worm-eaten candidates for the scrap heap that had been resurrected at the last minute by a nearly bankrupt nation desperate for ships. Among this number was HMS *Mermaid,* a sixth-rate, 613-ton, twenty-eight-gun frigate first commissioned at Hull on May 6, 1761, in the midst of the Seven Years War.[10]

In 1776 *Mermaid* was among thirty-five British warships still in port awaiting repairs and refitting, crews, guns, and every necessity required to field a man-of-war. By mid-July, however, the ship was nearly ready to begin convoy duty, escorting troops to America. By November 22 her first convoy of twenty sail had arrived at New York with recruits and provisions for General Howe's army. En route the old frigate had enjoyed the good fortune of capturing the ship *Grace,* and two more Americans, both bearing the name *Lyon,* all recently taken by the rebels.[11]

Following her arrival in America, under the command of Captain James Hawker, *Mermaid* was stationed off Nantucket Shoals, where on January 9, 1777, she captured the sloop *Dartmouth,* James Littlefield master. Already in desperate need of a refit, she sprung her bowsprit five days later and was forced to sail for the West Indies and the closest British naval base capable of providing the necessary repairs. At English Harbor, Antigua, she was refitted and again made ready for sea duty. On March 12 Captain Hawker was ordered to escort another convoy of troop transports to New York and there place himself under the command of Admiral Howe.[12]

En route to New York, *Mermaid* captured the merchant ships *Clarissa* (Noah Millar master, from St. Eustatia with salt) and *Escape* (Benjamin Weeks master, from Maryland with flour). On April 19, off the Virginia coast, she fell in with and recaptured the brig *Experiment,* from Philadelphia, laden with 1,400 barrels of flour. The brig had recently been taken by yet another *Lyon,* this time a Connecticut privateer commanded by Captain Timothy Shaler, and ran another of the privateer's prizes, the sloop *Hazard,* ashore. Then *Mermaid* encountered the privateer *Lyon* herself. The encounter was brief and decisive. The American was promptly driven ashore and destroyed at Long Beach, near Egg Harbor, New Jersey.[13]

After delivering her charges to New York, Captain Hawker again returned his ship to patrol duty, this time running between St. Georges Bank and the coast of Nova Scotia. In late May he fell in with the brigantine *Charles,* Jeffrey Tapley master, recently captured by Captain John Skimmer's privateer *Lee,* mounting ten guns and eighteen swivels, and sent her into Halifax. On June 5 he took the brig *Two Bettseys,* recently captured by rebel privateers, and two days later made a prize of the sloop *Elizabeth.*[14]

On June 16 Captain Sir George Collier, commander of HMS *Rainbow,* and at the time senior naval officer at Halifax, received intelligence that a party of rebels had landed at St. John's River and were preparing an invasion of Nova Scotia. When it was later learned that the invasion was actually to be launched from the port of Machias, Maine, he organized a successful preemptive strike on August 13. Sailing in company with *Mermaid, Blonde,* and the sloop *Hope* with Royal Marines, Collier was able to destroy the expedition before it could be launched.[15]

*Mermaid* returned to cruising off Nova Scotia for the remainder of the summer. On August 29 she recaptured the *Fanny,* John Wood master, which had recently been taken by the Massachusetts privateer *True Blue,* Richard Stiles commanding, and sent her into Halifax. By November the frigate was again patrolling off New Jersey and, as usual, with considerable effect. On November 18 she captured the twelve-gun Massachusetts privateer *Active,* John Foster Williams commanding, off Sandy Hook. Five days later she retook a recent enemy privateer capture called *Hope* and then set off after the privateer itself. She eventually captured the rebel and placed a prize crew of twenty men aboard. Unfortunately for Hawker and his men, *Active* was cast away on the New Jersey coast and the prize crew became prisoners of the rebels.[16]

For more than six months, *Mermaid* would continue to menace rebel commerce on the mid-Atlantic seaboard, especially along the Delmarva shores, without opposition. All that would change with the entry of France into the war. On April 13, 1778, a powerful French fleet under the command of the Comte d'Estaing sailed for America with the intention of blockading Admiral Howe, then ensconced in Delaware Bay. On July 7 the fleet belatedly arrived off the Delaware only to find Howe had departed. There was one consolation, however. HMS *Mermaid* was still at anchor in the bay, having been left there to warn and divert transports and victuallers from the estuary.[17]

When the van of the sixteen ships of d'Estaing's fleet arrived off Cape Henlopen, Captain Hawker correctly assumed that they belonged to the French navy. Sighting the enemy on the morning of July 8, he immediately weighed anchor and sailed due east, directly at the enemy, in a desperate effort to clear the Hen and Chickens Shoal and to escape into open water and then veer south before they arrived. The French quickly moved to cut off his flight by dispatching four fast warships in pursuit. Soon, the entire fleet followed. Forced to make a repeatedly dangerous series of short tacks because of a prevailing southwest wind that brought *Mermaid* ever closer to the shore, Hawker and his men drove their ship relentlessly onward, refusing to surrender. As the grim procession wore on, *Mermaid* ran aground on Fenwick Shoal. The end, either capture or destruction, seemed a foregone conclusion as the French closed in. Then several pursuers also ran aground, and the chase ground to a halt as the French struggled desperately to refloat their ships before their prey escaped. With all sails set, and through the use of his longboats and kedging, Hawker was able to get off first. At least five of the French fleet doggedly resumed the pursuit. Hawker ordered all of his guns and the small bower anchor tossed overboard and the water butts emptied to lighten ship, but for naught. The fast French warships began to gain ground. It was soon apparent to all that there could be no escape, as the English warship was trapped running along the inshore shoal line. Hawker resolved to drive his ship ashore and surrender her to the Americans rather than to the hated French. Thus, about 10:00 A.M., July 8, *Mermaid* was driven over the offshore bar of Fenwick Island, south of Sinepuxent, as two of the enemy's leading warships came on. The ship was immediately stranded and broken. After destroying his signals and charts, striking his flag, and cutting down the masts, Hawker ordered his crew to make for the shore. Before the French could board to formally claim their prey, an American vessel hove into sight and boarded first. The wreck had become an American prize.[18]

The officers and crew of HMS *Mermaid* faired better than their ship. Most were quickly taken by American forces and temporarily incarcerated at various locations on the Eastern Shore of Maryland. On July 16 Governor Thomas Johnson of Maryland instructed Commodore Thomas Grason of the Maryland State Navy to proceed with the galleys *Conqueror* and *Chester,* the boats *Plater* and *Emilia,* and tow several vessels across the Chesapeake to the port of Cambridge to take onboard the prisoners of war from the late frigate *Mermaid.* "The Prisoners are to be distributed amongst the Vessels with a View to convenience and security; Your own Disposition and Prudence, we flatter ourselves, will make it unnecessary for us to give particular Directions as to your Treatment of the Prisoners." From Cambridge, Grason was to proceed to Annapolis. By the onset of August, most of the prisoners, with the exception of a handful of sick, had been transferred to Philadelphia to await exchange for American seamen.[19]

And off Fenwick Island, not far from old Sinepuxent Inlet, the bones of the venerable warship *Mermaid* would slowly disappear beneath the ever-shifting sands of the Delmarva coast.

The career of *General Mifflin*'s consort, the sixteen-gun *Rattlesnake,* was flushed with far more success and fame. Her commander, David McCulloch, an expatriot Irishman, had little love for the British and had exercised his ship with considerable skill against them to prove it. Although no formal commission has been found for *Rattlesnake,* references to her activities indicate that, although fitted out at either Martinique or St. Lucia in the West Indies, she had apparently sailed on her first voyage as a Pennsylvania letter of marque about the beginning of 1777, and her first prize, a brig called *Hope,* was reportedly sent into the Delaware on February 19 of that year.[20]

Like most of the privateersmen during the early stages of the war, McCulloch had chosen to cruise in the target-rich waters of the West Indies, where friendly (albeit technically neutral) ports in the French Leeward Islands could provide necessary provisioning and repair facilities. From time to time *Rattlesnake* would operate in company with one or more other privateers, usually also bearing Pennsylvania commissions, to the great detriment of the English island trade.

About March 25 *Rattlesnake* made a stunning capture west of Barbados when she took a London brig called *Endeavour,* which was sailing from Africa with ninety slaves, ten tons of ivory, and other goods. Soon afterward, while in company with the privateer *Security,* Captain John Ord commanding, she had the amazingly good fortune to fall in with and take two British transports, six or seven merchantmen from Cork, Ireland, and two more Guinea slave ships, one of which had 511 slaves on board. Her remarkable luck continued when a lumber transport from Florida and three ships from Granada carrying sugar were easily snapped up. All were sent to the French port of St. Pierre, Martinique. Then came the capture of *Elizabeth,* while in company with *General Mifflin.* In very short order, *Rattlesnake* had earned the reputation of being "such a noted runner that she is said to be a terror to the English islands."[21]

Although the hunting was good, not every prize made it into a friendly port. On May 14, 1777, the *Pennsylvania Journal* reported that since *Rattlesnake* had left Philadelphia, it was said that she had taken at least eight prizes, only five of which had arrived safe in port. A case in point was one of her first captures, made on March 5, which had been the richly laden brig *Betsey,* Sam Gerrich master, bound from Surinam. McCulloch had placed a prizemaster and five men aboard to bring the ship into St. Pierre, but as the prize neared her new destination, she was retaken in an insurrection mounted by her former crew and carried into the nearby British-held island of Dominica. Some of *Rattlesnake*'s prey chose to fight. In late April or early May the *John of London* managed to beat off the privateer in a hard-fought engagement, inflicting serious damage to the rebel's bow and forcing her to limp into St. Vincent for repairs.[22]

About mid-May, manned by a complement of 121 crewmen, *Rattlesnake* began cruising with three other privateers, including the famed *Oliver Cromwell.* The only serious enemy opposition in the region was the sixteen-gun sloop-of-war *Beaver,* Captain James Jones commanding. The four privateer commanders fell upon a scheme to jointly attack the warship, but, as often was the case, other more "lucrative" offerings caused the plan to be aborted. Nevertheless, on May 17 *Beaver* and *Rattlesnake* nearly came to blows before the privateer made good her escape into Trinity Bay, Martinique. Her luck was better than that of *Oliver Cromwell,* which fell in with the warship two days later and after a spirited engagement was captured.[23]

By mid-June *Rattlesnake* and at least four other privateers had put into St. Pierre to refit. McCulloch had his vessel rerigged as a ship and added two more cannon to his battery, bringing up his fighting capacity to eighteen guns, all brass. By now McCulloch and his ship had achieved a swashbuckling notoriety. On September 8 a letter from an unidentified author obviously sympathetic to the Revolution was published in a Barbadian newspaper and later republished in England:

> The captain of the *Rattle-snake,* whom we here call the hero of the marine, is at this instant in chace of a sail that he has espied. What his success will be, it is impossible to determine: but certain it is, he is the boldest fellow that has made his appearance in these seas for some time. The *Rattle-snake* carries only 14 [*sic*] guns, is an excellent sailer, and has taken a prodigious number of prizes, the chief of which he has sold at Martinico [Martinique]. A short time since the captain, who is a native of Ireland, wrote word to captain Singleton of the *Bridgetown,* that if he did not take great care he would cut his ship out of harbour. Singleton, well acquainted with his disposition and courage, took, accordingly every precaution against this enterprising Neptune. Bets used to be often laid in Martinico, relative to the captures the above vessel would bring into any of the respective harbours. People would be looking out for her; and on her appearance with a prize, the joyful alarm was, *Le Serpent a Sonnettes!*—The beach would then be crowded with spectators, and the *Rattle-snake* enter the harbour in triumph.[24]

The career of the now-famed Pennsylvania privateer *Rattlesnake* would continue unabated for more than a year. Finally, in the late fall of 1778, she returned to the American coast. Divesting his ship of a number of guns, and taking on a large consignment of salt and rice at Charleston, McCulloch and a reduced crew of thirty-five sailed about mid-November to bring her home to Philadelphia for a well-earned rest and refit. Or so they had hoped.[25]

The night of November 21 was as black as it comes off the Virginia capes, but not so dark that the heavily laden *Rattlesnake* was invisible to a vigilant enemy cruiser. The fourteen-gun, 303-ton British sloop-of-war *Swift* was passing through the area en route to Sandy Hook, New Jersey. *Swift* was a newly built ship, ninety-seven feet long and twenty-seven feet abeam, launched at Portsmouth dockyard only the year before. But she was already a seasoned veteran of the war in America. When her commander, Captain Joseph Tathwell, was informed of the strange sail, he ordered an immediate pursuit but in the darkness quickly lost sight of his prey. The following morning, however, the quarry was again spotted, now making directly for the entrance to the Chesapeake.[26]

For McCulloch and his men, the only hope of escape from the heavily armed and manned *Swift* was to draw her into the bay, in which lay a recently arrived squadron of French warships. The chase was hot, and by afternoon, the dogged man-of-war gradually began to overhaul the American, which Tathwell was soon able to identify as a privateer. Throughout the day, as the deadly race continued, *Rattlesnake* refused to give up. Her pursuer was equally resolute to overtake her. By late afternoon the two ships were finally within firing range. The British opened with their bow chasers, albeit without visible effect. The prospects for *Rattlesnake,* however, with barely half as many men as her assailant and far fewer guns, seemed bleak. As *Swift* approached to within hailing distance, Tathwell called for the privateer to strike her flag. McCulloch responded defiantly that the British commander "might be damned, for he would not surrender."[27]

By now it was getting dark and the two ships were running almost neck and neck and perilously close to the notorious Middle Ground Shoal, in the center of the entrance to Chesapeake Bay and not far from Cape Henry. Tathwell decided to fire a broadside, come across and then fire the other, after which he would haul off and come to anchor. When the first broadside was unleashed, McCulloch apparently attempted to avoid the blow but struck ground, bringing his ship literally to a crashing halt. Before *Swift* could take advantage of the situation and bring her second broadside to bear, she also ran aground in the midst of her own yaw.[28]

Both vessels appeared to be hopelessly stranded. McCulloch and his men, sheltered by darkness, elected to escape ashore in their small boats after attempting but failing to set fire to their ship. Tathwell, however, was not about to give up. He ordered *Swift*'s guns and provisions tossed over to lighten ship, but the effort failed (presumably owing to the adverse sea conditions). In the morning the yards and topmasts were struck, and boats were launched to carry out and drop the anchors in a kedging effort, but these endeavors were quickly aborted by strong winds and high seas. The steady pounding soon proved too much. *Swift*'s hull opened, and she quickly bilged. All aboard knew that it was only a matter of time before the ship would break up beneath them. Their sole consolation was that they had watched the stranded privateer roll over on her beam end amid the waves. All presumed she would soon succumb to the same wrath of nature they all faced.[29]

Fortunately for the British, by the afternoon of November 23 the weather had moderated enough to permit a small party to reach shore. Unfortunately, they immediately fell into the hands of a band of local militiamen who promptly sent out for reinforcements. Within a short time, the rebels were joined by the garrison at Portsmouth, Virginia, comprised of a unit of the Princess Anne County Militia under Colonel Thomas Reynolds Walker. Walker dispatched a message to Tathwell and his remaining crew informing them that two field pieces were being brought up and two American frigates were already on their way to the scene. Having been stranded close enough to the shore to become a sitting duck, the British had little alternative but surrender. A preponderance of *Swift*'s men was thus sent ashore, having been unable to toss over either the ship's guns or provisions. Her commander had but one choice left to prevent either from falling into the hands of the Virginians. Being the last to leave his ship, Tathwell set her afire about 7:00 A.M. on the morning of November 24 and pushed off for shore. Soon afterward, HM Sloop-of-War *Swift* blew up in a violent explosion that sent her flaming bones arcing high over the Middle Ground. Soon after the explosion, the captain and ninety-one of his men found themselves prisoners of war, the former being comfortably lodged in Williamsburg, and the latter less amenably so onboard a prison ship in the James River.[30]

Although stranded, partly burned, and lying on her beam-ends near Cape Henry, *Rattlesnake* was not irretrievably lost but remained firmly aground. When inspected, it was determined that she might even be salvageable. Within several months, she had been patched up, refloated, refitted, and returned to active enterprise "to plague the British." No longer capable of service as the speedy privateer she had once been, however, she was nevertheless outfitted as an armed merchantman and convoy escort. Under the command of Captain William Cannon, she made several successful voyages to Aux Cayes in the West Indies and lived to see old age.[31]

Though the fates accorded *General Mifflin, Mermaid,* and *Swift* would be repeated countless times in the Western Hemisphere, and often on the Delmarva coast, during the remaining days of the American Revolution many hundreds more privateers would cause unending trouble for British commerce. Few, however, would be awarded the fame or notoriety achieved by "Le Serpent" *Rattlesnake.*

# 6

## The Infamous Tar

Lieutenant Colonel John Cropper, of the 11th Virginia Regiment of the Continental Army, was not an imposing looking man. At twenty-three years of age, however, he was one of the youngest senior general officers in the army. His high forehead was crested by a dark shock of hair swept back, exposing a premature widow's peak. His chin seemed a mite longer and more bulbous than perhaps it should have been. But, somehow, his presence commanded attention and obedience, for he led by example. In the fall of 1779, he rode on horseback over the rutted dirt road leading into Accomack after serving without a break in Washington's army for nearly three years. He was eager to see his wife and infant daughter and to look after his long-ignored interests and ancestral estate. Indeed, he longed for nothing better than to leave the war behind for the duration of the 190-day furlough he had been granted.[1]

As the eldest son of Sebastian and Sabra Corbin Cropper, John had been born on December 23, 1755, at Bowman's Folly, the family plantation in Accomack County, Virginia, not far from the entrance to Folly Creek (sometimes called Great Metompkin Creek), near Metompkin Inlet. He had married well, a local beauty named Catherine Bayly, in August 1776. Only four months later, as captain of the Shore Company, 9th Virginia Regiment, he had answered the call to war and left his home and newly pregnant wife to join Washington's army at Morristown, New Jersey.[2]

Now, as he made his way home, Cropper may have ruminated little about the tumultuous events he had witnessed over the past several years, significant as they were. In 1777 he had been promoted to the rank of major in the 7th Virginia Regiment, and in September of that year was wounded at the Battle of Brandywine. The following year he had been appointed by General Lafayette to the rank of lieutenant colonel in Daniel Morgan's 11th Virginia, and in June he had heroically led his men at the Battle of Monmouth. Both he and Morgan, who was also just twenty-three years old, had been in the thick of it on that hot and sultry day. Now, as he galloped homeward across the frozen turf, it was unlikely he was thinking of how his men had suffered for lack of water during the fight and just how furious Washington had been with General Charles Lee for his now infamous retreat from the field. Cropper had been with his own men the morning after the contest, dogging the enemy's retirement from the battle-field and making several captures, including the coach of a general officer. But battlefield glories meant little to him at the moment as he belatedly returned to his family and his beloved Accomack County.[3]

The homecoming reunion with Catherine at Bowman's Folly was undoubt-edly as joyous as that of any husband returning from battle to join his family could be. In this case, the joy was doubled when Cropper saw for the first time his little daughter, Sarah Corbin, who had been born a few months after his de-parture for the war, and was now more than two and a half years old. Yet the re-turn of the young warrior was destined to be anything but peaceful.[4]

Almost from the very beginning of the Revolution, the sparsely populated shores of the Delmarva coast had provided critical egress for patriot shipping and the war effort. As early as August 19, 1776, the Virginia Council of Safety had ordered that the harbors at Cherrystone, on the bay side of Northampton County, and Chincoteague, on the Atlantic side of Accomack, be fortified. American commercial and military shipping, at least that portion that was un-willing to hazard British blockaders cruising off the Delaware and Chesapeake, quickly began to employ Chincoteague, Virginia, and Sinepuxent, Maryland, as convenient, shallow-water harbors of refuge where the deep draft British cruis-ers dare not venture.[5]

The example had been set in July, when some of the first privateering prizes of the war were sent into both inlets. "Captain John [actually James] Campbell, Commander of the *Enterprize* Privateer, from Baltimore," it was reported in Maryland, "has taken and sent into Chincoteague, a brig loaded with Molasses; and a ship from Barbadoes, to England, is sent into Sinepuxent, on the 24th ult. When the Brig left Capt. Campbell, he was in chase of a ship, deeply laden, and expected to be in possession of her in a few hours. The prize which is safe arrived in Sinepuxent, is said to have on board a great Quantity of Spanish dollars, &c, &c. and was taken by Capt. Campbell the 18th inst." In September 1776 a prize taken by the Maryland privateer *Harlequin* landed her cargo safely at Chin-coteague. In mid-December the Continental Navy sloop *Independence,* laden with muskets and blankets for Washington's army, was chased by six enemy cruisers off the Delaware but escaped southward into that same inlet. Robert Morris, chairman of Congress's Secret Committee of Correspondence, setting a precedent, instructed that the cargo be offloaded there and carted across the peninsula to a landing on the Chesapeake side, from where it could be safely transshipped to the army.[6]

By January 1777 the Secret Committee had become convinced that the lower inlets of the Delmarva coast were so aptly suited and safe for entries that it began instructing secret agents and couriers returning from Europe to employ these ar-eas for their reentry. Typical were the instructions issued to one Captain Larkin Hammond, who was sailing for Nantes, France, in the schooner *Jennifer* with important dispatches for Silas Dean, Benjamin Franklin, and Arthur Lee, the

American commissioners to the Court of Louis XVI. Upon delivery of the dispatches, Hammond was to await the commissioners' orders and letters and then sail for America. When he returned, he was to "put in at the most convenient Port to the Southward of the Delaware; we think Chincoteague or some other on the back of the Eastern Shore the most likely for avoiding Men of War, and would therefore have you attempt getting into one of those Ports."[7]

With both the Delaware and Chesapeake under blockade, the use of Chincoteague and a formalized mode of transshipment across the peninsula soon became one of the more successful methods of evading enemy blockaders and landing supplies. The Secret Committee soon began to recommend Chincoteague and other remote Delmarva inlets as convenient places to put in to avoid enemy warships, and also as places where cargoes could be taken on by outbound shipping. In May 1777 Baltimore merchants Samuel and Robert Purviance informed a colleague in Massachusetts: "We are at present loading a Schooner for a Friend in your State with Flour & Bar Iron, which We send by Water from hence to the River Pocomoke, from whence the Goods are carried 12 Miles over Land to Chincoteague Inlet on the Eastern Shore of Virginia."[8]

The Purviances were delighted with Chincoteague and had enlisted a local agent named William Burdett to handle their affairs there. "This Place," they wrote, "has proved an Assylum for many Vessels inward bound, wh[ich] w[oul]d otherwise be lost: And of late we have fallen on the expedient of loading them there, tho at a considerable Expence. Should your Board [of War] be Necessitated by Want of Flour or Iron to run the Risque of attempting to get them in these perilous times, We would advise that the Vessels be ordered into Chincoteague and the Masters directed to apply to our friend Mr William Burdett, who will send us their Letters by Express—This Gentl[ema]n will see any Goods that we forward, Carted across & Shipp'd."[9]

Unfortunately, the dangerously shifting shoals of the Virginia barrier island shores were often as hazardous to patriot shipping as to enemy blockaders. One example was recorded by Lieutenant Joshua Barney, prizemaster of the Jamaican snow *Thomas,* laden with valuable mahogany and logwood, which had been taken in December 1776 by the Continental Navy warship *Andrew Doria.* Barney had been instructed to carry the snow into Philadelphia, but with myriad enemy cruisers about, one of which lay squarely in the Cape May Channel, he had opted for Chincoteague. His personal memoir of the events that followed clearly outlined the dangers of the area, especially during the winter:

> I parted with the Brig [*Andrew Doria*] having encountered bad weather. We were twelve days on the coast in which time we experienced 8 gales of wind; on Christmas night 1776 [we] got among the breakers on Chincoteague shoals with a gale at East; I was obliged to anchor in that dreadful situation, every sea broke over our vessel, my crew & self were obliged to get into the tops to prevent being washed overboard, where we remained several hours waiting for day light, at length the long wished day appeared, when we discovered the land right astern of us, at a short distance; the breakers mountains high; we expected every moment that our Cable would break & nothing but death stared us in the face; about ten O'Clock we saw a Sloop near us,

bound in, & in a few minutes she struck the ground; went to pieces & we saw no more of her or her crew, in the afternoon the wind changed & became moderate, we then got under way & the next day got into the harbour of Chincoteague, here I remained several day.[10]

British intentions in the spring of 1777 were something of a mystery to American strategists. What was certain, however, was that an army under General John Burgoyne was preparing to move from Quebec toward Albany, New York, to sever New England's communications with the southern states. The British in New York City, under Major General William Howe and his brother Admiral Richard Howe, were preparing for a major thrust either against Philadelphia or up the Hudson to meet Burgoyne. Whatever their objectives might have been, it was quite clear that a major naval force was already assembling in New York Bay under Admiral Howe. The inhabitants of the Delmarva coast may well have worried, for if the fleet sailed south, nowhere between Cape Henlopen and Cape Charles was likely to be safe. At the very least, small naval raiding parties were likely to begin descending like mosquitoes on the remote and largely unprotected coastal centers such as Metompkin, Chincoteague, Sinepuxent, and Lewes. Those same areas that hitherto offered refuge and sanctuary for patriot shipping would become death traps.

In early July, the Delmarva inhabitants' fears began to materialize. On July 4 the brig *Stanley,* Lieutenant Richard Whitworth commanding, and the schooner *Delaware,* commanded by a midshipman named Rogers, both being tenders now belonging to the ill-famed HMS *Roebuck,* began cruising off Chincoteague Inlet. Flying French colors to deceive the local pilots, they were soon able to bring one off and force him to lead them through the inlet. Soon they had entered Chincoteague Bay "for the purpose of taking any of the rebel ships lying within." Whitworth and Rogers were undoubtedly delighted to discover eight vessels swaying serenely at anchor therein, many of which were French. All were taken without a fight. Four of the vessels—the sloops *Polly,* Richard Wells master, *Mary,* William Le Frame master, *Sally,* James Le Mair master and owned by the Committee of Safety, all bound to Martinique in ballast, and an unidentified vessel, William Earles master, owned by Robert Morris's Philadelphia trading house Willing, Morris & Co., bound in ballast for St. Eustatia—were destroyed where they lay. Four more, including the brigs *Hero,* William Paul master, for Martinique, and *Sally,* Anthony Hill master, for St. Martin, the sloop *Jenny,* Robert Tuille master, for Curaçao, all with flour and tobacco, and the schooner *Polly,* John Ellis master, for Dunkirk, France, in ballast, were taken as prizes. When the jubilant raiders departed for New York, they took with them not only their four prizes but also forty prisoners.[11]

Word of the sinking of four vessels and the capture of four more raced up the coast. Colonel Zadock Purnell of the 3rd Maryland Independent Company, Worcester County, informed Maryland governor Thomas Johnson of the event. "I have rec[eiv]ed intelligence," he wrote hastily, "that two of the British Cruisers went into Chincoteague the day before yesterday & took possession of the Vessells in that port except two or three which were up some of the Creeks. The same attempt upon our Harbour [Sinepuxent] I think may undoubtedly be expected—I cou'd wish that a kind of Row Galley or Gundalo could be constructed which to act in Conjunction with our little Battery would I presume render us very secure, if your Excell[enc]y should approve of such kind of Vessell being stationed here we should want some Carpe[n]ters who would be able to direct & carry on the work."[12]

No naval protection would be forthcoming. A small battery to guard the entrance was the best that could be produced.

General Howe and fifteen thousand British and mercenary German troops departed from Staten Island, New York, on July 23 aboard 230 ships heading not for the Delaware but for the Chesapeake Bay, throwing the Continental government into a frenzy. Where were the British actually bound? On August 3 the slow, plodding armada was off Assateague. Twelve days later it entered the Chesapeake bound for the head of the bay, where the army would land to march on Philadelphia via the backdoor route. On August 30 Virginia governor Patrick Henry informed Governor Thomas Johnson of Maryland: "Two small Betterys are nearly finished at Sengoteague [Chincoteague] & Matompkin, where the trade of this & your State may receive some Assistance. Is there any Method by which Virginia can annoy the Enemy & thereby assist you?"[13] But it was too little and already far too late to hold back the flood of raiders, both loyalists and regulars, that would soon begin to inundate the middle and lower Delmarva shores.

With the Eastern Shore intersected on both Chesapeake and Atlantic sides by countless navigable waterways, all serving as veritable highways stemming from the British-controlled sea-lanes, no place was safe. As the Royal Navy began deploying armed tenders, row galleys, and other shallow-draft vessels rather than larger warships to menace coastal inlets and settlements, as during the early days of the war, the conflict along the Delmarva was assuming a new face. Uprisings by loyalists sputtered to life and were extinguished with the greatest of difficulty. Guerrilla warfare, replete with kidnapping, murder, and general mayhem, was becoming the order of the day. To make matters worse, operating from their bases in New York and, after late September, Philadelphia, British and loyalist seaborne raiders began to assail settlements, farms, and homesteads on the Delmarva coast with unnerving regularity. With escalating frequency the harried local militia was called on to protect the coastal population from an enemy that seemed to be everywhere and then nowhere. Time and again, sea raiders arrived at shorefront farmsteads to rob and burn houses and barns, purloin livestock and slaves, and whenever possible incite the general slave population to insurrection. When organized resistance was met, the raiders usually disappeared as abruptly as they had appeared.[14] Such was the unsettled situation in Accomack when young Colonel Cropper arrived home to enjoy his long-awaited furlough.

There would, unfortunately, be little time for pleasure.

. . .

On Sunday, January 17, 1778, there was a deep snow on the ground at Bowman's Folly, but it did not deter John Cropper from attending to pressing matters. He had, unfortunately, reached home only to find Accomack—and his own estate—in a virtually defenseless condition and had busied himself ever since to set his own house, if not the county's, in order. The danger of enemy raids was ever present. Only the evening before, a British cruiser had been reported probing Metompkin Inlet and had sent a boat in as far as Folly Landing, not far from his home, to cut out whatever vessels might be found there. Cropper had gone down to Folly Creek to check on a boat belonging to one of his neighbors, Major Southy Simpson, that had been hidden in the marsh. Fortunately, he discovered, the raiders had failed in their effort and had disappeared from the scene as quickly as they had appeared. He was convinced, however, that they would be back. If such an event occurred he fully intended to defend his plantation with or without support of the local militia. Thus, on January 23, he rode to Accomack Court House to secure the necessary arms, and was promised a number of muskets.[15] It would, unhappily, not be enough to deter the raiders who arrived, much as expected, by sea but far sooner than anticipated.

It was reportedly a motley crew that manned the New York privateer *Thistle,* a Bermuda-built sloop in the service of the British, commanded by a notorious loyalist captain named Thomas Byron Williams. Feared for his heartless, lightning-like depredations against the Delmarva coast, the captain and his surgeon, a man named Gramble, were well known about Accomack. Williams's vessel was said to be serving from time to time as a tender for the Royal Navy. Just who his masters were, however, meant little to the citizens of Accomack: most considered him to be little more than a pirate. Indeed, Williams's name, when mentioned in the conversations of patriots, was usually preceded by the derogatory sobriquet "Infamous Tar."[16]

Williams was apparently well aware of the recent return of the famous Colonel Cropper and had decided to pay him a visit. The captain thus entered into an agreement with a local Tory named Dutton to serve as a pilot to guide a landing party straight to Bowman's Folly. He picked the evening of February 12 to launch his surprise sortie in *Thistle*'s small boats. Rowing with muffled oars in the dead of night, the raiders entered Folly Creek entirely undetected and set foot ashore but a short distance from the colonel's home. With practiced stealth, they surrounded the estate. Then, with stunning alacrity, they rushed the house, spilling into the hallway and beating savagely on the bedroom door.[17]

Cropper was taken by complete surprise. Before he could even dress, much less mount a defense, the raiders had burst into his bedroom and seized him. In a heartbeat several others ripped the covers from the bed where his wife and infant daughter were lying, and for amusement proceeded to threaten and insult the terrified woman. Then commenced an orgy of destruction as the invaders smashed furniture and rifled through treasured belongings in search of loot, stealing jewelry or anything of value. Others ransacked the house in search of hidden booty. Another party proceeded to the slave quarters where Cropper's servants and field hands were lodged and marched them down to the beach, where they were taken aboard *Thistle* as prizes of war. The raiders discovered the cellar, amply stocked with wines and liquors, and before long the entire raiding party had become uproariously drunk.[18]

In the meantime, Cropper had been roughly imprisoned in a room guarded by a pair of British soldiers, both armed with muskets and standing at the outside of the door. Patiently he bided his time, waiting for an opportune moment to make his escape, as the two men began to quaff their share of the colonel's best liquor. Then, he quietly raised the latch and opened the door. Before the soldiers knew what was happening, he had jumped over them and vanished into the winter darkness. Wearing only his underclothes, Cropper ran two miles through the winter night to the house of a neighbor. Undoubtedly with some effort he aroused the man, who had also been a soldier, and persuaded him to provide guns and return with him to Bowman's Folly. Carrying three old Tower muskets, the two made their way back as expeditiously as possible in the dark to Cropper's house.[19]

As the two Virginians neared Bowman's Folly, the neighbor grew increasingly nervous. The colonel's house was now fully lit, and considerable noise could be heard coming from inside. Frightened by the prospect of encountering a superior number of the enemy, who might next descend on his own home if they recognized him or, worse, captured him, the neighbor lost his nerve, threw down his gun, and took to his heels. Undismayed, Cropper picked up the musket, and with all three weapons in his arms quietly approached the house. Since he certainly could not beat them with numbers, he tried one of the oldest tricks in the book. In quick succession he fired the old guns and shouted as loud as he could: "Come on, boys, we have them now." The bold deception worked flawlessly. The inebriated enemy, suddenly surprised by what appeared to be an obviously superior force, dashed from the house toward their boats and rowed to *Thistle* and safety without looking back.[20]

The colonel had returned just in time. Had he arrived a few minutes later he might well have found Bowman's Folly in ashes for the raiders had been laying a train of powder to it with the intention of blowing it up. Nevertheless, all of his furniture and crockery had been ruined, his belongings stolen, and liquor supplies drained or destroyed. Thirty of his slaves had been carried away. But thankfully his wife and daughter, who had been locked up in an outhouse, were safe. The arrival of the local militia the next day did little to dispel his uninhibited rage. Revenge against *Thistle* and her nefarious commander and crew, he vowed to himself, must soon be his.[21]

John Cropper began at once to plan his reprisal. With his wife understandably worried about another attack on Bowman's Folly, he was obliged to remove his family to another of his properties for safety, a place named Latin House, which was much nearer to the courthouse. When intelligence arrived late on February 24 that Williams in *Thistle,* accompanied by a small schooner commanded by a Lieutenant Morris, had just returned and was lying at the south end of nearby Cedar Island, he saw his opportunity. He immediately began to organize an expedition to intercept and take the enemy by surprise. It took a full day for Major Simpson and a small company of thirty-five militiamen, whose homes were dispersed throughout the region, to muster. Once assembled, however, they prepared to march immediately under Cropper's command, taking with them a single brass four-pounder field piece.[22]

At 8:00 A.M. Friday, February 26, probably employing Simpson's boat as a ferry, Cropper landed his small force on the north end of Cedar Island to avoid alarming the enemy, who was then ensconced off the opposite end. With all expedition they marched south toward Wachapreague Inlet, where *Thistle* and her consort reportedly lay at anchor. On their arrival, after an excessively fatiguing march across the snow-covered sands during which many of his company deserted, the colonel personally conducted a reconnaissance of the point. With absolutely no cover available, he deemed it a most unacceptable place to erect a battery. Finding it "to deceive my expectations in ev'ry respect" as a place "fit to mount an attack," he later wrote, and with his remaining men completely worn out from the march, his zeal for immediate vengeance was severely frustrated. Moreover, they had set off in haste, without a sufficient supply of provisions and water, and then been subjected to a storm of freezing rain while on the march. Cropper decided to pull back from the exposed position. "I determined to withdraw the gun as far as possible," he recorded that evening in his journal, "which was about one mile, left her there under the care of Major Simpson, and went off to the main almost dead w[i]t[h] fatigue."[23]

Having returned to Latin House, he was informed by a county militia officer the next evening that another neighbor, Colonel George Parker, had managed to land an iron four-pounder gun on the beach at Parramore Island, on the other side of Wachapreague Inlet, and was also "endeavoring to prevent the going out of the tenders." Rejuvenated by Parker's initiative, Cropper immediately set about rounding up some nearby residents, and was soon en route back to Cedar Island with a four-pounder iron gun in tow. This time he set about erecting a battery on the open beach, probably under the cover of darkness. With batteries on both shores at the outlet of Wachapreague, *Thistle* and her consort were trapped. When he discovered his predicament Thomas Byron Williams knew there was little choice but to fight or surrender. He chose to fight.[24]

John Cropper's account of the engagement that followed on Sunday, February 28, was remarkably terse: "3 o'clock the tenders made sail and engaged the fort on the beach, and passed out after an obstinate struggle, one of them having her hull and rigging torn to pieces." When the privateersmen who had nearly destroyed his home, threatened his wife and child, and inflicted so much misery and destruction on his neighbors fought their way past the battery, the young colonel was soon successfully revenged on his enemy. As *Thistle,* the scourge of Accomack, struggled to push through the inlet amid a storm of gunfire, she was repeatedly struck and soon sinking. The "Infamous Tar" knew capture was not an option. Desperately, his crew labored at the pumps as the inlet's waters surged through gaping shot holes, but to no avail.[25]

There is little record regarding the last minutes of the marauding privateer sloop *Thistle,* only that the militiamen of Accomack County, Virginia, standing on the cold shores of desolate Cedar Island, watched her sink with all hands aboard. Lieutenant Colonel John Cropper had indeed been revenged.

# 7

## Now That Is What I Call Combat

Captain the Honorable William Clement Finch, RN, stood at the taffrail of his command, HMS *Terrible,* and viewed with a mixture of pride and apprehension the British line of battle as it approached the Chesapeake capes on the morning of September 3, 1781. His ship, a seventy-four-gun third-rate two-decker assigned to the rearmost division of the fleet, was from all outward appearances as impressive, powerful, ponderous, and bellicose-looking as any in the nineteen-ship line. Indeed, she and her sister ships were without question the ultimate weapons of sea power, the mightiest engines of destruction humankind had yet devised, and the very backbone of the Royal Navy and the British Empire. When each vessel of the fleet was employed as an integral component of the whole, sailed and fought with efficiency, and maintained its own position in the line of battle without deviation in accordance with the long-accepted naval doctrine known as the "Fighting Instructions," the Royal Navy was difficult, if not impossible, to beat. Or so it was believed.

To suggest that *Terrible* was formidable was an understatement. She was, like all of her sisters, nothing less than a mightily armed and heavily populated floating fortress, a wooden, Brobdingnagian city on the sea. Like all maritime societies, that which abided aboard a Royal Navy man-of-war had its own traditions, customs, foodways, rules and laws, and social order quite separate from the terrestrial world. So it was aboard *Terrible,* whose reason for being was no different from the rest of the fleet: to impose British authority, might, and order through force of arms upon the high seas against both national enemies and rebellious subjects of the crown.

Below decks lay *Terrible*'s deadly business center, where two tiers of cannons could belch forth nearly a half-ton of death in a single broadside, with cannonballs the size of human heads. Then there was the grape shot, chain shot, bar shot, red-hot shot, nails, and a wide assortment of other piercing, cutting, gouging, and ripping junk that might be stuffed down a cannon's throat and fired cloud-like at an enemy. With more than thirty-five guns roaring in unison in an opening broadside, the murderous firepower of a third-rater such as *Terrible* can only be described as devastating.

The British fleet was under the overall command of Admiral Thomas Graves and was divided into three divisions. Sailing from New York, every captain in each division was well aware at this stage of the conflict that his mission was critical, perhaps even pivotal, to the war effort. All were cognizant of the sequence of events leading to their recent hurried deployment and their current mission. It had all begun on August 28 when Graves had learned that an enemy squadron of eight French warships and eighteen transports under Admiral Jacques Comte de Barras de Saint-Laurent had just sailed for the Chesapeake. The convoy, it was discovered, was transporting a large shipment of siege artillery to an Anglo-American force that was attempting to surround a British army at a little Virginia river port called Yorktown. It was up to Graves to intercept the French and to deliver supplies and two thousand troops to the besieged army. Success was critical indeed, but given the superiority of the British fleet and the historical inclination of the French to avoid a major sea engagement while outnumbered, few thought the mission could fail.

Finch alone might have had some trepidation regarding his ship and its role in the new campaign, despite her imposing appearance and muscle. At 1,644 tons she was an enormous vessel, even for her time. Built by Barnard at Harwich and launched on September 4, 1762, during the French and Indian War, she had served king and country well. Her overall length between perpendiculars was 167 feet and 47 feet abeam. As with all ships of her rate and size, her main armament was carried on two gun decks (although she had three decks running the length of the ship), and included twenty-eight thirty-two-pounders, thirty thirty-pounders, and sixteen nine-pounders, which could toss a total of 1,940 pounds of metal at a double broadside firing.[1]

The great majority of the ship's company, which numbered between six hundred and seven hundred men fit for action at any given time, were berthed on the second of her three decks. They slung their fourteen-inch-wide hammocks from the beams of the deckheads, and stowed them by day in netting troughs that lined the sides of the forecastle and quarterdeck. The netting troughs, during battle, doubled as barricades for the protection of sharpshooters. The crew ate their meals on the gun deck, on tables slung between the guns. With gunports usually kept closed while at sea to prevent water from coming in, there was little light on the gun deck except that which shaped a course through the hatch. Nor was there much circulation of air. In short, the company's living conditions aboard *Terrible* were crowded, smelly, and generally unpleasant. Of course, there was the added possibility of being injured or dying in combat. Yet the ship and her men had been an integral part of the seaborne walls that had kept England strong, her enemies timorous, and her vassals obedient.[2]

A year after the onset of the American Revolution, *Terrible* was listed, like many old veterans of the last war, out of commission. She had at the time been among thirty-three men-of-war (all but two being first- to third-raters) held in port ready to be commissioned "at the first order for the most difficult cruises." By June 1776 there were already eighty-seven warships patrolling in North American waters, a dozen cruising in the West Indies, thirty-four more under construction, and thirty-one undergoing, or desperately in need of, repairs. Still, some said that the navy, which also had to maintain patrols off the coast of Africa, in the Mediterranean, in the East Indies, off Newfoundland, and elsewhere with but a handful more ships, had been stretched entirely too thin. Only nineteen guard ships protected the English Channel. Three others were on long-term voyages of discovery. When the war in America escalated, the need for ships had become so great that eighteen ships that had been condemned as unfit and scheduled for destruction had to be called back into service. Yet, even with the largest and most efficient battle-tested naval force in the world, it had not been enough.[3]

From the very beginning of the war, England's most virulent rival for empire, France, knew practically everything about the ships of the Royal Navy—their organization, conditions, strengths, weaknesses, supplies, and operations. The French were well aware that during the dozen years of tranquility following the French and Indian War, the British navy had suffered from "false economies" at the Admiralty and outright profiteering by naval contractors. France's own navy had been virtually annihilated during the last conflict, yet by February 1778, when France formally allied herself to the revolutionaries in America, the French fleet had been completely resurrected. A proud King Louis XVI had declared the navy "the first service of the realm" and, under the Duc de Choisel's administration, had lavished enormous amounts of money on its growth and improvement. Thus, when France entered the fight her navy included no fewer than eighty new ships-of-the-line to be pitted against sixty-nine in England's largely antiquated, sea-worn battle fleet. At that time only eleven line-of-battle ships were then in American waters, although thirty-five more were listed as being readied for sea. Even the British recognized that the French ships were faster, more maneuverable, and better constructed than their own. French gunners, after a vigorous training program, were far more accurate at long-range fire. When Spain honored the Bourbon family compact the following year by joining in the struggle against England, sixty more ships-of-the-line were arrayed against the Royal Navy.[4]

*Terrible* was perhaps as representative of England's plight at sea as of her strength. Not until February 1777 had she been deemed ready to return to duty. Initially placed under the command of Captain Sir Richard Bickerton, she had been assigned to cruise off Spain and Portugal to protect trade against American privateers. On April 15 she took her first prize, the sixteen-gun Massachusetts privateer *Rising States,* James Thompson master. By July she was cruising in the Irish Channel. Over the next few years hard duty and little time for repairs would take their toll. Assignment to the disease-ridden West Indies, where both men and ships frequently fell victims to the elements, had been even more ruinous. When Finch had taken command, *Terrible* was in a tragic state of disrepair. The voyage with Admiral Hood from the West Indies to join the fleet at New York had been difficult in the extreme for both captain and crew. The ship leaked incessantly, and her men worked at the pumps the entire voyage simply to keep her afloat. As she sailed south with Graves, she bore the dubious distinction of being the third oldest member of the fleet (exceeded only by HMS *Shrewsbury,* built in 1758, and *Centaur,* formerly a French warship captured in

1759). Soon she would enter the most important naval battle of the American Revolution, indeed one of the most significant sea fights in history, with work parties laboring around the clock at the pumps even before the first shot was fired.[5]

The Battle of the Virginia Capes—and the ultimate fate of the Revolution and of HMS *Terrible*—actually had its origins in the highlands of New York, where General George Washington and his army had been firmly ensconced for months. It had long been the general's principal goal to drive the British from their New York City stronghold, even as two separate British armies, one under Major General Lord Cornwallis and the other under the American traitor Benedict Arnold, had been running rampant through the South. Washington had been desperate to counter the damage being inflicted in the lower Chesapeake Tidewater by Arnold and had sent troops under Major General the Marquis de Lafayette to pursue him. As the war in Virginia escalated, an undefeated but weary army under Lord Charles Cornwallis had marched north from the Carolinas to consolidate a quarter of British troop strength in North America. Failing to corner Lafayette's much smaller force, Cornwallis had retired with seven thousand British and Hessian soldiers to Yorktown to recuperate and await reinforcements and supplies from New York. It would prove to be an imprudent and fatal move.

Unknown to either Cornwallis or British headquarters in New York, far to the south in the West Indies a massive French fleet under the brilliant fifty-nine-year-old Admiral François-Joseph Paul Comte de Grasse, replete with fresh troops from Europe, was coming north. Washington pleaded with the French minister to the United States, the Chevalier de la Luzerne, that the fleet be directed to cooperate with the American army to trap Cornwallis. If the French navy could block the narrow gateway to the Chesapeake, cutting British army supply lines by sea, the American and French armies could march south from New York and carry out a surprise pincers movement to decisively destroy the best troops the British had. On August 14, 1781, Washington learned that de Grasse had agreed to put his fleet at the general's disposal. De Barras would sail from Rhode Island with additional troops and logistical support.

Since the beginning of the war, with little effectual support from the Continental Navy, the Revolution had been but one military disaster after another for the Americans and was barely able to sustain itself. Now, the French marine was finally in play on a grand scale. De Grasse would be heading for the Chesapeake with twenty-eight ships-of the-line, four frigates, and fifteen transports (that he had personally chartered on his own account), as well as three regiments of French infantry, 100 dragoons, and 350 artillerymen to reinforce Lafayette. He could linger about the Tidewater as late as October. Washington was now able to envision for the first time the possibility of combining superior land and sea forces in a concerted effort to eliminate a major component of the British army. Now assured of an entire French fleet, he acted without hesitation. In utmost secrecy, he dispatched instructions to Lafayette to contain and occupy Cornwallis.

He then dispatched the bulk of his own troops, as well as an allied French force under Lieutenant General Jean-Baptiste Comte de Rochambeau, on a forced march to Virginia, even as de Grasse was sailing north in a serpentine approach to avoid British detection.

De Grasse's absence in the West Indies quickly aroused British suspicions, and an expedition under Rear Admiral Sir Samuel Hood consisting of fourteen line-of-battle ships, including *Terrible,* was sent to find him. On August 25, Hood arrived in the Chesapeake and saw that it was empty. He pressed on for New York, where he soon joined Admiral Graves and his own force of five ships-of-the-line.

Vexed by constant attrition through battle, desertions, disease, and recruiting problems, the Royal Navy fleet was extremely undermanned. Press gangs were quickly deployed in New York City to forcefully round up at least four hundred colonists to fill out the serious manpower deficiencies. The impressment of a civilian population for the navy was unpleasant for all involved. One officer recorded that the procedure "furnished us with droll yet distressing scenes—taking the husband from the arms of his wife in bed, the searching for them when hid beneath the warm clothes, and, the better to prevent delay taking them naked, while the frantic partner of his bed, forgetting the delicacy of her sex, pursued us to the doors with shrieks and imprecations, and exposing their naked persons to the rude view of an unfeeling press gang."[6]

Only four days after Hood had peeked into the Virginia capes, de Grasse dropped anchor inside Chesapeake Bay, surprising and capturing several Royal Navy frigates in the process. With the arrival of the Franco-American army, Yorktown and Cornwallis's troops therein were quickly invested. The French immediately began to disembark their troops, and dispatch their transports up the bay to help ferry a significant portion of Washington's forces down to the York. At that moment, Graves was still ignorant of the whereabouts of de Grasse but informed Hood that he had learned that de Barras had just sailed from Rhode Island, presumably bound for the Chesapeake. The French squadron and its transports, he noted grimly, would have to be intercepted and destroyed. On August 31, with little time to make repairs to many of the vessels in the squadron that had just arrived from the West Indies, the combined fleet under Graves's overall command set sail for the Chesapeake, manned by 11,311 men and carrying 1,408 guns. Few envisioned that they were embarking on the pivotal naval campaign of the war.

The voyage was anything but smooth. As Graves's armada plowed southward, it was immediately apparent that many of the ships were having difficulty. No fewer than six were leaking badly. Only three days into the voyage, *Terrible,* perhaps the worst impaired of them all, raised a distress signal. The admiral ordered the entire fleet brought to. It was soon learned that the old ship had come all the way from the Leeward Islands with five pumps working constantly, and the situation was not improving. There was no alternative, however, but to continue on, for every ship would be needed.[7]

· · ·

On the Chesapeake, de Grasse found it expedient to post ships-of-the-line at the mouth of the James and York Rivers to blockade Lord Cornwallis and all of his transports. The action reduced the available French fleet to twenty-four line-of-battle ships, manned by 18,200 men and carrying 2,822 guns, to defend the entrance to the Chesapeake.

Early on the morning of September 5, a French picket frigate sighted the oncoming British and signaled their approach. Soon afterward, about 11:00 A.M., one of Graves's lookouts reported sighting masts just inside the entrance to the bay. The admiral, at first believing that he had cornered de Barras's small squadron, was delighted, but as he drew closer and discovered a virtual forest of masts, joy turned to dismay. Yet the element of surprise still remained on his side, and the French appeared to be at anchor and in total disarray.[8]

About noon, while at anchor in Lynnhaven Roads against a lee shore and within the confines of the Chesapeake, de Grasse was stunned to find himself the one surprised. A powerful enemy armada was coming on full bore. The danger of being locked in was imminent, and he quickly ordered his fleet to form a line of battle. An incredible flurry of activity followed, as sails were unfurled, guns readied, shot distributed, and anchor cables attached to buoys and slipped.

With the tide momentarily favoring the French, the movement to sail and form a line of battle, one proud Frenchman later wrote, "was executed with such precision and boldness, in spite of the absence of the best-drilled part of the crew, that the enemy, doubtless taken by surprise, at once wore so as to be on the same tack as the French fleet. It had the cape E. and E.N.E.; in this position, being to leeward, it awaited the enemy's attack. The issue of the expedition, the vacancy left by the crews employed in the debarkation, the fear of getting too far from the mouths of the York and James rivers, and the fear lest the English fleet, by its known superior sailing, should succeed in getting between these mouths and the French fleet, all obliged it to keep on the defensive. The enemy held the weather gage in excess."[9]

Despite his inferior numbers, Graves's line, bowsprit to stern in the finest tradition of the Fighting Instructions, still held the advantage of surprise and position, with a northeast wind at its back and soon an incoming tide. It was almost a stately cavalcade, exacting in its formation, a magnificent, exquisite demonstration of precision and military orchestration and, as events would prove, completely hollow. Hood's division led the English van, the admiral flying his flag aboard HMS *Barfleur,* with *Alfred* leading the line. The second division was in the center, with Graves's Union Jack flying stiffly at the mizzen peak above the ninety-gun flagship *London.* The third and rearmost division was commanded by Rear Admiral Samuel Francis Drake in *Princessa* and included, among others, *Terrible* and *Ajax,* another ship that had been fighting simply to stay afloat during the entire voyage from Antigua. As the lead vessel of the fleet approached the entrance to the bay, it became apparent that the Middle Ground Shoal and the narrow three mile-wide ship channel on its southwest side were significantly reducing the French fleet's ability to maneuver effectively. Moreover, though Graves could not have known it, almost half of de Grasse's officers and crew were occupied elsewhere, ferrying troops and artillery ashore. Some French vessels had barely enough men to man half their guns. As several warships in the French van attempted to form in line, it became immediately evident that de Grasse's force was still in some confusion. All that was required for an English victory was to assail the still-forming French fleet, order "general chase" to cut off each division as it emerged from the bay, and destroy it in detail.

Then, the incredible occurred; it was a decision that would alter the course of the battle and ultimately the history of the world.

As de Grasse came out of the bay at the head of the French line in his enormous hundred-gun flagship *Ville de Paris,* Graves ordered "line ahead" instead of an immediate attack. He thus permitted, before ordering a signal for close action, the French to emerge and begin forming a complete line of battle with their twenty-four ships. All advantage but the weather gage had been sacrificed to follow the edicts of the Fighting Instructions to engage a superior force. At 2:05 P.M., as *Alfred* approached dangerously close to the Middle Ground, Graves ordered the fleet to "wear," or pivot in place and reverse course 180 degrees. This maneuver placed Drake's division, with *Shrewsbury* in the lead and *Terrible* in the van, heading toward the open sea, with Hood's division in the rear, running almost parallel with the still forming French line. Drake's division, the weakest of all, would soon bear the preponderance of combat.[10]

*Terrible*'s desperately vulnerable condition was evident from the outset, even to de Grasse's officers. One French account later reported "the *Terrible,* which was pumping four pumps, not feeling in a condition to take part in the action, kept the windward of the enemy's line, athwart Drake, who signaled her to take her position, which she lost some time in doing. But the Rear Admiral soon persuaded her to take her place by sending her three cannonballs. Then it was that they tacked to the larboard as we did, and hoisted a great white flag astern; but they soon struck it and hoisted their own." Indeed, only a few minutes after the contest had begun, at 2:52 and then again at 3:09, signals were raised for the division to lead more toward the starboard, in the direction of the enemy. *Terrible, Montagu, Royal Oak, Princessa,* and *Alcide* were instructed to get back to their stations in line.[11]

For the next hour and a half the vans of the two fleets slowly closed in a V rather than parallel lines. Six and a half hours after the initial sightings, both lines were in perfect formation, even as the rearmost French vessels were still emerging from the Chesapeake. Thus, only the lead ships in both lines came close enough to engage. Unfortunately for the British, Graves now raised contradictory signals. Hoisting a white pendant and a blue-and-white checkered flag beneath to signal, "bear down and engage close," he ordered every commander in the fleet to turn and attack the nearest French warship. For some reason, he had neglected to bring down the signal flying for "line ahead," which superseded all other orders. Thus, the British center and rear maintained their elegantly straight line, even as Graves turned *London* in the center to confront the enemy. The result was total confusion and disarray in the English line.

At the vanguards of the two converging lines, the lead ships were but a musket shot apart as the first exchange of broadsides erupted. Damage to the British fleet was debilitating, especially to the spars and rigging. One half of all British casualties incurred during the fight, in fact, were aboard the lead ships, *Shrews-bury* and *Intrepid*. The rest of Drake's division, including *Alcide, Ajax,* and *Princessa,* nevertheless suffered greatly. When one of the French division commanders, Commodore de Bougainville in *Auguste,* waded brazenly into the fight and came close to boarding *Princessa,* Drake somehow managed to avoid him. The Frenchman immediately turned his guns on Captain Finch's now dreadfully injured *Terrible,* the weakest ship in the fleet. Within minutes a pair of cannonballs had crashed through an already-sprung foremast. Another pair buried themselves deeply in the wood. One of the shots, retrieved by carpenters after the fight, was weighed and found to be thirty-nine pounds.[12]

Damage to *Terrible* mounted as *Auguste* pounded away. *Terrible* returned fire relentlessly, but her own suffering was escalating. Several shots smashed her hull between wind and water. The ability to keep the water pumped out was soon being hopelessly compromised. The ship's pumps "being blown, and only kept together by tarr'd canvas, lead, and mouldings, the chains worn out, and but few links to repair them, pump leather all expended; she was making two feet, two inches of water every twenty-five minutes." Some officers were already despairing of her survival.[13]

"The British van was cut to pieces before Graves got into action at all," British critics of the admiral's performance later lamented.[14] "The two vans having come so close as to be almost within pistol shot," wrote one of the French participants, "the fire was long well sustained, and the affair seemed about to be decisive, when Admiral Hood made a signal to the English rear division, which he commanded, to bear down on the French rear. The admiral [de Grasse] witnessed this movement with pleasure and prepared to tack his whole fleet together, bearing N.N.W., which would inevitably have thrown the English line into confusion, but Admiral Graves anticipated him and signaled his whole fleet to keep the wind. The heads of the two fleets gradually fell off in consequence of this new order of the English admiral, and the fire ceased at 6½ P.M."[15]

Captain Finch assessed the damage to *Terrible* and was not optimistic as he watched his bloodied crewmen fighting the rising water in the hold. Graves was equally pessimistic. Not only was *Terrible* leaking badly, but *Ajax* was also in a similar state. *London* had been savaged, and most of the ships of both Drake's and Graves's divisions had suffered serious damage. Neither side, however, acknowledged defeat or gave up the field of battle, although it was clear that the British had suffered far worse than the French. If there was any glory to be had, it belonged to Bougainville for taking on both *Princessa* and *Terrible*. De Grasse would later pay the commodore a well-deserved accolade for his action against *Princessa:* "Now that is what I call 'combat'!" he declared exuberantly. "For a while I thought you were going to board!" Soon after the battle, the French commander in chief publicly declared to Generals Washington and Rochambeau that "the laurels of the day belong to De Bougainville . . . for having led the [French] van and having personally fought the *Terrible*."[16]

· · ·

The French fleet passed the night not far from the British line of battle, the fires in all the warships lighted. These beacons of triumph were not belied at day-break the next morning, for the French readily perceived that the British fleet, if not mortally injured, had been mutilated. Though only 90 men had been killed and 246 others wounded, against 209 French killed and wounded, the English ships had been devastated in their masting and maneuverability. Moreover, Admirals Graves and Hood were at icy odds with each other about what to do next, even as *Terrible* continued to fight the flood. The two national opponents, however, still in sight of each other making repairs, spent September 6 favored by a rather frail north wind that continued until 4:00 P.M. The breezes then blew in from the southwest, and the French again sought to approach Graves's battered armada. It was, however, too late to begin the affray anew, and both sides lay that night as the preceding.

For two days the fleets faced each other, separated by only seven or eight miles of ocean. Then sea conditions changed dramatically. "On the 8th of September," Graves later reported, "it came on to blow pretty fresh" with violent thunder and lightning. At 11:00 A.M., when standing against a head sea, *Terrible* made the signal of distress, and the frigates *Orpheus* and *Fortunee* had to be sent immediately to her aid.[17]

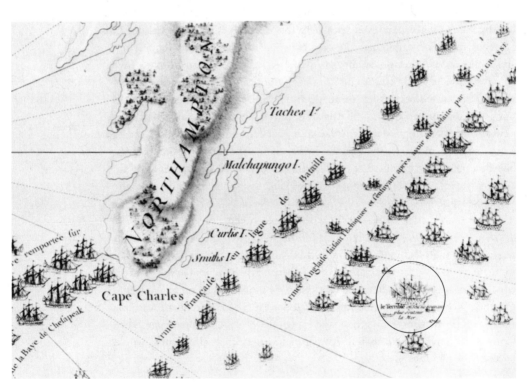

Detail from a French chart, published in Paris in 1782, showing a portion of the overall alignments of the British and French fleets during the Battle of the Virginia Capes. Note the position *(circled)* of HMS *Terrible* at the time of her loss. (William L. Clements Library, Ann Arbor, MI)

The following day the two fleets again began to maneuver, and Graves became even more acutely aware of just how crippled his squadron actually was. HMS *Intrepid* had lost her main topmast during the maneuvering and was about to lose her foreyard. Finally, on September 9, the two fleets lost sight of each other. De Grasse had abandoned the field to return to the Chesapeake, the protection of which he was obliged to insure at all costs. He would continue to maintain control of the entrance to the bay to ensure the trapdoor escape route for Cornwallis remained closed.

Captain Finch and his men were still working desperately aboard *Terrible* to keep the old warship afloat. On the same day that the French disappeared from the scene, the captain was obliged to inform Graves that even with all pumps working, his ship was now taking on water at the rate of six feet per hour. Not surprisingly, he was "apprehensive that the ship cannot be saved." By September 10 the rate had increased to eight feet an hour. In a drastic measure to lighten ship, he ordered five of the lower-deck guns thrown overboard "while it was still in our power to do so." Others were marked to follow. "Although we do not make quite so much water on this tack," he declared, "we make too much to give us any great hopes of being able to carry her into port."[18]

Finch's pleas for direction from the commander in chief brought an eight-man survey party headed by First Lieutenant Richard Ash. The surveyors examined *Terrible* and unanimously determined that it was "absolutely impracticable" for her to make port even with help from other vessels of the fleet. On September 11, the weather had calmed somewhat and Graves summoned Hood and Drake to a council of war aboard *London* to determine *Terrible*'s fate. "We are of opinion," they agreed, "to take out People and sink her." Accordingly, that evening the great ship was hastily stripped. Her crewmen, powder, and provisions were distributed around the fleet. A dozen of her marines, thirty barrels of powder, gunner's supplies, and the like were transferred to the flagship. Then a seacock was opened to let the Atlantic waters claim yet another victim. Incredibly, the ship refused to sink. The next evening, at 8:30 P.M., she was set afire and burned, becoming the only line-of-battle ship lost as a result of the Battle of the Virginia Capes.[19]

Graves limped back to New York with only eighteen ships-of-the-line. The drubbing had not only been humiliating, but its consequences would be far reaching. Though a second effort would be launched to rescue Cornwallis, it would arrive far too late. The cream of the British army and its German mercenary hirelings, hopelessly besieged by twenty thousand troops under Washington and Rochambeau, surrendered on October 19. The Battle of the Virginia Capes had, in denying him succor and a possible route of escape, guaranteed Cornwallis's fate, and ultimately American independence. The world would never be the same again.

Recriminations for the British defeat at Yorktown and the standoff naval engagement at the Virginia capes would soon reach epic proportions. The loss of *Terrible,* perhaps as symbolic as any other event in the futile campaign, aroused enormous ire throughout England. A hue and cry was raised over the deliberate destruction of the venerable warship. One writer in the *Political and Military Journal* caustically noted that simply "because she made six feet of water an hour" sinking her had been "a very wrong step. Sir Samuel Hood in coming from the West Indies never thought of destroying her, though she made the same quantity of water during that passage. Besides, there are other facts to go upon. After the action she made no more water than she did before it. But when it was deemed necessary to sink her, and the men were taken out, in order to hasten her sinking, they opened a large cock of nearly two inches in diameter, to let the water into her hold, and left her a whole night, yet with this assistance she would not go down; therefore the next day, that she might not continue to swim, and perhaps fall into the hands of the enemy, she was set on fire. If an able officer had been at the head of the fleet, the *Terrible* would not have been destroyed."[20]

The Franco-American triumph at Yorktown, which eventually obliged England to recognize American independence, is acknowledged as one of the most decisive battles of the world. But it was the Battle of the Virginia Capes that had ensured American victory, all thanks to confused flag signals and a stern adherence to Fighting Instructions written more than a century before. And no one would even remember the travails of HMS *Terrible*.

# Plunder till They Could Plunder No More

No one knows for certain when the first coins were found near the entrance to Indian River Inlet. Some say they were discovered by a vacationing Milford, Delaware, resident while surf fishing a year or so after the inlet had been dredged in 1930.[1] The earliest published account, however, states that coins had been found from time to time as far back as 1878, when a beachcombing tourist picked up two gold pieces and a Spanish-milled dollar in the surf line. The first well-publicized find, the one that began to focus the public's fascination on the area, was made at the height of the Depression, on February 22, 1937, when enrollees from a local Civilian Conservation Corps camp picked up several eighteenth-century English pennies and half pennies lying partially buried in the sand. Not surprisingly, a holiday treasure hunt ensued, organized by the corps' local educational adviser, Edward L. Richards. Within days the new finds had made the newspapers, whose reports conjectured that the coins were from the wreck of an old sailing vessel. Moreover, they revealed that coins had "been found in lesser quantities following storms and northeast winds for the past several years."[2]

A week after the CCC hunt, Major Lindsley L. Beach, a retired army officer, and two companions discovered in the surf line "an old sea chest," three feet square, bound in copper and weighing an estimated four hundred pounds. Ever since his retirement, the major had whiled away his hours beachcombing for anything of interest, and near the inlet he had already accrued a collection of nearly one hundred coins dating from 1774 to 1782. All had been English pennies or half pennies. But the sea chest was a beachcomber's dream. Before the incoming tide could halt their investigation, Beach and his companions had pried open one of the "compartments" of the heavy, barnacle-encrusted chest only to find it empty. Unfortunately, there was no holding back Mother Nature, and the chest soon disappeared beneath the incoming tide, never to be seen again. Major Beach was a patient man, however, and continued to patrol the lonely shoreline after every storm. On March 13, following another blow, he discovered a coin dated 1749, the earliest found, and another minted in 1775. The word was out. Soon afterward, youths from Ocean View retrieved more than 150 coins, and Captain A. C. C. Osborne, of the local Coast Guard station, and two of his men,

W. J. Cobb and S. B. Savage, found still more.[3] From that time on, the waterfront would bear the deliciously inviting sobriquet Coin Beach, a name that would one day draw tourists, curiosity seekers, and even treasure hunters from far and wide.

But one question was on everyone's mind: where did the coins come from?

John Elliott was an enterprising young man, a pioneer of sorts, born in 1762 in Northern Ireland into a family of means and property. Elliott family tradition holds that John's father had sent him on a family reconnaissance mission to America aboard the ship *Lazy Mary* in 1784. The great American Revolution had finally ended, and many in Ireland who still suffered under British rule longed for the same freedoms that had been won across the Atlantic. An ever-increasing westward flood of Irish emigration began. John's task was to get a feel for the land of opportunity, to see if it was indeed a place for the Elliott clan to begin a new life, free from oppression.[4]

The directives John's father had given him were clear. If, at the end of the year he thought the family should immigrate to America, he was to send coded instructions "to do some impossible thing." That way, if the missive were intercepted and read by authorities in Ireland, they would not deliberately prohibit John's two younger brothers, William and Simon, both of conscription age, from leaving the country. (All young men at the time were obligated to serve a number of years in British military service.) The Elliott family in Ireland was not without some small fortune and possessed a substantial house. John, of course, found America to be a land of more than promise, a place where a man was free to do as he pleased, worship as he chose, and travel anywhere he desired. He thus wrote to his family, outlining the "impossible thing." He wrote that he was incapable of building himself a house in America and entreated his parents to send theirs, clearly a most "impossible thing" to do. They understood that John was recommending that they move to America.[5] The entire extended family, including scores of cousins, nieces, nephews, uncles, and aunts, accepted the challenge immediately.

On July 9, 1785, the core Elliott family— the father, two sons, and five daughters—boarded the good ship *Faithful Steward* at the port of Londonderry. They were accompanied by 237 other passengers, many of them, such as the Lees, Stewarts, and Espeys, blood relations and all bound for the port of Philadelphia. More than one hundred of the passengers were women and small children.[6] The Lee clan, numbering fifty members, was as plentiful as any aboard. James Lee, born in County Donegal in 1759, was typical of the young family leaders charged with shepherding his own extended kin to the Promised Land. His party consisted of no less than three brothers, two beautiful sisters, three sets of uncles and aunts, thirty-three cousins, and assorted other relations.[7] Among the many Espeys aboard were Hugh and Mary Stewart Espey who, accompanied by their own five children, were sailing to join their eldest sons William and Hugh Jr., awaiting their arrival in Pennsylvania.[8] For all aboard the crowded ship, the allure of America was the same. As John McIntire Jr., one of the emigrants aboard, later stated, they were bound for "a country where the banner of freedom waved proudly; a country where heroes lived; where genius expanded to full perfection; where every good was possessed."[9]

*Faithful Steward* was a large three-masted vessel, 150 feet in length, 350 tons burthen, and said to be capable of enduring the worst the Atlantic could throw at her. John Maxwell Nesbitt, James Campbell, and William Allison, all Philadelphia merchants, owned the ship. Her commander, Connoly McCausland, was a rough, hard-drinking mariner who commanded an equally tough crew of twelve. The ship carried not only an overly large number of passengers, most of whom were squeezed into cramped, black quarters below decks, but also a "very considerable" amount of their property, sufficient enough to help securely establish them in the new nation.[10] Unlike many transoceanic voyages of the eighteenth century, *Faithful Steward*'s had been blessed with excellent sailing. Many on board later reported that they "had a very favourable passage, during which nothing of moment occurred, the greatest harmony having prevailed amongst them."[11]

By September 1, after a tedious voyage of a month and a half, they were nearing their destination, Delaware Bay, and everyone was buoyant with expectation. When a young couple named Gregg announced that it was also their first wedding anniversary and they wished to celebrate the occasion with a dinner, Captain McCausland readily gave his consent. The captain, mates, and a number of passengers, of course, were invited to join in the festivities. Following the meal, which was attended with considerable goodwill, there was a party with "music, dancing and every description of mirth." As evening fell and the spirits began to flow ever more freely, a "most intemperate carousal was the closing scene of the day." Among the most heavily intoxicated of the celebrants were the captain and the first mate, "who were borne insensible to their cabins."[12]

It was, unfortunately, a most inauspicious time for the ship to be without a commander, for even as McCausland and the first mate, Mr. Standfield, were being placed in their beds, a nasty wind had sprung up from the east. The ship's speed was accelerated through the water, driving her much closer toward the Delaware capes than the navigator had earlier computed when plotting his course after taking a sighting of the evening star. Second mate Gwyn, the only officer left sober and on duty, grew concerned. At 10:00 P.M. he nervously ordered the leadsman to take soundings and was stunned to find the ship skimming along through the darkness in only four fathoms. Instantly he ordered the helm thrown over and hauled all sails to bear off the bank, but it was too late.[13]

With a sickening grinding sound the ship struck bottom. Many aboard, lying in their crowded hammocks and bunks, were thrown to the floor. Two small children were instantly killed by the fall. In the pitch-black darkness below decks, sheer panic ensued. The horror can only be imagined, as husbands sought to find their screaming wives and children while others tried to rush topside all at once. Those who got there first were not encouraged, for in the obscurity of night they could see no land. Yet the ship was unquestionably stranded near the beach, for they could hear the frightening roar of breakers crashing against the unseen shore. Though they could not confirm it at that moment, their bow was indeed pointed landward and the sterncastle toward the open ocean. High waves, propelled by increasingly heavier winds, began washing over the stern and soon contributed to the panic.[14]

Second mate Gwyn instantly dispatched a seaman to awaken the captain. Mc-Causland was immediately shaken and roused from his drunken stupor, although inebriation still blanketed his senses. When informed of the situation, he growled ferociously, slurring his words, to the bearer of bad tidings: "The man that takes my command, I will hang in Philadelphia." The consternation and astonishment that prevailed is easier conceived than described. Young John McIntire later recalled "the shrieks of the women and the cries of the children were insufferable." The worst was still to come.[15]

By the onset of the first gray morning haze, it was ascertained that *Faithful Steward* had struck ground between 100 and 150 yards from the shore on the Mohoba Bank (also called by Irish immigrants Mahogan's Bay), four leagues south of Cape Henlopen and nearby Indian River Inlet. The ship was in desperate shape for throughout the seemingly endless night the waves had pounded her ceaselessly, breaking over her deck and carrying off anything and anyone that was not tied down. The incessant assault had already broken the ship's small-boats and longboat free during the night when a group of men had tried to reach the shore. A single vessel, sans occupants, survived but had been driven onto the beach, terminating any immediate hopes for an escape by boat. The crew made an effort to cut away the ship's masts lest she be forced over on her side, but when the masting fell into the sea, it remained firmly affixed to the wreck by a spider web of rigging that had not been cut. Then, without warning, the ship suddenly rolled onto her side. Many were thrown into the water and perished instantly; others, trapped below deck, drowned in utter darkness and confinement. Those men, women, and children who had somehow survived now clung to whatever purchase they could find, growing weaker by their ordeal but somehow still clinging to life.[16]

As one horrible disaster was unfolding, a second one, unseen, was just beginning nearby. A French brig from Ostend bound for Philadelphia had been caught in the same rough weather. Within sight of the stranded immigrant ship, the unidentified vessel had suddenly filled and foundered, driving her terrified crew to their boats. Although it was later learned they had managed to successfully shove off from the doomed ship without loss, their ultimate fate was unknown. All were presumed to have been lost.[17]

As daylight began to define the shoreline, four brave sailors aboard *Faithful Steward* plunged into the brine apparently hauling a line from the ship with them. Somehow they succeeded in swimming to the beach in a desperate attempt to retrieve the sole surviving longboat. All of the men reached the surf line and then labored heroically to manhandle the boat to the water. Once they had run lines out to *Faithful Steward*'s bow, they began to pull the boat along the line and through the waves. Then, when the little vessel was almost within reach of the ship, the rope gave way against the violent surge. The sea instantly swallowed the boat. And with it went all prospects of salvation for scores of helpless men, women, and children.[18]

With seemingly no other hope before them, many of those stranded on the wreck now abandoned all caution and tried to swim for the beach. Few succeeded as the sea was still running exceptionally high. Some struggled to hold onto pieces of the flotsam that were broken free by the violent action of the waters. Others, too timorous to venture forth, or not knowing how to swim, clung to the wreck as best they could. Some were simply swept overboard and drowned. Throughout that long, horrible day, as the ship was gradually being beaten to pieces, the cries for help, the weeping of women as their babies disappeared beneath the waves, and anguished screams of men at the loss of their wives, children, parents, sisters, brothers, cousins, nieces, and nephews rose above the sounds of the pounding surf.[19]

By late afternoon, the waves began to subside and the tide to ebb, encouraging fresh attempts by some to swim ashore. A few sought to climb along the masts that now lay half submerged in the water between the wreck and the shore, anything to get them a few feet closer to the beach. Some made it; others did not. Moved by his own family's entreaties to hazard the attempt, John McIntire Jr. climbed out onto a mast lying still attached to the ship only by a tangle of rigging lines, which brought him a few precious yards closer to the shore. At the tip of the mast, he leaped into the sea and swam with all his strength, until there was no more left in him. Miraculously, he was able to close with the beach, but had one of the ship's sailors who had already made it ashore not waded through the breakers to tow him in, he too would have perished.[20]

During the course of the day word of the disaster spread along the sparsely inhabited coast, and local residents began to arrive on the beach in ever-increasing numbers. Little girls and old women, farmers and watermen, and townsfolk from as far away as Lewes arrived to offer assistance.[21] Many with less than humanitarian interests sought to profit from the misfortune of the victims by scavenging the dead lying along the beach, within yards and clear sight of their relatives still struggling for their lives aboard the wreck. When John McIntire Jr. reached the beach, he was stunned as he watched the locals "stripping the lifeless bodies of their clothing, matching everything of apparent value, heaping the plunder on wagons and hauling it away." He was distressed as some inhabitants came "not to aid in the cause of humanity, not to rescue their fellow beings from the ruthless waves, not to console the bereaved or administer to their wants. No, but solely to plunder till they could plunder no more . . . Many looked with eyes of disappointment whenever they found a person both dead and naked, or alive and clothed; as, in either case, there was no hope of gain."[22]

Dazed, McIntire wandered aimlessly along the beach searching among the living and dead for his family. Suddenly he came upon his father, John Sr., who was alive but senseless. "We then lay together for some time in a state of almost equal inactivity," he later recalled, "while many persons continued to pass and repass along the shore, while numbers were still arriving from the wreck, and numbers [more] still uttering a cry for help. A cry terrific in the extreme, and a cry that has rung in my ears to the present day. Among those who came ashore in the night was a sister of mine. Adhering to a plank in company with another female she was discovered by two young passengers of her acquaintance who carried her to me. It was a meeting of inexpressible joy, though I learned she had received many wounds by collision with the ship's timbers."[23]

By the following morning, the beach presented a panorama of destruction as far north as Cape Henlopen. The bodies of drowned men, women, and children lay in the surf line washing to and fro with every wave. Other corpses, pale and bloated with water, lay higher on the sands, carried there by the last high tide. Clothing, sea chests, suitcases, and other personal items—the flotsam of humanity—as well as rigging, decking, and the artifacts of disaster that had yet to be scavenged, were strewn along with the bodies as far as the eye could see. Local inhabitants buried many of the dead in the sand where they lay; others were interred in common graves well above the normal high-water mark. On the shoal beyond, the broken and lifeless carcass of *Faithful Steward* shivered with every swell.[24]

When news of the disaster reached Philadelphia, several humane and public-spirited gentlemen of the city set about raising a subscription "for the relief of the unhappy people who were saved from the wreck, and there can be no doubt of their meeting with great success from the benevolent inhabitants, who have never been backward in generously affording assistance to the distressed." Though only seven women had been saved, many of the survivors were children. Several were taken in and raised by large landholders and important families in the neighborhood such as the Rodneys and Fishers. A man named Gordon temporarily took in the three surviving members of the McIntire family, John Jr., his father, and his sister Rebecca. But McIntire's mother, brothers, and another sister had been lost, leaving forever inscribed on his soul a vision of the despicable inhumanity he had witnessed on the beach on that terrible day.[25]

Several days after the disaster, while young John was recuperating in Lewes, he saw a man walking down the street wearing a vest that had once belonged to someone in his family. Enraged, he demanded its return. A fight ensued but was fortunately stopped by a justice of the peace before mortal damage could be inflicted. Young McIntire swore a formal oath attesting to his claim, and the garment was returned. There were, undoubtedly, other such incidents, but none was recorded.[26]

When the final death toll was in, the statistics were staggering. Of the 249 passengers and thirteen officers and crewmen aboard, there were only sixty-seven known survivors. One hundred and ninety-five people had lost their lives. The exact number, however, may never be known as it was later reported that several survivors eventually died from their injuries. Captain McCausland and his men all survived, but of the fifty members of the extended Lee family, only James and four cousins had made it ashore. Like the rest of the survivors, the disaster had left James in dire straits, for "as the passengers consisted chiefly of families, who had previously defrayed every expense of the voyage, with a design of settling in this country," all were now penniless, friendless, and beleaguered in a foreign land where the bodies of their dead families had been stripped of every dignity. James Lee would eventually make his way to Maryland, where he would be obliged to work as a common laborer, and then to Pennsylvania to live out the remainder of his life.[27]

The surviving McIntires also made their way to Pennsylvania, destitute and reliant on their own will to survive. Forty-six years later, John McIntire Jr. would record the bitter memories of that tragic day in a local newspaper and then die a forgotten man. Other families had suffered in like manner. Hugh and Mary Espey and two of their boys had been lost. Yet brothers Robert and John; John's wife, Jean Morehead; and a sister named Mary had been rescued, albeit at great cost. Mary died the next day of exposure, and Robert was crippled for life. He would live out the remainder of his days with his brother Hugh Espey Jr. near Harrisburg, Pennsylvania. Of the eight members of the Elliott family that had boarded *Faithful Steward* in Ireland, only Simon and William made it ashore alive. The family's chests full of valuables and every other belonging had been lost with the ship. But the Elliotts would go on and eventually settled with their brother John in Washington County, Pennsylvania. They would later marry and emigrate as pioneers again, this time to the Ohio and Illinois country.[28]

In the formidable history of the Elliott family and their extended kin in an America that they helped settle against all odds is recorded this sad ballad:

> The Elliotts and the Lees
> And Stewarts of great fame,
> They may lament and mourn
> For the lands they've left behind.
> They may lament and mourn
> As long as they have days,
> For the friends and relation
> Lie in Mahogan's bays.[29]

The loss of *Faithful Steward* would become one of the most enduring tales of the Delmarva coast. In time, it would be woven into the fabric of legend and associated with the numerous coin finds that would be made on the beaches near the loss site. By the late twentieth century, in the lore of Delaware, *Faithful Steward* had evolved into a veritable treasure ship, the lure of which would draw fortune hunters from near and far. Yet the historic proportions of the loss of so many lives, no matter how obscured by the distortion of time, could not be ignored.

In 1985 a deputy attorney general of Delaware named Peter Hess, representing the Delaware Natural Resources and Environmental Commission, drafted a resolution to memorialize the grievous loss of *Faithful Steward* with a historical marker at the approximate site of its destruction. The resolution was formally introduced to the Delaware General Assembly and readily passed. On Labor Day, September 2, 1985, hundreds of vacationers watched the formal dedication of the historic marker on what had been, two centuries before to the day, the scene of the worst single maritime disaster in Delaware history.[30]

# 9

## So Much for Attending Congress

On the first Monday in December 1790, the day on which the First Congress of the United States of America was to open its winter session at Philadelphia, a shining new era in the history of the world was about to commence. Congressman Aedamus Burke of South Carolina, who was to serve as one of the first elected representatives from his state to participate in the proceedings of that august body, anticipated that it would be one of the most important days in his event-filled life. Barely a year and a half earlier, on May 23, 1788, his state had been among the last to ratify the new Constitution of the United States but had done so overwhelmingly. Not long afterward, George Washington took the presidential oath of office on the steps of Federal Hall in New York City. On September 25, 1789, the Bill of Rights had been adopted. On August 31, 1790, Congress had authorized the transfer of government to the City of Philadelphia. It was a heady time for America and for the revolutionary Irish-American from South Carolina who had helped make it happen.

Aedamus Burke was born in Galway, Ireland, on June 16, 1743. Like many of his colleagues in the new Congress, he was a learned individual, a man of law, and a soldier. He had been educated at the theological college at St. Omer, France, before emigrating first to the West Indies and then to the colony of South Carolina. But it was in the great emerging seaport of Charles Town that he chose to put down his roots. It soon became his home, and he fought hard to preserve it, serving in the South Carolina Militia and later in the Continental Army during the Revolution. In 1778 he was appointed judge of the State Circuit Court and performed his duties with distinction until British forces overran the region. The following year he was elected to the South Carolina House of Representatives and served in that capacity for nearly a decade. In the meantime, he found time for military service when his country and state had called. When the courts were reestablished in South Carolina after the war, he was quickly reappointed to the bench and in 1785 was named one of three state commissioners to prepare the first digest of state law. It was, perhaps, natural that in 1788 he was chosen to serve as a member of the state convention assembled to consider ratification of the U.S. Constitution. Late in May, after seemingly endless debate, the South Carolina convention voted 145–46 for ratification.

Though Burke and many other antifederalists had opposed action on the issues of state's rights, he nevertheless pledged to support the new law of the land vigorously. He was soon elected to the U.S. House of Representatives of the First Congress. It was time to get down to business again, and Aedamus Burke looked forward to it with all his heart.[1]

Burke had allowed himself ample time for the trip from Charleston to New York, where he would conduct some business before traveling to Philadelphia. He had booked passage on the fastest and newest packet available, the sloop *Friendship,* commanded by Thomas Barlow, a veteran skipper. The sloop would depart Charleston on November 14 on a trip that was expected to take perhaps less than a week. Burke had calculated that would leave him plenty of time to attend to his business in New York, then take a stage to Philadelphia, find lodging in the city, and meet old friends before the winter session began.[2]

The embarkation at the city wharf had been inauspicious enough, but after passing Sullivan's Island at the entrance to the harbor, the first intimation of trouble began. Though almost instantly meeting with strong headwinds "and very boisterous weather," *Friendship* struggled to make headway up the coast for almost two weeks, usually keeping well off the land. It was an unpleasant voyage. Finally, on November 25, after many days of being unable to take a sighting, Barlow sailed west to get a shore bearing. A low, sandy cape shouldering a wide embayment sighted nearby proved to be Cape Henlopen. Thus assured of his position, the captain turned his bow toward New York. Unfortunately, not long after sighting the cape, "a fierce gale of wind from the north east," against which all progress was impossible, struck the ship. Barlow made a strategic decision to put back for Delaware Bay and find shelter, if possible, under Cape May.

While beating in for the cape, the crew spotted an unidentified brig also standing in with maintopsail hauled and other sails close reefed. It was apparently at the same moment the brig also observed *Friendship* and "thinking we were unacquainted in the bay" sought to come up and offer assistance. Voice communication between the two ships, despite their close proximity, proved to be almost impossible above the roar of the sea and wind. But after some effort Barlow was delighted to learn that the ship had a seasoned Delaware pilot onboard who suggested that *Friendship* follow them to a safe anchorage site.

For one ship to keep company with another in good weather was often difficult, but in a nor'easter within the confines of a shoal-pocked bay, it was nearly impossible. Nevertheless, *Friendship* managed to stay in the brig's company throughout the day. As evening came on, the stranger hung a light for the sloop to follow. "But the fury of the tempest increasing about night-fall, and pouring round us the spray of the sea like a torrent of violent rain . . . and the lowering cloudy weather adding to the darkness of the night," Burke later recalled to a colleague, "we lost sight of the brig." Desperately, Captain Barlow struggled to regain a glimpse of the shepherd, but in the doing, *Friendship*'s jib and mainsail were split.

"Our embarrassment was a serious one," recalled the congressman, "exposed [as we were] to a furious tempest in Delaware bay, during a long dismal night, surrounded on every side by shoals and breakers." Without a pilot or sails, Barlow was forced to put his ship before the mercy of the wind. Unfortunately, the gale was blowing directly for the Cape Henlopen Lighthouse, which "shone full in view before us remarkably bright."

Barlow, like most mariners who regularly plied these coastal waters, was well aware of the deadly sands that the noble light warned of, but he "knew not the place of direction of the shoals ahead." Everyone aboard was equally well aware of the danger. The only hope of saving their lives, they were told, was to be fortunate enough to beat over the first series of shoals without tearing out *Friendship*'s bottom, and come to anchor in the lee of them. If they could manage that, then perhaps they might be able to ride out the gale until the morning. Congressman Aedamus Burke now began to wonder whether he would ever have the opportunity of serving his country again.

While the captain and crew of *Friendship* mulled over the diminishing expedients available to them, the breakers of Cape Henlopen suddenly loomed out of the pitch-black night and into view. They "rolled furiously, and white as snow, over a shoal, which we since found to be called the Shears." All aboard held their breath as the sloop drove into the tumultuous surf and was then, miraculously, carried intact over the shoal. Twice the ship struck bottom, but suffered no apparent damage other than staving in her dead lights, and half filling the cabin with water.

As soon as the sloop had passed over, Captain Barlow ordered both anchors let loose. With cables stretched to the limit, *Friendship*'s fatal drive shoreward was stopped cold. It was but a tenuous reprieve from the inevitable, for about 4:00 A.M., the gale increased its fury. The sea swells stepped up proportionately, and the strain on the anchor lines could no longer be sustained. Suddenly, one of the lines snapped. The remaining anchor began dragging across a shoal, which in the gray dawn of morning was discovered to the lee.

"We saw now," recalled Congressman Burke, "that nothing remained but to slip our cables, and once more to put the vessel at the mercy of the sea and wind right afore it, and try to pass through the breakers, which reached and broke violently near a mile in upon the shore." If the passengers and crew of the sloop were ever to make it ashore alive, it was now absolutely necessary that *Friendship* beat over the inshore bar, through the breakers, and ground herself on the beach. The ship would certainly be lost, especially with the horrific surf conditions being what they were, but there was no alternative. In trying this last "experiment" *Friendship* struck bottom several times, but somehow successfully managed to beat over the breakers. She was carried high onto the beach at 9:00 A.M., "about two leagues to the northward of the light-house," near the point of Cape Henlopen. Salvation had been granted.

Within but a few hours, the wreck of *Friendship,* whose travails the evening before had been closely watched from the shore by a Delaware pilot, was visited by a boat from Lewes. A rescue was quickly effected, and the survivors were taken to the town where they were "treated with great kindness by the inhabitants." Captain Barlow and his men were heartily commended by the townspeople for their conduct in the drama. The natives "look on our escape as extraordinary—they ascribe it to our bringing the vessel to under the shoal; for had we ran in for the light house, there cannot be a doubt but we must have been certainly lost." Indeed, Burke learned, the brig that had rendered so much assistance only the day before, a vessel from Cape François laden with sugar and coffee, had herself been cast away entirely. Her remains had come to rest a mile to the north, high up on the sandy beach.

Following his first term in office as a member of the U.S. House of Representatives, Aedamus Burke would be obliged to decline a second term when the South Carolina legislature passed a law prohibiting a state judge (an office he continued to hold) from leaving the state. He would not abandon public service, however, and was soon elected a chancellor of the Courts of Equity, in which capacity he would continue until his dying day, more than twelve years later. But throughout his remaining years, Aedamus Burke would never forget that traumatic day of November 27, 1790, when he was cast away on the Delmarva coast in the fast packet *Friendship,* or his thoughts as his rescuers approached in the little Delaware pilot boat: "So much for attending congress, the first Monday in December, for a southern delegate."[3]

# IO

## The Captain Was in a Hilarious Mood

HMS *De Braak* could be termed a nondescript vessel at best, brig-rigged and classed by the British Admiralty as a sloop-of-war for commission and payroll purposes, though officially referred to as a brig-sloop. In 1795 she was a vessel quite new to the Royal Navy, yet anything but a novice to hard and dangerous sea duty. Although her origins are still clouded in mystery, *De Braak* is known to have served under two, possibly three, national flags during her long career. That she was built prior to 1781 and the onset of the Fourth Anglo-Dutch War, when she first appeared on Dutch navy lists as having been purchased by the Admiralty of the Maas, one of the five independent state navies of the Netherlands, is certain. Some authorities have suggested that she was specifically built for the Dutch naval service. A few have posed the theory that she was even American built, constructed well before her service on behalf of the Netherlands, perhaps during the closing days of the American Revolution, or that she had seen French service before being sold to the Dutch. Still others believed her to have been an English-built vessel, originally intended as a privateer, then captured by the French and sold to the Dutch in 1781. Whatever her origins were, her known history was fraught with action. Yet it was the mystery surrounding her tragic loss that would prove one of the most enduring legends of all on the Delmarva coast.[1]

What is certain is that while in Dutch naval service, *De Braak* was first documented as a cutter of 255 tons, mounting a single mast, and fore-and-aft rigged. With a deck of eighty-four feet, a keel length for tonnage of fifty-seven feet four-and-three-quarters inches, an extreme beam of twenty-eight-feet eleven inches, and a depth of hold of eleven feet two inches, she was typical of a class of very large, fast cutters constructed during the late eighteenth century and employed by the Dutch in the revenue marine, as privateers, or as naval dispatch boats. Most Dutch vessels in her class were planked with oak and pine from the Baltic. However, *De Braak*'s keel was constructed of elm, hinting at possible British or American origins. Her frames, stem, and sternposts were of white oak, possibly of British origin, or procured from such Baltic timber outlets as Memel, Danzig, or Stettin. Her interior components, such as partitions, bulkheads, and shot lockers, were of red pine, possibly from the Baltic port of Riga. Ships of her spe-

cific class employed in regular Dutch naval service, observing a tradition established in the seventeenth century, were usually given canine names. Her own
name meant "beagle," a fast and popular dog once highly coveted as a hunting
animal and often glowingly depicted in paintings by the Dutch masters.[2]

At the onset of the Fourth Anglo-Dutch War, *De Braak* was rated to carry
twenty guns but perhaps mounted somewhat fewer. Her initial service was under the command of a Lieutenant Bach. Her record while in the service of the
Netherlands unfortunately remains a gray area owing to the destruction of a substantial portion of the Dutch archives in a fire in the nineteenth century and
during the two world wars. The surviving archives provide only the sketchiest of
operational backgrounds.[3]

Between August 2 and 10, 1784, while under the command of Captain Alexander Gijsbert de Virieux, *De Braak* sailed out of Texel Roads for Malaga, Spain,
to rendezvous with the fleet of Rear Admiral Jan van Kinsbergen. Soon afterward, de Virieux was ordered to assume command of the thirty-six-gun frigate
*Jason,* and *De Braak* was placed under Captain Cornelis de Jong. On December
6, 1784, she joined a large squadron commanded by Captain Pieter Melvill at
Toulon, France. Melvill's fleet, presumably including de Jong and his cutter,
would not return to the Netherlands until 1787. The career of *De Braak* over the
next six years is virtually unknown. Indeed, not until February 25, 1793, when
she was placed under the command of a Lieutenant Johann Von Grootinwray,
are the threads of her life again woven into the fabric of history.[4]

Grootinwray's first assignment aboard *De Braak* was to be anything but uneventful. On February 1, slightly over three weeks before the lieutenant took
command, France declared war on England and Holland. Fifteen days later, a
French army division under the command of General Charles François du Perier
Dumouriez invaded the Netherlands. *De Braak* was immediately ordered to assist in the defense of the fortress city of Willemstad. On March 1, Dumouriez
was routed by an allied force of Dutch and Englishmen at the Roer River and
withdrew from the Low Countries.[5]

Many months later, on December 19, 1794, having been promoted to the
rank of full captain, Grootinwray was directed to escort a merchant convoy
bound for the Dutch South American colony of Surinam. The infectious bacil-
lus of revolution, however, had succeeded in spreading from France to the
Netherlands, and in January Willem V, Prince of Orange, was forced to flee and
establish a government in exile. *De Braak* was now instructed to sail from the
Texel to the North Sea and join a small Dutch squadron led by Captain Gerard
Corthuys to escort a convoy of merchantmen to the East Indies. Obliged to traverse the English Channel on the initial leg of the voyage, Grootinwray first visited the British port of Plymouth, arriving there on January 10, 1795, and then
proceeded on to Falmouth, on the coast of Cornwall. Here, he again stopped to
top off his provisions and take on wood and water before beginning the long
voyage ahead.[6]

The decision to put into Falmouth was, unhappily for Grootinwray and his
crew, to prove their undoing. The swirl of events and the shifting alliances during the dynamic ascendancy of Napoleonic France moved far too rapidly for

anyone to predict. It was not uncommon for one day's allies to be foes the next. While the diminutive warship lay at anchor in Falmouth Harbor, war was declared between England and the new Dutch Batavian Republic, a satellite of the French revolutionary government. Although Grootinwray could not have known it, his ship's fate was all but sealed.[7]

Moored adjacent to a big Dutch East Indiaman that had put in with her, and being in immediate danger of internment, *De Braak* was not alone in her predicament. Indeed, nearly half a dozen other Dutch warships and twenty-four merchantmen, presumably the convoy bound for the East Indies, had found themselves trapped by events. Grootinwray, like the other naval commanders, must have pondered his position with some pessimism. Fighting his way to the open sea was out of the question. His ship was lightly armed with only twelve guns, four-pounders and swivels, and was manned by an insufficient complement. She stood little chance of forcing her way past the great British men-of-war and forts guarding the harbor. There was no alternative but to await notification of the intentions of his country's former ally.[8]

The British Admiralty's reaction to the declaration of war, of course, was immediate. On January 20, 1795, His Majesty's warships were instructed to prevent all Dutch vessels in English ports from sailing, and to employ force of arms if necessary. In the days that followed, *De Braak* lay idle at anchor as negotiations were carried on between the British government and the Prince of Orange, who had fled to England, to determine her disposition and that of the other Dutch vessels in port. Their numbers and force were not taken lightly by the English, who saw them as a ready-made addition to the nation's hard-pressed navy. The Dutch naval flotilla was substantial and included the big, sixty-four-gun man-of-war *Zeeland;* the fifty-four-gun *Braakel;* the *Tholen,* of thirty-six guns; the *Pyl,* of sixteen guns; and the cutter *Miermin,* of fourteen guns. And, of course, there was *De Braak.*[9]

The disposition of the six warships remained undetermined for more than a year. Finally, on Friday, March 4, 1796, a dispatch was sent from Plymouth to London announcing the navy's intentions. "All the Dutch ships of war in this harbour," it stated, "consisting of one ship of 64, one of 50 guns, a frigate, and two sloops of war [*sic*], were yesterday taken possession of by the commanding officer of this port; the Dutch flag was taken down, and the British hoisted in its stead, and their crews were put on board the prison [ship] and some other ships of war in the harbour."[10]

At Falmouth, Captain Wooldridge, commander of the British fourteen-gun brig-sloop *Fortune,* was instructed to take *De Braak,* by then the lone Dutch warship at that port, under his charge. On June 13, 1796, the Admiralty officially ordered Wooldridge to take formal command of the little cutter. Grootinwray and his men were informed that they could either remain with their ship under the authority of the Prince of Orange, or return to their homeland as paroled prisoners of war. Sixty chose to return to the Netherlands, while five elected to remain.[11]

Having been ordered to bring the cutter around to Plymouth for refitting, Wooldridge noted that he would be obliged to strip his own crew of twenty-five men to carry out the order because the Dutchman was "very heavily rigged." The captain was also, no doubt, affected by the quite commonly held English aversion to the class of Dutch cutter he was charged with manning. Indeed, the cutter rig on craft greater than sixty-five feet in length was quite unpopular with the Royal Navy, no matter what the nationality of the vessel. They simply took too many men to work the sails. And *De Braak* was a full eighty-four feet in length. Nevertheless, when sternly instructed "to proceed to Plymouth," Wooldridge dutifully followed his orders.[12]

Five days later, the cutter was moved from Falmouth Harbor to a new anchorage in Carrick Roads preparatory to departure and placed under the command of a Lieutenant King, a petty officer, and four men. On June 27 an additional seventeen hands were taken on board. The remaining Dutch crewmembers still held aboard were removed. Then, in company with *Fortune* and the fifth-rate forty-four-gun frigate *Expedition, De Braak* sailed for Plymouth Sound. Despite encountering a strong gale at sea, she and her escort reached their destination safely the same day.[13]

On August 26 the Admiralty office determined that all of the Dutch warships that had been reassembled at Plymouth were to be surveyed to ascertain their condition, usefulness, and suitability for induction into the Royal Navy. The chief surveyor of the Plymouth Dockyard informed the Admiralty on September 1 that the required survey could not be completed unless the vessels were entirely unrigged and all of their guns removed. Only then could they be heeled, thoroughly inspected, and have their lines taken. A week later all of the vessels were reported to be in good condition. All had been found suitable for commissioning and were to be put into fighting trim within six weeks. On September 15, it was publicly announced that the vessels were "ordered to be got ready for commission immediately." *De Braak* would prove to be the lone exception. On September 10, following her survey, the Navy Board directed that *De Braak* be converted into a brig. She would then be reclassified and commissioned as a sloop-of-war. Nine days later the order was officially issued.[14]

The surgery necessary to convert a single-masted cutter to a brig would prove to be more than superficial. Once stripped of guns, stores, and furnishings, most of her rigging, including her mast, was removed. In dry dock, John Marshall, surveyor of the navy, took her lines and drew a set of plans showing her decks and hull configuration, noting them to be "as when taken." Another set of plans, labeled "as fitted," was then produced to show the required modifications.[15]

Before addressing the major alterations, the shipwrights were first obliged to replace or repair injured or deteriorated timbers. Working fast and efficiently, they afforded only enough time and attention to replace the worst dry-rotted timbers before proceeding to more significant alterations. Then they raised the gunwales and set to building port cabins for the captain's party, starboard cabins to serve as the clerk's office, and a toilet in the stern. They roofed cabins and added skylights. They replaced an aft ladderway with a hatch leading down to the breadroom and opened a glass "companion" forward of the hatch to permit natural light into the lower deck. *De Braak*'s original pumps were removed and a ladderway cut through the deck to the officers' quarters. A hood with hinged side and top was erected over it.[16]

While operating as a cutter, *De Braak* had employed a windlass, rather than a capstan, in her bow to raise anchor. The Plymouth shipwrights used an existing companion to install a new capstan much more suitable for her new brig rig. They installed wooden tubes for the suction pumps and pierced holes through the decks for installation of the mainmast and foremast. The lower deck was completely rearranged, with several cabins torn out and replaced by new ones to accommodate the ship's new lieutenant, master, captain's clerk, purser, surgeon, and gunner. Two more cabins were built forward for the carpenter and boatswain. A new shot locker was built, and a lead-lined fire-hearth pit constructed to receive a cast-iron "Brodie Patent" stove for cooking. So it went, with shipwrights working diligently to meet navy specifications and to field *De Braak* as quickly as possible.[17]

Finally, they had to sheath the hull in copper, a necessary expedient to prevent the disastrous effects of boring shipworms common to temperate and tropical environments and to discourage barnacle growth that might affect the ship's sailing, speed, and maneuvering efficiency.[18]

On September 30 the Admiralty instructed that *De Braak* be armed with carronades in lieu of the traditional long guns that had for years provided the deadly kick in a British broadside. These squat, large-caliber cannons represented the very latest in naval ordnance and one of the most important technological advancements in firepower of the Napoleonic Age—an innovation that would in fact influence the evolution of naval tactics during the remaining years of fighting ships under sail.[19]

Once fully refitted, armed, and manned, HM Sloop-of-War *De Braak* would prove to be a welcome addition to the hard-pressed Royal Navy in one of its bleakest hours. Her new commander, however, was something else.


It may be said that Captain James Drew was one of the least inspiring commanders in the Royal Navy, but he would nevertheless be awarded his own niche in history—for reasons he might never have considered.

Born on April 19, 1751, in the parish of St. Stephens, hard by the little village of Saltash, near the outskirts of Plymouth, James Drew was the youngest of seven children. With his brother John he had entered the Royal Navy and at the age of thirteen was enrolled on the muster of HMS *Burford* as a captain's servant. By the time he had applied for and received his lieutenant's license on June 18, 1771, at the age of twenty, he had served under no fewer than five commands in every subordinate position and aboard ships great and small. In 1775 he was serving aboard Vice Admiral Samuel Graves's flagship HMS *Preston* in Boston Harbor and witnessed firsthand the Battle of Bunker Hill, after which he gained the eternal enmity of the rebels by walking the grounds after the engagement shooting American wounded lying about on the battlefield. He would serve aboard various ships throughout the Revolution, albeit with little distinction but always moving up. By 1787 he had been promoted to post captain aboard HMS *Powerful*, the largest ship he would ever command. For some unknown reason, however, Drew was demoted almost immediately and served for the next four years in command of several small sloops-of-war, until his last ship, *Fly*, was paid off and he retired on half-pay. After fathering an illegitimate child by a housemaid, he fled to America and married into a socially prominent New York mercantile family. On April 10, 1792, Drew wed Lydia Watkins, daughter of John Watkins and Lydia Stillwell Watkins and niece of British Lieutenant General John Maunsell, in New York's Trinity Church, officiated by the Reverend Benjamin Moore, the future bishop of New York. The couple settled in Harlem Heights, even as war clouds again began to envelop Europe.[20]

With revolution brewing in France, James Drew sought a new command in the Royal Navy. The Navy Board was apparently not impressed with either him or his record and in 1795 he was still unemployed. By the spring of 1797, bankrupt England hovered on the brink of disaster as Napoleon Bonaparte swept through Europe and threatened invasion across the channel. At the peak of the crisis, fifty thousand men in 113 ships of the Royal Navy mutinied on an Easter morning. The mutiny spread to the Nore, the Thames, and many other outports of the nation to protest impossible living conditions, short pay, inedible rations, impressment, and brutalities of every kind condoned and committed by the officer corps. The mutineers demanded the worst officers be removed from command. The navy agreed and negotiated an end to the insurrection, then hung its leaders. It was then, during the waning days of the Great Mutiny at the Nore, that forty-five-year-old James Drew, a career plodder with a lackluster record and a less-than-sterling character, received a call to his last command, a tight-looking little brig-sloop called *De Braak*.[21]

On June 16, Captain James Drew boarded *De Braak* for the first time, only three days after she had been declared ready for service and her crew had begun to draw wages. Her new complement of eighty-five officers and men had already been entered into the muster and pay books. All that was necessary thereafter was for the brig to be provisioned and readied for service in the English Channel.[22]

Captain James Drew launched into his new command with unconditional zeal, for there was precious little time to whip both ship and crew into order or to fill the few remaining billets still vacant. On July 7 he was issued instructions to commence convoy duty on the English coast as soon as his vessel was in fighting trim. There were, indeed, innumerable reasons for haste, not the least of which was the Admiralty's desire to remove as many disaffected seamen as possible from the still mutinous atmosphere of Plymouth.[23]

On July 15 Drew ordered two new gunports cut in *De Braak*'s bow. The following day he wrote to the Admiralty, requesting that two bow chasers be sent for his battery. Four days later, a pair of six-foot, six-pounder long guns were brought aboard and rolled into position at the newly cut gunports. Drew intended to put the guns to good use. Although he had been assigned to convoy duty, what many officers considered the most tedious assignment in the navy, he saw it as an opportunity to take a few prizes. Chase guns were an absolute necessity for such work, for they offered, if not accuracy, range, which was a valuable asset in any pursuit. As the war continued to expand, there were prizes aplenty to be had, even in home waters, including the rich Spanish merchantmen sailing from the Americas with sugar, cocoa, copper, and, on rare occasions, gold and silver. With Napoleon's flirtation with Spain and Spain's hostility toward England, Spanish shipping had become fair game for every ambitious captain in the Royal Navy. As early as September 27, 1796, all British commanders had been instructed to detain every Spanish ship encountered. It was an order that James Drew, who had never taken a prize in his life, fully intended to obey. His primary mission, however, was another matter.[24]

The protection of seaborne trade, on which the prosperity and, indeed, the very survival of the British Empire depended, was of paramount importance in the war against Napoleon. Owing to the heavy demands on the main British battle fleets, there was a chronic shortage of ships and men suitable for the defense of the trade and supply routes that kept Britain afloat, in both home waters and overseas. In England's own backyard, British shipping was frequently subjected to the depredations of swarms of French privateers working the English Channel and ports along the Bay of Biscay. Others harried the American trade by lurking about the periphery of major U.S. outports. Now, with America's impending turn against France, Yankee shipping had also begun to suffer from the assaults of French raiders.[25]


By late summer James Drew was actively engaged in convoy service in the English Channel and the Irish Sea. On September 13, 1797, he reported to Admiralty Secretary Evan Nepean on *De Braak*'s safe arrival at the English port of Milford Haven with the Plymouth trade. Duty had extracted its toll, however. On September 27 the captain reported that one Lieutenant Percy Dove had been hospitalized and would be unfit for duty for the foreseeable future. He therefore requested that his own nephew, young Lieutenant John Drew, son of his brother Stephen, currently serving aboard HMS *Cerberus* under the command of another brother, Captain John Drew, be appointed in Dove's place. The request was approved. Nepotism in the Royal Navy was nothing new.[26]

Despite the onset of winter weather, *De Braak* remained almost continually at sea. In December the British Isles were ravaged by gales. The damage to both the military and the merchant marine was substantial. On December 11, HMS *Marlborough,* of seventy-four guns, was driven ashore at Plymouth, and a gunboat named *Love and Friendship* was bilged and sunk. A sloop called the *Four Sisters* was destroyed on the Ramshead, to the west of Plymouth. The channel ports soon became crowded with ships seeking refuge. Prognostications for the immediate future were dour. "The very high gales of winds from the Southward," reported the *Times* of London, "will occasion, we fear, ruinous losses and accidents at sea. We never recollect to have witnessed a more tempestuous gale."[27]

Reports of casualties flowed into London. "We had this morning," one such report stated, "a most tremendous hurricane of wind from South West. Several ships have left their anchors, and three ships are driven on shore in Stokes Bay, one of which is the Cadiz packet of Hull; she is driven up to high-water mark, but has yet received no material damage, she makes no water. The *Britannia,* of Minehead for Oporto, was enabled to get into the harbor [of Portsmouth] with the loss of one anchor. One other vessel on shore, we hear, is a yellow-sided brig belonging to Weymouth."[28]

The continuing storm did not overlook *De Braak.* On December 11 Drew reported that his ship had lost one of her masts and that she would have to put into port to make repairs. Ten days later, reports out of Portsmouth included the following: "Arrived the *De Braak* sloop of war, of 18 guns, Capt. J. Drew, from a cruise, with loss of main-mast, which appears to have gone by the board; but whether it was occasioned by a gale of wind or in an action, is not ascertained; there is a probability however, that it was by the latter, as a number of shot holes appear in several of her sails."[29]

That *De Braak* had engaged in a skirmish or firefight is possible. That the damage inflicted on her mast resulted from the weather, however, is certain. Drew noted, somewhat ruefully, that his ship's mainmast had been lost because she was simply overmasted in the first place, but it was only at the explicit direction of the Admiralty that he had come into Plymouth to refit.[30]

On December 24, while still in port, Drew was instructed to make repairs and then to take on provisions for three months of channel duty. An attack by Napoleon's armies was still uppermost in the minds of many Englishmen, and the protection of the channel and its trade was central to the British defense strategy. "The Invasion of England," noted the *Time*s of London, "is at present, in France, the order of the day." It was also the single greatest concern of the British Admiralty. Despite her initial orders, however, *De Braak* was not destined to remain in home waters for long, or to participate in the defense of the British Isles. On February 8, 1798, Drew's instructions changed: he was directed to take on provisions for a six-month ocean voyage.[31]

*De Braak*'s refitting, however, proved more extensive than had been anticipated. As late as February 17, 1798, the little brig was still in port, even though Drew had already received orders to proceed to Cork to "collect such Trade bound to North America" as might be ready to sail. Similar instructions had been issued to Captain Francis Pender, commander of the sixty-four-gun ship-of-the-line *St. Albans,* then outfitting at Spithead. On February 24, additional orders pertaining to the joint convoy were drafted and dispatched to Admiral George Vandeput, commander of the North American Station at Halifax, informing him that he was to take both *De Braak* and *St. Albans* under his command on their arrival there.[32]

It was the Admiralty's intention that *St. Albans* sail from Spithead on March 1 to convoy the American trade, mostly American-owned merchantmen, to American ports after rendezvousing off Cork with *De Braak,* which would be escorting the Irish trade. Drew was specifically ordered to "put himself and the Trade assembled" under Pender's command and protection. The whole fleet of nearly fifty vessels would then proceed to Delaware. From Delaware Bay, *De Braak* would turn south with those vessels bound for southern ports. *St. Albans* would sail north, escorting her own convoy of ships to Philadelphia, New York, Boston, and Halifax.[33]

Drew's instructions cautioned that care be taken not to part company with his charges. Owing to an infestation of the U.S. Middle Atlantic seaboard by French privateers, which had been preying on both British and American merchantmen, vessels bound for the Chesapeake Bay were to be escorted in by *De Braak* before the remainder of the fleet could be released to sail south. Vessels bound for Georgia and South Carolina were then on their own, although Drew was specifically instructed to "use his best endeavors to see [the ships] in safety off their respective ports." After having shepherded his flock to their destinations, he was then to turn north and make directly for Halifax.[34]

Orders notwithstanding, *De Braak*'s long tenure in port may not have been entirely due to her extensive refitting. On February 18, Drew informed the Secretary of the Admiralty, Evan Nepean, that his nephew, Lieutenant John Drew, was at sick quarters and requested a replacement. In securing a replacement, James Drew had unwittingly saved his nephew's life.[35]

But there were other, more serious, problems to attend. Drew complained of having trouble with "three of the most seditious and mutinous men in the Kings Service." Two of the men had been transferred to his ship from HMS *Saturn* and one from *Ramilles*. The crew of each vessel had, only the year before, been among the first to join the Great Mutiny at the Nore. Many men aboard *Saturn* and *Ramilles* had continued to offer resistance well after the revolt was concluded. Drew was fearful, therefore, that the three miscreants might "be capable of corrupting the minds of the Briggs company however well disposed at present, and which nothing but the energy of the Officers can counteract." Without the assistance of a lieutenant, the situation was serious. Drew promptly requested that a new lieutenant be appointed to fill his nephew's position and attend to the problem. Thomas Hickson, an Irishman, was assigned to the post.[36]

The mission at hand soon overshadowed Drew's problems with the few rebellious seamen. By the end of February, ten ships that were to sail under *De Braak*'s protection had gathered at Plymouth for the first leg of their voyage to America. *De Braak*'s final complement of seventy-three officers and men and twelve able Royal Marines was assembled. Although at least thirty-five of the men were west-country men from the counties of Devon, Wiltshire, and Cornwall, ten were from Ireland. There were also three from Greenock, Scotland, and one each from New York, Hamburg, Sweden, and Portugal. Six were from Gloucestershire and five from Warwickshire. The remainder were from various unidentified places throughout England.[37]

On March 1, with the east wind at her back, the little brig-sloop *De Braak* and her covey of merchantmen, briefly accompanied by the cutter *Cygnet,* finally sailed from Plymouth. Soon afterward, while stopping at Falmouth to pick up additional vessels, the convoy was temporarily brought to anchor by strong southwesterlies. Drew dutifully took a count of the fleet and reported the delay. Five days later, on March 7, the convoy was still anchored in Carrick Road, detained by westerly winds. Drew chafed under the delay. He had been informed that his immediate arrival at Cork was of "the utmost importance," and he fumed at the lethargy of the "heavy Convoy" he was charged with protecting. He quipped in exasperation, "I alone could get there shortly." His belated arrival at Cork, however, was not without some benefit, for an even larger fleet of merchantmen, more than twice the size of the one he had escorted out of the channel, had used the additional time to assemble and prepare for the long Atlantic voyage with him.[38]

Drew's belated departure was not an uncommon event during the age of sail, when men, materials, ships, and, most importantly, the weather all had to be in alignment before a convoy could leave port. Indeed, it was not until March 14 that *De Braak*'s co-escort, HMS *St. Albans,* and her own contingent of a dozen merchantmen were finally ready to sail.[39]

Once the *St. Albans* convoy had swept beyond the Lizard and Land's End, the southwesternmost tip of the Cornwall Peninsula, the voyage to the rendezvous point to meet *De Braak* and the Irish fleet off Cape Clear proved uneventful. Finally, on March 26, off Galley Head, Pender's little armada of merchantmen fell in with Drew and his own convoy, swollen now to thirty American and four British merchantmen, most of which had been picked up at Cork. Both Pender's and Drew's orders directed them to proceed under joint convoy "towards their places of destination (keeping during [their] course to the southward as circumstances point)." The combined fleet, numbering forty-four merchantmen and two warships, turned their prows southwestward.[40]

On April 1, off the Azores, Pender sighted two strange sails and signaled Drew to give chase. Within a short time, the suspect vessels were discovered to be HMS *Magnamine* and the privateer *Victory,* a French prize late of Boston. Soon afterward, the weather began to deteriorate. By the following day, the convoy was being buffeted about by increasingly turbulent winds. Although Pender could count all of the convoy ships, *De Braak,* bringing up the rear, began to fall ever further astern. By late April 2, Drew's ship was "almost out of sight . . . on a stern bearing NE by N45." Pender fired a signal gun to call her up in an effort to keep the convoy together. But the next two days of stormy weather aborted every effort to maintain order. By April 4, the flotilla had become so dispersed that only seven merchantmen were within sight of the big man-of-war. *De Braak* had disappeared.[41]

For the following seven weeks, the whereabouts and activities of Captain James Drew and his ship were unknown. Some legends have suggested that Drew, one of the Royal Navy's least illustrious "plodders," an adequate but undistinguished officer, took the time to make a brilliant raid on a Spanish treasure fleet and single-handedly capture between three and ten heavily laden treasure ships. Some wags would even claim that Drew was sailing under "secret orders" to harass the Spanish in the Caribbean. Others would say that *De Braak* had made for Kingston, Jamaica, to take aboard the payroll for His Majesty's garrison at Halifax and a cargo of gold for the Dutch West Indies Company. It mattered little to the wonderful yarn-spinners of later ages that the last great Spanish treasure Flota had sailed in 1778, a full twenty years before the final voyage of Captain James Drew. And only rarely did ships bearing the treasures of a not-so-new world depart from the Americas. The Halifax garrison was paid in local currency. The Dutch West India Company had long before ceased to exist. What mattered to the storytellers was that *De Braak* had utterly vanished for seven weeks.[42]

The first recorded reencounter with the long-lost brig occurred in the early hours of Friday, May 25, when the American sloop *President*, Captain Skidmore commanding, bound from Philadelphia, sighted and fell in with an unidentified armed vessel twenty miles south of Cape Henlopen. Skidmore, who had been informed the day before by a captain going into the Delaware that he had been chased off the capes by a privateer, was himself hailed by an unidentified brig, "which as he could not distinguish her colours, he took to be a French privateer." In a classic case of mistaken identity, Skidmore "immediately put about and stood in for the Delaware, in consequence of which seven shots were fired at him, but to no effect."[43]

The vessel from which the sloop *President* had barely escaped during the night, it would later be learned, had been *De Braak*.[44]

Ironically, James Drew had arrived off the Delaware capes only hours after Pender's departure. He had made, given the circumstances, the best time possible in reaching the appointed rendezvous point, but to no avail. His orders had been quite explicit: he was not to become separated from the convoy. One astute observer later noted, "As he was an officer with nearly thirty years service in the Royal Navy and had tried desperately to get appointed to a command, it is not likely that he went prowling for prizes." Nevertheless, his ship was not alone. According to accounts that were conveyed to New York several days later by one Vincent Low, *De Braak* had parted company with *St. Albans* somewhere off the Western Islands (the Azores) while in pursuit of a strange sail and had been unable to rejoin the convoy. Then, on or about April 30, she fell in with and captured a Spanish prize, sixty days out of Rio de la Plata in South America, bound for Cadiz. The prize, identified by Drew as *St. Francis dehaveren*, alias *Commerce de Londros*, and by Low and the media as *Don Francisco Xavier*, was laden with a substantial cargo of two hundred tons of copper bars, a quantity of cocoa, and other goods valued at a stunning £160,000 sterling. A prize crew, consisting of a prizemaster and approximately eleven sailors, was immediately placed aboard. Prizemaster Lieutenant Thomas Griffith, *De Braak*'s paymaster, was instructed to take "all possible care not to part company." In the event that the prize was separated from *De Braak*, he was "to repair to Cape Henry in the Chesapeak" and await Drew's arrival. At least fifteen Spanish seamen were taken prisoner, and most were transferred to the brig. It was a significant moment in the long and undistinguished naval career of James Drew, for the richly laden Spanish ship was to be his first and last prize.[45]

By the afternoon of May 25, the brig and her captive were prepared to enter the Delaware to refresh their water supplies. A pilot named Andrew Allen, master of the Lewes pilot boat *Friendship*, had soon come up and was taken aboard. Another pilot boat, commanded by Gilbert McCracken, hovered nearby. Onboard *De Braak*, Drew was eager to get on with the business at hand, although his concerns were no longer with conducting a convoy but with securing his prize. Better yet, there was the possibility that he might soon have a reunion with his wife, Lydia, in New York.[46]

For nearly a century after the catastrophe that claimed the life of James Drew and many of his men, a single American eyewitness account of the final moments preceding the loss of *De Braak* would be handed down from generation to generation, retold countless times, and become part of the oral history of Delaware. Although marred by editorial embellishments before finally appearing in print in 1887, at least part of pilot Andrew Allen's tale is worth recounting.[47]

When Allen was taken aboard the little British warship, after racing Gilbert McCracken for the business, Captain Drew immediately informed him that he was "constrained" to go into Lewes for water. "The captain," it was recorded, "was in a hilarious mood. He had enjoyed good luck, he said, and the pilot must drink to his health. But a storm was brewing in the southwest. Ominous clouds were looming behind Rehoboth; and so, while the captain had gone down into the cabin for another bumper, pilot Allen ordered the light sails screwed up. When the captain returned to the deck and noted what had been done he ordered the sails sheeted home again, and turning to Allen, with a violent oath, said, 'You look out for the bottom, and I'll look out for the spars.' "[48]

At about 4:00 P.M., *De Braak* entered Old Kiln Road, off Lewes, under mainsail and reefed topsail. There was an air of excitement as her officers and crew made ready to drop anchor about a mile from Cape Henlopen Lighthouse. The brig's six-oared cutter had already been deployed and lay alongside, waiting to carry the captain ashore to Lewes to secure fresh water. Nearby, the Spanish prize, by now with only a nine-man prize crew aboard, under the command of Lieutenant Griffith, prepared to do likewise. Drew's personal servant busied himself tying his master's scarf.[49]

Whatever freak weather condition it was that struck *De Braak* on that fatal day in May 1798—variously described as a "thunder gust," a "violent squall," or a "sudden flaw of wind" by those closest to the scene—its impact was devastating. Without warning, the brig suddenly heeled over on her beam ends so quickly that within seconds she was filling up with seawater through her open hatches. Those unfortunate souls who were below decks had absolutely no warning or hope of escape. The scene was one of pandemonium and terror as the sea poured through the hatchways, tossing goods, ballast, and bodies about indiscriminately. Topside, the heavy guns broke free and caromed across the deck, cutting down screaming men in their paths.[50]

Quarter-gunner Samuel Mitchell, among the fortunate survivors, later testified that he and thirty-two other men, including the boatswain, managed to scramble aboard the cutter lying alongside and reached safety on the Spanish prize, even as *De Braak* slipped beneath the sea. The captain, his lieutenant, purser, surgeon, gunner, carpenter, four midshipmen, clerk, cook, armorer, three men from the carpenter's crew, a steward, three ship's boys, eleven seamen, four marine privates, and twelve Spanish prisoners, forty-seven men in all, were lost in an instant.[51]

(Right) A raised marble portrait of Captain James Drew in St. Nicholas Church, Saltash, England, is the only known likeness of the ill-starred commander of HMS *De Braak*. (Photo by author)

(Below) The last minutes of HMS *De Braak* as she was capsizing during a thunder gust off Cape Henlopen, Delaware (Delaware State Museum, Dover; photo by author)

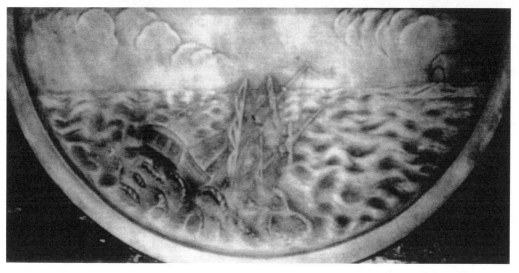

The only known contemporary portrayal of HMS *De Braak* appears as a raised detail in marble on the Drew Memorial in Saltash. In the distance to the right is an inaccurate representation of the Cape Henlopen Lighthouse, which the sculptor never saw. (Photo by author)

When Mitchell and the other survivors boarded *Xavier* and looked back to the spot where their ship had been just moments before, all that could be seen was her topgallant masthead standing proud above the water. A headcount on board the prize revealed that the prizemaster, boatswain, quartermaster, and thirty-one crewmen, as well as one sergeant, one corporal, and nine marine privates, were all that remained of *De Braak's* original complement. Of the captured crew of the Spanish prize, only three survived. Captain James Drew was nowhere to be seen.[52]

Somehow, several survivors eventually made their way to Philadelphia on foot and aboard *Don Francisco Xavier* to inform Phineas Bond, the British consul in the city, of the loss. The consul moved immediately to recover as much as possible. On July 21 HMS *Assistance* arrived off the Delaware to determine the feasibility of salvage and then rushed to Halifax, Nova Scotia, with news that *De Braak* might be saved. In mid-August HMS *Hind,* accompanied by the salvage brig *Vixen,* was dispatched to raise the wreck. Despite several days of concerted effort, the endeavor failed but lent credence to unfounded rumors. The British, it was said, had returned to raise the diminutive ship not for return to the Royal Navy—after all it was already a superannuated vessel by the standard of the times—but because of a purported treasure taken from a great Spanish galleon. It mattered little that the galleon fleets had ceased operations nearly two decades earlier or that *De Braak* had captured but one vessel, and that one bearing only a cargo of copper. Hadn't Spanish sailors come ashore with gold coins in their pockets? Soon, rumors began to circulate along the Delmarva coast that the brig had foundered with a vast treasure of Spanish gold, silver, and other riches. As time passed, this unfounded tale of the treasure of HMS *De Braak* would grow out of all proportion to the actual history of the ship to become one of the most famous legends of the Delaware coast and a mainstay of American treasure lore for nearly two centuries. By the late twentieth century, the value of the treasure was said to have been as much as $500 million.[53] Over the course of the next two centuries, many would spend their lives and millions of dollars in search of the purported treasure of *De Braak,* and all in vain. For it was all malarkey.

But more on that later!

# The Unfortunate Spaniards Waved
# Their Handkerchiefs

The workday had begun as usual for Captain Leon Rose, skipper of the Wanchese Seafood Company fishing trawler *Lady Cheryl,* as he deployed then hauled in his dredge net filled with fish. Working a short distance off Assateague Lighthouse hauling the net close to the bottom was usually pretty routine stuff. Though recent storms had stirred things up a bit on the smooth seabed, the last thing he expected in these waters was a bad snag. There were, of course, the myriad assortment of wrecks, but he knew the bottom like the back of his hand and meticulously avoided them. If he didn't, he well knew that the oversight could be costly, which was why this snag was different. The net came free, and he mentally noted the position so that he would not hit it again. Hauling it in, however, was not easy, for this time he had run into something big—very big—and it was coming up!

The mysterious catch in 1989 proved to be a heavily encrusted sea anchor, with a stock nearly twelve feet long. A portion of a wooden ship's bow was attached in a gritty concretion that had formed about it. Adhering to the matrix was an ancient pewter plate, battered and bruised, but intact. Barely discernible on the plate was an incised letter "J" and other inscriptions far too faint to decipher. Subsequent drags resulted in the recovery of the sternpost of a vessel and two bronze gudgeons.

Rose eventually sold the anchor and conglomerate to the proprietor of Payne's Sea Treasures, a curio shop on Ridge Road at Pony Swim Lane, Chincoteague, dealing in driftwood, old bottles, and other flotsam. The proprietor, a colorful and loquacious man who called himself simply "Captain Bob," positioned the anchor in front of his shop for all to see, and proudly displayed the pewter plate. "It's from a Spanish treasure ship, don't you know," he would say with a grin to anyone who asked about its origins. "They called her *Juno.*"[1]

Until the last week of October 1802 the voyage of the merchant schooner *Favourite* from Madeira and Teneriffe to Boston had been unremarkable at best. Then all hell broke loose. Though it was not unusual or unexpected to encounter heavy weather on the open North Atlantic at this time of year, the northwest gale that had begun to lash the merchantman as she approached latitude 37°N and longitude 67°W exceeded the worst that Captain Pourland or any of his crew had ever experienced. In a tempest such as this, anything could happen.[2]

On October 24, during a brief lull in the storm, Pourland observed a great ship, a man-of-war, bearing down hard on him from some distance. It was an observation that no doubt caused considerable concern. As the range between the two vessels narrowed, the captain made her out as a Spanish frigate, and she appeared to be laboring heavily in the enormous swells. A distress flag was flying at her masthead. Overtaking the schooner, the commander of His Most Catholic Majesty Charles IV's warship *Juno*, Captain Don Juan Ignacio Bustillo, signaled that he was in danger of imminent sinking. He requested that *Favourite* stay by him and "assist in getting the frigate to the nearest land," which in this case would most likely be near the Delaware or Chesapeake. Pourland replied his willingness to assist, though he might be diverted for some time from reaching his own destination. For a merchantman to escort a foreign warship into an American port was not exactly everyday fare, but the skipper of the big schooner most certainly acted out of humanitarian concern for fellow mariners in distress. Thus, it was quickly agreed that several Spanish officers and soldiers would be transferred to the schooner with provisions that might be required in an emergency and to address specific details concerning the escort.[3]

Within a short time the frigate's second-in-command, Don Francisco Clemente, a lieutenant of the African Regiment; Don Jose Maria Zorilla, a cadet; Don Antonio Malagon; and four grenadiers had boarded the schooner. They quickly related to Captain Pourland the tale of their sad odyssey and then set about formalizing the arrangements.

Clemente's story was, perhaps, as frightening as any seamen who dared challenge the elements cared to hear. The Spaniard's thirty-four-gun warship had originally sailed from Vera Cruz, Mexico, on January 15, 1802, in the company of the forty-gun frigate *Amfritrite*. She was laden at the time with a substantial quantity of specie and other treasure worth a hundred thousand dollars. Almost immediately the two ships encountered terrible weather that delayed their departure and later dismasted both ships at sea. They had been forced to seek refuge in Puerto Rico. For months they languished in the tropical waters of San Juan Harbor as bureaucracy and time-consuming repairs pushed a revised departure date well into the late hurricane season. Finally, on October 1, after an eight-month delay, *Juno* took aboard the Third Battalion of the African Regiment and made sail for home, again in company with *Amfritrite*. Captain Bustillo now had under his charge the lives of 420 crewmen and soldiers, as well as a number of men, women, and children passengers.

For days the voyage was blessed with settled, temperate weather, and the two ships maintained constant contact. On reaching the meridian of Bermuda, however, the winds increased, the skies darkened, and the seas, laced by continuous squalls, became turbulent. Captain Bustillo was not surprised, for at this time of year such conditions were common in these waters. What was disconcerting to him, however, was that during a particularly violent squall, the two warships had become separated.

For days the dirty weather continued unabated, with winds blowing from every sector of the compass. Bustillo first hoped to evade the storms by heading north rather than northeast, but there was no escape. With every passing hour the heavy seas continued to make the great man-of-war work increasingly harder, while mercilessly pounding her weakest joints. By the night of October 22, the ship had begun to take on water. With great waves buffeting her about, and a hardy wind now blowing from the northeast, Bustillo decided to ride it out with *Juno*'s topsail on all reef points. Within minutes a terrible tearing noise was heard. The sail had split. For a half hour the ship was unable to continue sailing until the mizzenmast was cut. Trouble, unfortunately, was escalating as the undiminished winds continued to extract their toll.

With the lives of everyone aboard at stake, the crew worked quickly to clear the deck of wreckage and check the cables, masting, and rigging. Yet nothing could stop the waters from washing over the sides or seeping through the leaks below deck. The caulker on duty informed the captain that there was seventy-four inches of water in the hold and every danger that it would be increasing. It was obvious to Bustillo that with only two pumps currently in operation, the race to stem the water increase might be entirely—and fatally—lost if something more was not done. He ordered a second set of pumps put into action. Both soldiers and sailors were organized into pump gangs and distributed around the ship, with specific shift times assigned to each to allow for rest periods. Thereafter "followed moments of great fatigue" for everyone.

The following day, October 23, *Juno* was allowed a short reprieve. The weather cleared somewhat, and Captain Bustillo took advantage of the respite to locate the origin of the major leaks and attempt to impede their deadly progress. Men were sent below to conduct a "scrupulous investigation." One can only imagine the difficulty faced by the brave seamen as they plunged into the dark, frigid water-filled hold, searching mostly by touch for the ruptures in the hull. After nearly a year aboard, they were guided only by a now-intimate knowledge of and familiarity with the ship's design. They were all too aware that unless they succeeded they might well have been surveying the insides of their own watery coffin.

The crew found major leaks in the boatswain's storeroom and quarters, which had caused the forward part of the ship to dip deeper than the stern. Buoyed by the discovery, melancholy thoughts of the previous night's hardships gave way to renewed confidence. Bustillo's every order was now followed with celerity and efficiency. All guns between the mainmast and the bow were jettisoned. The third and forth anchors were also thrown overboard. The storerooms were emptied and all supplies transferred to the stern. At the same time, Bustillo had a task force of caulkers and seamen attempt to plug the leaks, the most difficult mission of all.

Every possible method available was employed to stem the water. The crew stuffed oakum into the torn seams from the inside, but ocean water continued to pour in. They applied plaster, with equally negative results. Pulley blocks with lines attached to both sides of a spare sail were fastened to the opposite extremities of the main yard and the sail hauled over the side of the ship to cover the entrance of the leaks from outside, but to no avail. The flow of water into the ship continued to increase. Then, on October 24, *Juno* sighted and began to chase *Favourite*.

Captain Pourland and Lieutenant Clemente quickly got down to establishing a protocol for escorting the man-of-war into the closest American port. They decided on a plan for signals to indicate if the water in the hold of the frigate was increasing or diminishing. They also agreed on a tactical maneuver for *Favourite*'s approach to the warship if it became necessary to offload the people in a hurry. With a consensus on "sensible precautions" achieved, Captain Bustillo took heart for the first time in many days and believed he could actually make the coast of the United States. Encouraging his men, he set a course, albeit with a fresh southwesterly against him. The men at the pumps were given new life. It was, unfortunately, a false hope born of absolute desperation.

For the next three days the warship and her unlikely escort plodded slowly on, with the water in the hold slowly, insidiously overtaking the ability of the pumps to manage it. Then, in the early morning darkness of October 27, Bustillo signaled Pourland that the ship's pumps were no longer able to sustain the leaks. With her belly bloated with water, the ship was now barely able to move: the rudder had been lost and the water was still rising. Her bone-weary men were now forced to bail by hand in the bow and stern. A rig for steering with oars was assembled to replace the rudder. At midday, as *Juno* lumbered along in a southwesterly direction, Bustillo took a sextant reading and determined his position to be 38° latitude north and 69°56' longitude west, approximately three hundred miles off the Delmarva coast. Still the water rose.

About 10:00 P.M. the wind shifted to the northwest and erupted into yet another squall. The violence of the weather was devastating. The gaff peak was parted, and *Juno* was left with nearly bare poles, all but defenseless against the blows of the sea that drove her first one way then another, mile after mile after mile. Then, with a sudden crack, the mainmast, foretopsail, and yard (which had been used to jury rig a tiller) became the next victims as they were "wrenched" from the ship. The mainmast came down across the handrail and opened a clear portal for water to come over the sides and into the ship. The dying man-of-war frantically signaled *Favourite* for help. The schooner, however, was only able to safely run under the warship's lee to within barely a third of a cable's length, or about 240 feet. It was close enough to hear the anguished cries for help, the shrieking of women, the sobbing of children, and the pitiful laments of the doomed, but little more. With his schooner overcome by the wind, Pourland was convinced that if he attempted to bring his vessel round she would capsize. "The unfortunate Spaniards waved their handkerchiefs," it was later recounted, "and the ship rolled as if nearly full of water." Captain Pourland and his men, as well as the seven Spaniards who had earlier come aboard, could do little but "watch the ship disappearing below." *Favourite* remained incapable of maneuvering at all for the remainder of that terrible night.[4]

When the dawn of October 28 arrived, the crew of *Favourite* searched the horizon in vain for sight of the Spaniard. The ship had vanished forever from the surface of the sea. Convinced that his charge had indeed gone down with all 413 soldiers and seamen, and an unknown number of civilian passengers remaining aboard, a horrific loss by any standard, Pourland set a course for New England. On November 1, the schooner dropped anchor in Boston harbor. Testimony later offered by Lieutenant Clemente and his six compatriots attested to the order, composure, and discipline maintained aboard *Juno* at all times. "Everyone carried their duty." But it had not been enough.[5]

With the loss of *Juno* and her purportedly substantial cargo of specie, yet another legend had been born. Like that of the ill-fated *De Braak,* the lost ship's tale was destined to evolve and mutate over time. It was a story that would eventually generate innumerable treasure hunts, and nearly two hundred years later an international controversy that would influence the direction of global maritime law.

# 12

## Rothschilds among the Toilers of the Sea

Gathering in chattering, chirping bands, the reedy-legged birds of beach and marsh flee south from the Delmarva coast after summer. The perfume of salty foam blowing across the shore and cool breezes sweeping wavy trails across the dunes cannot mask the onset of another season. On the barrier islands the raccoons, rabbits, deer, and tiny horses arm themselves with shaggy manes against the coming chill of fall. Terrapins dig into the muddy bottoms of shallow creeks and sounds. Legions of waterfowl, ducks, and Canada geese darken the skies in ragged wedged formations as they wing their way south from summer nesting grounds. Their passage denotes the changing season, but many drop down for a winter of growing plump on the dusky colored roots of the slough grasses. In November, the crass voices of whistling swans crack through the late autumn air. It was then that sea disasters on the desolate shores of the barrier islands seemed the worst. And it was then that the wreckers thrived, even as men died and fortunes were made.

The famed English man of letters Dr. Samuel Johnson once wrote, not so facetiously, that "no man will be a sailor who has contrivance enough to get himself into jail; for being in a ship is being in jail with the chance of being drowned." Indeed, the life expectancy of seaman and ships alike was short and cruel. One late-eighteenth-century observer computed that for every sixteen sailors who died of all diseases, eleven perished by drowning or in wrecks, and one of every twenty-five British ships was lost each year. Even during those rare times of peace, more than two thousand Englishmen perished yearly in the mighty deep, "chiefly from shipwrecks, by which property to the amount of £3 millions annually is lost to the nation and hundreds of widows and thousands of children are thrown on the cold and precarious charity of the public." The average life span of the seaman was forty-five years. And the ill-defined, shoally coastline between Capes Henlopen and Charles was one of the most dangerous claimants of human life in English-speaking America.[1]

Between 1783 and 1800, more than 125 vessels are known to have met their end on the skeleton shores of the Delmarva coast. By the end of the twentieth century, over 2,300 ships and thousands of lives would be lost. Yet, as the saying goes, one man's loss was often another's gain, for in those early days of American history, many folks who settled on these isolated islands or on the mainland behind the sounds considered shipwrecks as an economic blessing and an important part of their livelihoods. With satisfactory evidence, authorities paid one pound per body to those who buried drowned sailors cast ashore. Ship timbers and lumber salvaged from stranded vessels or washed up on the beach provided building materials for island homes and docks and firewood for hearths. Local salvors might recover practically everything they needed for subsistence, and what they did not use might be sold or bartered on the mainland. Preserved meats, tropical fruits, sugar, molasses, lumber, notions, furniture, grain, lard, salt, alcoholic beverages (especially rum), salted fish, hides, cotton, bricks, and many other items including, in later years, oysters, coal, and new fuel products were often to be had in abundance. By the mid-eighteenth century, wrecking was already on the way to becoming an informal industry on the Delmarva coast and a boon to local economies, especially on Assateague and at Sinepuxent, as mainland stores and auctions sold off cargoes salvaged from wrecks at an accelerated clip. Wrecking soon became a quasiregular, albeit illegal, occupation for many. As the famed Worcester County historian Reginald Truitt once wrote, until the end of the nineteenth century "men, here and there, were called, not too openly, by such agnomens as 'Sugar', 'Silver', 'Banana', 'Molasses', 'Rum', and others (as in fictitious Rum Winton and Silver Jasper) according to their respective take-home booty which when in excess of family use, was sold or bartered for other commodities."[2]

Salvaging wrecks on the Delmarva coast, most notably at Assateague and Sinepuxent, started out, some proponents argued, to make use of cast-up articles and flotsam that would have otherwise gone to waste. The actual governance of marine salvage, relating not just to shipwrecks but to anything regurgitated by the sea, had deep roots in law well before the first colonists set foot in America. From medieval times the sea itself, "the packhorse of the King," was considered another of a monarch's chattels, just like countries, money, and his population of serfs and soldiers. In 1236 King Henry III of England granted a charter permitting an owner of wrecked goods to reclaim his property if done within three months of the time of loss, with the proviso that if there were any survivors, human or beast, the ship could not be deemed a loss. The proviso had a purpose: it ensured that wreckers would not seize and destroy vessels that might be refloated. In dangerous English coastal regions like Cornwall, the statute had the effect of becoming a permit for wreckers to murder survivors, to guarantee that the ship's loss was total. King Edward I infamously reiterated the act in the First Statute of Westminster. Not until 1771, after countless murders of shipwreck victims, was the "man or beast" ruling explicitly repealed![3]

The French in 1266 drafted the first identifiable sea code adopted by the English and most of Europe. It was known as the Rules of Oleron. The articles therein addressed not only acceptable maritime practices but also punishments for those who imperiled shipping for the purpose of profiting from shipwrecks. Corrupt pilots who "out of design to ruin ship and goods, guide and bring her upon the rocks, and then feigning to aid, help and assist the now distressed mariners" were to be hung at the place where they brought the ship to ruin. The gibbets were to "abide and remain to succeeding ages on that place" as a warning to other ships. Any lord who participated in such villainies was to be fastened to a stake "in the midst of his own mansion house." The house was to be burned, its stones pulled down, and the site converted into a marketplace for the sale of hogs and swine. Those who murdered shipwreck victims were to be seized and punished by plunging into the sea "till they be half dead," after which they were to be stoned to death.[4]

During the reign of King Henry VIII, the administration of wrecks was more formally codified. The Lord High Admiral of England was authorized to appoint vice admirals for each of the counties of the nation. In return for the submission of annual accounts, the vice admirals, in concert with designated nobles, were awarded rights to all shipwrecks in their counties. Corruption by the vice admirals forced passage of an act in 1713 authorizing customs officers and justices of the peace to order the rescue of distressed vessels; the act also provided for salvage awards as an incentive. In 1753, for the first time, an act of George II addressed the use of false lights to lure ships to their doom and declared it a felony punishable by death without benefit of clergy. It also made illegal the taking and concealing of wrecks and the offering of such wrecks for sale, which was punishable by seven years' indenture in America.[5]

In many ways the concept of marine salvage had been absolutely antithetical to the principles of common law, and even today it provides for a bountiful award to anyone who successfully "salves" (saves) marine property and cargoes from marine damage. Since the late seventeenth century, as in the counties of England, it was among the many duties of the British Vice Admiralty Courts in America to deal with problems concerning shipwrecks and the salvage of vessels and cargoes. In the absence of Admiralty adjudication, the colonial administrations frequently intervened.[6] Beaches and things cast up on them by the sea were still the king's purview. Abandoned or wrecked ships whose owners were unknown or dead belonged to the monarch, as did most all other valuable things cast up by the sea, such as whales, which provided food, oil, ambergris, and bone. That both whales and shipwrecks were numerous along the Atlantic seaboard was not ignored by the king of England. They were, wrote one eighteenth-century traveler, considered "to the great Advantage of those inhabiting the Sand-Banks, along the Ocean, where these Whales come ashore, none being struck or kill'd with a Harpoon . . . as they are to the Northward, and elsewhere; all those Fish being found dead on the Shoar, most commonly by those that inhabit the Banks, and Seaside, where they dwell, for that Intent, and for the Benefit of Wrecks, which sometimes fall in upon that Shoar."[7]

The issue of comprehensively addressing the administration of marine salvage on the Delmarva coast appears to have first been undertaken in Maryland in the late seventeenth century. On March 10, 1692, King William II of England awarded to Mainhardt, Duke of Schonburgh and Leinster, "Letters Patents for all Wrecks, Derelicts &ca Between the Latitudes of Twelve Degrees South and forty Degrees North for Twenty years." It was, of course, an open-ended, exclusive patent for salvage over an enormous area that extended from the central eastern seaboard of Brazil to Mantoloking, New Jersey. It mattered little to either the king or the duke that it overlapped Spanish, Dutch, French, and Portuguese territories well beyond any individual's abilities to administer. The colonial waters of the Delmarva, and Maryland in particular, however, were clearly within reach.[8]

Less than a year after the Duke of Schonburgh received his patent, on February 10, 1693/94, Colonel Francis Nicholson was appointed captain general and governor in chief of Maryland by King William and Queen Mary of England. By virtue of his executive position, the colonel was granted the lucrative post of vice admiral of Maryland, with jurisdiction over all bays, rivers, creeks, harbors, inlets, islands, and territories belonging to the province. He was also to administer His Majesty's Vice Admiralty Court in the province in all matters marine. Among his many responsibilities was to protect the monarch's interest in marine salvage, the rights to which now fell under Schonburgh's patent.[9]

The duke, who had apparently taken no action during the administration of Lionel Copley, the previous governor of Maryland, took the opportunity of Nicholson's appointment to formally apprise the new chief executive and vice admiral of Maryland of his own rights and interests granted by the Crown. Precisely one week after assuming office, Nicholson was reminded by the duke's agents of his requisite duties and his own monetary interests on the subject of salvage. "Wee have Agreed," they wrote, "to allow to your Self and others imployed by you out of any Wreck, Derelict &ca that you or they shall Discover, seize and secure one Tenth part of the clear profits thereof for you[r] Encouragement in this service."[10] Nicholson was granted absolute power of attorney as deputy and agent for the duke. On the nobleman's behalf, and by extension the monarch's, Nicholson's authority extended over "all and Every such Wrecks Jetsam ffloatsamlagan Goods Derelicts Riches Bullion Plate Gold silver Coyn Barrs or piggs of silver ingots of Gold Merchandizes and other Goods & Chattells whatsoever which at any time or times then-to fore had been or at any time or times then after should be left cast away Wreckt or lost in or Upon any of the Rocks shelves Shoales Seas Rivers or Bancks in America between the Latitude of Twelve Degrees South and fforty degrees North And which at any time or times within twenty years next after the Date of the said Indenture should betaken up gotten or Recovered by him the said Mainhardt Duke of Leinster his Executors Administrators or Assignes or his or their Agents or Substitutes as by the said Grant . . . within the Province of Maryland and all the Limits & Boundaries upon the Sea Coasts of the s[ai]d Province of Maryland."[11]

Nicholson was authorized to seize and take into his possession all wrecks and aforementioned items lost and to reimburse himself "all charges and allowances." In the event that he encountered any obstruction or opposition to the lawful execution of his mission, he was authorized to "Sue Implead and Imprison all & every person & persons whatsoever that shall detain possess dispose purloyn or imbeazle any of such Wrecks and premises before particularly mentioned." He was also to have the power to appoint deputies, agents, or servants as required to promulgate salvage.[12]

On March 28 the documents were signed, and at the same time a proclamation declaring Nicholson as governor of Maryland was authorized. The proclamation was formally read on July 27, 1694, in the capital of Maryland, St. Mary's City.[13]

Nicholson's administration over a colony sorely divided by religious dissension was one of the most difficult possible. It is not surprising that the issue of marine salvage would wait for more than a year for attendance. Finally, in the summer of 1695, one Edward Green, surveyor of Somerset County, submitted a petition for appointment as wreckmaster. On August 19, Green, who "Liveth convenient to the sea boardside in Somerset County . . . haveing a right to the greater part or share of those Marshes and Sand banks or beaches so termed Adjoyning the seaboard side or breakers of the main Sea within the said County of Somerset" had his petition read before the Council of Maryland.[14]

He requested that he, and he alone, be commissioned to seize "all Wrecks condemnable by Law also all drift Whales or other great ffish belonging to his Ma[jes]ty And the said ffish to Cut up and try for Oyle what can not be got from the bluber thereof it being a hardship." He also requested that "any Strangers or Inhabitants should have freedom to range the said beaches belonging to your pet[itione]r & cut the timber there-upon, Intreating that the Kings allowance may be moderate."[15]

Nicholson and the council acted immediately and issued Green a commission "to looke after those Matters" outlined in the petition with the stipulation that he render a "just & true" account "as well of all his proceedings & therefore profits" accrued at all times as well. He was to be accountable to His Majesty's Court of Vice Admiralty on the Eastern Shore for any other profits he or any other person "by means of any such Drifts or Wrecks heretofore made and unaccounted for." A bond for the same and for payment of that part belonging to the King or Vice Admiralty Court was to be posted. In return he was accordingly awarded powers "for the seizing all wrecks thither coming & by Law condemnable, as also to looke after all Whales & other Royall ffish which at any time may happen to be driven & cast up there, with liberty of trying for Oyle what can be got from the blubber of the same."[16]

Two days after his appointment, Green and an Eastern Shore plantation owner named John Edmundson put up a £500 performance bond to be deposited with the governor. Green was then formally appointed by the governor as the "only Officer under me for the taking seizing cutting up & trying the blubber, and making such other use & benefit as you shall think fit or possible can for the most advantage of all such drift whales Grampus's and other Royall ffish and of all or any other Drifts, Waftes, or Wrecks, whatsoever as shall at any time hereafter happen to come or be cast on the Seaboard Side w[i]th in the limits & Jurisdiction of this Province." He was also authorized to deputize and employ as many persons as deemed necessary. All magistrates, military and civil officers, and inhabitants within the province were ordered to permit him to conduct his business as he was authorized to do. They were also to "resist oppose & prevent all others, Strangers, intruders or interlopers whatsoever that shall presume at any time hereafter to intermedle or concern themselves therewith, without leave of Lycense so to do, first legally had and Obtained To have hand-hold the place and Office aforesaid."[17]

On December 11, 1742, Somerset County was divided, and Worcester County, whose eastern sea frontier constituted the entirety of Maryland's Atlantic seaboard, was born. By that time the office once held by Edward Green, nearly half a century earlier, appears to have fallen into disuse. In the frequent absence of a duly appointed wreckmaster, illegal wrecking would thrive as never before.

Without an effective, lawful authority, wrecking on the Delmarva coast soon became an occupation conducted, usually illegally whenever a maritime disaster struck. The proficiency—and competitive rivalries—of those involved in the profession grew over time to substantial proportions, as evidenced in the case of *La Galga* in 1750.[18] Whole extended communities were often involved in one stage or another, from the men who actually stripped the wrecks, to haulers who carried the salvaged goods overland to commercial outlets or private homes, and merchants who sold the goods and sometimes the wrecks themselves. On the sparsely populated coastal islands, in a region sometimes devoid of civil law and government, inhabitants carried on with their frugal, simple lives as farmers, fishermen, and tradesmen but always kept a keen eye open for the next unfortunate ship that might wash up on the beach.

There was often a fine practical line between wrecking and salving, but a world of legal difference existed between them. By the eighteenth century, under English law, wrecking was considered a malicious act with forethought by the perpetrators. Salving of a wreck and its goods from destruction was, on the books at least, deemed a selfless pursuit and was not illegal. But it was up to the salvor to report to the authorities all property that was saved so that the original owners might be informed. If the owners were located and demanded the return of their goods, the salvor was required to hand them over but would receive a just compensation and sometimes storage fees. If the owner could not be found or the owner was no longer interested in the goods, ownership of the property reverted to the salvor. To many, salving appeared to be little more than theft, but in the eyes of the law it was—and still is—considered looking after property until the owners claimed it.

Wrecking and salvage for profit in the colonial and early republic days was not, in practice, structured on humanitarian concerns but on taking charge of cargoes and wreckage as quickly as possible, before agents of the ship owners, rival claimants, or the law appeared on the scene. Unlike wreckers on the Outer Banks of the Carolinas, however, who were said to occasionally lure ships ashore with false lights, or those of Long Island, New York, who sometimes could not wait for a shipwreck victim to expire before cutting off a finger to remove his rings, the Delmarva salvors of the eighteenth and nineteenth centuries were seldom brutal. More often than not their work was laced with a streak of compassion. But profit was always the motive, and competition for wrecks was often heated.[19]

After the Franco-American victory at Yorktown, when independence was heavy in the air, Virginia moved aggressively to get its affairs in order regarding wrecking and salvage in state waters. The desolate barrier island chains of Accomack and Northampton Counties on the Delmarva peninsula had repeatedly suffered maritime tragedies, not only in the loss of life but also in the loss of valuable ships and cargoes, much of which fell into the hands of wreckers. Shipping concerns and insurers complained, as did those who rushed to the rescue, more often than not too late to be of help. Finally, in 1782, the state officially established an Office of Commissioner of Wrecks.[20]

The job of the commissioner of wrecks was to get to every shipwreck as soon as practicable and take command of the wreckage and cargo. The Virginia government thus took charge until the lawful owners could be located. In order to carry out his mission, the commissioner, acting on behalf of the state, was thus authorized to engage or hire people as necessary to do the work and secure transportation to haul away the goods from a wreck site. A levy of the cargo was paid the government for its services. If the vessel's owner was lost in the disaster, then the government would dispose of the goods along with the wreck itself at public auction, and the money would be placed in the government's general fund.[21]

Creating an official post was simple. Carrying out its mission was another thing. Problems erupted immediately, especially along the occasionally disputed Maryland-Virginia border on Assateague. As during the days of the *Galga* affair, Marylanders accused the inhabitants of Accomack of robbing wrecked vessels. The Virginians responded vigorously, assuming a virtuous attitude over their neighbors to the north who had as yet to reestablish a state office to deal with wrecks. A war of words ensued in the press. In 1784, the new commissioner of wrecks, John Teackle, in a letter to Virginia governor Benjamin Harrison, claimed that the good citizens of Accomack were foully criticized for supposed "robberies made on Wrecked vessels." In fact, he claimed, it was the Marylanders who considered it their privilege "to embezzle from wrecked vessels." They were responsible for the ill repute of the good inhabitants of Accomack. He went on to claim that this villainous employment on Assateague, whose shoals were already famed as the resting place of numerous valuable shipwrecks, provided so many opportunities for plunder that ghoulish Marylanders ensconced on the island frequently sent word to their accomplices on the mainland to join them when a wreck was near at hand. Some, it was rumored but never proven, even lured ships to their doom with false lights.[22]

The war of words continued without letup. In 1787 the survivors of the Maryland packet boat *Joseph and Peggy*, which struck a "reef of rocks" near Smith Island on May 9, were viciously robbed of the few valuables they had saved from the wreck. When news reached Annapolis, the editor of the *Maryland Gazette* exclaimed in derision at the wreckers by comparing them to the famed and bloodthirsty wreckers of the English coast: "The boors of Cornwall would have blushed at the behavior." The subsequent actions of the Delawareans at the wreck site of *Faithful Steward,* of course, were little better.[23]

Marylanders, like Virginians, were not above an occasional good fight, legal or otherwise, for the profits to be derived from a shipwreck, commissioner or no commissioner. For as long as there have been shipwrecks, there have been people fighting over them, both on the beach and in the courts. When the brig *Lively*, Captain Lawrence commanding, bound from Amsterdam to New York, became stranded in January 1795 "near the Delaware" but on the Maryland coast, probably in the vicinity of Sinepuxent, the scene was set for one such contest that may have helped influence Maryland legislative action.[24] There is little record of what happened to *Lively's* commander or his men, but it is safe to say that the wreck did not go unnoticed by the local inhabitants, nor apparently was her location forgotten. The wreck was duly reported and settled by the ship's insurer, Lloyds of London, and then all but forgotten—except by the wreckers.

Almost a year later, in January 1796, on the beach barely two miles from the site where *Lively* had grounded, a local resident named Schoolfield Parker discovered twenty-nine sealed pipes of gin, seven of which were snuggled in the sand at the breaker line with water washing over them. Now this was no small find, for each pipe was the equivalent of a hogshead of spirits, or 250 gallons. The *Lively* had in fact carried a lading of gin, and Parker had discovered some of it and was entitled to salvage it. The find was a valuable one, for 7,250 gallons of English gin on the open market would fetch a pretty penny.[25]

Parker, however, was in a quandary. Unable to remove the heavy containers from the beach by himself, he wrote his name on each of the seven pipes buried in the sand and rushed across Sinepuxent Bay to secure assistance. Though he quickly rounded up a number of neighbors and friends to aid him in his task and returned to the pipes of gin the same day, it was already too late. When he arrived at the site he discovered John Fassitt, whose home lay at nearby Sandy Point, and a number of others already engaged in hauling off the valuable pipes to a secure place.[26]

Parker was naturally furious and moved to prevent Fassitt from proceeding and attempted to take the gin back into his own possession. Fassitt retorted forcefully and prevented his rival from further interference. Parker retired to his own home, seething over the injustice of it all. Finally, on February 15, he again ventured forth and once more demanded Fassitt turn over his ill-gotten gains, but to no avail. Much to his chagrin, he now discovered that Fassitt not only had full possession of all twenty-nine pipes but had also paid the duty on them in an effort to provide grounds for legal title to them. Parker was not put off, and on March 23 he instituted a legal action for return of at least the seven pipes he had left his mark on. The action was delayed, however, until the September 1798 term of the General Court of the Eastern Shore, by which time Parker had died.[27]

For the next four months no action was undertaken. Not until January 8, 1799, could Parker's executors provide testamentary papers that would allow them to continue on with the suit. On February 4, the executors again brought suit against Fassitt, but not soon enough, for by that time he too had died. Nevertheless, the battle between the executors of the two claimants continued until the court finally made a ruling in September 1802, more than seven years after the loss of *Lively*. The plaintiffs moved that "the Court direct the Jury that if they should find that plaintiffs had a right to the gin, the plaintiffs were entitled to recover 'for money received' if Fassitt had converted the gin to his own use." The court refused the motion, and the verdict was for the defendant.[28]

It is uncertain if the highly visible and contentious case was directly responsible for moving the State of Maryland to act. But act the state did. In December 1799 the Maryland General Assembly passed legislation creating the office of wreckmaster in Worcester County, Maryland's sole Atlantic coastal county. In the preamble, justification for the act was given: "whereas from the exposure of the south-east bounds of Worcester county to the Atlantic ocean, many vessels have been and may hereafter be stranded on the sea-coast in the county aforesaid, and the goods, or other property, belonging to such vessel or vessels may be embezzled and stolen, to the great injury of the owners or insurers, and it would be highly expedient to appoint a wreck-master in said county."[29]

The act was specific in its articles regarding appointment, duties, powers, pay, penalties, deputations, and so forth. The governor of Maryland, Benjamin Ogle, with the advice and consent of his council, was authorized to nominate and appoint a "discreet and sensible person" who resided near the seacoast of Worcester County to serve as wreckmaster. The specific business of that officer, like his counterpart in Virginia, was to act "on the earliest intelligence" or at the request of any owner or commander of any vessel being in danger of stranding, or having already been stranded, to appoint a constable or constables nearest the coast where the vessel was in danger to summon as many men as necessary to offer assistance. The wreckmaster was authorized to impress into service any Maryland vessels and boats riding near the site "and such hands as they can conveniently spare" to provide assistance. Any commanding officer who refused to provide aid was to forfeit £100 to the owner of the ship in distress, with costs.[30]

For every vessel in distress attended to or cargo saved, the wreckmaster and the commanding officer of any vessel impressed into service, as well as any others who assisted, were to be paid "a reasonable reward" within forty days by the vessel owner or the merchant whose goods were saved. If the owner and/or merchant defaulted in payment, the vessel and goods would remain in the custody of the wreckmaster until charges were paid or security given for that purpose. In the event of a disagreement over payment, the commander, owner, supercargo, or factor would have legal recourse via the county court. In such cases, the interested parties would be given five days notice of time and place for determination by the chief justice of the district of the amount of compensation to be paid. If the amount was not paid within thirty days, the wreckmaster was authorized to sell any of the goods, wares, merchandise, or articles saved to the value of the judgment. If goods saved from a shipwreck and taken possession of by the wreckmaster went unclaimed, "a true description of the marks, numbers and kinds of such goods [were] to be advertised four weeks in the Easton, Baltimore and Philadelphia newspapers." If, after three months, no claimant had stepped forth, the wreckmaster was to dispose of the goods at public sale (except for perishables, which would be immediately disposed of). After charges had been deducted, all monies derived from the sale were to be turned over to the treasurer, who was to maintain an account for the benefit of the owners or insurers. After satisfaction of an auditor and receipt of his warrant, they would receive the residue.[31]

To prevent illegal wrecking, the act specifically forbade anyone but those empowered by the wreckmaster to board a vessel in distress without leave of the commanding officer. Anyone who molested the wreckmaster's agents during the saving of either a vessel or its goods, or endeavored to hinder the saving of such, or defaced cargo marks before they could be recorded, would be fined £50. All such fines were to be paid immediately, or security given within a month. Failure to pay up would result in corporal punishment "not exceeding thirty-nine lashes on his, her or their bare back." Moreover, the act authorized any commanding officer of a vessel in distress, or the wreckmaster, to repel by force any persons who sought to press themselves aboard a vessel without consent. Anyone caught with goods stolen from a vessel in distress was obliged to return the goods to the owner or pay a fine of four times the value of the goods. The worst penalty of all, however, pertained to intentionally causing a wreck: "if any person shall make, or be assisting in making, a hole in any vessel in distress, or steal any pump, materials or goods, or shall be aiding in stealing such pump, materials or goods, from any vessel, or shall willfully do any thing tending to the immediate loss of such vessel, such person shall be guilty of felony, and suffer death without benefit of clergy."[32]

Given the increasing regularity of shipping disasters on the Worcester County coast, the post of wreckmaster was a formidable responsibility and, at the same time, a potentially profitable sinecure. To curb the likelihood of corruption, any man appointed to the office of wreckmaster was to provide £1,000 bond and security "for the due and faithful execution of his office." In the event he should abuse his office and be convicted of either fraud or willful neglect relative to a vessel or cargo, he was to forfeit four times the damages of the aggrieved party and would be relieved of his post. Anyone who was associated with him in such actions would also have to pay a fine of £10. Commercial wreckers holding licenses or permits to conduct salvage, however, would continue to work.[33]

Over the years that followed, amendments and revised wording of the act would appear, reflecting nuances in the office, its mission, and expenses. In January 1807, the assembly passed two supplemental acts. The first clarified the authority of the wreckmaster to contract with laborers to assist in the job of wreck assistance and salvage. The wreckmaster himself was authorized to receive a sum not exceeding 20 percent of the property saved for his services "at the discretion of the county court, some one of the judges thereof out of court, or of the orphans court of the county."[34]

Apparently the office of wreckmaster was occasionally unoccupied, for another supplemental act noted that "it frequently happens that during the recess of the county court of Worcester county, the office of wreckmaster becomes vacant by death, resignation or otherwise." A newly appointed wreckmaster was required to give bond and security to the court; however, he was authorized to delay such until the new court was in session.[35]

With a revision of the Maryland State Constitution in 1851, the Worcester County wreckmaster became an elected official, placed in office every two years by the voters of the county.[36] In 1860 the Wreckmaster Act was again amended

A view of wreckers stripping a stranded wreck (*Harper's Magazine*, 1882; author's collection)

to address fines and payments. The fine for any ship's commanding officer who refused to assist in a rescue or salvage was placed at $500. The wreckmaster was to be paid $25 for the first day he took charge of a wreck, and $10 a day for every day thereafter. All others who assisted were to be paid two dollars a day. Independent wreckers who attempted to work on a wreck for profit without first securing authorization were to be fined $150, and if they failed to pay were still to receive the mandated thirty-nine lashes. Anyone who refused to give assistance to the wreckmaster was to be fined $25. Anyone who sought to sink or injure a vessel in distress would no longer have to face the death penalty but would be subject to between five and fifteen years' imprisonment in the state penitentiary.[37]

Further revision of the law in 1867 authorized the election of a wreckmaster in the county on the first Monday of November every two years. In 1920 the act was recodified. By 1930, the office of wreckmaster had existed for 131 years, with its parameters basically unchanged. Thirty-nine lashes was still the maximum punishment to be doled out for failure to pay fines for illegal wrecking. Fifteen years' imprisonment was still the maximum penalty for intentionally sinking or damaging a vessel in distress. There is no indication that either punishment was ever meted out.[38]

Delaware eventually established its own wreckmaster's office. Wrecking and salvage appear to usually have been left to the discretion of that office, but those issues were sometimes entwined with the actions of the U.S. Collector of Customs. Such involvement was not always to the liking of commercial wreckers, ship owners, underwriters, or the public. When the British bark *Medway,* bound from London for the Delaware, and the ship *John Sidney,* bound from Philadelphia for Liverpool, both went ashore on the shoals just south of Cape Henlopen on the night of October 25, 1872, the disasters caused some sensation. The public's interest, however, was not stirred by the loss of seven men from *Medway* or the saving of the twenty-eight crewmen, stewardess, and the captain's wife from *John Sidney.* It was the fate of the cargo of spirits that had washed up with the wrecks that intrigued them.

The press had a field day. "WRECKED FIRE WATER," read the headline in one newspaper. "From the wrecks of the ships *John Sidney* and barque *Medway,* near the Breakwater some weeks ago, there were picked up on the beach 60 barrels of Scotch whisky and 8 barrels of French brandy. The value is said to be some $15,000. There was a readiness to try some of its quality at once, but the wrecking master first took charge of it and stored it away, until Thursday. Collector Nolen of this district went to Lewes and claimed its custody, to secure the payment of about $5,000, import duties . . . As yet, the disposition of the spirits is not decided, Dr. Nolen having written to Washington for instructions to sell it. The wreckers are entitled to half its value for salvage, which will be to $7,500; the government wants $5,000, and the balance will be eaten up, (if not drank up) by other charges. Taking this view, the underwriters have given up any claims to it."[39]

The wrecking laws of Virginia, Maryland, and Delaware notwithstanding, both legal and illegal wrecking operations continued to thrive well into the latter half of the nineteenth century. One of the last, and perhaps most famous, of the Delmarva wreckers arrived late on the scene. His name was Nathan Cobb. A thirty-six-year-old native of Eastham, on Cape Cod, he was a shipbuilder by profession and the grandson of a colorful whaler who had twice been captured by pirates. In 1833 Cobb's wife, Nancy, was diagnosed with tuberculosis, and her physician suggested that she immigrate to a warmer climate. Nathan decided to move his family, including his three sons, Nathan Jr., Warren, and Albert, south. After stocking his schooner with supplies, clothing, lumber, and furniture, the Cobb family sailed from their native Massachusetts never to return.[40]

The voyage was at first smooth. Then, off the barrier islands of Virginia, bad weather drove the Cobbs into an inlet near the isolated little fishing village of Oyster. The New Englanders were welcomed with open arms and soon adopted the town and its people as their own. Nathan opened a general store, but after five years as a shopkeeper, he had had enough. The wreckers who frequented Oyster told tales of easy money. Thus, in 1838 he decided to become a professional (and lawful) salvor himself and turned his sights to the ship-killing shoals of the barrier islands. In 1839 he purchased Sand Shoal Island, eight miles from Oyster, from William "Hardtime" Fritchett for $150. Within a short time, he had dismantled his house in Oyster and moved it and his family to the island. Although he dubbed his new abode Cape Cod, the island quickly came to be known as Cobb's Island after its dynamic new owner.[41]

The island soon became the headquarters for Cobb's Salvaging Company. In 1840 Nancy Cobb died, and two years later Nathan remarried Ester Carpenter, a fair lass from nearby Hog Island. In 1866, when Ester passed away, Nathan married her sister, Nancy Richardson. In the meantime, his sons had joined the business, serving as the old man's wrecking crew. Business was exceptionally good, with a ship and cargo panning out $5,000 here, a three-masted bark for $4,000 there. Their tools of the trade were simple: a five-handed oar-powered Cape Cod fishing boat steered by an oarsman, anchors, hawsers, block and tackle, horses and sails. The work itself was both hard and dangerous. Ultimately, they would salvage no fewer than thirty-seven vessels, earning the Cobb family a small fortune and the sobriquet "Rothschilds among the toilers of the sea."[42]

Unlike other wreckers, the Cobbs were generally praised for their humanity and respect for human life. One contemporary wrote that the Cobbs "rescued at risk to their own lives many crews from sailing vessels driven ashore there. Often a crew of ten or twenty would be landed on the island from stranded vessels without a penny, and they were tenderly cared for as though they were millionaires. Money cut no figure with these people. The life saving service of the present day, with all the modern improvements, has done no more noble deeds than the Cobbs."[43]

Profit was the main objective for the company, however, and Cobb, ever the shrewd New Englander, never lost sight of it. One of the most important vessels to be salvaged by the company was a coffee bark called *Bar Cricket,* which had become stranded on a shoal quite near the Cobb household while en route from Rio de Janeiro in 1870. The Cobbs efficiently saved the crew and then salvaged both the vessel and its cargo. After a somewhat extended legal contest, Nathan was awarded 35 percent of the total value of the ship, $18,000, an exceptionally large sum for the times. Soon afterward, they salvaged the schooner *Henry Lee* and were awarded 40 percent of the vessel's value and an incredible 60 percent of its cargo value.[44]

The day of the Delmarva wreckers, however, was nearing a close, and Nathan Cobb knew it. In some areas, where lighthouses had been erected, wrecking had already fallen off. In 1833 a lighthouse had been built at Toms Cove, on Assateague, and in 1859 another on Fenwick Island at the Delaware border. These two lights, with one standing 154 feet above the Atlantic waters and the other 83 feet, could be seen at sea for nineteen miles and effectively warned mariners of the dangerous shoals. Then, in 1871, the government created the U.S. Life Saving Service, founded for the specific purpose of saving the lives of shipwrecked mariners on the coasts of the nation and securing their property when possible. Four years later the Life Saving Service began the construction of a chain of permanent lifesaving stations on the Delmarva coast and training its corps of intrepid surf men. At first only six stations were commissioned, one each on Smith Island, Cobb's Island, Hog Island, Cedar Island, and Assateague Beach, Virginia, and Green Run Inlet, Maryland. The first station erected on Cobb's Island was mysteriously burned, but another was quickly erected to replace it. Some suggested that the fire had been an act of deliberate arson carried out by persons with a vested interest in assuring the failure of the Life Saving Service on the island, namely the Cobb family, but its actual cause was never discovered.[45]

In 1876 more stations were commissioned at Cape Henlopen and Indian River, Delaware. By 1878 there were also stations established at Rehoboth Beach, Delaware; Ocean City, Maryland; and Pope's Island, Virginia. Within the next six years, additional stations were erected at Lewes, Delaware; North Beach, Maryland; and Wallops Island and Parramore Beach, Virginia. In 1889 the Metompkin Island Station opened in Virginia and two years afterward the Fenwick Island Station was in service in Delaware. The last two stations, Isle of Wight, Maryland, and Bethany Beach, Delaware, came on line in 1898 and 1908.[46]

Not surprisingly, when the government finally erected the second Cobb's Island Life Saving Station and manned it with a dedicated corps of men, the Cobb's Salvaging Company soon found its lucrative salvage fees disappearing. Yet Nathan Cobb and his boys were anything but defeatists. Wrecking had been a mainstay of the family economy for thirty-seven years and had made it prosper beyond all expectations. Fortunately for the Cobbs, they had also earned a reputation for their acumen at hunting waterfowl and shorebirds for New York restaurants and millinery markets and for serving as hunting and fishing guides for well-to-do northern sportsmen. The lower barrier islands, Cobb's Island in particular, and the waters surrounding them were rich in game and fish. Cobb thus decided to capitalize on the natural resources around him and his own reputation as a guide. Using the funds earned from the *Bar Cricket* salvage, he built a resort hotel, a rambling structure that expanded each year along with its wealthy clientele. It was a pivotal event for the Cobb family and the island bearing their name. The last of the old-time wreckers had finally called it quits, and a new industry had been born.

# 13

## Assailed by Overwhelming Odds

For the stolid watermen, farmers, and merchants of the lower Eastern Shore, news of the formation of the Provisional Government of the Confederate States of America on February 4, 1861, at Montgomery, Alabama, came as no surprise. The admission of Virginia into the Confederacy on May 7, while Maryland and Delaware held firm to the republic, however, presented a considerable conundrum for the small, dispersed rural population of the Delmarva coast. Like other citizens of the border states forced to choose sides, many simply wanted to go about their daily lives in peace. It was, of course, not to be.

The march toward open civil war had been swift. On April 15, following the capture of Fort Sumter in Charleston harbor and federal property elsewhere in the South, President Abraham Lincoln had issued a call for 75,000 militia to "repossess the forts, places, and properties which have been seized." Two days later, with the South lacking even the nucleus of a regular navy to wage war at sea, Confederate president Jefferson Davis issued a proclamation authorizing privateering. In an effort to strangle rebel commercial shipping, smuggling, and privateering, Lincoln responded on April 19 by declaring a blockade of the rebel coastline from Texas to South Carolina. Eight days later the blockade was extended to include Virginia and North Carolina. Lincoln warned that anyone molesting any U.S. ship, its persons, or cargo would be punished as a pirate.

Although the Confederate congress would not confirm Davis's call for privateers until May 6, everyone understood the rebel need for oceangoing cruisers to destroy Yankee commerce. The day after the Confederate government formally authorized privateering, three thousand applications for letters of marque inundated the new administration. Eleven days later, the first Confederate privateer, the little Charleston pilot boat schooner *Savannah,* was promptly captured by the USS *Perry.* Others such as the ex-revenue cutter *Aiken,* renamed *Petrel,* suffered an even worse fate when she was sunk on July 28 by the USS *St. Lawrence,* taking four of her forty-man complement with her.[1]

By the summer of 1861, the Confederate government's need for regular oceangoing naval cruisers was germinating through many coastal areas of the South. Confederates isolated on Virginia's Eastern Shore, many of them born and bred to the waterman's life, were not immune to the allure of privateering.

The myriad islands, sounds, and backwaters that laced the Delmarva coast, which had served so well for smugglers and pirates in colonial days, for blockade-running during the Revolution, and for illegal wreckers throughout, appeared to offer the perfect environment from which a rebel privateer might sally forth and return to hide in safety. If a small, fast craft could be secretly outfitted up some shoally, remote waterway, there seemed little the deep-draft Yankee gunboats could do about it. At the very least, the presence of such a vessel might tie up Union men and ships, denying their deployment in more important theaters of conflict.

The threat simply could not be ignored. On August 26, 1861, Maryland governor Thomas H. Hicks, a Union man through and through, wrote to Major General George B. McClellan regarding the danger. He worried that if sufficient attention was not paid to Virginia's Accomack and Northampton Counties, which bordered the undefended Atlantic shores of Maryland, the rebels there might be able to link up with sympathizers from Maryland, Delaware, Pennsylvania, New Jersey, and elsewhere. With some small arms and even an eight-gun battery, they might pose a formidable threat to the whole of the fully exposed Eastern Shore. He strongly recommended that a force be sent to nip things in the bud. Moreover, "the bay should be well guarded to prevent escape to the Western Shore; then the Chincoteague Sound, on the east northeast side of Northampton ought to be looked at too, or they will go to sea and pass outside the cape and come and land on the Western Shore of Virginia."[2]

The U.S. Army and Navy were well aware of the dangers inherent in leaving Accomack and Northampton unguarded by land or sea. For the navy, however, the problem was not easily resolved. Lincoln's blockade had stretched the sea service to its limits in both ships and manpower. The navy did its best, purchasing vessels of all kinds, often ignoring their decrepit conditions in order that they might be deployed for blockade duty as quickly as possible. One such ship was a 295-ton, three-masted screw steamer called *Louisiana*. Purchased on July 10, 1861, at Philadelphia for $35,000 by Rear Admiral Du Pont, this 143-foot-long ship was destined to find her first and most profitable employment as a blockader on the mid-Atlantic seaboard.[3]

Assigned to the North Atlantic Blockading Squadron under Flag Officer John M. Goldsborough and based out of Hampton Roads, *Louisiana* was placed under the able command of Lieutenant Commander Alexander Murray. On September 13, soon after coming on line, *Louisiana* experienced her baptism by fire, in company with the USS *Savannah,* when she exchanged shots with the Confederate Navy steamer *Patrick Henry* off Newport News, with neither side scoring a hit.[4] But it was in coastal blockade duty that Goldsborough thought Murray's ship would best serve, as she drew only eight feet six inches of water and could penetrate, albeit with difficulty, many of the shoally areas of the lower Delmarva coastline. Goldsborough promptly assigned her to blockade Virginia's Atlantic shores; her beat was to be from Cape Charles to the Maryland border—one ship to watch an unwatchable coast.

Fortunately for the Federals, the active Confederate forces of Virginia's Eastern Shore, like the population itself, were small in numbers and had to be occasionally buttressed, usually under cover of darkness, by small boatloads of troops running across from the Western Shore counties. Moreover, unlike on the Virginia mainland, antipathy or neutrality regarding secession by most of the general population seemed the rule, and occasionally motivated the few indigenous secessionists to intimidate their brethren. The consequences served to alienate some inhabitants and turn them toward the Union side. A few of these became informers and kept the Union command abreast of the motions of the local "Secesh" population and the arrivals of rebel reinforcements. In early October one such piece of intelligence, regarding a rebel privateer purported to be outfitting near Chincoteague, was passed to Commander Murray and demanded his immediate action without awaiting orders from Hampton Roads.

On the night of October 4, while conducting a routine reconnaissance patrol, *Louisiana* surprised, engaged, and destroyed two enemy dispatch sloops. Undoubtedly from prisoners captured during the expedition, Murray discovered a greater danger afoot: a large band of Confederates had been secretly outfitting and readying a fine privateer schooner in an isolated, little-used waterway called Cockrell Creek, not far from the fishing village on Chincoteague. There was no time to waste. He immediately set his warship in motion, pushed across the bar at Chincoteague Inlet before morning, and was soon approaching the shallow entrance of the creek.[5]

At precisely 9:00 A.M. on October 5, at high tide, two boats manned by twenty-two seamen under the command of Acting Master H. K. Furniss were dispatched with orders to take or destroy the unnamed privateer, by surprise if possible. Buoyed by the tide, while carefully avoiding shoals and snags as he moved through the shallow waterway, Murray followed behind the boats in *Louisiana* to provide large gun support if necessary. Suddenly the sound of heavy fire perforated the Sabbath stillness. As the pair of Federal boats had rounded a bend and spotted the privateer approximately three hundred yards ahead, they found themselves the targets of as many as 300 Confederate guns. Bravely, they ran the gauntlet and made directly for the rebel ship as a storm of miniballs peppered the waters around them like so many hailstones. "The boats," Murray later reported, "after passing through a terrible fire, finally reached the schooner" only to find her aground. Shouting above the noise of battle, Furniss directed his men to take immediate cover behind the stranded vessel. Quickly the men "made a breastwork of her and opened a deadly fire." The firefight was intense on both sides, but the outnumbered Federals showed the utmost "coolness and intrepidity when assailed by such overwhelming odds," albeit not without injury. Acting Master Hooker, one of the boat commanders, received a serious hit that took him out of the fight, while three more men sustained lesser wounds.[6]

Now the long-range guns of *Louisiana* chimed in, blasting great holes in the salt marshes and in the ranks of Confederates lying therein. It was the turning point in the sharp little contest. The combined firepower of the warship and the boat crews proved too much for the rebels, who were forced to retreat to some distant cover, carrying eight dead and wounded with them. The short but intense Battle of Cockrell Creek ended as abruptly as it had started. Almost immediately, the boat crews turned their attention to the privateer, which was soon ablaze, a rebel warship that would never sail.[7]

With the big guns of *Louisiana* to protect them, the two boatloads of seamen returned to their ship in triumph.[8] For their bold actions both Commander Murray and Acting Master Furniss were commended by the secretary of the navy and Admiral Goldsborough.

On the night of October 27, the brave men of *Louisiana* again proved their worth by conducting a reprise of their opening operation. Informed of the presence of several rebel vessels lying sequestered in Chincoteague Creek, Murray dispatched a small boat expedition aided by five volunteers from Chincoteague Island, this time without backup, into the shoally waterway. The sailors were again counting on surprise and left the warship under cover of darkness at 10:00 P.M. to capture or destroy the Confederate vessels reportedly anchored a mile or more up the creek. With as many as three hundred rebel soldiers believed to be lying nearby at a place called Horntown, the whole affair was conducted "with so much system and discretion that the enemy . . . was unconscious of the presence of our expedition." By 3:00 A.M., the raiders had returned as quietly as they had departed, having located and burned another enemy schooner and two sloops.[9]

Because of the support of the Chincoteague volunteers, and the avowed loyalty of the majority of the citizens of that place who had assisted the Union, or at least remained neutral, Admiral Goldsborough was inclined to support requests to permit their commerce with the North to proceed without interruption as before the war. "These people, 800 in number, have to depend mainly upon supplying Philadelphia and New York with oysters for their subsistence," the admiral informed Secretary of the Navy Gideon Welles. "They pray to be allowed to continue this occupation under any restrictions the Government may impose, and they tell me that unless they can secure this privilege they must either abandon their homes or starve. May I extend it to them? I feel confident that I can manage the matter so as not to prove detrimental to the public interests and at the same time be beneficial in a high degree to the indigent applicants. They have taken the oath of allegiance. It was administered to them by Lieutenant Commanding Murray."[10]

The hostile intentions of the several hundred diehard Confederates further inland notwithstanding, the Chincoteague Islanders were as good as their oaths for the rest of the war. To ensure their protection, however, the Union army would maintain detachments on the island, at Cherrystone, and at Drummondville, to the very end of hostilities. Rebel activities on the Delmarva would never again offer a major threat to Yankee control.[11] The waters offshore, however, were a different matter.


Federal authority now ranged the length and breadth of the Eastern Shore, but the Union would not go long without suffering losses of its own on the coast, both commercial and military—some by accident, others as casualties of war. The first of these was to be a well-armed warship named *Sumpter*.

Like many men-of-war in Federal service at the outset of the Civil War, USS *Sumpter* had already seen considerable commercial sea duty before being called into service by the U.S. Navy. Built at Philadelphia in 1853 as *Parker Vein* and re-named *Atalanta* five years later, this 460-ton wooden screw steamer had been purchased by the navy in 1859 for an expedition to Paraguay, South America.[12] At the outbreak of the Civil War, however, she was ordered to be repaired at the New York Navy Yard and readied for service in the North Atlantic Blockading Squadron. Classified as a fourth-rater, armed with a single twenty-pounder Parrott rifle and four big thirty-two-pounder long guns, she was renamed *Sumpter* on June 14, 1861.[13]

*Sumpter*'s career in the North Atlantic Blockading Squadron was active but undistinguished. Her one small claim to fame came on March 18, 1862, when she participated in the capture of the blockade-runner *Emily St. Pierre* off Charleston. Unfortunately, even this minor victory, shared with a number of other blockaders, was to be short lived, as the prizemaster was soon after over-powered by the runner's master and steward, who then escaped to Liverpool with their ship.[14]

On June 10, 1863, Acting Volunteer Lieutenant Peter Hays, *Sumpter*'s commander, was ordered by Acting Rear Admiral Samuel P. Lee to proceed with her to Yorktown, Virginia, and report for duty to Lieutenant Commander James H. Gillis, senior commander on the river.[15] Her new beat, Hays was informed, was to be patrol duty at the entrance to Chesapeake Bay, one of the most heavily trafficked wartime areas on the Middle Atlantic seaboard.

Two weeks later, on June 24, Lieutenant Hays found himself cruising on his newly assigned station, eight miles east-southeast of the Cape Charles Light. Though the night was foggy, all seemed in order. At 12:30 A.M., the officer of the deck, Acting Ensign Thomas W. Spencer, sighted an unidentified light, reported it to Hays, and asked if he should run for it. The lieutenant ordered him to make for the stranger to ascertain who she was. "We approached her very slowly, going through the water slowly." Hays later reported. "There was a heavy mist at the time and we were unable to distinguish an object with any degree of accuracy be-yond 200 yards." It was soon apparent, however, that the vessel was a steamship showing one light forward, one aft, and a red light apparently amidships.

As *Sumpter* closed, it was Spencer's intention to pass astern of the mysterious vessel, "but being deceived by the mist found he had not room, and endeavored to bring our ship upon a course parallel with hers, and [in] endeavoring to do so the vessels collided, our bow striking her about the fore chains. The shock was a very light one."[16]

The unidentified steamer immediately dropped astern as Lieutenant Hays hailed her but received no answer. Soon afterward, however, *Sumpter* herself was hailed and asked to send a boat, which Hays did immediately, supposing the stranger to be sinking. The boat returned soon after and reported her to be the transport steamer *General Meigs,* from New York to Port Royal, and that she was uninjured. The investigating officer also noted that the captain of *Meigs* had asked if a volunteer officer commanded the *Sumpter* and, being answered in the affirmative, replied in a derisive tone that "he thought some secesh officers were on board of her," whereupon he immediately resumed his course and disappeared into the fog.[17]

Hays now turned his attention to his own ship and anxiously queried the engineer of the watch if *Sumpter* was making any water. He was answered in the negative. Not content with the reply, he went forward to inspect what damage had been done to the bow, at the same time directing the carpenter and an officer to see if she was taking on any water anywhere in the forward section. Investigating the impact area, he was stunned. The ship, he discovered much to his dismay, "being very rotten, even that slight shock had the effect of wrenching the entire stem off her." *Sumpter,* he correctly surmised, had been fatally injured and would not remain afloat much longer. She had already settled more than five feet forward within the few minutes since the collision.[18]

Hays ordered *Sumpter* abandoned at once. The well-disciplined crew took to the boats in an orderly fashion and, as if it were only a drill, abandoned ship without incident. They lay by the mortally injured vessel for only five minutes before her bow was nearly under. Dame Fortune had indeed been with them throughout the crisis, for soon afterward they observed a sail close by and pulled for it. Their savior proved to be the merchant schooner *Jamestown,* Captain Laverett commanding, bound from Washington for Boston. Hays calmly informed the captain about the situation and asked him to return with *Sumpter's* crew to Hampton Roads.[19]

Twenty minutes after the schooner departed, *Sumpter* sank in about seven fathoms, leaving only her mastheads standing proud above the water to mark her burial site. Within hours her officers and crew had been returned to Hampton Roads, where they reported to Admiral Samuel P. Lee on board the USS *Minnesota,* flagship of the squadron. The next morning, *Sumpter's* commander, Peter Hays, and her paymaster, A. B. Robinson, reported via telegraph directly to Secretary of the Navy Gideon Welles on the loss. Robinson informed the secretary "nothing in my department was saved. All my books and accounts, the iron chest containing $2,070, with a small amount of provisions, small stores, and clothing, went down with the ship." Admiral Lee promptly ordered *Sumpter's* men transferred to the USS *Brandywine* for temporary accommodations until they could be distributed about the fleet.[20]

For nearly a year, the Delmarva coast appeared to be free of naval danger, as the lower peninsula was neutralized, Union power grew, and the North Atlantic Blockading Squadron improved in strength and experience—that is, until a fast and daring Confederate commerce raider suddenly appeared on the scene to wreak untold havoc.

The vessel in question, CSS *Florida,* was a sleek-looking ship, a sloop-rigged propeller steamer with three raked masts and two raked stacks that gave her a distinctively swift racing silhouette. Built by the British firm of William C. Miller and Sons, she had originally been purchased for the Confederate States Navy as *Oreto* early in the war from the firm of Fawcett, Preston & Co., of Liverpool, who had installed her engines. Though initially dubbed *Manassas* by the

Confederate Navy Department, her career, and that of the officers who commanded her, was to become legendary as *Florida*.[21]

*Manassas* was not a particularly big ship for her day, only 191 feet in length, but with an extremely narrow beam of only twenty-seven feet two inches, a depth in hold of fourteen feet, and a draft of thirteen feet, she was low enough in the water to permit her a speed of 9.5 knots under steam and 12 knots with canvas piled on. With a full complement of 146 to man her and fight her six six-inch guns, two seven-inch rifles, and single twelve-pounder howitzer, she was indeed a formidable cruiser, capable of both a running fight and, if need be, fast flight.[22]

Initially under the direction of a daring veteran commander, Lieutenant John Newland Maffitt, CSN, her career had begun under a cloud after leaving Britain thanks to an aborted attempt to take on coal from a tender at Nassau in the Bahamas. Nevertheless, Maffitt had somehow managed to secretly outfit her with stores and arms at an isolated islet called Green Cay, where she was finally commissioned on August 17 under the name *Florida*. With an already short complement reduced by yellow fever to just five able men, Maffitt made a desperate and heroic run for Cuba, where he too came down with the disease. Despite his and his men's condition, he then sailed from Cardenas, Cuba, to Mobile, Alabama, where, amid a barrage of naval gunfire, he ran her through a gauntlet of Union blockaders on September 4, entering the harbor intact and in triumph. There, for the next four months, the ship was carefully manned and outfitted.

On January 16, 1863, *Florida* escaped to sea and for half a year terrorized American shipping on the coasts of North and South America and in the West Indies, while managing to elude a large Union squadron sent out to destroy her. On July 27, 1863, in dreadful need of repair, she sailed for Brest, France, where she was again refitted, staying in port until February 1864. With Maffitt now completely broken in health, command was relinquished to a daring and accomplished young officer named Charles M. Morris, who pointed *Florida*'s bow toward the West Indies, taking a valuable prize en route and then bunkering at Barbados.[23]

On June 2, 1864, Morris received an important letter from the Confederate secretary of the navy, Stephen R. Mallory. The communiqué authorized him to draw $50,000 for cruising funds and offered a bold suggestion that he consider conducting a raid on New England shipping. Morris immediately headed north to commence a campaign against Union commerce that might earn him his own page in history, but to get there he had to first pass the heavily traveled, and now well-patrolled, shipping lanes between the Delaware and Chesapeake.[24]

When CSS *Florida* entered the waters off the Delmarva coast, she would encounter some of the most fruitful hunting of her career. Her campaign began on July 8, in latitude 37°28′N, longitude 72°W, as she approached Virginia waters and spotted the lumbering 335-ton New Bedford whaling bark *Goloconda*, bound for home from Talcahuano, Chile, with 1,800 barrels of whale oil. After easily overtaking and bringing the whaler to, Morris ordered her captain, two mates, and nineteen men to board his ship as prisoners. Then, after taking off what whale oil he needed, he burned the new capture. One can only imagine the blaze that the remaining whale oil aboard must have made.[25]

The Confederate raider *Florida* in Brest harbor (Library of Congress, Washington, DC)

At daylight the next morning, in latitude 36°43'N, longitude 74°11'W, the rebel raider sighted a small sailing vessel, which was also taken without difficulty. The capture proved to be the seventeen-ton New York schooner *Margaret Y. Davis,* returning home in ballast from Port Royal with a crew of seven after having delivered a government cargo. No sooner had the torch been put to the unfortunate little craft than the Confederates spotted yet another sailing vessel and set off in pursuit.[26]

The second chase of the day was as short-lived as the first, and within a few minutes, *Florida* had overhauled the schooner *William Clarke,* from New York. With a population of twenty-eight prisoners onboard from the late captures, however, Morris decided to spare his most recent prize and transferred to her the crews of *Goloconda* and *Margaret Y. Davis,* as well as some provisions for their use. It was a practical but dangerous move. He could ill afford to tend to so many prisoners and still carry out his mission, yet to release them would mean that as soon as they reached the nearest port, his strength and position off the Delmarva coast would be known. Soon every available Federal warship on the Atlantic seaboard would be out trying to run him down. At best he might enjoy only a few more days in the rich hunting grounds between the Chesapeake and Delaware before necessity required him to flee.[27] But he convinced himself that there was still time to get a few more good licks in against the Yankee merchant marine!

Morris now turned *Florida*'s prow toward Cape Charles and the entrance to Chesapeake Bay. The area, heavily patrolled by Union warships, was by the summer of 1864 perhaps the best-guarded Federal shipping lanes of any on the southern coast. A significant capture or two in the area, he knew, might instill enough panic among the Federals that it would draw off forces and sow widespread confusion and fear. The lieutenant's strategy was immediately rewarded when a steamer and a bark were discovered sailing close inshore of his cruiser. As *Florida* closed for the kill, Morris made out that his primary target, the steamer, was flying U.S. colors and moving on a southwesterly course, towing the heavily laden bark. By this time, however, the Yankee steamer had spotted the Confederate and was rapidly preparing to show her heels. Within a few minutes, Morris observed, she had cast off her towlines and pressed on toward the southwest under full steam while the bark turned in toward Cape Henry, perhaps hoping to find sanctuary in the midst of the Union fleet at anchor therein.[28]

*Florida* took up immediate pursuit of the steamer, but her quarry was fast and had enough of a lead that an easy capture seemed out of the question. Giving up the chase, Morris was obliged to settle for second best and turned his attentions toward the heavy, clumsy bark. In a desperate effort to elude the rebel raider, the bark suddenly altered her course again, this time for the Delaware. The exercise was almost laughable; lumbering along like a hog in the water, she was easily overtaken. The capture proved to be the 459-ton *Greenland,* of Brunswick, Maine, which had recently been chartered by the Federal government to haul nine hundred tons of anthracite to the U.S. naval base at Pensacola, Florida. From her officers, Morris learned that she had been under tow of the speedy steam tug *America,* which had been chartered at Philadelphia. Unfortunately for the rebels, *Florida* was by now in desperate need of fuel, yet her furnaces were unable to use anthracite. Time was running out, owing to the escape of *America* and the release of *Clarke,* so the rebel commander decided to burn his latest prize and shape a course directly for the Delaware "in hopes of falling in with some of the army transports bound into the James" from Philadelphia. Within a short time, *Greenland* was ablaze.[29]

The seamen of *Florida* would have little respite as they cruised in a northerly direction off the Maryland coast, for July 10 would prove to be one of the most hectic days of the voyage as Morris's plan began to bear immediate fruit. At 3:00 A.M. they spotted another bark not far off Parramore Island. Within minutes of the rebel crew having been roused from their slumber, the 469-ton bark *General Berry,* of Thomaston, Maine, had been captured. It was then learned that the U.S. Army had chartered the prize on July 6, only four days before her capture, to carry 1,166 bales of hay and 36 bales of straw from New York to Fortress Monroe for use of the military livestock. Morris ordered the provisions and crew removed and the ship set afire.[30]

No sooner was *General Berry* in flames than another sail was sighted, pursuit taken up, and another capture made. This time the prize was *Zelinda,* a 559-ton bark from Eastport, Maine, sailing from Matanzas, Cuba, in ballast for Philadelphia. Almost as soon as the latest prize was hauled to, another sail was sighted to the east. Having ordered an officer and prize crew onboard *Zelinda* with instructions for them to follow in *Florida*'s wake, Morris found the chase to be the New York schooner *Howard,* bound from San Salvador for home with a cargo of fruit belonging to English merchants. With so many captures, *Florida* again found herself overpopulated with prisoners, sixty-two in all. Morris decided to bond *Howard* for $6,000, place the prisoners onboard, along with provisions and water, and release her. *Zelinda* was then brought up, divested of what few provisions she had onboard, and set afire.[31]

*Florida* stood off to the east now and immediately sighted another sail. This time the vessel was the English schooner *Lane,* from Baracoa bound for New York, also with a cargo of fruit. Being a neutral ship, she was immediately released.[32] And none too soon. With four chases, three captures, and two sinkings in the space of ten and a half hours, the Confederates were undoubtedly heady from their success. But the next challenge would prove the most difficult of any encountered on the Delmarva coast, and one of the most valuable.

At 1:30 P.M. a large brig-rigged steamer was observed standing to the southeast. Morris ordered yet another pursuit and headed to cut off his prey, which, for all he knew, might be a man-of-war. About 2:00 P.M., as soon as he was close enough, he ordered a blue English ensign raised to mask his identity. The quarry, completely taken in, responded with American colors. For ten minutes *Florida* pressed on, closing to within firing range. At a distance of a thousand yards, Morris piped his men to quarters, ordered a shot fired astern of the chase, and raised the Confederate flag. Unlike the cruiser's previous victim, the big Yankee ship refused to heave to. The rebel fired two more shots from her broadside guns. The shells, however, were unloaded and filled with sand. Both were well directed and ricocheted off the water and directly over their target without injuring her. The effect was as hoped. This time the ship stopped and hauled down her colors. The prize proved to be a spanking new 810-ton propeller mail steamer called *Electric Spark,* of Philadelphia, bound from New York to New Orleans with mail, forty-two passengers, thirty-nine crewmen, and "a very valuable assorted cargo." Among the passengers were Union military officers, including Lieutenant Colonel J. A. F. Hopkins, of the 133rd New York Volunteer Regiment; Acting Master William P. Gibbs, USN, bound to join the USS *Pinola* off Mobile; and Lieutenant C. D. Waterman, of the U.S. Army Engineers.[33]

Morris immediately placed the prize under the command of Lieutenant S. G. Stone and a prize crew with orders to follow *Florida.* As the English schooner *Lane* was still in sight, he determined to overtake her and persuade her skipper to relieve him of his newest prisoners. The captain of *Lane* apparently had little interest in further involvement with the rebel cruiser and continued on his merry way. *Florida* aggressively pursued for two hours, however, and *Lane* finally hove to at 5:40 P.M. when the rebels fired a shot to windward. A Confederate officer was sent onboard with a proposal. "We were to pay $720 [in gold] for her deck load of fruit," Morris later reported, "which he would be obliged to throw overboard to make room for the passengers and crew, which she would land at Delaware Breakwater, then distant 73 miles." The schooner's captain was reluctant but agreed to the terms, and the prisoners were transferred without incident. As Morris watched a lone shark swimming lazily amid the trio of ships, the Union military officers were paroled on the spot.[34]

With keen interest Morris eyed the brand-new steamer he had just taken. If Lieutenant Stone and his prize crew could take *Electric Spark* south and run her into Wilmington, North Carolina, one of the few Confederate ports still open, she might prove a valuable addition to the Confederate States Navy. But the plan proved a mere chimera, for he lacked enough trained engineers to operate her engines. Two of his best firemen had been sent aboard, but they were firemen and not engineers competent to run the ship's power plant. Moreover, his acting second assistant engineer, a man named Jackson, "had just been dangerously wounded by the falling of a tackle from the maintop, striking him on the ankle joint, and Mr. Thompson [*Florida*'s chief engineer] said it would be impossible for him to spare one of the engineers of the vessel." Under these circumstances, Morris very reluctantly deemed it best to destroy the prize. But in the doing, he also intended on providing his erstwhile prisoners with a bit of disinformation to further confuse the Federals. He casually mentioned in front of the prisoners before they departed that he intended to make a tender of the prize and run her into Wilmington. The false information, of course, would eventually be relayed to Union authorities, who would then be obliged to divert additional shipping to intercept her. Once *Lane* was beyond the horizon, however, instead of burning the prize, which would give off telltale smoke, the Confederates would scuttle her before daylight by cutting all of her pipes and opening all of her air ports. It was a clever plan, and it worked, albeit not without tragic loss.[35]

*Florida* lay by her doomed prize throughout the evening as Lieutenant Stone and his men worked feverishly to send it to the bottom. One of those in his crew, Midshipman William B. Sinclair, a popular young officer, set the example. Quickly and efficiently the prize crew cut large gaps in at least six major pipe systems: the water rushed in and covered the fire room floor in a matter of minutes. At 8:00 P.M., their work having been completed, Stone and his men manned one of the cruiser's cutters and shoved off as *Electric Spark* quietly began to settle down by the head. Suddenly, as they were making their way toward the cruiser, a rogue wave swamped the little boat.

Morris's report to Confederate Navy secretary Stephen R. Mallory later described the tragedy that ensued: "The moment it was known that the cutter was in danger," he wrote, "a boat was sent to her assistance. On reaching her she found all of her crew hanging on the bottom of the boat, and Mr. Sinclair missing. Mr. Sinclair had nobly refused the assistance of the crew, ordering them to hang on the boat, and he would swim to the ship and would take care of himself. He was never seen afterwards, and I fear must have been seized with cramp or taken by a shark; one had been seen not long before swimming about the ship. Every exertion was made to find him, but to no avail. Mr. Sinclair was a most promising young officer, and esteemed and beloved by officers and crew. His death has cast a deep gloom over all."[36]

*Florida* lay by her ill-fated prize until 11:15 P.M., having taken from it only the mailbags and an iron chest belonging to the Adams Express Company. Morris knew that by now the steam tug *America,* which had escaped the day before, had had ample time to reach a Federal port and telegraph the news of the rebel cruiser's presence on the Delmarva coast. He was equally aware, from the late newspapers taken from his many prizes, that there were far more numerous fast and powerful warships at New York, Philadelphia, and Newport News ready for sea and capable of immediate pursuit than he had anticipated. Moreover, his own coal supplies were insufficient to get him to one of the few rebel coaling stations still open on the American coast. The "Anaconda" stranglehold, enforced by a triple line of Yankee cruisers all along the Confederate coast, was simply too formidable to challenge with *Florida*'s coalbunkers nearing empty. Deeming it prudent to be well off the coast before daylight, Morris abandoned all hopes of a raid on New England. A new course was set, under full steam, for the Canary or Cape Verde Islands. Once in the open Atlantic, he could ease up and proceed under sail, confident of escape.[37]

The raid of the CSS *Florida* on the shipping lanes off the Delmarva coast was over. "I had hoped to have been able to have made a much longer stay," Morris later informed Secretary Mallory, "and have gone up as far north as the fishing fleet before leaving; but my plans were all disarranged by the escape of the steam tug *America*. After that I deemed it prudent to send the prisoners off by every opportunity, and if possible to leave the coast without any supernumeraries to feed." He was proud that when he had chased *Electric Spark,* before he knew that she was not a gunboat, his crew "displayed the greatest eagerness for a fight. Should they ever be brought into action with the enemy they will give a good account of themselves."[38]

It was not to be. *Florida*'s career was nearly at an end, and it would make only one more capture. The daring cruiser eventually reached Teneriffe in the Canaries in safety and then sailed for the neutral port of Bahia, Brazil. On October 7, 1864, while anchored therein, with her commander and half of his crew ashore, the much-feared raider was caught defenseless by an audacious nighttime cutting-out operation directed by Commander Napoleon Collins of the USS *Wachusetts*. *Florida* was immediately secured and towed to sea (despite protests regarding the violation of Brazilian neutrality rights) and sent to Newport News, Virginia. Then, on the night of November 19, while at anchor there, she was "accidentally" struck by the army transport ship *Alliance* and sank nine days later in nine fathoms of water. Though Collins was court-martialed for his illegal cutting-out expedition into a neutral port, he had won lasting fame for ending the career of the daring raider, and he was eventually promoted. As for *Florida,* she had captured a total of thirty-seven prizes during her short but brilliant career. Eight of her victims had been taken off Delmarva, several of them within sight of land. The bones of six still lay in their watery graves, relics of a famed, but soon forgotten, naval episode of the Civil War on the Delmarva coast.[39]

# 14

## Unprecedented Disregard

When the USS *Montgomery* arrived at the remote Federal naval station at Key West, Florida, in early June 1861, her first wartime mission seemed simple enough: proceed to Apalachicola, on the coast of the Florida panhandle, cut off rebel communications, and establish and maintain "an effective blockade of that port against the entrance and egress of all vessels, excepting vessels of war of those nations in amity with the United States."[1] The imposition of the blockade at Apalachicola and, indeed, along the entire coastline of the Confederacy would be a learning experience for the navy, both militarily and diplomatically, as the extremely controversial wartime career of *Montgomery* and her officers and men would soon demonstrate.

The big three-masted, four-topsail schooner-rigged screw steamer was not physically unique, but she was a workhorse typical of the newer navy vessels charged with instituting and maintaining the blockade of the South. Built of white oak at New York in 1858 and first chartered by the U.S. Navy in May 1861, she was destined to suffer one of the most vexing careers in the fleet and a most ignominious end off the Delaware capes. Entered as a third-class man-of-war, armed with six guns, and placed under the captaincy of Commander T. Darrah Shaw on May 17, 1861, the 787-ton steamer was ordered to join the infant Gulf Blockading Squadron.[2]

Commander Shaw quickly proved himself to be an inadequate, timid commander at best and, in the eyes of his superiors, possibly a bit too sympathetic to the South. He was soon relieved of command and replaced by Lieutenant James E. Jouett, an aggressive officer destined one day for flag rank.[3] As the sorting out of good and bad commanders continued throughout the Union navy, so did the organizational development of Lincoln's so-called Anaconda Plan, the economic strangulation of the South by naval blockade. On January 20, 1862, navy secretary Gideon Welles ordered that the Gulf Squadron be divided into an Eastern and a Western Blockading Squadron. The dominion of the Eastern Squadron, to which *Montgomery* was initially assigned, commenced at St. Andrews Bay, east of Pensacola, and extended to Cape Canaveral, on the east coast of Florida. The squadron was to be commanded by Flag Officer William W. McKean and headquartered at Key West. Admiral David Farragut was to command the Western Gulf Squadron, which extended from St. Andrews Bay all the way to the Mexican border.[4]

Within a short time, *Montgomery* was transferred to the Western Squadron, even as Farragut worked to shape the command structure in the gulf to his own liking. He immediately sought to stiffen the blockade and demanded more aggressive commanders to do it. When Jouett was moved to take command of another blockader, *R. R. Cuyler,* the admiral's personal choice for *Montgomery* was Lieutenant Charles Hunter, a toe-to-toe bulldog who took over from Jouett on March 7, 1862. The coast of Texas was to be Hunter's backyard, and any and all intruders were fair game.[5]

With his ship assigned from time to time to various isolated stations on the Texas coast, Hunter quickly proved to be every bit the sailor Farragut wanted. While on patrol on April 5, passing San Luis Pass, south of Galveston, the commander had observed a rebel schooner inside the harbor. He immediately ordered an imitation Confederate flag raised at the fore along with a burgee bearing the name *Adolph Hugel,* and fired a gun to announce his arrival. His deception was total. A surprise cutting-out expedition into the fortified harbor resulted in the destruction of the blockade-runner *Columbia* and the capture of a sloop right under the nose of enemy batteries.[6] Farragut was impressed. The Confederacy was not.

Several of Hunter's more difficult cruising grounds were to be the entrances of the Brazos, Santiago, Boca Chica, and Rio Grande Rivers. There he would earn an enviable reputation as an officer of ability and action. The Rio Grande, which formed the border between Texas and Mexico, was a particularly sensitive sector owing to illicit trade carried out between the two areas. The Mexican port of Matamoras was especially employed by neutrals in profiting from that commerce, a burgeoning cotton trade, as well as serving as a sanctuary for Unionist refugees fleeing Confederate Texas.

Farragut was explicit in his instructions to Hunter. All vessels entering or departing Texas ports, except Matamoras, would be subjected to seizure. Those sailing from or to Matamoras would be liable to visitation and search. If found to belong to rebel interests, the cargoes would be seized. "But it is not the intention of our Government," said the admiral, "that we should interfere with or molest neutrals in their legitimate commerce with Matamoras more than is indispensable necessary to comply with the above instructions; that is, to ascertain the true ownership of cargo, and that it is not contraband of war destined for the aid and comfort of our enemies."[7] They were difficult orders to follow under any conditions.

On April 19, *Montgomery* arrived off the Rio Grande and commenced examination of the shipping.[8] On one occasion, while en route back to his own ship after an inspection, Hunter stopped to board an American schooner and met an agent from the American Consular Office in Matamoras with a letter from the U.S. consul, L. Pierce Jr. There were then about one hundred refugees from Texas in Matamoras, Pierce informed him, all loyal to the Union, including a score or more U.S. soldiers, many of whom were recently escaped prisoners from San Antonio. They were destitute of funds. Moreover, rebel commanders at Fort

Brown, a Confederate stronghold on the opposite side of the river, were trying "every possible means to recover them." The Mexican military commander of Matamoras had requested that they be removed to prohibit a possible international incident. It was outright dangerous, noted the consul, for the Unionists to remain in Matamoras any longer. "I take the liberty," he implored, "to ask if you could aid me in getting them off to some safe place."[9]

"Mexico," Hunter boldly replied, "is bound to protect these poor men, and if she fails in so doing it will be considered a very grave offense by our Government, and one which our people will insist upon being fully vindicated, and with the whole of our power if necessary. An American citizen, or anyone claiming to be such, shall have the full protection of his Government, so far as I have it in my power to give it to him." Proof of any agreements between the Mexican military commander at Matamoras and the rebel commander at Brownsville (which were rumored to exist) would result in the possible loss of Mexico's status as a neutral nation and in force being deployed against it by *Montgomery*. They were strong words indeed. "The military commandant of Matamoras is assuming a grave responsibility by doing anything inconsistent with our treaties with Mexico . . . we will consider all who aid the rebels in any way, directly or indirectly, as our enemies," he stated bluntly. As for the refugees, he instructed that they be escorted to the coast by a Mexican guard "and delivered to our boats, which will come to take them." *Montgomery* soon came to anchor less than a mile outside the breakers, on the Mexican shore, to be near where the distressed Americans might be brought onboard.[10]

Early on the morning of April 25 the refugees appeared on the beach at the location designated for their evacuation pickup. Not until the following morning, due to heavy surf, was *Montgomery*'s surfboat able to reach the shore and bring them off. Ultimately, fifty-one loyal Americans would be brought safely aboard.[11]

Throughout the summer, Hunter sailed with *Montgomery* between Scylla and Charybdis, rarely blessed with a full complement of seamen, often short of coal, water, and ammunition, but never failing to impose a strong American naval presence along the Texas-Mexico border. The hard, hot duty taxed both the warship and its men. But Hunter, who repeatedly upended the illicit rebel trade on the Rio Grande, made the most out of it and was thoroughly despised by both Texans and pro-Confederate Mexicans.

On August 2, with her boilers and machinery in a debilitated condition, *Montgomery* was finally ordered to Philadelphia and then to New York for overhaul.[12] Repairs were quickly carried out at the New York Navy Yard and by late September, the ship was again ready for duty with the West Gulf Blockading Squadron. On September 29 she departed for her old station, passing first through the Providence Channel, and arriving off Havana, Cuba, on the night of October 6. The following morning Hunter paid a courtesy visit to the American consul general, Mr. Shufeldt, returned to his ship about noon, and then sailed immediately.[13] The stage was now set for Texas revenge.

While skirting along the north coast of the island, barely two hours later and only nine miles out of Havana, Hunter spotted a steamer inshore and standing to the eastward of himself. Suspecting the ship to be a rebel blockade-runner, he turned *Montgomery* to the southeast in an effort to cut her off. Within ten minutes, the warship had come up to within two and a half miles of the stranger and fired a blank cartridge to bring her to. At that, the suspect ship quickly hoisted English colors but kept going. Hunter ordered a live shell loaded, but it jammed and the gun misfired. The projectile dropped less than six hundred yards from the warship. The stranger, however, was obviously intimidated, immediately stopped engines, then glided toward the shore seven or eight miles from the town of Mariel, and came to anchor so near the beach "that her stern touched." Later testimony by the runner's officers and crew stated the "master considered it prudent to run into Mariano Creek, and did so, anchoring about 300 yards from the beach."[14]

*Montgomery's* intended prey was the 417-ton steamship *Blanche,* sailing under British colors and registered on July 30, 1862. She was purportedly owned by George Wigg of Liverpool and bound for Havana with a valuable cargo of 583 bales of cotton taken onboard at Port Lavaca, Texas, on September 29. There "not being any blockading ship at the time off the entrance to Matagorda Bay," the steamer had sailed unimpeded across the Gulf of Mexico. On October 4, about thirty miles east of Cape Antonio, finding herself short of coal, she had crossed inside of the Colorado Reefs at Cayo Levisza and arrived at La Mulataon the following morning. There, she secured fuel and a coast pilot to bring her into Havana. On the morning of October 7, she cleared the Bahia Honda reef within a mile of the shore. About nine miles from the Morro Castle, *Blanche* observed a steamer to the northeast, apparently steering about northwest. At 1:30 P.M. she saw a Spanish frigate enter Havana harbor and immediately afterward noticed a second steamer had altered course and was bearing down on them. Within four or five miles distance, the stranger hoisted the flag of the United States.[15]

As *Montgomery* closed in, the Spanish pilot aboard *Blanche* went ashore and immediately returned with the *alcalde de mar,* the only Spanish official on the spot, and his son. The master, with his ship clearly anchored in Spanish territorial waters, immediately claimed the protection of the Spanish government.[16] At 2:30 P.M., ignoring diplomatic niceties entirely, Hunter dispatched two armed cutters with twenty men under Acting Volunteer Master Charles G. Arthur with instructions to board the stranger and examine her papers. If she was a rebel, or if her documentation was not in order, they were to bring her out. A half hour later, Arthur approached the steamer. Before he arrived, however, the *alcalde de mar* raised a Spanish flag above the English flag to show that *Blanche* was now "under the protection of the authorities and within the jurisdiction of her Majesty the Queen of Spain." Seeing the boarding party shove off from *Montgomery,* and now aware that the issue of national sovereignty was not likely to prevent the Yankees from boarding, the captain of *Blanche,* R. N. Smith, ordered his cable slipped and his ship driven hard ashore with her engines. A few minutes later, the first cutter bumped alongside and was met at the rail by Smith. Arthur asked him why he had run his ship aground, but the officer answered only with a shrug of his shoulders. What was his cargo, the naval officer queried? "Cotton," came the reply. "Don't you know that cotton is contraband of war?"

said Arthur rather angrily. "No, not that I am aware of, on board of a British ship, and in a neutral port," said the master. Then the ship's papers were ordered up, and found to include a certificate of ownership, a crew list, and shipping papers of a vessel called *Blanche* but whose previous name was *General Rusk,* which was reportedly bound from Indianola, Texas, for Havana. When the master of *Blanche* protested that his was a British ship boarded in neutral waters, the boarding officer was later reported to have replied that he cared little about the protection offered by the Spanish authorities or flag. His orders were to take her wherever he found her, and he intended on doing so. Her crew would be sent as prisoners onboard *Montgomery*. Furthermore, he "would not discuss as to his right to do so, but would leave that point to be settled afterwards by the two Governments."[17]

According to Confederate accounts, Arthur ordered all of *Blanche's* hands on deck, and placed sentries in all parts of the ship, threatening to shoot any of the crew who attempted to stir. Several pistols were fired to accentuate the seriousness of his warning. He asked the crew if they wished to enlist in the U.S. Navy, to which all replied in the negative. He then ordered *Montgomery's* assistant engineer to the engine room to try and get the ship afloat again. When the *alcalde de mar* protested in Spanish the violation of his country's territorial integrity and the insult to his flag, he and his son were ordered to leave. Failing to comply, both were forcefully manhandled to the ship's side. During the struggle one of the boarding party members struck the son in the face, and the two men were unceremoniously compelled to disembark with pistols aimed at them.[18]

Ensign Putnam, in command of the second cutter, had by this time also come alongside the steamer. The engineer worked diligently to get the steamer off the beach and under way. Soon the engine was operating and thrown into reverse. Slowly the steamer began to move. Less than ten minutes after having boarded, Putnam discovered that the ship was on fire. Almost instantaneously, smoke began to issue "from every crack and crevice from below" near the engine room. Someone shouted out that there was gunpowder aboard, "upon which the boarding officers and boat crews of the United States vessel made a rush for their boats." Putnam was immediately ordered to take one cutter forward and rescue the *Montgomery's* men cut off in that quarter, while Arthur shoved off in the second cutter with the remainder. *Blanche's* crew, looking out for themselves, succeeded in lowering the only boat that they had aft and scurried ashore.[19]

"The steamer," Arthur later reported, was by now "a complete sheet of flame, and not deeming it prudent to lie too near her, for fear of the explosion of her boilers, I ordered the boats to pull a short distance from her and lie by; we remained until her masts burned off and fell, and then made the best way to the *Montgomery*."[20]

Again the warship got under way, pressing along the Cuban coast, albeit a safe distance from land. It stopped several more vessels, all Cuban, but allowed them to go on their way. Ramon Arbela, the Spanish pilot taken from *Blanche,* was transferred to the last of the vessels stopped, a schooner, which was permitted to depart without further investigation. At 2:30 A.M., October 11, *Montgomery* dropped anchor in Pensacola harbor.[21]

The destruction of *Blanche* caused an immediate uproar in Havana and measurably swayed popular and official sentiment in favor of the Confederacy. As one Southern agent in the country put it, "The Confederate cause is more popular here now than it has been at any time since we began our struggle for independence."[22]

On October 10, even as *Montgomery* was steaming for Pensacola, several members of *Blanche*'s crew, including Captain R. N. Smith, William Scrimgeour, mate, and August Lawrence, seaman, submitted an official protest and description of the ship's destruction with the British acting consul general in Cuba, John Vincent Crawford.[23]

Rear Admiral Charles Wilkes, USN, commander of the West India Squadron, on learning of the incident after his arrival in Cuba for an official courtesy call immediately after the affair, was shocked and entirely repulsed. "This unwarrantable act," he later stated, "was at first laid to me by one of my squadron, and was promptly brought to my notice by the governor-general through his principal staff officer, shortly after I was informed of it by our consul-general. I of course at once denied any knowledge of it, or sanction of such an act and infringement of the waters of Spanish territory." He promptly requested an interview with the Spanish captain-general of Cuba, Governor Serrano, which was granted the following morning.

"This intercourse took place," Wilkes reported heatedly to Secretary Welles on October 13, "and resulted in my satisfying him that whoever committed the act, it would be disapproved of by my Government and due reparation made." The admiral soothed the governor by assuring him the act had been contrary to all instructions issued by Secretary Welles, "and would be visited upon the head of the officer whoever he might be." The perpetrator, he promised, would be sent home under arrest. The admiral's assurances that the guilty party would be brought to justice had the desired effect.[24]

The Confederate government agent in Havana, Charles J. Helm, for reasons later made clear, was not as quick to inform his own government of the incident and the obvious benefit it was likely to have for the Confederacy. Not until October 23 did he notify Judah P. Benjamin, the Confederate secretary of state, of the affair. The incident, he said, was "a piratical act more aggravated than the forcible abduction of our commissioners from the English mail steamer *Trent*" and an "unprecedented disregard of the rights of neutrals by a belligerent." Helm, however, had quickly informed the Confederate agent in Spain, Judge Rost, of "the outrage" and forwarded a complete report of it to the Spanish government in Madrid, as well as another to the agent in England, J. M. Mason. He also informed Secretary Benjamin that the governor of Cuba, General Serrano, who had "constantly urged upon his Government the propriety of an immediate recognition of the Confederate States" was returning home and would likely be of great service to the Confederacy there as well.[25]

Undoubtedly aware of the possible repercussions of his brash action, and as a normal course of action, Hunter had immediately prepared a full report to the Navy Department on the *Blanche* incident the same day it had taken place. Four days later, on October 11, at Pensacola, he composed a second report, this time to Farragut, and enclosed a deposition taken from one of *Blanche*'s passengers, an Englishman named Clement, in the event an attempt was made to charge *Montgomery* with the destruction of the steamer while in Cuban waters. Both reports and the deposition appear to have been delayed in delivery, purportedly owing to the lack of regular packet communications between blockading outposts and the far-flung Union bases in southern waters. It was a flimsy excuse at best. The commander, however, seemed well satisfied that he was in the right and that the loss of the blockade-runner had been caused by her own crew, for Arthur's report seemed clear in that respect. "During the time of our stay on board the *Blanche*," the acting master had immediately reported "not one of our men went below her deck, and she must have been fired by some of her own crew, and from the rapidity with which the fire spread, everything must have been in readiness beforehand. We had not been on board ten minutes before it was perceived she was on fire, and then the flames were bursting through her deck and sides." The order for the engineer to go below and get the engine started seemed to have been conveniently forgotten.[26]

The deposition taken from Robert F. Clement, who claimed to be a British subject, born in 1816 at Bath, England, thought a current resident of Indianola, Texas, indicated that the steamer had a provision charter signed by John V. Crawford, Her Britannic Majesty's acting consul general in Cuba, and that the vessel had originally been built in Delaware as the *General Rusk* in 1857. He had boarded the ship at Indianola on September 29 and was bound for Havana. He stated that Captain R. N. Smith "told me before I embarked on board the *Blanche* that he was determined to destroy the vessel rather than have her taken by a United States vessel; that it is my firm and entire belief and conviction that the said *Blanche* was fired by order of the captain, by the crew or officers on board her; that the said *Blanche* was laden with about 500 bales of cotton on board, which was put on board at Lavaca, in the State of Texas, United States."[27]

Hunter's suspicions that there would be fallout from the incident were soon proven correct. Within the month, Don G. G. y Tarrara, the minister plenipotentiary of Her Catholic Majesty the Queen of Spain, vigorously protested to Washington the violation of Spanish territorial waters. On October 28 Secretary of the Navy Welles ordered Farragut to conduct a full inquiry into the conduct of the American officers involved and to release a Spanish subject said to still be onboard *Montgomery*. Farragut responded to the secretary on November 25 (a delay in response undoubtedly caused by the slowness of communication by water) stating that Hunter had informed him "that he had already reported the affair to the [Navy] Department" and that the report of October 11 was merely for the admiral's information. He informed the secretary that the Spanish prisoner had been released the same day as the incident but nevertheless forwarded Hunter's report along with the deposition taken from Clement.[28]

As the *Blanche* incident continued to fester and grow many miles from the Gulf of Mexico, *Montgomery* continued her mission. On October 16, the big warship arrived off Mobile bar, and Hunter received instructions to cruise between Mobile Bay and Horn Island Pass.[29] *Montgomery* resumed her duty on station with vigor and participated in several aggressive actions, most notably capturing the 582-ton blockade-runner *Caroline* and the cotton-laden sloop *William E. Chester* off Mobile.

Unfortunately, neither Farragut's communications nor Hunter's dispatches regarding the *Blanche* incident had reached Washington in time to stem the angry Spanish demands for redress. Charges were made against Hunter. Secretary Welles, unaware that an account had been sent but was yet to come in, noted that the "question is one of grave importance" and was aggravated by Hunter's apparent failure to submit the report. By early December, the Spanish minister to Washington, by order of his government, had repeatedly brought the matter to the attention of the Navy Department. Because two months had passed without any reports from either the admiral or the commander having reached Washington, the secretary feared that the latter "has been delinquent and guilty of neglect." Welles wrote Farragut on December 9 that the subject "has now become of so serious a character that extraordinary measures are demanded." The Spanish government was "dissatisfied" with the delays and demanded "an explanation and satisfaction and a course of proceedings in relation to the alleged offense that will atone to Spain for the indignity which she thinks she has received." Under pressure from the Spanish, backed by a pledge from the U.S. State Department that a full investigation would be conducted, and in the absence of a report from either Hunter or Farragut, Welles informed the admiral that there was little alternative but to detach the commander from command and order *Montgomery* home for a full investigation.[30]

At New Orleans the next day, from aboard his flagship *Hartford,* Farragut sent off his own report of the investigation, unaware of the navy secretary's directive, penned over two thousand miles away the day before. The inquiry, carried out by three naval officers, cleared Hunter of all wrongdoing. Moreover, it declared him to be "an excellent and most vigilant officer . . . most anxious to do his duty." Nevertheless, on January 2, 1863, by order of the secretary of the navy, Hunter was forced to turn over command of *Montgomery* to his executive officer, Acting Master George H. Pendleton, and report to Washington for a full court-martial.[31]

Farragut was not pleased with the loss of the aggressive Hunter or his ship. They have "ordered *Montgomery* home, Hunter suspended," he wrote on January 5, "to gratify the Spanish Government; so look out upon the river for surprises."[32] His fears were well founded, for soon afterward, the rebel commerce raider CSS *Florida* would escape to heap enormous destruction on Yankee commerce on the high seas.

The admiral's investigation into the *Blanche* incident could not paper over the allegations of misdeeds. On January 8 Her Britannic Majesty's Envoy Extraordinary and Minister Plenipotentiary to the United States, Lord Lyons, dispatched a note to Secretary of State William H. Stanton claiming that Hunter had "obtained the signature of [an] Englishman, Clement, to the deposition which he made in Pensacola, secretly and surreptitiously, and that compulsion was exercised to induce him to sign the document." Clement, it seemed, later reported to the British consul in Havana that he had been repeatedly cross-examined on several consecutive days in Pensacola with the objective of forcing him to say that

*Blanche*'s crew had set fire to the steamer. Having threatened to keep him as a prisoner until he agreed to the statement, he claimed Hunter was thus guilty of extorting the statement from him. The British government demanded an apology and full compensation to Clement for his detention. Stanton, too, demanded an investigation, adding further to the captain's woes.[33]

On January 12 *Montgomery* came to anchor at the New York Navy Yard. Eight days later, Commander Hunter was formally charged with violating the territorial jurisdiction of a neutral government, and with scandalous conduct tending to the destruction of morals, and ordered to face a formal court-martial by the U.S. Navy. The court convened on February 16, 1863, and found the officer guilty of the first charge but not guilty of the second. The court adjudged that he be dismissed from naval service but recommended deserving of the clemency of the chief executive, Abraham Lincoln.[34] The United States, it was later claimed in Confederate circles, was obliged to pay Spain $200,000 in reparations.[35]

Then came a diplomatic bombshell. In March, Judah P. Benjamin, Confederate secretary of state, after some investigation of his own, glumly informed the Confederate representative in Paris, John H. Slidell, that *General Rusk*, while at Galveston in commercial service, had originally been impressed into Confederate service when the war began and was placed under the control of Major T. S. Moise, assistant quartermaster for the Department of Texas. Moise, it seems, was a rather scandalous miscreant and had recently been court-martialed, convicted, and dismissed from the service, after which he promptly proceeded to enter into a fraudulent cabal with four other swindlers, Robert Mott, Nelson Clements, J. L. Macauley, and Macauley's brother. Under cover of procuring supplies for the Confederate military, Moise had transferred (without authority) *General Rusk* to his associates without bothering to inform or pay the government. He then authorized them to transfer the ship's registry to fly a British flag "by collusive transfer to some British subject." She would then be employed as a runner between Havana and the Confederacy for his and his associates' benefit without stipulating for any freight or charter money in favor of the government or taking bond (though assigned by his associates for $50,000, a third of the value of the vessel).[36]

It was a masterful sleight of hand. The vessel was taken to Havana and somehow had been placed under a British flag, possibly through the aid of Charles J. Helm. She made one successful and immensely profitable voyage and was on her way for a second to Havana when she was destroyed. One of the parties to the fraudulent conspiracy against the Confederate government, claimed Benjamin, "has gone to Europe for the purpose of claiming as owner the whole amount of the indemnity accorded by the Government of the United States to that of Spain." Benjamin thus instructed Slidell that he take proper measures to have the payment of the sum made out to the government, even though Spain had not officially recognized the Confederacy.[37]

The scandal continued to grow even as the new embarrassment to the Confederate government was slowly being realized. On June 3 it was reported at Havana that the Spanish minister in Washington (without knowing the whole story) had been instructed by his government to demand a formal apology and payment to the owners of *General Rusk* for the value of the steamer and cargo. The demand was made, and the federal government, also ignorant of the true background of *Blanche,* formally disavowed the act of the commander of *Montgomery* and promised payment. The Confederate agent at Havana, Charles J. Helm, however, informed Secretary Benjamin: "Should the money be paid and the subject be referred back to this colonial Government, I anticipate no difficulty in arresting payment, at least until after the recognition of the Confederate States."[38]

Damage to the Union war effort was significant. The career of a patriotic, aggressive, and talented, albeit politically insensitive, naval officer had been destroyed in the ongoing diplomatic effort to ensure nonintervention by foreign powers. A vitally needed man-of-war had been removed from active service for months on end, pending resolution of the controversy. Her absence on the line permitted the escape of numerous blockade-runners, as well as a terribly destructive rebel commerce raider. And national humiliation was visceral. The apology to the government of Spain was explicit in the actions of the navy against Hunter, but payment of reparations would never be made. On July 3, 1863, with the conclusion of the Battle of Gettysburg in a Union victory, rebel hopes for any formal diplomatic recognition of the Confederacy by either England or Spain would be dashed, and with it the indemnity sought for the loss of a stolen ship on an isolated Cuban beach called Mariel.


The subsequent military career of *Montgomery,* though noteworthy and at times heroic, would never erase the embarrassment caused by the *Blanche* affair. Reassigned to the North Atlantic Blockading Squadron, the big warship would face myriad enemies and engage in some failed expeditions, not the least of which was the hapless pursuit of the Confederate raiders *Tacony* and *Florida.* Her career with the blockading fleet off North Carolina would prove far more productive. There she would cooperate in several spirited chases and important captures, including such blockade-runners as *Ceres, Bendigo, Dare, Pet,* and *Bat.* In November 1864, after undergoing much-needed repairs at Norfolk and while cruising off the Chesapeake capes, she unsuccessfully chased the Confederate raider *Tallahassee* before returning to blockade duty off Wilmington, North Carolina. On December 22 she served as the admiralty observation ship for the first assault on Fort Fisher, arguably the mightiest rebel bastion on the Confederate coast, guarding the Cape Fear River access to the last major rebel port open to commerce. On January 15, 1865, she participated with distinction as a combatant in the final and successful assault on the fort and later in actions against minor defensive posts on the river. But for all of her service, the stain of the *Blanche* affair would remain indelibly etched on her record.[39]

*Montgomery* remained on station off the Cape Fear until the end of May 1865. By then the war was over, and the weathered veteran sailed for Hampton Roads, and then on to the Philadelphia Navy Yard where, on June 20, she was formally decommissioned. Less than three weeks later, on August 10, like many of her battered and noble sisters, she was sold at auction to commercial interests. On April 1, 1866, she was redocumented as a commercial freight hauler.[40] For the next eleven years she would lead a colorless, nondescript existence, but one that was apparently lucrative for her owners.

The subsequent mundane service of the merchant marine was, in many ways, as hard on *Montgomery* as her military career had been. In 1869 it was necessary to completely overhaul her, and the following year she required a brand new screw. Constant sea service in the name of profit proved every bit as strenuous as blockade duty, and the repeated, heart-stopping pursuits of blockade-runners and commerce raiders during the war. In 1872 she had required additional repairs, and two years later had been surveyed and classed one-and-a-half by the New York Board of Underwriters. Despite it all, she had acquitted herself well for her owners and those who required her services.[41]

If *Montgomery* had a soul, she would no doubt have detected some irony in having eventually found gainful employment under the flag of the New York and Havana Line that regularly returned her to the coast of Cuba. When the old warhorse cleared New York on Friday, January 5, 1877, bound for Havana, it had all the appearances of yet another milk run.[42]

The voyage at first had proceeded without incident, although the winter seas were becoming obnoxiously heavy. Captain Thomas Winters, a veteran officer, had followed his usual routine. Discipline among his crew was very good, and the only thing he worried about was the boisterous weather. By midnight a thick fog mingled with rain had set in, but as the ship's lights were all up and burning, no one seemed apprehensive.[43]

At 1:30 Sunday morning, approximately thirty miles off the Delaware capes, *Montgomery*'s lookout spotted something moving through the mist. At first, judging from its rig and faint display of lights, he thought it to be a schooner, and piped up a warning to the helmsman. Immediately the wheel was put to the starboard in an attempt to quickly cross the approaching vessel's bow. Then the stranger burst out of the fog—it was no slow-moving schooner but in fact the steamship *Seminole,* of the Boston and Savannah Line, bearing down at a deadly nine to ten knots.[44]

If *Montgomery* had been caught by surprise, there was no less consternation aboard *Seminole.* Onboard the latter, the watches had been set for the night as usual, and the watch below had turned in. Then, shortly after two bells had been struck, sounds of confusion reigned on the deck, and cries were sounded, "as if an accident of some kind had happened or was impending." Crewmen sleeping in their bunks below decks in both vessels were jarred to action and rushed to pull on their trousers and boots and get topside.[45]

Collision was now unavoidable as *Seminole,* with a large lading of cotton aboard, closed bow on with *Montgomery.* Everyone on deck stood stunned, watching the crash as it unfolded through the mist almost as if in stop motion. *Seminole*'s bow struck just abaft *Montgomery*'s pilothouse, crashing in the bulwarks and slashing open her side from the rail to below the waterline. There was a slight recoil. The second mate's room was penetrated and stove in, with the officer, a man named Aschell, pinioned by pieces of the wreck but still alive. His pitiful screams for help went unanswered as everyone now looked to his own survival.[46]

Steward E. O. Laughlin, who had been sleeping half dressed in his berth, had been roused by the shudder of the crash, the loud blowing of whistles, and confused cries from the deck, and he rushed topside to see the two vessels locked together at a point just opposite the foremast of *Montgomery*. He stood for a moment drinking it all in. Four Spanish passengers were working desperately to cut away one of the ship's lifeboats, while all around them chaos ruled. The pitiful cries of the wounded man trapped below pierced the night. The steward could see that *Seminole*'s bow had driven nearly halfway through his own ship. Then he watched in horror as the cotton steamer slew, or swung around, opening a wide breech that allowed "a flood of water to pour into the hold."[47]

By this time, Captain Winters had also rushed onto *Montgomery*'s deck, shouting to his men to jump aboard *Seminole* while they could. He and his first mate, J. W. Savage, and six others, including Second Steward Frank Lewis, Messman Joseph Close, Stokers Patrick O'Brien and Hugh Doherty, and Seamen J. S. Nickardon and Fred Longuard, made the successful leap for life. Two or three others who followed, just as *Seminole* began to back off, "fell short of their mark and leaped into the sea, to meet death almost instantly."[48]

Barely four minutes after the fatal impact, *Montgomery* was settling rapidly by the head. She lunged forward and, "with a single glide, without listing a particle, sank beneath the waves," taking many of those aboard with her. "By their agonizing cries," one observer from *Seminole* later remarked, "it appeared to me that a large ship's company were struggling for life, but their voices were soon hushed." Among them had been eight of *Montgomery*'s crewmen and the four passengers. Those who went down with the ship included Second Officer Aschell; John O'Brien, oiler, of New York, "a married man, whose mother and sister are living"; James Granger, oiler; John Morgan, fireman, of New York; Thomas Scott, stoker, of New York; James Dung (Deering), stoker, of New York; Albert A. Smith; Alice Phillips, cook; Thomas Stockburn, waiter, of New York; and the four unidentified Spaniards.[49]

Immediate rescue of many who had not perished with the ship was imperative, for most would succumb to hypothermia in the freezing Atlantic waters within a very few minutes. "There was quite a high sea running at the time," remarked one of the men engaged in the attempt, "and the *Seminole*'s boat forward on the starboard side was with difficulty steered away, launched, and manned, and sent to aid any that might be floating on any part of the wreck. But there was little left to mark the spot where the ill-fated steamer had gone down." When the boat returned, three survivors had been picked up. Chief Engineer John McEwen and bandolier Henry Osborne had been found clinging to the upturned keel of a small boat, while Quartermaster John Monroe was taken from a floating hatch eight minutes later.[50]

E. O. Laughlin was also struggling for survival in the frigid ocean. Despite the blackness of night, he soon managed to discern the forms of other men near him in the water, although he could not distinguish their faces. For half an hour he swam about in the frigid sea, hoping to find some purchase. Suddenly, out of the night, he spied a dark object floating near him, lunged for it, and caught the side of a boat that had floated free of the wreck. Six hands, belonging to three of his mates, helped pull him aboard. Though undoubtedly weakened by his cold swim, Laughlin nevertheless took an oar and with his comrades began to pull the boat toward the lights of *Seminole*. En route three more men were found and rescued, making seven saved in the lifeboat: Laughlin, First Assistant Engineer R. H. Jenkins, Fireman James Morton, Seaman/Fireman James Callender, Seamen John Lehman (Luman), P. O. Strum, and John Haskis.[51]

As soon as *Seminole*'s captain was convinced that all the surviving members of *Montgomery*'s crew had been picked up and ascertained that his own ship had sustained little injury, he turned for Boston, his original destination. Despite the catastrophe, *Seminole* arrived in Boston harbor almost on schedule on the afternoon of Monday, January 8. There she disgorged the survivors who, before their return to New York two days later, were reportedly treated kindly by the inhabitants.[52]

Thirty miles off the Delaware capes, the controversial old warrior *Montgomery* had finally found peace.

# 15

## Suits of Ice

There were between thirty-five and forty vessels, mostly barks, brigantines, and schooners, and a few tugs and steamships, lying at anchor under the protection of the Delaware Breakwater on the night of Sunday, March 11, 1888. Many had been en route to various destinations with cargoes of sugar, lumber, ice, molasses, and other commodities and had come in to seek shelter from increasingly heavy seas. It was raining a bit as the evening came on, with airs braced by a crisp, moderate breeze blowing steadily from the southeast. Most crews aboard the vessels under the breakwater had already battened down their hatches and buttoned up for the night. Few, if any, apprehended the slightest menace.[1] Nevertheless, at the Lewes Life Saving Station, Keeper John A. Clampitt, a veteran of innumerable storms and rescues, going into his fifth year as station captain, kept a watchful eye on the weather gauges. A few miles to the east, at the Cape Henlopen station, Keeper Theodore Salmons, always on the alert for sudden weather changes, ordered his men to be extra vigilant during their evening patrols. Just in case.

For many crewmen aboard the vessels at Delaware Breakwater, both Clampitt's and Salmons's wariness would prove to be their salvation. Few could have known that for days a low-pressure system originating as far west as the Rocky Mountains had been racing east across the United States with incredible velocity and would soon crash head on into a major storm system pushing north from the Carolinas. No one could have foretold that the collision of these two systems on the Delmarva coast, with Delaware Breakwater being squarely in their paths, would produce a hurricane-force blizzard and loss of life and property hitherto without precedent on the Eastern seaboard.

Four vessels typical of the lot lying in the so-called protected anchorage that fateful night included the steam tug *Lizzie Crawford,* Captain Enos Kane; the 178-ton Somers Point, New Jersey, wrecking tug *Tamesi,* Captain Charles Townsend; the little 102-ton Philadelphia steamer *George G. Simpson,* Captain Hardy Holt; and the brig *Startle,* Captain Burns. All were snugged up together at the steamer pier at Lewes when the first hint of trouble made its appearance. The wind, which had been fresh all day, had been increasing in force somewhat as evening came on, but no one seemed worried. Few noticed as the moon and stars were slowly enveloped behind a black mantle of clouds. Shortly before midnight, all of the vessels sheltered by the strong stone shield of the breakwater began to swing nervously on their anchor cables. Then, it happened.[2]

Like most of his men, Captain Charles Townsend of the tug *Tamesi* was stunned when, at about seven bells into the first watch, a tempest suddenly burst forth with demonic fury in but a matter of minutes. "We did not have the faintest idea that we were going to have a storm until it came right down on us," he later reported. "Everybody was naturally taken unawares." His chief engineer, George Robinson, described it as "the first roar of a cyclone." The wind, braced with leaden sheets of rain, struck hard from the north-northwest, then shifted dramatically to southwest "and assumed the proportions of a hurricane."[3]

Out of the eastern darkness, great black waves began to break heavily against the ships and threatened to dash them to pieces. Crews rushed up from below decks to further secure their vessels as best they could. On some, it was impossible for mates to hear orders over the din of confusion and the roar of the storm. On others, voices of desperate men begging for assistance went unheard or unanswered, as rain suddenly turned to blinding snow and sleet.[4]

At the steamer landing *George G. Simpson* was jammed between *Lizzie Crawford* and the pier, and *Crawford* herself was blocked in by *Tamesi,* which was unable to move on account of having no steam up in her boilers. Though both *Simpson* and *Crawford* had fenders out, the wind hammered them mercilessly against the pier, adding to the confusion. With the seas washing over their upper decks and the battering increasing in intensity with every passing minute, escape to open water was imperative. Making it happen was something else for their crews, as "the atmosphere was piercingly cold, freezing the wet on one's clothes until they were caked with ice."[5]

Despite the degenerating conditions, *Simpson*'s mate, George Robinson, was a model of decorum, until the steam pipe of a donkey engine that kept the pumps working was suddenly ruptured, that is. The shrill scream of the escaping steam stunned and frightened him. Rushing onto the deck, he stumbled on some lumber that had been blown onboard from the pier and tumbled overboard into the freezing cold water. Instinctively, he grabbed for any purchase he could find. His fingers miraculously encountered a tender rope, with which he managed to haul himself back aboard. Though shivering with cold, he shut off the steam to the donkey engine to prevent a scalding. By now, Captain Holt had begun to deftly maneuver his ship away from the pier, despite her tightly packed proximity to neighbors and the gyrations of the sea.[6]

Aboard *Tamesi,* Captain Townsend and his men had been working like demons to build up a head of steam. Then, as the big wrecking tug finally began backing away, there was a crashing of timbers and the terrifying sound of escaping steam that almost rendered the raging noise of the blizzard inaudible. The bow of *Simpson* had somehow been turned and rammed squarely into the center of *Tamesi,* ripping an enormous gap in her side and tearing open the sides of her boiler. Townsend shouted above the storm, ordering his men to jump onto the nearby pier and save themselves. Within seconds, all were able to scramble onto the pilings and temporary sanctuary, with the captain himself being the last to abandon ship as it drove ahead entirely unmanned. Then, as the captain clung precariously to a slippery piling, both he and his men watched *Tamesi* go down in shallow water near the beach a half-mile from the pier.[7]

In the meantime, *Simpson* had continued her own erratic course, with some aboard now in an absolute state of panic. Two crewmen, Mate Eli Walls and William Fletcher, "gallantly breasted the storm tossed stream side by side until they reached the piling around the pier," even as their ship was pulling off. Their yells for assistance were quickly answered as a tangle of arms and hands belonging to *Tamesi*'s men dragged them up to their own safe perch.

Chaos and fear reigned supreme among those left aboard *Simpson*. Robinson later recalled, "by that time we were able to get out towards the Breakwater . . . The sight was an awful one. The *Simpson* was plunging, rolling and diving. The sea, which was increasing in fury with the wind, [was] threatening to swamp the boat. To add to our peril she began leaking badly. The donkey engine was useless, and there was only a hand pump. It was impossible to keep her free. The captain, fireman and myself did all we could to keep her afloat by bailing with buckets." There were now only four persons aboard the ship, Captain Holt, his terrified wife, fireman John Lynch, and Robinson.[8]

*Lizzie Crawford* was the next to suffer. No sooner had the *Tamesi* and the two *Simpson* crewmen clambered onto the pier than *Crawford* was smashed by a horrendous wave. It propelled the ship clear through the pier, shaving off her housing and decking as she was driven obliquely toward the beach. Heavy pilings, any one of which could kill a man, "were snapped off like pipe stems" and dropped on the deck of the tug like so many matchsticks. The boat was instantly swamped. Her fireman fell overboard, and the engineer, without a thought to his own life, jumped in to rescue him. Fortunately, both were driven onto the beach and saved. Soon their ship was lying stranded and broken, a shambles of a wreck, not far from where the men had come ashore.[9]

Those who had made it to the pier, now eleven in number, would soon discount their luck, for when *Crawford* had been driven through, she cut a wide, clear gap that isolated and stranded them on the end. The steamboat pier had been all but destroyed by the storm and *Crawford*. Battered by the sea, it soon parted again in several places with great, ice-covered chunks crashing into the surf. Amazingly, at the still-standing extreme end were the survivors, huddled together in abject terror, completely isolated from the world, but still alive.[10]

In the meantime, without a working pump, *Simpson* was taking on water rapidly and in imminent danger of sinking. Observing another vessel about a mile away anchored near the "Stone Pile" (as the breakwater was not so affectionately called by bay pilots), Holt and Robinson sought to temporarily stabilize their ship and bring her within rescue range of the stranger. "Seeing that there was only one chance left," the mate later stated, "I managed to get for'ed and threw the anchor over, veering away all the chain we could, about thirty-five fathoms." The anchor failed to grab, and *Simpson* was swept helplessly along past the breakwater but fortunately close to the other vessel, which proved to be Captain William Mimford's big wrecking tug *Protector*. Seeing the oncoming steamer's desperate situation, Mimford ordered a line thrown, but as soon as it was taken

Though later saved, the tug *Lizzie Crawford* lies a stranded and battered wreck. Note the remains of the Lewes pier in the background. (Purnell Collection, Delaware Public Archives, Dover)

on board *Simpson* and run around a bitt, it parted. The effort had served, however, to halt the vessel's progress just long enough to get another line to her starboard side. This time it held![11]

Quickly, the sinking tug warped alongside her savior. Waiting for their chance to jump, "for the *Simpson* was now rapidly filling," all aboard, one by one, transferred to *Protector*. The first to go was Mrs. Holt, caught in the arms of Mimford and his engineer. Robinson and Lynch followed in rapid succession, all landing safely. Captain Holt was not so fortunate.[12]

"The waves kept running higher and higher," Holt later recalled, "and when I jumped they were running as high as a three-story house. I remember jumping and that's all I do remember. When I came to myself I was lying in the cabin and all hands were rubbing me and trying to force medicine down my throat. I had fallen on the deck and struck my head on one of the stanchions cutting my head open. Everybody but my wife thought I was dead, and they tell me I was unconscious for half an hour. When I regained my senses the *Simpson* was at the bottom of the bay in six fathoms of water and her deck houses had been washed away."[13]

Men of *Tamesi* and *Simpson* still clung to the end of the pier. Their foothold on the open structure was precarious at best, and the blizzard threatened them with a death from freezing or exposure. From their lonely perch, with ice-flecked seas breaking relentlessly over them, they watched the destruction of scores of ships and lives pass before them as if in a macabre pageant. "I was in a position to see almost everything that happened in the harbor," recalled Townsend, "and I believe that more than twenty persons were drowned or lost their lives in the storm. I saw the *Simpson*'s wheel and pilot-house ashore on the beach." At one moment, an unidentified three-masted schooner passed the breakwater headed for the shore with all of her crew hanging in the rigging. One of the seamen aboard had already frozen to death. The others were encased in clothes frozen fast to their bodies, seriously frostbitten, and visibly suffering. At another instant a large Norwegian bark, sheathed in ice, was dismasted and driven hopelessly before the wind toward the beach. No one was seen alive aboard the ghostly wreck.[14]

Then a two-masted schooner was hurled shoreward, with all of her hands lashed to the main mast. No one could hear their screams of mortal anguish or pleas for divine intervention above the gale. "While near the pier the wind increased and started the main mast from its braces. The change was so great that the mast tottered and fell, and all the men, with two exceptions, lashed themselves to the foremast. Two of the crew were unable to extricate themselves in time from the wreckage and were washed overboard and drowned. The others were rescued from their dangerous situation by the [Cape Henlopen] life savers."[15]

"About an hour afterwards every man [on the pier] was clothed in a suit of ice," Townsend later reported. "The wind was blowing at a terrible rate and we suffered agonies from the cold. The waves cut right through the pier in three places and then we feared that we were saved from drowning only to die in the water later . . . Every man was as near frozen to death as he possibly could be without actually dying, and we were compelled to remain quiet on account of the weakness of the pier. We huddled together and hardly exchanged a word after the first few hours. Then we became hungry, but not a word passed our lips for twenty-three hours. There we were almost on land, but actually cut away from all communication from it."[16]

Throughout the night the storm persisted, destroying, capsizing, sinking, or driving ashore ship after ship until beach, breakwater, and harbor were littered with the detritus of seafaring humanity and industry. Death and suffering were everywhere. There was no sanctuary. The schooner *Paul and Thompson* was a case example. Commanded by Captain Josiah Mathews, and manned by a crew of five, the 204-ton vessel was a veteran of twenty-one years in the trades, home ported at Perth Amboy, New Jersey, and no stranger to dirty weather.[17] She had been on a routine voyage from the James River for New York with a cargo of lumber and put in at Delaware Breakwater to take shelter from the storm. When the great gale began in earnest, however, another schooner moored nearby named *George W. Anderson,* also bound for New York with lumber, dragged her anchor and drifted into *Paul and Thompson,* staving in her bow and causing her mainmast to fall. The latter immediately filled and capsized onto her beam-ends, but not before her captain and crew made it safely to *Anderson.* Two hours later, with both anchors out and still dragging, *Anderson* was driven onto the beach and completely destroyed.[18]

Rescue for many stranded crewmen by the lifesavers from the Delaware coast stations seemed an impossible hope. The early morning north foot patrol from the Cape Henlopen station, which kept vigil as far as the point of the cape itself, was astonished at the wreckage strewn along the beach and at the intensity of the ninety-mile-per-hour winds, which had literally pushed him back to the station house. Keeper Salmons, informed about the massive amounts of wreckage floating ashore, at once assembled his men and equipment to march back to the cape and perform the impossible. The snowfall had been extraordinary, and the trek north to the point through the driving blizzard was difficult in the extreme.[19]

At the Lewes Life Saving Station, John Clampitt and his men made their first attempt to reach the beach before dawn, but they were driven back by hurricane force winds stippled with sleet and snow, and returned to the station literally crawling on hands and knees. During a brief lull, the predawn gunmetal-gray sky, though threatening, suggested a second window of opportunity might be in the offing. The team again bravely set out, this time hauling their surfboat, breeches buoys, and line-throwing Lyle gun, and reached the beach just as the storm resumed its fury. The landscape before them was appalling. At first count no less than twenty schooners and two, perhaps three, steamers had been driven ashore and wrecked, sunk, or were in the process of sinking at or near the breakwater. On many hulks, men more dead than alive and covered in ice clung to the masts, rigging, or tops of cabins. A few were lashed to the sides of vessels lying on their beam-ends. The scene was one from the lowest levels of Dante's hell.[20]

Fifty or more volunteers from Lewes began to fight their way to the beach to assist in the desperate work of saving lives. Dragging their rescue apparatus behind them, the lifesavers headed for a vessel that appeared to be in the most serious condition, a three-masted schooner that had been driven onto the bar a mere eight hundred yards north of the Lewes station. The vessel was the 169-ton *Allie H. Belden*, home ported at South Dennis, Massachusetts, but last from Boothbay, Maine, ironically with a cargo of ice. She was going to pieces fast, with monstrous seas breaking clearly over her. Her terrified crew had climbed high into the rigging, where they were rapidly freezing to death.[21] Stranded nearby lay the spanking new pilot boat *Ebe W. Tunnell*, which, for the time being at least, was not in immediate danger of breaking up. It was now about 5:00 A.M., and Clampitt chose the hardest and most endangered of the two to rescue.

Clampitt's men quickly rigged their Lyle gun and managed to send a whipline over the *Belden* and within arm's-length of her captain. With hands already frozen stiff, the schooner's skipper could not hold onto the line, which was instantly blown from his grasp. A second shot went across the jib boom. It too could not be reached by a sailor in the rigging before the sea carried it away. A third line was prepared but was frozen stiff. When the gun was fired, the line snapped like a broken icicle. The storm now increased to an even greater intensity and the lifesavers could barely see more than a few feet before them. Still they persisted, firing two more lines but each time failing in their objective.[22]

Clampitt resolved on a new strategy. With all of the few remaining lines now frozen stiff, the Lyle gun was no longer an option. The surf conditions could best be described as atrocious, and a direct boat launch through the breakers was dangerous, if not impossible, even for the most experienced of his team. Keeper Clampitt nevertheless instructed his men to prepare the surfboat. He then sig-

The ice-covered hulk of an unidentified schooner stranded by the "Blizzard of '88" near the Delaware Breakwater (Purnell Collection, Delaware Public Archives, Dover)

naled *Tunnell* to cast a line ashore. With the pilot boat crew pulling the line and his own men pulling at the oars, he hoped, the surfboat just might be able to make it through the huge breakers on the beach. Yet, pull as they might, the men could not punch through, and the boat was mercilessly beaten to the lee of *Belden* and then back onto the beach. Again they tried, and again they were hammered back by the freezing waters and winds. Though wearied and wet, Clampitt ordered yet another attack. This time the lifesavers, assisted by the volunteers from Lewes, waded the surfboat to the windward of *Belden* and then shoved off. The plan was rewarded with success, but the effort had so completely exhausted the men that they were obliged to come to anchor outside the breakers to recuperate their energy. Then, by alternately rowing and anchoring, they slowly moved by degrees toward the schooner.[23]

About two in the afternoon, nine hours after the rescue had begun, the surf-boat finally reached *Belden*. The gallant lifesavers, themselves now more dead than alive, managed to board the ice-sheathed schooner with considerable difficulty and found four nearly lifeless bodies frozen to what was left of the encrusted rigging. Two more of the crew, they discovered, had failed to survive the horrors of the night and had been swept to their deaths just as the rescue had begun. The survivors, hideously frostbitten, were removed and carried to the Lewes station house where Dr. Hall, the local physician, attended to them.[24] Clampitt's cold and weary men, rather than rest, next focused their efforts on the rescue of *Tunnell*'s crew.

In the meantime, Keeper Theodore Salmons's Cape Henlopen lifesavers had already arrived on the scene. Finding Clampitt's men totally embroiled in the *Belden* rescue, they borrowed the Lyle gun and the line, which had been thawed and dried at the station, and returned to the cape, where several more wrecks had been reported. En route they encountered a small, forty-five-ton pilot boat schooner called *Enoch Turley* stranded near the breakwater. Seven men were waving and shouting from the boat after every successive breaker that washed over them. Salmon ordered the Lyle gun prepared and on the first shot sent the whipline directly across the pilot boat. Within an hour, the breeches buoy had rescued all seven badly frostbitten crewmen, who were then dispatched to the Lewes station house for treatment.[25]

Salmon's next objective was the big New York schooner *William G. Bartlett*, which had stranded on the most exposed point of the cape itself. Unfortunately, the last of the shot lines had been used in rescuing the *Turley* crew. The lifesavers, who had set out without their own heavy surfboat, were thus obliged to march against the blizzard to the nearby Marine Hospital, where another was kept, and then haul it back to the wreck site. It is perhaps impossible to comprehend how that indefatigable band of heroes was able to drag the three-thousand-pound carriage-mounted boat across the snow-covered beach into the teeth of the murderous storm. But they did. En route, they encountered three young seamen belonging to *Bartlett*'s crew, floundering in the swash of the surf, desperately trying to reach the shore. With considerable courage, the surf men plunged into the freezing water and retrieved the men, all within inches of certain death, and hauled them onto the beach and salvation.[26]

Though their own uniforms were by now frozen stiff, the lifesavers returned their attentions back to *Bartlett*. Hauling the surfboat to the water's edge, they somehow successfully deployed it. With incredible difficulty, they managed to pull through the breakers and reach the schooner, lying nearly eight hundred yards from the beach. Three more men were found. Two were in critical condition from exposure and a third, the steward, had already frozen to death. All had been in the rigging for eighteen hours, fully exposed to the elements.[27]

The storm continued without letup. "It was," reported one veteran sea captain who counted himself lucky to live through the night and next day, "the worst storm I have seen in thirty-five years. You couldn't look to windward, it would cut out your eyes."[28]

Four stranded and sunken schooners lay amid floating ice following the "Blizzard of '88." Few would be saved. (Purnell Collection, Delaware Public Archives, Dover)

By midday of March 12 various reports had begun to filter into Lewes, all bad. The first news in stated that two schooners had been sunk, and twenty-one more had been driven ashore and wrecked on the beach, while an additional twenty-five were lying near the breakwater flying distress signals, all in danger of sinking.[29]

An unknown tugboat with a coal-laden schooner barge in tow was reported down with all hands off the Hen and Chickens Shoal, to the immediate south of the cape. Keeper Dag Joseph at the Cape Henlopen Lighthouse had watched as *C. B. Hazeltine,* with 1,190 tons of coal and a crew of five, from Port Richmond, had been driven to their doom. "No human power," he later reported, "could have saved her, even had aid been possible, and in a short time she was among the terrible breakers that were leaping high into the air over what was probably the most fatal and dangerous shoals on the middle Atlantic coast." In less than five minutes she had disappeared completely. Not long afterward the British bark *Brimiga,* laden with sugar from Bahia, Brazil, met the same fate not far from where *Hazeltine* had been destroyed.[30] Then a report came in that the tugboat *Philadelphia* was believed lost off the Delaware capes with all hands.

As the hours passed, the damage reports worsened, increasing the toll to twenty-eight vessels stranded, many so high up on the beach that salvage would be impossible. Some reports were stating that between twenty-two and twenty-five lives had been lost at the breakwater alone by drowning and hypothermia. Nearly a dozen men were still stranded on the steamer pier, cut off from food and communication and freezing to death where they stood. The privations of even those fortunates who had managed to reach safety were terrible to behold. Many who had struggled onto the beach were drenched to the skin. The sub-Arctic temperatures had glaciated their garments, giving them the appearance of being clad in silvery medieval armor rather than clothing. "The men," one report noted, "were literally encased in ice and the blinding snow which followed the gale added to their awful sufferings. More than sixty persons were bound hand and foot by the ice and a large majority of these are now badly frostbitten and confined to their beds with heavy colds."[31]

The damage elsewhere along the Delmarva coast had been inestimable. "Twenty-five oyster dredging boats," reported the *New York Times,* "were capsized in Chincoteague Bay, and cast ashore there, and it is reported that fourteen bodies of drowned seamen had washed ashore, six of them lashed to the rigging of the capsized vessels." On Chesapeake Bay, more than one hundred vessels were in distress or reported lost. The storm was cutting a swath of destruction as far north as Maine, killing many scores of men, sinking hundreds of vessels, and devastating countless maritime facilities, waterfront communities, and homes.[32]

At Cape Henlopen, by late evening of March 12, the winds had finally begun to abate. Then, as suddenly as it had been halted, all about the frozen scene of the Delaware Breakwater life began to stir anew. At the end of the ruins of the steamer pier, after twenty-three hours of exposure to the worst that nature could throw at them, eleven men had to be physically wrenched free of their Arctic cocoons by rescuers. When help arrived to recover their bodies, they had to be lifted like ice-covered logs into the boats. But they were alive![33]

Although the damage to shipping had been extraordinary, some vessels had somehow managed to ride out the storm, and like *Protector,* save many lives. One such boat was the little tug *George W. Pride Jr.,* which had performed several rescues and had done so without incurring any damage except the loss of her port anchor. Grief and relief were doled out in equal proportions. *Protector* had proved an agency of mercy not only for the *Simpson's* men but for other storm victims as well. One schooner, flying her ensign down, had been driven past the tug and stranded on the beach. From 3:00 A.M. Monday to 3:00 P.M. Tuesday, her crew had clung to the rigging and endured enormous suffering in the cold, until Captain Mimford and his men had bravely rescued them from almost certain death. The praise for the good captain, who had saved many lives, was substantial. When *Protector* finally offloaded her cargo of wreck victims, the citizens

The Cape Henlopen Lighthouse viewed from the west. From this lighthouse, Keeper Dag Joseph watched the destruction of *C. B. Hazeltine* and her crew of five. (General Collections, Public Buildings, Delaware Public Archives, Dover)

Cape Henlopen Life Saving Station, from which Keeper Theodore Salmons and his heroic band of lifesavers rushed forth to the rescue of scores of stranded and freezing mariners during the "Blizzard of '88" (Post Card Collection, Delaware Public Archives, Dover)

of Lewes were stunned and elated to learn that Captain Harding Holt and his wife, who had initially been reported as having drowned in *George G. Simpson,* were among them. Yet many others ashore still waited patiently to learn if their loved ones had survived or perished. That evening, every pew in the three churches in town was filled by mourners, as well as by those giving thanks.[34]

On March 15, with the storm barely over, the harbor was literally choked with debris. The good citizens of Lewes, while still caring for the near frozen survivors lodged in their homes and at their own expense, began to take stock and clean up. That afternoon, a number of prominent vessel owners and several members of the Philadelphia Maritime Exchange chartered the Red Star Line steamer *Juno* to carry them down to the Delaware Breakwater to ascertain the total damage and loss of life. Among their number were Edward R. Sharwood of the exchange, William Brockie Jr. of the Insurance Company of North America, and Captain Benjamin Robinson, part owner of *Simpson* and brother of George Robinson. The latter had come down to find and collect the body of his sibling who, he was told, had gone down with his ship.[35]

Captain Robinson's first stop was at the Lewes Life Saving Station, where he called on an old acquaintance, Captain Thomas J. Truxton, keeper of the Rehoboth station, who had come up to lend a hand. "Have you recovered my brother's body yet?" he queried.

"Your what?" responded Truxton with a grimace.

"My brother's body. I came to take it home."

"Your brother's body is up at the hotel," replied the keeper with a wide grin. "Just now your brother is taking his breakfast."

Within minutes, the two Robinsons were enjoined in an emotional reunion they would never forget.[36]

Initial estimates of the loss to shipping were placed at between $400,000 and $500,000. Yet it appeared that the financial cost to insurers, though considerable for the times, would not be as bad as first anticipated. An officer of one prominent marine insurance company had even declared before the disaster was over: "I do not think that the insurance companies will suffer much loss from the storm. Most of the vessels which have been lost or disabled are coastwise vessels. The insurance on the hulls of such is so high that few of them are insured. The larger vessels detained at the Breakwater seem to be all right. As soon as a gale like this comes they put their bow to the wind and anchor, and lay in that position until the gale subsides. Most of the risks placed by the Philadelphia companies and the other companies represented here are on the large steamers and their cargoes."[37]

For the next week, as other vessels that had survived the storm at sea began to arrive in port, additional news of shipping losses off the Delmarva coast and in Delaware Bay began to trickle in. One captain surmised that the damage had been as horrific at sea as within the breakwater. "I believe," he said, "that all schooners that passed through the Capes since the beginning of the storm have been lost." The report of one Captain Howes, of the steamer *Dessoug,* from Savannah, seemed to verify it when he commented that on Wednesday, while sailing nine miles south-southeast of Cape Henlopen, he saw a battered victim of the late tempest, a large unidentified bark with yards on her foremasts and trucks painted white, sink before his eyes. Elsewhere, the bark *Vanadas* was reported ashore at Bombay Hook, while the pilot boats *Henry Edmunds* and *E. C. Knight,* both belonging to Philadelphia, were reported missing at sea.[38]

At Parramore Island, down the coast, the big three-masted schooner *Esk,* bound from Sombrero Island for Norfolk with a cargo of guano and thirty-two black laborers, had come to grief on the beach where she was quickly buried beneath the sand and snow. There were no survivors.[39]

Soon wreckers would go to work on the "sorry spectacles" lying about the Delaware Breakwater and Cape Henlopen, and the detritus of destruction would gradually disappear. So it went, day after day, until the news of losses finally began to ebb, and life at the entrance to Delaware Bay resumed its normal routine.

• • •

An unidentified schooner capsized off Lewes, Delaware, during the "Blizzard of '88" (Purnell Collection, Delaware Public Archives, Dover)

With his head wrapped in bandages, cuts clearly disfiguring his face, and his frostbitten skin turning black in many places, Hardy Holt, late skipper of the ill-fated *George G. Simpson,* and his wife boarded the train at the Lewes station bound for Philadelphia and home. Charles Townsend, *Tamesi*'s captain, boarded another car en route to the same city. Not long afterward, Engineer George Robinson of *Simpson* would appear before his own spouse and was at first recognized by her as a specter and then as flesh and blood risen from the dead. Each man would soon tell his story to the press and the world about the worst storm in the recorded history of the Delaware capes, the "Terrible Blizzard of '88." None believed such a horrific tempest could ever happen again in their lifetimes.

But they were wrong. And for many of them, they were dead wrong.

# 16

## Chips of Wood on the Angry Waves

Monday, September 8, 1889. Captain D. A. Risley sat in the cabin of *J. & L. Bryan,* a superannuated schooner that had served as both his home and command for many years, and allowed himself a last moment of relaxation. He had just finished supervising the always-dirty job of loading 550 tons of coal at Greenwich Wharf, on the Philadelphia waterfront, and in minutes would be departing to deliver it to Salem, Massachusetts. His crew of six were nearly all new hands, with all four of his seamen hard-working, tough, and reliable men.[1] That was good, for experience told him that there would be little time to deal with weak-kneed sluggards on the voyage ahead. These final few moments dockside would likely be the last he would be able to call his own for the next week or so. Carefully, he picked up the packet of letters sitting on his table, each addressed to him in the same elegant feminine hand and bound together by a delicate blue ribbon. He considered untying the ribbon and again perusing his greatest personal treasure. But he demurred. He had read the letters at least a hundred times before, but he promised himself that when he returned he would reread them once more. Carefully, he put them back in their special place and looked at his pocket watch. It was time to go.

The first real premonition that dirty weather was brewing off the Delaware came after sunset when a strong wind from the northeast began to lash the waters off Cape Henlopen into angry, foaming waves. Great dark clouds, heralds of impending peril, were soon enveloping the sky and squeezing out the light. Though the weather was thick and foreboding, for most of the shore-bound citizens of Sussex County, Delaware, it did little to hinder business as usual. By early the next morning, September 9, the Merchants Exchange was open down on the Delaware Breakwater, and at Lewes the morning rituals of unshuttering shop windows and unlocking business doors proceeded as normal. The pilot boat *Ebe W. Tunnell,* which, like her consort tug *Enoch Turley,* had been recovered from a watery grave after the fatal blizzard of 1888, had put out to sea just before first light. Besides a crew of eight there were several well-known veteran pilots aboard, including John Barnes, Lewis Bertrand, James Rowland, and Harry

Hickman. By midmorning, a considerable distance out in the Atlantic, she had already spoken to an incoming vessel, but assistance had not been requested. It would be the last time anyone saw her afloat or her crew and the pilots alive.[2]

By midday it was apparent that the coast was in for a stiff nor'easter. At first, at least around the population centers, the storm was deemed quite moderate and injury was light. At Wilmington, the only serious damage was some knocked-down trees, and at Dover the peach crop was badly smashed. Up at Kitts Hammock the water had been blown across the wide beach clear up to Melvin's Hotel, a well-known resort establishment. Nearby, some summer beachfront cottages had been damaged. Aside from the properties directly affected, however, no one seemed worried. Then, shortly before the first light of Wednesday, hell arrived for breakfast.[3]

At 4:00 A.M. "the storm burst out in all its fury," as great, smashing, dirty green waves began to assail the shores without letup. A foamy sheet of water, three feet deep, pressed onward by the storm surge, was soon covering the land to the very abutments of Lewes itself and within a few feet of the houses at the edge of town. The little cluster of buildings called Hugheyville, closer to the cape and only a quarter mile away, was completely inundated. Some old-timers were already declaring that it was the highest tide experienced since 1867. Here and there carts drawn by pairs of horses accustomed to "water driving" could be seen slowly wading against the flood as more than two hundred people fled Hugheyville for higher ground before it got worse. It was not long before conditions met their expectations. "The long continuance of the gale created tremendous seas that swept over the protecting stone bulwarks," one observer remarked, "and even the half mile of meadows that reach between the town of Lewes and the beach have been for the past twenty-four hours covered with water." Telegraph communications with the breakwater were destroyed by 9:00 A.M. Soon, all contact with the coast was entirely shut down except by boat, and then only at one's hazard. And the storm was just getting started. For those brave enough to venture out, their gum coats and sou'wester headgear "made but a slight protection to the bitter cold rain and sand that came from the bay like sharp particles of glass, each piece of sand stinging as it struck." Encompassed within the protecting arms of the Delaware Breakwater were between sixty and one hundred vessels that had sought shelter from the storm. As in 1888, with so many vessels clustered so closely together, it was a prescription for disaster.[4]

Captain John A. Clampitt and his lifesaving crew at the Lewes station, like their colleagues at the Cape Henlopen and Rehoboth Life Saving Stations, had anticipated the gathering storm early and prepared their slender resources to combat its inevitable consequences. The need for their services was not long in arriving. By 4:00 A.M., the first report of a vessel ashore had already come in. Others followed in quick succession and would continue to do so well into the following day. At the breakwater, the ship captains and their crews fought bravely to prevent the almost certain destruction that faced them on the beach. To many it seemed that every boat in the harbor must surely sink. Great ships, noted one observer, "rolled like mere chips of wood on the angry waves and soon vessels became mixed up in an inextricable mass."[5]

By evening the damage to shipping was heartbreaking. A correspondent for the *Philadelphia Inquirer*, unable to get closer to the scene of destruction than Lewes, penned a description viewed from his upstairs room in the Verdin House, where water now twelve feet deep in places lapped less than thirty feet from the boardinghouse steps.

> It is impossible to give the extent of the damage done to shipping at this point by the storm, which has raged for the past forty-eight hours and is now unabated. The wind is blowing seventy miles an hour at this time (9 P.M.), and there are seventeen sails ashore, with a full score more fast drawing into the breakers . . . The oldest sailors here say there has never been a storm at this point to compare with this. The crews of six-teen of the wrecked vessels are now at the Verdin House, being cared for by the pro-prietors . . . As I write a terrible sight is being witnessed by the dozen brave men on shore composing the life saving crew of Lewes Station . . . A three-masted schooner is ashore just outside the inner bar and is fast going to pieces, with her crew of ten men clinging to the rigging . . . The lines which the brave life-saving crew have shot over her are tangled in such a manner as to make it impossible to use the [life] car. It is a terri-ble sight to witness, and yet no human power can save them. In the morning their bodies will possibly be washed ashore and receive burial in the sand along the water.[6]

By the morning of September 11, it was prognosticated, as many as thirty ves-sels would be piled up on the beach. One old captain at the Verdin House, whose own schooner had been stranded just above the government pier, said ominously that "if the wind continues blowing as it now is for ten hours [more] not a sail of the sixty remaining in the harbor will be afloat." Some observers now claimed "it was the most furious storm known to the oldest inhabitants." By midday at least two score vessels had been counted as beached, with twenty-seven of them driven upon the shore a hundred feet above the low-water mark. Both wooden piers at Lewes were washed away, and all the way to Rehoboth the beach was strewn with shipwrecks. At Hugheyville, the last refugees out reported that the Marine Hos-pital there had been severely damaged, and commercial piers belonging to Brown and Company and the Leuce Brothers had been swept out to sea. At Lewes, the pier that had been destroyed by the Blizzard of '88 and only recently rebuilt was once again a complete wreck, and most of the nearby outbuildings had washed away.[7] The Maritime Exchange station on the breakwater had been entirely gut-ted, and the greatest part of the property there had been lost. The men in the sta-tion had been saved by the timely arrival of the tug *Argus*, Captain Barnard, of the Red Star Line, which had taken them off and then landed them on the beach. Others were not as fortunate. It was at first thought that between twenty and fifty lives had already been lost in the bay and directly off the Atlantic coast, as many men were seen clinging to the rigging of fast-sinking vessels, frantically yelling for help. "It was," remarked one chronicler of the scene, "a terrible sight to witness, but no human power could save them. Their bodies were washed ashore . . . and were buried in the sand."[8] It was far from over.

The gale, blowing from the north-northeast, continued without pause before mercifully moderating. But news of horrible disasters and heroic efforts kept streaming in. The tales of the schooners *Kate E. Morse, William F. Parker,* and Captain Risley's *J. & L. Bryan,* all lost on Fourteen Foot Bank, were typical.

*Kate E. Morse* was a large schooner, owned by Morse and Co., of Bath, Maine, and like *J. & L. Bryan* had loaded with coal at Greenwich Point, Philadelphia. On Sunday, September 7, she had left the wharf bound for Boston. Onboard was Captain C. W. Crocker, of Machias, Maine; the mate, A. W. Clark; steward Frendenth G. Flinn; and a crew of six, three Philadelphians and three Bostonians.[9]

"The weather was bad when we arrived at the Breakwater," recalled the steward, but as the ship had been securely anchored, Captain Crocker deemed her well situated to ride it out. One of the ship's anchors had been planted in ninety feet of water, the other in fifty. But there was no accounting for the fickleness of fate. When the storm appeared to be approaching its apex, about 2:00 P.M. on Tuesday, *Morse*'s cables parted and she was carried helplessly before the fierce wind out of the east for nearly several hours. About 5:00 P.M. Captain Crocker found his ship being pushed toward the treacherous Hawks Nest Shoal, on the edge of Fourteen Foot Bank, and southeast of the Brandywine Shoal in Delaware Bay. Suddenly, with a terrific bump, the ship grounded squarely on the shoal and was soon forced over on her beam-ends with giant waves washing entirely over her. With her deck practically submerged and no purchase to be had on her naked sides, the crew lashed themselves to the rigging.[10]

Early the following morning another vessel identified by the lettering on her transom as the Philadelphia schooner *William F. Parker,* under the command of Captain Phil Wheaton, appeared out of nowhere and stranded on the same shoal. She lay within thirty yards of Captain Crocker's schooner, and her tragic end would soon be played out directly in front of those pitiful souls who clung for their lives to *Morse*'s rigging. "In the distance we saw the *Parker* on the shoal near us," recalled steward Frendenth Flinn, "and we soon beheld seven men lashed to the rigging. They were clinging to it as hard as possible. After awhile a particularly large wave came and the whole seven went under." Just as suddenly, six of the men reappeared, still clinging ferociously to the rigging. The seventh man had disappeared.[11]

About 6:00 A.M. another vessel hove into view, perhaps a mile distant, and all aboard the two stranded schooners took heart. The stranger proved to be the tug *Argus,* but as the seas pounding the shoal had become so dangerous, her captain decided not to hazard his own ship and men in a rescue attempt.

Throughout the day, the gale continued, and the beating absorbed by the men aboard *Parker* became unbearable. Finally they could stand it no longer. The crew of *Morse* watched in utter disbelief as one of *Parker*'s men tore away the lines that bound him to the rigging and, with a wild yell, consigned himself to the sea and whatever flotsam he might encounter. In a few minutes another followed his example, then another and another, until the last man, the captain, was seen to throw himself overboard and disappear in the angry billows. Those on *Morse* were horror-stricken at the sight they were compelled to view. Then *William F. Parker* herself began to break up.[12]

"The last we saw," said Flinn of the *Parker*'s men, "was two of them who were on two floating spars lashed. One looked to be the mate, as he wore a coat, and another a sailor. The latter was washed off the spar, then on again and then off, and never in all my life did I see anything so heartrending as that man's fight for his life. Slowly he would slip away from the spar, until at last he had nothing but his shoulder to the mast and then a big wave came and washed him away. It seemed to take the last bit of courage out of us [on *Morse*] when we saw him go."[13]

The survivors on *Morse* cursed their luck and the tug *Argus* for not at least sending a boat. "They left," recalled one angry seaman, "and had a lifeboat been sent to us after they reached shore the whole of the *Parker*'s crew could have been saved." Yet no one could afford to worry about what had just transpired, for holding on against the constant battering and the still relentless fury of the storm required almost superhuman effort. "Every time the *Morse* would go up and come down it would thump us against the rigging, and for twelve hours after we saw the [last] man on the *Parker* go down we remained and suffered." Throughout the night that followed, the storm howled and beat against them. And throughout the night the heroic Captain Crocker "kept his courage, and frequently urged his men to keep up heart, as he still had confidence that some one would come from the shore and render aid."[14]

Not far to the north, the little Philadelphia tug *A. L. Luckenbach* was putting into Salem Cove on the New Jersey side of the bay. Having learned of the disaster unfolding at the capes and on the bay itself, she had left Philadelphia Tuesday night under the command of Captain Henry A. Williamson to offer assistance. On Wednesday morning, with the storm having subsided somewhat, she proceeded but a short distance down when she encountered a heavily battered schooner called *Lizzie D. Babcock* making for safety. *Babcock*'s master grimly informed Williamson that there was a waterlogged schooner "drifting" in the vicinity of Fourteen Foot Bank, "a total loss and all hands on board drowned." From the style of the craft it was estimated she may have had seven men aboard, but from every appearance all on board had perished. He also informed that another vessel, identified as *J. & L. Bryan,* was wrecked and appeared to be drifting to the southwest with her crew in the rigging. *Luckenbach* immediately proceeded down to see what could be done.[15]

About 10:00 A.M., Williamson spotted the wreck of *Morse* and, not a hundred yards away, what little remained of *Parker*. Between 2:00 and 3:00 P.M., after hours of clawing her way into position, the tug finally hove in close to *Morse*, still lying on her beam-ends. The little steamer's arrival came none too soon. All of the schooner's men, after more than forty hours lashed to the rigging, were exhausted and had all but given up. Several "had already made ready to throw themselves overboard." Unfortunately, the sea was running so high that, try as he might, Williamson dared not bring his tug closer than twenty yards from the wreck. His mere presence, however, served to offer *Morse*'s beleaguered crew renewed hope, and their resolve to hold on immediately escalated. Williamson promptly dropped anchor and attempted to deploy a small boat but in so doing drifted across a shoal and broke his windlass, preventing him from retrieving his anchor until nightfall.

Williamson refused to give up and lay by *Morse* throughout the night. Early in the morning, he again attempted a rescue. He still could not field his small boats. Nevertheless, he maneuvered the tug as close as possible to the wreck, dropped anchor within one hundred feet of her, and threw lines with leads on the end to sailors clinging to the rigging. Once they had grasped the lines, they were directed to coil them about their bodies and jump overboard. Then, one by one, they were hauled over to *Luckenbach*. When the last man was finally safely on board, all were taken into the warm engine room and revived. Their recovery had been timely, for almost as soon as the last crewman had leaped into the sea, *Morse* broke up, and in a short time nothing remained but a few of her shattered bones floating on the water.[16]

Captain Williamson at once steered his boat toward the Lewes Life Saving Station. En route, between the Brandywine and Brown shoals, "one of the most dangerous places on the shore," he encountered an abandoned and waterlogged vessel, with her flags still up and Union down. She proved to be the schooner *William O. Snow*, lately commanded by Captain William B. Crosby, owned in Bath, Maine, and bound from Norfolk for Providence with a load of coal taken on at Philadelphia. Examination revealed her to be in fairly good condition. It was readily apparent, however, that the crew had taken to the mastheads for, as Williamson later testified, "you could see where they had tarpaulins to protect them . . . I think there is no doubt the crew of the *Snow* have all perished. From appearances they have got in their yawl boat and been drowned, and that is the way they would come to save themselves."[17]

*Luckenbach* arrived at Lewes about 2:00 P.M. The exhausted and half-starved crew of *Morse* were taken ashore and made as comfortable as possible. Reflecting the appreciation of the late schooner's entire crew, Frendenth Flinn heaped accolades on their rescuer: "The captain of the tug deserves all praise. He never left us all that weary night and his manly courage saved our lives."[18]

When *Luckenbach* reported her efforts to the Lewes Life Saving Station, Williamson learned of the sad fate of the crewmen of *William O. Snow*. The schooner's yawl, broken in half, had just washed ashore near the pier. It was conjectured that the crew had jumped into the boat, and were subsequently drowned. The tug *Argus,* which had just brought in the crew rescued from the Maritime Exchange, all of whom had been isolated for days on the breakwater, immediately turned about and set out in search of the missing men. That afternoon, she would relocate *Snow* and about 3:00 P.M. shipped the schooner's anchors and towed her to the Brandywine Shoal. There, in shallow water, Captain Barnard, set about pumping the wreck out. After three hours, more than four feet of water had been removed and the schooner was hauled to Philadelphia. The bodies of her crew would never be found.[19]


Captain D. A. Risley's schooner *J. & L. Bryan* was a "strongly built" vessel owned in Somers Point, New Jersey, and operated out of Philadelphia.[20] On the evening of Monday, September 8, soon after setting out from Greenwich Wharf, Risley had seen the storm coming and sought to prepare for it by taking up an anchorage on the mudflats of Morris River. Even the best preparations were no match for the tempest that beset his ship, relentlessly driving it down to Delaware Bay. "When the storm struck us [the next morning]," recalled Otto Kaiser, the mate, "all necessary preparations were made for safety, but our anchor slipped after a half hour and we were soon at the mercy of the sea." Just before dark one of the masts "came crushing across the boat and several of us had narrow escapes from death in that way. When the steering apparatus broke we saw that our only chance was to lash ourselves to floating debris." It had taken less than an hour for the schooner to founder on the shoals and start breaking up. The captain and steward, Frederick Freeman, and two seamen lashed themselves to a mast, while Kaiser, a black West Indian seaman named Pete Nelson, and another man bound themselves by lines wrapped around their wastes and tied to the cabin hatch.[21]

By 6:00 P.M. everyone was prepared to die. Suddenly, four lumbering coal-laden barges, later identified as *Tonawanda*, *Wallace*, *Consilda*, and *St. Cloud*, floated into view, accompanied by the struggling little tug *C. W. Morris*. All were in obvious trouble. Then, as quickly as they had appeared ghostlike out of the storm, they were gone. Though no one could have known it, all four barges were doomed. For the men lashed to *J. & L. Bryan*, the sighting had seemed a mere apparition amid a much greater nightmare.[22]

Soon after the barges had disappeared, an enormous wave struck the wreck, driving Kaiser, Nelson, one of the new crewmen, and the cabin hatch to which they were lashed from the ship and into the water. The three men drifted into the evening darkness, holding onto the makeshift raft for dear life. They watched in awe as the mainmast of their ship tumbled into the deep and disappeared along with Captain Risley and their shipmates who had lashed themselves to it. The waves were mountainously high, and with each summit that crashed down on them, the ropes they had around their waists cut into their flesh ever more deeply.

"It was a terrible night," Kaiser later recalled. "Almost every few minutes we would be in the midst of debris and then up against the side of a vessel. The unknown man was on one end of our raft. I was next to him and Nelson on the other side of me. Several times the raft was on top of us, and one time for fifteen minutes we were submerged and only by superhuman effort did we turn ... The unknown man finally got tangled up in some debris and was drowned, and then we made an effort to keep his body with us, but for our own safety we were compelled to cast it adrift. To add to the horror of the night we saw two vessels go to pieces, and I believe every soul on board met death in that howling hell of waters."[23]

Kaiser and Nelson had been watching the death throes of *Parker* and *Morris*. From their peculiar vantage point they had seen the *Parker*'s men drop into the sea, one by one, until Captain Wheaton himself disappeared. "We watched the floating debris," noted Kaiser, "to see if there was anything we could see of the men, but was unable to see what became of them." Somehow the two men managed to survive the night. At dawn they could see the breakwater and realized they were mercifully drifting inshore instead of out to sea. Between 9:00 and 10:00 A.M. they were thrown by the waves onto the beach about two miles from Lewes, and a full seventeen miles from the scene of the wreck. They were bruised and battered, their hands swollen and torn from pulling on their ropes, but otherwise uninjured. Slowly they hiked to the Lewes Life Saving Station, where they related their tragic tale.[24]

For Otto Kaiser it had been his second narrow escape in two years, for during the Blizzard of '88 he had been rescued from the wreck of the *Elizabeth S. Lee* in the same port he had just washed up on.[25]

It was unfortunate that the disaster that had befallen many vessels on Delaware Bay had not occurred within the assistance radius of the lifesavers of Lewes, Cape Henlopen, and Rehoboth, all of whom had been expecting and preparing for the worst. They had, of course, gotten what they expected as the coastline, particularly in the vicinity of the Delaware Breakwater, was littered with scores of wrecked and stranded vessels.

No one was surprised when the first patrol to get out on the morning of Wednesday, September 10, reported a large Italian bark called *Il Salvatore* hard aground near the Iron Pier, about a mile distant and east of the station. She had been en route from Philadelphia for Cagliari, Italy, with a lading of oil but had made the mistake of trying to ride out the weather at the breakwater. Captain Clampitt ordered the surfboat immediately run out, but the tempest and flooding were so great his men could not manually drag it to the wreck site. The captain immediately ordered a team of oxen brought up from the Rehoboth station, eight miles to the south, and then set off to personally discover the condition of the unfortunate Italians. Accompanied by the first dim, gray light of dawn, and a number of local volunteers picked up along the way, he arrived on the scene to discover the bark pressed hard into the pier and rapidly breaking up. He quickly shouted orders for the Italians to abandon ship and leap for the pier. Within minutes, the entire crew had escaped with but trifling injuries. By this time, the lifesavers from the Cape Henlopen station had arrived on the scene and helped accompany the shipwreck victims to the Lewes station.[26]

No sooner had the Henlopen crew reached the Lewes station with the Italians than another storm victim, the two-masted schooner *Charles P. Stickney,* was seen to have snapped her anchor chains and driven ashore a mile to the west. The lifesavers expeditiously moved to field the beach apparatus on its cart, but breaking waves had obliterated the boat run. Incredibly, the station house itself, normally forty feet above high water, was under assault by the sea and steadily being undermined. Thinking quickly, the lifesavers swiftly dismantled the cart, passed the pieces through the back window of the station, reassembled it outside, and were soon on their way to the stranded schooner. *Stickney,* fortunately, had grounded barely seventy-five yards from the shore, and the first effort to get a line to her with the Lyle gun was a success. Her crew of six were quickly rescued in the breeches buoy and sent back to the station. Within minutes after their departure, the schooner had virtually disintegrated.[27]

About a quarter mile west of the station, Captain Benjamin Latham's fishing schooner *Gertrude Summers* had also been driven ashore after her chains parted, not far from the site of another, much older, wreck that had lain on the beach for some time. The lifesavers, however, had been obliged to make some hasty repairs to the beach apparatus and had returned to the station before being able to begin the rescue of the *Summers* crew. Unfortunately, because of the disposition of the earlier wreck, they found it impossible to position their equipment in the normal manner. Undismayed, they carried the Lyle gun into the second story of a neighboring boathouse and fired the line through the window to *Summers*. With the waves breaking not only over the top of the schooner but against the sides of the boathouse as well, both were in imminent danger of destruction. The lifesavers worked quickly to get the breeches buoy rigged even as the sea poured through the windows and obstructed their efforts. One by one, the crewmen of *Gertrude Summers* were hauled from their ship and into the second story window of the boathouse, until all aboard had been saved. After Captain Latham was finally ashore, he informed his rescuers, with a cheerful wink, that he had survived no less than four previous shipwrecks and was happy to say "he had fooled Davy Jones once again."[28]

After another brief visit to the station to repair some badly damaged shot lines, Clampitt and part of his crew rushed to the relief of the next storm victim, the oceangoing fishing schooner *J. F. Becker*, which had dragged her anchors and stranded not far from *Summers*. When the lifesavers and a number of local volunteers appeared on the beach, the desperate fisherman fastened a line to a timber, threw it overboard, and watched as it was driven by the waves toward the rescue party. Clampitt's men quickly retrieved the timber end of the rope. A whipline and boatswain's chair was then rigged to run between the schooner and the shore to be hauled back and forth by Clampitt and his men. The nine fishermen aboard *Becker* were thus handily saved.[29]

With the wind and rain refusing to abate, and the beach still flooded by the storm surge, Clampitt and his indefatigables pressed on to their next rescue. The coal-laden schooner *Norena*, with a crew of eight, had been among those anchored at the breakwater to ride out the storm. About noon her anchor chains had parted, and she had been driven onto the outer bar west of the lifesaving station, about two hundred yards from shore but not far from the wreck of *Becker*. Clampitt quickly assessed the situation and chose a diminutive sandy hill from which to operate. By now, his crew were almost robotic in their motions in getting the Lyle gun set up, armed, and aimed. On the first shot, the line whisked directly across the stranded vessel and a hawser was soon set up. This time, however, because of the heavy seas, a closable life-car was deployed rather than the open breeches buoy. After three perilous trips, the entire crew was safely ashore.[30]

Despite the horrible storm, with its hurricane winds, driving rain, and terrifyingly high seas, the arduous work of saving lives was by now becoming an almost by-the-numbers ritual. Repair the gear, move on to the next shipwreck in line, establish a base, set up the Lyle gun, and effect the rescue.

By this time many curiosity seekers had begun to brave the storm to witness the drama unfolding on the beach. Some offered to render what assistance they could. Thus, when Clampitt, his surfmen, and the party of volunteers who were assisting him arrived at the wreck sites of the schooners *Byron M.* and *Alena*

The Lewes Life Saving Station near the end of the nineteenth century (Purnell Collection, Delaware Public Archives, Dover)

*Covert,* a half mile west of the station, he was delighted to discover a rescue effort already under way. The crews had thrown ladders overboard to run lines to the shore. A boatswain's chair was already in operation retrieving eight men from *Alena Covert.* The lifesavers quickly set up their own breeches buoy and rescued six crewmen from *Byron M.* The surfmen next turned their attentions to the schooner *Eunity R. Dyre,* which had come ashore a third of a mile west of the station, and without delay they rescued five more crewmen in the breeches buoy.[31]

As evening was approaching, the team of oxen Clampitt had sent for from Rehoboth finally came in, hauling a new outfit of gear. The lifesavers quickly turned their attention to the schooner *Mina A. Read,* which had become stranded shortly after noon a quarter mile northeast of the station. She was in a deplorable state, with the waves breaking over her, and her seven crewmen and the wife of the steward, the only woman aboard, lodged in the rigging. Again the Lyle gun was readied, but there was only one shot left. The worn and frayed shot line, which had already been spliced several times, parted and the shot was lost. While the Lewes lifesavers considered their next move, reinforcements from the Rehoboth station under Keeper Thomas J. Truxton arrived with fresh gear. This time, a line reached the wreck, but the whipline became hopelessly fouled.[32]

With darkness upon them and the storm continuing unabated, using the surfboat to reach *Read* was now out of the question. Utterly exhausted and not having eaten all day, the lifesavers gave up for the night. Clampitt, however, insisted

Wreck of the Italian bark *Il Salvatore* against the end of the Iron Pier. With her stern completely torn off, the vessel was a total loss. (Delaware Bay Pilot's Scrapbook, Small Manuscript Collection, Delaware Public Archives, Dover)

The disintegrated remains of the schooner *Charles P. Stickney (lower left)* lie on the beach near the Lewes Life Saving Station. Four stranded but relatively intact vessels await assistance nearby. (Delaware Bay Pilot's Scrapbook, Small Manuscript Collection, Delaware Public Archives, Dover)

that a patrol be maintained on the beach until morning, when they might renew their efforts. They slept little throughout that fierce night, but with the dawn pitched in with renewed vigor. The Atlantic surf had moderated somewhat, and the surfmen decided to attempt a lifeboat launch, hitherto deemed impossible, to save the crewmen of *Read.* Each attempt to deploy the vessel met with frustrating defeat. The worn-out crewmen onboard the schooner, who by this time had been in the rigging for eighteen hours, struggled to clear the whipline that had fouled the attempt the night before. Finally the rescue moved forward and was crowned with success. The steward's wife was brought ashore in the breeches buoy, and then, in three successive trips, the remainder of the crew followed. Less than an hour later, the schooner broke into three sections and was totally lost.[33]

There was no shortage of wrecks demanding attention. About midday, a small tug appeared off Lewes with a signal raised for assistance. But there were so many victims of the storm in need of immediate aid that lifesavers could only wave her off. The lifesavers next moved to the Philadelphia schooners *Addie F. Bacon* and *Major William H. Tantum,* which were approximately six hundred yards apart, east and west of the station. Keepers Theodore Salmons and Thomas Truxton and their combined crews from the Cape Henlopen and Rehoboth stations attended to *Tantum,* which lay two hundred yards from the shore, while Clampitt's men assisted *Bacon.* Despite difficulties encountered on each front, where both the surfboat and a life car were employed, the rescues were successful.[34]

Broadside of a sandbar and just west of the lifesaving station lay the wreck of the schooner *J. D. Robinson,* laden with coal and stranded below the Iron Pier not far from another schooner called *Nettie Champion.* All three station crews working together quickly extricated *Robinson's* crew of eight. But *Champion,* in less danger of breaking up, would have to wait her turn, for in the meantime a report had come in of yet another ship ashore, a very large oceangoing vessel, on the point of Cape Henlopen with a substantial crew in far more serious peril. Keeper Salmons and one of his men immediately set off to investigate. While en route, passing the Iron Pier, they observed in the harbor seven men paddling furiously for the shore in a hurriedly constructed raft. With the waves threatening to sink them at any moment, Salmons roused four local volunteers, launched the Lewes surfboat, which had been left behind at the pier the previous day, and speedily effected the rescue.[35]

Leaving the rescued men in the hands of the volunteers, Salmons pressed on for the cape, where he discovered the newly reported wreck, mastless, approximately two hundred yards offshore and with enormous waves crashing over her. The great, unidentified ship proved to be *William R. Grace,* named in honor of a former governor of New York, and owned by the firm of Flynn & Co. of New York. She had been bound from Le Havre, France, for Philadelphia with a cargo of empty oil barrels and twenty-nine persons aboard. "She was brought to anchor off Henlopen," it was later reported, "in hopes of out riding the storm, but the anchors dragged and the hurricane drove the vessel far upon the beach." To prevent capsizing, the crew had cut away her masts and then, undoubtedly aware of their proximity to the Cape Henlopen Life Saving Station, patiently (at first) awaited rescue. Exposed as *Grace* was to the full force of the Atlantic, however, on the very point of the cape, it was soon deemed "impossible for a boat to reach her." The crew quickly became disconsolate and began to succumb to exhaustion.[36]

Salmons immediately sent a messenger to Lewes requesting assistance from the other two teams and then headed down the coast to his own station, about a mile distant, to get the necessary equipment for yet another rescue. At the station he rendezvoused with Clampitt and Truxton and their men, just returned from the rescue of *Bacon* and *Tantum.* Together they bulldogged their way along the flooded beach, directly into the teeth of the nor'easter, hauling their cart and apparatus behind and fighting for every step. Then, just as they arrived, they watched in horror as *Grace's* crew attempted to lower a small boat to land, a desperate measure undertaken by desperate men. The dinghy immediately filled and sank, fortunately before anyone had boarded.[37]

The surfmen were now faced with a dilemma. They could neither use the boat nor were they likely to get a line secured to the wreck since there were no spars left standing for the crew to secure it. Moreover, the elevation of the highest point on the ship was not enough to employ a breeches buoy in the usual manner and keep it or its passenger safely out of the water. Nevertheless, the first shot by the Lyle gun carried a line directly over the ship and it was immediately secured. The whipline and hawser were soon hauled off and fitted to the ship's railing. Then, twenty-five persons were hauled off in as many trips. Each rescue was a harrowing episode, with the breeches buoy one minute skimming through killer waves and the next through the vortex of the hurricane winds. The captain, who was extremely ill, his wife, and an exhausted crew were taken ashore and then painfully made their way to the Cape Henlopen station. There they were warmed and fed, and clothed by donations of the Women's National Relief Association and from the surfmen's own sparse wardrobes.[38]

Four men—the mate, carpenter, steward, and an elderly sea captain who had been onboard as a passenger—remained aboard *Grace* hoping that the vessel might yet be floated by the tide and they could claim right of salvage. But it was not to be. "The vessel was high and dry this morning," the *Philadelphia Inquirer* reported the next day. "She is now in a dangerous position at the point of the cape and should a northeast wind strike her, she will certainly go to fragments. Her masts and most of her rigging are entirely gone, and the boat is racked from top to bottom." The *New York Times,* in a slightly varied report, added that the ship ultimately "was driven well up on the beach and firmly embedded in the sand, and is not likely to be broken up by the surf . . . she is badly strained and is beached so high that it will be impossible to float her again." The four would-be salvors aboard were removed soon afterward by wreckers.[39]

The work of the lifesavers was not yet over. Even as the rescue of the *Grace's* crew was under way, part of the team broke away to attend to the brigantine *Richard T. Green,* which had gone ashore at daybreak several hundred yards west of the Lewes station while bound for Boston with a cargo of logwood from Jeremie, Haiti. Eight crewmen and a local pilot were handily rescued.[40]

Finally, it was *Nettie Champion's* turn. For nearly two days the men aboard the schooner, lying close to the wreck of *J. D. Robinson,* had patiently awaited salvation that some among them thought would never come. The vessel, they real-

The dismasted hulk of *William R. Grace* of New York, 1,900 tons, high and dry on the point of Cape Henlopen, was eventually deemed a total loss. (Delaware Bay Pilot's Scrapbook, Small Manuscript Collection, Delaware Public Archives, Dover)

ized, simply lay too far offshore for rescuers to get a line to her. The surfmen soon fell upon a leap-frogging plan to make their way back out to the wreck of *Robinson* with their Lyle gun and fire a line from her deck to *Champion*. Within a short time, the surfmen had put their boat out and were soon boarding *Robinson* and hauling their gear behind them. A line was tossed to them from *Champion*'s jib boom, hauled in, and made fast. The breeches buoy was then deployed, and soon, despite the great hazard of the ongoing hurricane, her seven crewmen were standing on the deck of *Robinson*. All hands then embarked in the surfboat and, working along a line that had connected the schooner with the shore, were landed safely.[41] Thus was concluded the last rescue of the storm.

At 6:00 P.M. the lifesavers were able to finally set out for their respective stations, drenched to the skin, bone-weary, and hungry. Though at least twenty-nine and possibly as many as fifty lives had been lost on the Delaware Bay, 194 had been saved on the shores and in the nearby waters adjacent to the Rehoboth, Cape Henlopen, and Lewes Life Saving Stations. The lifesavers had provided shelter, food, and even their own clothing for the victims of the ships that had been assisted, as well as for the rescued crews of other storm victims such as *Kate E. Morse, Consilda,* and *S. A. Rudolph.*[42] Captain Clampitt of the Lewes Life Saving Station, who had selflessly orchestrated the majority of rescues, had nothing but praise for his tiny band, and a few recommendations on how their efforts might have been improved.

"It was the worst we have ever had on this coast, and it is Providential that no lives were lost on the beach," he later told a reporter. "The sea was never so angry before or never so high. The six men at this station have to their credit no less than 142 lives saved, and every one of these men were taken from the riggings of the vessels as fast as they were beached and in the face of one of the darkest nights and fiercest of storms. They never seemed to tire, and for two days they worked, never taking a wink of sleep and eating their meals in their hands, but they did not complain. Their work was made doubly hard on account of insufficient accommodations by the government. We need here badly two more lifeboats and two horses to haul the life car out of the water and along the beach. Much valuable time was lost by a lack of these, and much needless work imposed upon tired men."[43]

The heroism the lifesavers had exhibited soon became the focus of national attention and could not go unrewarded, as had happened so often in the past. On October 10, the general superintendent of the Life Saving Service, S. I. Kimball, issued the following letter of commendation to Keepers Clampitt, Salmons, and Truxton:

> Gentlemen: The gallant conduct shown by yourselves and by the crews under your command during the great storm of September 10 to 12 last has been noted by this office. Upon that occasion, notwithstanding an unusually high tide that flooded the beach so as to seriously embarrass your efforts, you combined your crews and gave efficient aid to no less than twenty-two vessels, taking off by boat thirty-nine persons, and by line apparatus one hundred and fifty-five, a total of one hundred and ninety-four persons, not a life being lost from any vessel that came within the scope of your actions.
>
> In this successful work you showed a zeal, a discretion and an ingenuity in availing yourselves of the resources at your command worthy of the highest praise. Undaunted by the perils you encountered, you and your crews manfully worked throughout each day and well into the night without food, enduring extreme fatigue. Such service as this does honor to all engaged in it, to the Life-Saving Service, and to the country. It is the desire of the Secretary of the Treasury to recognize as far as lies in his power the worth of your achievements and he has accordingly directed that the pay of each of you be increased to the maximum amount that can be allowed by existing law to officers of your grade, namely, eight hundred dollars per annum, to take effect from the date of the official oath of each. The official notices of this increase are enclosed herewith.
>
> It is a matter of deep regret that no means exist for compensing in a similar manner the brave surfmen who constituted your crews on that occasion. As they already receive the maximum salary allowed by law, this cannot be done, although the successful results are in equal measure due to their resolute bravery and faithful endurance.[44]

Despite the heroism that captured the admiration of the American public, in the aftermath of the event the inevitable search for someone to blame, a scapegoat, was substantial. Much criticism was laid at the feet of the government and the inadequacy of the Delaware Breakwater itself. Though the breakwater had emerged relatively unscathed, with the exception of a few railings being knocked out, the whole value of the anchorage as a sanctuary was now deemed questionable, as the two monumental storms, in 1888 and 1889, had so clearly exhibited. The breakwater, noted the *New York Times,* which "by reason of its conformation, is capable of affording safe anchorage to only about forty vessels, was crowded with nearly one hundred craft, not half of which could secure adequate protection from the terrific gale."[45]

An early estimate of the damage, initially placed at $750,000, was staggering for the times. Later estimates, that the loss to vessels and property at the breakwater might reach as high as $5 million, were entirely unacceptable. "Of the twenty [*sic*] vessels on the beach here today, it is questionable if ten of them will ever be floated again. Most of them are so firmly embedded in the sand that the expense of removing them would far exceed their value." The *Summers, Stickney, Rudolph, Timour, Hooper, Dyer, Tantum,* and *Grace* were all total losses with cargoes valued at $450,000. The loss of other vessels was expected to reach $200,000. And more than $100,000 would hardly pay for the losses of *Bryan, Morse, Parker,* and the barges *Tonawanda, Wallace, Consilda,* and *St. Cloud.* When the finally tally was in, a terrible total of forty-three vessels were counted as lost or stranded all along the Delaware coast.[46]

By the time wrecking crews had begun to mobilize, on September 14, agents representing insurance companies and ship owners were already descending locust-like on Lewes. Although it was at first expected that several of the stranded vessels at the breakwater might be readily refloated, the overall news was not good. Worse, it was soon revealed that most of the vessels, as in 1888, were uninsured. "A singular thing about the vessels beached," noted one Philadelphia newspaper "was the absolute lack of insurance. Out of all the vessels sunk it is said that only three or four have any insurance on them." The ship *Grace,* valued at $100,000, was among this number, and the loss to its owners would be total.[47]

The true extent of the damage was far greater than at first observed, as updates on other losses continued to come in. The beach, as far south as Rehoboth, and as far north on the Delaware as Wilmington, was lined with debris and wreckage attesting to far more casualties than anyone expected or originally counted. Some of the shipwrecks were identifiable and some were not. At Rehoboth, the schooner *Sarah C. Clarke,* of Bridgeton, New Jersey, had been driven ashore with no one aboard. The pilot boat *Edmunds* had been blown clear across Delaware Bay and stranded on the New Jersey shore. The *Atalanta,* a Norwegian bark, had been beached and broken up at the Iron Pier, and the British bark *Thomas Keller,* from Philadelphia for London, had ended up not far away in like circumstances with no hope of getting off. Sadly, for the close-knit pilot community of Lewes, the pilot boat *Ebe W. Tunnell* and all aboard, most of them survivors of the Blizzard of '88, including some of the town's most esteemed pilots, had been destroyed. As far up the Delaware as Slaughter Beach, eight miles from Milton, at least one three-masted schooner and several fishing yachts were ashore.[48]

News of the losses farther off the Delmarva, though late in coming in, was nevertheless equally devastating. The tale of the Norwegian bark *Sorriden,* originally bound from Falmouth, England, for Haiti, was a case in point. The crippled ship had been picked up on the afternoon of September 14 a few miles from the Delaware capes by the tug *Rattler* and towed into the breakwater. Her fore and topmasts had been blown away during the storm, and two of her men, the second mate and steward, had been washed overboard but not before she had encountered a number of unfortunates worse off than herself. Off Cape Henry she had picked up a dozen men who had been in an open boat for twelve hours after their own ship, the Norwegian bark *Freya*, had foundered in the hurricane. The following day, they had rescued five men from the waterlogged and sinking schooner *C. H. Lister*, which had just lost its captain overboard. Soon afterward she had sighted an abandoned four-masted schooner floating bottom up, before succumbing to storm damage herself.[49]

Destruction to coastal communities and resorts along the Delmarva, all the way from Wilmington to Cape Charles, had been substantial. In many places the "mammoth" sand dunes that lined the coast between Cape Henlopen and Rehoboth, "which have existed as long as the oldest frequenters of the resort can remember," had been washed away by the storm surge. At Ocean City, Maryland, the telegraphic office had ceased to function. The large columns support-

Wrecks such as that of *Timour*, stranded a quarter mile west of the Lewes Life Saving Station, became the subject of considerable curiosity to visitors following the 1889 storm. (Delaware Bay Pilot's Scrapbook, Small Manuscript Collection, Delaware Public Archives, Dover)

ing the porches of the hotels and cottages there had been washed away, doors and windows broken down, and furniture was seen floating everywhere along the beach. During the height of the storm the seas were reported to be breaking on the second story of the posh Atlantic Hotel and Congress Hall. Waves six feet deep were running through the hotels, and the furniture was floating in many of the rooms. The dancing pavilion at the hotel was demolished, and the roofs of several cottages and their porches had been blown away. Not a vestige of a bathhouse remained on the beach. The Ocean City Life Saving Station was so badly damaged that it had to be deserted. At the worst of the storm, a special train had to be sent to the town to rescue the dwellers on the beach. The rescue work was accomplished "by a large number of stout men holding hands and wading through waist deep water." They brought the ladies to the train cars one by one, seated on their hands, and saved them all first. "Several times the rescuers were knocked down. Mr. Stokes, one of the rescue party, was washed out to sea, but an incoming wave threw him back in. The last occupant of the beach, who left last night, expected that all of the cottages and portions of the hotel would be washed away." The damage, it was reported, would amount to many thousands of dollars.[50]

At Rehoboth, during the peak of the tempest, the incredibly high storm surge broke directly over the Bright Hotel and the Douglas House, while Surf Avenue was completely washed away. Excursion boats running to the resorts had ceased operations. At Kitts Hammock, not far from Dover, waterfront hotels had been badly flooded. The resort hotel at Cedar Beach was surrounded by water, and all of the beach houses had been washed out to sea. On the Delaware at Slaughter Beach, hundreds of fishing shanties had been washed away, with many fishermen barely escaping with their lives.[51]

Hardly had the winds died down and the seas subsided than calls for improvements of the Delaware Breakwater were being made in the national press. "The plan of a refuge inside the capes of the Delaware is a noble one but wrongly executed," stated one editorial in a Philadelphia paper.

> The place now is a trap for shipping. Vessels run in there to avoid a coming storm, and are wrecked at their anchors, while their crews are drowned. Almost every great storm makes victims at the Breakwater. There have been little or no loss of life from the present storm anywhere except at the Breakwater, and there it has been fearful. The great, rich, enterprising Government of the United States should remedy this state of things without delay. It is possible that something will be done in this direction by the coming Congress, as the appalling loss of life and property by this storm will still be fresh in memory when it meets, and surely some of the Congressmen whose constituents have vital interests depending on a safe harbor inside the Capes will be thoughtful enough to bring up the subject. The government should do this work for its own benefit as well as in return for the enormous revenues it derives from the commerce to which the desired works would afford an important help. The government's own vessels are likely to have frequent need to take shelter there, and certainly the structure should be built for the encouragement of commerce, if for no other reason. Our com-

mercial bodies should bring to bear all the influence they have to secure a new break-water at the earliest date possible.[52]

Even the staid *New York Times* was appalled. The 2,500-foot-long breakwater, which had been created in 1828 at a cost exceeding $2 million and later enlarged with a stone 1,500-foot-long ice breaker extending obtusely from the main breakwater, had originally been designed to protect the harbor from floating ice. Between 1828 and 1860 the structure had been adequate to provide protection for twenty to twenty-five vessels under its walls, but the rapid increase in the coasting trade had overtaxed its capacity, and innumerable three-and four-masted schooners, as well as many foreign vessels, both steam and sail, would come in at the least sign of degenerating weather. "It is a rare day when at least fifty sails cannot be counted at anchor off the Lewes shore." Improvement was imperative.[53]

In 1892, bowing to public pressure and the lessons so persuasively demonstrated by the disastrous storms of 1888 and 1889, the federal government completed the construction of an enormously improved sanctuary dubbed the Harbor of Refuge, which, when combined with the extant Delaware Breakwater, provided one thousand acres of safe anchorage. It was not a perfect solution, for losses would still be suffered from time to time. Yet, never again would Mother Nature claim such an enormous number of victims at one time at the dangerous mouth of Delaware Bay.[54]

Not long after the terrible hurricane of 1889 had passed, a seaman was examining the incredible damage sustained by his ship, *Thomas F. Bayard,* when the tip of a bright blue ribbon standing out amid the sand and wreckage that covered the deck caught his eye. Bending over to pick it up, he discovered the ribbon still bound a packet of letters addressed in a delicate, feminine hand. They bore the name and address of one Captain D. A. Risley, late commander of the ill-fated schooner *Byrne,* who now lay asleep in the deep a full twenty miles away. How the letters came such a long way to end up on the deck of *Bayard* in such perfect condition "is one of the many singular things of this great storm."[55]

# 17

## Poor Pussy

The weather reports reaching the New York Navy Yard on the morning of October 9, 1891, were not encouraging as Lieutenant W. E. Cowles conducted a last-minute inspection of the Presidential Yacht *Despatch*. Captains of incoming vessels had nothing but discouraging news to relate concerning the awful storms that had plagued the Atlantic for the last two weeks. No fewer than two terrible gales had developed into full-fledged hurricanes that had caused unending concern for the safety of many ships at sea, and the weather had yet to settle down.[1] Cowles, however, had little choice in the matter, for when the commander in chief summoned, he had to go. *Despatch* would have to be at the Washington Navy Yard by October 11, storm or no storm, even if Neptune himself stood in the way.

The voyage was to be an auspicious one, for *Despatch* had been called back to the capital city to take onboard President Benjamin Harrison, Secretary of the Navy Benjamin Tracy, and a number of high-ranking naval officers for a more-than-routine cruise. The ship was scheduled to convey them down the Potomac to the new naval proving grounds at Indian Head, Maryland, where they were to witness projectile testing of revolutionary nickel-steel armor plates for use in new warships. It was also scheduled to be the ship's last official voyage after serving for nearly eleven years as the presidential yacht. Being old and out of repair, with her machinery weakened by constant use and her boilers almost played out, she was to be placed out of commission at the Washington Navy Yard and replaced by the dispatch boat *Dolphin,* which was even then being outfitted at Norfolk.[2]

Cowles undoubtedly had little time to reflect on the illustrious career of his ship as she steamed out of old Wallabout Bay and into the East River, but he, if not all seventy-four of the officers and seamen aboard, likely knew it by heart. George Steers had originally built the ship in 1873 as a private yacht for a well-known New York stockbroker named Henry C. Smith at a cost of $200,000. Smith's orders to Steers had been for him to construct the "largest and handsomest yacht afloat," which he had more than accomplished. At 200 feet long on deck, 25½ feet abeam, 15½ feet depth of hold, and with a draft of 19½ feet, the ship was said to easily be the largest private yacht afloat in the world. She was a roomy seven feet between decks and had a net tonnage of 490, a displacement of

560 tons, and a coal capacity of 124 tons. Her indicated horsepower was 515, and during her heyday her speed had officially been clocked at 12½ knots, although Cowles had once seen her reach 15 knots. Her first owner had christened her *Americus*.[3]

Smith did not retain ownership for long, for soon after the vessel had been delivered, he experienced financial reverses that compelled him to place *Americus* up for auction at New York. The U.S. Navy liked the ship for her speed, construction, and luxury. Her timbers were fine seasoned oak and mahogany, and her 174-foot keel was of oak. Her cabin was the largest and the finest the navy had seen. A unique feature of her outfit was seats that could be transformed into berths when occasion required. Moreover, she was a bargain that could not be passed up. The service snapped her up for less than half the price Smith had paid only a few months earlier.[4] *Americus* was formally commissioned as the U.S. Navy warship *Despatch* on November 23, 1873, and placed under the command of Lieutenant Commander F. Rodgers. Altered for naval service, she was substantially lightened and armed with three twenty-pounder Parrott guns (which were later replaced by a single breech-loading six-pounder), and manned with a complement of eighty-one men.[5]

In December 1873 *Despatch* was assigned to the North Atlantic Station and, with a cargo of ammunition, joined the American fleet assembling at Key West, Florida, in anticipation of war with Spain. The casus belli centered on the seizure of the American steamer *Virginius* by the Spanish cruiser *Tornado* for allegedly "filibustering" (illegal privateering) in Spanish waters. *Virginius* had been hauled into Santiago de Cuba and was immediately condemned by the Spanish. The capture became an international incident that sent the United States to a war footing when fifty-three of the steamer's passengers and crew were condemned as pirates and summarily executed by the Spanish. Fortunately, after protracted diplomatic negotiations, 102 survivors were delivered to the USS *Juriata*. *Virginius* was then to be turned over to Captain W. D. Whiting, chief of staff of the North Atlantic Fleet, who was to be conveyed to Bahia Honda aboard *Despatch*. On his arrival Whiting took charge of *Virginius,* after which the purported pirate steamer was taken under tow to Key West. It had been an auspicious initiation into naval service for *Despatch*. She served thereafter in the fleet as a dispatch and relief vessel, participating in squadron drills until April 24, 1874, when she returned to the Washington Navy Yard.[6]

For the next three years *Despatch* operated from her base at Washington carrying out special duty assignments and from time to time operating in conjunction with the North Atlantic Fleet along the eastern seaboard of the United States and in the Gulf of Mexico. Occasionally she was employed in towing the aging fleet of Civil War–era ironclad monitors from place to place and in spar torpedo experiments at Newport, Rhode Island. Owing to her splendid outfit and roominess inside, she was even used on several occasions to transport the Secretary of the Navy and Senate committees, which undoubtedly led to her only foreign assignment.[7]

In 1877 the Russo-Turkish War was already well under way when *Despatch* was assigned to transport the American minister, Ambassador Mayard, to Constantinople. Departing for the Mediterranean on April 20, she arrived at her destination on June 14 to find the Turkish capital in a state of turmoil and internal political unrest. Although assigned to serve the American embassy as a dispatch vessel, she would remain at anchor off the city for thirteen months, as much a symbol of the American presence in that far corner of the world as a means of immediate escape from the city for the U.S. delegation should it be required. Finally, in 1879 she was detached from the mission and returned to her home port, where on July 9 she was placed out of commission to take on new boilers. Recommissioned on June 8 of the following year, she was employed as a practice ship and cruised the east coast with cadet engineers from the Annapolis Naval Academy. Then, on October 19, 1880, she received new orders and perhaps the highest honor an American naval vessel might achieve. The flag of the commander in chief, the president of the United States of America, was to be raised on her for the first time as the presidential yacht, although she would conduct other services as required. Though temporarily out of commission at Washington from September 23 to October 19, 1880, for the next eleven years she would operate principally in the Potomac River and Chesapeake Bay and along the East Coast from Norfolk to Maine, engaging in many unique duties. She was often used by the president, the secretary of the navy and other members of the cabinet, congressional committees, members of naval boards conducting inspections, and for assorted ceremonial assignments. From time to time she carried dispatches and men to the fleet and along the East Coast, towed into port or destroyed badly injured ships and wrecks, and escorted new naval vessels during their sea trials. From mid-December 1881 to early June 1882 she was employed in surveying Samana Bay and the Yuna River, Cuba.[8]

During her long career serving the president, *Despatch* would welcome aboard many distinguished guests as her passengers, both foreign and American, while no fewer than five presidents or former presidents—Hayes, Garfield, Arthur, Cleveland, and Harrison—would tread upon her decks. Grover Cleveland would twice be her passenger, once during the funeral rites for the late President Ulysses S. Grant in 1885 and again at the unveiling of the Statue of Liberty in October 1886. Her ceremonial duties were numerous. In 1888, for instance, she represented the Navy Department at the launching of the new cruisers *Yorktown* and *Baltimore* and the dynamite boat *Vesuvius* at Philadelphia.

At the centennial celebration of Washington's inauguration in April 1891, *Despatch* carried President Benjamin Harrison, Vice President Levi Parsons Morton, and a distinguished assemblage of statesmen, military leaders, and civilians from Elizabethport to the foot of Wall Street, New York, occupying the foremost position "in the finest naval pageant" the country had ever seen. During her special services, she also carried foreign celebrities, including Emperor Don Pedro of Brazil, King Kalakaua and Queen Kaplolani of Hawaii, and British dignitaries such as Sir Joseph Chamberlain, Lord Chief Justice Coleridge, and the Duke of Argyle.[9]

The boats carried by *Despatch* were as historic as the ship itself was. Her whaleboat and gig had been used in the expedition of the *Bear* and *Thetis* and were employed in the rescue of the starving Greely expedition in the Arctic re-

USS *Despatch,* ca. 1874 (The Mariners' Museum, Newport News, VA)

gions at Cape Sabine, Ellesmer Island, in 1884. The gig was named *Dorothy,* after the young daughter of Secretary of the Navy William Collins Whitney. The yacht's barge, which was decorated on the bows with the naval symbol of the United States, was named *Queen Kaplolani,* as that royal lady was the first to use it and the flag of her country the first to fly from its staff astern. Her furnishings were elegant, and during her later service her silverware and china alone were valued at $30,000.[10]

It was on the decks of *Despatch* that Senator Evarts once made his famous retort to Lord Chief Justice Coleridge of England. The yacht was taking a resplendent party of diplomats and dignitaries, both foreign and domestic, down the Potomac, when Coleridge remarked to the senator that he doubted the anecdote that told how President Washington once threw a dollar across the river. He thought the distance too great. "My lord," the senator replied without missing a beat, "you must remember that a dollar went further in those days than it would go now."[11]

For all its ceremonial importance, like every vessel afloat, *Despatch* was not impervious to accidents. She had been aground on several occasions, once when Secretary Tracy had been aboard. "Much enjoyment was had at his expense," it was later noted in the press, "by claiming that he was in command ex-officio, and therefore should be subjected to a court of inquiry." Tracy, however, was anything but gun shy. As recently as August 1891 the secretary had seen fit to cruise along the New England coast in the presidential yacht to review the fleet, after which the ship put into New York for what would prove to be the last visit of her long and illustrious career.[12]

As the crew cast off the lines at the Navy Yard wharf, no one paid much attention to the pair of frisky, well-fed collies or the Maltese cat that had for years served as pets and mascots onboard *Despatch* or Secretary of the Navy Tracy's pet dog Docksey, which for some unknown reason was onboard for the trip. The mascots had been lucky charms that had seen the ship through not a few difficult seas. But when a frazzled stray black cat, undoubtedly a denizen of the garbage-filled alleys of the Brooklyn waterfront, jumped aboard, some of the more superstitious sailors became uneasy. The uninvited guest, several groused, was an omen of bad luck and bode only ill fortune, yet when she disappeared below decks as the ship pulled away from the shore, it was already too late to capture her and throw her off. The midnight-colored vagrant would remain aboard.[13]

As *Despatch* steamed down the East River without incident, and then east toward the New York narrows, all thoughts of the uninvited guest were lost in the well-orchestrated rhythm of work. Within an hour, the ship had passed through the narrows, and then out to sea, intending to go down to Cape Charles, turn into Chesapeake Bay, proceed up the bay to the Potomac, and thence to Washington. In about forty-eight hours at most she would be lying at her familiar old berth at the Washington Navy Yard, ready for her last presidential assignment before retirement. As she entered the open Atlantic, however, it was obvious that the recent weather reports had not been far off the mark. Foul winds and an ugly sea had again picked up. Cowles consulted the other officers onboard, Lieutenants York, Neel, and Mulligan, Paymaster Heap, Chief Engineer Ogden, and even Assistant Surgeon Gatewood, and decided to hug the coast, thereby escaping any bad weather that might have been kicked up farther out as a byproduct of the latest hurricane from Bermuda, which had already been making things disagreeable and dangerous all along the Atlantic coastline.[14]

The voyage along the New Jersey coast proceeded as normal, but with the onset of evening, after *Despatch* had passed Delaware Bay, a thick fog set in, forcing Lieutenant Cowles to reduce speed. Then sour weather arrived, with treacherous winds that were soon reaching gale force, and high seas "with a decided land swell." By midnight, sea conditions were atrocious.[15]

Aware that he was approaching the notorious killing shoals of Assateague, Cowles paced the deck, constantly scanning the dark horizon for signs of the Winter Quarter Shoal lightship or the great red and white spire of the Assateague Island light. The island, he knew, was "one of the most inhospitable-looking places on the Atlantic coast." Fronting the sea for more than thirty miles and sparsely inhabited, its most dominant feature was a line of high sand hills which overlooked the ocean, and from which one could see a long line of breakers and seemingly endless tracts of low-lying marshes and meadows. In the middle of the southern end of the island, which had an average breadth of about a mile and a half, stood the great lighthouse itself, and a little further down was the Assateague Beach Life Saving Station. The beacon on the island was marked on the charts as a white light, but it was well known to mariners that on certain foggy or rainy nights what was normally a white light often appeared to be of an orange, almost red tint. "And this," it was later reported, "is how it seems to have appeared to Lieutenant Cowles, who evidently mistook it for the light on the Winter Quarter Shoals lightship, at least a mile and a half from the Assateague lighthouse, which carries a red light."[16] Cowles's error was to prove for *Despatch* a most fatal one indeed.

It was about 3:00 A.M. on the morning of Saturday, October 10, when disaster struck. Most of the crewmen were asleep below. The ship had been proceeding at a reduced speed of eight knots owing as much to her weakened machinery and played-out boilers as to her commander's caution, and, unsuspected by all, a mile and a half off course. The light on Assateague Island, Cowles later reported in his own defense of the events that ensued, was on the charts as a white light but did not "burn as a white light on Saturday morning. It was red." Then he discerned to his immediate horror where he actually was, but it was already too late. *Despatch* suddenly struck a submerged bank of sand head on and was instantly turned by the seas broadside onto the shoal, from which there would be no salvation.[17]

A contemporary artist's view of the wreck of the USS *Despatch* appearing in *The Illustrated American* soon after the actual stranding on Saturday, October 10, 1891. Although the illustration shows an officer, presumably Lieutenant Cowles, directing the salvage of jetsam, little was saved by the crewmen but the clothes on their backs. (The Mariners' Museum, Newport News, VA)

"I never saw worse surf," recalled the lieutenant later. He ordered out an anchor, which, after some considerable difficulty, prevented the ship from thrashing around, but by then she had already beat well upon the shoal. "I knew no power on earth could save her. Water poured into the engine-room, and the ship was shattered from stem to stern."[18]

Although neither Cowles nor any of his men knew precisely where they were at the time, the ship had struck about three miles north of the south end of the island, two miles south of a large sand dune called Sheep's Pen Hill, and seventy-five yards from the beach. Despite their predicament, each member of the crew, though expecting "that in a short time . . . he would be choking in the breakers," remained calm as navy discipline prevailed. Cowles ordered distress flares fired, and three discharges of the ship's gun to alert anyone ashore of the ship's situation. As fate would have it, the wreck had occurred only two and half miles east by north of the Assateague Beach Life Saving Station, and a diligent beach patrolman spotted the flares. By 5:00 A.M., despite the storm, the lifesavers, under the command of Captain James T. Tracy, keeper of the station, arrived after a two-hour trek hauling their boat across the sands, boarded the stranded ship, and at 9:20 A.M. commenced landing the crew. By 11:00 A.M., thanks to a respite in the winds, and after making ten trips in the station lifeboat and in *Despatch*'s own whaleboat, the rescuers had taken off all hands, the ship's three mascots, and Secretary Tracy's dog Docksey, without injury.[19]

"I was reluctant to get out and leave the ship," Cowles later recalled, "but it had to be done, and we escaped in our own boats and in that of the life-saving crew." The escape, however, was not without incident, for just as the last boat was leaving, the ship made a sudden list. The ship's launch, which was still in the davits, suddenly disappeared when her last davit and the yardarms reached the water. The sea was now rolling with increased anger, and a stiff wind was blowing from the northeast at twenty miles an hour. The ship's crew, which had reached the beach with little more than the clothing on their backs, looked with long faces toward the wreck.[20]

"It was a remarkable sight," one of them later said, "to see the ship roll, slow and graceful, so near the shore as she lies, listing toward the sea, apparently endeavoring with each surge to reach the shore, but old Neptune holds her in a tight grasp. Now and then, a crash is heard in the high wind and sea, a davit loosens its hold on shattered planks, [and] mouldings, chairs, tables, boxes, etc. spread themselves over the watery surface." It was, indeed, the opinion of all hands that by daylight the next morning, there would be nothing left to see but wreckage strewn along the beach.[21]

News of the disaster spread quickly, first by word of mouth on the island, then to Pocomoke City on the mainland, and from there by telegraph to the outside world. The first report to reach Washington was simply that the presidential yacht was ashore, broadside on the shoals and fast going to pieces but the officers and crew had been saved. No one yet knew precisely how much peril the ship or its men were in. Rumors immediately began circulating. Secretary of the Navy Tracy, it was reported, had also been onboard. Captain Tracy (no relation to the secretary) soon dispelled such tales in a succinct telegram to the superintendent of the Life Saving Service, S. I. Kimball, while informing him that the wreck was full of water, listing off shore, and fast breaking up. Half of the ship's complement, including her commander and most of the officers, had been carried to the Assateague Life Saving Station, where they "are making out as well as circumstances will allow." The other half, owing to an inadequacy of space and supplies at the station, had been obliged to erect a makeshift shelter from sailcloth and the ship's two boats.[22]

"The unfortunate men," it was later reported, "had a hard time of it on the island. Suffering from exposure to a terrible storm, with no clothing except that in which they reached the shore, and drenched to the skin, they were compelled to eat and sleep, and get what little shelter they could, in a place not fit for dogs. Many of the poor fellows had no shoes. But naval routine and discipline were observed just as on board ship, and the men never grumbled, although they were sorely in need for some time of supplies. All that had been saved from the pantry were several boxes of bread, and all that was saved from the medicine chest was a small bottle of brandy, which did not last long among seventy-odd men continually exposed to a cold and driving storm on a lee shore day and night."[23]

There was unfortunately little mention of the gallant lifesavers who had risked their own lives for the shipwrecked sailors, or that their entire day-to-day existence was conducted in "a place not fit for dogs." It was later reported that the lifesaving crew had, in fact, saved all of the seamen's clothing and all of their boats except one cutter. Lacking essential supplies, however, many seamen began retrieving anything that floated ashore. Finally, several days later Paymaster S. L. Heap, undoubtedly through the assistance of Captain Tracy, was able to arrange for a merchant on Chincoteague Island to bring up an ox-cart filled with provisions.[24]

*Despatch*'s back had been broken by midday of October 10, and the ship was listing off shore twenty to thirty degrees. Captain Tracy signaled Washington that no further assistance could be rendered her, but by then several tugs had already been ordered up from Norfolk, including the wrecking steamer *North America,* to survey the hulk and salvage whatever might be saved. The USS *Yantic* was being sent down from the Brooklyn Navy Yard to recover the crew as soon as she could get under way.[25]

A report was dispatched to the Navy Department by a Lieutenant Wadsworth, inspector of the Life Saving Service, as follows: "*Despatch* is broken up forward of engines, upper works are washed off. But little material is coming ashore here. Officers and crew are well and being made comfortable at station. Will remain until weather abates. *Yantic* was off station Sunday night, but has not been seen since. Thick weather, heavy gale, very high surf." Contrary to Wadsworth's account, however, locals from Assateague and Chincoteague began to appear on the scene, hoping, some said, to scavenge whatever they could that might float ashore, even though it was technically government property. If the media were to be believed, there was apparently much to be had. The reporters from big city newspapers who began to arrive about this time called the locals "born wreckers" who had to be restrained in their nefarious endeavors, and ridiculed them as "odd people."[26]

"The whole beach for over three miles is strewn with wreckage," reported the *Baltimore Sun,* "and it looks as though hundreds of people are along to observe every new object of interest which floats ashore. One man rushes down to clutch a box of cigars, another a box of candles, another one a can of ham. Then here dashes a handsome chair, a large refrigerator tosses about and with one high surge lands high and dry with the hinges broken." The *Peninsula Enterprise,* a local newspaper on the mainland, responded vehemently, claiming that the out-of-state reporters, especially those from New York, possessed "vivid imaginations" and that there was no need for the navy to protect the wreck from the locals.[27]

But a single living thing remained on board *Despatch,* and it soon caught the eye of every sailor standing on the beach—a solitary black cat clinging tenaciously to the highest part of the wreck, near the stern where the savage waves had not yet reached. "Poor pussy," noted one commentary on the event, "with an air of dejection, sat on the highest point she could get. She waited for the end and was apparently resigned to her fate." The end came that night, for on Monday morning her body, battered and lifeless, was discovered on the beach.[28]

By the morning of October 12, the search for a scapegoat had already begun. The navy only awaited Lieutenant Cowles's official report of the loss before it would appoint a court of inquiry to determine who, if anyone, was responsible for the accident. But for a scandal-hungry public that was not enough. It was soon being reported in the *Baltimore Sun,* without any substance, that the "disaster is accounted for by the absence of a lightship at Winter Quarter Shoal, which was taken away a short time ago to be overhauled, and the steersman, supposing the Assateague Light was the lightship's beacon, was misled. The lightship . . . is now in Wilmington, Delaware undergoing repairs."[29]

The U.S. Lighthouse Board, which was responsible for the lightship, was quick to respond, claiming the charges were patently unfair. The board denied "that the loss of the U.S.S. *Despatch* is in any way due to the absence of the regular light ship at Winter Quarter shoal for needed repairs for the reason that a relief ship, the schooner *Drift,* showing the same kind of light, has been stationed there ever since, ample notice of the change having been given six weeks ago." The board then released the text of a dispatch from the head lighthouse inspector, Commander P. E. Harrington, to verify its statement: "PHILADELPHIA, Oct. 13.—Lighthouse board, Washington, D.C.—I believe Winter Quarter light vessel *Drift* is on her station and has not been off of it. I have had reports of her being off of her station or her lights being out and upon visiting her by the tender found her all right. Her light can be seen seven miles with naked eye in clear weather. Newspaper report arises probably from vessels having passed her in hazy weather without seeing *Drift* or light. As soon as I can get services of tender I will have her visited again. P.E. HARRINGTON."[30] The board's prompt rebuttal to the rumors immediately put to rest all charges.

By Wednesday, October 14, the navy rescue ship had yet to arrive, for, unbeknownst to Cowles, the ship had suffered an explosion in its engines while passing the Delaware coast. Concerned over the plight of his men, the lieutenant ordered camp broken. Then, in single file they traipsed across the marshes toward

Chincoteague and caught a boat to the island. After marching through town in military order, merrily singing "The Girl I Left Behind," they posed for pictures at the railroad wharf, raised a hearty cheer for Captain Tracy and his men, issued a few short speeches, and boarded the little steamer *Widgeon* bound for Franklin City. By the time the ship originally sent to rescue them had reached Delaware Bay to make repairs, the crewmen of *Despatch* had already arrived at Philadelphia.[31] Lieutenant Cowles and four of his men remained behind to protect what little had been saved from the wreck: the ship's boats, the gilded eagle from the ship's bow, several flags and some furniture, a life buoy, and several blankets. On October 19, Cowles departed the Delmarva coast by train bound for Washington to face the inevitable investigation and court-martial.[32]

The court-martial went better than Cowles might have expected. The accident, despite the report from the U.S. Lighthouse Board to the contrary, was pinned on a supposition that the light in the Winter Quarter Lightship at the time of the stranding was "entirely out, or was burning dimly." Moreover, after the stranding it had been impossible, he argued, to "have got [the ship] out of the pocket she was in and off the shoals" because of her weak machinery and bad boilers. The court deemed the lieutenant's actions during the event to be proper, and he was fully exonerated from all blame. In 1892 he was promoted to lieutenant commander, and two years later married Anna Roosevelt, sister to Theodore Roosevelt, the future president of the United States. By 1908, W. E. Cowles had achieved the rank of rear admiral.[33]

Captain Tracy and his crew of lifesavers, who had garnered little praise in the press for their prompt and efficient services, received only a note of thanks for the hospitality they had extended to the seventy-five men of the late Presidential Yacht *Despatch*. As for the ship itself, which had last been valued at the time of loss at $135,000, she was sold for salvage on November 12, 1891, barely a month after the disaster. No record of her recovery has been found, although in 1905 brass items belonging to the ship and valued at $165 were reportedly washed up on the shore, the last known relics of a once truly grand ship of state.[34]

## 18

## Five-Poler

The bottom is sandy and dark, and the few stubby, worm-eaten frames protruding from it betray little of their past. They are the bones of a century-old sailing vessel that once plied the Norfolk and New England coal trade. They belonged to a ship that, in her heyday of elegance and grace, helped make a fortune for her owners. Now lobsters and fish hide in her ruins. Not far away, resting in nearly one hundred feet of water, lies another wreck, more substantial in her bulk remains but upside down and broken. She appears as little more than a skeletal framework of disintegrating steel hull plates and bulkheads. Amid her disarticulated ruins stand the shambles of enormous boilers, towering almost twenty feet off the bottom, which are the only reasonable indicator of her once-formidable size. The remnant of the great ship's bow lies curiously bent at a slight angle, perhaps turned askew forever by the impact as she hit bottom on that fatal day when she plunged to her death. It was, in a sad way, a historic day of sorts, when one of the largest American five-masted schooners in history, among the last of her unique breed, collided with the largest American freighter afloat. It was a day that all but heralded the end of the great age of sail.

William F. Palmer had not started off his professional life in the shipping business. Born shortly before the start of the Civil War, he had early on chosen the life of a simple New England schoolteacher. Yet his intelligence, drive, and desire demanded far more from him. By the 1890s he had progressed to become headmaster of the prestigious Bristol Academy in Taunton, Massachusetts, a grimy, industrial town but also a leading New England shipbuilding center. Among its many distinctions, the town had recently earned some notoriety as a center for the bituminous coal trade, which apparently set Headmaster Palmer to thinking.[1]

Palmer was an industrious and inquisitive man of many talents. One of the skills he mastered during his tenure at Bristol Academy was the art and science of naval architecture. By 1899 the headmaster was forty years old and had moved on to become the principal of Malden High School in Malden, Massachusetts. By then, as with many men at midlife, he had begun to reconsider the direction of his career and fortunes. The following year he made the fateful decision to move from schoolteacher to shipper. He resolved not only to start a ship-ping company from scratch but determined that he would also build his own ships. He was as persuasive as he was aggressive and soon found backers, not the least of whom was Captain Lorenzo Dow Baker, one of the most famed and suc-cessful shipping magnates in all New England.[2]

Success was immediate for the novitiate coal shipper following the launching of his first vessel, a distinctive-looking four-masted schooner named *Marie Palmer,* at Bath, Maine, in 1900. Over the next eight years, Palmer would launch no fewer than fifteen schooners, all but two being five-masters, primarily em-ployed as colliers, and each bearing "Palmer" as the last part of its name. The first part, according to rumor, was named in honor of each new ship's primary backer. If that was true, William Palmer apparently had at least eight rich wom-en supporting his endeavors.[3]

All of the Palmer vessels had been constructed at Bath, Waldoboro, or Rock-land, Maine, except for one built in Boston. The largest of the fleet, arguably one of the largest of her class ever constructed, had been the five-masted *Elizabeth Palmer,* built on the Kennebec River at Bath in 1903 by the firm of Percy and Small. The firm was one of four major shipbuilders in that port who led the na-tion in the construction of four-, five-, and even six-masted schooners such as *Wyoming, Edward B. Winslow,* and *Eleanor A. Percy.*[4] *Elizabeth Palmer* was the ninth vessel designed and ordered by Palmer, who sold shares in her ownership for $2,125 each. When completed, the ship was deemed to be one of the largest sailing vessels of her time, measuring 300 feet in length, 48 feet abeam, and 28 feet depth. Her registered tonnage was reported at 3,615 gross and 2,440 net. Like all vessels in the Palmer fleet, her trademark color, unusual for ships em-ployed in the coal trade, was cloud white.[5]

William Palmer and his associates did extremely well with the first vessels of the fleet, but by 1906 work for sailing schooners in the coasting trades had be-gun to fall off rapidly owing to the efficiency of larger, faster, and more pre-dictable steam-powered freighters. Even as the last Palmer ships were sliding off the ways, many sailing vessels were already being dismasted and converted to schooner barges. Yet Palmer pressed on. In 1908, following the launching of his fifteenth and last ship, the *Fuller Palmer,* the former schoolmaster-turned-shipper vested ownership of his flotilla in a corporation called The Palmer Fleet, with Boston as its home port. The following year he died, and the firm of J.S. Winslow and Company, of Portland, Maine, took over the majestic armada of white colliers. In a pragmatic move, the ships were repainted black with white trim and their decor altered to reflect their true mission in life, namely the dirty business of hauling coal under sail. They would be the last of their breed, for by the early 1920s, they would be entirely supplanted by the more profitable steel-hulled, coal-fired, and even diesel-powered freighters many times their own deadweight tonnage capacity.[6]

Standing in sharp contrast to the "five-polers" was the American-Hawaiian Line freighter *Washingtonian,* built in 1914 at Sparrows Point, Maryland, at a cost estimated at between a half million and a million dollars. She was, in fact, one of the most expensive American freighters ever built to that time. Weighing

The launch of the majestic five-masted schooner *Elizabeth Palmer,* one of the last and largest of her kind, at Bath, Maine, in 1903 (The Mariners' Museum, Newport News, VA)

*Washingtonian* was the largest American flag steam freighter of her day. (W. B. Taylor Collection, The Mariners' Museum, Newport News, VA)

in at 6,650 gross tons, this coal-fired steamer was 407 feet in length, 53 feet abeam, and 28 feet deep, and home ported (for registration purposes) at New York. She was the largest freighter under the American flag. Designed specifically to carry salmon from the Pacific Coast fisheries of Oregon and Washington to markets on the Eastern seaboard, her hold was equipped with the latest in modern refrigeration plants. Her maiden voyage, however, possibly owing to a decrease in demand for salmon, would not be to Oregon or Washington, but to the Hawaiian islands, where she was instructed to take aboard a cargo of raw sugar at Honolulu bearing a market value of approximately $1 million.[7]

On December 30, 1914, *Washingtonian* departed Honolulu with nearly ten thousand tons of sugar and miscellaneous merchandise aboard. She sailed with a crew of forty under the command of Captain E. D. Brodhead. A long-time employee of the line, Brodhead had earned his master's license about 1911 and was considered an able navigator. The ship reached Balboa, Panama, without incident on January 17 and passed through the Panama Canal two days later, bound for the Delaware Breakwater.[8]

Sailing in the opposite direction on January 10, from Portland, Maine, with a stopover in Boston, and bound for Norfolk was the *Elizabeth Palmer.* The big schooner, flying along in light ballast, was temporarily under the command of Captain George A. Carlisle, of Boothbay, Maine, who was standing in for her normal skipper, an ailing New Englander named Wallace. Carlisle commanded a crew of thirteen, including one woman, the wife of steward John Andrews. The ship was under full sail and intended to take on a cargo of coal at the Virginia port intended for Portland.[9]

Thus was set the scene for a tragic and symbolic collision between the waning age of sail and the nascent era of the steam freighter.

A "somewhat heavy sea" was running off the Delmarva coast during the predawn hours of January 26, 1915, but the night sky was clear with a comparatively gentle wind blowing. A slight haze hung over the water like a damp sheet. Seeking to make the most of his schooner's sailing capacity in the light breezes, Captain Carlisle had piled on as much canvas as possible and his ship "was speeding like an express train." By 3:30 A.M. *Palmer* was "bowling along at a good eight knots with all possible drawing sail set" off Fenwick Island, about twenty miles south of the Delaware Breakwater, heading on a southwest by south course. Suddenly, out of the night a massive dark shape appeared off the port bow—another vessel, a steamship, heading in a northeast by north direction, directly opposite that of the schooner.[10]

The oncoming steamship proved to be *Washingtonian,* which was moving at a steady twelve-knot clip. Captain Carlisle was well aware that the international navigational rules of the road stated clearly that a steam vessel must yield right of way to a vessel under sails at all times, and thus kept to his course. But the oncoming ship failed to slow down. Suddenly, it became painfully apparent "that the steamer was moving in a direction that would have taken her across our bows, and that our lights were seen too late to avoid us." On the bridge of the steamer, Captain Brodhead, two quartermasters, and a seaman were on watch, but none realized that the great schooner, with all sails set, was moving as fast as eight knots, which proved to be a tragic misjudgment, for she was definitely on a collision course.[11]

"We struck the *Washingtonian* head-on," Carlisle later reported, "making a hole in her almost amidships, the force of the impact smashing in the bow of the schooner." The terrible force of over three thousand tons striking the steamer just forward of the engine keeled her over to her port, trephining a great hole in her side, which instantly caused her to fill with water. Crewmembers who had been sleeping soundly only moments before were tossed from their bunks. *Elizabeth Palmer* "immediately broke away and went ahead about a mile before [her] course was checked." The schooner's jib boom and foretopmast had gone by the boards on impact, and she too began to take on water, but Captain Carlisle was initially optimistic. "I thought," he later reported, "the schooner would keep afloat."[12]

It was soon obvious to all aboard the steamer that she would sink in a matter of minutes. A wireless distress signal was immediately dashed off, even as all hands were ordered to the two lifeboats. Unfortunately not everyone made it. Herman Meyer, a water tender, was last seen rushing about the deck, "and it is presumed by his mates that he went below for some of his effects and was caught by the inrushing water." Several others, panic stricken, jumped or fell into the frigid sea, but the majority took to the lifeboats and survived. Barely ten minutes after the collision, the largest steam freighter to that date to ever fly the American flag slipped beneath the waves bow first, unceremoniously turning turtle as she descended.[13]

Approximately a mile away, *Elizabeth Palmer* was also suffering her own death throes, as water rushed through splintered seams. By 4:30 A.M. the big schooner's decks were awash as she gradually sank to her topgallant bulwarks. Captain Carlisle had little choice but to order all aboard into the motorized lifeboat and head for the Fenwick Island Life Saving Station, believed to lie a mile and a half away. As the only person to escape from either ship with any belongings whatsoever, he carried with him little more than a few shirts and collars that he had managed to stuff into a pillowcase. "The top of the rail," he would later report, "could still be seen level with the water when we came away."[14]

Fortunately the short wireless distress signal sent by *Washingtonian* had been picked up by the Old Dominion Line steamer *Hamilton,* which was cruising only a few miles distant bound for New York. Within an hour, Captain Brodhead and thirty-nine of his men were picked up. Captain Carlisle and his own crew were also recovered just before 6:00 A.M. Even the men who had jumped or fallen into the sea from *Washingtonian* were saved, albeit not by *Hamilton* but by the crew from *Lightship no. 72,* then stationed off Fenwick Island. They had been rescued none too soon, for they were nearing extreme hypothermia when pulled from the water with their clothes frozen stiff about them. They were immediately taken to the lightship and given warm drink. Finally, all were transferred to *Hamilton,* and Brodhead mustered the *Washingtonian* men for roll call. It was then that the absence of Herman Meyer was first discovered.[15]

Having received news of the collision, and as yet entirely unaware that *Elizabeth Palmer* had already gone down, a wrecking company tug called *I. J. Merritt* was dispatched from Norfolk on the night of January 26 "to pick up the schooner . . . and if possible tow her to this port." In the meantime, *Hamilton* had again turned her prow toward New York, where she arrived about the same time *Merritt* was departing Norfolk.[16]

Unquestionably aware that according to the recognized rules of the road, the responsibility for the collision, and the loss of Herman Meyer, rested with himself for failing to yield right of way to a vessel under sail, Captain Brodhead was deeply affected by the loss of his ship—and career. Lawsuits were almost a certainty. By the time *Hamilton* arrived at New York, reporters swarmed the waterfront anxious to go aboard and interview the commander of the largest freighter to ever go down under an American flag. The first person aboard, however, was J. D. Tomlinson, marine superintendent of the American Hawaiian Line, who spoke with the captain in private and prepared a brief statement for the press, merely outlining what everyone already knew: "there was a haze and confirmed Capt. Carlisle's report that the *Washingtonian* had been struck amidships on the starboard side," and Herman Meyer had probably drowned, being the only victim of the disaster. Captain Brodhead and all of his men, not surprisingly considering the circumstances, refused to speak to the press and were immediately sent home by Tomlinson.[17]

The physical and financial loss to both shipping firms was estimated at $2.125 million, of which only $125,000 belonged to J. S. Winslow and Co. The loss to the American Hawaiian Line had been devastating, not only to the ship's owners but also temporarily to the world sugar market. Claus A. Spreckles, president of the Federal Sugar Refining Company, was quick to address the impact the sinking of *Washingtonian* might have on world sugar supplies and prices. "The loss of 10,000 tons of sugar would not ordinarily have any effect on sugar prices," he said, "but at present, conditions are by no means ordinary. The Cuban crop, upon which this country depends for its chief supply is about 200,000 tons behind last year in point of production, owing to rains. In addition, the scarcity of shipping room has recently become an important feature of the sugar market. Owing to the [First World] war, the world's supply of sugar is abnormally low, and we can ill afford to lose a single ton. Well informed shipping interests say there is not sufficient tonnage available to take care of more than 40,000 tons a week of Cuban sugar, and this country will soon be demanding from 50,000 to 80,000 tons a week for its normal requirements, not to mention what will be needed by England and France."[18]

With the loss of *Elizabeth Palmer,* the original fifteen vessels that once comprised the majestic Palmer Fleet had been reduced by accidents and sinkings to only eight vessels. Many saw those that remained as little more than relics of a glorious bygone era when sail commanded the high seas. Within six years the last of the Palmer four- and five-polers would be gone, and steel-hulled, fuel-powered freighters would rule. Though the tragic collision of the two ships had fortunately not been encumbered by great loss of life and was quickly forgotten in the swirl of far more shattering world events, the accident was symbolic, as the new technology replaced that which had governed navigation on the high seas for the last five thousand years.

Today what little remains of *Elizabeth Palmer,* worm-eaten and disintegrating, is little visited. The dark and battered hulk of *Washingtonian,* however, constitutes one of the most visited wreck sites on the eastern seaboard where lucky sport divers can snag a good-sized lobster and touch an emblematic moment in history without even knowing it.

# 19

## The Rules of Engagement

The evening of July 12, 1921, was filled with a frenzy of activity and expectation at the Army Air Base at Langley Field, Virginia. As usual, General William "Billy" Mitchell was in the thick of it as his airmen readied their aircraft for the first round of bombing tests the next day more than sixty miles off the Virginia capes. For Mitchell, the army, the United States, and the world, the tests would prove epochal.

The days following the end of World War I had been both heady and troubling for the U.S. military. The conflict had brought enormous advances in naval, air, and land warfare technology, and the world political stage was still in the process of absorbing them. Mitchell, who had organized and led the first thousand-plane bombing raid in history, had been a strong advocate for ongoing experimentation in military aviation. He believed that air power could be effectively used not only on land but also at sea, and he had been a leading champion of strategic and tactical aerial bombing. But more importantly, he believed that air power could be used to trump sea power. It had been an uphill struggle, for few in either branch of the U.S. military believed aircraft were suitable for more than combat reconnaissance, let alone being employed as ship killers. Mitchell, however, would not be denied.

As part of German war reparations, the United States had received a number of ships belonging to the German high seas fleet that had survived the hostilities. The vessels, which had been taken in by the U.S. Navy, in accordance with treaty obligations had been scheduled to be scrapped or sunk at sea. Several high-ranking officers in both the army and navy suggested that the ships be employed as targets in aerial bombing tests. The navy, whose interest in improved armor plating for its battleships and other capital vessels, agreed. The sea service hoped to determine under controlled conditions precisely how much injury near misses and direct hits might have on battleships and how they could best be protected.[1]

The navy began testing on one of its own obsolete battleships, the USS *Indiana,* but chose to employ placed charges rather than explosives dropped from aircraft, as some leading military experts questioned the ability of an airplane to accurately deliver bombs on a target. The tests, though carried out as planned, proved inconclusive. It was at this point that the navy decided to conduct additional tests using the ex-German navy warships as targets. The army had also been considering using the German ships for its own test program and was preparing to request some ships from the navy. Duplication of effort, then as now, was not a widely accepted approach when it came to government money. Public outcry and congressional pressure soon compelled the navy to invite the army to join in its testing.[2]

With the two rival services obliged to cooperate in the field tests, a period of heated debate over management, methodology, control, procedure, inspection, and so forth ensued, and Billy Mitchell was in the very center of the fight. From the outset, the general argued vociferously that it was the navy's intention to restrict aerial operations to such an extent as to ensure failure and thus disprove the value of aircraft in naval warfare. His constant public haranguing soon led the navy's chief of the Bureau of Aeronautics, Admiral William Moffett, to submit a memo to the secretary of the navy entitled "Publicity Propaganda of General Mitchell Running Contrary to President's Policy." Mitchell refused to be reined in.[3]

Despite the interservice wrangling, final plans for the tests on the German warships were completed in May. The plans were comprehensive and filled with specifics as to the number of aircraft that would be permitted in each sortie, the anchorage site for each target vessel, the number and size of bombs to be dropped, scheduling, inspection of damage, and so forth. One of the preliminary experiments, to be conducted prior to the tests, called for an obsolete American battleship, the USS *Iowa,* to be operated by radio control at sea. She was to be bombed with dummy explosives so as to prevent harming the expensive radio control equipment. The army refused to participate, excusing itself with the justification that dummy bombs had no purpose. Why even bother dropping them if you couldn't study the results? The army had the last laugh in the matter. When the tests were carried out, the ship was lost and an army blimp had to locate it. The navy took small satisfaction in that only two out of eighty bombs dropped had actually struck their target, supporting the sea service's contention that aerial bombing could never be an exact science. Mitchell not only questioned the navy's ability to hit a target but also implied that the poor results of the bombing runs had been intentional.[4]

On June 20 the navy proceeded on with the testing against its first ex-German warship, the *U-117,* moored approximately seventy miles northeast of Virginia Beach in 230 feet of water. Some observers may have felt elated when a dozen U.S. Navy Curtiss F-5Ls began their approach to the old sub. Under her former commander, Otto Dröscher, she had been responsible for sinking no less than twenty-four Allied ships during the war. She went down in less than sixteen minutes. The navy crowed about its bombing expertise but was quick to note that the tiny U-boat was unarmored. The bombing had proven nothing, for the ship was not only unarmored but also immobile. Two days later, two more submarines, *U-140* and *U-148,* also stationary, were sunk off the Virginia capes, this time by naval gunfire.[5] Then it was Billy Mitchell's turn.

The composite air fleet Mitchell selected to employ on the first stage of his own operations included a dozen Sopwith Experimental SE-5 pursuit planes be-

*U-117* and *U-140* awaiting their fate (National Archives, Washington, DC; photo courtesy of Michael Pohuski)

General William "Billy" Mitchell's air force unit arrayed in review at Langley, Virginia, before embarking on their historic mission (National Archives, Washington, DC; photo courtesy of Michael Pohuski)

longing to the First Provisional Pursuit Squadron, all armed with twenty-five-pound Cooper bombs. His small bomber force was commanded by Major Davenport Johnson and comprised three units, the 14th, 50th, and 88th Bombardment Squadrons, totaling twenty-eight Martin 4-B and De Haviland 4-B bombers, with each plane carrying six one-hundred-pound bombs. Three dirigibles and two Caproni airplanes were also available for the project, although only one of the latter would be deployed. An army surveillance squadron made up of ten flying boats commanded by Captain C. H. Reynolds was to be deployed for reconnaissance, while four De Haviland 4-S planes under the command of Lieutenant J. H. Hodges would record the operation from the air using both still and motion-picture cameras. General Mitchell would personally participate in the exercise, flying in his own plane. A backup force was also mobilized but stood in reserve, "on the alert and ready to proceed instantly if necessary against the 'enemy fleet.'" The U.S. Navy would deploy a pair of seven-plane squadrons during the tests, mostly seaplanes based at Hampton Roads. Thus, a total of seventy-one U.S. Army and Navy aircraft were readied to participate in the largest exercise of its kind to date in American history.[6]

With the exception of the army surveillance squadron and the navy's small force, all of the aircraft employed were land-based planes. They would be flying far out over the Atlantic with no available place to put down in case of emergency. It was thus imperative that perfect mechanical performance, navigation, timing, and operational management be achieved. Although a string of navy destroyers had been assigned to take station at every seventh mile from Thimble Shoal Lighthouse in the Chesapeake to the first of the five target ships, along with a number of seaplanes and flying boats, the flight would nevertheless be dangerous.[7]

The first target, the destroyer *G-102,* like all of the vessels ultimately chosen for destruction during the impending demonstrations, had once belonged to the Imperial German Navy and had been acquired as a war prize by the United States, via the British, following the surrender of Germany in October 1918. She had been anchored approximately sixty miles east of Cape Charles to await her denouement. Two miles away, two more ex-German destroyers, *S-132* and *V-43,* awaited their turn on Friday, July 15, as did the heavy cruiser *Frankfurt,* which was scheduled to be sunk on the July 18. Some distance farther away, the magnificent dreadnought *Ostfriesland,* deemed by many as unsinkable, was scheduled for the July 20–21 operation. Already in place and stationed from one to three thousand yards away around the first target were the great bulldogs of the Atlantic fleet, Battleship Division Five, including the USS *Delaware, North Dakota,* and *Florida,* and at least five destroyers, including the USS *Dickerson, Sicard, Leary, Schenck,* and *Herbert.*

General Mitchell, who had personally planned and would superintend the whole air operation for the army, was a fastidious commander. At forty years of age now, he had learned from grim experience in the Great War to leave nothing to chance, for he was not a strong believer in serendipity. He also knew that several navy ships were filled with reporters and dignitaries from the world over.

His men's and his own performance would be under the microscope of not only the War Department but the entire world. No major warship had ever been sunk by aerial bombardment. If he succeeded, the very methodology of making war would be forever altered.

There would be two arms of the operation ahead, with his army fliers all departing from Langley Field and the navy contingent flying out of Hampton Roads. For the army, it would be a straightway course of eighty-five miles to the first target ship. Each army plane would have enough fuel to reach its destination, approximately a half hour's flying time over the target itself, and the return flight home. The total distance would be approximately two hundred miles per flight. The first to have a crack at the *G-102* would be the fast little Sopwiths, then the De Havilands. The navy planes would also have an equal shot at the target and, he knew, they were now determined to outperform the army before the eyes of the nation and the world. Interservice rivalry had never before been so blatant or intense.[8]

When the first group of surveillance planes took off from Langley about 8:00 A.M., followed immediately afterward by the fast pursuit planes, the weather conditions over the Atlantic could not have been better. As the V-formation of Sopwiths pressed eastward, however, they began to encounter occasional cloudbanks and light drizzles. Then, as the first surveillance planes arrived over the target on schedule at 9:00 A.M., the Sopwiths, farther behind, encountered surprisingly dense, low cloudbanks and a heavy thunderstorm. None was deterred.[9]

On the blue-green seas below, the fleet watched and waited in anticipation. Aboard the U.S. Navy transport ship *Henderson,* Air Commodore L. E. O. Charlton, of the British embassy in Washington, stood transfixed amid the naval air attaché's staff watching the surveillance aircraft begin their condor-like circling half a mile away above the ex-German warship. The air and naval attachés for France, Italy, Portugal, China, Japan, Brazil, and Chile stood by their own interpreters, anxious not to miss a word of the proceedings as the Sopwiths finally arrived in V-formation and then peeled off to circle the target.[10]

The destroyer *G-102* before her destruction (National Archives, Washington, DC; photo courtesy of Michael Pohuski)

At precisely 9:30 A.M. the speedy army pursuit planes began strafing the target with twenty-five-pound Cooper bombs. The little bombs had been designed to wound crewmen and drive them from the decks of a ship so that when the bombers arrived they would encounter no opposition. Their sweep was comparatively low, and out of forty bombs dropped, twenty had been direct hits.[11]

Above the fray, General Mitchell circled in his own De Haviland. He had arrived almost unnoticed with the first surveillance group and had stayed to studiously observe the Sopwiths in their attack. With the Sopwiths' departure, he dropped down close above *G-102* to personally survey the damage. The destruction was significant. The stern, in particular, had been badly mauled, and little else escaped some form of injury. Had there been an actual crew aboard the ship, it was clear that not a man would have been left standing topside.[12]

Minutes passed. Then, at 10:00 A.M. the 14th Bomber Squadron appeared, flying in a tight V-formation, followed by two seven-plane squadrons of navy seaplanes and army De Havilands, one on each side. For the next ten minutes, twenty-eight bombers maneuvered to begin their attack approach. Each of the planes was loaded with six three-hundred-pound demolition bombs. Then the assault began at an altitude of 2,000 to 2,500 feet. The navy planes first dispatched bomb after bomb, forty-four in all. Not until 10:20 A.M., however, was the first hit made. Shortly afterward, a bomb ricocheted off the destroyer's bow just as it was inundated by a wave. Then, an army bomber, with the fourth three-hundred-pounder dropped, made a second direct hit. It struck amidships of the funnels and wrought such destruction that the destroyer lunged forward, kicked her stern in the air, and began to sink immediately. For a single, critical moment, everyone could see the damage. The ship had been split entirely in half lengthwise, her bridge a shattered heap. At the moment of impact, Mitchell himself was directly above the ship.[13]

From the navy command ship, a signal was raised calling the attackers off. The army planes had been operating at far faster speed than the navy's, which had been dropping their loads from such heights as to be deemed totally ineffective by the observation team. The navy later claimed that the bombs "became 'duds' from the height at which they were dropped" and "the attack with heavy bombs did not come up to expectations." But there could be no denying the results. In very short order *G-102* had become the first major warship in history to be sunk by aerial bombardment.[14]

When Mitchell again circled for a close inspection, less than twenty-five feet above the sinking target, he must have smiled. One three-hundred-pound bomb had been enough "to make a ruin of the German boat, which had an evil record." But the second three-hundred-pounder had completed the execution. It mattered little who had dropped it. *G-102* was going down fast. At 10:40 A.M., within two minutes of the last hit, the destroyer had disappeared from sight in fifty fathoms of water, leaving only a great elliptical oil slick on the surface and splintered floating wreckage to mark her grave.[15]

It had taken the aviators only twenty minutes to sink the German warship in what was soon being reported as "the most interesting and spectacular" joint army-navy experiment of all time. The army fliers had used fewer than half of their bombs. The attack force had carried a total of 168 bombs, of which only fifty-one had been dropped, while the pursuit squadron had dropped only forty-four Cooper bombs.[16]

The aftermath of the test was heated discussion, with most navy supporters seeking to downplay the results as mere luck. Mitchell was ebullient. The attack, he said, was absolutely conclusive. "In less time than it takes to tell it, their bombs began churning the water around the destroyer," he later wrote. "They hit close in front of it, behind it, opposite its side and directly in the center. Columns of water rose hundreds of feet into the air. For a few minutes the vessel looked as if it was on fire, smoke came out of its funnels and vapors along its deck. Then it broke completely in two in the middle and sank down out of sight." He did not mince his words. "All our methods and systems for bombing had proven correct."[17]

The average flying time for the army planes, which had the farthest to come, had been two hours and forty minutes for the round trip to and from the target. The return flight had faced twenty-two-mph headwinds before reaching shore, and all of the planes returned safely. Three planes had been forced to make emergency landings over land, but not one of them had been lost in the water. The importance of having successfully attacked an enemy warship, on the open ocean far from land, was not at first appreciated. Doubters commented that under war conditions major warships, such as a heavy cruiser or dreadnought, would use powerful antiaircraft guns to stop an attack. "It is to be feared that these tests will change few preconceived opinions of the sea service," suggested the *Times*. "That would be unfortunate, for the aviation menace is real." Yet the testing had just begun.[18]


The Army's First Provisional Air Brigade marshaled in review at Langley Field on Thursday, July 14, for the benefit of foreign air and naval attachés, congressmen, and other guests of the U.S. Navy who had witnessed the previous day's tests or would soon watch the experiments ahead. In the afternoon, members of Congress, the press, and others in the reviewing party were given an opportunity to ride in pursuit, light, and heavy bombers to get a bird's-eye view of Langley Field.[19]

At the conclusion of the review, Colonel M. T. Milling, commander of Langley Field, addressed the assembled visitors and spoke candidly of the army airmen's ambitions for the utilization of aircraft in coastal defense work. He noted that while the army's heavy bombers were now capable of carrying a 2,400-pound high-explosive bomb, the largest ever developed for the army's air arsenal, an even more devastating 4,000-pound bomb was in development as was the aircraft to carry it. The current heavy bomber force would soon be termed as little more than light bombers. The audience, attempting to digest the significance of the colonel's statement, was stunned. It seemed incredible, but given the rapid improvements in technology, anything now appeared feasible. The colonel went on to predict that in the event of an enemy naval attack on the U.S. coast, the army would be able to muster in less than twenty-four hours all of the planes east of the Mississippi for mobilization on the Atlantic at the point of attack, and within thirty-six hours all of the planes east of the Pacific. Moreover, within a few years, the army would be able to safely project its air power more than 150 miles out from the shore for bombing attacks. The implications for naval coastal defense strategy, which was hitherto dependent on heavily armored warships, were obvious if the colonel's predictions were true.[20]

The navy was not happy but could muster only a muffled rebuttal. "So far nothing has been proved in the tests but the ability of airmen to hit and destroy a rather small target drifting at sea." Major line-of-battle ships, they kept repeating as if by rote, could never be challenged by air power alone.[21]


Friday morning, July 15. The ex-German destroyers *S-132* and *V-43* lay at anchor barely several hundred yards apart, and two miles from the resting place of *G-102*. It was the navy's turn now to display its awesome firepower and show the world how to sink an enemy ship the right way. To accomplish the mission no less than four battleships—the USS *Delaware, North Carolina, Florida,* and *Pennsylvania;* six destroyers—the USS *Dickerson, Bagley, Sicard, Leary, Schenck,* and *Herbert;* two minesweepers—the USS *Virco* and *Quall;* and a tender, the USS *Lebanon,* would participate in the exercise. Command of the operation was accorded to Rear Admiral A. H. Scales. *Dickerson* and *Bagley* would serve as observation vessels to conduct inspections of the targets after each attack. The USS *Henderson* was assigned to carry the congressmen, senators, U.S. Navy and Marine officers, foreign naval attachés, and newspapermen to witness a highly choreographed show.

The "rules of engagement" were quite straightforward. The two target vessels would first be attacked by two destroyers, steaming at high speed, at a range of five thousand yards. Ten rounds of ammunition per gun were to be allotted. If either of the target vessels remained afloat after the attack, two battleships would commence shelling. The battleships were to be allowed twenty rounds per every secondary gun of one broadside. It was assumed that none of the targets would be left within minutes of the opening of the initial battleship barrage. In the unlikely event the dreadnought's bombardment failed, the targets were to be finished off by depth charges planted on their decks by *Virco* and *Quall.*[22]

The weather conditions for the operations were anything but favorable. Intermittent showers and thirty-knot winds would provide a difficult environment for the 9:00 A.M. turkey shoot. Not until late morning, however, was the environment deemed suitable to begin the exercise. Finally, at precisely 11:05 A.M., the first destroyer division, traveling in column formation with *Dickerson* leading *Sicard, Leary, Schenck,* and *Herbert,* began standing down southward of the target at a speed of thirty knots with orders "shoot to sink." Unfortunately, the seas were "so rough that it rolled both destroyers and targets and provided the gunners with anything but a steady firing platform, and made the test difficult." An order went out from the flagship to postpone the assault.[23]

For the next two hours the destroyers circled the targets in a great arc before again bearing down for their next try, though by the rules of engagement only two among them would be allowed to actually fire their guns. At 1:15 P.M., at a range of six thousand yards, the USS *Leary* finally opened the attack, with *Herbert* joining soon afterward. At first the two warships concentrated fire on *V-43* from their three starboard four-inch guns, then they assailed *S-132* as well. For the next thirty minutes as they steamed southward, closing to within 3,500 yards, they continued the assault unabated. Then, in the midst of the shooting, a slow-moving three-masted windjammer appeared on the scene, apparently disregarding all signals to turn away, and was soon in danger of getting in the line of fire. The bombardment was halted until the ship finally sailed off. Incredibly, as if on cue, another large unidentified vessel, this time a steamer, appeared seemingly out of nowhere behind the line of firing ships, causing even further delay before finally disappearing.[24]

The attack resumed at 2:55 P.M. with *Herbert* unloading only three shots in nine minutes, all well over the targets. Not until the eighteenth shot had been fired was a hit observed. However, another hit soon evinced bellows of smoke from both funnels of the target. *Herbert's* last shot, her thirtieth, was a "beauty" that landed on the bridge of *S-132* and kicked up an even greater cloud of debris and smoke. Finally, after the two warships had used up the authorized ammunition allowance, the attack was terminated. The Board of Observers, all naval officers, attempted to put the best face on what the press deemed a poor display of marksmanship, and boldly proclaimed that "these shots would have done serious damage to the target vessel if she had been under steam, with officers and crew aboard."[25]

Soon after the Board of Observers passed alongside *S-132* they radioed their observations to Commander Jules James, the official censor aboard the transport *Henderson:* "Three hits along water line, amidships and forecastle on starboard side; one on bridge; one on stack; one on last stack; six hits altogether; vessel in sinking condition." The navy put the best spin it could on a disappointing demonstration. There was no doubt, the observers stated, that *S-132* would gradually have sunk as a result of *Herbert's* gunnery. But the fact was obvious to all: neither of the immobile target ships had yet been sunk, even by almost point-blank fire![26]

While the Board of Observers lay alongside *S-132*, *Delaware*, *Florida*, *North Dakota*, and *Pennsylvania* were readying for their part in the game, "the rules providing that if either target remained afloat after the *Leary* and *Herbert* had fired, each must be subjected to gunfire from battleships." The dreadnoughts were ordered to approach from a distance of not less than ten thousand yards (five nautical miles) and to open fire anytime outside of five thousand yards using secondary battery fire only. Each ship was to employ all seven of its starboard five-inch guns with an allowance of twenty rounds per secondary battery gun on one broadside, or 140 shots each for *Florida* and *Delaware,* the two ships authorized to conduct gunnery tests. The actual range at which they began shooting was about ten thousand yards. They closed to within eight thousand yards when they were abeam of the targets.[27]

*Florida* opened the attack on *V-43* at 4:20 P.M. by firing an impressive 140 shots in only twelve minutes, "but the guns so enveloped the target in smoke that after the first dozen hits it was impossible to count the rest." A short twenty-nine minutes after *Florida* had unleashed her five-inch guns, *V-43* suddenly hoisted her stern perpendicularly in the air and went down by the bow.[28]

The column of four battleships now steamed toward their second target, *S-132,* and began firing at 5:54 P.M., stopping eight minutes later after all 140 shots had been expended. Their target had already been slowly sinking, with her decks awash, from the earlier attack of the destroyers. When the battleship bombardment commenced, the first three salvos riddled her hull so badly fore and aft that she could not long survive. At precisely 7:07 P.M. *S-132* joined her sisters on the bottom of the Atlantic.[29]

Though the operations off the Virginia capes had lasted nearly seven hours, the actual firing time had been just forty-nine minutes. Yet it had taken two destroyers and two battleships to sink two stationary destroyers. The demonstration, much to the navy's dismay, failed to ignite the same incredulity as the performance of the air attack the day before. "While today's gunfire attacks were effective," remarked the *New York Times,* "the show staged by the navy, except when the battleships *Florida* and *Delaware* were shaking up the sea area for some miles around with the thunder of their many salvos, was a mild performance compared with the spectacular performance of the sinking of the *G-102* on Wednesday by army aircraft aerial bombing attack."[30]

The ex-German battle cruiser *Frankfurt* was carefully inspected as she quietly awaited the hour of her projected demise. Like her late sisters, she too had been anchored some sixty miles off the Virginia capes to face an air assault, thirty-two planes in all, which would be dropping as many as 108 bombs ranging in size from 250 to 600 pounds. If they failed to finish their attacks, the cruiser was to be shelled, as with *V-48* and *S-132,* by the Navy's Atlantic fleet destroyers. If that failed, she was to be sunk by depth charges placed around her hull.[31]

The navy's air arm this time included five divisions of aircraft, piloted by both navy and Marine Corps pilots. The aircraft consisted of F-5Ls, F-2Ls and Martin Bombers. The Army Air contingent was made up of eleven light and six heavy bombers. The accepted plan was to divide the attacks into two phases. During the first phase, the army, navy, and marine planes would drop lighter bombs ranging from 250 to 300 pounds each.[32] As before, the target ship would be surrounded by the Atlantic fleet, which carried an even larger body of diplomatic and political observers than before, as well as some of the highest-ranking military leaders in the United States.

Although the attack was again scheduled to begin at precisely 9:00 A.M., the arrival of the first squadron on the scene, the navy's 4th Division, consisting of four planes commanded by Lieutenant Commander J. H. Strong, did not begin their bombing runs until 9:12 A.M. Seven minutes later, amid a cluster of four 250-pound bombs, the first hit was registered on the cruiser's foremast. Another wave of planes appeared, and then a third consisting of three Marine Corps aircraft, but they did little damage.[33]

Next it was the army's turn. A fourth assault was made at 10:46 A.M., this time by one of the army's light bomber squadron planes commanded by a Lieutenant Kirksey. The lieutenant's bombing was superb. Seconds after loosing his six three-hundred-pound bombs, blanketing the sea in the immediate vicinity of the target, a great flash of fire issued from the ship. Deck wreckage was thrown hundreds of feet into the air, and enormous clouds of soot were flushed heavenward from the cruiser's three great funnels. With Kirksey's bombs expended, a signal was raised for the Board of Observers to inspect the damage. Before the inspectors' ship, the USS *Shawmut,* had come alongside, General Mitchell, who had been watching the attacks most of the morning, flew within a few feet of the target, conducted a "series of bulls eye surveys of the damage done to the target," and then returned to the sky to let the navy do its own assessment. The inspectors quickly determined that while the army's hit had been "spectacular," it would not sink the cruiser. The small bombs had inflicted little structural damage but had killed innumerable animals that had been tied to the deck to simulate a crew.[34]

The last wave of the light bomber phase of the assault was not to begin until 1:30 P.M., to permit the myriad dignitaries, military brass, and politicians to enjoy a delicious luncheon as guests of the navy. Then it was again the navy pilots' turn to show their stuff. Three light bombers armed with five-hundred-pound bombs and belonging to the First Division dropped their loads close to the cruiser but caused no damage. Aboard the fleet, even as the navy's planes conducted their ineffective attack, many naval officers who had long espoused the belief that aircraft could never sink a capital ship were delighted but focused their belittling remarks on the army's air service. "Imagine that baby under steam and able to fight off the airmen," said one, alluding to the general failure of the planes to make many hits. Another was almost giddy. "Gee," he said sarcastically, "I'm feeling safer every minute."[35]

It was now time for the heavy bomber phase to commence. As before, the navy would lead off, this time with three Martin bombers commanded by Lieutenant Commander Harold Bartlett, all armed with six-hundred-pound bombs. Bartlett himself led the attack. His first bomb "landed between the first and second smokestacks of the cruiser, burst with a large show of flame, and . . . tore up the deck of the target near these stacks." Within two minutes the other two planes dropped three more bombs in a salvo, one of which hit abaft the mainmast. Three minutes later, the division rounded up its work by dropping the last of the bombs, without registering a hit.[36]

Again, like a bird of prey, Mitchell swooped down to inspect the target, as the naval inspectors were making their belated way toward her. They arrived well after the last navy attack had been completed and determined that the hits had penetrated through the stern and exited the hull above the water line without doing great damage. They reported, even before nearing the target, "that while severe damage had been done to the deck and upper works of the *Frankfurt,* the hull seemed intact. No water was entering it, and up to the very edge of the attack by the army and navy bombers, with six-hundred-pound bombs loaded with TNT, it was the belief of the members of the board that it would be useless to go ahead with the rest of the aircraft attacks." But as *Shawmut* drew alongside

*Frankfurt* it was already too late! A squadron of army bombers had just been spotted coming in from the west.[37]

In the half hour it had taken *Shawmut* to ferry the observers to the target ship, a stream of orders and counter-orders flooded the airwaves between Langley and the fleet. Messages were sent from *Shawmut* directing the army bombers not to approach the target area, ninety-seven miles from their base, but to await further orders before proceeding. Minutes later the orders were countermanded. Not wishing to give anyone in the navy a chance to second-guess the countermanded directive, a squadron of six army Martin heavy bombers with six-hundred-pound bombs took off immediately, even as Bartlett's bombers were leaving the target area. Aboard the "gallery" of battleships, destroyers, and other naval vessels, thousands of officers and enlisted men lined the decks in white uniforms "waiting for the next move in the game." Momentarily believing that the aerial bombardment had been called off, plans even went forward aboard the fleet to sink *Frankfurt* by destroyer attack or by bombs placed aboard the target ship by a wrecking party from the USS *North Dakota*. It was at this juncture, while members of the prospective wrecking party were being assembled to sink the cruiser "by the time bomb route," that the army bombers commanded by a Captain Lawson brought the operation to a sensational finish. But not before some last minute obstruction from the navy arose.[38]

The ex-German heavy cruiser *Frankfurt* under attack for the last time (National Archives, Washington, DC; photo courtesy of Michael Pohuski)

The stern of *Frankfurt* seen moments before she disappeared beneath the Atlantic (National Archives, Washington, DC; photo courtesy of Michael Pohuski)

As Lawson's planes approached *Frankfurt,* dense clouds of smoke rose from the aft funnel of *Shawmut,* a prearranged signal for the bombers to withhold their attack until further orders. The signal was intended to prevent *Shawmut* from being accidentally bombed while the inspection was under way. In truth, the navy was doing its best to stop the attacks. High in the air, General Mitchell seethed with anger at what he felt to be a deliberate delaying tactic. For his land-based bombers to fly nearly a hundred miles from Langley over the sea, where "gasoline meant everything to them" and then be held up by the navy's delayed inspection infuriated him. Nevertheless, the Board of Observers proceeded at what seemed a snail's pace, while the six army bombers circled repeatedly around the target, unable to land and eager to attack. At 4:00 P.M., a half hour after his arrival, Lawson radioed *Shawmut:* "Must begin bombing within fifteen minutes; fuel limited." Unless permitted to attack by 4:15, his planes would have to return to base. Even if they were allowed to attack, the bombing operation would have to be truncated. Finally, reluctantly, *Shawmut* signaled to "proceed to attack."[39]

The V-formation of bombers immediately reformed into a single column and began circling in an ever-closing arc around the target. The two lead planes, Nos. 14 and 17, at precisely 4:15, opened the attack by dropping two six-hundred-pound bombs, one of which scored a devastating blow to the deck near the forecastle gun. Then came another direct hit. The remaining bombs, nine in number, which were dropped by only four planes, fell into the sea near the ship. As these bombs exploded, the concussion wave caused by the detonation in the water was felt against the sides of the vessels of the fleet at a distance of several thousand yards simultaneously with the appearance of the big spouts of water kicked up by the explosions. Then, one of the bombs went into the water directly alongside the hull and sealed the fate of *Frankfurt.* The concussion from the explosion broke the cruiser's back and immediately caused her forward compartments to fill with water. The great German warship was soon sinking fast by the bow. Her aft smokestack was riddled and leaning, and the deck between her funnels was a mass of wreckage. Within minutes the ship was listing heavily to port. Then, in the blink of an eye, her stem stood perpendicular to the water, showing her rudder in a final salute as she gracefully slipped into the depths.[40]

Though only four planes had dropped most of their bombs, eleven in number, in only ten minutes, their work had been done so effectively that "they soon called a halt to the expectation of those among the navy officers present who had insisted that the *Frankfurt* could not be sunk by aircraft bombing attack." For the navy, the swift, undeniable success of the attack had been entirely unexpected. As the army bombers headed home in triumph, with barely enough fuel to get them to Langley, a division of big navy N-C airboats arrived and circled like a gaggle of leaderless Canada geese. *Shawmut* signaled for them to return to base.[41]

General Mitchell could now support his contention "respecting the ability of bombing aircraft to deal with capital and other types of naval vessels." The attacks had lasted all day until the "army brought the operations to a sensational finish." It had taken the navy nine hours and thirty-seven minutes and 26,850 pounds of bombs to destroy a couple of light warships. It had taken Mitchell scarcely half an hour and fourteen six-hundred-pound bombs to sink a heavy cruiser, with the killer bomb actually sinking the ship by concussion rather than direct contact. Only later was it revealed that when the Board of Observers had boarded *Frankfurt,* they had discovered nine unexploded navy bombs, all duds built by the navy for the navy. "Such an exhibition," noted the *New York Times* with some indignation, "demands an investigation into the Naval Ordnance Department."[42]

News of the spectacular sinking of *Frankfurt* raced around the world. But at Langley, everyone knew that on Wednesday the biggest challenge of all was still to come, when they would sally forth for one last test, to sink the mighty ex-German dreadnought *Ostfriesland,* one of the largest, most devastating killing machines ever built by man. This time, however, they would not use six-hundred-pound bombs, but thousand- and two-thousand-pounders in what some expected to become the most "spectacular" event in naval and air history.

# 20

## Billy and the Battleship

The navy had been infuriated by General Billy Mitchell's actions during the *Frankfurt* experiment. His pilots, they fumed, had deliberately ignored the pre-arranged signals to halt their attack simply to provide the general with a dramatic demonstration that he could market to the world. He had made a special effort to record every operation with still and motion picture cameras. When *Frankfurt* was sunk, he had the film flown to New York so that it could be processed and shown in theaters at the earliest possible moment. Unfortunately, the plane carrying the film crashed en route and the pilot was killed.[1] In the meantime, the admirals comforted themselves with the assurance that *Ostfriesland* would be different.

The battleship *Ostfriesland* was in many ways unique. Built in 1909 for the German navy under specific instructions of Grand Admiral Alfred von Tirpitz to be as unsinkable as possible, she was, for her time, a marvel of naval architecture and engineering. Her hull had been divided by heavy bulkheads into numerous watertight compartments, longitudinal as well as traverse. She wore three skins of iron amidships and two fore and aft of her machinery to protect her from mines and torpedoes. She was of the same naval generation as the USS *Florida,* which would be present at her execution. The big dreadnought had been part of the first German battle squadron to take an important role in the Battle of Jutland, at which she was credited with helping sink several British vessels. During the engagement she had struck a mine, inflicting damage that would most certainly have sunk a lesser vessel. But *Ostfriesland* had been kept afloat by pumps and eventually reached Wilhelmshaven intact. At the end of the war she had been taken to Britain as a war prize and was eventually turned over to the United States. On May 18, 1920, at Rosyth, England, she was commissioned into the U.S. Navy, and under American officers and crew sailed for New York where she was placed out of commission at the New York Navy Yard on September 20.[2]

. . .

General John J. "Black Jack" Pershing was perhaps the greatest bona fide American hero to come out of the first World War. He was a no-nonsense military man, a West Point veteran who had fought in the Indian Wars and the Philippine insurrection and led the expedition against Pancho Villa. For his leadership as commander of the two-million-man American Expeditionary Forces in Europe he had been given a new title, General of the Armies, created specifically for him, and named army chief of staff. For Pershing, the formal military establishment and by-the-book regimen formed the parameters within which high command had traditionally operated. Innovation was something to be looked at critically and accepted only with the greatest caution, especially as it related to air power. Now the general was about to confront one of the most innovative military concepts of his career. Accompanied by Secretary of War Weeks, Pershing would witness the final phase of testing off the Virginia capes, the aerial assault on the *Ostfriesland* on July 20, the last German warship allocated to the United States now left afloat.

Pershing was well aware that, under an agreement made by President Woodrow Wilson at Paris, the *Ostfriesland* must be sunk at sea on or before Sunday, July 24. He was equally cognizant that his own army "birdmen" believed that they could "turn the trick" on the battleship if allowed to use heavy bombs. But

The ex-Imperial German battleship *Ostfriesland* soon after her acquisition by the U.S. Navy. Sunk during an aerial bombardment test off the Virginia coast by the U.S. Army and U.S. Navy in 1921, her demise was destined to usher in a new era in aerial and naval warfare. (The Mariner's Museum, Newport News, VA)

it had been the navy's game, to which the army had been invited only as a courtesy. Mitchell had agreed to the testing but had vigorously opposed the restrictions and format of the proceedings, which had originally restricted the size of bombs he might use. When it came to the attack on *Ostfriesland,* he had insisted the bombing would have to start with nothing less than 250 to 600 pounders at a minimum, and preferably thousand pounders or more. But the newspapers were already touting what everyone already knew: "It is not the expectation that the *Ostfriesland* will be sunk by any bombs lighter than 1,000 or 2,000 pounds. Naval officers are insisting that the fliers will never sink the *Ostfriesland* at all." Despite Mitchell's eagerness to move right on to the heavy bombs, Pershing was adamant about procedure. The two-thousand-pound bombs would not be dropped until Thursday. If the dreadnought remained afloat after that, she would be attacked by the USS *Pennsylvania's* main battery of fourteen-inch guns at a range of no less than eighteen thousand yards. Some doubted that either aircraft bombs or battleship guns would even do the trick, and the ex-German warship would have to be sunk by depth charges deployed by a party from the USS *North Carolina.*[3]

On the morning of Wednesday, July 20, the battleship *Pennsylvania,* flagship of the Atlantic fleet, hosted an illustrious retinue of visitors. Fifty of the most distinguished guests were to be entertained at a luncheon by Admiral Hillary P. Jones, commander of the fleet, and to witness the tests from his quarterdeck. These included Pershing; Secretary of War John Wingate Weeks; Secretary of the Navy Edwin Denby; Colonel Theodore Roosevelt, assistant secretary of the navy and son of the late president; Admiral Robert E. Coontz, chief of naval operations; Major General John A. Lejeune, head of the U.S. Marine Corps; eight U.S. senators, twelve members of the U.S. House of Representatives, and other high federal officials; General Benito Aboglio of Italy; and naval and air attachés from numerous foreign embassies in Washington. Special guests included aircraft pioneer Glenn L. Martin and Colonel John W. Joyes of the Army Ordnance Department, who in 1913 had been the first Americans to experiment with aerial bombardments.[4]

At Norfolk the marine and navy pilots were eager to be off to dump their small twenty-five-pounder bomb loads, which the army flyers derisively called "pumpkins" because they had just about as much destructive capability against an armored warship. Owing to low clouds, poor visibility, and rough seas, the navy declared it was too dangerous to send the planes out. The cloudy weather continued until finally it was decided that the tests be called off and the fleet turned toward Hampton Roads.[5]

For the next hour and a half, the fleet plowed homeward through heavy seas, "much to the disgust of the distinguished party that had gone from Washington to see the tests." Then came an unexpected radio message from General Mitchell: he was ready to attack and would soon be on the way despite the weather. The message was clear. If the army could chance the weather, then the navy would have to as well, simply to save face. The entire fleet turned about and steamed back to the target area, and the first wave of naval and marine aircraft, five planes in all, took off from Hampton Roads.[6]

At 1:40 P.M., having less distance to fly, the Marine Corps bombers arrived first on the scene with their six-hundred-pounders, followed soon afterward by a navy squadron carrying thousand-pounders. For the next hour and eighteen minutes, the bombing was intense and the hit rate was considered very good. The target was, after all, quite immense. Of the fifty-eight bombs that had dropped, thirteen of them, weighing 4,410 pounds, fell upon the deck of *Ostfriesland*. Much to the embarrassment of the Bureau of Naval Ordnance only four navy bombs actually exploded. As had occurred during the previous test, the majority of the bombs were duds that "crumpled up without exploding." When the Board of Observers conducted their inspection, it was discovered that one of the live hits had been on the after-waist turret on the port side, but the only damage had been to rip up a short piece of the decking. The other live hits had been amidships at the aft funnel and did little more than char the deck. The demonstration had proved yet another embarrassment for the sea service. The army bombs had all dropped in the waters alongside the ship.[7]

While the *Shawmut*'s team of observers went about their business examining the disintegrated fragments of the Bureau of Naval Ordnance duds, and the negligible damage, four army bombers and a division of three navy F-5Ls circled overhead with a total of nineteen thousand-pound bombs. Finally, at 3:44 P.M., the signal to attack was made from one thousand feet, through extremely low cloud cover at six hundred feet. In a single column, the navy planes dropped their loads, making three hits, only one of which exploded. Two more duds struck the quarterdeck, penetrated through to the next deck, and splintered into pieces. Two minutes after the assault had ended, a lone F-5L carrying a six-hundred-pound bomb began its approach.[8]

The single bomb was the last hit of the day, striking the starboard side on a coal chute in front of the forward twelve-inch gun turret. It exploded and tore up several feet of deck, sending fragments through to the next deck but failing to penetrate the protective lower deck. "The explosion from this bomb," noted an observer, "was not as great as it should have been." The side armor of the turret near where the bomb struck had been previously removed by the navy for use in ballistics tests and even with this armor removed the turret was not injured.[9]

Further testing for the day was summarily canceled. A nasty northeast squall had already careened along the coast before turning east a half hour earlier and was heading directly toward the target area. The decision to halt the exercise was a wise one for the blow would indeed provide both the navy and army fliers with a few hair-raising experiences. Three of the dirigibles assigned to the offshore tests were forced to make a detour northward toward the Eastern Shore of Maryland and did not reach Langley Field until 11:15 P.M., having been in the air for fifteen hours. General Mitchell and another army reconnaissance plane, which had spent several hours flying over *Ostfriesland,* were forced to turn southward on their return trip and make a detour that took them to Currituck Sound, North Carolina. They finally returned safely to Langley Field late in the evening, but only after covering a distance of six hundred miles that required several refuelings. Four of the big army bombers somehow headed home straight through the storm and landed safely at Langley Field. A fifth had oil trouble and was forced to land west of Cape Henry but later returned safely to base.[10]

For the advocates of battleship supremacy it had been a great day, with the consensus of most being that the central cores of such ships were absolutely safe against six-hundred-pound bombs. "The real vitals of a battleship lie behind the side armor and under the protective deck." For the army aviators at Langley, the issue was still open. Yet all of the tests to date had clearly demonstrated the superiority of the army's ordnance. When nine out of thirteen bombs the navy dropped simply disintegrated on impact, the event did not go unnoticed by the press.[11]

The Board of Observers was nevertheless convinced that *Ostfriesland* could never be sunk with six-hundred-pound bombs. Her hull was intact and taking on no water when examined late in afternoon. Her protective armored deck had not been pierced. Her hull plating, as far as known, had not been opened by any heavy explosions of bombs that fell into the water near stem and stern. Whether *Ostfriesland* would be immune to one- and two-thousand-pound bombs was a question that would have to await the next day's testing to be solved once and for all. If she withstood these attacks, as the navy brass believed she would, the USS *Pennsylvania,* flagship of the Atlantic fleet, would simply haul off with her main battery of sixteen-inch guns and try to sink her with the least expenditure of ammunition.[12]

Secretary Weeks and General Pershing had already seen enough and were convinced that further air attacks would prove futile. They departed the fleet in the evening aboard the destroyer *Dahlgren* bound for Point Comfort. Assistant Secretary Roosevelt, who had spent the previous evening "roughing it" by sleeping on one of the upper decks of the transport *Henderson,* had also seen enough and departed onboard a destroyer for Hampton Roads, where a plane waited to take him back to Washington for "more important business." Navy secretary Denby, however, resolved to see the tests through, to be there and savor the correctness of his and his colleagues' judgment: a battleship could never be sunk by aerial bombardment alone.[13]


Billy Mitchell's aircraft had caused little apparent damage to the exposed superstructure and armor plating of the mighty *Ostfriesland.* Indeed, most of his six-hundred-pound bombs had fallen into the water close to the ship's sides. Most observers had chalked it up to poor marksmanship, but it had, in fact, been by plan. Instead of seeking to penetrate the deck armor, Mitchell gave his men instructions to hit *Ostfriesland* if they could but in any case to drop their bombs as close as possible along her waterline. His true objective had been to shake open the seams of the dreadnought by concussion below the armor belt and send it toppling into the sea, regardless of the character of its armored exoskeleton. But six-hundred-pound bombs had not been powerful enough. There was, he was betting, a far better chance with the thousand-pounders. Indeed, he was ready to risk his career by publicly announcing on July 21 that two-thousand-pound bombs would most certainly do the trick. The navy immediately countered with what was becoming the fallback argument that a battleship would normally be protected by intense antiaircraft fire, and that flying between 1,500 and 2,500 feet would be suicide for attackers. Mitchell retorted that his men, indeed any good flyers, would be willing to take that chance as "their altitude is determined not by the guns of the target, but of the concussion of their own bombs."[14]

When the first rays of sunlight broke over the Atlantic on July 21 and the fleet again gathered in its now customary semicircle around the target, it became immediately obvious to all that the damage wrought by the six-hundred-pound bombs the previous day had been far more severe than the Board of Observers had initially detected—especially from those dropped in the waters beside the ship. *Ostfriesland* had gone down substantially by the stern during the night. Again the inspectors boarded the ship and this time discovered that Mitchell's bombing had indeed opened underwater seams and the ship's aft section was already down by two feet and still taking on water. Such observations mattered little to the navy brass aboard *Pennsylvania*. One high-ranking naval officer was overheard to say that the odds were still a thousand to one against the German dreadnought being sent to the bottom by Mitchell's aerial bombardment.[15]

Tension filled the ranks of both navy and army participants and observers, for everyone knew that Mitchell considered the rules established by the navy for the day's bombing experiment to be overly restrictive. The actual operations were to begin at 8:00 A.M., and bombs could only be dropped one at a time. Mitchell reneged and his planes arrived early with a laconic directive that they "not be interfered with by naval aircraft."[16]

Five army bombers arrived over the target area at 8:23, each carrying a single thousand-pound bomb, as well as several range bombs. Minutes later, four small bombs were loosened over the target to establish range. Then, at precisely 8:30, traveling in a single column circling overhead, the bombers began the attack. The first dropped was a direct hit on the starboard side of the forecastle. The second splashed into the water 150 feet off the port bow. The third fell onto the starboard side near the aft funnel, sending debris flying skyward and inflicting considerable damage on the deck. The fourth scored a direct hit in the same part of the ship and sent billows of pitch-black soot flowing from all three funnels. It broke away part of the aft structure just back of the funnel and, it was later claimed, would have disabled the after-fire room if it had been in boiler service. The final thousand-pounder fell into the water seventy yards off the starboard beam.[17]

Having effectively scored three hits out of five tries, the five aircraft were ordered to cease bombing as the board "ruled that enough hits had been made to warrant calling off the rest of the 1,000 [pound] bomb attack." All three hits had caused severe damage to deck equipment and superstructure, but the board declared that because none had even pierced the armor-protected deck, none of them would have sunk her. The next to final phase of the aerial testing had been completed, and the battleship *Ostfriesland* had been injured but she was still afloat. The navy called for a halt to bombing for further assessment of damage, but the army was having none of it. Mitchell was determined to finish the job in a most spectacular way as he considered the attacks already too far along to halt.[18] Everyone was poised for the final episode, one that would either change the course of history or terminate the brilliant career of the U.S. Army's most outspoken commander, General Billy Mitchell.

Captain A. W. Johnson, USN, was commander of the Atlantic fleet air force stationed aboard the observation ship *Shawmut* and was nervous when he radioed the order to Langley Field, 97½ miles away, to dispatch its force of army bombers with their mammoth two-thousand-pound bombs. Six minutes later, at 10:58 A.M., Colonel T. D. Milling, commander at Langley, replied that the bombers, six Martins and a single Handley-Page, were on their way. The lone division of aircraft was sighted approaching the target area at 12:05 P.M. Within ten minutes they had formed into the usual column for attack. As before, the lead aircraft dropped a small bomb as a range finder, which hit the water 150 feet ahead of *Ostfriesland*'s bow. The next plane dropped the first two-thousand-pounder at 12:19, which hit the water close in to the starboard bow, causing a terrific underwater explosion.[19]

The two-thousand-pound bombs, each carrying over a thousand pounds of TNT, were huge. Eleven and a half feet in length and a little over a foot and a

A column of water erupts from off the starboard midships of *Ostfriesland* with a near hit. Concussion from such hits is credited with sinking her. (National Archives, Washington, DC; photo courtesy of Michael Pohuski)

half maximum diameter, as they fell they could easily be seen by the naked eye from the deck of *Henderson* and those of the dozen or more American warships two miles from the target. Nose and tail fuses assured the function of the army ordnance in exploding on contact without delay. Unlike the navy's weapons, the army bombs had no suspension lugs and were carried under the plane by steel slings passed under their cylindrical bodies at their centers of gravity. But the most important advantage was that the army fliers were excellent marksmen.[20]

The third plane now made its approach, but its bomb hit the water three hundred feet from *Ostfriesland*'s bow. A range correction was called for. The next plane dropped a small range-finding bomb that hit one hundred feet off the starboard bow. Then, a third two-thousand-pounder plummeted from the sky and scored a bull's-eye hit on deck in the forward point of the bow called "the eye of the ship." The explosion was devastating. A monumental burst of fire and smoke leaped heavenward, tearing a great hole out of the starboard side of the forecastle. At 12:26 the fourth big bomb was dropped and entered the water close in on the port side of the target and abreast of the mainmast behind the funnels. The entire Atlantic fleet physically shuddered at the concussion as the explosion lifted the ship upward and threw a heavy fall of water on the deck, "which flowed like Niagara over the starboard side."[21]

There was no respite now for the helpless giant of the late German navy as the fifth bomb, "the one that began to put the ship under," fell a minute later, a little further back in the water near the stern on the port side quarter. The bomb exploded "with terrific effect, sending up a great sheet of water that fell clear across the quarterdeck." Immediately, the nose of the ship rose, and she began to sink by the stern. The two big guns in the after turret, which had been thrown out of alignment by one of the morning shots, disappeared. The ship was going down quickly, and her water line was rising on the forward starboard quarter. "When a death blow has been dealt by a bomb to a vessel," Mitchell would later write, "there is no mistaking it." Yet, the army pilots showed no mercy and left nothing to chance. Another bomber dropped the sixth bomb at 12:32, which struck the water less than fifty feet from the starboard stern. Within two minutes of the last strike, the battleship was listing heavily to port with all of her decks awash.[22]

At 12:39, *Ostfriesland*'s afterdecks went under as her bow stuck boldly out in the air, like the great jaw of a posturing dictator. Then she quickly rolled over on her port beam-ends and turned turtle, exposing most of her bottom from the mainmast area forward. A minute later the great hulk slipped down stern first toward the ocean bottom in three hundred feet of water until only the inverted bow was visible, glistening in the early afternoon light with seawater and barnacles. When the stern reached the bottom, fifty feet of the bow could still be seen, and the sinking momentarily stopped. For endless seconds the bow seemed to stand frozen in time as if "to bid a last farewell to all her sister battleships around her." Then it suddenly dropped forward and disappeared. "It was," noted one observer, "as if the Washington Monument had been placed slantingly in the sea, with its base ploughing into the sand, and the apex for a few seconds remaining exposed before cutting through the water to the bottom of the ocean." As the old warship died, the lone Hadley-Page, carrying the last big bomb, attacked and

A view from one of Billy Mitchell's reconnaissance planes as *Ostfriesland* begins to roll and go down by the stern (National Archives, Washington, DC; photo courtesy of Michael Pohuski)

dropped it as "a parting funeral salute to what was once the pride of the German navy." The bomb "struck in the water, penetrated deeply and burst with a force that helped shove *Ostfriesland* faster to the bottom." For some minutes after the disappearance of the dreadnought, the air escaping from her compartments rose to the surface, kicking up billows of white frothy water over her grave, as if the sea itself were boiling. Then all was quiet.[23]

Onboard *Henderson,* Major General Charles F. Menoher, director of the Army Air Service, radioed a message of congratulations to Mitchell, who was circling overhead. The airman swung his plane down and sped close around the transport, tipping his wings in salute, followed closely by another army De Haviland. The gallery of generals, senators, representatives, foreign military attachés, and others on board waved and shouted their congratulations to the aircraft as their planes spun around the transport in a victory lap, and then headed west.[24]

Though considerable damage had been inflicted upon *Ostfriesland* during the morning attacks with thousand-pound bombs, it was conceivable that under combat conditions the ship might still have made port as her steering gears, boilers, pumps, and machinery had not been touched. But no amount of intact machinery and pumps could have saved her from the two-thousand-pound bombs "dropped with such skill in the water close along both port and starboard sides of the target this afternoon." The question of whether a modern battleship could be sunk by an aircraft bombing attack had been solved in double-quick time, indeed in only twenty-five minutes.[25]

The army, with the noteworthy exception of Pershing, crowed. General Williams, army chief of ordnance, sounded the keynote comment after the bombing. "A bomb was fired today that will be heard round the world," he said. "It is a heavier explosive charge than has ever been delivered against a battleship. Its sinking of the *Ostfriesland* means that the capital ship now faces a new menace that must be guarded against every possible study and effort . . . Today we have seen a 2,000-pound bomb, half of whose weight represented TNT explosive, dropped alongside a battleship after having been carried by an airplane 100 miles from base out to sea. The thing done today was the carrying of a mine of unprecedented size out that distance in land planes and putting it down successfully. Stop and think what that all means."[26]

General Menoher stated he believed the sinking of *Ostfriesland* had brought to the forefront a new menace to the battleship that the army, navy, and Congress would have to take immediate steps to address. "A cold material fact has been demonstrated," he said. "That fact is that the battleship can be sunk by the aerial bomb. That's the real lesson of this affair."[27]

The navy did its best to put a positive spin on things. Navy secretary Denby, forcing a smile in front of the news cameras, said of the army flyers: "I congratulate them with all my heart." Admiral W. A. Moffett, director of naval aeronautics, was far more candid: "The lesson is that we must put planes on battleships and get aircraft carriers quickly . . . We must put aviators on all our battleships to enable them to be ready to ward off air bombing attacks in the event of war."[28]

Undersecretary of the Navy Roosevelt seemed far less concerned. "I once saw a man kill a lion with a 30-30 caliber rifle, under certain conditions," he commented haughtily, "but that does not mean that a 30-30 rifle is a lion gun." It was his opinion that airplanes were a splendid auxiliary arm, but he cautioned that "they should not be considered capable of superseding more recognized means of attack and defense." He claimed with a wink that he was anxious to avoid the attitude of deprecating their work but would by no means admit they were superior to battleships.[29]

Glenn L. Martin, the pioneer who had been the first to experiment with aerial bombing in 1913, was among the most prescient of those who had watched the tests. "It is evident, with the large percentage of hits and the size of bombs to be carried hereafter," he stated almost as soon as the last tremors from the falling ordnance had disappeared, "that no fleet afloat is safe if it loses control of the air. Control of the air is vitally necessary. Each country must have sufficient air force to safeguard its capital ships. An enemy by gaining control of the air can now carry its own peace terms into the heart of any country. The sinking of *Ostfriesland* will be epoch making. Future development as I now see it should be one of preparedness with proper air forces paralleled with development of offensive aircraft, with a defensive development, which means that we must have airplane carriers as quickly as they can be obtained and all aircraft equipment necessary to combat such a formidable arm of offense . . . It is evident to every one who attended the demonstration that history is being made."[30]

Martin was not afraid to make a few prognostications. "The future bombing fleet of the air," he predicted, "will be made up similar to the present sea fleet. It will have its capital airships in the form of immense bombing planes loaded with 1,000-pound to 2,000-pound bombs and will be surrounded with various pieces of combat and reconnaissance planes to take care of the capital bombing planes of the sky the same as capital battleships of the surface fleet must be protected." He then revealed that he had just completed designs for an even newer and larger Martin bomber capable of carrying 7,500 pounds of bombs and four tons of gasoline per plane, enough fuel for a radius of a thousand miles at 100 mph. The history of warfare would forever be changed.[31]

When Billy Mitchell returned to Langley Field, he did so as a conquering hero to his men and the army establishment in and around Tidewater Virginia. Even officers of the navy doffed their caps to him as a man who had made good his predictions by achievement. The destruction of *Ostfriesland* had been recognized as almost instantly wiping out "all alibis" of side-deck protective armor. The general had personally flown more than two thousand miles during the week of the *Frankfurt* and *Ostfriesland* tests, making his own damage assessments after each attack and honing the approach for his next try. The accomplishment of his brigade was indeed remarkable, as each army plane had to fly a minimum of two hundred miles on every sortie. None of the bombers had been fitted with pontoons like many of the navy aircraft, which had to fly shorter distances. Yet there had been no loss of life.

In the weeks that followed, the world seemed to spin ever faster. Mitchell's sinking of a battleship from the air had set naval planning and strategy in every major industrialized seafaring nation of the world on its ear. An almost instantaneous reassessment of just who might become America's enemy in the near future was begun. The sinking of the German warships soon proved an embarrassment to Capitol Hill as well as the navy. Before the tests had even begun, the U.S. Congress, in its most recent navy bill, had already killed any hopes of the construction of aircraft carriers. Indeed, the navy possessed but a single active so-called carrier, the USS *Langley,* a converted collier once called *Jupiter.* The press had a field day. "It is the joke of the service," said the *New York Times,* "because its maximum speed is twelve knots. As Congress made an appropriation for this ark of an aviation ship that everybody knew would be obsolete as soon as she was fitted up to carry planes, ignorance of the sore need of the Navy could not be pleaded when the Senate proposal was rejected." The British already had an aircraft carrier fleet of six ships capable of doing twenty-five to thirty-one knots, the largest of which was the 735-foot-long, 19,100-ton *Furious.* Japan was already building its first of a squadron of battle cruiser–speed carriers with each capable of accommodating up to thirty aircraft.[32] Many foresaw either of those nations as America's next major opponent. Moreover, control of the Atlantic and Pacific would never again be a matter for ships alone.

The controversy between Mitchell and the navy did not end with the tests. Mitchell's accusations against the navy for designing the experiments in such a way as to provide a major hindrance to aviators were well known. He now charged that the sea service had placed the tests along the hundred-fathom line to force army aircraft to fly a greater distance than the navy's own planes and, perhaps, cause an embarrassing crash or two. The navy feebly countered by asserting that the test results were invalid because of Mitchell's violation of the rules. Because *Ostfriesland* had been sunk so quickly, the data they had sought to acquire could not be gathered. The general, they said, had destroyed the battleship in such a spectacular fashion for one purpose only—to sway public opinion.[33]

On August 19 a final opinion of the Joint Army and Navy Board on the bomb tests was issued. The board, of which General Pershing was senior member, submitted its findings to Secretary of War Weeks and Assistant Secretary of the Navy Roosevelt. The announcement was stunning in the scope of its inability to digest the important lessons that had been produced by the recent tests, with or without Mitchell's grandstanding. The battleship was "still the backbone of the fleet . . . so long as the safe navigation of the sea for the purpose of transportation is vital to success in war." Despite the results of the tests, the board declared, "the introduction of the airplane has not revolutionized modern naval warfare," nor had it rendered the battleship obsolete. The congressional committee that had killed the acquisition of aircraft carriers and witnessed the tests that proved them wrong unanimously concurred.[34]

If ever there had been a more backward-looking moment in American military history, this was it. General Mitchell was livid and refused to be silenced. In mid-September he delivered his own report of the bombing operations to his superior, General Menoher, who had warned him to "speak softly." Mitchell refused to be muzzled. By September 13 the memorandum had been leaked to the world.

The document was sensational in its opposition to the official line. The equations for naval warfare had been irrevocably altered. "Air forces with the types of aircraft already in existence or in development," Mitchell asserted, "operating from shore bases, were now capable of finding and destroying all classes of seacraft under war conditions with negligible losses to aircraft. It was unnecessary to destroy hostile naval forces at a distance from a shore greater than twenty-five miles in order to protect the coast as that exceeded the range of the most powerful naval guns. Aircraft, acting from suitable air dromes, could destroy any class of surface seacraft on the high seas." Moreover, they could operate under conditions when seacraft were helpless and could safely protect the shores of any coastline. Yet during the navy's orchestrated tests, the aircraft were only allowed to deploy bombs, not torpedoes, gas, gunfire, or mines, all weapons that Mitchell deemed could readily be delivered by air against both land and sea forces of an enemy. They had not been permitted to attack the targets as they would have under combat conditions and were never allowed to employ more than a tenth of the total brigade available for the attack. Had the army aircraft been permitted to conduct the operation, as Mitchell had wanted, none of the targets would have survived for more than ten minutes in a serviceable condition. Indeed, his First Provisional Air Brigade, the cost of which did not exceed that of a single destroyer, could have put the entire Atlantic fleet out of action in a single assault. "The problem of destruction of seacraft by airplanes is finished." It was now imperative to provide an air organization and strategy for defending not only American coasts and cities but also the heartland of the country against hostile air attack. The recent maneuvers had shown that an enemy who gained control of the air—which gave him control of the sea—could deploy aircraft from aircraft carriers onto any islands, which could not be attacked by artillery or troops, to launch air assaults on the great population centers of the nation, "extending even to Chicago, St. Louis and other Middle Western cities," which could be bombed with high explosives and kill citizens with gas and incendiary devices.[35]

When it was published on September 14, Mitchell's vision presented a terrifying scenario that stunned the American public. Yet he had concluded his memorandum with four significant and prescient recommendations to address the problem: (1) that the U.S. government establish a separate air force specifically for frontier and coastal defense; (2) that the navy be specifically equipped for offense on the high seas and not for coastal work; (3) that navy control should cease two hundred miles from shore, leaving protection of the land and coastal defense to the army and air force; and (4) that the various services should coordinate and form a working understanding between them. "The present system, a heritage of our early wars, has clearly demonstrated that the present lack of cooperation is a serious fault . . . In this connection, an efficient solution of our defensive needs will not exist until a department of national defense is organized with a staff common to all services. Sub-secretaries for the Army, the Navy and the Air Services must be created."[36]

Mitchell's farsighted statements, many of which flatly contradicted the accepted dogma, were embarrassing to both the military and political establishments. "Those in high political circles," it was soon being said in the press, "believe that there may be a housecleaning in the Air Service." They were correct.[37]

Over the next few years, the military would conduct more aerial bombing tests on warships, and, as before, General Mitchell would be there to preside over operations and publicly goad the government into taking action. A keen observer of the growing might of the Japanese empire on the Pacific Rim, he predicted that that nation could launch an air attack from mighty aircraft carriers against the Hawaiian Islands and the new American naval base at Pearl Harbor. But by then the establishment had endured him too long.

In April 1925 General Billy Mitchell was reduced to the rank of colonel and transferred to a minor post as air officer in San Antonio, Texas, where he would no longer garner the public's attention—or so it was hoped. Yet he continued to remain critical of the poor state of preparedness of the infant Air Service. The battle of wills between the War Department and the irrepressible officer could not long be sustained. In December 1925 Mitchell was court-martialed for insubordination and suspended from active duty. He chose to resign and on February 1, 1926, retired to his farm at Middleburg, Virginia. From there he continued to employ his fame and reputation to promote air power. On February 19, 1936, General William "Billy" Mitchell died.

Less than five years later, on December 7, 1941, from a fleet of aircraft carriers hundreds of miles from their target, the Imperial Japanese Navy launched its devastating air attack on the American Pacific fleet at Pearl Harbor, sinking or placing out of commission almost every capital ship in port and bringing America into World War II, just as the sinking of *Frankfurt* and *Ostfriesland* and the prescient general had foretold. And nobody had listened.

In 1949 General Billy Mitchell was posthumously awarded a special Congressional Medal of Honor by General Carl Spaatz, chief of staff of the newly established United States Air Force.

# 21

## Chopping the Bank Right Off

They were a hardy lot, the pound-net fishermen who harvested the bounty of the deep a mile or more off the shores of the little seaside resort town of Ocean City. The first of them had emigrated from Cape May, New Jersey, in 1896, a little over twenty years after the founding of the new Maryland resort. Most were independent operators whose whole lives during the season centered on bringing in hardheads, trout, porgies, butterfly fish, and sometimes flounder three or four times a day for local buyers or for consignment to markets in New York, Philadelphia, and Boston.

By the beginning of the 1930s a sizable commercial fishing community had firmly taken root on the south end of town. There a cluster of unpainted, wooden fishing camps lined the beach astride the southern spur of the Baltimore, Chesapeake & Atlantic Railway. It was a low and often wet area where no less than nine individual company camps were maintained not far from the railroad fish-loading platform.[1] It was also a dangerously exposed location, frequently flooded during heavy weather, that offered little sanctuary save for a usually sanded-up southern egress into Sinepuxent Bay called Sandy Point Inlet and a rarely used shoally one called Sinepuxent Point, five miles south of town. Being little more than a depression in the sand, Sandy Point was seldom used, though from time to time, and as recently as 1907, groups of private investors had tried but failed to open it. Nevertheless, with commercial fishing boats being launched directly off the beach, the demand for a sheltered and deep commercial anchorage had begun to grow with the town. Not until 1929 had the State of Maryland seen fit to appropriate $500,000 for such a project, contingent on the availability of federal funds. Sadly, the effort had died aborning, stymied by the onset of the Great Depression.[2]

Yet, as Ocean City and the fishing community slowly grew in economic importance, so did their political clout. In 1931 Senator Millard E. Tydings and Representative R. Alan Goldsborough led a large delegation from the Eastern Shore to press Congress for $281,000 for the project. They argued that a permanent inlet near Ocean City would provide a secure anchorage for as many as a thousand boats, hailing from as far away as New England, to work the offshore fishing grounds. With an inlet convenient to a railhead, they could more efficiently speed their hauls to Baltimore, Philadelphia, New York, Boston, and other markets. The economic benefit to Ocean City, Worcester County, and Maryland was obvious, but the bill failed to pass.[3]

It was a well-known fact that if one wished to know the next day's weather on the Delmarva coast, all one had to do was ask a waterman. Until the late nineteenth century, weather predictions had been largely a matter of conjecture except by those whose livelihoods depended on their knowledge of winds, waves, and tides. Based on keen observations of swells, wind intensities, temperature variations, the roar of the waves, indeed, the very mood of the ocean itself, watermen confidentially claimed they could predict even the slightest of weather changes.[4]

By the third decade of the twentieth century, meteorological science had developed an impressive array of tools to assess weather patterns and predict major storms well in advance of their arrival. Information regarding a storm's origins, tracking, intensity, and dissipation had been immensely improved by the utilization of the telegraph, telephone, radio, balloons, and modern recording devices.[5] The seaside mariners of the Delmarva, however, often stuck to their intuition, for when it came to big storms, few paid attention to the weather bureau. Had the average vacationer at Ocean City, Rehoboth, or Lewes bothered to read up on the subject of hurricanes and tropical storms or pay attention to the worried chatter of the commercial fisherman in early August 1933, many might have headed for the mountains instead of the beach.

The word "hurricane" is said to have been derived from "Hurrakan," which in the language of the Indians of Guatemala meant "storm god." Unquestionably the most powerful and destructive weather events produced by Mother Nature, hurricanes are generally accepted to mean only those tempests whose winds exceed 75 mph or, as the famed hydrographer Francis Beaufort once called them, winds "that no canvas could withstand." Hurricane breeding grounds in the Western Hemisphere usually begin a hundred or more miles north of the equator, and generally extend over the western Atlantic and Caribbean Sea. The life of a hurricane from origin to dissipation varies, but it usually averages twelve days, during which time winds as high as 200 mph can occur, with gusts stepping up velocity to 40 percent or more. A hurricane with 100 mph winds is a stupendous beast that can drive waves up to 50 mph with swells and crests hundreds of miles in advance of the tempest itself, causing devastating flooding in coastal areas even before the storm strikes. Coiled like a snake, most tropical storms that collide with the Delmarva coast (fewer than one a year on average), range from one hundred to four hundred miles in diameter but usually are little more than gales (with winds 39 to 74 mph) or the fringes of storms that have already dissipated or deflected further south. Hurricanes pitch their shade on the beach as previews of worse to come, first as stiff, gusty winds. Then, as the eye of the storm advances, on an average of about 12 mph, the winds increase by degrees until they become gales. Soon they reach hurricane proportions.[6]

• • •

For the two hundred guests of the Atlantic Hotel in Ocean City, their mid-August vacation at the beach had been disappointing. From at least August 19 it had rained, more or less without letup. By August 20 the seas had kicked up something ferocious, and the incessant pounding of the surf had achieved a decibel level none had ever experienced. It was reported that the roar was so loud that it could be heard from as far inland as Snow Hill and Berlin. Though the guests at the Atlantic, among Ocean City's oldest hotels, had little idea of what lay in store for them, the commercial fishing community had already begun to prepare for the worst. For many in Sinepuxent Neck and in the St. Martins region of Worcester County, Maryland, great reliance had traditionally been placed in accessing the roar of the sea. The watermen were well aware that a reverberation such as they were now hearing suggested that storm swells and waves, possibly as high as thirty-five feet, some old-timers said, might soon be striking their shores, perhaps two hundred miles in advance of the actual storm itself. Few realized, however, that not one but two storm systems, one a murderous high-pressure nor'easter and the other a tropical hurricane, were about to converge over the Delmarva. Meteorologist John R. Weeks of the U.S. Weather Bureau described the weather condition as a "tropical disturbance of great intensity west of Bermuda, and a high-pressure area over New England and the lakes region combined." Together they would change the course of regional history.[7]

The weather patterns over the United States during the first weeks of August, monitored by the U.S. Weather Bureau, had been unusual. In the Northwest, a disturbance had formed inland, bringing with it extremely unseasonable weather over the northern Rocky Mountain region, the northern Plains States, Oklahoma, and the Missouri Valley. Unseasonable storms, dropping six inches of snow along the Continental Divide, had closed mountain passes in Montana, while icy rains had fallen from Wyoming to New Mexico, sending temperatures skidding toward freezing. Then the front had driven east, bringing rains to the Atlantic states from New England to the Carolinas. The East was already in ferment when, on Sunday, August 20, the nor'easter had descended upon the Atlantic coast from Boston to Cape Hatteras, striking New Jersey, from Sandy Hook to Cape May, with tragic consequences. At least seven persons had died, while scores of small craft had been destroyed.[8]

The nor'easter, originating out of New England, had struck the Delmarva coast as well, bringing with it torrential rains that dropped six inches of water on Ocean City and eight inches at Berlin in just twenty-four hours. One Ocean City waterman, Captain John Elliott Sr., would recall years later: "It rained continuously like you never saw . . . Every stream emptied into Sinepuxent Bay, Assateague Bay, Isle of Wight Bay, and Assawoman Bay was full and overflowing with more rainwater than I ever knew."[9] The storm, with its high-pressure front, then swerved into the Chesapeake, sinking a dredge named *Point Breeze,* belonging to the Arundel Corporation, in Cut Off Channel near Seven Foot Knoll and caused at least one drowning, while forcing bay shipping to flee for shelter. Fortunately, twenty-seven of the crew had found refuge on a nearby scow and were rescued by the Coast Guard.[10]

The worst was yet to come. The tropical disturbance, swirling out of the Caribbean, the acknowledged "mother of violent West Indian hurricanes," was reported approaching the mid-Atlantic seaboard. The storm, which was first observed on August 17 some one hundred miles east of Puerto Rico, had strengthened into a bona fide hurricane the following day. By August 21 it was centered about 220 miles south-southwest of Bermuda and working slowly NNW with wind velocity registered at 80 mph.[11] Though the alarm was sounded, most ignored the warning. Few hurricanes lived long enough to reach north of the Carolinas, they said. Indeed, the last time a major "north of Hatteras" hurricane had struck the Delmarva coast was way back in 1888.

On Tuesday, August 22, morning newspapers along the East Coast reiterated the danger. "Storm flags flew from Boston to Cape Hatteras this morning," reported the *Washington Post*, "as the Atlantic Coast battened down its movables in anticipation of dangerous gales predicted by the Weather Bureau as a result of a West Indian disturbance."[12] The vacationers in the Atlantic Hotel at Ocean City, as at most resorts on the Delmarva coast, were not yet impressed. They soon would be.

A tropical storm is much like a top that spins furiously in a counter-clockwise direction yet changes its geographic position quite slowly, almost deliberately. The pressure of such a tempest is exceptional and can be highly lethal owing to the vacuum effect it creates on its lee surface. For a hurricane with 100 mph winds it is forty-five pounds per square foot. At 150 mph it is 112 pounds. The velocity of hurricane winds varies with the power of the pressure area and inversely with a storm's center, but they can wreak a swath of destruction unparalleled by anything the hand of man has ever created.[13] In the late night hours of August 22–23, the tropical storm that struck in a slightly oblique northwesterly direction along three hundred miles of Atlantic coast smashed against the beaches of North Carolina and Virginia and then rolled slowly up the shores of the Chesapeake Bay and the Eastern Shore.

The Outer Banks of North Carolina suffered the initial elemental frenzy when a roaring storm surge, well in advance of the tempest itself, broke across the beach at Nags Head, demolishing resort homes, blocking roads, and cutting off all communications with the mainland. Elizabeth City, on the mainland, was soon paralyzed. Between 3:00 and 4:00 A.M., August 23, the beast made landfall at Nags Head with a central pressure reading of 28.50 inches.[14]

The first news of possible losses at sea came in during the early afternoon when the Coast Guard cutter *Modoc* dispatched a report that a message from the Diamond Shoal lightship had been intercepted about 2:00 P.M. The lightship, stationed off Cape Hatteras, reported that it had been swept six miles off its position during the morning by an 80 mph wind. Then the message faded and died.[15]

On the coast, one of the first verifiable victims of the tempest was the four-masted Maryland schooner *G. A. Kohler*. The big 3,365-ton, 212-foot-long vessel had sailed under the command of Captain George H. Hopkins from the pier of Redman-Vane Company, Baltimore, on Sunday, August 20, bound to Cap-Haïtien for logwood. She had been beached two miles south of Gull Shore Coast Guard Station, and twenty-eight miles north of Cape Hatteras. Fortunately, despite the raging storm, nine men and one woman aboard were rescued by the Coast Guard, but their ship was a total loss.[16]

When the storm smashed into Virginia on August 22, it was with unrelenting force preceded by incredibly turbulent seas. On the following day even worse wind-whipped torrents shrieked out of gray heavens, swelling meek runlets and mild, meadow-flanked creeks to devastating flood. At Virginia Beach, no stranger to violent storms, the impact was awesome.

The travails of little Jean Ruggles, a fourteen-year-old who had been visiting the oceanfront cottage of Francis Buchanan, were typical of many visitors to Virginia Beach. The Buchanan family had been playing host to Jean and several other guests when they were warned of the approaching storm. Though they had resolved to ride it out, as did many of their neighbors, lashing winds soon forced them to abandon the elegant framed cottage and seek refuge nearby at the posh Cavalier Beach Club and Hotel. Only minutes after they scuffed from the cottage, it succumbed to the storm and was blown in its entirety into the ocean.[17]

Unfortunately, the refuge offered by the Cavalier was to prove temporary. Soon after the first refugees arrived, the entire protective Cavalier Shores seawall was ripped to pieces and swept to sea. Then the main Virginia Beach seawall fell victim to the sledgehammer blows of the surf. Soon, the approaches to the Lesner Bridge at Lynnhaven Inlet north of town were severed, cutting off Cape Henry and all the residents of Virginia Beach from Norfolk. Within hours the Cavalier Beach Club had been completely destroyed, with parts of the wreckage swept by the waves clear across Atlantic Avenue, the town's principal street, which was by then under five feet of water. Once again little Jean and the other terrified storm victims were forced to seek refuge. Some found sanctuary in a ferry terminal at Willoughby Beach and others in private homes that were still standing. Yet rescuers were already en route. Wading in water up to their armpits, a body of resolute U.S. Coast Guardsmen fought through swirling currents in utter darkness to take people from tottering cottages, even as the winds ripped roofs and porches off all about them, hurling them into the ocean. Eventually, seventy residents and guests, including Jean Ruggles, were saved from what was left of the once-prestigious Cavalier Shores.[18]

Not far to the west, the two grand wings of the Nansemond Hotel at Ocean View were undermined by the waves and outrushing waters, and occupants there were forced to evacuate as well. The local boardwalk and its bulkheads were completely splintered.[19]

The assault on Hampton Roads ravaged seawalls, hotels, and cottages but also produced "ghastly stories of wholesale destruction." The eye of the hurricane passed over Norfolk at 9:00 A.M., and twenty minutes later the pressure fell to 28.08 inches, one of the lowest pressure readings ever registered in Virginia. Blowing at gale force ashore but hurricane force at sea, the storm pushed a high tide before it directly into the roads with battering-ram brutality. Harbor shipping was unable to dock when waves inundated waterfront piers. Communication lines were ripped away; vacationers on the shore were forced to flee from crumbling beach structures, traffic stalled entirely, and the whole power grid shut down when the electric-generating station was flooded. For the first time in fifty years, owing to winds of up to 80 mph, the Norfolk-Portsmouth ferry suspended operation.[20]

In Norfolk, city newspapers and many industrial plants were forced to shut down when coursing tidewaters five feet deep flooded streets and cellars, broke windows, and swept porch furniture into the newborn currents. Rafts and other improvised forms of transportation were used in the morning, with the former providing the sole means of moving through Norfolk's business district. At Newport News, Phoebus, and Buckroe Beach the story was much the same. Cottages along nearly a mile of the shore at Buckroe had already been ripped apart during the predawn hours and blown into a tangled mass of debris. Many occupants, fearful of an unknown fate in the darkness outside, remained in those houses still standing until daybreak, when a general evacuation of the resort was made through heavily inundated streets. National Guard officers at Buckroe and Phoebus begged for help, reporting that lives and property were seriously threatened while their own resources were stretched to the limit. Virginia governor John Garland Pollard requested the U.S. War Department to furnish all necessary assistance, even as concrete highways and roads sank from sight, bridges washed away, railroad lines ruptured, and all of civilization's intimate and vital arteries of travel and communication were being indiscriminately mangled. The Virginia National Guard was ordered mobilized, and the U.S. Army moved to dispatch assistance to sorely stricken Phoebus and elsewhere.[21]

At the onset of the storm, late on August 22, Major General Paul B. Malone, commandant of the U.S. Army Third Corps Area, which embraced Virginia, Maryland, the District of Columbia, and Pennsylvania, had wisely placed his command on alert. He ordered all officers to remain on duty throughout the night to maintain radio communications with distressed points in the corps area. Nevertheless, the city of Newport News was soon isolated from contact with the outside world, both physically and electronically. Power cables and telephone lines were blown down, while streetcar tracks were washed out in countless places. Ferry services from the town were suspended. As the disaster intensified, Malone repeatedly attempted to telegraph his superior in Washington, Brigadier General Samuel G. Waller, adjutant-general of Virginia, for permission to take National Guard tents, cots, blankets, and other supplies to the relief of storm victims at Phoebus and Buckroe Beach, but efforts to get the message through proved futile. Though assistance was eventually dispatched from as far away as Fort George G. Meade in Maryland, it would not arrive for days.[22]

Among the many strategic points with which General Malone had attempted in vain to communicate with was Fort Monroe, the most important military base in Tidewater Virginia. At 5:50 P.M., the base commander, Brigadier General Joseph P. Tracy, radioed that wave and wind damage there had been severe.[23]

"Worst storm last night and this morning in the history of Fort Monroe has caused havoc here," he reported the next day.

> Antiaircraft guns park demolished and antiaircraft guns damaged. Officers beach club partly demolished and noncommissioned officers' club wiped out. Noncommissioned officers' wooden quarters swept off foundation. Some cantonment buildings occupied by Virginia National Guard slipped from foundation and partly demolished. All temporary buildings housing tractors, trucks and mobile searchlights wrecked. Magazines flooded. Tide poured into old fort, but dike hurriedly built kept flood out of barracks. Waterfront piers and half of railway trestle demolished. Highway bridge connecting fort to mainland badly damaged. Many trees down all over post. Post without electric current preventing operation of pumps and sewage ejection. Waves washed across and inundated the entire post. National Guard troops and large class of reserve officers have been housed in regular garrison. Expect high tide at 10 tonight, but hope that shift in storm will prevent much further damage. Hospital full of refugees, but no casualties so far.[24]

By late afternoon on August 23 the water had barely subsided enough to permit resumption of some vehicular traffic in a few areas of the lower Virginia coast. That brief recession, even though the winds were still blowing, enabled the navy, Coast Guard, and local fire and police departments to unite in rescuing flood victims in inaccessible areas. Every available boat was called into service. "Motorized" police were dispatched from Richmond to Newport News and Phoebus. Within hours approximately one hundred families marooned at Willoughby Beach, many standing on their rooftops, were rescued. Coast Guardsmen were obliged to take many people out of second-story windows at Willoughby and Ocean View, where furniture drifted aimlessly in canals that had once been streets. Fatalities, unfortunately, were inevitable. During the morning a fallen power line electrocuted three men in Portsmouth, and a man named Oscar Dockery drowned while trying to tow a boat ashore. In Suffolk a downed high-tension wire electrocuted a thirteen-year-old boy. Two more people drowned at Willoughby, hardest hit of the surrounding communities.[25]

In Hampton Roads and in the lower Chesapeake enormous damage was done to the shipping. The Norwegian freighter *Linghaug* was driven ashore on Craney Island. Some vessels, such as the tug *Bald Rock*, bound from New York to Norfolk, had failed to appear. Farther out in the bay, the fishing fleets of Tangier and Smith Islands had been all but wiped out. On the James River, at historic Jamestown Island, where the first English settlers landed, a bridge connecting with the mainland was submerged and the island flooded. Thirty people had to be rescued by boat. On the York River, historic Yorktown was termed "a desolate waste." The water in the river had risen ten feet above normal and, lashed by a sixty-mile-gale, destroyed most of the lower town. The beach and concession buildings met the full force of the waves, and nothing was left intact except a brick bathhouse. In the shopping and shipping section all buildings except brick structures had been destroyed. The Baltimore Steamship Company docks were wrecked, and both the Yorktown and Gloucester ferry slips had been carried away. The long dock of the hotel company and the fishery docks were almost a total loss. A large ice plant and the shipping depot of the local fish company were under water. All small craft anchored in the stream had been carried away.[26]

By the evening of August 23, the first damage estimates began to come in: $1 million at Virginia Beach, $1.5 million at Ocean View and Willoughby, $2 million at Norfolk. All were very preliminary figures. At Norfolk, thousands of small boats on the streets provided the only mode of transportation. The Virginia Electric and Power Company plant and its two largest turbines, which supplied the Hampton Roads power grid, were still under water even as the Norfolk City Fire Department struggled to pump it out. The ground floor office of the *Norfolk Ledger-Dispatch* was covered by fourteen inches of water, and staff members, trying to get publication back on line, worked in bare feet or boots. Of the 27,000 telephones in the city, 25,000 were out of order after lines had been felled by thousands of uprooted trees. Out of the thirty-eight square miles in the Norfolk area, ten were still covered by water, contributing to an almost complete intercity disruption of communications between Norfolk, Portsmouth, Newport News, Hampton, Phoebus, Virginia Beach, Ocean View, and Willoughby.[27] And the storm had not yet even begun to dissipate.

The roaring storm, it was reported in the *Baltimore Sun,* was now marching "with tattered banners of cloud up the Chesapeake and the Delaware Bay into the verdant fruitlands of the Delmarva Peninsula." Now, more than four thousand square miles of the Eastern Shore would soon find itself absolutely isolated.[28]

Some of the most harrowing tales of distress and hardship were reported in lower Accomack County, Virginia, where the county courthouse served as both a refuge and information center. Throughout the storm, bedraggled, worn-out men, women, and children had filtered in, many having endured a night and day of absolute terror on tiny isolated wooded hummocks and islands along the Atlantic coast. On Wallops Island, forty-five women and children had been rescued from a fishing lodge clubhouse and carried by Coast Guardsmen to a place of apparent safety on a pine-covered hummock on the only immediate elevated terrain on the mainland. Thinking they were safe, they soon found themselves trapped by the rising tide and forced to take refuge in the tops of pine trees. As the deadly waters surged beneath them with unrelenting force, the refugees were obliged to lash themselves to the treetops. For a full thirty-six hours the women clutched their children to their breasts and watched the breakers roll through the woods, shaking their precious refuges with every new wave.

One man who occupied a house on a small island off Chincoteague awakened to find the water coming into his bedroom on the second floor. Quickly, he placed his wife and baby into a small skiff, covered them with a blanket so they would not panic at the sight of the sea, and shoved off for the mainland. He eventually safely alighted Noah-like in the barnyard of a farmer in upper Accomack County.[29]

In the town of Oyster, Mrs. Jessie Davis, while clinging to her roof, had her two-year-old child torn from her arms by the sea. At Hacksneck, a falling tree crushed a man. On Monkhorn Island, the island's owners, Larimer Cushman and his wife, were driven to the roof of their hunting lodge, where they clung to a flagpole for hours until rescued by the Coast Guard. Reports coming in from Hog Island suggested that as many as two hundred residents had been forced to flee. Even the Coast Guard stations at Wachapreague, Parramore, Metompkin, and Cobb Island had all been abandoned, and none too soon. Within hours, the storm surge had swept across all of the barrier islands of Accomack and Northampton Counties, leveling most signs of humanity before it. The elegant hunting and fishing lodges that drew sportsmen from all over the Eastern seaboard and beyond disappeared in the twinkling of an eye. Most would never come back. The famed Cobb family hunting and fishing resort, along with several family members, ceased to exist.[30]

Many Baltimoreans had attempted to drive to the rescue of their families vacationing at Ocean City and other coastal resorts, but the floods had turned all back. The first reliable information on the paralysis of the Delmarva did not reach Baltimore until the night of August 24, when an agent of the Associated Press named H. Skipworth Gordon Jr. returned from a dangerous nine-hour two-hundred-mile driving survey of the Maryland Eastern Shore. His report was dismal.[31]

Fruit orchards, with countless trees ripe with peaches, apples, and pears, were beaten down, and crops were devastated. Every river and creek on the peninsula had overflowed, forcing thousands of people to second floors of their homes or to seek refuge on higher ground. Highways were flooded, in some places as much as four feet deep. "The whole fertile peninsula," reported the press, "appeared ravished by the winds and the rain, as its myriad rivers large and small—the Pocomoke, Nanticoke, Choptank, Chester, and Elk among others—felt the frantic pulse of life from their drainage sheds and sped berserk toward the bay and sea." All along the coast, ships were beached, smaller craft wrecked, villages and hamlets inundated by mammoth waves, and the highway system and bridges torn asunder or ruined by swollen streams.[32]

By midday of August 23 the Maryland Eastern Shore south of the town of Northeast, in Cecil County, was cut off from the outside world, with only a few scattered reports being produced by hobby wireless operators. In Easton, the three hangars at the Tred Avon Airport and several planes were demolished. At Cambridge riverfront homes were under water. Civilian Conservation Corps Camp No. 1318 nearby was completely destroyed. The bridge at Greensboro was wiped off the map. At Denton and Dover, the Choptank bridges were under water. Federalsburg was flooded by nearby Marshyhope Creek. In Delaware, whole towns such as Cardova, Greenburg, and Goldsboro were completely inundated. All roads to Elkton had been flooded except the one to Ocean City. Rescue and salvage work everywhere was still all but impossible. By nightfall "the entire southward pointing finger of the Delmarva Peninsula, south of a line running from east to west through Rehoboth, Bridgeville and Easton, was mute beneath the weight of its disaster."[33]

On the Chesapeake the waters were "lashed into a turmoil" by a six- to nine-foot surge with crests as high as twelve feet that virtually sank or stopped all traffic. A report from Crisfield was devastating. Practically the entire fishing fleet had been destroyed. A report to Maryland governor Albert Ritchie was succinct: "Islands near town completely isolated from mainland. Smith and Deal Islands had bridges washed out, and all roads leading to them covered with water. Islands as far south as Point Lookout cut off from mainland. Hooper's Island bridge between Charity Point and town of Fishing Creek carried away. Bridge between Pan's Point and Bluff Point washed out, with whole neck in that area under water. All boats in Hooper Island group appeared to have been smashed. Neck between Honga river and Fishing Bay in bad shape with large areas flooded and bridges washed away."[34]

Neither were the northern and western shores of the Chesapeake spared. The tidal surge on the Chesapeake had been huge, as the main line of the storm slithered up the western shore in Maryland. As the surge was forced into the narrowing confines of the Potomac River and became a tidal bore, literally a wall of water, an entire amusement park at Colonial Beach, on the Virginia side of the river, was destroyed. By the time the surge reached Alexandria it was twelve feet above normal low tide, and it flooded the town's entire waterfront strand, including the Ford Motor Company plant and the Torpedo Factory, under six feet of brine. At Washington the water reached 11.3 feet above normal low tide. On the Anacostia River, a train was swept off a bridge, killing ten people. Solomons Island, at the mouth of the Patuxent River, was completely inundated. Upriver, four soldiers died when their car was swept into the Little Patuxent.[35] Even Annapolis, the capital of Maryland, was totally isolated as the storm increased in violence. The Severn River bridges were completely inundated, and the few reports reaching Baltimore told of many residents marooned on the waterfront being removed from their homes by boats.[36]

At Baltimore, where the winds were reported at only 52 mph and the storm was considered mildest, great trees were toppling all over town. Traffic was snarled, and much of the waterfront of the inner harbor was flooded. Along Light Street, the city's main waterfront thoroughfare, water was six feet above the pilings. All the city's main bridges and their approaches were inundated. Interurban bus transportation halted completely. All bay ferry services were discontinued. Baltimore and Ohio Railroad officials reported that the company's tracks between Baltimore and Washington were blocked by high water and washouts, and trains had to be rerouted over the Pennsylvania Railroad. The Pennsylvania reported that its own trains were running far behind schedule. Telephone and telegraph communications suffered frequent interruptions owing to fallen poles and broken lines. Communications were out completely at many points beyond Baltimore, especially connections with the Eastern Shore and southern Maryland.[37]

On the upper bay near Baltimore four barges were torn from their moorings, with two of the barges stranded and the other two lost. Hundreds of yachts and small boats were also lost, sunk, or damaged beyond repair. The destruction or sinking of private and commercial craft along the Patapsco River waterfront was traumatizing. At the Maryland Yacht Club alone, no fewer than fifteen expensive yachts were destroyed.[38] Along Jones Falls and Gwynn's Falls, rising waters trapped or drove families out of houses. Shore cottages at Dundalk were reported afloat. Soldiers were dispatched from the Holabird Quartermaster Depot to aid the occupants. Coast Guardsmen were summoned to the rescue of families marooned on Miller's Island, where, according to some reports, parents had to hold their children on their shoulders to keep them safe from the rising tide, which was already shoulder deep. Families were also reported similarly marooned at Essex and surrounding points. The Back River Bridge was under water.

As more reports began to filter into the army's Third Corps Area headquarters from remote inland centers of the Eastern Shore, the news was as distressing as any from the coast. When an unidentified wireless operator radioed that the Maryland town of Salisbury, situated on the Wicomico River twenty-five miles from the sea, was in "serious condition and practically wiped out," the report was at first discounted. The fact that several small milldams on the river above the town had been weakened and were in danger of bursting was overlooked. Yet the town's situation was critical. The Du Pont Highway, the major artery between the town and Dover, fifty miles to the north, and numerous collateral roads were impassable because of high water, washed-out bridges, and gaping ruptures in the pavement. A bridge on the south side of town was partially destroyed, while one leading into the north section of the city was obliterated. Then, the milldams began to burst. Tuesday night, the pond at Leonard's Mill had risen until the Salisbury-Delmar highway was flooded. The pond backed up behind a twenty-two-foot fill of the New York, Philadelphia, and Norfolk Railroad until it broke through the obstruction and washed into the Isabella Street Dam. Four hundred feet of the main highway between Salisbury and Easton were carried away in an instant. Then, three more dams burst. High water soon began to flood some sections of the town and surrounding countryside. Only one dam remained, the battered Isabella Street Dam, which, if it failed, would inundate much, if not most, of the business district.[39]

Salisbury's utility commission met in an emergency session at noon and decided on a bold plan to redirect the overflow around the city and relieve the pressure on the Isabella. By that time the river had already backed up behind the dam into the homes and buildings along the banks, forcing residents to flee. Every able-bodied man in Salisbury soon turned out to dig a large ditch to divert the Wicomico onto the main highway between the town and Ocean City. Though the effort was initially successful, the town now found itself entirely cut off from communications with the outside world.[40] Then the dam broke.


Ocean City, twenty-five miles to the east of Salisbury, was in even worse shape, but no one except those already trapped therein seemed to know how bad, as all communication had been severed. Before the telephone lines had gone down, however, it was reported that many summer residents vacationing in the resort, having spent an uneasy night listening to the mounting power of the storm, had begun to evacuate about six in the morning of August 23. Waves sweeping across the strip of land on which the town was situated stranded many motorists in their tracks and began pushing across into Sinepuxent Bay. The wind was blowing at between 60 and 70 mph. Then all contact was lost. The little information that escaped in the ensuing hours, however, was disconcerting. Everyone reckoned the worst when an amateur radio operator in Baltimore, F. H. Warnsmann Jr., received a cryptic message from an operator in the resort saying the town "needs help bad."[41]

Somehow, the only bridge connecting the city to the mainland, though in danger of collapse and frequently swept by waves, was still standing. A few refugees who had managed to evacuate about 2:00 P.M. and make it to Elkton were the last to leave. They reported that mountainous waves as high as twenty to thirty feet had been battering the boardwalk, sweeping sections of it into side roads, closing down streets, shutting off electricity, and fouling water supplies before spilling into the sound to the west of the city. Distilled water in bottles was being peddled door to door by some enterprising souls willing to brave the storm. The battering had continued throughout the early part of the day as a general exodus slowly filtered across the causeway bridge. The natives of the city stood fast, but visitors who could flee did so. "People got out first by automobile, then by foot," it was reported the following day. "The bridge shook under fleeing cars. It was hard to evacuate. Many cars, flooded under as much as four feet of water, simply blocked places where roads had once stood. The electric gas pumps were out of commission and there was only one operating pump in town." Nevertheless, all who could get out of the resort took their own vehicles, escaped in their friends' cars, or in the few buses still running back and forth between Ocean City and Berlin.[42]

Throughout the day angry combers continued to tear out great sections of the boardwalk, in some instances depositing fifty-foot chunks, with lampposts intact and upright, many yards inshore. Sand and spray from the waves were carried a block from the beach onto Baltimore Avenue, while the houses fronting on the bay soon found themselves surrounded by water.[43]

The refugees who escaped during the morning later reported that by midday, when the Sinepuxent Bridge was in great danger of giving way, police were only allowing cars to cross one by one. No one was being permitted back into town unless they could provide a good reason. The last resorters who attempted the crossing said that at the time seawater was churning over the running boards of their automobiles. The Pennsylvania Railroad Bridge over Sinepuxent Bay had already been demolished by giant waves. Then some visitors began to flee by boat. Berlin, a few miles distant, was inundated not only by water but by refugees as well. Nevertheless, at least four thousand persons, two-thirds of them out-of-town visitors, now found themselves marooned in Ocean City, a place many thought would surely be swallowed whole by the sea.[44]

By evening, the lower end of the boardwalk had been entirely washed away. Eventually, the largest part of the three-mile-long boardwalk would disappear. Many private homes were already in ruins and abandoned. One vacated ground-floor apartment resembled a recent archaeological excavation site. A copy of Theodore Dreiser's *American Tragedy* lay on the threshold, sand was level with the bedsteads, and an empty baby's crib stood on a heap of sediment. In fact, many buildings fronting the ocean were filled with layers of sand driven up from the beach, even as the underpinnings of hotel and cottage porches were blasted away in other places by the erosive waves. At the Idlewild Hotel the waves beat in the ground-floor windows and flooded it. Guests at the Colonial Hotel were evacuated when the waves grew to dangerous proportions. The guests were placed in quarters farther back from the beach, until they too became untenable. The cellar floor of the George Washington Hotel was completely wrecked when its portion of the blocking boardwalk frontage simply disappeared into the sea. At the Atlantic Hotel the first floor was flooded, and a barbershop therein was eviscerated by the waves. Despite the storm, the owner of the Atlantic, where there had been some two hundred guests on August 22, found only thirty the next day. That night, in what can only be described as a bold display of Eastern Shore bravado, because a dance had been scheduled, a dance was held.[45]

The deluge churned by the mad northeast wind did not spare the Delaware coast. Though it battered Wilmington and New Castle County, it was much more severe below Dover and in Sussex where wind-leveled trees fell across wires, cutting off communication. Some towns were without gas and electric power. Railroad tracks were inundated, dams were blown out, and crops leveled. In Sussex, where 70 mph winds and sheet rain laced the countryside, crop loss was believed to be total. Practically every road in the county was under water. The entire coastal sector of the state was simply smashed to bits. Rehoboth Beach, it was reported, was "almost torn away by the fury of the ocean," and the little town was evacuated only with great difficulty. At some points the ocean and bay had met. Historic old Cape Henlopen, "pointing its snub nose northward at the mouth of Delaware Bay" was said to have been all but erased by the waves. At Lewes, the gale was providing the town with one of the worst lashings it had experienced in years.[46]

The waters of Delaware Bay and River were equally destructive. The gale had whipped up tremendous waves, which were slashing all of the beaches, causing enormous destruction to property. Boats moored along the bay were torn loose and hammered to bits. At Milford, the military installations at Fort Salisbury had to be evacuated "as the water rose round the houses on the reservation and licked the edges of the fort itself." At Frederica, on Browns River, the dams gave way. At Bowers Beach and Slaughter Beach, the flooding drove residents to the second floors or roofs of their houses and inundated highway escape routes. Inshore between Kitts Hammock and Lewes, thousands of acres of land were flooded. In the capital at Dover, dwellings and pavements were torn asunder by trees uprooted by the wind. At Leipsic, residents worked desperately to lay sandbags to stem the flooding Leipsic River from washing away the shoreline. Woodland Beach and Bayview Beach, and the shores of the Chesapeake and Delaware Canal, were under water, causing damage to innumerable structures. At New

Castle, a big U.S. Army Corps of Engineers tugboat named *Liston* was reported missing with four crewmen. A search was immediately launched. Braving the downpour and churning seas, the U.S. Engineers tug *Camden* courageously put out for a search of the river and bay but was forced to return empty handed.[47]

Though Wilmington was largely spared, inland towns such as Laurel and Seaford, both on small waterways, suffered inordinately. In the little village of Laurel, thirty homes were flooded, and five of them on Lindbergh Avenue were washed away as the waters of a once-docile tributary of the Broad River called Rossakatum Branch swept through the town. The twenty-foot-high wall of water funneling through had literally decimated seventy-five feet of highway and carried off half a dozen bridges. Local firemen worked feverishly to rescue scores of families marooned in their homes, while those fortunates whose houses were on higher land were giving aid to the flood victims.[48]

By the morning of August 24, relinquishing its grip on a stricken Eastern Shore, the storm that had howled in from the Atlantic Ocean for thirty-six hours began to yield to clearing skies and fitful sunlight. It was time to take stock and regroup. The region was still cut off from the rest of the world, with floodwaters still covering tens of thousands of acres. Indeed, even many sections of the Western Shore of Maryland and Virginia were still isolated. In rural southern Maryland, which had suffered from considerable flooding, the state police had to be called out to prevent looting.[49]

In Tidewater Virginia, and along the shores of Accomack and Northampton Counties, rehabilitation and relief services, aided by nearly a score of local, state, and federal agencies, began the long struggle to restore damaged homes and businesses and, wherever possible, the salvage of crops. Virginia representative S. Otis Bland went to Washington to be assured that the National Red Cross, the Civilian Conservation Corps, the Public Health Service, the Public Works Administration, and other federal agencies had a true picture of the situation. Governor Pollard ordered a commission to survey the damage and report quickly and precisely as to what immediate aid was needed, and to make recommendations to the state and federal public works committees just what projects should be developed as precautions against similar disasters in the future.[50]

Rehabilitation would be costly and difficult. At Norfolk thousands of persons lined up for inoculation against typhoid fever when it was feared that the water supply had been contaminated. Even the beginnings of the cleanup were fraught with obstructions when thunderstorms and waves still rolling in at record highs caused unending delays. Throughout many towns, fishing boats and pleasure craft, which had washed into main streets, now lay strewn about amid unroofed houses and some buildings that had been turned end on end. Power lines and telephone cables lay strung about like wet spaghetti around uprooted trees. Public services were at a standstill.[51]

On the Eastern Shore of the state, from Saxis Island down along Onancock, Pungoteague, Nandua, and Occohannock Creeks, towns were still inundated and household furniture ruined. At least ten people in the region were known dead. On the coast at Chincoteague, Wachapreague, Willis Wharf, and Oyster, wharves were wrecked, hundreds of boats sunk, and seafood processing plants razed. Damage to farm crops was incalculable.[52]

There was some good news amid the bad, as bands of refugees, many believed to have been lost, continued to trickle back to civilization. The forty-five women and children who had been forced to lash themselves to the tops of pine trees, though threatened with hunger and exhaustion, had steadfastly clung to their perches until there was a pause in the storm. During the lull, they escaped with their children to Wishatt's Point and were given food and medical treatment by Coast Guardsmen from the Wallops Island Station, who had had to abandon their own base.[53]

A band of fifty haggard refugees from an isolated storm-ravaged strip of land fifteen miles south of Norfolk, between Back Bay and the Atlantic, who had abandoned their wrecked homes and sought shelter in the ruins of the Little Creek Coast Guard Station, had also struggled to reach civilization. The day after the storm they managed to walk to the outskirts of Virginia Beach, where they were supplied food dropped from airplanes.[54]

The damage in Maryland was more readily ascertained than in Virginia. Governor Ritchie was the first state executive to order an assessment of the ruin on the afternoon of August 25, even before contact could be made with his state's most isolated sectors. He had also begun immediate measures to provide whatever state assistance could be generated for thousands of homeless refugees.[55]

A contingent of six Maryland National Guard planes under the command of Major Charles D. Masson was dispatched to conduct an aerial survey of the tidewater regions of the state to determine what relief measures would be necessary. The planes took off from Logan Field at 1:45 P.M. and returned at 6:00, each of them having covered separate territories of about 340 miles. Manned by a dozen airmen, the squadron flew over two thousand miles, blanketing an area south of Marydel, east of the Chesapeake Bay, as far south as Crisfield and east to Ocean City. Aerial photographs of the landscape were taken to show state officials the extent of the damage. Throughout the Eastern Shore, with miles of farmlands under water, the property destruction was enormous. Roads were washed away and bridges carried off by swollen rivers. They found that the islands off Crisfield and south of Cambridge were still entirely cut off from civilization. A subsequent survey of the bay by an Annapolis Naval Academy seaplane reported that Hooper, Taylors, and Bloodsworth Islands were flooded and had suffered severely. As information from bay watermen in the state began to filter in, it was soon apparent that nearly every wharf on the Western Shore, and the majority on the Eastern Shore, had been destroyed or badly damaged.[56]

The aerial survey of Ocean City, which was still cut off from the whole world, was particularly illustrative of the damage incurred. "Road near Sinepuxent Bay covered by two to three feet of water," it was reported. "Large section of beach washed away, with bay running into ocean. On west of town many houses and boats destroyed. Railway tracks running toward Berlin washed away for a distance of 3,000 feet . . . In southern section of resort many buildings in the amusement park destroyed with about 4,000 feet of boardwalk washed away. Larger hotels and most of beach cottages appeared to be all right. Southern section of town hardest hit."[57] Ironically, while many people were digging their automobiles out of sands that had drifted like snow above the hubcap level, and others cleared wrecked homes and the basement bars of hotels fronting the beach, a few who had come to the resort for the beach had already begun to romp again in the surf at the first glimpse of sun.

Captain George Cobb, a member of the Maryland National Guard squadron that flew over the resort, had a quite personal interest in his mission—his wife and son had been vacationing there when the storm struck. The plane in which Cobb rode as observer was flying directly over the resort when, to his amazement, he spied his family sitting on the battered porch of a hotel. The plane circled over the beach at low altitude and the captain dropped a note to his wife. The message was instantly picked up, and his family waved that they were all right. People swimming in the ocean also waved to the plane as it passed.

Even as some folks quickly returned to their normal lives, news streamed in that many others never would. Late on the night of August 25, more bad tidings from Ocean City reached Washington and Annapolis: Captain H. L. Birch and his assistant, H. I. Mason, representing the entire personnel of the Green Run Coast Guard Station, sixteen miles south of the resort, were missing. An overturned lifeboat, marked "Green Run Coast Guard," led Ocean City Coast Guardsmen to believe Birch and Mason had been lost in attempting to cross to the mainland during the storm. Moreover, the bodies of two African American youths were found floating nearby in the bay west of the station. The two boys had been missing since Wednesday when they tried to swim to the mainland from a duck-blind raft.[58]

Some islands in the Chesapeake remained isolated, even those normally connected by bridges to the mainland. The storm-driven seas had smashed the Hooper Island Bridge, even as the island itself was inundated. The first refugees from that place reported that coffins had been washed up out of cemeteries, boats wrecked or foundered, and packing houses blown down. Moreover, the islanders were now badly in need of food. Dorchester County commissioners set out at once by boat laden with supplies for the island. On their arrival they learned that at least four islanders had been lost.[59]

The cost to the state was not just in property. As in Virginia, the fear of epidemic was uppermost in many minds. Dr. Robert H. Riley, state director of health, ordered all county health officers in the impacted area to be on guard against epidemics arising from polluted water supplies. The state conservation commissioner, Swepson Earle, followed with the gloomy assessment that the amount of debris, mud, and sand washed from the banks of Maryland shores would seriously affect oystering in shoal waters for the foreseeable future.[60]

The August storm of 1933 was deemed by later historians of the event to have caused the greatest damage to the seaside of Maryland, and by extension the entire Delmarva coast, up to that time. The final estimate of damage ranged between $30 and $40 million. In rural Worcester County alone, the loss was estimated at $800,000 "in a time when money values were much higher" than today. Of forty-one oyster houses in the county, which had been readied for the coming season, only eight badly damaged establishments were left standing. Though the accompanying winds had barely reached hurricane strength in some areas, indeed achieving an official reading of only 70 mph at Norfolk, 82 mph at Cape Henry, and 88 mph at Norfolk Naval Air Station, waves and tidal surge had been devastating. The total loss of life reported on August 25 stood at forty-seven—thirteen in Maryland, twelve each in Virginia and Pennsylvania, eight in New Jersey, and two in New York.[61] Word of additional fatalities would later trickle in.

If there were any bright spots, they were in the countless acts of heroism and selflessness exhibited by average citizens, civil servants, and the military alike. The Coast Guard had been outstanding in its professionalism and dedication. In the Baltimore-Washington metropolitan area alone, 195 lives were saved by rescues from sinking craft or by towing helpless victims to port, including five large excursion vessels. Scores more were saved in the bay, and along the Atlantic coast from North Carolina to New Jersey. Innumerable acts of gallantry undoubtedly went unreported.[62]

Many more were the tales of steely resolve against overwhelming odds. The fate of the Old Dominion Line veteran passenger steamer *Madison* and her unflappable commander, Captain W. S. Heath, stands out among them. *Madison* had departed New York for Norfolk with thirty-seven passengers and a crew of sixty when she immediately encountered the advance fringes of the storm off Sandy Hook, New Jersey. Fortunately, the stoutly built ship was no foreigner to adversity. During twenty-two years of service she had survived a ramming by a fruit steamer in 1912, entanglement in a steel antisubmarine net in Hampton Roads during World War I, grounding in a dense fog off Norfolk, and a fire at New York in 1928.[63]

At 5:45 A.M. on August 23, however, she encountered seas the likes of which she had never faced before and began shipping water over her port quarter, badly damaging the saloon housing amidships. The captain persevered, keeping his bow headed in toward the wind and waves in an effort to ride out the storm. Then, at 7:20, a gigantic rogue wave, estimated by witnesses at an incredible seventy feet in height, loomed out of the darkness. At that moment, Captain Heath and First Officer Z. S. Baranowski were standing in the pilothouse and saw it coming, "a giant roller that towered even above the smokestack of the vessel." The monster wave broke over the starboard bow, carrying away the second-class quarters and railing around the forecastle deck. Quartermaster James Corbett, off watch at the time, was in his quarters and lost. Second Mate L. Lawrence, who had gone aft to lash down a lifeboat that had been wildly careening back and forth in its davits on the starboard side, was also swept away. Immense quantities of seawater flooded staterooms, hallways, and other sections of the ship. Heath immediately ordered an S.O.S. sent out over the wireless.[64]

Purser C. W. Ruddocks, who was in charge of the passengers below deck, rushed into action. Praising the courage of his charges, he later reported: "There were no signs of hysteria. We had been battling high seas ever since we left New

York Tuesday afternoon and many of the passengers were suffering from seasickness. Most of them were in their staterooms. Only three persons were in the social hall on the promenade deck when . . . a gigantic wave sent a great section of the starboard railing smashing through the side of the hall. One man was sitting on a bench along the side of the room. How he escaped is a mystery. He wasn't even scratched . . . Immediately orders were sent out for all passengers to come into the social hall. Despite the fact that one side of the hall was smashed in, it was still the driest part of the vessel. Everybody was nervous—but everybody held their heads. Several of the passengers knelt in prayer."[65]

The S.O.S., which was repeated constantly throughout the morning, was picked up at Coast Guard headquarters in Norfolk, and the cutter *Carabassett* and destroyer *Upshur* were dispatched to take off passengers and crew if necessary. Captain Heath, however, was steadfastly resolved to weather the storm if he could until help arrived and grimly continued to head into the wind. Not until 7:30 P.M. did *Upshur,* the first rescue craft, find the stricken steamer twenty-seven miles southeast of the Chesapeake Lightship. Forty minutes later, in an effort to help calm the turbulent waters, the destroyer began to spread oil on the sea. Under escort of the warship, *Madison* then shaped a course for the lightship and from there toward Old Point Comfort in the Chesapeake. A little after 2:00 A.M., August 24, with the assistance of a tug, Captain Heath brought his ship smoothly up to Pier 5 on the Norfolk waterfront.[66]

The ship was in ruins, with her forward deckhouse and sections of her railing and superstructure swept away, scores of cabins smashed, and many of her lifeboats gone. Yet, owing to the superb seamanship of both captain and crew, the steady courage of the passengers, and a dose of good luck, there were, besides the two men swept overboard, only three other casualties, all hospitalized. Captain W. S. Heath, a modest man, had saved the day, and his passengers and crew knew it. Yet, as soon as the ship docked, he slipped away amid the rousing cheers of passengers who credited his ability with preserving their lives. "All we could do," he said, "was to keep her headed into the wind and attempt to ride it out."[67]


There was, perhaps, a single redeeming product of the storm: it had irrevocably altered the future of the little Maryland resort town of Ocean City by doing something the governments of the city, state, and nation could not. It had opened a brand new inlet into Sinepuxent Bay and expanded a second, while formally converting the long Assateague Peninsula into an island.

The birthing process of the new inlet had not been without pain or cost. During the night of August 22–23, the turbulent waters of Sinepuxent Bay had already begun eating out a section of the causeway leading to the bridge connecting the peninsula with the mainland, threatening to maroon those residents who had not fled before the storm. Though the causeway and approaches to the bridge were flooded, they had remained passable to automobiles, buses, and pedestrians for several hours during August 23. Then, late in the afternoon, the evacuation had been suddenly halted when a major section of the causeway was torn out by the waves. By the morning of August 24 the gap in the causeway had been conquered by a primitive ferry system consisting of two fishing skiffs hauled back and forth on ropes. The enterprising Elliott Brothers Fishing Company had set up the system. Later, a barge, which had been moored nearby, was commandeered to form a floating bridge over the break. Men with their trousers rolled and women with their skirts held high or clad in bathing suits waded through a half foot of water for nearly eight hundred yards, ignoring the battered and destroyed houses that flanked the flooded road on either side. In some of the houses, "occupants had clung on tenaciously and could be seen sitting in their doorways, often with wreckage at their feet, watching the flow of aquatic pedestrians pass by." Yet even the causeway break failed to distract from the grand works that Mother Nature had just created elsewhere: a brand new inlet at the south end of town.[68]

Sinepuxent Bay, which had been filled to the brim after days of heavy rain and seawater spilling across the strip of land that separated it from the Atlantic, had already sought to relieve itself even as the storm was passing. Normally there were two tides a day, flood and ebb, as the ocean rose and fell, but on August 23 no tides flowed into the shallow inlet five miles south of town, as the bay was already filled by days of precipitation. Now, mountains of water locked in the bay had picked the lowest spots on the strip to flood back toward the ocean, and it never stopped. Two low, weak points succumbed, one at the south end of Ocean City at the fishing camps at Sandy Point, where the ocean had once come across and worn down the beach, and the vestigial remnant of old Sinepuxent Point inlet miles below town.[69]

By the morning of August 24, as the sun attempted to break through the clouds and the winds subsided, recalled one local resident, "You could hear the inlet, and [it] was chopping the bank right off. It had cut the railroad right out. It was just wild. We were panicky then. We really didn't know what was going to happen to us." Only one fishing camp survived as the waters continued to slice away at the banks for the next four or five days, carrying debris ranging from twisted railroad tracks to heavy cement septic tanks from the camps, and turning them end over end as they rolled out to sea. The new inlet south of the city was already at least fifty feet wide and eight to fifteen feet deep, and the other five miles to the south, though very shallow and destined to sand in again, was a thousand feet wide.[70]

Captain Elliott surveyed the site where his and many other fishing camps below Ocean City had once stood. There was little left now besides the ruins of the old railroad pier. Though none of his boats and nets had been lost, he must have instinctively known in his heart that the heyday of pound-net fishing off the town was over. Four or five days later, when the tides were more amenable, and the currents rushing through the newly cut and ever-expanding inlet calmed a bit, he brought one of his boats through. He was the first man to do so, but he would certainly not be the last.[71]

Within two days of the storm's passing the realization of what nature had given Ocean City was becoming self-evident. "For seven years," the Associated Press reported, "residents of Ocean City have sought State and Federal aid for building an inlet from the Atlantic to Sinepuxent Bay, but without avail. The cost was placed at $750,000. Today there are two inlets, dug overnight by Wednesday's storm and without financial backing." Although initial estimates by Mayor William W. McCabe placed the cost of storm damage to the town at between $350,000 and $500,000, everyone seemed more interested in how to make the new inlet permanent.

It would take nearly two years for the Public Works Administration to produce the emergency funding needed, but by July 1935 the federal government was finally able to put up over $780,000 to build a concrete seawall on the new inlet's north side. Seven months later, another allocation went to pay for two great stone jetties on the Atlantic side to preclude migrating sands from washing in. As time passed, the shoreline north of the jetties expanded owing to the backwash of sand. The accretion soon became so great that the boardwalk had to be elevated and so wide that the city was able to build a municipal parking lot for the countless vacationers who would soon be descending every summer. And come they would.[72] From then on, the devastating tempest that had swept the peninsula would be known as "The Great Inlet Storm of '33." Assateague would become Delmarva's longest island, and Ocean City would become the greatest vacation resort on the entire Delmarva coast.

# 22

## Unterseeboot

December 7, 1941. Admiral Karl Dönitz, German commander in chief of U-boats, read the message from the teleprinter at his headquarters in L'Orient, France, with a mixture of delight and concern. At 1930 hours Central European Time, the Japanese Empire had opened hostilities against the United States as "strong air formations attacked Pearl Harbor." A mighty carrier strike launched across 3,200 miles of the Pacific Ocean had all but wiped out the U.S. Pacific fleet in the surprise assault. Now, Adolf Hitler's Germany, Japan's treaty ally since September 27, 1940, would also have to fight the sleeping giant across the Atlantic.[1]

If the Japanese success had proved anything, it was that the United States was both weak and ill prepared for war, and the art of surprise was still among the best tactics in a sea fighters' chest of tricks. Dönitz, a strategist without equal in the chronicles of undersea warfare, was well aware, however, that once fully aroused, America might well prove a difficult adversary. It was imperative that the German Submarine Service, the Kriegsmarine, the only German force capable of laying the war at America's doorstep, had to strike as soon as possible. The Atlantic frontier of the United States was unquestionably among the busiest sea-lanes in the world. Yet they were at best only lightly protected by an inadequate and antiquated naval and air defense shield and must therefore be hit before Yankee industrial might could be organized to support strong countermeasures. After all, it was American industry that had kept England, the only major thorn in Hitler's left flank, in the war. American lend-lease ships had helped keep British supply lines open, and her "false neutrality" had caused unending difficulties for the Nazi war effort.[2] Now it was time for revenge. Dönitz alone would take the war into America's home waters.

Undersea warfare had ripened and matured quickly during the long years of the last Great War, supposedly "the war to end all wars," and no nation had excelled at it better than imperial Germany. The German *Unterseeboot,* or U-boat, as it became known, had very nearly tipped the scales in Germany's favor during that terrible conflict. Many had come to consider the Kaiser's dreaded submarines as little more than evil sea beasts, appearing suddenly from the murky depths to prey upon the defenseless seafarer. Now, the German Kriegsmarine, under Dönitz's leadership, once again had an opportunity to secure victory by using tactics developed and refined in the very cauldron of combat. This time, he vowed, things would be different.

Dönitz prided himself on his pragmatism. Owing to the early success against individual ship operations, and the Allies' subsequent employment of sophisticated armed and guarded convoy systems, he had come to rely on an aggressive submarine squadron approach known as the "wolf pack." In this system, several U-boats would take up positions at approximately fifteen-mile intervals in a long line across possible Allied convoy routes. When one of the U-boats sighted a convoy, it would immediately notify the others of the enemy's speed, course, and other pertinent data. The wolf pack would then close around the convoy from all points and destroy it in detail.[3]

Yet the technology of antisubmarine warfare also had advanced substantially since the last war. The British invention of Asdic, an echo-sounding device that could find objects underwater but not on the surface, had significant ramifications for German strategy. Though U-boats were faster and more maneuverable on the surface, they were now obliged to hunt at night, when their low silhouettes were practically impossible to see and close-in point-blank targeting was possible. Thus, he realized that the war in American waters must be one of stealth carried out in the dark of night.

When the United States declared war on the Axis powers, Dönitz's fleet consisted of ninety-one operational submarines, only five of which were in the Western Hemisphere, all in Canadian waters. To compensate for the tremendous number of U.S. merchant ships already afloat, and to offset the anticipated increase in ship production by American industry, a kill rate of unparalleled proportions would be required. Dönitz calculated that no less than 800,000 tons of shipping a month would have to be sent to the bottom to win. Speed and surprise were imperative to capitalize on the early days of conflict with the United States, before an adequate convoy system could be adopted and while commercial shipping was still traveling alone and without protection along the coast.[4]

Three days after Pearl Harbor, Dönitz requested 112 long-range type-IX U-boats with which to devastate the American merchant marine. Every type-IX submarine was armed with fifteen torpedoes, each being twenty feet in length and weighing 3,528 lbs. The majority of the torpedoes were driven by battery-powered motors and were capable of moving at thirty knots but left no wake. Hitler, however, fearing an Allied invasion of Norway, distributed his navy accordingly and allowed Dönitz but six boats for the opening assault, of which only five would eventually put to sea. Undismayed, the admiral proceeded to formulate Operation Paukenschlag—Operation Drumbeat—to deploy five boats between Cape Hatteras and the St. Lawrence. All commanders were directed to avoid any and all contact while en route, although they would be permitted to attack ships of ten thousand tons or larger if conditions allowed. With only the individual commanders informed of their destinations, the task force would sail for Newfoundland and from there turn southwest. Then the slaughter would begin.[5]

· · ·

The U-boat terror descended like the Wagnerian Furies on the entirely unprepared and defenseless Allied shipping lanes of the American coast on January 13, 1942. The first victim in U.S. waters was the Norwegian-owned, Panamanian-registered *Norness,* a 9,577-ton, 494-foot-long diesel screw motor-tanker. The unfortunate ship was torpedoed by *U-123,* Kapitanleutnant Reinhard Hardegen commanding, off Montauk Point, Long Island. During the first week of the onslaught, as the type-IXs spread themselves southward from New York to the Caribbean, more than 150,000 tons of shipping would be lost, along with nearly five hundred seamen. During the coming months, additional U-boats would be sent to North American waters, mostly shorter-range type-VIIs, which were dispatched into Canadian waters that were three hundred miles closer to Europe than the United States. Those patrolling off Canada experienced poor hunting owing to the winter weather. Finding their fuel consumption to be less than expected, many turned south and penetrated as far as Cape Hatteras, with devastating consequences for Allied shipping. The Delmarva coast, unfortunately, would prove to be one of the richest killing grounds in the Western Hemisphere.[6]

During the first ten days of Operation Paukenschlag it seemed that the waters off the Delmarva were somehow sacrosanct, as shipping went down off New York, New Jersey, and North Carolina with frightful regularity but none between the Delaware and Chesapeake. Not until January 25 would the first victim of a U-boat attack, the Norwegian tanker *Varanger,* be sunk off the mouth of Delaware Bay, twenty-eight miles east of Wildwood, New Jersey. It was the first instance of a Paukenschlag attack off the U.S. with no fatalities.[7]

On January 25 the first indication of the German presence in Virginia waters came when the American tanker *Olney* struck a submerged object off the Virginia capes while en route to Fall River, Massachusetts. While the ship was stopped dead in the water to examine for damage, a crewman sighted a torpedo headed straight for her. Orders to get under way were issued instantly, but too late. The undersea missile, fired by *U-125,* struck and detonated just as the ship began to move to shallow water. Fortunately, the damage was slight and *Olney* eventually made New York, where she unloaded and made repairs. The near catastrophe served ample notice that a whirlwind of death and destruction was about to descend on Delmarva's own waters.[8]

Two nights later, the 7,096-ton Atlantic Refining Company–owned tanker *Francis E. Powell,* Captain Thomas James Harrington commanding, en route from Port Arthur, Texas, to Providence, Rhode Island, was sailing off Chincoteague, Virginia, a dozen nautical miles southeast of Winter Quarter Light Vessel, when her time came. Without warning, about 2:43 A.M., a torpedo fired by the *U-130,* Ernes Kals commanding, tore into the ship's port side, slightly aft the midships deckhouse between tanks number 4 and 5. Captain Harrington, a native of Baltimore, immediately assessed the damage. The explosion had ignited a fire in the pump room. With his ship's back broken, her amidships section was sagging badly and was soon awash. Her radio antenna, a large portion of catwalk, and a considerable section of the port rail had been carried away. One of the ship's four lifeboats had been destroyed. More disturbing was the telltale odor of 80,024 barrels of leaking gasoline and fuel oil that might explode at any moment.

Harrington ordered "abandon ship." Within five to ten minutes, twenty-nine officers and crewmen had put the three operable lifeboats over the side. At the last minute, for some unknown reason, Harrington decided to return, possibly to retrieve and toss overboard codes and confidential papers. Then, as he hurriedly descended the rope ladder into one of the boats, the tanker suddenly pitched, instantly crushing him to death between the boat and the ship's hull. In frantic desperation to get away from the sinking tanker lest they be pulled under by suction, the lifeboats started rowing hard. Six men in one of the boats, however, thinking only of their skipper, bravely attempted to recover his body. Suddenly, a huge wave picked up their boat and deposited it on the tilted deck of the sinking ship. In haste they jumped over the side and fortunately were picked up by another lifeboat. Literally rowing for their lives to escape the ring of oil that now encircled the wreck, which might ignite at any second, the two remaining and badly overcrowded boats failed to notice the enemy sub just fifty yards away. Owing to the darkness, they had been entirely unaware of the proximity of the U-boat, whose catwalk was out of the water, until they were within mere feet of her. As they closed with the unseen warship, one of the crew looked up and suddenly saw the looming con of their assassin. "They seemed to be waiting for us to shell us, but they didn't," said John D. Axeson, one of the crewmen, days afterward. Within seconds of a collision, the lifeboats reversed course and, like frightened water bugs, scurried off to hide in the darkness. For the next seventeen hours, the boat carrying Axeson and ten others floated aimlessly in the freezing winter Atlantic. At 7:00 A.M., *Francis E. Powell* passed into history. A fast Coast Guard rescue vessel was dispatched to recover the survivors and was unsuccessfully chased while en route by the slower U-boat. A passing ship called *William Fairbanks* picked up the remaining seventeen survivors and carried them to Lewes. Captain Harrington and three of his men were the first of many to sacrifice their lives on the Delmarva coast in World War II.[9]

The survivors of *Powell* were indeed more fortunate than later victims of the U-boat offensive. The British freighter *Tacoma Star,* manned by eighty-five officers and crewmen, and seven Naval Armed Guard members, had departed Newport News bound for Great Britain on January 30. The following night a short distress call was received from the ship, reporting that she was sinking. Then nothing. An immediate air and sea search was launched but to no avail. Her disappearance remained a mystery until after the war when German records told of her sad fate. Ambushed at 37°33'N, 69°21'W, just three hundred miles east of Chincoteague by the *U-109,* Kapitanleutnant Heinrich Bleichrodt commanding, *Tacoma Star* had gone down with all hands.[10]

All along the Eastern seaboard, the German U-boat offensive was just beginning to take an enormous toll. By mid-January it was becoming apparent to the Germans that organized defense of the Atlantic coast was nonexistent. Nazi submarines, which had been instructed to keep a fair distance from the beach, began to operate with impunity close in. One sub, the *U-123*, had closed to within viewing distance of New York's city lights. In time, the long-range U-boat offensive would be kept in continuous motion thanks to the utilization of supply tankers, known as "milch cows," which supplied fuel in midocean to marauding wolf packs.[11] Off the Virginia capes the attack on the 6,836-ton Socony Vacuum Oil Company tanker *Rochester* suggested the almost casual attitude enemy commanders were beginning to assume by assailing Allied shipping even in broad daylight.

Built in 1920 at Sparrows Point, Maryland, and manned by thirty-three officers and men, *Rochester* was sailing less than twenty miles northeast of Cape Charles on January 30 when a torpedo ripped into her side about 11:00 A.M. The explosion instantly disabled the ship's engines, damaged her radio equipment, and left her helpless in the water. Captain A. L. Clark, her master, after observing the enemy sub surface barely half a mile away, was well aware that it would only be a matter of minutes before she administered the coup de grace. In the meantime, hurried repairs had been made to the ship's transmitter and a rushed S.O.S. was sent. The captain then ordered "abandon ship." Three of his dead crewmen, killed by the explosion, would have to be left behind. A fourth seaman would die a week later.[12]

As Captain Clark and the rest of the survivors clambered aboard two lifeboats, they watched in horror as a gun party climbed out onto the deck of the submarine. Oberleutnant zur See Herman Rasch, commander of the *U-106*, had boldly decided to finish his prey off in broad daylight from the surface. The Americans quite naturally feared for their lives until a German sailor vigorously motioned for them to row away from the tanker. Once the lifeboats were clear, the Germans fired thirteen rounds at *Rochester*, most striking her port side near the waterline. Amazingly, the ship remained afloat. A quarter hour later, they watched as the U-boat commander adeptly maneuvered his boat to the starboard side of the ship where another torpedo was loosed. This time, the tanker took a death roll onto her side. About noon she sank by the stern but refused to go down completely. Oberleutnant Rasch, however, did not wait to see her final demise as he turned his prow southward. Within hours two U.S. Navy planes had arrived on the scene in response to the distress signal. The ill-fated *Rochester* was still visible, pointed heavenward with her bow still exposed. The men in the two lifeboats indicated by hand gestures that the submarine had headed south. By 3:00 P.M. the survivors had been rescued by the U.S. destroyer *Roper* and were then taken to Norfolk.[13]

The arrival of *U-106* on the Virginia coast was bad enough. The arrival of *U-86*, Kapitanleutnant Walter Schug commanding, which had been hunting off Nova Scotia, to cooperate in a mini-wolf-pack effort would prove even more costly for Allied shipping. Their first victim was one of the largest and fastest merchant ships in the world, the 15,355-ton Swedish steamer *Amerikaland,* owned by Axil Bastrum and Sons and, ironically, built in 1925 in Hamburg, Germany. The 561-foot-long steamer, manned by a crew of thirty-eight under the command of Captain Ragnar Schultz, was sailing in ballast, steering a zigzag course and showing no lights to avoid U-boat attack, when first sighted on February 2 by *U-106*. The weather at the time could not have been worse, with turbulent seas and a blinding snowstorm under way.[14]

Oberleutnant Rasch was not the only vessel stalking the giant merchantman. *U-86* was also in the area and had sights on Rasch's quarry. Communicating by radio, the two U-boat skippers decided to team up. Rasch, being the more combat experienced of the two, would lead the attack after dark.[15]

Though the big merchantman followed evasive maneuvers all along, it was not enough to protect her against the veteran U-boats. The first torpedo that hit *Amerikaland* struck a bit forward of the bridge, but the blow was not fatal. A second, however, followed immediately afterward. Captain Schultz, having already lived through one sinking in 1917, during World War I, had been in bed when the attack came but jumped into action immediately. Having survived naked for nearly nineteen hours in the freezing Atlantic the last time around, he was not about to suffer the same again. Within seconds of the blasts he was in the radio room overseeing the third mate as he dashed off S.S.S. and S.O.S. signals relaying their position. There was no reply. He then went to the control center for a damage report. Five men had died, and, without orders to do so, the crew was already abandoning ship in utter panic. Rushing topside, Schultz saw a pair of lifeboats being lowered and joined in the exodus. Moments later a third lifeboat with six men aboard was lowered under the direction of the third mate.[16]

By this time it was snowing hard, but like water gliders the three boats pulled hard to swiftly distance themselves from their ship. As before, the dark silhouette of a U-boat, this time *U-86,* appeared on the turbulent waters. Yet the crew of *Amerikaland* could distinguish neither the enemy nor their own ship owing to what had become a full-fledged blizzard. In pregnant silence thirty-six men awaited the denouement. In an instant they heard two earsplitting blasts, then all but the wind and sea was silent.[17]

Though only a few miles from the Delmarva coast, *Amerikaland*'s crewmen, with the exception of Captain Schultz, were now faced with the greatest challenge of their lives. Crowded in three small boats on the open Atlantic at the height of winter, amid freezing temperatures, high winds, and tempestuous seas, many prepared to meet their maker. Within a short time the three lifeboats became separated by wind and water. For nearly four days the boat commanded by the third mate drifted aimlessly about until sighted by a Dutch freighter named *Castoria.* The survivors were rescued and taken to Curaçao. On February 6, the second boat, with seventeen survivors and the corpse of a crewman who had died of exposure, was spotted by the Brazilian steamer *Taubate* and taken to Recife, Brazil, where they arrived on February 22. There were a total of eleven men in Schultz's boat, which the resourceful and courageous captain managed to rig with a sail and slip into the shipping lanes of the Gulf Stream. Though most aboard were pessimistic about their lot, Schultz reminded them that he had survived a worse ordeal and repeatedly bolstered their spirits. On February 7, five days after the sinking, the captain's boat was picked up by *Port Halifax,* a British ship, and taken to New York.[18]

• • •

One of the most successful German U-boats hunting off the Delmarva coast was *U-103*, a type IX-B long-range submarine commissioned on July 5, 1940. Commanded by Kapitanleutnant Werner Winter, this killing machine was destined to sink no less than thirty-one ships during her forty-two months of wartime service. Four of them would go down between Virginia and Delaware.[19]

*U-103*'s first victim was the Standard Oil of New Jersey tanker *W. L. Steed*, Captain Harold McAvenia master, bound from Cartagena, Colombia, with 66,000 barrels of fuel oil. After nearly three weeks at sea, *Steed* was nearing her destination when she encountered sour weather and snow. Captain McAvenia was forced to reduce speed even though he knew he was in submarine-infested waters, but he observed all precautions, having repeatedly practiced his men for the event of a possible U-boat attack. Though a light was observed on the starboard quarter, which heightened tensions aboard, nothing more could be seen through the snowstorm. At 12:40 A.M., February 2, the ship passed Isle of Wight Shoal on her port, and proceeded on her northerly course ten miles off Fenwick Island, where she was struck on her starboard side by a torpedo fired by *U-103*. The hit was forward of the bridge and was devastating in that it immediately ignited the cargo of fuel oil. Thanks to the training Captain McAvenia had given his crew, all thirty-eight abandoned ship safely in four lifeboats. Pulling away from the ship as quickly as possible, they watched as the submarine surfaced and prepared to finish off her prey with a deck gun. They counted seventeen rounds fired before *Steed* exploded in a horrendous burst and then sank. The submarine briefly turned toward the lifeboats and then disappeared into the swirling, stormy darkness.[20]

The 6,182-ton tanker *W. L. Steed,* torpedoed and shelled by *U-103* on February 1, 1942, went down with all but four of her crew of thirty-five. (The Mariners' Museum, Newport News, VA)

Captain McAvenia's assiduous training, unfortunately, could not have prepared the crew for the brutal difficulties ahead. Though less than a dozen miles from the Delmarva coast, the four lifeboats were unable to fight the brutal, freezing gale that first separated them and then blew them eastward. HMSC *Alcvantara* picked one of the boats up on February 4 with only three of the five aboard still clinging to life. A second boat was recovered two days later with only two of the fifteen men aboard still alive. The two survivors had somehow managed to build a small fire in a water bucket to ward off death by freezing. The British ship *Raby Castle* picked up a third boat near the Virginia capes on February 11 with three dead and one man barely alive. The sole survivor died soon afterward and was buried at sea. The fourth boat, with several bodies aboard, was spotted near the site of the sinking by a South American steamer. Owing to the sighting of a periscope by a nervous crewman, the steamer left the area immediately without recovering the dead.[21]

It was probably fortunate for the South American steamer that she had moved on, for Kapitanleutnant Winter had indeed lingered in the area. Two days after sinking *W. L. Steed*, while cruising just a few miles east of Chincoteague, he sighted a 3,598-ton Panamanian-register ship belonging to the United Fruit Company named *San Gil*, Captain Walter W. Koch commanding. Onboard were forty-one crewmen and a single passenger. When the U-boat's torpedo struck the port midships, forward of the engine room bulkhead, the explosion was horrendous, tearing a great hole in the hull, bringing down the radio antenna, and killing two men in the engine room. On the bridge Captain Koch ordered "abandon ship" and then proceeded to drop the ship's manifest overboard in a weighted bag. Fortunately, the radio operator, Robert Thorpe, managed to rig an emergency antenna and send off an S.O.S. and the ship's position. "Torpedoed, sinking fast. Can't receive." In a matter of minutes, as the submarine surfaced a thousand feet from her victim and her gunnery crew prepared to administer the death blow with their deck gun, *San Gil*'s crew managed to scramble aboard the lifeboats. Eleven of the fifteen shots fired at the helpless giant struck home, but the ship refused to sink. Perhaps a little unhappy that he was obliged to waste another of his precious torpedoes to complete the job, Winter circled around to the freighter's opposite side and at 12:35 A.M. finished her off with a single blow. With her back broken, the freighter quickly broke up and sank in 130 feet of water. As with *Steed*, Kapitanleutnant Winter taunted his victims by bringing *U-103* to within fifty feet of the lifeboats before veering away into the freezing night.[22]

Less than seven hours later, at 7:00 A.M., *U-103* sighted the twenty-one-year-old oil tanker *India Arrow*, an 8,327-ton New York–register ship owned by the Socony Vacuum Oil Company. Laden with 88,369 barrels of diesel fuel, she was running entirely blacked out, with no navigational lights showing. For Winter, it was obvious his next intended victim was fully laden as indicated by her low silhouette against the coastal horizon at Indian River Inlet, a little under twenty miles to the west. The tanker was en route from the Texas oil town of Corpus Christi bound for New York City, her home port.[23]

The sinking of *India Arrow* followed much the same tragic sequence as those before her: a torpedo slamming into her stern quarter killing two men in the engine room, burst fuel lines, and an explosion in the starboard boiler, stunned crewmen rushing onto the deck, frantic attempts to tap out an S.O.S. in the radio room just as power was extinguished, and spewing fuel oil spreading a thick gooey slick around the ship. Less than five minutes after the explosion, Captain Carl Johnson ordered "abandon ship" and then hopped into the starboard midships lifeboat even as the tanker's stem began to settle. Unfortunately, the little boat was quickly assailed by a fist of the sea and dashed against the 468-foot-long sinking hulk, spilling the captain into the frigid water. As other crewmen rushed to the port midships lifeboat, the sinking ship suddenly lurched. Though several men were tossed clear by the jolt, the lifeboat, still lashed to the falls, and the men in it were poured from the tilting deck into the sea and disappeared. At the last moment, radioman Edward Shear leaped into the sea and struggled to hold onto a floating hatch cover. Within minutes, a lifeboat with three survivors had picked up Captain Johnson and began to search for others in the water. Ten minutes after the first torpedo strike, the survivors in the lifeboat watched *U-103*'s conning tower, starkly silhouetted by the blazing oil, as she surfaced two hundred yards from her victim. By this time, the ship's stem rested on the seabed two hundred feet down, but her buoyant bow was still poking obscenely skyward at an angle above the surface. Terrified to move lest they draw attention to themselves, twelve shivering men in a cockleshell lifeboat watched transfixed as the submarine gun crew methodically delivered half a dozen explosive shells into the bow of their ship at two-minute intervals. As the snow continued to fall, the shelling set the oil-soaked sea ablaze in a fire that Captain Johnson later estimated might have been seen twenty miles away. Twenty-six of their mates were still aboard, dead or dying, or already dead in the water.[24]

Though the dozen men in the boat, most of them shoeless and some of them largely undressed, raised a sail and tacked toward shore, they made little progress against the winter winds. Two tankers passing in the night, fearing a Nazi trick, fled at the sight of the lonely S.O.S. flashlight signal the survivors blinked in utter desperation. Though their rations and drinking water had been contaminated by fuel oil, they somehow manfully struggled and succeeded in fending off the Atlantic cold for three days. Finally, barely twelve miles off Ocean City, New Jersey, they were picked up by the fishing boat *Gitana* and carried to the Atlantic City Coast Guard Station where they were fed, clothed, and revived. That same day, the USS *Tormaline* sighted the bow of *India Arrow* still projecting proud from the water—but not for long. Her loss would eventually be tallied at $1.3 million.[25]

Undoubtedly elated over making two kills in a single day, Kapitanleutnant Winter headed southeast to await his next victim. On the morning of February 5, twenty miles off Metompkin, Virginia, he found her. In a cruel twist of fate, the ship he sighted through the crosshairs of *U-103*'s periscope proved to be the 8,403-ton *China Arrow,* sister ship to *India Arrow,* laden with thousands of barrels of Number Six fuel oil and bound from Beaumont, Texas, for New York

City with a crew of thirty-seven. Like all those that had preceded her, she was sailing alone and unarmed, weaving the pathetic zigzag pattern, as per navy instructions, that was supposed to make a U-boat attack more difficult. The weather had finally cleared a bit but still wore a dirty gray overcast.[26]

This time Kapitanleutnant Winter would attempt to finish off his prey in one blow. At 11:15 A.M. he fired off two torpedoes into the starboard side of the American tanker. The monumental explosions decimated the main deck, devastating the bridge control to the engine room and the radio antenna and blowing off the rudder. Fires were ignited in the cargo area and engine room. *India Arrow*'s master, Captain Paul Browne, unable to communicate with the ship's aft, dispatched his chief engineer to the burning engine room, where he was able to smother the fire. Elsewhere, several crewmen attempted to jury-rig a radio antenna just as the U-boat surfaced five hundred feet off the starboard quarter. The order to abandon ship was given immediately. Again, the routine that was becoming all too familiar to the German submariners was set in motion. *U-103*'s deck gun was unlimbered. As three lifeboats pulled away from the tanker, the gunners commenced peppering their victim with fifteen to twenty rounds, watched the ship go down by the stern, and then slithered off beneath the gray Atlantic waters. On the morning of February 7, thirty-seven survivors in three lifeboats tied together were spotted by a navy patrol plane, which guided the USCG cutter *Nike* to them.[27]

Thus was concluded the rampage of *U-103*. Unfortunately, the U-boat campaign of terror was just beginning for the Delmarva coast.

# 23

## Like a Knife Gutting a Fish

In the first weeks and months of America's baptism by fire in the Atlantic theater, the Nazi submarine offensive off the shores of the United States would claim an astonishing toll in shipping and lives. In February alone, a handful of U-boats destroyed approximately 145 ships. The following month, another 150 would go down. The litany of casualties bloodied off Delmarva's shores during these dark days was heartbreaking. They included the liberty ship *Ocean Venture,* sunk on February 8 with fourteen crewmen lost; the passenger liner *Buarque,* torpedoed east of Cape Henry on February 15; the freighter *Azalea City,* sunk the following day by *U-432* off Virginia; the neutral Brazilian freighter *Olinda,* sunk east of Chincoteague by the same sub on February 18; the Canadian freighter *Gypsum Prince,* torpedoed barely three miles off Lewes on March 4 with the loss of six lives; the Norwegian freighter *Hvoslef,* torpedoed twice and sunk in two minutes off Fenwick Island, taking with her five men on March 11; the ore carrier *Trepca,* torpedoed and sunk by *U-332* off the Chesapeake capes with the loss of four men on March 13; the British tanker *San Demetrio,* sunk nearby two days later by *U-404* with the loss of nineteen men; the Panamanian freighter *Equipoise,* destroyed March 26 just east of Cape Henry along with thirty-eight of her fifty-three officers and crew; the tug *Menominee* and two of three barges she was towing, *Allegheny* and *Barnegat,* on March 31 off Parramore Island; the American tanker *Tiger,* sunk on the same date as *Menominee* off the Virginia capes with the loss of one life; *David H. Atwater,* laden with 3,911 tons of coal, sunk entirely by shellfire off Chincoteague by *U-552* on April 2, taking with her twenty-four officers and seamen; the Argentinean tanker *Victoria,* struck and sunk by a torpedo fired by the *U-201* well off the Virginia capes on April 18; and the British freighter *Empire Drum,* torpedoed without warning on April 24 east of the entrance to the Chesapeake.[1]

The American defenses were totally inadequate. Ships continued to use their radios freely, occasionally mentioning their positions and revealing themselves to the deadly ship killers lying below at day and calmly hunting inshore after sunset. Lighthouses and navigation buoys were still displayed and shining brightly. Shorefront towns continued to remain lit at night as if peace still reigned over the world. Antisubmarine defenses remained primitive and ineffective. Indeed,

While en route home from Aruba, the SS *Tiger* was torpedoed by *U-754* off the Virginia capes. Though her stern was aground in sixty feet of water while her bow remained afloat, relief efforts to salvage the ship proved in vain, and she was written off as a total loss. (The Mariners' Museum, Newport News, VA)

not a single casualty would be inflicted on the aggressor in American waters until April 14, when the USS *Roper* finally sank *U-85* off Nags Head. Admiral Dönitz, though not achieving his goal of sending 800,000 tons of American shipping a month to the bottom, had reached 60 percent of his target with but a tiny portion of the fleet he had hoped to deploy and was elated.[2]

America struggled desperately to bring itself to a fully organized war footing during the early months of 1942. The North Atlantic Coastal Frontier—that is, the seaways extending 200 miles from the Atlantic seaboard of the United States—was partitioned for operational purposes into five frontiers encompassing more than seven thousand miles of coastal waters. The Delmarva coast sat squarely in the center of the largest of these, designated the Eastern Sea Frontier (ESF), which extended from West Quoddy Head, Maine, on the Canadian border, to St. Johns, Florida. At the onset of hostilities, Admiral Ernest J. King was appointed to command all ships, fleets, and other forces defending the North Atlantic Coastal Frontier. King in turn appointed a fellow Annapolis Naval

Academy classmate, Admiral Adolphus "Dolly" Andrews, commandant of the Third Naval District operating out of New York, to take charge of the ESF.[3]

Admiral Andrews had little to work with. Of the twenty vessels assigned to defend practically the entire Atlantic seaboard of the United States, some were so old they had been commissioned before World War I, while others were in such poor shape they were simply unreliable. At the outset his fleet would have been laughable if its reason for being had not been so deadly serious. It consisted of a 165-foot Coast Guard cutter, three World War I–era 200-foot-long *Eagle* Boats, six 125-foot Coast Guard patrol boats, four antiquated 110-foot subchasers, four small converted yachts, and two gunboats. A conscription campaign to secure the services of private yachts (including several owned by the likes of the Rockefellers and Vanderbilts), fishing boats, and small sailing craft did little to stem the U-boat onslaught. It was almost an embarrassment when the British agreed to loan America two dozen trawlers for patrol duty barely two years after lend-lease. Andrews's air arm, which included 105 U.S. Army and Navy aircraft, was equally limited. The only operational long-range aircraft were several dirigibles, some of which were unarmed. With few radios to go round, the military relied on carrier pigeons to convey reported sightings of U-boats. Radar was simply unavailable, and even training in ship recognition was foreign to most aircrews. Nevertheless, airbases were soon in operation at Chincoteague, Langley, Oceana, Creed, and Pungo in Virginia. Armed blimps were stationed at Elizabeth City, North Carolina. Ocean City, Maryland; Cape Henlopen, Delaware; and Cape May, New Jersey at least facilitated the thin air patrol capability. Coast Guard beach patrol units, on horseback and afoot with dogs, were employed to prevent enemy agents from landing on the desolate beaches between Cape Henlopen and Cape Charles.[4]

Protection of all inland waters, including the interior channels near the entrance to both Chesapeake and Delaware Bays, was given to the U.S. Army. The establishment of strategic encampments and artillery bases and stations and the placement of minefields and antisubmarine nets at harbor entrances were also army responsibilities, although the navy did not relinquish full jurisdiction over minefields to its rival service.[5]

At the eighteen-mile-wide entrance to the Chesapeake, the army minefield that was eventually deployed consisted of 365 controlled-contact mines placed between the tip of Cape Charles and the northern edge of the main channel. Another twenty-two groups of controlled mines, totaling 418 units, were spread about in the channel northeast of Fort Story, on Cape Henry. Six more groups, in two lines, were planted near Thimble Shoal Light. Controlled from shore points, the mines were harmless until remotely armed at night, during periods of low visibility, or whenever a commander deemed it necessary to do so. Artillery positions mounting sixteen-inch guns were erected at Fort Story on Cape Henry and Fort Custis on Cape Charles, and on Fort Wool in Hampton Roads. Mobile defense units were established at various posts from Manteo, North Carolina, to the Delaware capes. All along the rolling dunes and scrublands of the Delmarva coast from Fenwick Island to Henlopen, fire-control towers were strung at intervals along the beach. At Fort Miles on Cape Henlopen and across Delaware Bay on Cape May, military installations, concrete gun emplacements, and watchtowers were erected to guard against submarine intrusion or enemy landings. Like the Chesapeake, the channels of the Delaware were festooned with a dizzying array of mines and nets.[6]

Not surprisingly, accidents happened. One such incident occurred during the height of the U-boat offensive, on February 16, 1942, when the tanker *E. H. Blum* was making her cautious approach into the Chesapeake. Though her identity was recognized, for some unknown reason she failed to respond to radio calls and was thus denied entry. The night was foggy and all mines had been armed, but the nineteen-thousand-ton ship was not given directions or warning. With communications apparently down, she continued on. Blundering into the minefield, she soon struck a mine, which blew up and broke the ship cleanly in half. Though the bow was towed ashore, and the other half was later salvaged and rejoined to it, the lesson was endemic to the hazards of the antisubmarine war that was being waged.[7]

The seamen and ships of the merchant marine were not the only ones to suffer casualties off the Delmarva in the early days of the war. The U.S. Navy, spread oil thin along the coast, would also fall victim to the Nazi torpedo. On February 28, 1942, the USS *Jacob Jones* (DD-130), a Wickes-class flush-deck "four piper" destroyer built in 1919 at the New York Shipbuilding Corporation yards at Camden, New Jersey, was proceeding south on patrol out of New York, under the command of Lieutenant Commander Hugh Black, when her rendezvous with destruction occurred. Ironically, her namesake had been another destroyer that had been torpedoed in 1917, and whose crew had been devastated by the ship's own depth charges going off as it sank. The *Jackie,* as her crew affectionately called her, had been loaned to the ESF from the fleet Admiral King had held in reserve for use in the Pacific, owing to the vigor of the U-boat offensive. She had been detailed for an unspecified period, the first ship so assigned on a regular basis. As it turned out, the loan would be one of the shortest on record.[8]

Death came at 5:00 A.M., while the full face of the moon was still shining down on the Atlantic. Though running blacked out at fifteen knots, she was taking no evasive actions, as was usual procedure. *Jacob Jones* became the proverbial sitting duck silhouetted against the predawn sky. In rapid succession, two portside explosions went off, one under the bridge in the forward magazine and the second under the stern. The blast forward lifted the entire ship out of the water, ripped off the bridge, and separated ninety feet of the bow forward of number-two boiler room from the midships. The bow immediately sank. All but one of the ship's officers, a desperately wounded ensign, and nearly a hundred enlisted men perished in an instant. Incredibly, though the sides of the stern had caved in and the after part of the ship above the keel plates and shaft was disappearing, the fantail was still connected to the main body of the vessel. Amid innumerable small fires, twenty-five men who had survived the explosions amidships, though constantly slipping on the oil-covered deck, struggled mightily to break loose lifeboats that had become stuck in their cradles and filled with debris, but in

USS *Jacob Jones* in her heyday (National Archives, Washington, DC; photo courtesy of Michael Pohuski)

vain. Unable to secure a purchase on the slippery deck, they resorted to the life rafts, all of which had to be cleared of detritus before being pushed into the sea. Until now, watertight integrity between the compartmentalized sections of the hull had preserved the center of the ship from sinking, even as men struggled in the 38°F water to grab on the rafts. Suddenly the stern rose perhaps forty feet in the air and then disappeared beneath the sea.[9]

History was about to repeat itself. For the men in the water and clinging to the sides of life rafts, the second round of disaster came moments after the stern went under. The aft section had been laden with depth charges, which were detonated by the water pressure as the stern descended. The incredible concussion waves of so many detonations at once proved fatal for those in the water and on rafts nearest the sinking ship. Most died instantly. Those further away suffered serious internal trauma. Five hours later an army patrol plane spotted several rafts amid floating wreckage and vectored in the USS *Eagle 56* to pick up survivors. Of the original crew of 145, only a dozen men were plucked from the sea and transported to Cape May, with one of the survivors dying en route. The USS *Jacob Jones* bore the sad distinction of becoming the first U.S. warship sunk during the war in continental American waters, less than forty miles from Cape Henlopen.[10]

As the German offensive continued to inflict slaughter on Allied shipping, the U.S. Navy struggled to bring some order from chaos with the few resources at hand. Merchant ships were armed and navy gun crews were placed aboard to defend them. Instructions were provided to freighters, tankers, and other commercial vessels regarding evasive maneuvers and running blacked out at night (the U-boat's prime hunting time). Protocols for entering and departing mined harbors were instituted. The government failed to adopt some obvious procedures during the early days of the enemy offensive, however, such as ordering total blackouts along coastal areas to prohibit enemy subs from targeting passing ships silhouetted against the horizon. In March 1942, at the height of the U-boat attacks, Virginia's governor, Colgate Whitehead Darden Jr., angered at the government's unwillingness to order coastal blackouts, tried to take action on his own. Both the government and Virginia's own business community, unfortunately, rebuffed him on the grounds that it might instill panic among the general population and harm local commerce if the lights in beachfront towns were extinguished at night.[11] Politics had trumped security and common sense in the name of public morale and business. It came as poor consolation for the mariners whose lives were sacrificed thanks to a brightly lit horizon.

It wasn't that the government had not learned its lessons from the U-boat offensives in World War I and how to counter them, namely through the adoption of the armed convoy system to protect shipping. It was simply that it still lacked the wherewithal to provide enough armed ships do so and still maintain a strategic naval reserve for both the Pacific and Atlantic theaters while America girded herself for combat. Yet, as Admiral Dönitz had feared all along, once the Yanks got rolling, it would be difficult, if not impossible, to stop them. The advantages earned by the aggressive German U-boat offensive in the early days of the war would be for naught. When American convoy operations began, there could be no turning back.

The first convoy, forty-five ships strong, designated KS-500, departed Hampton Roads on May 14, 1942. Another bound north, designated KS-100, sailed from Key West, Florida. The voyages were timed so that passage through critical submarine-infested choke points would occur during daylight hours when U-boats were most vulnerable to attack. It was by no means foolproof, but it was a start. From then on, until the end of the war, coastal shipping traveled close to shore in convoys escorted by warships or other armed vessels. The shallow depths discouraged all but the most aggressive U-boats from attacking because they could not elude discovery or depth charging by escort vessels as readily as in deep water. Moreover, as experience had already shown, rescue of survivors of torpedoed ships close to shore was usually faster and more successful.

Once the convoy system was adopted, only two more merchant vessels would fall victim to direct enemy submarine attack off Delaware, Maryland, or Virginia in World War II. The first of these, the Norwegian freighter *Moldanger,* laden with animal hides, wool, and vegetable oil, was ambushed on June 25 while en route from Buenos Aires to New York City, several hundred miles off Virginia Beach, by the *U-404,* Kapitanleutnant Otto von Bulow commanding. The ship and twenty-three of her men were lost. The second, *Swiftscout,* would come only days before the war ended.[12] Undefeated and ever obedient to their Führer, however, the Germans were not through with the Delmarva just yet.

By the late spring of 1942, as the Kriegsmarine's halcyon days of U-boat successes along the ESF appeared to be on the wane, Dönitz resolved to counter with one last-gasp effort against the Delmarva—offensive mine warfare. The shipping lanes leading into the Chesapeake and Delaware Bays were perfect avenues to deploy one of the most insidious ship killers of all, the submarine mine.

When Kapitanleutnant Horst Degen, commander of *U-701,* sailed from the occupied port of Brest, France, in mid-May 1942 on a top-secret mission, he did so carrying not only torpedoes but fifteen magnetic mines ingeniously fitted into the boat's five torpedo tubes. He arrived on June 12 at the entrance to Chesapeake Bay, where he was to deploy his deadly weapons. Degen's orders were to remain submerged for twenty-four hours, taking note of the most-used traffic routes, and then to plant his mines in the most appropriate areas. From the latest nautical chart of the Virginia capes he noted that shoals extended at least eight miles south of Cape Charles and that the one and only deep-water channel into the bay was barely two miles wide. He grimaced to also observe that it was clearly within the defensive perimeter of Cape Henry. Air and sea patrols crisscrossed the area day and night. Minefields and antisubmarine netting obstructed passage. His mission was formidable, if not impossible, but Degen was not to be denied.

Approaching the shores of Virginia Beach at night, *U-701*'s lookouts could clearly discern cars and people on the shore, and then the brilliant glow of the Cape Henry Lighthouse. Soon they were actually in the Chesapeake Bay, within the American defense perimeter. About 1:00 A.M., a blacked-out trawler passed within 150 yards of the submarine without seeing her. Slowly Degen maneuvered his boat across the channel, deploying a mine from a torpedo tube every sixty seconds. A second pass was made and more mines were dropped to the bottom. Each mine was designed to remain dormant for sixty hours after deployment, to allow the U-boat's escape, after which it was automatically activated. When a ship passed nearby, a magnetic contact in the detonator would be generated and an explosion would ensue, sinking the ship and causing havoc. Though another patrolling trawler caused a brief revision of plans, Degen was again able to effectively escape detection. At dawn the U-boat submerged, her mining mission completed after many silent hours, and prepared to depart the Virginia capes for new hunting grounds off Cape Hatteras. Her legacy of death and destruction had been sown with legendary German efficiency.[13]

On the evening of June 15, a diminutive convoy of merchantmen, sailing in single column formation, was making its approach into Lynnhaven Bay. The fifth ship in line was the 11,615-ton Atlantic Refining Company tanker *Robert C. Tuttle,* Martin Johansen master, laden with 42,000 barrels of crude oil. Just why none of the lead ships had triggered a mine is unknown, but the *Tuttle* did. The explosion that claimed the life of the relatively new tanker erupted on her starboard side, instantly breaking her back aft the midships housing. Forty-six crewmen escaped aboard three lifeboats, but one man did not, as their ship sank in fifty-four feet of water and thousands of barrels of spilled oil set the sea ablaze.[14]

The sixth ship in line was the 547-foot-long *Esso Augusta,* laden with 120,000 barrels of gas oil, belonging to the Standard Oil Company of New Jersey. Stunned by the explosion of *Tuttle* and believing a submarine to be in the area, *Augusta*'s master, Captain Eric R. Blomquist, ordered all hands to battle stations. The engine room was signaled full speed even as the wheel was turned hard right to begin zigzag maneuvers. Within mere seconds, another explosion just three hundred yards off the port bow spread a plume of water skyward in an area where there were no vessels. Though the captain could not have known it at the time, one of the mines in the field had somehow been prematurely triggered or was set off by undersea turbulence caused by the first explosion. Suddenly the area was filled with aircraft and ships dropping depth charges all about as the convoy continued its evasive maneuvers. An uneasy hour passed as *Augusta* pressed on until, without warning, another powerful explosion went up immediately aft the port quarter. The blast stripped the ship's rudder cleanly off.[15]

A sleek U.S. Navy destroyer escorting the convoy, the USS *Bainbridge,* began again to scour the area for enemy U-boats, dropping depth charges in her wake as she proceeded. Another mine exploded close by her path, damaging the warship's rudder and propeller and forcing her to retire to Norfolk. It was now clear to the lead and middle sections of the convoy that the culprits were probably mines and not enemy torpedoes, and they were in the very midst of the minefield.[16]

In the meantime, not far to the south, the tail of the convoy was coming up under the protection of the Royal Navy armed trawler *Kingston Ceylonite,* recently loaned to the United States. Apprised of the commotion ahead and assuming the convoy to be under direct U-boat attack, her commander, Lieutenant W. McK. Smith, RNR, ordered the 448-ton ship to abandon her flock and press on to the waters off Virginia Beach. As she raced headlong into the danger zone, vessels already in the area signaled that there might be German mines in the area. Before the trawler could respond, however, she triggered a horrendous explosion that sent her to the bottom in less than three minutes, along with eighteen crewmen and two officers, including Lieutenant Smith.[17]

The losses were quickly and officially attributed to German mines, and on June 16, the day after the disasters, the navy dispatched a clutch of minesweepers from the Coast Guard base at Yorktown. By the following day, the "all clear" was issued and egress was again opened into Chesapeake Bay. Unfortunately, owing to a procedural error, one of the three areas that were to have been swept had not been, while another had actually been "cleared" twice. The result would prove deadly.

On that same morning the 7,117-ton Ore Steamship Company collier *Santore,* Captain Eric Nyborg master, one of the first ships to sail after the channel had been declared free of enemy mines, departed the Chesapeake to join a southbound convoy. At 7:45 A.M., while steaming off Virginia Beach, her port side was suddenly peeled open like a can of tuna by a tremendous explosion. Within three minutes the ship rolled onto her side, forcing forty-three crewmen and Naval Armed Guardsmen to jump into the sea, all of who were soon picked up. Three others did not make it into the water and perished.[18]

The Germans did not ignore the approaches to Delaware Bay, which were being laced with magnetic mines by another sub, *U-373.* Fortunately, only a single victim, a salvage-and-rescue tug named *John R. Williams,* which had been leased to the navy by the Great Lakes Dredge and Drydock Company, was claimed by the Nazi mines off Delaware. On June 24 *Williams* had been engaged in freeing several stranding victims from Fenwick Island Shoal. While en route back to the Delaware capes, approximately seven miles east of Rehoboth Beach, she was suddenly lifted out of the water by an immense explosion amidships and sank immediately. Only four men, all of whom had been on the fantail at the moment of detonation, were plucked from the water by a navy patrol boat. The remainder had perished with the ship. The Coast Guard immediately issued a warning that the area between Cape Henlopen and Cape May, Macries Shoal, and Fenwick Island were off limits to all shipping, including pleasure craft and fishing vessels. The area was soon cleared by minesweepers.[19]

As for the *U-701*, she would go on to sink two more ships and damage another off North Carolina before finally being sunk on July 7, 1942, by U.S. Army Bomber Squadron 396. The *U-373* would survive until June 8, 1944, when she would be sunk by the British in European waters. There would be no further victims of German mines on the Delmarva coast in World War II.[20]

The German U-boat offensive, at least off Delmarva's shores, was all but over. Confronted by an increasingly effective American convoy system, constant and intensive air and sea sweeps, as well as exigencies elsewhere, Dönitz was forced to call an end to aggressive action against the Eastern Sea Frontier. For the Germans the statistics revealed the failure of the campaign. In April there had been only twenty-three sinkings, four in May, and thirteen in June. In July only three ships had gone down, and none would be sunk for the remainder of the year. On July 19, Dönitz ordered the last two U-boats patrolling the ESF to conduct a tactical withdrawal, and eight days later he terminated the campaign on the Atlantic seaboard. Unfortunately, the U.S. Navy would suffer the loss of two warships, not through combat or submarine attack, but by accident. The losses were no less painful.[21]

The USS *Moonstone* was the first such disaster. Originally built as a luxurious private yacht named *Lone Star* for one George Gall Bourne, she was first home ported at Greenwich, Connecticut. Later sold to Frederick H. Prince, of Aiken, South Carolina, this incredibly elegant vessel was eventually moved to Newport, Rhode Island. On February 10, 1941, at the height of the U-boat offensive, Prince sold her to the U.S. Navy for $80,000 for conversion into a patrol boat. The Gibbs Gas Engine Company of Jacksonville, Florida, undertook an accelerated refitting program, and the ship was commissioned into the Navy as *Moonstone* (PYc-9) on April 10, 1941. On August 30, 1943, after service on the Panamanian Sea Frontier, the 469-ton, 171-foot-long former yacht reported for temporary duty on the Atlantic coast.

On the night of October 15, 1943, *Moonstone* was conducting routine antisubmarine patrol duty under the command of Lieutenant Walter Robert Scott Curtis approximately twenty-six miles southeast of Indian River Inlet. Though a heavy fog lay over the Atlantic, to avoid observation by any U-boats that might be in the area, she was running on a northerly course at seven knots without navigational lights or sounding fog signals. The lookout was keeping a keen eye searching for the southern channel buoys marking the entrance to Delaware Bay. At 11:18 P.M. the soundman notified the officer on the con, Lieutenant Frank Walther, that he had a contact bearing 315 degrees. Standing on the port wing of the bridge, Walther peered hard into the fog. Within seconds he was able to discern the silhouette of an oncoming ship and ordered the rudder hard right. In the pitch darkness, he groped for the searchlight switch, but it was too late; the approaching vessel was already upon him. The silhouette proved to be the USS *Greer* (DD-145), bound from the Brooklyn Navy Yard to Hampton Roads in company with the USS *Upshur* (DD-144) and USS *Vixen* (PG-53), all running with lights blacked out on a routine training mission. Although Walther could not have known it, onboard *Vixen* was the commander in chief of the U.S. Atlantic fleet, under escort of *Greer* and *Upshur*.

*Moonstone*, which was not outfitted with radar, had already been on *Greer*'s scope for eleven minutes and had first been reported at a distance of four miles. The destroyer quickly altered course to place herself between *Vixen* and the unidentified stranger. Though already skimming along at thirteen knots, a fatal decision to maintain speed was made. *Moonstone*'s position was continuously plotted, but it was not until 11:20 P.M., barely sixty seconds before collision, that *Greer* could actually see the patrol boat through the fog. At that moment reverse engines were ordered and general quarters sounded, but to no avail. Like a knife gutting a fish, the destroyer cut through the patrol boat's port side, slicing cleanly through the superstructure to the pilothouse and into the forward section to the keel. Crewmen jolted by the impact were already spilling into the water when Lieutenant Curtis, who had been in his room, reached the deck. The order to abandon ship had to be passed by mouth, as the alarm was no longer working. Fortunately, the gunner's mate had presence of mind to secure the depth charges on deck, which had been set to detonate at seventy-five feet, to prevent them from exploding when the ship sank, as had occurred during the *Jacob Jones* disaster.

Many crewmen leaped overboard, while others were flushed in by waters rushing through the gash. Before Curtis could issue further orders or the lifeboats could be launched, the ship sank under him. Within three to four minutes of the collision, *Moonstone*'s bow had already slipped down as her stern cantilevered upward at a thirty-five-degree angle and then disappeared as well. To avoid being pulled down by suction caused by the sinking ship, *Greer* quickly backed off. Two searchlights were immediately turned on, and a whaleboat was lowered to search for survivors in the fog. For the next forty-five minutes, forty-seven men struggled in the chilly Atlantic, clinging to anything that floated before finally being rescued. Following the rescue, *Greer* returned to New York the following day and landed the survivors.[22] The incident was quietly written off as a war loss. The commander in chief's voyage was otherwise unimpeded.

USS *St. Augustine* was another warship originally built as a private yacht. Like *Moonstone* before her, she was strikingly beautiful, with low, sleek lines and splendid attire. Named *Viking* by her original owner, banker George E. Baker Jr., her elegance was attested to by maritime historian Erik Hofman: "She was one of the most comfortable, roomy, seaworthy yachts ever built. Her turbo-electric drive gave her smooth, quiet performance, with exceptionable maneuverability."

At the time of her construction, yacht owners, designers, and crews were reluctant to depart from the sailing ship appearance they were accustomed to, so clipper ship bows, bowsprits, jibs, masts with yards, and counter sterns decorated with gilded trailboards and counters were retained, often in modified form, for nearly the whole steam yacht era. A superbly carved Viking figurehead graced her bow, shouldered by elegant gilded and hand-carved trailboards. *Viking* was among the last classic steam yachts to be built. Her large windows with steel shutters containing deadlights could be closed in a seaway yet gave good light under calm conditions. Baker was a wealthy and ardent deep-sea fisherman, and for nearly eight years he and *Viking* followed the fish, with the ship going out of commission only in January and February for a few weeks' maintenance and overhaul. In the summers she would go to New England, Nova Scotia, and the St. Lawrence, and in the winters to the West Indies, the west coast of South America, and the Galapagos Islands. In the fall and spring she would often steam off to the Mediterranean. In 1937, at the height of the Great Depression, Baker started her on a round-the-world cruise, albeit with just enough fuel capacity to go on one engine economically from Panama to Tahiti. There she refueled 76,000 gallons from nearly 1,500 drums by hand! On the way to Australia, her wealthy, globe-trekking owner became ill and diverted *Viking* to Honolulu, Hawaii, where he died. Baker's estate sold the yacht in 1938 to Norman B. Woolworth, cousin to heiress Barbara Hutton, who renamed her *Noparo*. Woolworth retained ownership for less than two years.

On December 5, 1940, the U.S. Navy purchased what was the most unlikely and ornately attired vessel to ever become a modern warship and assigned it to the Bethlehem Steel Corporation for conversion at the Boston Navy Yard. *Viking* was delivered to the navy at New London. On January 9, 1941, she was renamed and a week later formally commissioned as *St. Augustine* (PG54/A4), in honor of the Florida city, but she retained her distinctive Viking figurehead. Initially operating out of the First Naval District, she was later reassigned to the Eastern Sea Frontier and operated out of Tompkinsville, New York, escorting convoys between New York City and the Caribbean.

On the morning of January 6, 1944, while under the command of Lieutenant Parker Hatch, *St. Augustine* was escorting Convoy NG-588, consisting of the USMS tanker *Tydol Gas* and the Coast Guard cutters *Argo* and *Thetis,* out of New York harbor. Several vessels were scheduled to join the southbound ships off the Virginia capes. Soon after departing New York and swinging south at Ambrose Light, *Augie,* as her crew called her, encountered heavy seas. A frigid gale was blowing although the sky remained crystal clear. As evening fell, a bright, full moon lit the heavens and sea below. Steaming along at ten knots in the obligatory zigzag pattern, *St. Augustine* was in the lead, with the two cutters and tanker following behind on a straight course at 7.5 knots.

At 5:30 P.M., as the convoy was steaming southward, a lone tanker bound for Trinidad named *Camas Meadows* was departing the Delaware capes, proceeding out at a heady sixteen knots. Five hours later, sixty miles south of Cape May, *St. Augustine*'s radar man reported a blip on his screen. Altering course to investigate, the gunboat sighted the tanker at a distance of approximately twenty miles

The elegantly carved figurehead and trailboards denote the more genteel services of *St. Augustine* as the private yacht *Viking* in 1929. (The Mariners' Museum, Newport News, VA)

USS *St. Augustine* in camouflage (The Mariners' Museum, Newport News, VA)

and continued to track her for the next thirty minutes as the range between the two ships closed rapidly. Following normal wartime procedures, both ships were running blacked out. As the range between the two converging vessels narrowed to three thousand yards, the lookouts on *St. Augustine* finally discerned the silhouette of the tanker. She was moving on a course that would take her directly across the track of the convoy.

Onboard *Camas Meadow* the third mate had also spotted *St. Augustine,* which was then flashing a challenge with a hand-held Aldis lamp. Although he failed to see the first signal, when the patrol boat switched on running lights he realized at once that the craft was attempting to communicate. A second challenge via Aldis lamp was spotted but the third mate was unable to decipher the message. Fearing a U-boat trick, he sent for the signalman to interpret the signals. As the two ships continued to close to within half a mile the officer of the deck aboard *St. Augustine* quickly plotted and ascertained that the tanker and patrol boat were on a collision course. He immediately ordered hard aport, but too late. The tanker, whose own officer of the deck was not on the bridge, simply continued on course at sixteen knots. Though the patrol boat was making only two-thirds ahead, she responded slowly to the helm, too slowly to pass the tanker.

The turn propelled her directly across the bow of the tanker but without enough speed to make the pass. At that moment, Lieutenant Hatch came onto the bridge and realized the error in the officer of the deck's judgment, and he ordered full left rudder, which the helmsman was already holding, and full ahead on the starboard engine. Before the directive could be executed, however, the skipper changed orders and called for full speed ahead in a last ditch attempt to charge past the tanker's bow. Then, in an instant pregnant with horror, he shouted over the speaker system, "Stand by for collision."

The bow of *Camas Meadow* sliced through the midships hull of *St. Augustine* at 11:25 P.M., cutting obliquely through the bulkhead and penetrating the crew's quarters. The ship's boilers were instantly decimated, causing the engine room and fire room to fill with blistering steam. The superheated water seared the lungs of some and instantly scalded the bodies of others. As the bow pierced the berthing area, bursting pipes and filling it with searing steam, men attempted to flee forward into the officers' galley to escape through a hatch leading to the main deck.

At that same moment, confusion aboard *Camas Meadows* led some to believe their own ship had been torpedoed. A radio message sending the code "S.S.S." was sent out to that effect at 11:32 but was soon revised to "Have collided with another craft" and stated that men were in the water.

Now *Camas Meadow*'s engines were reversed and the ship slowed as she pushed the patrol boat sideways like a rag doll. As she backed clear of the wreck, the obscene open gash in *St. Augustine*'s side was fully revealed. Seamen aboard the tanker watched in stunned silence as half naked men, some without lifejackets, rushed about the deck of the patrol boat.

Onboard the navy vessel, Lieutenant Hatch ordered "abandon ship." Lifeboats crashed into the sea even as water began to swish across her fantail. More than one hundred desperate men struggled to stay alive in the winter waters, some heroically taking measures to ensure the safety of others. As on *Moonstone,* the gunner's mate had waded to the depth-charge racks, risking his own life and chances for survival, to set each charge on safe and prevent explosions as the ship sank. Within minutes, bathed in moonlight, *Augie* lay on her beam-ends and was soon pointing heavenward.

Aboard *Argo,* the officer of the deck watched in horror as *Augie's* bow rose precipitously out of the water before she went down by the stern. All hands aboard *Thetis* were ordered on deck to prepare for rescue operations. *Camas Meadows* got off the first call for assistance, and ESF headquarters ordered all available rescue craft dispatched. Within a short time a veritable armada of vessels was en route, including the USS *Allegheny, SC 1321, CO 93314, SC 1354,* and *Point Judith.* Planes and blimps would also be sent to assist in the search for bodies. Unaware of the identity of the sunken vessel, headquarters even dispatched orders for *St. Augustine* to participate in the rescue effort. Not until 1:15 A.M., January 7, would ESF be informed that the collision had been between *Camas Meadows* and one of the very vessels assigned to the search.

With surface temperature hanging at 32°F and water temperature at 38°F, the loss of life was appalling. Not until two hours after the sinking were the last survivors brought in. They were terribly few in number. Of her original crew of 145, twenty-six men had been taken up by *Argo,* and thirteen by *Thetis.* Of those recovered by the latter, only seven survived. The remainder of the crew, nine officers and 106 crewmen, had gone down with the ship or died in the water from shock, hypothermia, and exhaustion. When rescue vessels and aircraft finally began to arrive on the scene, a daylong search for bodies commenced. In the end, sixty-seven corpses were recovered from the sea. Survivors were taken to Cape May where they were treated and hospitalized.

A court of inquiry was immediately convened and was present when the haggard remnants of *Augie's* crew were brought to the section base at Cape May. The investigating board ruled that neither ship was blameless. *St. Augustine* had failed to properly estimate the speed and course of *Camas Meadows* and should not have altered its own course so as to place it across the bow of the tanker. Moreover, had the signalman on *Camas Meadows* been more vigilant, the disaster might well have been avoided.[23]

During the closing days of the war, Adolf Hitler ordered one last suicidal offensive against North American shipping. A total of three vessels were assailed off the Virginia and North Carolina coasts. It was indeed a sad event, for the war in Europe was all but over by April 18 when the final U-boat victim was sunk off Virginia by *U-548.*

It was 7:00 A.M., and the tanker *Swiftscout* was passing the Delaware capes when she developed engine trouble and stopped to make repairs. Everything seemed in order, and no one anticipated any danger. After all, it was generally agreed that the Atlantic coast had been free from U-boats for at least two years. Two hours later, Captain Peter Kasares, the tanker's skipper, ordered the voyage south resumed. Then the unthinkable happened. At 9:25 a torpedo ripped into the ship's port side. The explosion instantly broke her back, causing the main decks to sag, as bow and stem were lifted out of the water. But the ship remained afloat.

Spotting the U-boat's periscope, *Swiftscout*'s gun crews, rather than panic, courageously opened fire from guns mounted on the tanker's bow and stern. The U-boat skipper, Kapitanleutnant Erich Krempl, thus wisely chose to keep his boat safely submerged as he maneuvered her into position to fire another torpedo. At 1:35 P.M. the second undersea missile struck the tanker somewhat aft of the first hit. This time, the ship began to fill rapidly and was soon sinking stern first. Ten minutes later, the bow had also slipped under, but residual air pockets caused it to reappear several times, bobbing like a cork, before finally succumbing to the laws of physics.

The forty-six crewmen of *Swiftscout* hastily took to the lifeboats after the second torpedo hit, but not before a distress call was sent from an emergency transmitter placed in one of the boats. The survivors were taken up by the tanker *Chancellorsville* at 6:50 P.M. and later transferred to a Coast Guard vessel in Lynnhaven Roads. Fortunately, there had been but a single fatality in the attack, the last U-boat victim on the Delmarva coast.

A few days later, *U-548* attacked the Norwegian tanker *Katy*, but the ship was only damaged and made Hampton Roads on her own power. On April 30, four American warships, the USS *Coffman, Bostwick, Thomas,* and *Natchez,* assailed the submarine and sunk her off Cape Hatteras. There were no survivors.[24] Seven days later Germany surrendered. The long U-boat nightmare on the Delmarva coast was finally over.

# 24

## A Long Shudder

It was a polyglot crew of seamen—Germans, Norwegians, Finns, Spaniards, and Sudanese—that bedded down for the night in the gymnasium of Ocean City Elementary School, on Baltimore Avenue and Third Street. The extraordinary events that had delivered them to the town were already making national headlines, and their presence was causing something of a sensation in the little seaside resort. Only a few hours earlier they had been besieged by a gaggle of reporters from the *Washington Post, New York Times,* and *Baltimore Sun.* The journalists tried to extract from the foreigners, who spoke little or no English, the dramatic details on the tragic loss of their ship, the Liberian-register tanker *African Queen,* earlier in the day. The men had at first been subdued when they were ferried ashore from the wreck by an airlift fleet of noisy helicopters from several different military services. Several hundred curiosity-seekers had watched the landing operations. A few of the crewmen had smiled broadly as they trooped past the "rubberneckers," but most displayed little emotion reflecting their narrow escape from death.[1]

Soon after coming ashore they had been briefly quarantined in the white-framed Coast Guard station on the Ocean City boardwalk pending the arrival of U.S. immigration and public health officials. But shortly after their captain, Kai Danielsen, of Kristiansund South, Norway, the last to leave the ship, had been brought ashore, they were transferred to the school. The local civil defense agency had helped secure their lodgings, and several kindly town folk provided homemade meals for them. A few of the mariners, however, had fanned out to find the few taverns that were still open in the resort town during the winter season, and only returned to their temporary lodgings after securing trophies in the form of numerous six-packs of beer.[2]

Reporters had been amused during the so-called interviews as one crewman chased the late ship's mascot under a cot. The animal in question was a small white furry pup acquired at a bar in Naples and called "Napoli" by some and "Bos'n" by others. The capture had unfortunately come too late to save the seaman a clean-up task. All of the men of *African Queen* were clearly exhausted, especially Captain Danielsen, who had been up for the better part of two straight days and now peered at the world through heavy-lidded bloodshot eyes. The weary and depressed captain did his best to express his gratitude in broken English for the work of his rescuers. But when a reporter asked how the ship had been lost, he glared at the man and said with a touch of Scandinavian sarcasm: "The ship broke in two. That's what caused the trouble." At 10:00 P.M. it was lights out. It was the end of a most horrific day.[3]

*African Queen* was an oil tanker of unexceptional design, size, or service. Built in Kiel, West Germany, in 1955 by the firm of Kieler Howaldswerke, the 22,340-dead-weight-ton, 590-foot-long ship had been owned by a syndicate of Norwegians called African Enterprises Ltd. and was registered for tax purposes in Monrovia, Liberia. At the time of her loss, she was operated by the Packet Shipping Company of New York under charter to the Socony Vacuum Oil Corporation and was bound from Covenas, Colombia, with 21,000 tons, about 200,000 barrels, of Venezuelan crude, valued at $700,000. The Coast Guard later estimated value of both ship and cargo at between $5 million and $7 million. After an uneventful 2,100-mile voyage, manned with a complement of forty-five officers and seamen (who had just spent Christmas aboard), she was only hours from her destination on the Delaware to deliver her cargo to the Socony Mobil Oil Company refinery at Paulsboro, New Jersey, when disaster struck.[4]

Captain Danielsen had been at sea for twenty-seven of his forty-three years. Life in the merchant marine had been both rewarding and hard, especially during the late war, and the tall, slump-shouldered officer looked twenty years older than his true age. He had been the skipper of *African Queen* for barely a year but had for some undetermined reason taken an almost paternal interest in her. He was not the only one aboard with a personal concern for the ship. Third engineer Axel Loeck had helped build her at the shipyard in Kiel and was particularly fond of the vessel that had his sweat in its veins.[5]

Danielsen was no stranger to the Atlantic seaboard and was well aware that the shipping lanes off the Delmarva coast were a major corridor employed annually by hundreds of ore carriers, tankers, and other ships. He was also aware that there were, even at this late period in the mid-twentieth century, a number of still largely uncharted "humps," or shelves of sand, sometimes extending several miles offshore just west of the shipping lanes. Local watermen knew them like the calluses on their hands, but skippers of the large foreign bottoms that regularly plied these same waters were far less knowledgeable about them and usually gave them a wide girth. Unfortunately, Mother Nature occasionally took a hand at confusing even the best mariners about their locations, sometimes with fatal consequences. Such was the case with poor Captain Danielsen.[6]

*African Queen,* though barely three years old, was no stranger to dirty weather, and she appeared to be taking on the rain, high winds, rough water, and heavy Atlantic swells off the Delmarva with almost cavalier nonchalance in the pre-dawn hours of December 30, 1958. Captain Danielsen was nevertheless a cautious man. Having been awakened by the turbulent seas, which he later attributed to a "gale force" storm, he was disturbed that he was unable to spot shore lights or navigational aids where he thought they normally should have been. A firm believer in "better safe than sorry," he thus ordered the ship's speed reduced to four knots. The big tanker had a depth between deck and keel of thirty-two feet, and it was imperative that his deep-hulled ship, even when trimmed in the normal manner for winter sea conditions, proceed with all wariness.[7] Slowly but resolutely the tanker plowed ahead through the darkness.

Shortly before 6:00 A.M., like many of his fellow crewmen, nineteen-year-old Detlef Leetz, a red-bearded seaman from Emmerich, Germany, had been asleep but was awakened by what he later described as "a loud grrmp" and the watch excitedly shouting, "All hands on deck!" The sound was not heard in the pilot-house where Danielsen had been keeping a keen watch for lights ashore. He did, however, hear the troubling sounds of the engines laboring hard and then noticed a distinct lack of forward motion. The ship, he instantly realized, was aground. Her bow had somehow slipped onto a shoal, though her stern and propellers were still free, pushing her relentlessly onward into the sediments. Without hesitation, he pulled the engine order telegraph to the stop position. The steam pressure that fed the ship turbines was then discharged until her massive propellers finally idled in their bearings. As soon as the propellers stopped, Danielsen rang for full astern to back her off and struggled to hold her steady while reiterating the order for all hands on deck.[8]

James Law, a thirty-one-year-old Welsh resident of Germany, having been asleep in his bunk, had also been jarred awake by the impact. At first thinking it little more than rough weather, he began to slip back into slumber until awakened again, this time by the watchman. "What are you doing in bed?" the watchman screamed. "We're aground."[9]

Another crewman, Gunther Molberg, of Hamburg, Germany, had been relaxing after coming off the 4:00 A.M. watch. He later reported that he had heard a "boom" and went topside to see what was going on, only to hear shouts of "The ship is up! The ship is up!" and knew she was aground.[10]

It is uncertain whether or not Captain Danielsen knew his precise position at the time of the stranding, or the depth of water he was in. In fact, his ship was first reported as having gone aground in twenty-seven to thirty feet of water on an unmarked "hump" on or about Gull Shoal approximately thirty miles south of the Delaware, nine to ten miles east-southeast of Ocean City. He sent out word of his situation at 6:10 A.M. to the Coast Guard through a portable transmitter but said that the ship was in no immediate danger. The call, unfortunately, did not get through. For the moment, Danielsen was more concerned with getting off the hump than talking. For the next hour he worked to pull her off but in vain.[11]

Again the sound of laboring engines was heard, and then suddenly a loud "heavy cracking" rent the air at the moment the ship pulled free. The great hull separated forward of amidships and began to jackknife. The bow "whipped around" to starboard at a forty-three-degree angle even as the stern continued to pull away on a straight course. Then, as the separated portions, still attached by only a few mangled hull plates, began bumping together, the forward compartments were gutted, "ripping one tank after another." Tons of Venezuelan crude began to spill into the Atlantic as the last sheets of steel holding the two sections together finally tore apart. "I told the crew to run to the afterpart," the captain later said, "which I knew from previous experience would be more likely to stay afloat." Fortunately, no crewmen had been in the bow section that had broken off. It was now about 7:58 A.M. and using an emergency transmitter aft, the captain sent out the first S.O.S. requesting assistance. This time it was received by the Fifth District Coast Guard Command. Unfortunately, no one seemed to know the ship's position.[12]

Engine repairman Paul Kunath had been stunned when the ship stranded. His pet cat Suzy had "started screaming like a little child." In an instant he had been ordered by the chief engineer to check the engine room to see if any repairs could be made. Then the ship "shuddered like crazy" and the lights went out. He could feel the ship tilt to one side and rushed up to the deck to witness the disaster unfolding before him.[13]

Soon the bow, driven by the turbulence of the sea, was creased and folding back along the starboard side of the stern. Danielsen ordered ten-inch-thick ropes placed between the bumping sections to prevent the metal sides from throwing off friction sparks. "But even so, I could see smoke from the heat when the two hulls struck," he later said. Crewmen were ordered to stop smoking. Boilers were shut down and lights extinguished. The oil tanks were flooded with foam to lessen the fire danger. "I knew the situation was desperate," the captain later reported. "I was afraid any minute the ship would catch fire." The danger of igniting the oil-covered sea itself was now very real. With the bow battering against the side plates of the stern, that section too was holed and leaking. A breach between the machinery spaces and the wheelhouse was quickly opened. The engine room walls were mercilessly ruptured, and everyone therein was now forced by the flooding to abandon their posts.[14]

Incredibly, as the bow slowly slipped past the fantail, everyone aboard was still alive and there was not the least hint of panic. No one could know when or if help would arrive since the ship's precise position was known only to be "somewhere between Norfolk and New York." Though they were in danger of going down at any moment, the crew simply huddled on the aft stem section and waited patiently.[15]

Word of the catastrophe was radioed up and down the Middle Atlantic seaboard, and the Coast Guard and U.S. Navy rushed into action. Search-and-rescue operations were supervised out of the Third Coast Guard District, where central command orchestrated all communications from Governors Island, New York. Search planes belonging to the U.S. Navy were immediately ordered into the air from Floyd Bennett Field in Brooklyn, New York, and Elizabeth City, North Carolina. At 8:36 A.M., only thirty-eight minutes after the S.O.S. had been received, the aircraft from Floyd Bennett Field sighted the two wallowing sections of the wreck and radioed their positions. Within a matter of minutes, from New York to North Carolina, an enormous and extremely well-coordinated rescue effort was launched. The noisy swirl of armed forces helicopter blades was soon heard at Brooklyn and at Lakehurst, New Jersey, Patuxent

The bifurcated wreck of *African Queen,* 1958. Note the upturned bow in the distance (*far left*). (The Mariners' Museum, Newport News, VA)

Naval Air Station, Maryland, and the Chincoteague Coast Guard Station and Quantico Marine Base, Virginia. The Coast Guard cutter *Agassiz,* buoy tender *Sassafras,* and smaller rescue craft and patrol boats from stations at Cape May, Lewes, and Ocean City were soon en route.[16]

Nine U.S. Navy, Coast Guard, and Marine Corps helicopters from five states rushed to rescue forty-five crewmen from the stern of *African Queen.* The first service to appear on the scene were several Coast Guard aircraft and surface vessels. Soon the entire multiservice fleet had arrived, with the initial rescue operations supervised by a navy seaplane, which had landed nearby, and then by a Coast Guard amphibian. Though surface temperatures were an unseasonably warm 50°F or more, with rough four- to eight-foot-high seas swirling around the wreck and the wind blowing at twenty to twenty-five knots from the north-northeast, the approach by water was deemed too dangerous to effect a ship-to-ship rescue.[17]

It would have to be done by the helicopters circling above the wreck and operating in relays, taking off five men at a time. Each helicopter was equipped with a harness device, which was lowered onto the stern of the ship and strapped around a wreck victim who was then hoisted up. The operation proved to be a masterpiece of interservice cooperation and traffic management, though each chopper could carry, besides crew, only five passengers at a time. The first crewman rescued was a Sudanese cook and galley hand who was dropped onto the beach at the Ocean City lifeboat station at 10:45 A.M., little more than two hours after the wreck had been sighted and four hours after the S.O.S. had gone out. Though at this time of year the beachfront was normally devoid of crowds, the noisy rescue operations had attracted hundreds to the boardwalk. Operating in assembly line fashion, the fleet of helicopters had removed forty-three tired and cold men by shortly after noon. Only one minor injury—a crewman who had suffered a bump on the head when being lifted from the tanker's deck—had been reported. Captain Danielsen and first mate Jorgen Jorgensen, of Tonsberg, Norway, remained aboard until a little after 1:00 P.M. (when salvage rights were secured by their employers) and then transferred to a Coast Guard lifeboat and finally to the cutter *Agassiz,* which landed them at 3:15 P.M.[18] The Coast Guard's seagoing tug *Cherokee* was assigned the task of standing by the wreck to warn other vessels off and prevent further collisions.

Within hours of the rescue, the bow section of *African Queen* had pulled completely free of the firmly grounded stern and begun drifting out to sea. Late that night, it also grounded on a shoal. Captain Danielsen counted his blessings, for had the vessel split amidships rather than only a hundred feet or so from the bow, seven or eight of his men might have been trapped. Coast Guard officials, as well as the men of the ship, expressed their vast relief that the rescue had been effected in the face of a constant threat of fire from the spilling oil. One crewman called it "almost a miracle" that the oil had not burned. Though he, like most of his mates, had come ashore bearing only a small handbag that contained a camera, shaving gear, and a few articles of clothing, they were all alive and well. Most of the men, according to a spokesman for the Socony Vacuum Oil Company, would be transferred by bus to New York the next morning and sent home, although a few would immediately ship out again on other vessels.[19]

While the captain and crew of the late tanker *African Queen* finally slept, Paul Preus, one of the ship's agents and a personal friend of Danielsen, arrived at Ocean City to represent his firm's interests. He called the captain's supervision of the crippled ship a "tremendous feat of seamanship" and noted that it was remarkable that no lives had been lost and fire had been prevented. Yet there was no immediate explanation for the accident. He knew that the crewmen reported that they had no warning of the impending crisis before they felt a "long shudder" pass through their ship before dawn. But none of that mattered now, for uppermost in his mind was salvage.[20]

The last day of 1958 arrived with rough seas and bracing winds at the *African Queen* wreck site. A heavy slick of oil surrounded the wreck area for thousands of feet in all directions, and it was feared that unfavorable winds might wash it ashore at Ocean City with obviously detrimental prospects for the coming tourist season. During the night the oceangoing salvage vessel *Curb,* belonging to the Merritt-Chapman & Scott Corporation of New York, had arrived on site with the intention of conducting a preliminary survey of the two sections of the wreck, which now lay a thousand feet apart. *Cherokee* was no longer required to stand by the hulk. It was soon clear that another gale, which had descended on the region replete with twenty-five knot winds and eight- to ten-foot seas, would delay putting anyone aboard the stricken ship, and no plans could be made until a preliminary survey had been completed. *Curb* had been dispatched even before Danielsen abandoned the bridge, but her work would last for many weeks during which a full-scale inquiry into the cause of the disaster would be launched by the Liberian government.[21]

For the next month and a half, as winter weather, storms, ice, and a paralyzing cold hindered salvage operations, the work progressed in fits and starts. The company installed a great wooden patch on the stem and anchored the bow to prevent it from again floating off, but little else was accomplished. By the middle of February, Merritt-Chapman ordered the salvage operations suspended to await better weather but soon deemed the project a liability and abandoned the hulks to the mercy of the wind and sea. With the very real threat that the weakened stern hull plates might rupture, spilling tens of thousands more tons of oil into the Atlantic, African Enterprises Ltd. formally abandoned the ship. It was a move clearly intended to relieve the company of any future legal obligations regarding both the vessel and its cargo and to protect the firm from any potential lawsuits that might ensue. Ownership was passed to Lloyd's of London, which paid off the claim and promptly abandoned the ship as well.[22]

*African Queen,* without a legal owner, was up for grabs. As soon as its status was made known, a virtual feeding frenzy ensued, first among commercial fishermen and clammers. Anything and everything that could be readily removed was appropriated, even Captain Danielsen's clothing and the personal belongings of the crew. The tanker's motorized lifeboats were stripped from their davits. Steel cable, pumps, furniture, the ship's gyroscope, radar gear, radios, marine paint, fittings, bathroom hardware, and so on were quickly pirated. From above, the scene resembled nothing so much as a colony of ants swarming over the body of a dead bug while stripping it of its every appendage. With scores of men hustling and sometimes fighting over anything that might be transportable, mini turf wars soon erupted. One scrapper even laid claim to the entire bow and prohibited anyone from coming aboard, guarding his prize like an angry rottweiler until associates ashore could arrange to have it towed to Norfolk for scrapping. The salvor's tenacity unhappily cost him his life when a storm tore the bow from its moorings, turned it upside down and carried it more than a mile from its anchorage before it sank. The claimant's body was never recovered.[23]

Two who were initially more successful than the rest were Lloyd Deir and Beldon Little, both self-employed Norfolk metal workers. It was their avowed goal not just to strip the ship of all transportable items but to salvage it in its entirety. Though they knew little, if anything, about ships and salvage, they were extremely proficient in welding, machinery and engine repair, rigging, and heavy equipment operations. Operating "out of pocket," they worked without letup for the next six months, welding patches, pumping out water, and gradually returning buoyancy to the stern section. As they worked, the oil within slowly seeped into the sea. By September, having expended more than $55,000 of their own funds, they deemed *African Queen* ready to be towed into dry dock at Norfolk. The towing cost them an additional $55,000.[24]

It was for Deir and Little a triumphant day when their prize, recovered almost single-handedly by the two enterprising salvors, was hauled into Hampton Roads by the tug *Mary L. McAllister.* The hulk was soon put up for auction with a $250,000 minimum bid required to open. There were no takers. A second auction was called for. This time the starting bid was only $25,000, and the bidding was unhurried and nothing like the two salvors had hoped. When it was all over, the tanker's stern was sold for $134,000. Their half a year's work had yielded the two salvors, after expenses and commissions, less than $12,000 profit apiece, less than they would have made at their regular jobs.

Their troubles, however, were far from over. Waiting in the wings was one Gifford Warner, who asserted that he held prior salvage rights to the wreck, having posted a notice laying claim to it. The case was heard in Norfolk Federal District Court by Judge Walter Hoffman and promptly dismissed, finally concluding the woeful saga of *African Queen.*

# The Trouble with Treasure

The urge to swim like fish beneath the seas is as old as humankind itself. The desire to explore and reap the bounty of the submarine world, to seek out and recover its riches and curiosities, be they natural or the historical detritus of past civilizations, also has been around for a long time. One of the most alluring attractions of the undersea world has been the countless unfortunate vessels whose bones lay eternally resting therein. Through the ages, the industry of wrecking, salvage, and the pursuit of sunken treasures have been a colorful adjunct to maritime industry. For undersea work, at least since the late eighteenth century, such endeavors have largely been limited to deep-sea diving specialists using hard-hat surface-supplied air and industrial-strength salvage equipment. The invention by Jacques Yves Cousteau and Emile Gagan in 1946 of the demand-valve self-contained underwater breathing apparatus, commonly called *scuba,* dramatically changed the equation. Scuba's introduction to the public in the early 1950s immediately gave birth to a new sport focusing specifically on public access to an exciting frontier that was now to be explored, enjoyed, and sometimes exploited by millions. For the commercial salvor, industrial diver, oceanographer, and marine scientist, it provided a welcomed new addition to an ever-enlarging arsenal of work tools. For the treasure hunter, it provided the key to accessing a vast repository of untapped and potentially enriching targets hitherto inaccessible. For the professional archaeologist and historian, it made possible a new field of intellectual and scientific endeavor, a nascent discipline called underwater archaeology. It was for all a new era of discovery.

Not surprisingly, with so many competing interests in the underwater world, and particularly in shipwrecks, conflicts were bound to arise. Beginning in the mid-1960s, the most contentious issues began to erupt between the historic preservation community, including archaeologists, historians, and cultural resource managers, who subscribed to the premise that historic shipwrecks were archaeological and cultural properties that belonged to the public and must be preserved and studied in the public interest, and a burgeoning community of treasure wreck hunters, who believed that shipwrecks were to be exploited for profit as they had been for centuries. Although the first major skirmishes in

America were fought in Florida, perhaps nowhere else were the major battles more pivotal on a national and international scale than on the Delmarva coast.

Treasure hunting, wrecking, and salvage have, as we have already seen, been for-profit endeavors that have enjoyed a long history on the Eastern Shore. Many ships have, of course, gone down there with substantial cargoes that were exploited both legally and illegally for monetary gain and, in many cases, subsistence by whole communities. In the process, innumerable folktales have emerged regarding shipwrecks laden with eye-popping cargoes of gold, silver, jewels, and chests of coins. Among the most famous and enticing to treasure hunters were *La Galga, Faithful Steward, De Braak,* and *Juno.* It is not surprising that even today treasure hunting thrives on the Delmarva coast. With roots that go back to the first salvage attempts on *La Galga,* it began in earnest not long after the loss of HMS *De Braak.* It is a tale of the all-consuming lust for silver and gold that drives men beyond reason, fueled by human curiosity, dreams, high-risk Yankee capitalism, speculation, avarice, chicanery, controversy, fame, and an adoring media.

The origins of the rumors that began to circulate soon after the capsizing of HMS *De Braak* on May 28, 1798, are uncertain. Perhaps they arose from the Spanish gold coins that several survivors of the disaster paid their bills with at Lewes. Perhaps it was the interest the Royal Navy had exhibited by conducting a short and ill-fated effort to recover its property from the seabed. Perhaps it was a garbled account that mixed the value of *De Braak's* Spanish prize, *Don Francisco Xavier,* with unfounded reports of treasure brought ashore by former Spanish prisoners. Whatever it was, the tale, like most treasure stories that evolve with every telling, was simply too delicious to forget. And with the masthead of the sunken ship standing proud above the waves in Old Hore Kill Roads for months on end, no one was likely to do so for long.[1]

Gilbert McCracken, a Lewes pilot who had lost a race with Andrew Allen out to the warship when she first arrived, recorded the location of the wreck and about 1805 tucked it away in his family Bible. The record, which McCracken most likely had made so that he might recall a potentially hazardous navigational obstruction (the mast had, after all, been projecting out of the water), was destined to become the inspiration and primary source guide thereafter for many efforts to relocate the ship.[2]

The first salvage permit to recover the supposed treasure was sought from the U.S. government by one Captain Charles Sanborn following the Civil War. In 1867, Sanborn, who was reportedly "a noted submarine diver," was said to have conducted his research at Halifax and claimed to have discovered that the ship carried "an immense amount of treasure, consisting of gold and silver bars and precious stones." Before his project could get under way, however, he died. Yet word of his research served to lend credence to what had otherwise been little more than a local folktale. Thus it was that the legend of the *De Braak's* so-called treasure took root and really began to grow.[3]

The first actual search effort to locate *De Braak* was conducted thirteen years later by McCracken's grandson Samuel, who used the locational notes Gilbert had left in the family Bible. With backing from a Connecticut-based organization called the International Submarine Company (ISC), Samuel secured a salvage permit from the U.S. government and began a futile search that ultimately drove him to penury. In 1886, Dr. Seth Pancoast, a Philadelphia teacher, physician, and mystic, managed to secure control of the ISC and launched his own three-year-long campaign to recover the purported treasure from the ill-fated, and by now legendary, warship. With the assistance of the U.S. Navy, a professional hard-hat diver, and a steamboat called *City of Long Branch,* Pancoast directed one of the first systematic bottom surveys by a diver in the Western Hemisphere. Pancoast managed to keep investor interest high, even with dismally negative results, by occasionally creating tantalizing tidbits about the most recent finds, always connecting them to the famed shipwreck. Most were products of his own fertile imagination designed to spur investor confidence and support, a not-uncommon tactic of modern treasure hunters![4]

In 1888, as the charismatic Pancoast entered his final year of investigation, noted historian John Thomas Scharf's *History of Delaware* first appeared in print. Scharf had been captivated—and entirely taken in—by the treasure hunter's search for the now famous shipwreck and included in his book the by now well-embroidered treasure story as entirely factual. The book would incite dozens of subsequent expeditions and the expenditure of literally millions of investment dollars in the hunt for a treasure that never existed.[5]

The first to take a chance after Pancoast was the famed Merritt Wrecking Company of New York, which was contracted by the Ocean Wrecking Company, an ISC spin-off, in 1889. Over the next century no fewer than a dozen major expeditions would be mounted, and countless minor and undocumented efforts as well. Among the notable operations fielded were those led by Ralph Chapman in 1932 and 1933; the Braak Corporation in 1933; Charles N. Colstad in 1935 and 1937; Archie and Weldon Brittingham, Charles Johnston, and Rod King in 1952; William H. Boyce and Robert Howarth in 1955; William Strube in 1962 and 1963; D&D Salvage in a five-year program between 1965 and 1970; Tracy Bowden Associates in 1970; and Seaborne Ventures, Inc., in 1980.[6]

Even as investors poured an unending stream of venture capital into the ocean, scholarly research was publicly revealing that there had never been a treasure aboard *De Braak.* If there was any wealth to be found at all, it was the archaeological value of the wreck itself, an encapsulation of maritime culture and society during the Age of Napoleon and Nelson that could help define just who we as a modern civilization are and how we got here in the first place. In 1967, even as treasure salvors were tearing up shipwreck after shipwreck in search of *De Braak,* Howard I. Chapelle of the Smithsonian Institution and Lieutenant Colonel M. E. S. Laws published the first scholarly work debunking the treasure legend. Three years later, Mendel Peterson, director of exploration at the Smithsonian, presented an address at the Lewes Historical Society declaring for the first time on record that *De Braak* and, indeed, many other shipwrecks on the

Delmarva coast, were definitely of historical and archaeological significance and should not be destroyed by those in pursuit of treasure. The treasure hunters paid little heed and proceeded to demolish at least a dozen eighteenth- and nineteenth-century shipwrecks in search of the fabled booty. With every effort, every new press release, every news story, and every new hapless investor, the purported treasure grew in size.[7]

By the mid-1980s the wreck of HMS *De Braak* had served as a magnet for treasure hunters for more than a century, but it was not the only such attraction on the Delmarva coast. In 1980, several search efforts had been launched to find other supposed treasures lying between Cape Henlopen and Cape Charles, the most notable of the lot being conducted by a company called Seaborne Ventures, Inc., led by a professional Florida treasure hunter named Dennis Standefer. A veteran in the field, Standefer had mounted extensive campaigns in Mexico and Central America and had even earned for himself a place in John S. Potter's popular *Treasure Diver's Guide.* Thanks to the notoriety of Potter's book and others like it, two other supposedly coin-laden ships lost near Indian River Inlet, the 1785 wreck of *Faithful Steward* and *Three Brothers,* said to have gone down in 1775 while carrying military payroll in gold, silver, and copper coins destined for the British military command in Philadelphia, had begun to rival the tales of *De Braak.* It mattered little that neither British nor American military or civil records made mention of the loss of a *Three Brothers,* much less the loss of a valuable payroll. When lumped with *De Braak,* the allure of these two alleged treasure-bearing shipwrecks almost within hailing distance of each other had piqued Standefer's interest.[8]

In August 1980, Standefer arrived on the Delmarva coast. He entered the arena with panache. His objective was to search for *De Braak* in Old Hore Kill Roads of Lewes, *Faithful Stewart* and *Three Brothers* between Indian River Inlet and Dewey Beach, and an unidentified wreck a mile and a half below the inlet. He was financed by a wealthy Georgetown, Delaware, building contractor who had also supported the famed treasure hunter Mel Fisher, discoverer of the richest treasure wreck to that date in American waters, *Nuestra Señora de Atocha,* and by other well-heeled investors. By October 8 he had secured three exclusive leases from the State of Delaware, each covering a mile and a half of water, at a cost of $1,000 per site. Delaware's share of the treasure was to be 25 percent.[9]

The array of equipment eventually deployed by Seaborne Ventures was formidable and included the latest side-scan sonar and magnetometers. Standefer was betting that the systems might literally be worth their weight in gold. To facilitate excavation of the yet-to-be-found shipwreck sites, Seaborne rented a 275-foot barge at a cost of $3,000 per day from the McClean Dredging Company of Baltimore. The barge, which was expected to arrive during the second week of October, was to serve as a platform from which clam-bucket dredging of likely sites could be carried out. Standefer said he expected the project would cost as much as $500,000. Unfortunately, his actual research had apparently been as limited as that of his predecessors, relying heavily on the same old folktales.[10]

Nevertheless, with leases in hand and his investors footing the bill, Standefer began immediately. He decided to begin test-dredging operations off the Dewey Beach site the next day, on Thursday, October 9. Barry Schatz, who handled the company's publicity, informed the press of Standefer's strategy and noted that treasure hunters normally did not expect to find much treasure close to shore. Seaborne would rehearse its operations for the next several days by working a site some believed to be *Faithful Steward,* which from the 1930s on was said to be the source of the coin finds on Coin Beach, before moving up to Cape Henlopen for the big one, HMS *De Braak.*[11]

The McClean barge was towed into position and anchored a mere twenty yards from the beach, stern pointed shoreward, bow toward the open sea. It apparently mattered little to Standefer whether or not a shipwreck lay below (for there had been no verification of one), only that operations get under way as quickly as possible. The world was watching. Within an hour after establishing a four-point moor for the barge, the gigantic clam bucket had bitten into the sandy bottom, gouging out massive holes, and had brought its load to the surface to be deposited and sifted on deck.[12]

Two days after the beginning of operations, reporters and cameramen from a local television station arrived on the scene to begin filming the treasure hunt for a local show called *Prime Time.* As if on cue, the first major artifacts, two gold five-guinea pieces and a handful of copper coins, were found. The following day, Sunday, as cameras rolled, another two gold five-guinea pieces and more coppers were plucked from the mud. By October 13, five days after dredging had begun, nearly two hundred badly deteriorated coppers; four gold coins, dated 1752, 1756, 1759, and 1766; a brass navigational divider; a few brass spikes; a fistful of silver and brass shoe buckles; some copper sheathing; and several bits of slate and iron had been recovered.[13]

The Delaware State Wetlands Office was impressed by the finds. "The coins," one ranking official exclaimed, "look like they just fell into the water yesterday" and were worth between four and five thousand dollars. Despite the excitement of the state, the media, and everyone else, the salvors seemed strangely unimpressed by the recovered items. Was the site related to *Faithful Steward?* Was it some other wreck, or merely a random debris field? Had the coins been salted? Admittedly, there were numerous artifacts, but no timber from a shipwreck. At a cost of $15,000 in barge-rental alone, the return so far had not been profitable. At the end of the fifth day, Seaborne spokesman Barry Schatz was almost blasé about the work. "We found a lot of junk," he said. "If we don't find something big soon," he promised, "we'll move up to the *De Braak* site off Lewes." That evening, the effort off Indian River Inlet was terminated.[14]

Though a brief survey effort was launched soon afterward off Cape Henlopen, the weather refused to cooperate, and the project was closed down for the season. Dennis Standefer would not be back the following year. Others would.

As he prepared to depart from Lewes, Schatz was asked by a news reporter to define the driving motivation of a treasure hunter. "Gold and gleaming wealth," he replied, "have always been a powerful motivation. The entire Spanish New World was built on that obsession. In fact, the Spanish destroyed three of the world's most innovative civilizations because of it—the Aztecs, the Mayans, and the Incas. But there is more than the gleam of gold here. It is the lure of the past itself, the desire to link the present to a bygone time. It's the same kind of catharsis that an artist seeks. And like the artist who must believe in the importance of connecting his work, a treasure hunter is an optimist, a man who believes in the importance of himself to the flow of time. All the treasure hunters I know are big egotists. I don't mean that in a bad way. They are people who are driven. They are people who would appear to have blinders on. That's what causes them to hope, sometimes against all hope, that there's as much gold in a ship's store as there is in its legend."[15]

And the legend of *De Braak* had become one of the fastest-growing legends in history—dollarwise, that is.

By 1984, when yet another effort was launched, this time by a Reno, Nevada–based firm called Sub-Sal, Inc., the treasure of *De Braak* was estimated by the company's president, Harvey Harrington, to be worth half a billion dollars! Harrington secured a permit from the State of Delaware, which again allocated to the state 25 percent of the value of any treasure or artifacts raised. Utilizing the latest side-scan sonar technology and the services of veteran remote-sensing technicians, Sub-Sal succeeded where all others had failed. In April, the long-sought wreck of HMS *De Braak* was finally discovered and positively identified by a carronade, an anchor, a number of coins, and other items that were brought up, albeit in violation of the parameters of the state search permit.

Following the discovery, a legal procedure was initiated on July 26 in Wilmington U.S. District Court when the salvor filed suit against the wreck, the accepted protocol in matters of salvage. The suit, "Sub-Sal, Inc. vs. *De Braak,* Her Appurtenances, Furniture, Cargo, etc.," was signed by Chief Justice Walter K. Stapleton, and Sub-Sal was designated the wreck's legal custodian.[16] The law of salvage in 1984 was predicated on the legal definition of salvage, which is the rendering of aid to vessels and their cargo in distress at sea, regardless of whether afloat, shipwrecked, or sunken. The law of salvage allowed the salvor the right to just compensation for such services rendered, taken on behalf of the owner, to the property salved by allowing a lien to be placed against the property but did not divest the owner of legal title to the property. The lien was enforceable in the appropriate admiralty court in whatever jurisdiction the action was undertaken. The salvor, in turn, was required to care for the property in question as long as it was in his possession on the grounds that he had rescued it for the benefit of the owner but did not become the owner himself by virtue of the act. The lien was simply a guarantee that the salvor would be rewarded for saving the property and that the reward would be satisfied out of the property saved. The salvor did not have the right to simply keep the property he had saved but had the responsibility to bring it to a safe place. If the salvor and the owner failed to agree on a proper reward, they were obliged to place the property in the custody of the admiralty court for a determination of the reward. Wrecked and/or sunken property was subject to the salvage services of the first salvor on the scene. World admiralty principles agreed to in a 1910 international convention stated that a "no cure-no pay" policy should apply, that is a salvor may not be remunerated for services unless successful. Unfortunately, no provisions had been established expressly addressing historic or archaeologically relevant shipwrecks. And when such questions were finally engaged during the 1970s, the court battles that ensued had ruled in favor of salvors, often based on other precedents, such as the law of finds.[17]

In the case of abandoned property, the law of finds, rather than the law of salvage, was sometimes considered applicable. The law of finds allowed the admiralty court to confer outright ownership of the property to a finder. Most often this law was employed when an owner expressly and publicly abandoned property or when items were recovered from an ancient or unknown shipwreck and no one came forward to claim them. This law, however, was usually disallowed in favor of the law of salvage, the purpose, assumption, and rules of which were directed toward the preservation and protection of maritime property.[18]

The court appointed Dr. Terry Edgecombe, a friend and acquaintance of Harrington's, to serve a formal arrest warrant on the wreck. Two days after Sub-Sal had become legal custodian, Edgecombe dived on the site and placed a plastic, watertight envelope tethered by a short span of rope to one of the ship's carronades. The document read: "A warrant shall be issued for the arrest of *De Braak,* her appurtenances, her furniture, her cargo and apparel." Thus, Sub-Sal had formally effected legal possession of one of the most famous shipwrecks on the Delmarva coast. Despite legal challenges by competitors, the company's jurisdiction over the site was upheld, and salvage commenced from a thirty-eight-foot fishing boat called *Seneca.*[19]

As one of the most widely publicized treasure salvage operations in modern American history began, the nation watched in delight on the evening news. As the salvors raised cannons, a ship's bell, spirit bottles, and everyday accouterments of shipboard life of a late-eighteenth-century Royal Navy warship, the public's imagination was ablaze. But what really enraptured the fever of enterprise was the recovery of a thirty-eight-pound lump of concreted coins and a foot-tall chalice believed to be silver. What the public did not see was the behind the scenes actions that repeatedly violated state and federal laws. When human remains were discovered, they were illegally disposed of to prevent a slow-down of work. Large, ugly, or poorly preserved artifacts such as the ship's Brodie stove (one of only two ever found), requiring expensive conservation costs if recovered, were simply dumped into the sea when state agents were not present. When no further treasure was forthcoming, some recovered artifacts were illegally employed as collateral for bank loans to keep the project going. Other artifacts, of questionable authenticity, were used as props to raise investment funds. An expandable gold ring, said to be Captain James Drew's mourning ring, inscribed to the memory of his late brother Captain John Drew, commander of HMS *Cerberus,* who drowned on January 11, 1798, was recovered at a critical financial juncture and gained national press coverage—and further backing. Though Christie's of New York authenticated the artifact, other authorities noted that as an expandable ring it would have been the first known of its kind in the period.[20]

For Harrington, however, the incredible cash drain, exacerbated by the failure to find any real treasure, was taking its toll. His company was in tatters. Finally, in 1985, a real estate developer named L. John Davidson, a major financial supporter of then-governor of New Hampshire John Sununu, secured the blessing of Delaware governor Michael Castle with Sununu's support, control of Sub-Sal, and a new permit to work the site. He immediately infused the project with fresh funds and a gravitas hitherto lacking. He introduced industrial salvage techniques to the operation on a scale never before employed. Thousands of artifacts began to stream toward the surface and into an old fish-rendering factory on Cape Henlopen that had been secured to serve as a storage facility and conservation area. Armed guards carrying machine guns patrolled the grounds. Still, the discovery of actual treasure trove proved elusive, despite the reported expenditure of nearly a million dollars.[21]

Exasperated, Davidson began to subscribe to the suggestion that the treasure had not been found because it lay not in but beneath the ship's hull, an estimated 20 percent of which was still intact. A plan was set in motion, and agreed to by the state, to raise the hull onto a specially fabricated cradle by tunneling under the wreck and rigging lift lines and then moving it to one side on the bottom. Then excavation of 2,600 cubic yards of sediment using an industrial clam bucket operation could then be carried out at the site where the wreck had previously lain. The plan was eventually amended by its originator, archaeologist Walter Zacharchuk, who had been hired by Davidson as a consultant at the state's insistence. If they were going to all that trouble to simply move the whole hull fifty feet, why not bring it up? On August 11, 1986, under the watchful eye of thousands of curiosity seekers lining the shore, hundreds of small boats surrounding the area, and the national news media hovering in the skies above, the massive operation commenced. A 150-foot barge carrying a crane capable of lifting 300 tons, two auxiliary barges, and a seagoing tug were moved into position.[22]

The fates did not cooperate. Rigging the lines had been a nightmare. Then, when word came that a storm front was moving in, Davidson revised the plans in an instant. Delaying the operation for seventy hours until the storm passed was deemed out of the question owing to the additional operational costs. Moreover, the whole nation was watching. There was, he felt, simply no time to bother with a cradle as required by the State of Delaware. Spreaders would have to be quickly placed to distribute the weight. Wire shrouds that were to have been rigged across the top of the wreck to prevent spillage of artifact-laden sediments lying therein would be abandoned. The wreck would be brought up with only the original steel cables rigged under the naked hull.

The sequence of events that ensued has been termed the greatest maritime archaeological disaster in American history. The lift began at 8:30 P.M. at slack tide. Instead of being raised a foot and a half per minute as originally planned, the ship's fragile bones were raised at a gut-wrenching thirty feet per minute. Then a friction brake on the crane failed just as the keel of HMS *De Braak* broke the surface. For forty-five minutes the hull was awash and beaten by the swells, with countless artifacts being swept back into the deep. Finally the recovery resumed, and a seventy-foot-long, twenty-two-foot-wide section of ship emerged from the black sea, hanging with its starboard side almost vertical. Archaeologists watched in horror as artifacts of all kinds were seen to splash back into the bay along with a black, oozy mixture of mud and water. The disaster then was promoted to catastrophe as the cables beneath the hull began to slice through the ancient, soft, worm-eaten wood "like a knife through hot butter." More artifacts spilled into the water. At 10:30 P.M. that which remained was lowered onto the hull of a waiting barge, breaking the keel and deadwoods even further.[23]

The barge carrying *De Braak*'s remains proceeded toward Roosevelt Inlet. Within days Sub-Sal initiated its massive clam-bucket dredging of the entire wreck area. The industrial-strength operation can only be described as brutal. Artifact-bearing spoils were dumped aboard a barge where they were consolidated by a small front-end loader, smashing many fragile objects in the process. On their return to shore, the spoils were again clam bucketed and dumped, this time onto an industrial gravel separator running up to the rendering plant site, thereby breaking thousands more of the delicate relics. Workers, searching desperately for signs of treasure, picked away furiously to separate artifacts from the glop before the sediments reached a dump area dubbed "Mount Davidson." Thus, thousands of artifacts that had been intact before the recovery were broken or severely damaged during "the pick" and the subsequent clam-bucket operations. No treasure other than a coin or two was found. The battered hull was eventually moved to a water-filled coffer, where it remained until March 28, 1990, when it was finally transferred at state expense to a specially constructed wet-storage building at Henlopen State Park, where it remains to this day, locked up and out of sight.[24]

Though approximately 26,000 artifacts were brought up during the three-year-long salvage of HMS *De Braak,* at a cost of more than $3 million, fewer than 650 coins were recovered, most belonging to the purser's funds allocated for purchasing supplies. Christie's of New York appraised the monetary value of the whole collection, including the hull, artifacts, and coins, at $298,265.[25]

On February 4, 1992, after considerable litigation between the State of Delaware and Sub-Sal, U.S. District Court in Wilmington awarded title to the wreck's remains to the state, in whose waters the ship was deemed embedded. Citing the Federal Submerged Lands Act of 1988, which established title to and ownership of all lands lying beneath navigable waters of a state, including seaward boundaries three miles from a coastline, Judge Caleb Wright ruled the wreck lay in Delaware territorial waters. Though the law had given Delaware title to the land, it did not establish that title to the actual shipwreck and artifacts therein resided with the state. Instead, the court had relied on the common law of finds. Judge Wright, citing precedents, noted that *De Braak* had been abandoned in 1798 and its location on the Delaware coast had remained unknown until 1984 and concluded the law of finds was applicable. He rejected salvage law theory but subscribed to the theory that "disposition of a wrecked vessel whose very location has been lost for centuries as though its owners were still in-existence stretch[es] a fiction to absurd lengths." Ownership of abandoned property, according to the common law of finds, he declared, is generally as-signed without regard to where the property is found except that when aban-doned property is embedded in the soil, it belongs to the owner of the soil.[26]

If there was one redeeming quality about the whole "De Braakle," as the affair was termed by some, it was that the botched recovery had drawn national atten-tion to a visible archaeological disaster on a scope hitherto unseen and unheard of. Historic preservationists, archaeologists, and the museum community, which had been lobbying at the state and national level for years for the passage of historic shipwreck preservation laws, were galvanized. Employing the *De Braak* recovery disaster as a worst-case scenario, they vigorously and successful pressed for congressional action, which had been stalled on Capitol Hill for more than a decade. And it worked.

On April 28, 1988, President Ronald Reagan signed the Abandoned Ship-wreck Act of 1987 into law. It was the first federal act explicitly addressing the management and preservation of historic shipwrecks in national history. It allo-cated to individual states that initiated their own shipwreck preservation pro-grams authority over all such sites in state waters. Of the three states making up the Delmarva coast, only Maryland took the initiative to institute an under-water archaeology program and a management agenda to evaluate historic wreck sites before they could be destroyed.[27] Delaware, perhaps embarrassed by the whole *De Braak* affair, and Virginia, which had closed its own internation-ally recognized underwater archaeology program down two decades earlier as being a waste of taxpayer's money, simply looked away. The rest of the nation, with a few exceptions—most notably Delaware and Virginia—embraced the new national legislation as a means to protect its historic underwater sites.

As a consequence, the treasure hunts on the Delmarva coast would continue unabated, fueled by the lure of Spanish gold. The consequences, however, would this time bear the fruits of international controversy.

# 26

## Treasure Redux

Donald Stewart was a bear of a man, a rotund, white-haired chap with a passion for tall tales. Some would call him charismatic; others called him a liar and a charlatan. He liked to tell folks that he was a retired U.S. Navy captain and had come to the shores of the Delmarva coast from his home in Roland Park, Baltimore, to look for artifacts. A garrulous, acknowledged self-promoter, Stewart liked to call himself a "marine historian" who had been instrumental in helping save the USS *Constellation*. As president of the Atlantic Ship Historical Society (ASHS), a nonprofit corporation, he was active in maritime preservation efforts and in promoting undersea exploration—especially when there was a reporter in the vicinity. In 1977, when he made a grandiose announcement that he intended to formally arrest every shipwreck in Chesapeake Bay and boldly proclaimed he would excavate every one of them, he made front-page headlines in Baltimore. He even included in his target inventory a fictional Spanish galleon that he said had been captured by pirates and was then lost in 1700 off Kent Island. That he invented wrecks when no such vessels had existed simply to spice up a good story, especially when it suited his fund-raising purposes, was apparent only to some. If he didn't know the answer to a question regarding a famous ship, he made it up. But there was always the ring of truth, especially because it was being given by the head of a purportedly century-old historical society that claimed to have single-handedly saved *Constellation*. It mattered little that the society was almost a one-man organization, and that the city of Baltimore and many others might have had a say in saving the famed old warship.[1]

Nevertheless, shipwrecks had long been a source of fascination for the charming old man, and when he secured the leadership on *Constellation* as executive secretary for restoration, he quickly began to employ it as his bully pulpit to secure support to search for and exploit them. Fascinated by the prospect of ancient artifacts lying beneath the sands off the Delmarva coast, he often stated that he had collected bits and pieces of information on shipwrecks for more than two decades, "much of it requiring translation and intensive study of old records from Spanish archives." According to the garrulous old man, at least 633, and as many as 1,500, vessels had gone down off the peninsula. But he had a particular interest in a sixty-gun galleon called *La Galga,* the flagship of a ten-ship armada, which, he said in May 1980, had been lost with $30 to $40 million worth of gold, silver, and gems. He even claimed to have visited the Spanish archives in Seville to research her. In August he grandly announced that the ship carried 327 bars of silver, each weighing seventy pounds; twelve chests of worked silver coins and rubies; and emeralds, turquoise, and diamonds totaling 1,300 carats, valued at 4.25 million pesos, as well as animal skins, red dye, hardwood, bottled spirits, worked jewelry, tobacco, spirit oil, and quintals of copper. By November, the valuation had jumped to $540 million, and she had become "one of the richest vessels to sail from the New World," as part of "the second richest [fleet] ever to sail from the New World during the 325 years of Spanish conquest and colonialism." *La Galga,* he noted, was the personal property of the king of Spain, and her commander was "one of his most trusted admirals, friend since boyhood."[2]

"She was hit by a hurricane," Stewart said, "with seven ships being lost from the Florida Keys through Delaware. I believe three of those ships, including the warship, went down off the Delmarva coastline . . . I know within a mile radius the site where the remains of that ship are located," in less than one hundred feet of water.[3]

That the Flota was only seven ships strong might have been chalked up to a verbal slip. That *La Galga* was not a galleon and had carried fifty not sixty guns, and was definitely not carrying anything close to half a billion dollars worth of treasure, or that Daniel Houni, her commander, was a captain and not an admiral and had never been a personal friend of the king of Spain, most certainly was not. But it didn't matter. It all made for a wonderful story and sounded great to investors.

That Donald Stewart was zealous is undoubted. That he became convinced by his own embroidery of a tale, a sizable enlargement of the actual records of events, is likely. Whatever the motivation was, he moved from Baltimore to Ocean Pines, a mainland development near Ocean City, to ostensibly and publicly be closer to his objective, the eventual salvaging of *La Galga.* In vivid promotional conversations around Ocean City, the gregarious treasure hunter readily stimulated the interest of others in his quest. And with a tax-exempt nonprofit corporation as sponsor, the incentives were considerable. The setup was an investor's dream, at least for a tax write-off. ASHS's Baltimore-based attorney, Raymond J. Cardillo, would file a legal claim on the shipwreck and all of its contents with the Office of the Attorney General of Maryland. The society would then turn over the actual salvage operations by contract to a newly formed corporation called Sub-aqueous Exploration and Archaeology, Ltd. (SEA, Ltd.). Cardillo was given a seat on the salvage company's board; Stewart would be named as executive vice-president, and one of the investors, Dr. Richard Passwater, of Ocean Pines, would be named president.[4]

The State of Maryland was to be "offered" a 20 to 25 percent share of all recovered artifacts, including any treasure, "in order to avoid a prolonged legal battle over ownership of the shipwreck and its contents." Another 20 percent would be turned over to the society, with representative pieces put on display for the public and used as displays in a series of nationwide lectures Stewart said he was planning. The remaining 55 to 60 percent would go to the investors. To protect publication interests in a story that was already capturing the public's imagination, Stewart informed the press "he has copyrighted the complete story of the voyage, the ships, their commanders and their cargoes and obtained plans of the ship . . . [and] will retain publication rights as a portion of his share of the venture."[5]

Between March and August more than $100,000 from local businessmen, realtors, and even the editor of a weekly newspaper had been raised to find and salvage the wreck. By fall the overall project expenditure had skyrocketed and was predicted to cost about $500,000. The largest investors, Ocean Pines realtors Richard K. and Robert J. Firth, called the operation a "business venture," clean and simple, and believed the odds were "60 to 40 in our favor." Stewart claimed the odds "better than in an Atlantic casino."[6]

To conduct fieldwork, the company purchased a thirty-five-foot boat named *Bloodhound,* which arrived at the Bayside Boatel in West Ocean City on August 25 with Stewart at the helm, accompanied by William J. Atkinson, a retired merchant marine captain who was to command the vessel during the search. The boat was a broad-beamed craft, originally built for lobstering. She was now outfitted with two new engines, sonar, and eventually a magnetometer loaned by Charles Garrett, of Dallas, Texas, owner of Garrett Electronics, to locate ferrous metals, such as cannon, lying on or beneath the ocean bottom. The search was scheduled to begin on September 8 or 9. Once the wreck was found, no later than November it was hoped, an eighty-four-foot vessel would be hired to conduct the salvage.[7]

That the intrepid *Bloodhound,* paid for by investor money, actually conducted at least a limited search for *La Galga* in the fall of 1980 is certain, although the records of her operations were never released. That she failed to fulfill Stewart's dreams by locating the now-famous shipwreck, however, is also certain. When the search was over, the head of ASHS claimed to have located a wreck "at the exact site I said it would be" and vowed to return the following spring to begin salvage operations. But he began to hedge his statements. If the site did not prove out, he would relocate his search. In the meantime, *Bloodhound* would continue "patrolling along the coast . . . to pinpoint the locations of other shipwrecks for future exploration."[8]

The truth was hard to conceal, and investors were becoming increasingly upset. Stewart responded aggressively with proclamations that he was expanding his efforts to locate four more treasure ships. On January 28, 1981, in an effort to stave off charges that money was being misappropriated, SEA and ASHS aggressively employed the search and filed suit against an unidentified wrecked and abandoned vessel believed to be the *San Lorenzo de Escorial,* "her tackle, armament, apparel, cargo and other effects pertaining to her." They also arrested an unidentified wreck believed to be the schooner *Santa Clara,* another believed to be called *Santa Rosalea,* and a fourth believed to be *Royal George.* The arrests were publicly advertised in the classified section of the *Baltimore Sun* on March

20, 1981. Three of the four were said to be Spanish treasure ships and one an English privateer.[9] Again, it mattered little that at least two of the vessels, *Santa Clara* and *Royal George,* may have been creatures of Stewart's fertile imagination. The bubble was about to burst and a legal nightmare was about to begin.

Several months after SEA, Ltd., sought salvage rights to the ships, the State of Maryland filed a motion in U.S. District Court to dismiss the suit, declaring that the ships were in submerged land within the three-mile limit of state territorial waters and therefore belonged to the state. The challenge had the effect of initiating a three-way legal dispute. Before U.S. District Judge Norman P. Ramsey could rule on the issue of state or federal jurisdiction, a former diver for SEA, Ltd., John L. Amrhein Jr., who had lost $17,000 of his own money invested in the company, filed another motion to intervene. He claimed not only that no wrecks had been found at the sites described in the suit but that one of them, the *San Lorenzo de Escorial,* had never existed. Moreover, he charged that none of the vessels named in the suit had been found by SEA, Ltd., nor, in fact, had any other vessel of any kind. The only finds had been "several sewer pipes and junk." On December 21, Judge Ramsey ruled that the federal court lacked jurisdiction over the submerged wrecks and that state and federal law fully supported the Maryland assertion that the State of Maryland has first claim to any vessels and cargo found in its territorial waters. Acknowledging that SEA, Ltd., was by then penniless and dormant, Dr. Passwater declared that Judge Ramsey's decision "would have been our death knell if we weren't already dead."[10]

Ramsey denied Amrhein's motion to intervene. Amrhein's lawyers responded by filing a civil suit in the Worcester County Circuit Court against the founders of SEA, Ltd. Others involved in the federal suit's outcome were more concerned with the issue of state and federal rights. Judith A. Arnold, an assistant attorney general for Maryland, explained that from the state's point of view it meant that salvage divers would thereafter have to get permits from the Board of Public Works to excavate for sunken ships on the ocean or bay floor and that the Maryland Geological Survey, which then administered archaeological properties on state lands and bottomlands, would have to approve salvage procedures.[11]

The professional salvage community howled. For SEA, Ltd., however, the issue had become moot. Stewart had by that time become invisible. The company was entirely in Dr. Passwater's hands and was by then "in the process of dissolving." The ships to which it sought salvage rights had not been located. With $200,000 having been invested and spent, and no money available to continue the search, it had all but died.[12]

Dr. Passwater predicted "there will probably be no more salvage attempts for a decade or two." Yet there would be future attempts, including three years of efforts by Amrhein, who formed his own company called Ocean Recovery Operations, Inc. (or ORO, for the Spanish word for gold). After much research and several years of off-and-on fieldwork, he eventually came to the conclusion that *La Galga* lay buried not in the seabed but beneath a marsh eight hundred yards west of the beach in an inlet that had filled with sand. The wreck, he believed, lay two miles south of the Maryland-Virginia border, within the Chincoteague National Wildlife Refuge and was therefore within the jurisdiction of the U.S. Fish and Wildlife Service. When queried about the possibility of recovery, Dennis Holland, the refuge manager, said, "We have no plans to do any excavation. What is there will be preserved for the future."[13]

The parade of wreck hunters seeking *La Galga* was just beginning to peak, and some were becoming quite sophisticated and comprehensive in their research endeavors. In 1983 yet another group, the Alpha Quest Corporation of Ocean City, was ready to leap into the fray. The consortium of investors included a local real estate developer named Richard L. Cook, a condominium developer named Eugene R. Parker, and Robert Taylor, a former dean of Georgetown University's Dental School. Their search for historic, treasure-laden vessels, Cook later reported, had been triggered "by small clusters, called 'spills,' of late 18th-century and early 19th-century South American and Spanish gold coins washed up on the beach over the past 34 years." In truth, Cook was as undoubtedly as interested in finding *La Galga* as his predecessors. Having carried out substantial research in the Maryland Hall of Records in Annapolis and later, by proxy, in the archives of the United Kingdom and Spain, he was convinced he could find the long-sought-after man-of-war. When a local resident on Assateague, living near the Maryland-Virginia border, found blackened discs in the sand while beach-combing, a find that proved to be Spanish coins minted in 1745 and 1746, he was elated. Further examination of the beach revealed bottle shards, ship fragments, and other indications of a possible eighteenth-century wreck.

The legal terrain, however, was about to change. With the passage of the Federal Abandoned Shipwreck Act of 1987, Maryland's revisions of its own antiquities regulations, and the creation and institution of the Maryland Maritime Archaeology Program (MMAP) under the Maryland Historical Trust, the promulgation of salvage efforts on historic shipwrecks, especially for the purpose of treasure hunting, was likely to be curtailed sharply. However, as with all new laws and programs, it was going to take time before the kinks had been worked out. In the meantime, for many treasure hunters, it was business as usual.

In May 1989, acting on the advice of the new Maryland state underwater archaeologist, the head of MMAP, Cook contracted a respected marine archaeologist named Daniel Koski-Karell to serve as a technical adviser and remote-sensing technician. Having then chartered Captain Daniel Tilghman's fishing boat *Stallion* and using the latest technology—magnetometry, underwater remote television, hand-held metal detectors, and Loran electronic navigation system—he set out with several divers to locate the wreck of *La Galga*.

Diver James Karl was the first to encounter an indication of a possible site, a battered lead scupper. Ship timbers and other suggestions of a wreck convinced Cook he had found *La Galga*, "the first Spanish man-of-war found north of Florida." Together with Koski-Karell, he produced a substantial and impressive record of his archival research and photos of several artifacts. However, there was little in the way of treasure to speak of, so Cook moved on.[14]

Tantalized by the evidence of coins found on the beach at Ocean City, which dated between 1772 and 1827, Alpha Quest began planning another search. This time the hunt was to be centered along the waters off 18th Street, barely a cannon shot from the T-shirt boutiques and pizza palaces of the Ocean City boardwalk. When a winter storm had scoured out a section of sea floor off the town and revealed "the outline of what he thinks might be an early sailing ship," which was publicized in the local press, shipwreck fever once again gripped the Atlantic beaches. A remote-sensing technician was contracted to conduct a magnetometer survey and discovered "a possible cannon array consistent with an armed sailing vessel."[15]

By the late summer of 1989, Alpha Quest declared itself ready to begin excavation of a vessel it believed to have been the ship *Hawk,* William Carhardt master, which had sailed from Havana on Christmas Day 1798 and sank off Maryland's shores on January 5, 1799. Purportedly having dispatched researchers to major libraries in England and Spain and up and down the East Coast from Philadelphia to Charleston, and making the usual claims to have already spent more than a million dollars on research and permit requests, the company was poised to commence. The project directors planned to begin in September a small-scale exploratory excavation of selected hotspots lying within a square mile of ocean bottom close to shore, between Talbot Street and 37th Street. On August 30, a permit to start was issued by the Maryland Board of Public Works to disturb wetlands in the search area, and an interim survey permit from the Maryland Historical Trust, which technically administered historic shipwrecks in state waters by virtue of the Abandoned Shipwreck Act of 1987 and newly revised state regulations, was expected within a matter of days. Once the site was located, Alpha Quest declared its objective was to negotiate an agreement with the state "that will permit it to keep seventy-five to eighty percent of the value of any coins or other artifacts found."

"We're not exploring for treasure here, by any means." Cook stated publicly. "I don't right now have any aspirations to any great treasure." The Trust was not so certain. Then, Alpha Quest mysteriously ceased operations, even as other organizations stepped in, hoping to fill the void with untold riches that prior searchers had failed to find.[16]

One such firm was called Quicksilver, Inc. The Virginia Beach–based company's chairman of the board was Glynn Rogers, and its goal, reportedly as early as 1987, had been the location of the remains of the Spanish man-of-war *Juno.* For over a decade the company sporadically conducted its research well beyond state waters. In September, newspaper accounts stated, it had finally retrieved as far as forty miles out "the stem post of an old ship, the part that holds the rudder" believed to belong to *Juno.* Other artifacts found by Quicksilver or by others, such as a 2,500 pound bell located thirty miles offshore, also believed to have been on *Juno,* as well as a brass lantern and a musket stock recovered by one Earl Novak, had stimulated public interest. "Our research is immense," Rogers said. "We are convinced it sank in deep water."[17] Other treasure hunters with an interest in finding both *La Galga* and *Juno* disagreed.

· · ·

Ben D. Benson was an amiable sort for a thirty-eight-year-old millionaire, with thinning brown hair, a boyish face, a childhood brush with cancer and two heart attacks behind him, and a personal mission. The former Michigan timber company executive was definitely a go-getter. He had dropped out of school in the ninth grade, run away from home, made his break at fifteen by stealing the family Oldsmobile, and then embarked on his first venture into real estate with spunk, a new credit card, and a good dose of luck. At seventeen, though underage, he had joined the navy and worked as a sonar technician on a fast-attack submarine. After getting a hardship discharge owing to "allergies," he launched back into the business world by engaging in both the oil business and real estate. By 1991 he was running a two-hundred-employee timber company on Michigan's Upper Peninsula, which he sold for $13 million after his heart attacks. He arrived at Assateague in the late summer of 1996 to search for shipwrecks. "His dream," one commentator reported, "was to dive for gold bearing galleons in the Caribbean," but after acquiring some of the necessary technology to conduct remote-sensing subsea research—a magnetometer and side-scan sonar—he had decided to first test the gear off Virginia's Eastern Shore. He needed, however, a target. He thus hired a legal secretary to examine records in the Accomack County Courthouse. She returned with accounts of both *Juno* and *La Galga,* and his course was set. He began his first quest in September 1996.[18]

After examining the corroding anchor ensconced in front of Payne's Sea Treasures shop in Chincoteague and the pewter plate kept on display there, recovered by Captain Leon Rose 1,500 yards off Assateague, Benson was convinced the anchor was a spare that had been carried on the deck of *Juno.* Glynn Rogers disagreed vehemently, but the former timber executive was not to be deterred by a competitor. By 1997, certain that he too had located *Juno,* albeit just 1,500 yards offshore, and *La Galga* as well, he had formed a new company, Sea Hunt, Inc., of Manchester, New Hampshire. The company was named after the famed Lloyd Bridges television undersea adventure series. As the guidelines of the Abandoned Shipwreck Act had given title of historic vessels lying within state waters to the states, in this case Virginia, he promptly applied to the Virginia Marine Resources Commission for a permit to recover artifacts from each site. On Tuesday, March 25, by a unanimous vote, the commission approved the issuance of a permit for him to retrieve artifacts from two six-mile-square areas in the shoally waters off Assateague Island National Seashore to determine if the two finds were, in fact, *Juno* and *La Galga.* The permits were purportedly the first ever granted by the Commonwealth of Virginia for underwater recovery of historic property. By terms of the agreement, the state would receive 25 percent of the value of whatever was found, and would get first choice of any items deemed of historic value. It all seemed cut and dried.[19]

Benson was among those who subscribed to the theory that the ancestors of the famed Chincoteague wild ponies had been carried aboard *La Galga* and that *Juno* had been carrying a large cache of gold and silver when she went down. In August 1997 he established permanent headquarters on Marsh Island, at the foot of a swing bridge that provided access to the town of Chincoteague, with his twenty-one-year-old, thirty-five-foot ex–Coast Guard vessel, equipped with the latest technologies, tied up just outside. From there he would begin remote-sensing operations and preliminary hands-on evaluation of targeted sites. Then would come the recovery.[20]

On September 9, barely four hundred yards from shore, he made contact with a site he believed to be none other than the wreck of the ill-fated Presidential Yacht *Despatch*. The following day he posted an advertisement in the *Chincoteague Beacon* offering a $1,000 reward to anyone who might come forward "with the most interesting coin, artifact or story relating to items found on Assateague's shore." Less than a week later, while diving a mile north of Chincoteague Inlet and 1,500 feet from the beach, he recovered a Spanish coin and wood fragments from a mound of sand and mud that he sagaciously declared covered the remains of *Juno*. Moreover, he informed the media, the buried hull was intact. About the same time, not far away, just below the Maryland-Virginia line and only two hundred feet from the beach, he discovered fragments of another wreck that he declared was from the disarticulated remains of *La Galga*.[21]

The sites needed verification. To physically search for relics he was certain lay buried beneath the sands, Benson stated that he would have to remove huge swaths of overburden with a blower, then excavate smaller holes using an airlift, after which his divers would simply "feel around for objects." Although the archaeological community heartily frowned upon the use of such large area provenance-destroying disturbance systems and unsystematic groping for artifacts, the State of Virginia, which had closed its own underwater archaeology program down more than two decades earlier, seemed not the least disturbed. After all, the treasure hunters retorted, no professional archaeologists had ever paid a hoot to the sites before the wreck hunters had appeared on the scene. The Virginia Institute of Marine Science, a branch of the College of William and Mary, reviewed the methodology for possible environmental damage to marine life and the ocean bottom, and the scientists found no problem. "Any disturbance of the bottom would be expected to be reburied by natural movement in this highly dynamic area and therefore no long-term effects are expected," concluded VIMS marine scientist Thomas A. Barnard Jr. The potential destruction of any archaeological context was not even addressed. According to the press, what most concerned the Virginia Marine Resources Commission was the effect the excavation would have on the tourist season! The company was thus restricted from working closer than a half mile from shore between May 1 and August 15. Benson was miffed and declared his work would thus have to be halted until October. But his troubles were just beginning.

Unexpectedly, Benson received a phone call from the U.S. Department of Justice expressing its concern for the site. Because his purported sites were within federal waters directly adjacent to Assateague Island National Seashore, they requested that he meet with representatives from both the Justice Department and the National Park Service, which administered the national seashore, to secure a permit from them. Not surprisingly, the National Park Service (NPS), which was worried about the potential destruction of the archaeological record, raised further questions regarding Benson's survey and recovery methodology, as well as safety issues at Assateague, further delaying the project's start. The government agency representatives, however, assured him that he would have his permit within the week. Then weeks turned into months.

In fact, the government was increasingly ill disposed to allow a treasure salvor with no archaeological expertise to work in federal waters on what might prove to be incredibly significant archaeological sites. Of particular concern was the salvor's plans to use the downwash of a ship's propeller, known in treasure hunting circles as a "prop wash," which they charged was the equivalent of running a bulldozer to clear an archaeological site simply to get to the treasure. Though it wasn't said, the "De Braakle" was still fresh in everyone's minds.

Soon they began to reexamine the issue within the parameters of sovereign immunity provisions of admiralty law—that is, that state-owned vessels remain the property of the state no matter where and when they are lost—and the U.N. Law of the Sea Convention, by which Spain might still have legal rights to the ship as Spanish government property. The NPS thus took the unprecedented measure of informing the Spanish embassy that Spain might be a party of interest in the matter. At first the Spanish demurred but eventually responded positively. "I think the discussions were in the context of trying to work cooperatively with Sea Hunt," said Carolyn Zander Blanco, the Justice Department attorney who often represented the NPS in shipwreck matters, while later trying to explain the unconventional invitation. "These are the public's resources," she said. "If they're abandoned, they're held in trust for the public. It's as though somebody would take a tree out of the national park for their own gain and deprive the rest of us of that resource."[22]

By November, Benson had proclaimed to the world that his company had already expended between $250,000 and $500,000 in electronically mapping and detailing "hundreds of bits and pieces of suspected ship debris" in the two transects and had taken on three employees. He projected an expenditure of another $1 million before he was done, adding a prophetically accurate note: "Most treasure hunters pour more money into the sea than they ever take out." Some officials challenged the estimates as overly inflated. In addition, the hunt was beginning to take on some aspects of a race. In March 1998, Sea Hunt's principal rival, Quicksilver, Inc., announced it had discovered the wreck of *Juno* forty miles offshore.[23]

But it wasn't Quicksilver that worried Benson. He paid little heed to his competitor's claim. Fearing, however, what he believed to be delaying tactics by the U.S. government at the instigation of the archaeological community, and even a rival claim by the Spanish government, he went to federal court to secure sole salvage rights to permit excavation of his finds.[24]

On March 12, 1998, Norfolk U.S. District Court Judge J. Calvin Clarke Jr. granted Sea Hunt preliminary salvage rights to the alleged *La Galga* and *Juno* wreck sites, the latter of which Benson proclaimed to the media might be carrying as much as 700,000 coins and twenty-two tons of silver worth half a billion dollars. To some it seemed the ghost of *De Braak* had arisen in another form. The salvor would be allowed to "arrest" the wrecks in the usual manner in order to remove them from the purview of the federal courts. Clarke then issued an injunction, a restraining order, against NPS and the Justice Department to prohibit any interference with the treasure hunter's "research." To do so, they would have to take it to court.[25]

The legal wrangle was just beginning to heat up. By May, the Spanish government formally asserted ownership of the wrecks, citing the internationally accepted provisions of sovereign immunity accorded all national naval vessels of any state. Raphael Conde de Saro, Spanish deputy chief of mission at the Spanish embassy in Washington, DC, made his country's interests quite clear. Both *Juno* and *La Galga,* he informed the press unequivocally in late March, "are the property of Spain and were commissioned by the Spanish Navy and therefore were at all moments Spanish warships."[26] The local treasure hunt was now emerging from its chrysalis as a full-blown international controversy.

The Spanish claim was not made without precedent. The official policies of the governments of both the United States and Spain, in line with much of the world, regarding warships, naval auxiliary vessels, and other state craft owned and employed by a national state in noncommercial service at the time they sank, was that they were state vessels no matter where or when lost. The foundations for this policy, as it was being newly applied to historic shipwrecks, were based on both current international admiralty law and ancient and accepted principles of coastal states throughout the world. The United Nations Convention on the Law of the Sea (LOS), entered into force on November, 16, 1994, and had 106 signatory parties as of August 1996 (when Benson began his campaign). It recognized that the sovereignty of a coastal state extended beyond its land territory and internal waters to the adjacent territorial sea but could extend no more than twelve nautical miles from the baselines from which the breadth of the territorial sea was measured.[27] Though the United States had yet to sign the LOS convention it had vigorously observed in principle its provisions regarding sovereign immunity. Moreover, international admiralty law, as codified in Articles 95 and 96 of the convention, also recognized that state vessels and their associated artifacts, whether sunken or not, were entitled to sovereign immunity regardless of their location. Moreover, such sites wherein human remains existed or might exist were to be considered war gravesites. The sovereign immunity provisions of admiralty law thus provided a state the right and authority to retain custody of all its naval vessels and aircraft, and human remains, regardless of their locations when lost. Such vessels were recognized as historical artifacts of special importance and entitled to special protections. The LOS also authorized national coastal states, such as the United States and Spain, to presume that the removal of archaeological and historical objects from the seabed of its contiguous zone, without state approval, would result in the infringement of its customs laws and thus might exercise the control necessary to prevent and punish infringements.[28]

The long-established practice of national states, including the United States and Spain, endorsed and confirmed the established rule of law that title to national state vessels lost only by capture or surrender during battle and before sinking, by international compact, or by the deliberate act of abandonment, sale, or gift by the sovereign state was in agreement with the principles of international law and the law of the flag state governing the abandonment of government property. Upon the conclusion of hostilities, belligerents could not acquire title to such vessels through the act of sinking them.[29]

Most importantly, national coastal states could not acquire right of ownership to a sunken state vessel of any other national government by reason of its being located on or embedded in land or the seabed over which it exercised sovereignty or jurisdiction. Access to such vessels and their associated artifacts located on or embedded in the seabed of foreign waters, territorial seas, or contiguous zones was subject to coastal state dominion in accordance with international law. One prominent example of this was a precedent-setting agreement between the French Republic and the United States regarding the wreck of the CSS *Alabama,* which was sunk in battle by the USS *Kearsarge* on June 19, 1864, during the U.S. Civil War, approximately nine miles off Cherbourg. In this case the United States asserted and maintained ownership over the wreck, though sunk in foreign waters.[30]

Access to sunken state vessels and their associated artifacts located on or embedded in the seabed of twenty-four miles from the shore baseline was subject only to flag state control. It was also accepted by the United States, Spain, and the international community that, except for opposing combatants during hostilities, no person or state may salvage or attempt the salvage of sunken state vessels or their associated artifacts, wherever located, without the express permission of the sovereign flag state, whether or not the vessel was a war grave. Also, upon the conclusion of hostilities, sunken vessels containing crew remains were to be entitled to special respect as war graves and could not be disturbed without the explicit permission of the sovereign.[31] Thus was the premise established for Spain's claim to *La Galga* and *Juno.* Whether it would hold up in a U.S. court, however, remained to be seen.

If Benson had a mission, it was more than equaled by that of the National Park Service, which was now prepared to go to the mat, for it believed that the United States or any flag state was entitled to employ any and all legal mechanisms to prohibit unauthorized disturbance of a state wreck site, including debris fields, or salvage of the wreck itself. It had long been accepted NPS policy regarding historic shipwrecks (and a principal tenet of nautical archaeology) that disturbance of any wreck site was necessarily a destructive process. In every instance, when a recovery had been initiated, no historic wreck site could be fully restored or replicated. Any recovery that disturbed such sites denied authorized entities the opportunity of scientific discovery, study, and analysis.[32] The course seemed clear to federal officials. Whether it be sunken vessels of the U.S. Navy or the Spanish navy, it was clear to both governments that Spanish ownership of the purported wreck sites of *La Galga* and *Juno* had a good chance of holding up in court.

In February, Conde wrote to the NPS to formally state that it was his government's belief that the two ships belonged to Spain. "I would like to inform you," he wrote, "that the Spanish Authorities are very interested in closely following any operations that might affect these vessels. Both are the property of Spain and were commissioned by the Spanish Navy and therefore were at all moments Spanish warships."[33]

For the first time in memory, Spain had claimed ownership of Spanish government shipwrecks in American waters, and the U.S. State Department, Department of Justice, and National Park Service agreed. The claim, if upheld, was likely to have incredibly far-reaching effects for all coastal states in the United States wherein foreign vessels might lie. Citing Conde's letter, the NPS requested the VMRC to suspend the salvor's permits.

Benson was undoubtedly stunned. Spain had never before tried to claim other Spanish treasure wrecks in American waters, he said, citing the example of treasure hunter Mel Fisher and his landmark battles for ownership of the famed treasure ship *Nuestra Señora de Atocha*. Conde countered that Spanish archival records had revealed that whatever treasure had been aboard *Juno* had been transferred to another ship before the disaster. The treasure notwithstanding, he reiterated, both ships and their contents were still Spanish government property. Soon, the national archaeological community chimed in supportively, adding that Benson's salvage plans would disturb a historic gravesite on public lands and pointing out that there had never been any positive archaeological identification other than strong circumstantial data that the wrecks were *Juno* and *La Galga*. Benson's reply was curt: "Nothing he had found proved they weren't."[34]

In a move perhaps unprecedented in U.S. history, the NPS filed suit on behalf of Spain for ownership of the shipwrecks in an effort to preserve what it considered might be two historic shipwrecks. "We're not opposed to careful study of shipwrecks. What we oppose is destruction without a good reason," said Kevin Foster, director of the National Maritime Initiative for the NPS. Conde added: "Why should a memorial be disturbed? For what reason?" Benson had a ready answer. "Because my curiosity is up . . . The reason I got into this is because I like being on the sea and I like history. I wasn't expecting a monumental battle, but right now I'm hooked."[35]

Judge Clarke was unconvinced by the NPS's case and declared that the United States had no right to represent Spain in that country's claim to the two vessels. "The United States takes the unique position in this case of holding itself out as counsel for Spain. The Court has been unable to uncover any precedent for this position, and the United States has cited none," the judge wrote. Moreover, the federal government could regulate the salvaging of the vessels. The rulings essentially threw out the issue of who owned the ships because, as the judge said, "if Spain wants to claim that it never abandoned them, it must come back to court within 90 days and represent its own interests." The ruling was significant in that it clearly supported the tenets of the Abandoned Shipwreck Act of 1987, which gave states willing to accept the responsibility clear title to abandoned historic shipwrecks within three miles of their coasts. The government's court action directly assaulted that beachhead, which had actually been intended to preserve historic shipwrecks.[36] The ruling left little doubt that Virginia owned shipwrecks in its waters. The only question was whether Spain would actively attempt to make its case again for never abandoning ships and thereby retaining ownership of them. As for the VMRC permits, Robert W. Grabb, the commission's habitat chief, said that barring a successful court challenge, they would be allowed to stand.[37]

"Spain would have to start all over again, without U.S. representation," said Norfolk attorney David K. Sutelan, one of the lawyers representing the salvor. "We're about back to Square One." The media, which had always embraced treasure stories, for the most part supported the ruling. One newspaper, the *Virginian-Pilot,* came down squarely in Benson's court. "The Spanish claim is set to freeze out legitimate salvors from the tremendous wealth and historic artifacts contained in countless wrecks surrounding American coasts."[38]

The salvor's lawyers and professional treasure hunting advocates alike, anticipating a court challenge by the Spanish on their own behalf, pounced on the Park Service's missteps. "Are we going to see a Spanish salvage ship coming into American territorial waters to search these wrecks? Somehow I doubt it," said Sutelan. Peter Hess, a Delaware attorney specializing in shipwreck and treasure wreck cases, noted that normally diplomatic matters were handled by the U.S. State Department, not other federal agencies. "Is the U.S. Justice Department," he asked, "now in charge of our foreign policy?" Benson himself believed there was credible evidence that a scheme had been launched to gain control of the wrecks to get around the Abandoned Shipwreck Act of 1987 and the intent of Congress. "It seems," he noted caustically, "that piracy is alive and well."[39]

Spain decided to appeal its case by challenging Virginia's claims to *La Galga* and *Juno* again on the grounds that both vessels were warships of that nation and thus, under the tenets of recognized sovereign immunity, had never been abandoned. Represented by Washington, DC, attorney James A. Goold, the Spanish suggested that Sea Hunt's activities could even jeopardize diplomatic relations with Spain and U.S. rights to retrieve its warships near foreign shores. Judge Clarke, however, was about to issue a ruling worthy of Solomon.

In the spring of 1999, in a thoroughly surprising move, the court ruled that, in accordance with a 1763 treaty ending the French and Indian War, Spain had ceded all that it possessed in North America east of the Mississippi—in effect surrendering all that it owned prior to 1763—including *La Galga,* which sank thirteen years earlier. *Juno,* however, did not fall under the treaty's terms because it did not sink until 1802. In April, Judge Clark declared *Juno* to be the property of Spain and *La Galga* to belong to Virginia, which could do with it as it saw fit. Benson could not be compensated for the loss of $1.5 million he claimed to have spent on *Juno.* Moreover, all artifacts he had recovered from that purported wreck site belonged to Spain. The ship was to be considered a maritime grave that should not be desecrated, although the salvor was quick to point out that no human remains had yet been encountered. "Is there any justification for tampering with or for going into or recovering such a ship?" responded Conde. "How would you feel if people decided that Arlington Cemetery would be a good place to go in with a metal detector?"[40]

Benson was thunderstruck. The yearlong legal process had cost him $100,000 for the services of the high-powered Richmond law firm of Mays and Valentine. Spain, however, was not about to accept half a loaf and appealed the *La Galga* decision. Attorney Goold argued that the 1763 treaty did not embrace sunken ships and that an earlier treaty, signed in 1667 by Spain and Great Britain, proclaimed that neither side would take ownership of its rival's sunken vessels. The case truly became international when Great Britain filed a brief with the court supporting Spain's position. Benson's lawyers retorted, citing that the Adams-Onis Treaty, negotiated in 1819 and ceding East and West Florida to the United States territorial government, had awarded all Spanish possessions to the United States. In another brief, filed by Emory University law professor David J. Bederman in both Virginia's and Sea Hunt's behalf, called Spain's arguments about destroying a military gravesite nothing more than "inflammatory bluster" and stated his view that either by treaties ending hostilities with the American colonies or apparent inaction over the previous two hundred years, Spain had no just claim to the ships. "However you cut it, we say these ships are abandoned."[41]

By May 1, 2000, as the appeals were being presented to a panel of judges from the Fourth Circuit Court of Appeals in Richmond, the punches began flying even more fast and furious. Virginia solicitor general William H. Hurd waded in saying both vessels had been expressly abandoned by Spain because they had never been claimed. Spain again retorted that the ships had not been abandoned because they were never taken off the official register of the Spanish navy. Not surprisingly, the Justice Department backed Spain in the precedent setting move because it had become U.S. policy, not just on historical wrecks, to maintain ownership of such properties no matter where they lay. Simply put, the United States did not want other countries claiming thousands of American vessels and military aircraft sunk in foreign waters. Chief Judge J. Harvey Wilkinson once more accosted the Spanish case. The Spanish government, he charged, had been encouraged by federal agencies in an effort to thwart a private salvage company's bid to uncover the wrecks. "You and Spain," he said, "came into court at the last minute and essentially blindsided them and ambushed them." But this time a panel of judges would make the decision.

Then an attorney for Spain, David Beltran, lowered the boom with a bit more history and the final word in the case. Citing yet another treaty between Spain and the United States, signed in 1902 but stemming from the loss of the USS *Maine* in 1898 from a mysterious explosion, which protected the rights of each nation to its warships even when sunk in foreign waters, he was vociferous in arguing that the treaty must be upheld in the decision of the court. The panel, which was no less critical of Virginia and the salvor than it had been of the federal government, was well aware that their decision would have national ramifications on the future of state and national policy regarding submerged national properties. They would not, however, be judging the case on the grounds of historic merit but on the issue of sovereign immunity, specifically as it related to war graves. The panel adjourned for more than two months to consider its verdict.[42]

Finally, on Friday, July 21, 2000, the federal appeals court announced its ruling. Both *Juno* and *La Galga* belonged to Spain. The 1902 treaty had been the clincher. Another far-reaching precedent regarding the knotty issues of ownership and management of shipwrecks in U.S. waters had been resolved, but not along the lines anyone could have predicted. Chief Judge Wilkinson, after considerable review, had sided with Spain, ruling that the treaty was essential to protecting the integrity of military gravesites. The sites could not and would not be disturbed again. After more than three and a half centuries of maritime disasters and another century of treasure hunting on the Delmarva coast, a legacy of unexpected importance and a precedent of international significance had been forged.[43]

But the tale was not quite finished.

In late 2004, a U.S. Army Corps of Engineers dredging project off Roosevelt Inlet, near Lewes, Delaware, was undertaken to provide soil for a beach nourishment program. Unexpectedly, the dredging operation encountered a massive debris field of eighteenth-century artifacts from an unknown shipwreck as it pumped more than 165,000 cubic yards of sand ashore. With the assistance of a Philadelphia maritime cultural resource management firm called Dolan Research, which had been hired by the corps, a preliminary archaeological survey was undertaken in February 2005. In April a more formal investigation field investigation by Dolan archaeologist Lee Cox was launched in the fourteen-foot-deep water. Dubbed the Lewes Maritime Archaeological Project by the State of Delaware and administered for the Delaware Division of Historical and Cultural Affairs by Daniel R. Griffith, the project quickly escalated in importance as investigation of the probable wreck area was carried out immediately east of the Roosevelt Inlet navigation channel. Though no remnant of the vessel's structural fabric was initially discovered, more than 38,000 artifacts from at least five countries, including South Africa and China, were recovered. An incredibly wide range of artifacts, including tobacco pipes, pieces of a chamber pot, shoe buckles, ceramic dishware, stoneware jars and jugs, a musket trigger guard, personal attire, and millstones, were systematically excavated and removed for stabilizing and cataloging. The most intriguing artifacts were at least nine miniature soldiers and a sailing ship possibly employed by strategists of the eighteenth century in tabletop war games. Within days Griffith proclaimed that the Roosevelt Inlet shipwreck site, which appeared to date from the period 1769 to 1775, was rivaling in magnitude HMS *De Braak*. Designated state site 75-D-91A, it was soon afterward nominated to the National Register of Historic Places.

In September 2006 the Delaware Department of State contracted with Southeast Archaeological Research, Inc. (SEARCH) of Jonesville, Florida, to conduct a phased archaeological study of the site. Utilizing state-of-the-art magnetometry, side-scan sonar, and a differential global positioning system to collect magnetic and sonar data from the wreck area, it was determined the wreck site was concentrated in a single area and not spread widely across the bay bottom. Fabric of the ship's architecture itself was discovered and artifact concentrations pinpointed. Systematic underwater exploration and hydroprobing of the site in the low-to-zero visibility environment by marine archaeologists was undertaken to determine the extent of the surviving hull, which proved limited. A controlled test excavation was then conducted utilizing a prefabricated stainless-steel grid system and an airlift system.

From the preliminary findings of the archaeological survey it was determined that the vessel was laden with a large shipment of containers, including German and possibly English stoneware, bottles, earthenware plates, straight pins, seed beads, tobacco pipes, and antimony ingots. The ship showed some signs of old age, indicated by several lead sheathing patches and a possible gunport also covered with sheathing, indicating that the ship may have once been in naval service. Archival research suggested the wreck may be all that survives of an eighty-foot, three-masted English merchant ship called *Severn,* James Hathorn commanding. Bound for Philadelphia from Bristol, England, the unfortunate merchantman reportedly foundered off Lewes in 1774. It is conjectured, however, that the skipper may have run his sinking ship aground near the shore to prevent loss of life. Research in British archives found that a Royal Navy vessel, HMS *Severn,* commissioned in 1747, was sold out of service twelve years later, and may have entered commercial service under the same name. Yet the project had only begun.

Within a short time, between the spring of 2005 and the fall of 2006, the State of Delaware had been moved to action by the discovery and investigation of a major historic shipwreck. This time the motivation was neither gold nor silver but the simple need to know, in the pursuit of history itself. Belatedly following in the footsteps of neighboring Maryland, Delaware had finally laid the groundwork for adoption of a state historic shipwreck assessment, preservation, and management program.

Though Virginia continues to ignore its own vast submerged cultural resources, more than two-thirds of the Delmarva coast, at least as far as the future of its maritime heritage goes, may never be the same again.

## Chronological Index to Vessel Losses on the Delmarva Coast

*Henry B. Hyde,* 1884 (The Mariners' Museum, Newport News, VA)

*Date.* All dates are given year first, then month and day. When only the month of a wreck's reportage is available but not the precise day of loss, only the month is given. When it is known that the loss occurred prior to the listed month or day, the month/day is given followed by "p" in parentheses indicating "prior to" ca. = circa. When the month is unknown, a dash appears. When data from two or more sources provide conflicting dates, both are given, with the alternative given in a brackets. Unk = unknown.

*Vessel.* Formal vessel names appear in italics. A name in parentheses following a vessel's listed name indicates either an alternative given in conflicting reports or a previous name. Numbers in parentheses following vessels listed as unidentified indicate the number of vessels lost. A number in parentheses followed by a plus sign that indicates more than the given number of vessels were lost. The nationality of a vessel, when known, is given after a vessel name as follows: Arg = Argentinean; Br = British; BrCol = British Colonial; Braz = Brazilian; Du = Dutch; Eng = English; Fr = French; Ger = German; It =Italian; Ire = Irish; Jam = Jamaican; Nor = Norwegian; NB = New Brunswick; NS = Nova Scotian; Pan = Panamanian; Port = Portuguese; Rus = Russian; Sp = Spanish; Swed = Swedish; Urg = Uruguayan; Yugo = Yugoslavian.

*Type.* The following abbreviations indicate the vessel by type: Bark = Bark; Barkt = Barkentine; BB = Battleship; Boat = Boat; Brg = Barge; Brig = Brig; Brig/Slp = Brig-sloop; Brigt = Brigantine; Clip = Clipper Ship; Cr = Cruiser; Cut = Cutter; CSch = Centerboard Schooner; DE = Destroyer Escort; Drg = Dredge; Dry = Floating Drydock; Frg = Frigate; Frt = Freighter; FV = Fishing Vessel; GaS = Gas Screw; GaY = Gas Yacht; Gbt = Gunboat; HBrig = Hermaphrodite Brig; K = Ketch; LS = Lightship; LtB = Lightboat; Ltr = Lighter; M = Merchantman; MoW = Man-of-War; MS = Mine Ship; OlS = Oil Screw; OlY = Oil Screw Yacht; Ore = Ore Carrier; PB = Pilot Boat; PGbt = Patrol Gunboat; PSch = Pilot Boat Schooner; Pink = Pink or Pinky; Pkt = Packetboat; Pr = Privateer; PY = Patrol Boat Yacht; Sch = Schooner; SchY = Schooner Yacht; SchB = Schooner Barge; Scow = Scow; Shallop = Shallop; Ship = Ship; Skj = Skipjack; Slp = Sloop; SpW = Sloop of War; SlpY = Sloop Yacht; Snow = Snow; SoL = Ship-of-the-Line; StC = Steam Collier; StP = Side-wheel Steamer; Str = Steamer; StS = Propeller/Screw Steamer; StW = Stern-wheel Steamer; StY = Steam Yacht; Sub = Submarine; TB/D = Torpedo Boat Destroyer; Ten = Tender; Tkr = Tanker; Traw = Trawler; Trsp = Transport; Tug = Tugboat; U = Unknown; Y = Yacht. The type of a vessel followed by a P indicates use as a privateer or pirate.

*Manner.* The following abbreviations indicate the manner in which the vessel was lost: A = Abandoned; AB = Aerial bombardment, fleet reduction; AR = Artificial reef; AS = Abandoned and stranded; AS&I = Abandoned, stranded, and destroyed by ice; A&F = Abandoned and foundered; B = Burned; BP = Burned by pirates; B&F = Burned and foundered, B&S = Burned and stranded; B-WL = Burned as war loss; BrU = Broken up by weather; BU-FR = Blown up, fleet reduction; BU-WL = Blown up as war loss; C = Collision; C-WL = Lost in combat as war loss; CA = Noted only as "cast away"; Cap = Capsized; C&S = Capsized and stranded; Exp = Explosion; F = Foundered; I = Indian attack; Ice = Ice; L = Noted only as "lost"; NG = Naval gunnery, fleet reduction; NT = Naval testing; RA-WL = Ran ashore as war loss; S = Stranded; S&B = Stranded and burned as war loss; Sc = Scuttled by crew; S&F = Stranded and foundered; S-WL = Stranded or driven ashore as war loss; ScP = Scuttled by pirates; Sc-WL = Scuttled as war loss; U = Cause of loss unknown; W = Noted only as wrecked; WL = war loss; ? = Uncertain.

Vessels indicated as lost by collision are sometimes followed by numbers in brackets. These refer to the collision key numbers indicating the vessel or object collided with (see list at end of appendix). The letter R in brackets indicates that the vessel was either fully recovered or raised at a later date. When R? appears the recovery of the vessel was projected but the record is incomplete regarding its final disposition.

*Location.* The position of the vessel at the time of loss is usually given in geographic reference and distances from landmarks that have been cited in official reports, insurance records, published accounts, etc. Occasionally multiple locations for the same wreck are provided owing to conflicting data from multiple sources. Most early references are landmark-based citations, but late-nineteenth-and twentieth-century references are often given in longitude and latitude and, in more recent times, in Loran. Whenever more than one source is available, all sources are cited even if they do not agree. LSS = Lifesaving Station.

| Date | | Vessel | Type | Manner | Location |
|------|------|--------|------|--------|----------|
| 1632 | Sept | Unidentified | U | I | In the Delaware |
| 1654 | — | Unidentified | Ship | W | Virginia |
| 1657 | — | Unidentified | U | W | Vicinity of Cape Henlopen, DE |
| 1664 | — | *Eustatia* [Du] | Ship | F | Off Lewes, DE |
| 1670 | — | *Good Hope* | Ship | S | Assateague Island |
| 1687 | Aug 7 | *Society* | Ship | W | Eastern Shore coast of Virginia |
| 1689 | Aug 26 | HMS *Deptford* | K | W | Near Cedar Island, VA |

| Date | | Vessel | Type | Manner | Location |
|------|------|--------|------|--------|----------|
| 1695 | Mar 1 | *Boston* [Fr] | MoW | L | 43 miles off Delmarva, 38° 10′ N |
| 1698 | Feb 2 | *Princess Ann* | Ship | S | Assateague Beach |
| 1699 | July 26 | *Maryland Merchant* | Slp | S | Willoughby Point, VA |
| 1700 | Apr 22 | *George* | Slp | BP | Virginia capes |
| | Apr 26 | *Pennsylvania Merchant* | U | BP | Off Cape Henry, VA |
| | — | Unidentified | U | ScP | Off Virginia capes |
| 1702 | Feb | *Elizabeth* | Ship | L | Winter Quarter Shoals |
| | Sept | Unidentified | Ship | S | Southward of Cape Henry, VA |
| 1703 | Nov | *Betty* | Slp | S | In Lynnhaven Bay, VA |
| 1704 | Oct 21 | Unidentified | U | L | Cape Henry, VA |
| 1705 | June 21 | Unidentified | Brigt | S-WL | Off the Virginia capes |
| 1706 | Nov 6 | Unidentifieds (14) | U | L | North coast of Cape Charles, VA |
| 1708/9 | — | Unidentifieds (3) | U | B&S | In Delaware Bay off the capes |
| 1709 | Apr | *Garland* | Ship | S | On Assateague Beach, 38° 20′ N |
| 1711/12 | Jan 8 | Unidentified | Snow | Ice | Brandywine Shoal, Delaware Bay |
| 1711/12 | Jan 22 | Unidentified | Ship | Ice | Delaware Bay |
| 1712 | Oct 20 (p) | Unidentified | Slp | S | Delaware Bay |
| 1713 | Oct 27 | *Carleton* | Frg | S | Delaware Bay |
| 1721 | Nov 13 | Unidentified | Pink | S | Middle Ground, Chesapeake Bay, VA |
| | Nov 15 | Unidentified | Slp | L | Near Virginia |
| | Nov 15 | Unidentified | Brigt | L | Near Virginia |
| | Nov 22 | *Content* | Slp | S | Cape Charles, VA |
| | Nov 25 | Unidentified | Ship | S | Cape Henry, VA |
| 1723 | July 29 | *Robert and James* | Slp | S | 20 miles S of Sinepuxent, MD |
| 1724 | June 9 | Unidentified | Brigt | S | Cape Henlopen, DE |
| 1725 | Oct 4 | *Great York* | U | S | Delaware Bay, "on the Bank" |
| 1728 | Dec | Unidentified | Ship | F | In 7 to 8 fathoms, inside Virginia capes |
| 1729 | Jan | Unidentified | U | S | On the Sheres (Shears), Delaware Bay |
| | Feb | Unidentified | Ship | F | Just within the Virginia capes |
| 1734 | Sept 13 | *Guernsey* | Snow | S | Assateague Beach |
| 1738 | Apr 4 | *Richmond* | Ship | F | Middle Ground, Chesapeake Bay, VA |
| 1739 | Jan 3 | Unidentified | Ship | S | Lynnhaven Bay, VA |
| | Sept 17 | *Mary and Louise* | Snow | S | Assateague Beach |
| 1740 | July 9 (p) | *Lucy and Nancy* | Ship | L | On the Eastern Shore of Virginia |
| 1741 | Apr 14 (p) | *Murdock* | U | S | In Virginia |
| | Aug 21 (p) | *Sea-Nymph* | U | S | On Hog Island, on the Virginia coast |
| 1744 | Mar | *Dauphin* | Brig | S | Winter Quarter Shoals |
| | Aug | *Tartar* | Ship-P | Cap | Off the Delaware capes |
| 1745 | Mar 27 | Unidentified | Sch | F | Middle Ground, Chesapeake Bay, VA |
| | Dec 31 | *Success of Glasgow* | Ship | S | Middle Ground, Chesapeake Bay, VA |
| 1746 | Apr (p) | Unidentified | Ship | F | Just within the capes of Virginia |
| | Oct 14 | *Delaware* | Brigt | S | Hen and Chickens Shoal, DE |
| | — | *Glasgow* | U | B-WL | Smith Island, near Cape Charles, VA |
| | — | *Prince George* | U | S-WL | Smith Island, near Cape Charles, VA |
| 1747 | Mar 21 | *Raleigh* | Brig | S | Willoughby Point, Chesapeake Bay, VA |
| | Mar | Unidentified | Slp | S | Virginia capes |
| | Sept | *Happy Return* | Snow | S | Hen and Chickens Shoal, DE |
| | Oct 14 | *Delaware* | Brigt | S | Hen and Chickens Shoal, DE |
| | Oct/Nov | Unidentified | Slp | L | South of the Delaware capes |
| | — | Unidentified (1+) | U | U | Delaware Bay and Delaware River |
| 1748 | May | Unidentified (2) | U | S-WL | Delaware capes |
| | June 3 (p) | *Charming Sally* | U | F | 24 leagues from the Virginia capes |
| | Oct 14 | *Delaware* | Brigt | S | Hen and Chickens Shoal, DE |

| Date | | Vessel | Type | Manner | Location |
|---|---|---|---|---|---|
| 1749 | Aug 25 (p) | *Lamplugh* [*Tamphough*] | U | L | On Virginia coast near Cobb Island |
| | Oct 7–8 | *Amity's Goodwill* | U | S | Virginia coast |
| | Oct 7–8 | *Bess* | U | S | Virginia coast |
| | Oct 7–8 | *Earl of Stair* | U | S | Virginia coast |
| | Oct 7–8 | *Elizabeth* | U | S | Virginia coast |
| | Oct 7–8 | *Free Mason* | U | S | Virginia coast |
| | Oct 7–8 | *Greeny* | U | S | Virginia coast |
| | Oct 7–8 | *Osgood* | U | S | Virginia coast |
| | Oct 7–8 | *Rawleigh* | U | S | Virginia coast |
| | Oct 7–8 | *Rothery* | U | S | Virginia coast |
| | Oct 7–8 | *Thistle* | U | S | Virginia coast |
| | Oct 7–8 | *York* | U | S | Virginia coast |
| | Oct 7–8 | Unidentifieds (1+) | Ship | S | Virginia coast |
| | Dec 19 (p) | *Albany* | U | F | Outside the Virginia capes |
| 1750 | Apr 7 | *Brothers* | Ship | S | Pungoteague Shoals, VA |
| | July | *Ocean Bird* | U | S | Sinepuxent, MD |
| | Aug 28 | *La Galga* | Frg | S | Near Green Run Inlet, MD |
| | Aug 28 | *La Merced* | Snow | S | Machipongo Shoal, VA |
| | Aug 29 | Unidentified | Ship | S | On the Virginia capes |
| | Aug 29 | Unidentified | U | S | Near the Virginia capes |
| | Aug 29 | Unidentified (2) | Slp | L | On the Virginia capes |
| | Nov 6 (p) | *Humphrey* | U | L | On the coast of Virginia |
| | Nov 6 (p) | Unidentified | U | L | On the coast of Virginia |
| | — | *Lockerman* | U | L | On the coast of Virginia |
| 1751 | June 21 (p) | *King's Fisher* | M | S | Wallops Island, VA |
| | Nov 15 (p) | *Speedwell* | U | S | In Virginia |
| 1752 | Oct 22 | *Peggy and Nancy* | Ship | S | Willoughby Point, VA |
| 1753 | Jan 23 | *Lucy* | Ship | L | Middle Ground, Chesapeake Bay, VA |
| | Jan | Unidentified | U | S | Middle Ground, Chesapeake Bay, VA |
| | Nov 29 | *Baltimore* | Ship | F | Great Gull Shoal, off Assateague Island |
| 1754 | Oct 14/15 | Unidentified | Slp | S | On Sinepuxent, 20 miles S of Cape Henlopen, DE |
| | Oct 14/15 | Unidentified (2) | U | S | 20 leagues S of Cape Henlopen, DE |
| | Oct 14/15 | Unidentified (6–8) | U | S | Between Cape Charles and Cape Henlopen |
| | Nov 5 | *Beaumont* | Snow | F | Off the Virginia capes |
| | — | *Pearl* | Ship | S | Vicinity of Cape Charles, VA |
| 1755 | Dec 25 | *Penguin* | Slp | F | Lynnhaven Bay, VA |
| | Dec | *Patowmack* | Sch | F | Lynnhaven Bay, VA |
| | — | Unidentified | Sch | W | Assateague Island, MD/VA |
| 1757 | Mar (p) | *Pusey* | U | S | Reedy Island, DE |
| | Apr 22 (p) | *Cornelia* | M | F | Between Cape Henlopen and Cape May |
| | Nov (p) | *Sally* | U | S? | On Brandywine Shoal, Delaware Bay |
| | Nov 11 (p) | *Duke of Cumberland* | Pr | L | 9 leagues S of Cape Henry, VA |
| | Nov 11 (p) | Unidentified | Brig | L | South of Cape Henry, VA |
| | Nov 11 (p) | Unidentified | Snow | L | South of Cape Henry, VA |
| | — | *Lydia* | U | F | Near Cape Henry, VA |
| 1758 | — | Unidentified | Slp | W | Assateague Island |
| 1759 | Oct 16 (ca.) | *Adventure* | Snow | F | Off the Virginia capes |
| 1760 | Feb (p) | *Molly* | U | F | Delaware River |
| | Mar 16 | Unidentified | Ship | S | At the Delaware capes |
| | Mar 16 | Unidentified | Brig | S | At the Delaware capes |
| | Sept 13 | *Endeavor* | Ship | S | On Chincoteague Shoal, VA |
| | Nov 1 | *King of Prussia* | Brigt | F | Off the Virginia capes |

| Date | | Vessel | Type | Manner | Location |
|---|---|---|---|---|---|
| | Nov 7 (p) | *Neptune* | Ship | S | 25 miles S of Cape Henry, VA |
| | Nov 7 (p) | *Thomas and Richard* | Ship | S | 25 miles S of Cape Henry, VA |
| 1761 | Feb 19 (p) | Unidentified | Brigt | S | 20 leagues N of Cape Charles, VA |
| | Aug 7 (p) | *Russell* | U | L | "Coming out of Virginia" |
| | Sept | *Good Intent* | Sch | F | Entrance to Chesapeake Bay, VA |
| 1762 | Apr 6 (p) | *Phaeton* | U | F | 40 leagues off the Virginia capes |
| | Nov 11 | HMS *Marlborough* | MoW | F | 10 leagues off coast of Maryland |
| | — | *Sally* | U | S | Vicinity of Cape Charles, VA |
| | — | Unidentified (2) | M | S | Vicinity of Cape Charles, VA |
| 1763 | Feb 4 (p) | *Vaughn* | U | S | In the Delaware |
| | June 23 | *Earl of Albemarle* | U | F | Off the Virginia coast |
| | Nov 1 (p) | *Pitt Packet* | M | F | Delaware Bay |
| 1764 | Jan 17 (p) | *Countess of Leicester Packet* | U | F | Between North Carolina and Virginia |
| | Jan 17 (p) | Unidentified | Sch | F | Between North Carolina and Virginia |
| | May 22 | *Kitty* | Sch | S&B | Assateague Island |
| | Nov 25 | *Friendship* | Sch | S | "A little Southward of the Capes of Virginia" |
| | Nov 29 | *Fortune* | Brig | S | Assateague Island |
| 1765 | Jan 1 (p) | *Brothers* | U | L | Virginia capes |
| 1766 | Jan 25 | *Charles Town* | U | L | On Brandywine Shoal, Delaware Bay |
| | July | *Rogers* | U | S | Middle Ground, near Cape Charles, VA |
| | Oct 9 | Unidentified | Slp | S | Between Chincoteague and Sinepuxent |
| | Oct | *Ranger* | Ship | S | On Cape Henry, VA |
| | Dec 4 (p) | *Dunlop* | Snow | S | Willoughby Point, Chesapeake Bay, VA |
| | Dec | *Norfolk* | Ship | S | On Cape Henry, VA |
| 1767 | Jan | *Liverpool* | Ship | S | 5 miles S of Cape Henry, VA |
| | Feb 12 (p) | Unidentified | Slp | F | Between Cape Henry and Cape Henlopen |
| | Feb | *Lockhart* | U | S | South of the Virginia capes |
| | Mar (p) | *Royal Hunter* | U | L | Delaware River |
| | Apr 23 (p) | *Tartar* | U | F | Off the Virginia capes |
| | Aug 18 (p) | Unidentified | Ship | CA | Near Chesapeake Bay |
| | Oct 16 | Unidentified | PB | L | At the Virginia capes |
| | Oct 16 | Unidentified | Slp | L | At the Virginia capes |
| | Oct 16 | Unidentified | Slp | S | Lynnhaven Bay, VA |
| | Oct 30 | *Britannia* | Sch | S | 2 leagues S of Cape Henry, VA |
| | Oct | *Margaret and Rebecca* | Sch | S | 20 miles S of Cape Henry, VA |
| | Oct | Unidentified | Sch | U | Off the Virginia coast |
| | — | *Mercury* | K | F | Off the Virginia capes |
| | — | Unidentified | Slp | F | Between Cape Henry and Cape Henlopen |
| 1768 | Apr 28 (p) | Unidentified | Slp | S | Assateague or Sinepuxent, MD |
| | Apr 28 (p) | Unidentified | U | S | Assateague or Sinepuxent, MD |
| | July 7 (p) | *Charles* | Snow | S | Cobb Island, VA |
| | Aug 18 (p) | Unidentified | Slp | CA | Near Chesapeake Bay |
| | Oct (p) | *Kildare* | U | L | Delaware River |
| | Dec 8 (ca.) | *Molly* | Snow | S [R] | Willoughby Point, Chesapeake Bay, VA |
| | Dec 22 (p) | Unidentified | U | S | Outside the Virginia capes |
| 1769 | Mar 5 | *Deerhound* | Sch | S | Assateague Island |
| | Aug | Unidentified (1+) | U | S | Virginia capes |
| | Sept 21 (p) | Unidentified (1+) | U | S | Outside the Virginia capes |
| | Sept 21 (p) | Unidentified | U | S | Eastern Shore of Virginia |
| | Nov 2 | *Randolph* | Ship | S | Cape Henry, VA |
| | Dec | *Betsey* | Snow | S | "A little to the southward of our capes" [DE] |
| 1770 | May 24 (p) | *Gorrell* | Brig | S | 3 leagues N of Cape Charles, VA |
| | Aug 7 (p) | *Boyne* | U | S | On the coast of Maryland |

| Date | | Vessel | Type | Manner | Location |
|------|------|--------|------|--------|----------|
| 1771 | Jan 4 (p) | *Commerce* | Ship | S | "Near the Capes of Philadelphia" |
| | Mar 9 | *Queen of the May* | Brigt | Cap | "A Mile within the pitch of Cape Henlopen" |
| | Apr 9 | Unidentified | U | S [R?] | Lewes, DE |
| 1772 | Jan 3 (p) | *Kitty* | U | L | Off Cape Charles, VA |
| | Feb 27 (p) | *Margaret* | Ship | S | South of Cape Henry, VA |
| | Mar 26 (p) | *Charming Molly* | Brigt | S | 2 miles below Willoughby Point, VA |
| | Dec 19 | *Phoenix* | U | S | Machipongo Shoals, N of Virginia capes |
| | Dec 20 | *Donald* | Ship | S | On Hog Island, near Cape Charles, VA |
| | Dec 23 | *Jane Pierre* | U | F | Near Cape Henry, VA |
| | — | *Canceaux* | U | B | Off Assateague Island |
| 1773 | Mar | *Guardoque* | Ship | S | Cedar Island Shoal, VA |
| | May | Unidentified | U | S | Coast of Princess Anne County, VA |
| 1774 | June 14 (p) | *Severn* | U | S | In Delaware Bay |
| | Oct 1 | *Annapolis* | Brigt | L | Off Delmarva coast |
| | — | *Fanny* | Brig | AS | Off Cape Henry, VA |
| 1775 | July 5 (p) | Unidentified | Trsp | F | East shore of Princess Anne County, VA |
| | Sept 2 | *Hibernia* | U | S | 10 leagues S of Cape Henry, VA |
| | Sept 4/5 | *Minerva* | U | L | In the capes of Virginia |
| | Sept 28 (p) | *Sally* | Slp | S | Between Sinepuxent and Cape Charles |
| | Oct 21 (p) | *Live Oak* | U | L | Hog Island, VA |
| 1776 | Mar 27 | *Polly* | Slp | Sc-WL | Hore Kill Roads, 1 mile NW of Cape Henlopen |
| | Mar 27 | Unidentified | Slp | Sc-WL | Hare Kill Roads, 1 mile NW of Cape Henlopen |
| | Mar 28 | Unidentified | PB | S-WL | Cape Henlopen, DE |
| | Mar 28–29 | *Dove* | Slp | WL | Off Cape Henlopen, DE |
| | Mar 29 | *Betsey* | Slp | WL | NNW of Cape Henlopen, DE |
| | Mar 29 | *Dolphin* | Slp | WL | NNW of Cape Henlopen, DE |
| | Apr 5 | *Sally* | Sch | S-WL | Off Cape Henlopen, DE |
| | Apr 7 | *Farmer* | Sch | S-WL | 7 to 8 miles S of Cape Henlopen, DE |
| | Apr 22 | *Dolphin* | Sch | S-WL | About 12 leagues off Cape Henlopen, DE |
| | Apr 22 | Unidentified | PB | S-WL | About 12 leagues off Cape Henlopen, DE |
| | Apr 30 | Unidentified | U | S-WL | Near Cape Henlopen Lighthouse, DE |
| | May 6 | Unidentified | Shallop | B-WL | Bombay Hook, DE |
| | May 7 | Unidentified | Sch | S-WL | Near Newcastle, DE |
| | May 22 | Unidentified | Sch | B-WL | Mouth of Delaware Bay |
| | June 15 | Unidentified | Sch | B-WL | 2 miles off Cape Henlopen Light, DE |
| | July 15 | *Sarah and Elizabeth* | Slp | B-WL | Off Cape Henlopen, DE |
| | Aug 6 | *Susannah* | Slp | Sc-WL | 4 miles NW of Cape Henry, VA |
| | Aug 7 | Unidentified (2) | U | Sc-WL | Cape Henry, VA |
| | Aug 7 | Unidentified | Slp | S | Chincoteague Shoal, VA |
| | Oct 29 | *Two Brothers* | U | B-WL | Off Cape Henlopen, DE |
| | Dec 25 | *Patience* | Sch | S | South of Cape Henry, VA |
| | Dec 25 | Unidentified | Slp | S | Chincoteague, VA |
| 1777 | Jan 10 | HMS *Roebuck*'s cutter | Cut | F | 16 leagues off Cape Henlopen, DE |
| | Jan 20 | *Farmer* | Ship | B-WL | Cape Henry, VA |
| | Jan 20 | Unidentified | Sch | B-WL | In Indian River, DE |
| | Feb 14 | *Hope* | Sch | B-WL | Cape Henry, VA |
| | Feb 17 | *Molly* | Slp | B-WL | 9 leagues off Cape Henry, VA |
| | Feb 19 | *Esther* | Brig | B-WL | Between Virginia capes |
| | Feb 27 | *Nancy* | Sch | B-WL | 41 leagues off Cape Henry, VA |
| | Mar 3 | *Ninety Two* | Sch | Sc-WL | In Atlantic off Cape Henry, VA |
| | Mar 5 | *Hannah* | Slp | Sc-WL | In Atlantic off Cape Henry, VA |
| | Mar 8 | *Betsy* | Slp | B-WL | 38 leagues off Cape Henry, VA |
| | Mar 8 | Unidentified | Sch | Sc-WL | 22 leagues off Cape Henry, VA |

| Date | | Vessel | Type | Manner | Location |
|---|---|---|---|---|---|
| | Mar 14 | *Dolphin* | Slp | B-WL | In Atlantic off Cape Henry, VA |
| | Mar 17 | *Hanover* | Brig | B-WL | Off Cape Henlopen, DE |
| | Mar 18 | *Two Sisters* | Sch | B-WL | In Atlantic off Cape Henry, VA |
| | Mar 22 | *General Mercer* | Slp | Sc-WL | 28 miles off Cape Henry, VA |
| | Mar 26 | *General Mifflin* | Brig-P | S | Vicinity of Sinexpuxent, MD |
| | Apr 2 | *Industry* | Brig | B-WL | 8 leagues off Cape Henry, VA |
| | Apr 4 | *Friendship* | Sch | Sc-WL | 7 leagues E of Cape Henry, VA |
| | Apr 4 | Unidentified (2) | U | B-WL | 11¾ leagues SE of Cape Henlopen, DE |
| | Apr 4 | Unidentified | Sch | Sc-WL | 11¾ leagues SE of Cape Henlopen, DE |
| | Apr 5 | HMS *Perseus*'s longboat | Boat | F | Off Cape Henlopen, DE |
| | Apr 11 | *Morris* | Ship | BU-WL | Hen and Chickens Shoal, DE |
| | Apr 13 | *Elphinstone* | U | B-WL | Delaware Bay |
| | Apr 15 | *Susannah* | Sch | Sc-WL | 12 leagues SE of Cape Henry, VA |
| | Apr 22 | *Esther* | Ship | RA-WL | On Cape Henry, VA |
| | Apr 23 | *Betsey* | Slp | RA-WL | On Cape Henry, VA |
| | Apr 26 | Unidentified | Sch | S&B | Cape Henlopen, DE |
| | May 5 | Unidentified (2) | Slp | RA-WL | 5 miles S of Cape Henry, VA |
| | May 6 | Unidentified | Brigt | S | Virginia capes |
| | May 6 | Unidentified | Slp | S | Virginia capes |
| | May 26 | Unidentified | U-P | RA-WL | South of Cape Henry, VA |
| | June 1 | *Hawke* | Sch | S | Near Sinepuxent, MD |
| | June 19 | Unidentified | Brigt | S | South of Cape Henry, VA |
| | June 24 | *Delaware* | Slp | B-WL | Virginia capes |
| | June–July | Unidentified (6) | U | WL | Off Cape Charles, VA |
| | July 4 | *Polly* | Slp | WL | In Chincoteague Inlet, VA |
| | July 4 | *Mary* | Slp | WL | In Chincoteague Inlet, VA |
| | July 4 | *Sally* | Slp | WL | In Chincoteague Inlet, VA |
| | July 4 | Unidentified | Slp | WL | In Chincoteague Inlet, VA |
| | July 19 | *Sally* | Sch | Sc-WL | About 2 miles NE of Cape Henry, VA |
| | July | Unidentified | Sch | B-WL | NE by E 2 miles off Bombay Hook, DE |
| | Aug 27 | Unidentified | Slp | B-WL | Within the Virginia capes |
| 1778 | Feb 27 | *Thistle* | U-P | WL | Wachapreague Inlet, VA |
| | Apr | CN *Independence* | Brig | S | On the Virginia coast |
| | Apr | *Liberty* | U | S | On the Virginia coast |
| | Apr | *Mars* | Snow | S | Cape Henry, VA |
| | May 29 | Unidentified | Slp | S-WL | Cape Henlopen, DE |
| | July 8 | HMS *Mermaid* | Frg | S-WL | Assateague Island, North Beach, MD |
| | Aug | Unidentified | Slp | S | Near Chesapeake Bay |
| | Nov 20–21 | HMS *Swift* | SpW | S&B | Near Cape Henry, VA |
| | Dec 25 | *Endeavor* | Slp | S-WL | Delaware Bay |
| | — | Unidentified | Ten | CA | Cape Henlopen, DE |
| 1779 | Jan 13 (p) | *Hotham* | U | CA | Cape Henlopen, DE |
| | Feb–Mar | *Nautilus* | Brigt | RA-WL | 30 miles S of Cape Henry, VA |
| | May (ca.) | VSN *Dolphin* | Gbt | WL | Off the Virginia capes |
| | Sept 25 (p) | *Polly* | Sch | S | An inlet on the Eastern Shore of Virginia |
| | Sept | *Irish Hero* | U-P | RA-WL | Off Northampton County, VA |
| 1780 | Jan 20 | CN *Baltimore* | Brig | S | On Cape Henry, VA |
| | Jan | Unidentified (1+) | U | S | "As far southward as the Eastern Shore of Maryland and Virginia" |
| | Feb | Unidentified | Brg | S | On Cape Henry, VA |
| | Aug | *Chance* | U | S | Overfalls Shoal, Delaware Bay |
| | Dec 1 (p) | *General Green* | Ship-P | L | "In the Delaware" |
| | — | *Victory* | Brg | C-WL | Off Metomkin Inlet, opp. Folly Creek, VA |

| Date | | Vessel | Type | Manner | Location |
|---|---|---|---|---|---|
| | — | HMS *Magdalen* | Sch | WL | Parramore Island, VA |
| 1781 | Sept 5 | HMS *Terrible* | SoL | C-WL | Off Cape Charles, VA |
| 1782 | Feb 2 | *Diligente* [Fr] | Frg | S | On the point of Cape Henry, VA |
| | Feb | Unidentified | Brig | S | Willoughby Point, Chesapeake Bay, VA |
| | Dec 27 | Unidentified | Cut | WL | Near Cape Charles, VA |
| | Dec 29 | Unidentified | Ship | B-WL | Near Cape Charles, VA |
| 1783 | Feb 12 (p) | *Digby* | U-P | RA-WL | Near Cape Charles, VA |
| | Mar 3 | *Morris* | U | Cap | Off the Delaware capes |
| | Apr | *Mentor* | U | S-WL | "Within the capes of Delaware" |
| | Apr | *Prince William Henry* | Ship-P | RA-WL | Virginia |
| | Oct (p) | *Success* | Ship | L | Cape Henlopen, DE |
| | Oct 7 | *Count de Ducat* | Brig | L | Cape Henlopen, DE |
| | Oct 7 | *Patriot de Roum* | Brig | L | Cape Henlopen, DE |
| | Oct 7 | *Sophia* | Brig | L | Cape Henlopen, DE |
| | Oct 7 | Unidentified | Brig | L | Cape Henlopen, DE |
| | Oct 7 | Unidentified | Slp | L | Cape Henlopen, DE |
| | Oct 7 | Unidentified (3) | Sch | L | Cape Henlopen, DE |
| | Nov 12 | *Philadelphia Packet* | Brig | S | On Sinepuxent Bar, MD |
| | Nov 12 | Unidentified | Sch | Cap | Off Sinepuxent Bar, MD |
| | Dec 12 (p) | *Tabitha* | U | S | On Eastern Shore, Northampton Co., VA |
| | Dec 25 | *Adventure* | Sch | L | Off Wreck Island, VA, N of Cape Charles |
| | Dec 25 | Unidentified | Snow | S | Off Wreck Island, VA, N of Cape Charles |
| | Dec 30 | *St. Eustatia* [Du] | U | F | Off Gull Shoal, near Assateague |
| 1784 | Jan 1 | *Merchant* | Sch | S | Cape Henlopen, DE |
| | Jan 7–14 | *Betsy* | Brig | S | "On bar between Morris Listen's and Reedy Island," DE |
| | Feb 9 (p) | *Liberty* | Brigt | S | Lynnhaven Bay, VA |
| | Feb 12 | *Alexander* | Brig | S | "On the bar near the mouth of Lewistown Creek," DE |
| | Feb 13 | *Minerva* | Ship | S | 2½ miles S of Cape Henlopen Light |
| | Mar 10 | *Maria Johanna* | U | S | On the inside of Cape Henlopen, DE |
| | Apr 8 (p) | Unidentified (3) | U | S | On Assateague Island |
| | Apr 30 | *Mary and Betsey* | U | S | Between Cape Henry and Williamsburg, VA |
| | May 28 (p) | *Cox* | U | S | On Assateague Island |
| | June 8 | *Peace* | Ship | S | Hog Island, VA, N of Cape Charles, VA |
| | Nov 2 | *Brilliant* | Trsp | S | ½ mile N of Hen and Chickens Shoal, DE |
| 1785 | Feb 23 | *Le Courier* | Brig | S | "On the inlets of Accomack county," VA |
| | Feb 24 | *Tabitha* | U | L | Near Cape Henry, VA |
| | June 14 (p) | *Grange* | Ship | S | Off Cape Charles, VA |
| | Aug 20 | *Ariel* | Brigt | S | Assateague Island |
| | Sept 2 | *Faithful Steward* | Ship | S | On "Mohoba Bank near Indian River" Inlet, 100 yards off shore |
| | Sept 2 | Unidentified | Brig | F | At the Delaware capes |
| | Sept 22–25 | *Nancy* | Brig | L | On or off the coast of Virginia |
| | Sept 22–25 | Unidentified | Brig | L | Lynnhaven Bay, VA |
| | Sept 22–25 | Unidentified | Ship | L | On or off the coast of Virginia |
| | Sept 22–25 | Unidentified (30+) | U | CA | On the Virginia coast |
| | Sept 24 | Unidentified [Du] | Ship | AS | Off the Virginia capes |
| | Sept 25 | *Crown Royal of Prussia* | Ship | AS | Off the Virginia capes |
| | Sept 25 | Unidentified | Ship | W | Off the Virginia capes |
| | Sept 30 | Unidentified | Slp | S | Cape Charles, VA |
| 1786 | July 25 | *Maryland Packet* | Sch | S | On Cape Henry, VA |
| | Sept | *Mary* | Brigt | F | Off the Virginia capes |

| Date | | Vessel | Type | Manner | Location |
|---|---|---|---|---|---|
| | Dec 9 | *Return* | Slp | CA | Near Cape Henlopen, DE |
| 1787 | Apr 9 (p) | *Nonsuch* | U | L | Off the Virginia capes |
| | May 9 | *Joseph and Peggy* | Pkt | S | "On a reef of rock," near Smith Island, VA |
| | May 10 | Unidentified | U | L | 36° 36' N, 74° 17' W |
| | Dec 9 | *Return* | Slp | F | Near Cape Henlopen, DE |
| 1788 | July 16 (p) | *Santa Rosalea* [Sp] | U | S | At the Delaware capes |
| | Aug 22 | *Marquis de Seignelay* | U | F | Off the coast of Maryland |
| 1789 | Jan 27 (p) | *Lydia* | U | L | Between Virginia and North Carolina |
| | Aug 10 (p) | *Aurora* | Brigt | Sc | Eastern Shore, VA |
| | Oct 30 | *Pomona* | U | L | In Delaware River |
| 1790 | Feb 11 (p) | *Kitty and Alice* | U | L | Near Cape Henry, VA |
| | June 26 (p) | *William* | M | S | Near Cape Charles, VA |
| | Nov 27 | *Friendship* | Slp | CA | In Delaware Bay, 2 leagues N of Cape Henlopen Lighthouse |
| | Nov 27 | Unidentified | Brig | S | 1 mile N of *Friendship* wreck, Delaware Bay |
| | — | *Lovely Ann* | U | L | Near Cape Charles, VA |
| | — | *Fanny* | U | L | Near Cape Charles, VA |
| | — | *Jane and Dianna* | Ship | L | Near Cape Charles, VA |
| 1791 | Jan 28 (p) | *Flora* | U | S | 25 miles N of Cape Charles on Hog Island |
| | June 17 (p) | Unidentified | Sch | L | South of Cape Henry, VA |
| | Oct 11 (p) | *Swan* | U | S | On Hog Island, VA |
| | Dec 2 | *Nancy* | M | F | Middle Ground, Chesapeake Bay, VA |
| 1792 | Feb 10 (p) | *Rainbow* | U | L | Near Cape Henry, VA |
| | Feb 10 (p) | *Betsy* | U | S | "In the Delaware" |
| 1793 | June 7 (p) | *Industry* | M | F | In Delaware Bay |
| 1794 | Feb 18 (p) | *Peggy* | Ship | L | "In the Delaware" |
| | Feb 18 (p) | *St. Joseph* | Ship | F | "In the Delaware" |
| | — | *Harmony* | U | A | Near the Delaware capes |
| 1795 | Jan 9 (p) | Unidentified | Ship | S | In the roads of Delaware Bay |
| | Jan | Unidentified | Frt | S | Smith Island, VA |
| | Feb 20 (p) | *Lively* | Ship | L | "Near the Delaware" |
| | Aug 21 (p) | Unidentified | Sch | S | Off Cape Charles, VA |
| | Aug (p) | Unidentified | Ship | F | 30 miles S of Delaware capes |
| | Oct 3 | *Marathon* | Brig | F | Gull Shoals |
| | Oct 3 | *San Miguel* | U | F | Gull Shoals |
| 1796 | Mar 22 (p) | *Favourite* | M | F | "Near the Delaware" |
| | Mar 22 (p) | *Minerva* | U | L | "Near the Delaware" |
| | Mar 22 (p) | *Henry and Charles* | U | S | "Near the Delaware capes" |
| | — | *Lively* | Brig | S | Assateague Island |
| 1797 | Feb 2 (p) | *John* | Ship | W | Near Cape Henlopen, "in the Delaware" |
| | Dec 27 | HMS *Hunter* | SpW | W | On Hog Island, VA |
| 1798 | Feb 20 | *Antony Mangin* | Ship | L | North of Cape Charles, VA |
| | Mar 6 (p) | *Inclination* | U | S | On Hog Island, VA |
| | Mar 21 (p) | *Union* | Slp | F | Off Hog Island, VA |
| | May 25 | HMS *De Braak* | Brig/Slp | Cap | Old Kiln Roads, Delaware Bay |
| | — | *New Jersey* | U | L | "In the Delaware" |
| 1799 | Jan 5 | *Hawk* | Sch | S | "A little above Sinepuxent Inlet," MD |
| | Jan 5 | *Ocean Bird* | U | F | On shoals near Sinepuxent, MD |
| | Jan 25 (p) | *New Jersey* | U | S | Delaware Bay |
| | May 31 | *Sally and Nancy* | Brig | B | Near Cape Henry, VA |
| | Dec | *Lisbon* | Sch | CA | On Chincoteague Shoal, VA |
| | — | *Richard* | U | F | A few days out of Baltimore, MD |
| | — | *William* | Sch | F | Off Cape Henry, VA |

| Date | | Vessel | Type | Manner | Location |
|---|---|---|---|---|---|
| 1800 | Feb 1 (?) | *Jamlikehen* | Brig | S | 1 mile S of Cape Henry Lighthouse, VA |
| | Apr 18 (p) | *Admiral Parish* | U | S | Near Cape Henlopen |
| | Apr (p) | *Susannah* | Ship | W | "In the Delaware" |
| | June 16 | Unidentified | Brigt | B | Off Cape Charles, VA |
| | July 29 (p) | *Iphigenia* | Brig | S | Near Winter Quarter |
| | July | Unidentified | Brig | S | 30 miles S of Cape Henry, VA |
| | July | Unidentified | SLP | S | 30 miles S of Cape Henry, VA |
| | Nov 25 (p) | *June* | U | L | On Hog Island, VA |
| | Dec 11–12 | *Betsey* | U | S&F | Middle Ground, Chesapeake Bay, VA |
| 1801 | Mar 19 | *Musgrave* | U | S | On Chincoteague Shoal, VA |
| | June (p) | *Constellation* | M | F | "In the Delaware" |
| | July 31(p) | *Suffolk* | U | S | On the Virginia capes |
| | — | *Adriana* | U | Ice | Delaware Bay |
| 1802 | Jan 7 (p) | *Rising Polly* | Sch | S | On Assateague Island |
| | Feb 5 (p) | *Adriana* | U | Ice | "In the Delaware" |
| | Aug 30 | *Beaulieu* [Fr] | U | S | Assateague Island |
| | Aug 31 (p) | *Jupiter* | Sch | F | Tail of Middle Ground, Chesapeake Bay |
| | Sept 7 (p) | *Rover* | Sch | F | 16 miles outside the Virginia capes |
| | Oct 28 [29] | *Juno* [Sp] | Frg | F | 40 miles E of Assateague Island, VA |
| | Dec 25 | *Union* | U | F | Near Cape Henlopen, DE |
| 1803 | Jan 13 | Unidentified | Slp | S | South of Cape Henry Lighthouse, VA |
| | Feb 2 | *Postillion* | Sch | F | Great Gull Shoal, MD |
| | Mar 26 | *Determinee* | MoW | F | Fenwick Shoal, DE |
| | Aug 29 | *Jupiter* | Sch | F | Off the Chesapeake capes |
| 1804 | Aug 12 | *Debby* [*Phoebe?*] | Slp | F | Off Chincoteague, 30 miles N of Hog Island, VA |
| | Dec 8 (p) | Unidentified | U | F | 3 leagues above Hog Island, VA |
| | Dec 11 (p) | *Fortune* | U | Cap | Delaware Bay |
| | Dec 20 | *President* | Slp | S | Smith Island, VA |
| | Dec 25 | Unidentified | U | Cap | Off the Virginia capes |
| | — | *Samuel Smith* | Ship | W | South of Cape Henry, VA |
| 1805 | Jan 1 | *Aurora* | Ship | S | Cape Henry, VA |
| | Jan 1 | Unidentified | Sch | W | 37° N, 74° W |
| | Jan 3 | *Courier* | Brig | CA | On Parramore Island, VA |
| | Jan | Unidentified | Ship | S | On Cape Henry, VA |
| | Jan | Unidentified (1+) | U | S | South of Cape Henry, VA |
| | Mar 15 | *Farmer* | Sch | S | On Hog Island, VA |
| | Mar 19 (p) | *Fanny* | U | L | "On the Delaware" |
| | Apr 10 | *Nancy* | U | F | 9 miles N of Sinepuxent, MD |
| | June | *Nancy* | U | F | 2 miles SE of Fenwick Island, MD |
| | Sept | *Adventure* | Brig | S | "In the Pitch of Cape Henry" |
| | — | *China* | M | F | Delaware Bay |
| 1806 | Jan 8 | *Nestor* | Ship | S | Lynnhaven Bay, VA |
| | Jan 8 | Unidentified | Slp | S | Lynnhaven Bay, VA |
| | Aug | Unidentified | U | W | 37° 35' N |
| | Aug–Sept | *Richmond* | Sch | Cap | Off Chincoteague, VA |
| | Sept 11 | *Charming Mary* | Sch | F | 4 leagues N of Chincoteague, VA |
| | Sept 25 | Unidentified | Sch | S | 30 miles from the Virginia capes |
| | Sept | *Atlantic* | Ship | S | Cape Henry, VA |
| | Sept | *Impetueux* | SoL | B-WL | Near Cape Henry, VA |
| | Sept | *Martha Bland* | Brig | S | Cape Henry, VA |
| | Sept | Unidentified | Sch | AS | Off Chincoteague, VA |
| | Oct 21 | *Shepherdess* | Ship | S | 12 miles S of Cape Henry |
| | Oct | *Messenger* | Sch | W | Virginia-Maryland coast |

| Date | | Vessel | Type | Manner | Location |
|---|---|---|---|---|---|
| | Dec 15 | *Warrington* | Ship | S | Cape Henry Lighthouse, VA |
| | Dec 15 | Unidentified | Sch | S | Lynnhaven Bay, VA |
| | Dec | Unidentified | Sch | S | South of Cape Henry, VA |
| 1807 | Feb | Unidentified | Brig | S | Willoughby Point, Chesapeake Bay, VA |
| | Mar 31 | *Jane Anne* | U | S | "In the Delaware" |
| | Mar 31 | *Nanina* | U | S | "In the Delaware" |
| | Mar 31 | *Sally* | Brig | S | Near Bombay Hook, Delaware Bay |
| | Apr (p) | *Betsy* | Sch | S | Reedy Island, in the Delaware |
| | Apr (p) | *Friendship* | Sch | S | Lewes, DE |
| 1808 | Jan (ca.) | *Nancy* | Brig | S | Oyster beds, Delaware Bay |
| | Jan | *Regulator* | Sch | S | Cross Ledge, Delaware Bay |
| | Jan 31 (ca.) | *William Murdock* | U | L | Near the Virginia capes |
| | Aug 22 | *Tentacao* | U | S | Cape Henry, VA |
| 1809 | Feb (ca.) | *Camillus* | Brig | S | Reedy Island, Delaware Bay |
| | June (p) | *Elizabeth and Benjamin* | U | S | In Delaware Bay |
| | Aug 31 | *Robert* | U | S | In Lynnhaven Bay, VA |
| | Dec 21 | *Angelica* | U | Cap | Off Cape Henlopen, DE |
| | — | *Portland* | Brig | S | Morris Listons, on the Delaware |
| 1810 | Jan (ca.) | *Mary* | Brig | S | On the Overfalls, Delaware Bay |
| | Feb (ca.) | *Concordia* | Sch | S | Collins Ditch, Delaware Bay |
| | Feb (ca.) | *Cyrus* | Brig | S | Collins Ditch, Delaware Bay |
| | Feb (ca.) | *Eliza* | Brig | S | Appoquinimink, DE |
| | Feb (ca.) | *Huntress* | Sch | S | Appoquinimink, DE |
| | Feb (ca.) | *Nancy* | Sch | S | Deep Creek, Delaware Bay |
| | Feb | *Clementina* | Sch | Ice | Delaware Bay |
| | Feb | *Jane* | Ship | S | Morris Listons, on the Delaware |
| | Mar (ca.) | *Growler* | Brig | S | On Joe Flogger Shoal, Delaware Bay |
| | Mar 14 | Unidentified | U-P | S | Smith Island, VA |
| | Mar 30 | *Resolution* | U | S | At Cape Henry, VA |
| | June 7 | Unidentified | Sch | F | Off Delaware capes in 50 fathoms |
| | Nov 26 | *Henry* | Brig | S | Middle Ground, Chesapeake Bay, VA |
| | Dec 3 | *Plyades* | U | S | Assateague Island |
| | Dec 22 | *Humming Bird* | Sch | F | Off the Delaware capes |
| | Dec 23 | *Athens* | Sch | S&B | Sinepuxent, MD |
| | Dec | *Growler* | Brig | S | On Brandywine Shoal, Delaware Bay |
| 1811 | Jan 1 (p) | *Lucy* | U | L | Near Cape Henry, VA |
| | Apr 11 | *Heroine* | U | S | On Hog Island, VA |
| | Apr 21 (p) | *Hiram* | Brig | L | On Hog Island, VA |
| | Dec (p) | *Minerva* | U | L | "Between Philadelphia and New York" |
| | Dec 23 | *Liberty* | Ship | S | Lynnhaven Bay, VA |
| | — | *Matilda* | Ship | W | N side of Delaware Bay |
| 1812 | Jan (ca.) | *Juliet* | Sch | S | Near the point of Cape Henlopen, DE |
| | Jan (ca.) | *Lydia* | Ship | S | On the beach at Lewes, DE |
| | Jan (ca.) | *Perseverance* | Sch | S | On the beach at Lewes, DE |
| | Jan (ca.) | *Three Brothers* | Brig | S | Under Cape Henlopen, DE |
| | Jan | Unidentified [Sp] | Sch | S | Lewes, DE |
| | Feb (ca.) | Unidentified | Sch | S | Lewes, DE |
| | Feb | Unidentified [Sp] | Slp | S | "Near the pitch of Cape Henlopen," DE |
| | Aug 17 (p) | Unidentified (2) | Brig | S | South of Cape Henry, VA |
| | Oct 12 (p) | *Eagle* | Sch | S | 15 miles S of Cape Henry, VA |
| | Nov 30 | *Gorham* | Brig | B-WL | Off Hog Island, VA |
| | Dec 9 (p) | *Mary Ann* | Brig | S&B | 3–4 miles SE of Cape Henry Lighthouse, VA |
| | Dec 14 (p) | *Union* | Slp | S-WL | 3 miles W of Cape Henry Lighthouse, VA |

| Date | | Vessel | Type | Manner | Location |
|------|------|--------|------|--------|----------|
| 1813 | Jan | *General Apodaca* | Brig | S | Cape Henlopen, DE |
| | Feb 22 (p) | *Esther* | Sch | S | Lynnhaven Bay, VA |
| | Feb 24 (p) | *Esmeraldo* | Ship | S | Ragged Island, VA |
| | Apr 9 (p) | *Tamerlane* | Ship | L | Near Cape Henry, VA |
| 1814 | June | Unidentified (2–3) | U | WL | Within Indian River, DE |
| 1815 | Jan 22 | *Industry* | Slp | S | Near Lewes, DE |
| | Jan 29 | *Friendship* | Ship | Sc-WL | Delaware Bay |
| | Mar | USS *Helen* | Sch | S | Lewes, DE |
| | May 21–31 | *Hope* | Slp | S | On Chincoteague Shoal, VA |
| | June 24 | *Columbia* | Ship | S | Willoughby Point, Chesapeake Bay, VA |
| | June 30 | *Warrior* | Brig | S | On Isaac Shoal, VA |
| | July 21–22 | *Adventure* | Ship | S | Willoughby Point, Chesapeake Bay, VA |
| | Sept 2 | *Friends* | Sch | Cap | 20 miles S of Cape Henry, VA |
| | Sept 2 | *Olive Branch* | Sch | L | On Smith's Inlet, VA |
| | Sept 2 | *Richmond Packet* | Slp | S | On Smith's Inlet, VA |
| | Sept 2 | Unidentified | Slp | L | On Smith's Inlet, VA |
| | Sept 2 | *Experiment* | Slp | Cap | 38° 02' N, 73° 15' W |
| | Sept 2–4 | *Union* | Sch | S | South end of Hog Island, VA |
| | Sept 4 | Unidentified (7) | U | S | South of Cape Henry, VA |
| | Nov 11 | *Union* | Sch | S | Willoughby Point, Chesapeake Bay, VA |
| | Nov | *Friendship* | Sch | L | Willoughby Point, Chesapeake Bay, VA |
| | Dec | *Dispatch* | Brigt | S | Below Cape Henry, VA |
| 1816 | Sept | Unidentified | Sch | S | Joe Flogger Shoal, DE, 10 or 12 feet water |
| | Oct 7 | *George* | U | F | 38° 40' N, 74° 30' W |
| 1817 | Feb (ca.) | *Friends* | Brig | S | ½ mile inside of Cape Henlopen, DE |
| | Mar (ca.) | *Helen* | Sch | S | Lewes, DE |
| | Mar | *Amanda* | Brig | S | Delaware Bay |
| | Sept | *Levant* | U | S | Willoughby Point, Chesapeake Bay, VA |
| | Nov 5 (p) | *General Jackson* | U | L | "On the Coast of Maryland" |
| 1818 | Feb | *Alpha* | Ship | S | The bar off Lewes, DE |
| | Feb | *General Scott* | Brig | S | On shores of Delaware Bay |
| | Feb | *Roderic* | Brig | S | On shores of Delaware Bay |
| | Feb | *St. Helen* | Sch | Ice | Delaware Bay |
| | Mar 24 | *Clotilda* | Brig | S | 5 miles S of Cape Henry, VA |
| | Mar (ca.) | *Ann Maria* | Brig | S | Cape Henlopen, DE |
| | Apr 5 | *Pandora* | Sch | CA | 15 miles S of Cape Henlopen, DE |
| | Dec 27 | *San Vicenzo Fliorengo* | U | F | Fenwick Shoal, DE |
| | Dec 30 (p) | *General Andrew Jackson* | Sch | S | On Smith Island, VA |
| 1819 | Nov 8 | *Emulation* | U | S | Willoughby Point, Chesapeake Bay, VA |
| 1820 | Jan 22 | *Victoria* | Brig | A | 37° 40' N, 72° 00' W |
| | Jan 28 (p) | *Stag* | U | S | ½ mile S of Cape Henry Lighthouse, VA |
| | Oct 16 (p) | *Two Friends* | Sch | S&F | Off N end Smith Island, VA, Cape Henry bearing WSW |
| | Nov 6 (p) | *Benelia* | Slp | S | On Hog Island, VA |
| | Nov 6 | Unidentified | Brig | S | On Hog Island, VA |
| | Dec 1 | *Rising Sun* | Slp | S | SE of Willoughby Pt., Lynnhaven Beach, VA |
| | Dec 13 (p) | *Union* | Slp | S | On Lynnhaven Beach, VA |
| 1821 | Jan 5 | *Teazer* | Sch | S | Machipongo, VA |
| | Jan 5 | Unidentified | Sch | S | "Royal Shoal near the Swash," VA |
| | Jan 7 | Unidentified | Sch | S | Metomkin, VA |
| | Jan 16 | *Gypsey* | Brig | S | Wreck Island, 7 or 8 miles N of Smith Island, VA |
| | Feb 2 | *General Washington* | Slp | S | 14 miles S of Cape Henry, VA |

| Date | | Vessel | Type | Manner | Location |
|------|------|--------|------|--------|----------|
| | Feb 8 | *Orleans* | U | Ice | Delaware Bay |
| | June (ca.) | *Mary and Betsy* | Sch | S | Lewes Bar, DE |
| | Sept | *San Lorenzo* | Ship | W | Assateague Island, MD |
| | Sept (ca.) | *Newbern* | Brig | S | Bombay Hook, Delaware Bay |
| | Sept (ca.) | *William and Catharine* | Sch | S | Bombay Hook, Delaware Bay |
| | Sept (ca.) | *Washington* | Brig | S | Bombay Hook, Delaware Bay |
| | Sept (ca.) | Unidentified | Slp | L | Bombay Hook, Delaware Bay |
| | Oct 12 | *Reserve* | Sch | S | On Sinepuxent Beach, MD |
| | Nov 16 (p) | *Hind* | Sch | S | On Hog Island Shoals, VA |
| | Dec 19 | *Sophia* | Sch | S | Wash Woods, VA |
| 1822 | Jan 6 | *Diana* | Slp | S | Willoughby Point, Chesapeake Bay, VA |
| | Jan | *Irene* | Brig | S | Lewes, DE |
| | Feb (ca.) | *Concordia* | Brig | S | Mispillion, Delaware Bay |
| | Apr 22 (p) | *Grace of Ballycastle* | Brig | S | 6 miles S of Cape Henry, VA |
| | May (ca.) | *Seaman* | Slp | S&F | Overfalls, Delaware Bay |
| | June (ca.) | *Polly* | Sch | S&F | Joe Flogger Shoal, Delaware Bay |
| | Oct 22 | *La Plata* [Sp] | M | L | Near Cape Charles, VA |
| | Dec 28 | *Alert* | Brig | S | 1 mile N of Lewes, DE, $\frac{1}{2}$ mile from beach. |
| | — | *Janus* [Du] | Ship | S | On Cape Henry, VA |
| | — | *Seaflower* | Slp | S | Near Cape Henry, VA |
| | — | *Alert* | U | S | Near Lewes, DE |
| 1823 | Jan | Unidentified | Brig | S | Near Virginia–North Carolina line |
| | Mar 18 (p) | *Union* | Sch | S | Lewes Roads, DE |
| | Apr (ca.) | *Polly and Sylvia* | Sch | S | Lewes, DE |
| | Apr (ca.) | *Regulator* | Sch | S | 8 miles S of Indian River, DE |
| | June 9 | Unidentified | Sch | S | 8 miles S of Indian River, DE |
| | Nov 7 | *Lawrence* | Sch | S&B | Sinepuxent Beach, MD |
| | Nov 12 | Unidentified | Sch | S | Wash Woods, VA, 18 miles S of Cape Henry |
| | Nov 19 | *Mary and Achsa Ann* | U | S | On Hog Island Shoal, VA |
| 1824 | Mar 10 | *Liverpool* | Ship | L | Below Cape Henry, VA |
| | Dec 9 | *Adeline* | M | W | At Cape Henlopen, DE |
| | Dec 28 | *William King* | U | L | At Wash Woods, VA |
| | — | *Mary and Ann* | U | S | Hog Island Shoal, VA |
| 1825 | Jan (ca.) | *McDonough* | Sch | S | Lewes, DE |
| | Feb 15 | *Franklin* | Sch | S | On Cape Henry, VA, near the lighthouse |
| | Feb 20 | *Jay* | Slp | W | Off Smith Island, VA |
| | Feb 24 (p) | Unidentified (1+) | U | S | Between Cape Henlopen, DE, and Chincoteague, VA |
| | Feb 28 | Unidentified | Sch | S | On Cape Henry, VA |
| | Mar 8 | *Ocean* | Slp | S | Sinepuxent Beach, MD |
| | Mar 14 | *Ceres* | Sch | S [R] | Smith Island, VA |
| | Mar 21 | *Betsy* | Brig | S | Inside Cape Henry, VA |
| | Mar 24 | Unidentified | Sch | S | 3 miles N of Hog Island, VA |
| | Apr 2 | *Ceres* | Sch | S | Willoughby Point, Chesapeake Bay, VA |
| | Apr 2–3 | Unidentified | Sch | S | At the Ship Shoal, VA |
| | Apr 2–3 | Unidentified | Sch | S | On Assawoman Beach, VA |
| | Apr 5 | Unidentified (2) | U | S | At the Ship Shoal, VA |
| | Apr 7 (p) | Unidentified (2) | U | S | Below the Ship Shoal, VA |
| | Apr 7 (p) | Unidentified | Sch | U | 3 miles below Willoughby Point, VA |
| | Apr 7 (p) | Unidentified | Brig | U | 4 miles N of Smith Island, VA |
| | Apr 7 (p) | Unidentified | Sch | U | 4 miles N of Smith Island, VA |
| | Apr (ca.) | *Spartan* | Slp | S | Lewes, DE |
| | May (ca.) | *Louisiana* | Brig | S | Joe Flogger Shoal, Delaware Bay |

| Date | | Vessel | Type | Manner | Location |
|---|---|---|---|---|---|
| | May 13 | *Expedition* | Slp | S | Sand Shoal Inlet, VA |
| | May 25 (p) | *Sea Horse* | U | Cap | "In the Delaware" |
| | June 4 | *Ann Maria* | Sch | S | Near the Pleasure House, coast of Princess Anne County, VA |
| | June 4 | *George* | Sch | S | Near wreck of *Ann Maria* |
| | June 4 | Unidentified | Slp | S | 5 miles S of False Cape, VA |
| | June | *Betsy* | Slp | A | Cape Henlopen, DE |
| | June | *Emmeline* | U | F | Within Delaware Bay |
| | June | *Fame* | U | S | Within Delaware Bay |
| | June | *Herald* | Sch | S | Near Blackbird Creek, DE |
| | June | *Lewis Calpier* | PB | S | Cape Henlopen, DE |
| | June | *McDonough* | U | S | Within Delaware Bay |
| | June | *Uno* | U | F | Delaware Bay |
| | June | Unidentified | Brig | S | Cape Henlopen, DE |
| | June | Unidentified (9) | U | S | Lewes, DE |
| | June | Unidentified (32) | U | S | Cape Henlopen, DE |
| 1826 | Mar 30 | *Esperanze* | Sch | S | On Hog Island Shoal, VA |
| | Apr 1 | *Mary Jane* | Slp | S | On Hog Island, VA |
| | Aug | *Cicero* | Sch | S | On Brandywine Shoal, Delaware Bay |
| | Oct | *Amelia* | Sch | S | Lewes, DE |
| | Nov 4 | *Neptune* | U | S | On Rehoboth Beach, DE |
| | — | *Samarang* | Sch | F | Off Gull Shoal, MD |
| 1827 | Jan 10 | *Chili* | Slp | S | Hog Island, VA |
| | Jan 15 (p) | *William Porter* | Sch | Ice | Near Reedy Island, in the Delaware |
| | Feb 21 (p) | *Three Daughters* | Sch | W | "Near Lewiston Roads," DE |
| | Aug 25–26 | *Flag* | Slp | Cap | Middle Ground, VA |
| | Oct 12 | *James and David* | Slp | S | Near Cape Henlopen, DE |
| | Nov 15 | *Convoy* | Sch | S | At Machipongo Inlet, VA |
| | Nov 27 | *Fly* | Sch | S | On south part of Hog Island, VA |
| 1828 | Jan 2 | Unidentified | Brig | S | At Chincoteague Beach, VA |
| | Jan 4 (p) | Unidentified | Brig | S | On Assateague Point, VA |
| | Jan 12 | *Austerlitz* [Ger] | U | F | Off Assateague Island |
| | Apr 4 (p) | *American Hero* | Slp | S | Sand Shoal Inlet, 15 miles N of Smith Island, VA |
| | Dec 14 (p) | Unidentified | U | F | Off the Delaware capes |
| | — | *Santo Leocardia* [Port] | Ship | F | Off Fenwick Shoal, DE |
| 1829 | Feb 28 | Unidentified | Brig | S | At Goose Hill Flats, VA |
| | Mar 12 (p) | *Eastern Shore Packet* | U | L | Off Virginia capes |
| | June 16 | Unidentified | U | S&F | 10 miles S of Chincoteague, VA |
| 1830 | Feb 8 | *Complex* | Sch | S | "At Lewiston Roads," DE |
| | Mar 5 (ca.) | Unidentified | U | S | Machipongo Shoal, VA |
| | Mar 13 (p) | *Uniao* | Ship | A&F | 75 miles from Cape Henry, VA |
| | Aug 19 | *Good Intent* | Sch | Cap | 12 miles within Cape Henlopen, DE |
| | Aug 19 | *Jubilee* | Sch | Cap | Cape Henlopen, DE [?] |
| | Sept 2 (p) | Unidentified (18) | U | S | Cape Henlopen, DE |
| | Oct | *Advance* | Slp | S | Cape Henlopen, DE |
| | Dec 1 | *Samaratin* | Brig | S | Fenwick Island, Worcester Co., MD |
| | Dec 14 (p) | Unidentified | U | S | Off Carver's Inlet, VA |
| | Dec 28 (p) | Unidentified | S | A | 60 miles off Delaware capes |
| 1831 | Jan 14 | *Samuel* | Slp | S | Near Wachapreague Inlet, VA |
| | Jan 14–15 | *Mary Ann* | PB | S | "Opposite the Tan Yard" at Lewes, DE |
| | Jan 14–15 | *Thomas A. Morgan* | PB | S | "Opposite the Tan Yard" at Lewes, DE |
| | Jan 15 | *Alexandria* | Sch | S | "Abreast of Green Bank" near Lewes, DE |

| Date | | Vessel | Type | Manner | Location |
|---|---|---|---|---|---|
| | Jan 15 | *Bevan* | Brig | S | "Abreast of Green Bank" near Lewes, DE |
| | Jan 15 | *Chadwick* | Ship | S | On Cape Henry, VA |
| | Jan 15 | *William D. Borden* | Sch | S | "Abreast of Green Bank" near Lewes, DE |
| | Feb 13 | Unidentified | Brig | S | Carver's Inlet, VA |
| | Mar | *Republican* | Sch | S | Sand Shoal Beach, VA |
| | Apr | Unidentified | Sch | S | Near Lewes, DE |
| | Dec | *Caravan* | Ship | S | On Wachapreague, N of Hog Island, VA |
| | Dec | Unidentified | Brig | S | 41 miles NNE of Cape Charles, VA |
| | Dec | Unidentified | Sch | S | Virginia coast |
| 1832 | Mar | *Indian* | Slp | S | Cape Henry, VA |
| | Mar | Unidentified | Brig | S | 8 miles S of Cape Henry, VA |
| | Mar | Unidentified | Slp | S | 12 miles S of Cape Henry, VA |
| | Mar | Unidentified | Sch | S | 3 miles N of Cape Henry Lighthouse, VA |
| | Apr 15 | Unidentified (7) | U | S | Along the Virginia coast |
| 1833 | Jan 9 | *Chancellor* | Sch | S [R?] | In Lynnhaven Bay, VA |
| | Feb 14 | *Swift* | Sch | S | Middle Ground, near Cape Charles, VA |
| | Apr 4 | *Anacreon* | Ship | S | On Hog Island, VA |
| | Apr 23 | *Waccamaw* | Sch | C [1] | Below Smith Island, VA |
| | Nov 26 | *William* | Sch | S | Near Cape Henry Lighthouse, VA |
| | Dec 16 | Unidentified | Sch | F | Off Chincoteague, VA |
| | Dec 20 | Unidentified | Ship | S | On the N end of Hog Island, VA |
| | Dec | *Thompkin* (*Metompkin*) | U | AS | ENE of Cape Henry, VA |
| 1835 | Jan 12 | *Sabat* | U | S | 5 miles S of Willoughby Point light boat, VA |
| | Jan 29 | *Bon Homme Richard* | U | S | On Hog Island beach, VA |
| 1836 | Mar 29 | *George Washington* | Slp | S | On Machipongo Shoals, VA |
| | Apr 4 | *Neptune* | Slp | S | On Machipongo Shoals, VA |
| | May 24 | Unidentified | Sch | S | 5 miles S of Cape Henry, VA |
| | May 31 | *Douglas* | Brig | S | South of Wash Woods, VA |
| 1837 | Jan 28 | Unidentified | Sch | AS | 20 miles off Cape Henry, VA |
| | Mar 18 (p) | Unidentified | Sch | S | Near Cape Charles, VA |
| | July | *Carolinian* | Sch | S&F | In Lynnhaven Bay, VA |
| | Aug 19 | *Harmonia* | Brig | S | 20 miles S of Cape Henry, VA |
| | Aug 19 | Unidentified | Sch | S | 20 miles S of Cape Henry, VA |
| | Aug 19 | Unidentified (11) | U | S | Between Cape Henry and Cape Hatteras |
| | Aug 20 | *Eagle* | Slp | S | 15 miles S of Cape Henry, VA |
| | Oct 9 | *Mary* | Sch | S | South of Wash Woods, VA |
| 1839 | Mar 15 (ca.) | Unidentified | Sch | S | South of Wash Woods, VA |
| | Mar 23 | *St. Thomas* | Sch | S | 9 miles S of Cape Henry Lighthouse, VA |
| | — | *Retribution* | Ship | F | Assateague Beach |
| 1841 | Jan 15 | *Nancy Jane* | Brig | S | On the beach below Berlin, MD |
| | Jan 23 | *Castel* | Brig | S | 50 miles S of Cape Henry, VA |
| | Mar 16 | *Emily* | Sch | S | 5 miles E of Willoughby Point, VA |
| | Mar 22 | *Leander* | Sch | S | "Northward of Smith's Island light," VA |
| | Apr 21 (p) | *Legislation* | Sch | S | On Chincoteague Shoal, VA |
| | June 17 | *Millesent* | Sch | S | On Cape Charles, VA |
| | Nov 16 | *Gentle Return* | Sch | S | "On the spit off Cape Charles," VA |
| | Dec 1 [16] | *R. E. Loper* | Brig | S | Sinepuxent Shoal, MD |
| 1842 | Feb 8 [9] | *Cadet* | Sch | S | Near Delaware Breakwater |
| | Feb 13 | *Frances Stanton* | Bark | S [R] | 10 miles S of Cape Henry, VA |
| | Feb 21 | *E. Buckman* | Sch | S | On the bar near Lewes, DE |
| | Apr 5 | *Richard Thompson* | Sch | S | Hog Island, VA |
| | Apr 23 | *Columbia* | Sch | S | Carter's Bar, near Sand Shoal Island, VA |
| | July 12 | *Sarah Lee* | Bark | S | In Lynnhaven Bay, VA |

| Date | Vessel | Type | Manner | Location |
|------|--------|------|--------|----------|
|      | July 20 | *Frances Taylor* | Sch | S | On Chincoteague [Shoal?], VA |
|      | Nov 29 | *Lycurgus* | Sch | S | 20 miles S of Chincoteague, VA |
| 1843 | Jan 31 | *Victory* | Sch | S | 25 miles below Berlin, MD |
|      | Feb 8 | *Leo* | Sch | S | Off Chincoteague Shoal, VA (also given as off Lewes, DE) |
|      | Mar 28 | *North Carolina* | Sch | W | Near Berlin, MD |
|      | Aug 3 [9] | *Atlantic* | Sch | S | On the point of Cape Henlopen, DE |
|      | Sept 11 [13] | *Betsey Richards* | Sch | W | N slope of the Delaware Breakwater |
|      | Sept 11 [16] | *Forrester* | Brig | S | Near Fenwick Island, DE |
|      | Nov 30 (p) | *Enoch Turley* | PB | S | Off Indian River Inlet, DE |
| 1844 | Apr 13 | *Jno. M. Clayton* | Sch | CA | "Abreast of Cape Henry light," VA |
|      | Sept 2 | *Banner* | Sch | S | On Joe Flogger Shoal, Delaware Bay |
|      | Oct 19 | *Edward Prebble* | Brig | S | On Wreck Island, VA |
|      | Oct 21 | *David Rogers* | Sch | S | On Joe Flogger Shoal, Delaware Bay |
|      | Oct 21 [30] | *Walter* | Ship | S | Joe Flogger Shoal, Delaware Bay (also given as Indian River Beach, DE) |
|      | Dec 11 | *Samuel Ingham* | Sch | S | On "the Dry Isaacs to the southward of Smith's Island," VA |
| 1845 | Jan 13 | *Mail* | Sch | S | Near Cape Charles, VA |
|      | Jan 31 | *Candace* | Sch | F | Machipongo Shoal, VA |
|      | June 5 | *Emilee (Emilie)* | Bark | W | 36° 45' N, 75° 40' W |
|      | July 25 | *Jane and Rachel* | Slp | S | On Cape Charles, VA |
|      | Oct 4 | *Globe* | Bark | S | 9 miles S of Cape Henry, VA |
|      | Oct 22 | *Two Brothers* [Fr.] | Sch | S | On Delaware Breakwater |
|      | Nov 21 | *Four Brothers* | Sch | S | On "Watchaprig Bar" N of Hog Island, VA |
|      | Dec 25 | *Mary* | Sch | S | Stony Point, DE |
| 1846 | Jan 14 | *Nancy Jane* | Brig | F | On beach opposite Berlin, MD |
|      | Jan 17 | *Joseph Turner* | Sch | S | "Half a mile inside of Cape Henlopen" |
|      | Jan 18 | *James T. Hatfield* | Sch | S | 30 miles S of Cape Henlopen, DE |
|      | Feb 6 (p) | *Hannibal* | Sch | S | On Hog Island, VA |
|      | Feb 16 | *Democrat* | Sch | A | Near Smith Island, VA |
|      | Mar 16 | *Susannah and Phoebe* | Slp | S | Metomkin Beach, Accomack County, VA |
|      | Apr 8 | *Paul Jones* | Sch | S | 4 miles S of Cape Henry, VA |
|      | May 7 | *United States* | Sch | S | On the outer point of Cape Henlopen, DE |
|      | May 19 (p) | *Thaddeus* | Sch | S | On the Ice Breaker, near Lewes, DE |
|      | June 13 | *John M. Clayton* | Sch | Cap | Wilmington, DE |
|      | Sept 8 | *Walter R. Jones* | Brig | S | 1 mile S of Smith Island Lighthouse, VA |
|      | Sept 9 | *J. R. Sands* | Sch | S | Near Cape Henry, VA |
|      | Sept 9 [10] | *James R. Marks* | Sch | S | 2 miles S of Cape Henlopen, DE |
|      | Sept 9 [10] | *Olive Branch* | Slp | S | On the outer bar near Lewes, DE |
|      | Sept 13 (p) | *Harrisburg* | Brig | S | 4 miles S of Lewes, DE |
|      | Sept 15 | *Caucassian* | Sch | S | On Cape Henry, VA |
|      | Sept 18 | *Edward Adams* | Brig | S | Bar W side of Delaware Bay near Mispillion Light |
|      | Sept 18 | *Edward Blake* | Brig | S | Bar W side of Delaware Bay near Mispillion Light |
|      | Sept 18 | *Genius* | Brig | S | Bar W side of Delaware Bay near Mispillion Light |
|      | Oct 13 | *New Harbour* | Sch | F | Off Cape Henry, VA |
|      | Oct 27 | *Emma Louisa* | Sch | S&F [R] | In 7 fathoms, mouth of Chincoteague Inlet, VA |
|      | Nov 6 | *Mary Ann* | Sch | S | Willoughby's Point, VA |
|      | Nov 6 | *Pacific* | Sch | S | 20 miles S of Cape Henry, VA |
|      | Nov 6 [9] | *Solon* | Sch | S | 12 miles S of Berlin and Green Run Inlet, MD |
|      | Nov 27 | *Blanchard* | Brig | S | Hog Island, VA |
|      | Dec 16 | *Dahlia* | Brig | S | Cape Henry, VA |
|      | Dec 17 [18] | *Elizabeth* | Sch | S | "Afore the Mole" near Lewes, DE |

| Date | | Vessel | Type | Manner | Location |
|---|---|---|---|---|---|
| | Dec 18 | *Chattahoochee* | Brig | S | Foot of the causeway opposite Lewes, DE |
| | Dec 18 [19] | *Patuxent* | Sch | F | At Delaware Breakwater |
| 1847 | May 12–13 | *Grand Turk* | Brig | W | Near Cape Henlopen, DE |
| | July 26 | *Fair Play* | Sch | W | Cape Henlopen, DE |
| | Sept 14 | *Director* | U | W | Delaware harbor |
| 1848 | Jan (ca.) | *Reefer* | Sch | L | On Joe Flogger Shoal, Delaware Bay |
| | Apr 28 | *Edwards* | Ship | W | Cape Henlopen, DE |
| | Apr 28 | *Mary F. Lutherrus* | U | F | 15 miles NE of Cape Henlopen Light, DE |
| | June 28 | *Emiline* | Sch | S&F | On Hog Island, VA |
| 1850 | Feb 20 | *Antelope* | StP | S | On Hog Island, VA |
| | June 26 | *Mountaineer* | StP | S | Cape Henlopen, DE |
| 1851 | Dec | *John* | Bark | S | At Hog Island, VA |
| 1852 | May 26 | *Chincilla* | Brig | S | "6 miles below Fassitt's Ocean House nearly opposite Berlin, MD" |
| | Aug 29 | Unidentified | HBrig | F | 6 fathoms "near the Ledge" off Lewes, DE |
| 1853 | Jan 13 [?] | *J. W. Concklin* | Sch | Cap&S | Near Lewes, DE |
| | Jan 27 | Unidentified | PB | F | 38° 10' N, 74° W |
| | Feb 19 | *Champion* | Brig | S | On Chincoteague Shoal, VA |
| | Feb 19 | *Edwin Johnson* | Bark | S | Near the breakwater at Lewes, DE |
| | Feb 24 | *Mary L. Balch* | Sch | S | On Chincoteague Shoal, VA |
| | Apr 14 (p) | *John Franklin* | Sch | Cap&S | Fenwick (Phoenix) Island, DE |
| | May 2 (ca.) | *Ceylon* | Sch | S | Near Cape Henry, VA |
| | May 24 | *Columbia* | Sch | C [2] | 7 miles off Sinepuxent, MD |
| | June 4 | *General Hersey* | Sch | S | At the point of Cape Henlopen, DE |
| | June 4 | *Hannah Clarke* | Sch | S | At the point of Cape Henlopen, DE |
| | June 4 | *James and Lucy* | Sch | S | At the point of Cape Henlopen, DE |
| | June 19 | *Bladen* | StP | S | On Chincoteague Shoal, VA |
| | Oct 22 | *Harward* | Bark | S | On Wachapreague Shoal, VA |
| | Oct 29 [31] | *Buena Vista* | Brig | S | Inside Cape Henlopen, DE |
| | Nov 13 [15] | *Charlotte* | Brig | S&F | Delaware Breakwater |
| | Nov 17 | *Albany Packet* | Sch | W | Near Indian River, DE |
| | Nov 28 | *Eliza* | Bark | S | Near Cape Henry, VA |
| | Nov 29 | *Delhi* | Brig | S | Near Delaware Breakwater |
| | Dec 23 | *H. S. Bradley* | Bark | S | Brandywine Shoal, Delaware Bay |
| | Dec 23 | *Patrick Henry* | Brig | S | At Delaware Breakwater |
| | Dec 23 | *Matagorda* | Bark | S | Near Cape Henlopen, DE |
| 1854 | Apr 14–17 | *Lenity* | Sch | S | Lewes, DE |
| | Apr 14–17 | *Octavia* | Sch | S | Lewes, DE |
| | July 11 | *Craveiro* | Sch | S | Opposite Fenwick Island, near Berlin, MD |
| | Oct 23 | *Hibernia* | Ship | S | 3 miles S of Indian River, DE |
| | Oct 2 | *Mattapony* | Sch | F | "On the ice-breaker . . . at the [Delaware] breakwater" |
| | Oct 30 | *Eastern Belle* | Bark | S | On Cape Henry, VA |
| | Nov 13 | Unidentified | Brig | F | Off Cape Henry, VA |
| | Dec 27 | *Mary Jane* | Sch | S | Lynnhaven Bay, VA |
| | — | *Mary Turcan* | Sch? | F | Approximately 36 miles E of VA-NC border |
| 1855 | Jan 5 | *Osceola* | Brig | S | Fenwick Island |
| | Jan 22 | Unidentified | Sch | Cap | 12 miles SE of Chincoteague, VA |
| | Jan 22 | Unidentified | U | Cap | 15 miles NNW of Cape Henlopen, DE |
| | Jan 25 | *Charles S. Olden* | Bark | S | 5 miles S of Fenwick Island |
| | Jan 25 | *Elenor* | Brig | S | 43 miles N of Fenwick Island |
| | Feb 9–10 | *Blythewood* | Bark | S | On the West Flats, below Hawk's Nest Shoal, near Lewes, DE |

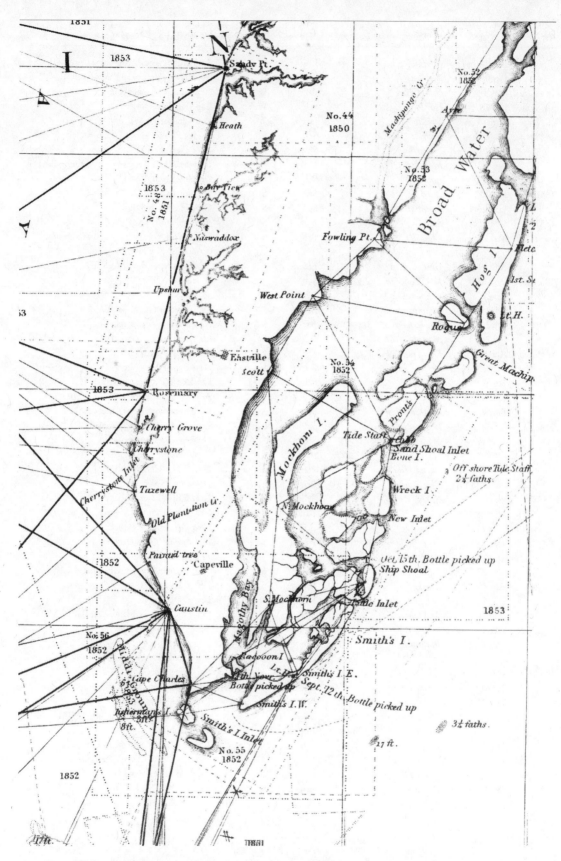

Detail from an 1855 U.S. Coast Survey chart showing the barrier islands of Virginia (author's collection)

| Date | | Vessel | Type | Manner | Location |
|---|---|---|---|---|---|
| | Feb 10–11 | Selah (or Selax) | Sch | S | "Outside of [the] Pitch, Cape Henlopen" |
| | Feb 14 | Lejok | Sch | L | On Cape Henlopen, DE |
| | Feb 21 | Autumn | Sch | S | On Indian River Bar, DE |
| | Feb 23 | Leo | Sch | S | Willoughby Point, Chesapeake Bay, VA |
| | Mar (p) | William Wirt | Ship | S | Near Cape Henry, VA |
| | Mar 10 | Julia Payson | Brig | S | Cape Henry, VA |
| | Mar 11 | Alcyona | Sch | S | Near Chincoteague, VA |
| | Mar 12 | Shibboleth | Brig | F | 36° 30′ N, 72° W |
| | Mar 14 | Unidentified | Ship | S | Indian River Inlet, DE |
| | Apr (p) | C. L. Allen | Sch | S | 15 miles S of Cape Henry, VA |
| | Apr 9 | Unidentified | U | Cap | 45 miles ENE of Chincoteague, VA |
| | May 5 | Vanus | Brig | C [3] | Off the Delaware capes |
| | May 11 | Adrian | Sch | C [4] | Delaware Bay |
| | May 12 | Little Tom | Sch | C [5] | Off Bombay Hook, Delaware Bay |
| | Sept 22 | Porpoise | Brigt | S | North Beach, Assateague, MD |
| | Sept 23 | John M. Clayton | U | F | Off the breakwater at Lewes, DE |
| | Oct 2 | Queen | Sch | AS | Off the Delaware capes |
| | Oct 3 | Commodore Stewart | Brig | S | Cape Henlopen, DE |
| | Oct 7 (p) | Charles Edwards | Brig | S | Cape Henlopen, DE |
| | Oct 20 | Lion | U | L | Hog Island, VA |
| | Dec 23 | Catherine H. Bacon | Sch | S | Assateague Island, MD |
| | Dec 30 | Mecklenberg | Sch | W [R?] | Near Chincoteague, VA |
| | — | Arcturus | Brig | F | SE of Cape Henlopen, DE |
| | — | Energy | Sch | F | At the breakwater, Lewes, DE |
| | — | J. R. Folsom | Ship | F | 12 fathoms off Hen and Chickens Shoal, DE |
| | — | Merak | Sch | S | Outside the Delaware capes |
| | — | William | Ship | S | Hen and Chickens Shoal, DE |
| 1856 | Jan 5 | Clotilda | Sch | S | Inside Cape Henlopen, DE |
| | Jan 5 | Cropper | PB | S | Atlantic coast of Maryland |
| | Jan 5 | Eliza Manning | Sch | S | In Lynnhaven Bay, VA |
| | Jan 5 | Fish Hawk | Sch | S | In Lynnhaven Bay, VA |
| | Jan 5 | John Silliman | Sch | S | Inside Cape Henlopen, DE |
| | Jan 5 | Unidentified | Sch | S | Atlantic coast of Maryland |
| | Jan 9 | John C. Dobbin | Sch | S | Near Indian River Inlet, DE |
| | Jan 17 | Don Nicholas | Sch | W | Off the Virginia coast |
| | Jan 18 | Unidentified (2) | Sch | S | 20 miles below the Virginia capes |
| | Jan 28 | Mecklenberg | Sch | S | 10 miles N of Chincoteague, VA |
| | Feb 9 | Leon Racer | Bark | S [R] | Near Cape Henry, VA |
| | Feb 16 | Arcadian | Brig | S | Assateague Island, at Green Run, MD |
| | Mar 28 | Mary Warren | Sch | S | Wachapreague Shoal, 15 miles N of Hog Island, VA |
| | Mar 30 | J. M. Warren | Sch | L | Near Cape Henry, VA |
| | Apr | Sidney | Sch | C [6] | Off the mouth of the Delaware |
| | Apr | Sylvina | Brig | L | Near Fenwick Island |
| | May 22 | Shoal Water | Sch | L | Near Cape Henry, VA |
| | May 28 | Henry T. Wood | Sch | S | Off Cape Charles, VA |
| | June 14 | E. I. Dupont | StP | S | Near Indian River, DE |
| | July 10 | Selah Brig | Brig | W | In Delaware Bay |
| | July 13 | W. P. Moore | Bark | S | Near Cape Henry, VA |
| | July 24 | Red Jacket | Tug | F | Off Chincoteague, VA |
| | Aug | John Crier | Ship | S | Fenwick Island |
| | Sept 1 | Glenview | Sch | S | Near Cape Henry, VA |
| | Sept 1 | Maria Perkins | Brig | S | At Cape Henry, VA |

| Date | | Vessel | Type | Manner | Location |
|------|------|--------|------|--------|----------|
| | Sept 8 (ca.) | T. H. Hughes | Sch | S | 12 miles S of Cape Henry, VA |
| | Sept 8 (ca.) | Washington | Sch | S | 12 miles S of Cape Henry, VA |
| | Sept 8 (ca.) | Wasp | Brig | S | 4 miles S of Cape Henry, VA |
| | Sept 8 (ca.) | Monmouth | Sch | S | 12 miles from the Virginia capes |
| | Sept 8 (ca.) | John Allmack | Sch | S | 22 miles S of Cape Henry, VA |
| | Sept 27 (ca.) | Mecca | Sch | S [R?] | Isaac Shoal, N of Cape Charles, VA |
| | Oct 16 | City of Savannah | StP | F | Near Cape Henry, VA |
| | Oct 18 | John Randolph | Sch | S | 18 miles S of Cape Henry, VA |
| | Nov 21 | Rattlesnake | Sch | W | Near Cape Henlopen, DE |
| | Dec 8 | H. W. Godfrey | Sch | AS | 37° N, 73° W |
| | Dec 20 | Jersey | Ship | S | Wash Woods, 30 miles S of Cape Henry, VA |
| | Dec 27 | Whitehall | Brig | AS | 38° 07' N, 72° 15' W |
| | — | Kate Helen | Sch | S | Cape Henry, VA |
| 1857 | Jan 28 | Herschel | Ship | S [R?] | On Willoughby Bar, Chesapeake Bay, VA |
| | Jan | Trade Wind | Sch | F | Delaware Breakwater |
| | Feb (p) | Georgia | Ship | S | Near Cape Henry, VA |
| | Feb (p) | Jersey | Ship | S | Wash Woods, 30 miles S of Cape Henry, VA |
| | Feb 2 | Lavacca | Brig | Ice | Delaware Breakwater |
| | Feb 2 | Oregon | Brig | AS&I | At the point of Cape Henlopen, DE |
| | Mar (p) | William D. Shurtz | Sch | AS | Off Cape Henry, VA |
| | Apr 27 (p) | Volant | U | L | Eastern Shore of Maryland |
| | May 21 (p) | D. C. Foster | Sch | W | Off Delaware Breakwater |
| | May 21 (p) | Unidentified | Boat | Cap | Off Delaware Breakwater |
| | June 30 | Gosport | Ship | S | Near Cape Henry, VA |
| | Sept 12 | Penobscot (ex-Norfolk) | StP | F | Near Hog Island, 10 miles S of Chincoteague |
| | Sept 12–13 | John H. Rhoads | Brig | S | 5 miles S of Cape Henry, VA |
| | Oct 4 | Jane Ingraham | Sch | S | On Sand Shoal, VA |
| | Nov 13 | Nebraska | Sch | F | Horseshoe Shoal, Chesapeake Bay, VA |
| | Dec 5 | Eva Dorathey | Ship | S | 3 miles S of Cape Henry, VA |
| | Dec 9 | Gratta | Bark | S | On Cape Henry, VA |
| | — | Amazon | StP | S | Cape Henlopen, DE |
| | — | Wide Awake | Sch | S | Lewes, DE |
| | — | Unidentified | Sch | S | Assateague Island, Green Run Inlet, MD |
| 1858 | Feb 16 | Ella | Sch | C [7] | Lewes, DE |
| | Aug 29 | Eureka | Brig | F | Off Sinepuxent, MD |
| | Oct 29 | A. J. Ward | Sch | Cap | Off Chincoteague, VA |
| | Nov 3 | Wissahiccon | Sch | S | On Cape Henry, VA |
| | Nov 13 | James Lawrence | Sch | S | Brandywine Shoal, Delaware Bay |
| | Nov 24 | Matilda E. Webb | Sch | S | On Dawson Shoal, VA |
| 1859 | Mar 26 (ca.) | Octavia | Bark | S | 25 miles S of Norfolk, VA |
| | May 10 | Eliza E. Parker | Sch | W | North side of Delaware Breakwater |
| | Dec 20 (ca.) | Unidentified | Ship | S | South of Cape Henry, VA |
| 1860 | Feb 5 (p) | Frank Day | Sch | S | Near Lewes, DE |
| | Feb 16 (p) | N. Smith | Sch | C [8] | Off Chincoteague, VA |
| | Feb 16 (p) | B. S. Johnson | Sch | C [9] | Off Chincoteague, VA |
| | Mar 19 | Swan | Bark | S | At Cape Henry, VA |
| | Apr 30 | Roger Stewart | Ship | F | 37° 10' N, 71° 45' W |
| | Aug 8 | John McMakin | StW | B | Lewes, DE |
| 1861 | Feb 9 | Victory | Clip | W | Near Cape Henry, VA |
| | Oct 4 | Unidentified (2) | Slp | B-WL | Near Chincoteague, VA |
| | Oct 5 | Unidentified | Sch | B-WL | Cockrell Creek, Chincoteague, VA |
| | Oct 27–28 | Unidentified | Sch | B-WL | Chincoteague Creek, VA |
| | Oct 27–28 | Unidentified (2) | Slp | B-WL | Chincoteague Creek, VA |

| Date | | Vessel | Type | Manner | Location |
|---|---|---|---|---|---|
| | — | *Juniper* | U | S | Winter Quarter Shoals |
| 1862 | Feb 25 | *R. B. Forbes* | StS | S&B | 25 miles below Cape Henry, VA |
| | May 4 | CSS *General Beauregard* | Sch | B-WL | Ragged Island, VA |
| | Aug 24 | USS *Henry Andrew* | StS | S | 15 miles S of Cape Henry, VA |
| | Aug 30 | *Clifton* | Sch | S | On Cape Henlopen, DE |
| | Nov 7 | *Amelia* | U | S | Lewes, DE |
| | Nov 7 | *Antietam* | Bark | S | Lewes, DE |
| | Nov 7 | *Kedron* | Sch | S | Lewes, DE |
| | Nov 7 | *Volant* | Sch | S | Lewes, DE |
| 1863 | Jan 2 | *International* | Ship | S | Near Hog Island, VA |
| | Jan 22 (p) | *Christiana Knight* | Sch | S | Below Lewes, DE |
| | Jan 22 (p) | *Deliverance* | Sch | S | Below Lewes, DE |
| | Jan 22 (p) | *Greenland* | Sch | S | Below Lewes, DE |
| | Jan 22 (p) | *James Tilton* | Sch | S | Below Lewes, DE |
| | Jan 22 (p) | Unidentified | Sch | S | Below Lewes, DE |
| | Jan 22 | Unidentified | Sch | S | Outside of Cape Henlopen, DE |
| | Feb 12 | *Beronda* | Brig | S | On the point of Cape Henlopen, DE |
| | Apr 2 | USS *Alligator* | Sub | F | En route from Norfolk to Port Royal, SC |
| | Apr 4 | *Patroom* | StS | S | Delaware Breakwater |
| | May 4 (p) | Unidentified | Sch | S&F | Delaware Breakwater |
| | June 15 | *Umpire* | Brigt | B-WL | 37° 40' N, 70° 31' W |
| | June 19 | *Guiding Star* [Br] | Sch | S | Delaware Breakwater |
| | June 24 | USS *Sumpter* | StS | C [10] | 8.5 miles SSE of Smith Island Light, VA |
| | — | *John Wesley* | Sch | S | Hog Island, VA |
| 1864 | Jan 16 | *Thomas Swan* | StS | S | Cape Henry, VA |
| | Feb 11 | *G. M. Partridge* | Sch | S | Near Cape Henry, VA |
| | Mar 22 | *Alabama* | Sch | F | Inside of Cape Henry, VA |
| | Mar 22 | Unidentified | Sch | S | Cape Henry, VA |
| | Mar 30 | Unidentified | StS | F | 65 miles NE of Cape Henry, VA |
| | Apr 1 | *Fair Haven* | StS | S | Cape Henry, VA |
| | Apr 3 (p) | *Clara Ellen* | Sch | S | Near Lewes, DE |
| | Apr 3 (p) | *John Crystal* | Brig | C [11] | Near Lewes, DE |
| | Apr 3 (p) | *Richard Vaux* | Ship | C [12] | Near Lewes, DE |
| | Apr 3 (p) | *Sea Crest* | Ship | S [R] | Near Lewes, DE |
| | Apr 3 (p) | *Susan* | Brig | S | Lewes, DE |
| | Apr 3 | *Sea Witch* | Sch | S | 1½ miles from Lewes, DE |
| | Apr 6 (p) | *Maria Foss* | Sch | S | Lewes, DE |
| | Apr 6 (p) | *Orion* | Sch | S | Lewes, DE |
| | Apr 6 (p) | Unidentified | U | S | Lewes, DE |
| | Apr 6 (p) | *Ravenna* | Barkt | S [R?] | At Cape Henry, VA |
| | July 8 | *Goloconda* | Bark | B-WL | 37° 28' N, 72° W |
| | July 9 | *Margaret Y. Davis* | Sch | B-WL | 36° 43' N, 74° W |
| | July 9 | *Greenland* | Bark | B-WL | 36° 56' N, 74° 51' W |
| | July 10 | *Electric Spark* | StS | Sc-WL | Atlantic Ocean, 35 miles off Maryland |
| | July 10 | *General Berry* | Bark | Sc-WL | Atlantic Ocean, 35 miles off Maryland |
| | July 10 | *Zelinda* | Bark | B-WL | 37° 33' N, 74° 20' W |
| | Dec 31 | Unidentified | U | F | Off Delaware Lightship, DE |
| 1865 | Jan 15 | *Melville* | StS | U | 38° N, 74° W |
| | Aug 22 | *Francis* | Sch | S | Joe Flogger Shoal, Delaware Bay |
| | Aug 24 | Unidentified | Sch | S | Brandywine Shoal, Delaware Bay |
| | Nov 25 | *Nellie Pentz* | StP | F | Lynnhaven Bay, VA |
| 1866 | Jan 7 (p) | Unidentified | Sch | F | Off Delaware capes |
| | Jan 18 (p) | Unidentified | U | F | 38° 10' N, 74° 30' W |

| Date | | Vessel | Type | Manner | Location |
|---|---|---|---|---|---|
| | Apr 11 | *Sally Gay* | Sch | S | Delaware Breakwater |
| | Oct 14 | Unidentified | Sch | S | 12 miles S of Fenwick Island, DE |
| | Oct 30 | *Fanny* | Sch | S | Joe Flogger Shoal, Delaware Bay |
| | Dec 31 (p) | *Cortes* | StS | S | Delaware Breakwater |
| 1867 | Jan 1 | *Canton Briton* | U | F | Delaware Breakwater |
| | Mar 21–22 | *Aurora* [It] | Bark | S | Delaware Breakwater |
| | Mar 21–22 | *Schultz* | Bark | S | Delaware Breakwater |
| | Nov 11 | USLHS *General Putnam* | StP | C [13] | 1 mile above Newcastle, DE |
| | — | *Croton* | StP | C [14] | Cape Henry, VA |
| 1868 | July 29 | *Mary E. Kellinger* | Sch | F | On Middle Ground, in 3 fathoms, Chesapeake Bay |
| | Aug 15 (p) | *E. L. Marts* | Sch | S | Metomkin Shoals, VA |
| | Oct 1 | *Blanche* | Sch | S | 12 miles S of Cape Henry, VA |
| | — | Unidentified | Sch | S | 15 miles S of Cape Henry, VA |
| 1869 | Jan 11 | *Boaz* | Brig | S | 2 miles S of Cape Henry, VA, in 16 feet |
| | Jan 11 | *Busy* | Bark | S | South Cape Henry, VA |
| | Jan 15 | *Antelope* | Sch | S | Near Cape Henry, VA |
| | Aug 31 (p) | *Ann Eliza* | Ship | S [R?] | 6 miles N of Cape Charles, VA |
| | Sept 27 | *Jessie L. Leach* | Sch | S | At Cape Henry, VA |
| | Dec 9 (p) | Unidentified (2) | Sch | S | Fenwick Island, DE |
| 1870 | Feb 24 | *J. W. Everman* | Sch | S | On the point of Cape Henlopen, DE |
| | Feb 27 | *Conquerall* | Brig | S | Joe Flogger Shoal, Delaware Bay |
| | Mar 29 (p) | Unidentified (2) | Sch | S | Indian River, DE |
| | Mar 29 | *Marlins* | Brig | S | Lewes, DE |
| | Apr 15 | *Carrie M. Rich* | Sch | S&F | Indian River, DE |
| | Apr | *Crest of the Wave* | Clip | W | Wreck Island, 15 miles N of Cape Henry, VA |
| | May 27 | *J. E. Simmons* | Sch | S | Cape Henlopen, DE |
| | June 1 (p) | *Varuna* | Sch | S | Joe Flogger Shoal, Delaware Bay |
| | Sept 2 | Unidentified | HBrig | S | Joe Flogger Shoal, Delaware Bay |
| | Sept 18 | *Rollerson* | Brig | W | Outside of Delaware Breakwater |
| | Nov 3 | *White Cloud* | Barkt | W | On Delaware Breakwater |
| | — | *Bar Cricket* | Bark | W | Cobb Island, VA |
| | — | *Henry Lee* | Sch | W | Cobb Island, VA |
| 1871 | Jan 19 | *Redington* | Sch | S&B | South of Cape Henry, VA |
| | Jan 21 | *Black Brothers* | Bark | S&F | On Winter Quarter Shoals, VA |
| | Mar 22 (p) | *Lizzie Watson* | U | S | ½ mile off Joe Flogger Shoal, Delaware Bay |
| | Apr 8 (p) | *Mary L. Tyler* | Sch | S | 1½ miles S of Fenwick Island |
| | May 19 (p) | *Ocean Bird* | Sch | AS | 25 miles from Cape Henlopen, DE |
| | Nov 25 (p) | Unidentified | Sch | S | Scott's Ocean House, Worcester Co., MD |
| | Dec 5 | *Village Queen* | Sch | S | On the point of Cape Henlopen, DE |
| 1872 | Feb | *Wando* | StP | F | 40 miles S of Delaware Lightship |
| | Mar 2 | *Rose* | Sch | S | Near Chincoteague Island, VA |
| | Mar 2 | Unidentified | U | S | Near Green Run Inlet, MD |
| | Mar | *Huffman* | Sch | S | Off Coffin's Beach, Worcester Co., MD |
| | Mar | Unidentified (2) | U | S | Off Coffin's Beach, Worcester Co., MD |
| | Mar | Unidentified (3) | U | S | Scott's Ocean House, Worcester Co., MD |
| | Oct 8 (p) | *William Wallace* | Sch | C [15] | Off Lewes, DE |
| | Oct 24 (p) | *John Watts* | Ship | W | Off Cape Henlopen, DE |
| | Oct 25 | *Midway* (*Medway*) | Bark | S | On Hen and Chickens Shoal, DE |
| | Oct | *John Sidney* | Ship | S | 10 miles S of Cape Henlopen, DE |
| 1873 | Jan 5 | *Morning Light* | Brig | S | Cape Henlopen, DE |
| | Mar 5 | *Maggie McDonnell* | Sch | S | On Indian River Inlet, DE |
| | Mar 8 | *Horace Adler* | Sch | F | Off Chincoteague, VA |

| Date | | Vessel | Type | Manner | Location |
|------|---|--------|------|--------|----------|
| | Mar 20 | *Jene Sassen* | Bark | S | Northern point of Indian River Inlet, DE |
| | Aug 27 | *Philadelphia* | StP | S | Hog Island, VA |
| | Sept 17 (p) | *Jason* | Sch | S | Brandywine Shoal, Delaware Bay |
| | Oct 9 | *J. Polledo* | U | S | Hen and Chickens Shoal, DE |
| | Nov 23 | *Five Fathom Light* | U | S | Fenwick Island Shoal, DE |
| 1874 | Feb 17 (p) | Unidentified | Brig | S | 18 miles S of Fenwick Island, DE |
| | Apr 25 | *Ocean Belle* | Brig | S | Brandywine Shoal, Delaware Bay |
| | Apr 25 | *Sea Breeze* | Sch | F | On Broadkiln Bar, DE |
| | Apr 25 | *W. B. Morgan* | Sch | S | Mispillion Creek, DE |
| 1875 | Jan 2 (p) | *E. C. Boyce* | U | S | Lower end of the Delaware coast |
| | Jan 22 | *C. E. Scammell* | Sch | S | 3 miles N of False Cape LSS, VA |
| | Jan | *Cienfuegos* | Bark | F | 2 miles S and 4 miles E of Cape Henlopen |
| | Feb 5 (ca.) | *Sabra* | Brig | S | Below False Capes, VA |
| | Feb 27 (p) | Unidentified | Slp | Ice | Delaware Breakwater |
| | Mar 13 (p) | *Ellen Holgate* | Sch | C [16] | Reedy Island Light, Delaware River |
| | May 8 | *S. I. Wines* | Sch | C [17] | 14 miles SSE of Chincoteague Light |
| | Oct 28 | *Eugene Borca* | Sch | S | SW point of Chincoteague Shoal, VA |
| | Nov 2 | *Mary E. Parks* | Sch | C [18] | 8 miles due E of Sinepuxent, MD |
| | Nov 11 | *Thomas C. Worrell* | Sch | C [19] | Winter Quarter Shoals, Assateague Island |
| | Dec 7 | *N. C. Price* | Sch | S | 1/2 mile S of Assateague Beach LSS, VA |
| | Dec 18 | *Anthony Kelley* | Sch | S | South of Hog Island, VA |
| | — | *Rambler* | SlpY | S | Abreast of Winter Quarter Shoals |
| 1876 | Jan 12 | *Aeolus* | Sch | S | S of Hog Island Shoal, VA |
| | Feb 2 | *Henna* [Nor] | Bark | S | Summers Shoal, SE of Overfalls, Delaware Bay |
| | Feb 2 | Unidentified (5) | U | S | Cape Henlopen, DE |
| | Mar 18 (p) | *Ann E. Cake* | Sch | S | On the point of Cape Henlopen, DE |
| | Aug 3 | *A. J. Pope* [Ger] | Bark | S | 15 miles S of Cape Henlopen, DE |
| | Sept 17 | *Charles P. Sinnekson* | Sch | L [R?] | 6 miles S of Cape Henlopen, DE |
| | Sept 19–20 | Unidentified (1+) | U | S | Western shore of Indian River, DE |
| | Sept 19–20 | Unidentified | U | S | Indian River Inlet, DE |
| | Oct 16 | *John S. Lee* | Sch | S | Dawson Shoal, Wachapreague Inlet, VA |
| | Dec 1 | *Ocean Bell* | Sch | U | Green Run Inlet, Assateague Island, MD |
| 1877 | Jan 7 | *Montgomery* | StS | C [20] | Off the Delaware capes |
| | Jan 12 | *Alice* | StS | B | At wharfside, Chincoteague, VA |
| | Jan 20 | *Delphin* | Sch | S | Cobb Island, VA |
| | Jan 20 | *Lella* (*Lilla*) | Bark | S | 3 1/2 miles S of Cape Henry Lighthouse, VA |
| | Jan 23 | *T. A. Nicholls* | StC | Ice | "In the Brandywine" |
| | Jan 27 | *George T. Treadwell* | Sch | S | Chincoteague Shoal, VA |
| | Feb 19 | *M. E. Demer* | Sch | C [21] | 36° 40′ N, 74° 72′ W |
| | Mar 26 | *Robert S. Graham* | Sch | S | 5 miles off Ocean City LSS, MD |
| | Mar 26 | *Galathea* | Bark | S | On S end of Smith Island, VA |
| | Mar 26 | *Pentzer* [Nor] | Bark | S [R?] | At Cape Henry, VA |
| | Mar | *Matilda* [Br] | Sch | S [R?] | Cape Henry, VA |
| | Mar | *Winchester* | Ship | S [R?] | Cape Henry, VA |
| | Apr 9 | *Sirena* [It] | Bark | S | Lewes, DE |
| | Apr 13 (p) | *Walton* | Sch | W | On Delaware Breakwater |
| | Apr 25 | *William P. Clyde* | StS | S | Chincoteague Point, VA |
| | May 2 | *Mary Wood* | Sch | S | Rose Island Bar, VA |
| | May 20 | *Armenia Bartlett* | Sch | S | Little Machipongo Bar, VA |
| | May | Unidentified | Bark | S | Sandy Shoal, VA |
| | Sept 7 | *Vashti Sharp* | Sch | S | Fenwick Island (Phoenix Island, Delaware Bay) |
| | Oct 22 | *Alveretia* | U | W | Cape Charles, VA |
| | Nov (p) | Unidentified (6) | U | U | Delaware Breakwater |

| Date | | Vessel | Type | Manner | Location |
|---|---|---|---|---|---|
| | Nov 1 | *Harriet Thomas* | Sch | U | Virginia Beach, VA |
| | Nov 18 | *James Anderson* | Sch | S | 1 mile ESE of Cedar Island LSS, VA |
| | Nov 25 | *Ossipee* | Brig | S | 7½ miles S of Assateague Beach LSS, at Ragged Point, VA |
| | Nov 25 | *Frank Jameson* (*Johnson?*) | Sch | S | 100 yards E of Smith Island LSS, VA |
| | Dec 3 | *Winged Racer* | Sch | S | 1½ miles ESE of Cobb Island LSS, VA |
| 1878 | Jan 1 | *Montevue* | Sch | S | South end of Wreck Island, VA |
| | Jan 3 | *R. K. Vaughn* | Sch | S | 3 miles S of Fenwick Island Light |
| | Jan 4 | *Francisco Bella Gamba* [It] | Bark | S | ½ mile N of Cape Henry LSS, VA |
| | Jan 6 | *J. J. Spencer* | Sch | S | 1½ miles SE of Hog Island LSS, VA |
| | Jan 23 | *Southern Belle* | Bark | S | 1½ miles S of Dam Neck Mills LSS, VA |
| | Feb 21 | *St. Bernardo* [It] | Ship | S | Lower Reedy Island, Delaware River |
| | Mar 7 | *North Point* [Jam] | StS | S | ½ miles S of Ragged Point, Assateague LSS |
| | Apr 6 | *Sophia Wilson* | Sch | C [22] | 7 miles ESE of Hog Island, VA |
| | Oct 22 | *Alveretia* | U | S | Cape Charles, VA |
| | Oct 22 | *Spray* | U | S | Fisherman's Inlet, VA |
| | Oct 22 | *A. S. Davis* (*A. C. Davis*) | Ship | S | 8 miles S of Cape Henry, VA, LSS No. 2 |
| | Oct 22 | *Emily G. Ireland* | Sch | S | Delaware Breakwater |
| | Oct 22 | *John Barbour* | Ship | S | Delaware Breakwater |
| | Oct 22 | *Lilla Rich* | Sch | S | Delaware Breakwater |
| | Oct 22 | *Long Branch* | Brig | S | Joe Flogger Shoal, Delaware Bay |
| | Oct 22 | *Stal* | Bark | S | Delaware Breakwater |
| | Oct 22 | *W. G. Fowler* | Tug | W | Below Reedy Island, Delaware Bay |
| | Oct 22 | *Wm. G. Boulton* | Tug | F | Dan Barbour Shoal, Delaware Bay |
| | Dec 1 | *Peerless* | Sch | S | 5 miles WSW of Smith Island LSS, VA |
| | Dec 2 | *Flora Curtis* | Sch | S | 3 miles from Assateague Beach LSS, VA |
| | Dec 23 | *Emma G. Edwards* | Sch | S | 2 miles S of Turner's Shoal, VA |
| | Dec 28 | *Tunis* | StS | S | 1 mile S of Cape Henry LSS, VA |
| | — | *Francis French* | Sch? | S | Off Green Run Inlet, MD |
| | — | *Rebecca Knight* | Sch? | S | Off Green Run Inlet, MD |
| 1879 | Feb 18 | *Moses Day* | Brig | S | Green Run Inlet, Assateague Island, MD |
| | Mar 2 | *Admiral* | Bark | S | 1 mile S of False Cape, VA |
| | Mar 3 | *James M. Vance* | Sch | S | 2½ miles N of Seatack LSS, VA |
| | July 26 | *John Rose* | Sch | S | 2½ miles N of Green Run Inlet, MD |
| | Aug 18 | *Stephen Bennett* | Sch | Cap | Off Chincoteague, VA |
| | Oct 6 | *Babel H. Irons* | Sch | F | Delaware Breakwater |
| | Oct 6 | *Bessie Morris* | Sch | F | Delaware Breakwater |
| | Oct 6 | *E. B. Wheaton* | Sch | F | Delaware Breakwater |
| | Oct 6 | *Firenze* | Bark | S | Delaware Breakwater |
| | Oct 6 | *Helen Rommell* | Sch | F | Delaware Breakwater |
| | Oct 6 | *Jesse Wilson* | Sch | F | Delaware Breakwater |
| | Oct 6 | *M. A. McGahan* | Sch | F | Delaware Breakwater |
| | Oct 6 | *M. E. Smith* | Sch | F | Delaware Breakwater |
| | Oct 6 | *Maggie McDonald* | Sch | F | Delaware Breakwater |
| | Oct 6 | *Matilda* | Brig | F | Delaware Breakwater |
| | Oct 6 | *W. G. Dearborn* | Sch | F | Delaware Breakwater |
| | Oct 19 | *Ellie Bodine* | Sch | W | 4½ miles S of Smith Island, VA |
| | Nov 3 | *W. E. Heard* | Bark | F | Due E of Cape Henry, VA |
| | Nov 8 | *Champion* | StP | C [23] | Off Cape Henlopen, in 14 fathoms, Loran 26849.2, 42735.9 |
| | Nov 21 | *Francis Burrett* | Sch | S [R] | 120 miles SW of Absecon Light, NJ, possibly in Virginia water |
| | Nov 26 | *Jason* | Bark | S | 1½ miles SE of Hog Island LSS, VA |

| Date | | Vessel | Type | Manner | Location |
|------|------|--------|------|--------|----------|
| | — | *E. A. Barnard* | Brig | S | 3½ miles N of Ocean City LSS, MD |
| 1880 | Jan 8 | *Alice Lee* | Brigt | S | 3½ miles S of Cedar Island LSS, VA |
| | Jan 11 | *Ada M. Hallock* | Sch | S | On or near Hog Island, VA |
| | Feb 2 | *Cho* | Brig | S | Broadkiln Bar, DE |
| | Feb 2 | *Quango* | Brig | S | Plumb Point Shoal, near Cape Henlopen |
| | Feb 8 | *Emma* | Slp | Ice | Off Chester Creek, in Delaware Bay |
| | May 9 | *Swiftsure* | StS | F | 4 miles S of Smith Island LSS, VA |
| | Aug 18 | *North Carolina* | Bark | S | ½ mile N of Little Island LSS, VA |
| | Aug 29 | *H. Houston* | Brig | F | 36° 57' N, 74° 20' W |
| | Sept 25 | *Woodruff Sims* | Sch | S | 1 mile S of Seatack LSS, VA |
| | Oct 22 | *Giambatista Primo* [It] | Bark | S | SE of Hog Island Shoal, VA |
| | Nov 5 | *Sandringham* | StS | S | 250 yards S of Cape Henry LSS, VA |
| | Nov 7 | *Sallie Coursey* | Sch | S | 4 miles SW of Smith Island LSS, VA |
| | Nov 14 | *John S. Higgins* | Sch | S | 1½ miles S of Cedar Island LSS, VA |
| | Dec 7 | *Robert W. Brown* | Sch | S | 2½ miles E of Cobb Island LSS, VA |
| | Dec 19 | *Madora Francis* | Sch | S | 3 miles SW of Fox Shoal off Assateague Beach |
| | Dec 26 | *Wanderer* | StP | C [24] | On the iron pier at Lewes, DE |
| | Dec 29 | *Elizabeth White* | Sch | S | Carter's Shoal, VA |
| | Dec 29 | *Elysia A.* | Sch | S | Dawson Shoal, VA |
| | — | *Peerless* | Sch | S | 5 miles SW of Smith Island LSS, VA |
| | — | *W. T. Harwood* (*Howard*) | Bark | S | At the iron pier at Lewes, DE |
| 1881 | Jan 20 | *Kwasind* (NB) | Bark | S | North end of Parramore Beach, VA |
| | Jan 28 | *D. Ellis* | Sch | S | Turner's Shoal, Chincoteague, VA |
| | Feb 10 | *Joanna H. Cann* (NS) | Bark | S | 2½ miles S of Seatack LSS, VA |
| | Feb 21 | *Dauntless* | Slp | S | Fox Shoal, Chincoteague Inlet, VA |
| | Mar 3 | *Syringa* | Bark | S | On outer bar, Green Run Inlet, MD |
| | June 9 | *Joseph and Franklin* | Sch | S | 2 miles N of Cape Henlopen LSS, DE |
| | July 11 | *Annie D. Merritt* | U | S | 2 miles N of Ocean City, MD |
| | Aug 8 | *William Allen* | Sch | S | Cedar Inlet, VA |
| | Sept 4 | *Scindia* | StS | S | Outer bar, S end Hog Island, VA |
| | Oct 5 | *Ada F. Crosby* | Bark | F | 37° 30' N, 72° 20' W |
| | Oct 9 | *Mary Ann* | Slp | S | Cobb Island, VA |
| | Oct 19 | *Zulu Chief* | Slp | S | Hog Island Bar, VA |
| | Oct 22 | *G. B. Claxom* | Slp | S | New Inlet Bar, near Cedar Island, VA |
| | Nov 4 | *John McDonald* | Sch | S | Carter's Bar, VA |
| | Nov | *Salas* [Br] | Brig | F | 38° 04' N, 74° 04' W |
| | Dec 9 | *George H. Chapman* | Slp | S | 4½ miles N of Hog Island LSS, VA |
| | Dec 14 | *Agustino C* [It] | Brig | S | On Smith Island Beach, VA |
| | Dec 19 | *George Washington* | Slp | S | On Hog Island, VA |
| | Dec 22 | *Carrie Hall Lister* | Sch | S | 1½ miles S of Cobb Island LSS, VA |
| 1882 | Jan 1 (ca.) | Unidentified | Brig | S | On Dawson Shoal, VA |
| | Jan 2 | *Jova Rycardo Boro* | Sch | S | 2 miles S of LSS No. 8, off Chincoteague, VA |
| | Jan 7 | *Albert Daily* | Sch | S | Smith Island, VA |
| | Jan 9 | *Sagitta* | Bark | S | Cobb Island Inlet, VA |
| | Jan 10 | *Sallie W. Kaye* | Sch | S | Fenwick Island |
| | Jan 21 | *Alfred* | Brig | F | Off the coast of Delaware |
| | Jan 24 | *Chancellor* | Sch | S | 1½ miles N of Green Run Inlet, MD |
| | Jan 24 | *Henrietta* | Sch | S | Wachapreague Inlet, near wreck of *Jova Rycardo Boro* |
| | Jan 31 | *Dolly Varden* | Sch | S | 3½ miles ENE of Assateague Beach LSS |
| | Feb 21 | *Dauntless* | Slp | S | 3½ miles SW of Assateague Beach LSS |
| | Mar 1 | *Hannah M. Lollis* (*Lollie*) | Sch | S | 1 mile E of Pope's Island LSS, MD |
| | Mar 23 | *Martha Collins* | Sch | S | 3½ miles N of Ocean City, MD |

| Date | | Vessel | Type | Manner | Location |
|---|---|---|---|---|---|
| | Apr 19 | *Josephine* | Sch | C [25] | Bend of the "Ice Breaker," Lewes, DE |
| | June 4 | *Maggie Bell* | U | S | Near LSS No. 7, Wallops Island, VA |
| | Sept 26 | *Katie Collins* | Sch | S | Boyd Shoal, Delaware Bay, inside channel |
| | Sept 27 | *W. N. Gesner* | Sch | F | 3 miles N of Mispillion Light, Delaware Bay |
| | Nov 3 | *Fourche* | Slp | S | Near Cape Charles, VA |
| | Nov 19 | *William L. White* | Sch | C [26] | ESE of Five Fathom Bank in 35 fathoms |
| | Nov 20 | *George White* | Sch | S | 1 mile NNW of Wachapreague LSS, VA |
| | Dec 3 | Unidentified | Ship | S [R?] | Cedar Island, VA |
| | Dec 4 | *Excelsior* | StS | C | Thimble Shoals, entrance to Chesapeake |
| | Dec 4 | *Maddalena Seconda* [It] | Bark | S | 1 mile NE of Wachapreague LSS, VA |
| | Dec 7 | *Anthea Godfrey* | StS | S [R?] | $3\frac{1}{2}$ miles SE of Cobb Island, VA |
| | Dec 30 | *Beston* | Sch | S | False Cape, 25 miles N of Cape Henlopen |
| 1883 | Jan 7 | *Albert Dailey* | Sch | S | 3 miles NE by E of Smith Island LSS, VA, 250 yards offshore |
| | Jan 8 | *Wyoming* | Sch | S | 5 miles N of Green Run Inlet LSS, MD |
| | Jan 9 | Unidentified | Scow | F | ESE of Chincoteague, VA |
| | Jan 9 | Unidentified | StS | F | Off Ocean City, MD |
| | Jan 10 | *Sallie W. Kaye* | Sch | S | 250 yards off shore, $5\frac{1}{2}$ miles N of Ocean City LSS, MD |
| | Jan 12 | *Julia Grant* (*Julia Grace*) | Sch | S | North of Green Run Inlet, MD |
| | Jan 12 | *Elizabeth M. Buehler* | Sch | S | North of Green Run Inlet, MD |
| | Jan 20 | *Alpin* | StS | S | $3\frac{1}{2}$ miles N of Green Run LSS, MD |
| | Feb 15 | *Minnie Hunter* | Bark | S | $\frac{1}{2}$ mile NE of Beacon Lt, Cape Henry, VA |
| | Mar 7 | *Worlverton* | Barkt | S | 5 miles SE of Assateague Beach LSS, Chincoteague, VA |
| | Mar 11 | *Jane Emson* | Sch | S | Myrtle Island, VA |
| | Apr 16 | *Lizzie Thompson* | Sch | A | 10 miles SE of Cape May Lightship, off Delaware Bay |
| | Aug 19 | *Amaryllis* | StS | S | N end Carters Bar, near Hog Island, VA |
| | Sept 7 | *Sarah Francis* | Sch | C [27] | Fishing Bank, off Cape Henlopen, DE |
| | Oct 6 | *A. M. Payne* (*Page*) | Sch | S | Isaac Shoal, VA |
| | Oct 23 | *Antelope* | Brig | W | 4 miles NW of Cape Henlopen LSS, DE |
| | Nov 12 | *O. C. Cleary* | Brig | C [28] | Delaware Bay, 5 miles SW of Cape May, NJ |
| | Dec 16 (ca.) | *Seven Sisters* | Slp | F | In the breakers at Assawoman Inlet, VA |
| | Dec 21 | *Chiswick* | StS | S | N end of island, Hog Island Shoal, VA |
| | Dec 23 | *Lillie A. Warfield* | Sch | F | Chincoteague Bar, Chincoteague, VA |
| 1884 | Jan 5 | *William T. Elmer* | Sch | S | Hog Island Shoal, VA |
| | Jan 10 | *Lizzie Jane* | Slp | S | $\frac{3}{4}$ mile E of Assateague Beach LSS |
| | Jan 15 | *Lewis A. Rommell* | Sch | S | 3 miles N of Little Island LSS, VA |
| | Jan 25 | *John S. Detwiler* | Sch | Ice | Upper and Cross Ledge Shoal, Delaware Bay |
| | Jan 26 | *Albert C. Page* | Sch | S | $2\frac{1}{4}$ miles N of Dam Neck LSS, VA |
| | Feb 28 | *Samuel Fish* | Sch | S | On inner Carter's Bar, near Hog Island, VA |
| | Mar 8 | *Addie Todd* | Brigt | C [29] | 10 miles off Delaware Lightship |
| | Mar 30 | *Celia* | Sch | S | 2 miles ENE of Cobb Island LSS, VA |
| | Mar 30 | *Riverdale* | Sch | S | Delaware Breakwater |
| | Apr 4–5 | *Anna Dole* (*Anna Dale?*) | Sch | S&F | On Dawson Shoal, VA |
| | Apr 27 | Unidentified | Slp | S | Near Trout Channel, Dawson Shoal, VA |
| | June 27 | *Hattie Paige* | CSch | S | $\frac{1}{3}$ mile W of Lewes LSS, DE |
| | July 23 | *Bradshaw* | Slp | S | Assawoman Inlet, VA |
| | July 27 | *Sallie Mair* | Sch | F | 10 miles SE of Hog Island, VA |
| | Oct 14 | *Sarah Shubert* | Sch | S | Stingray Point, near Parramore Beach, VA |
| | Oct 18 (ca.) | Unidentified | Sch | S | Near Wachapreague Inlet, VA |
| | Nov 6 | *John M. Rodgers* | Slp | S | $\frac{1}{2}$ mile SE of Assateague Beach LSS, VA |

| Date | | Vessel | Type | Manner | Location |
|------|------|--------|------|--------|----------|
| | Nov 15 | *A. D. Scull* | Sch | S | On outer bar of Hog Island, VA |
| | Dec 6 | *Margaret A. May* | Sch | S | 200 yards offshore, 3½ miles N of North Beach LSS, MD |
| | Dec 9 | *Jerusha M.* | Sch | S | 2 miles E of Lewes LSS near Cape Henlopen |
| | Dec 16 | *Bedabedec* | Sch | S | Williams Shoal, VA |
| | Dec 27 | *Lena* [Nor] | Bark | S | SE of Hog Island, VA |
| 1885 | Mar 22 | *A. M. Bailey* | Sch | S | 1 mile N of Seatack LSS, VA |
| | Mar 22 | *John M. Rogers* | Slp | S | On Cape Henlopen Beach, DE |
| | May 21 | *Rescue* | Sch | S | On Chincoteague Bar, VA |
| | July 26 | *Melita* | Sch | S | 2 miles S of Cape Henlopen LSS, DE |
| | Sept 20 | *Sallie Solomon* | Sch | S | On Isaac Shoal, VA |
| | Sept 25 | *Woodruff Sims* | Sch | S | Virginia Beach, VA |
| | Oct 4 | *Ann T. Sipples* | Sch | F | 30 miles E of Chincoteague, VA |
| | Oct 15 | *Samuel McMonamey* | Sch | F | Delaware Bay |
| | Oct 23 | *Murciano* | StS | S | North end of Wallops Island, VA |
| | Oct 24 | *Skylark* | Sch | S | North end of Carter's Bar, VA |
| | Dec 25 | *Davy Crockett* | Slp | S | 1¼ mile N of Seatack LSS, VA |
| | Dec 27 | *Lena Hunter* | Sch | S | 1¾ miles S of Cape Henry LSS, VA |
| 1886 | Jan 4 | *Adolphus* | Ship | S | The Shears, Delaware Breakwater, 38° 52' 00" N, 75° 07' 50" W |
| | Jan 12 | *Wm. G. Boulton* | Tug | Ice | Fourteen Foot Bank Light House Shoal, Delaware Bay |
| | Jan 17 | *Serpho* | StS | S | 3 miles S of Little Island LSS, VA |
| | Feb 3 | *Anthea Godfrey* | Sch | F | Lynnhaven Bay, VA |
| | Feb 3 | *Col. Stafford W. Razee* | Sch | S | Seven Pines, Lynnhaven Bay, VA |
| | Feb 5 | *Emma Aery* | Sch | S | On Carter's Bar, VA |
| | Feb 25 | *Rebecca J.* | Slp | S | South end of Cedar Island, VA |
| | Mar 2 | *Leona* | Sch | S | Outer bar of Hog Island, VA |
| | Mar 3 | *Two Brothers* | Slp | S | 1¾ miles NNW of Parramore Beach LSS, VA |
| | Mar 24 | *A. F. Kinderberg* | Sch | S | Dawson Shoal, Wachapreague Inlet, VA |
| | Mar 31 | *Mair and Cranmer* | Sch | C [30] | 7 miles S of Cobb Island, VA |
| | Apr 2 | *Julia A. Roe* | Slp | S | Chincoteague Inlet Bar, VA |
| | Apr 4 | *Brinkburn* | StS | S | Fenwick Island Shoal, DE |
| | Apr 16 | *Bertha A. Watts* (NS) | Sch | S | 2 miles SSE of Popes Island LSS, MD |
| | Apr 26 | *J. W. Everman* | Brg | F | Off Cape Charles, VA |
| | Aug 5 | *Edwin J. Palmer* | Sch | S | Williams Shoal, Chincoteague Bar, VA |
| | Oct 9 | *James E. Kelsey* | Sch | S | 2 miles NE of Wachapreague LSS, VA |
| | Oct 23 | *Howard N. Johnson* | Sch | S | SE point of Cobb Island, VA |
| | Oct 30 | *John Gibson* | StS | S | Outer bar of Hog Island, VA |
| | Oct 31 | *Fred* | Slp | S | North end of Parramore Island, VA |
| | Dec 5 | *Cocheco* | CSch | S | 1⅓ miles N of Cape Henlopen, DE |
| | Dec 5 | *Emma* (*Emily*) *A. Bartle* | Sch | S | ½ mile S of Wallops Beach LSS, VA |
| | Dec 8 (p) | *Banoverd* | Sch | S | Metomkin Beach, VA |
| | Dec 12 | *Ruth T. Carlisle* | Sch | S | 4¼ miles NE of Ocean City LSS, MD |
| | Dec 30 | *Pirate* | StS | S | 2 miles NW of Cape Henry LSS, VA |
| | Dec 30 | *Westway* | Brig | S | Hen and Chickens Shoal, DE |
| | Dec 31 | *Bertha* [Ger] | Slp | S | At Fenwick Island, MD |
| | — | *Eureka* | Sch | S | On Cape Henry Point, VA |
| | — | *William E. Hewlett* | Sch | S | At Lewes breakwater |
| 1887 | Jan 4 | *Helena* | Sch | S | North Beach, MD, 3½ miles SSW of LSS |
| | Jan 8 | *Elizabeth* [Ger] | Ship | S | 14 miles from Cape Henry, VA, between LSS Nos. 3 and 4 |
| | Jan 9 | *Elliot B. Church* | Sch | F | Off the Delaware capes |

| Date | | Vessel | Type | Manner | Location |
|---|---|---|---|---|---|
| | Feb 18 [17] | *Quattro* | Bark | S | Ocean City, MD, $5\frac{1}{2}$ miles NNE of LSS |
| | Mar 8 | *Rhein* [Ger] | StS | S | On Hog Island, VA |
| | Mar 11 | *Orville Horwitz* | Sch | U | Winter Quarter Shoals, VA |
| | Apr 3 | *Bayliss Wood* | Sch | C [31] | Cape Henlopen, DE |
| | Apr 5 | *Nellie Potter* | Sch | F | 6 miles NW of Cape Henry LSS, VA |
| | Apr 29 | *Sadie Bell* | Slp | Cap | At Fisherman's Island, VA |
| | May 10 | *Uranus* [Ger] | Ship | S | $1\frac{1}{2}$ miles N of Rehoboth Beach LSS, DE |
| | June 3 | *James E. Kelsey* | Sch | S&F [R] | Williams Shoal, Chincoteague Inlet, VA |
| | June 11 | *Joseph Baymore* | Sch | AS | 80 miles NE of Cape Henry, VA |
| | June 14 | *Gladiolus* | Tug | F | Fishing Banks, Delaware Bay |
| | Sept 18 | *Hygeia* | StS | S | $\frac{1}{2}$ mile SE of Cobb Island LSS, VA |
| | Oct 10 | *Manantico* | Sch | S | $1\frac{1}{2}$ miles N of Seatack LSS, VA |
| | Oct 10 | *Mary D. Cranmer* | Sch | S | $1\frac{1}{2}$ miles S of Dam Neck LSS, VA |
| | Oct 10 | *Carrie Holmes* | Sch | S | 1 mile N of Cape Henry LSS, VA |
| | Oct 10 | *Harriet Thomas* | Sch | U | 1 mile S of Seatack LSS, VA |
| | Oct 31 | *Edith B. Everyman* | Sch | U | Cape Henry, VA |
| | Nov 2 | *Harvester* | Bark | S | Near Cape Charles, VA |
| | Nov 17 | *Bessie Morris* | Sch | S | $2\frac{1}{2}$ miles SSE of False Cape LSS, VA |
| | Nov 20 | *Deutchland* | Ship | F | 2 miles SSE of Little Island LSS, VA |
| | Dec 6 | *Bertha* | Sch | F | 2 miles below Hog Island Gas Buoy |
| | Dec 8 | *Samuel Crawford* | Sch | F | Hog Island, VA |
| | Dec 18 | *Mattie W. Atwood* | Sch | S | Off Ocean City, MD, 38° 20' N, 74° 20' W |
| | Dec 19 | *Catherine W. May* | Sch | S | SE of Cape Henry, VA |
| | Dec 21 | *D. and E. Kelley* | Sch | F | On or near Fenwick ["Phoenix"] Island, MD |
| | — | *A. L. Dora* | Bark | S | On beach, $\frac{1}{2}$ mile NE of Lewes LSS |
| 1888 | Jan 1 | *Ada Gray* | Bark | S | $2\frac{1}{2}$ miles SE of Little Island LSS, VA |
| | Feb 10 | *Mascotte* | Barkt | U | On beach at Rehoboth, DE |
| | Feb 12 | *Gray Eagle* | Bark | W | Little Island Beach, VA |
| | Feb 12 | *Mascotte* | Barkt | S | Rehoboth Beach, DE |
| | Feb 13 | *Earnmoor* | StS | S | Metomkin Inlet, N end of Cedar Island, VA |
| | Mar 8 | *John Young* | Sch | S | Dawson Shoals, VA |
| | Mar 12 | *Abbie P. Cranmer* | Sch | S | On the beach at Delaware Breakwater, $\frac{1}{2}$ mile E of Lewes LSS |
| | Mar 12 | *Allie H. Belden* | Sch | W | 800 yards N of Lewes LSS, Cape Henlopen, DE |
| | Mar 12 | *Brimiga* [Br] | Bark | W | Hen and Chickens Shoal, DE |
| | Mar 12 | *G. B. Hazeltine* | SchB | W | Hen and Chickens Shoal, DE |
| | Mar 12 | *E. A. Seward* | Sch | S | On the beach at Delaware Breakwater |
| | Mar 12 | *Earl P. Mason* | Sch | S | On the beach at Delaware Breakwater |
| | Mar 12 | *Ebe W. Tunnell* | PB | S [R] | On the beach at Delaware Breakwater |
| | Mar 12 | *Enoch Turley* | PB | S [R] | On the beach at Delaware Breakwater |
| | Mar 12 | *Elizabeth M. Lee* | Sch | S | On the beach at Delaware Breakwater |
| | Mar 12 | *Elliott L. Dow* | Sch | S | On beach at Delaware Breakwater, near the iron pier |
| | Mar 12 | *Esk* [NS] | Sch | S | 2 miles S of Paramore Beach LSS, VA |
| | Mar 12 | *Eva Lynch* | Bark | S [R] | On the beach at Delaware Breakwater |
| | Mar 12 | *Flora A. Newcomb* | Sch | W [R] | At the iron pier, Lewes, DE |
| | Mar 12 [14] | *George J. Simpson* | Tug | F | Delaware Breakwater |
| | Mar 12 | *George W. Anderson* | Sch | W | Lewes, DE |
| | Mar 12 | *Index* | Sch | S [R] | On the beach at Delaware Breakwater |
| | Mar 12 | *Lizzie Crawford* | Tug | S [R] | On the beach at Delaware Breakwater |
| | Mar 12 | *Isabella Alberto* | Sch | S | On the beach at Delaware Breakwater |
| | Mar 12 | *Lizzie V. Hall* [*Wall*] | Sch | S | On the beach at Delaware Breakwater |
| | Mar 12 | *Paul and Thompson* | Sch | C | 1 mile E of Lewes LSS, DE |

| Date | | Vessel | Type | Manner | Location |
|---|---|---|---|---|---|
| | Mar 12 | *Pennsylvania* | Sch | S | On the beach at Delaware Breakwater |
| | Mar 12 | *Providence* | Sch | S | On the beach at Delaware Breakwater |
| | Mar 12 | *Rebecca M. Smith* | Sch | S | On the beach at Delaware Breakwater |
| | Mar 12 | *Tamesi* | Tug | S [R] | ¹/₂ mile from the iron pier at Lewes, DE |
| | Mar 12 | *William G. Bartlett* | Sch | S | 3 miles NNW of Cape Henlopen LSS, DE |
| | Mar 12 | *Zephyr* | Bark | S [R] | Delaware Breakwater, 1¹/₂ miles E of Lewes LSS |
| | May 2 | *Jan Melchers* [Du] | Sch | S | Near Fenwick Island Shoal, DE |
| | May 6 | *Eureka* | StS | C | 36° 45′ N, 74° 52′ W |
| | May 12 (p) | Unidentified | Sch | Cap | 50 miles SE of Cape Henlopen, DE |
| | May 12 (p) | Unidentified | U | F | 45 miles SE of Cape Henlopen, DE |
| | May 12 (p) | Unidentified | Sch | L | 39 miles SE of Cape Henlopen, DE |
| | May 15 | *Olustee* | Bark | S | Isaac Shoal, VA |
| | July 4 [5] | *Elizabeth de Hart* | Sch | W | On the point of Cape Henlopen, DE |
| | July 13 | *Lady of the Lake* | Sch | S | Dawson Shoal, VA |
| | Aug 22 | *Governor Jackson* | Sch | U | Winter Quarter Shoals, VA |
| | Sept 5 [6] | *Lewis Clark* | Sch | W | Cape Henlopen, DE |
| | Oct 17 | *Neva Mag* | Sch | AS | Off Cape Henry, VA |
| | Nov 25 | *Emma* | Sch | S | 1 mile N of Rehoboth Beach LSS, DE |
| | Nov 25 | *Hannah* | Bark | S | ¹/₂ mile WNW of Lewes LSS, DE |
| | Nov 25 | *Helen* | Sch | S | Near the iron pier, Lewes harbor, DE |
| | Nov 25 | *Lizzie Jane* | Slp | W | 14 mile N of Cobb Island, VA |
| | Nov 25 | *Morro Castle* | Bark | W | At Breakwater, 1¹/₂ miles NE of Lewes LSS |
| | Nov 25 | *William D. Marvel* | Sch | S | Lewes harbor, DE |
| | Nov 27 [25] | *Ella* [*Emma*] | Sch | S | Rehoboth, DE |
| | Dec 18 | *George H. Brent* | Sch | W | Delaware Breakwater |
| | — | *Jane Melcher* | Ship | F | Fenwick Island Shoal, DE |
| 1889 | Feb 1 | *Mary and Emma* | Slp | S | 20 yards NW of Hog Island LSS, VA |
| | Feb 18 | *E. L. Pettingill* | Bark | S | 2 miles N of Dam Neck Mill, LSS, VA |
| | Mar 3 | *William B. Wood* | Sch | S | Near Wachapreague, VA |
| | Mar 14 | *Agnes Barton* | Brig | S | ¹/₄ mile N of Dam Neck Mills LSS, VA |
| | Mar 15 | *G. W. Bentley* | Sch | S | 1¹/₄ miles S of Cape Henry LSS, VA |
| | Mar 20 | *Benjamin C. Terry* | Sch | S | ³/₄ mile N of False Cape LSS, VA |
| | Mar 23 | *Conserva* | StS | U | 2¹/₄ miles S of Seatack LSS, VA |
| | Apr 6 | *Carrie A. Buckman* | Sch | F | On the point of Cape Henlopen, DE |
| | Apr 6 | *Sunrise* | Brg | W | Delaware Breakwater (38° 52′ N, 75° 02′ W) |
| | Apr 6–7 | *Benjamin F. Poole* | Sch | S [R] | Near Seatack, VA |
| | Apr 6–7 | *J. O. Fitzgerald* | Slp | S | ³/₄ mile off Bone Island, VA |
| | Apr 7 | *Northampton* | Sch | S | Winter Quarter Shoals, VA |
| | Apr 8 | *Charles P. Sinneckson* | Sch | S | Ocean View, VA |
| | Apr 8 | *Independence* | Slp | S | Cape Henlopen, DE |
| | May 23 | *Patriot* [Nor] | Bark | W | 1¹/₄ mile NNW of Lewes LSS, DE |
| | Aug 10 | *Harry Doremus* | Sch | S | Metomkin Bar, N end of Cedar Island, VA |
| | Sept 10 | *Allie & Eva Hooper* | Sch | S | Delaware Breakwater |
| | Sept 10 | *Addie B. Bacon* | U | W | Delaware Breakwater |
| | Sept 10 | *Alena Covert* | Sch | S | Delaware Breakwater |
| | Sept 10 | *Anna and Ella Benton* | Sch | S | ¹/₂ miles NE of North Beach LSS, MD |
| | Sept 10 | *Atalanta* [Ger] | Bark | S | Below the iron pier at Lewes, DE |
| | Sept 10 | *Bayard* | PB | S | Delaware Breakwater |
| | Sept 10 | *Byron M.* | Sch | S | Delaware Breakwater |
| | Sept 10 | *Charles P. Stickney* | Sch | S | Delaware Breakwater, ¹/₂ mile W of Lewes LSS |
| | Sept 10 | *Ebe W. Tunnell* | PB | L | Off Delaware coast |
| | Sept 10 | *Eliza Ann Hooper* | Sch | S | ¹/₂ miles W of Lewes LSS, DE |
| | Sept 10 | *Eunity R. Dyer* | Sch | S | Delaware Breakwater |

| Date | | Vessel | Type | Manner | Location |
|---|---|---|---|---|---|
| | Sept 10 | *Gertrude Summers* | Sch | S | Delaware Breakwater |
| | Sept 10 | *Il Salvatore* | Bark | S | On iron pier, 1 mile E of Lewes LSS |
| | Sept 10 | *Henry M. Clark* | Sch | S | Delaware Breakwater |
| | Sept 10 | *Kate E. Morse* | Sch | F | Fourteen Foot Bank (Hawk's Nest Shoal), DE |
| | Sept 10 | *J. D. Robinson* | Sch | S | 200 yards W of Lewes LSS, DE |
| | Sept 10 | *J. S. Beckar* [ *J.F. Beckler?* ] | Sch | S | Delaware Breakwater |
| | Sept 10 | *J. and L. Bryan* | Sch | F | Fourteen Foot Bank (Hawk's Nest Shoal) |
| | Sept 10 | *Major William H. Tantum* | Sch | S | At breakwater, ¼ mile E of Lewes LSS, DE |
| | Sept 10 | *Maud Seward* | Sch | S | Delaware Breakwater |
| | Sept 10 | *Mima A. Reed* | Sch | W | ¼ mile E of Lewes LSS, DE, at breakwater |
| | Sept 10 | *Nettie Champion* | Sch | S | Below the iron pier at Lewes, DE |
| | Sept 10 | *Norena* | Sch | S | At breakwater, ¼ mile E of Lewes LSS, DE |
| | Sept 10 | *Richard T. Green* | Brig | S | Delaware Breakwater |
| | Sept 10 | *S. A. Rudolph* | Sch | S | Delaware Breakwater |
| | Sept 10 | *Sarah C. Park* | Sch | S | 2 miles N of Rehoboth LSS, DE |
| | Sept 10 | *Thomas Keiller* | Bark | S | On the beach at Lewes, DE |
| | Sept 10 | *Timour* | Brg | S | At breakwater, ¼ mile W of Lewes LSS, DE |
| | Sept 10 | *Tonawanda* | Brg | F | Brandywine Shoal, Delaware Bay |
| | Sept 10 | *Walter F. Parker* | Sch | F | Fourteen Foot Bank (Hawk's Nest Shoal), DE |
| | Sept 10–11 | Unidentified | Bark | F | Shears Shoal, Delaware Bay |
| | Sept 10–12 | *Casilda* | U | S | Cape Henlopen, DE |
| | Sept 10–12 | *Drooks* | Sch | F | At Slaughter's Beach, DE |
| | Sept 10–12 | *Sarah S. Clark* | Sch | S | 2 miles N of Rehoboth Beach LSS, DE |
| | Sept 10–12 | *St. Cloud* | Brg | F | Delaware Breakwater, Delaware Bay |
| | Sept 10–12 | *Wallace* | Brg | F | Brandywine Shoal, Delaware Bay |
| | Sept 10–12 | *William O. Snow* | Sch | A [R] | 7 miles up Delaware Bay |
| | Sept 10–12 | *William R. Grace* | Ship | W | On the point of Cape Henlopen, DE |
| | Sept 12 | *Orris V. Drisko* | Sch | S | Lewes, DE |
| | Sept 13 | *E. and L. Byrne* | Sch | F | Brandywine Shoal, Delaware Bay |
| | Oct 5 | *Amy Dora* [Br] | StS | W | 37° 33' 18" N, 75° 38' 12" W |
| | Oct 23 | *Frank O. Dame* | Sch | S | 2 miles N of Little Island LSS, VA |
| | Oct 23 | *Henry P. Simmons* | Sch | S | 1½ miles NE of Wash Woods, VA |
| | Oct 23 | *Rover* | Sch | F | Off Ocean View, VA |
| | Oct 26 | *Welaka* | Sch | C [32] | 800 yards NE of Cape Henry LSS, VA |
| | Oct 29 | *Cleopatra* | StS | C [33] | 8 miles off the Delaware Lightship (Five Fathom Lightship) |
| | Oct 29 | *Crystal Wave* | StS | C [34] | 8 miles off the Delaware Lightship (Five Fathom Lightship) |
| | Nov 15 | *Lizzie Jane* | Slp | S | S of Metomkin Inlet, VA |
| | Nov 20 | *Agnes Manning* | Sch | C [35] | Off Fenwick Island |
| | Nov 20 | *Manhattan* | StS | C [36] | Off Fenwick Island, Loran 27007.4, 42419.6 |
| | Nov 25 | *George L. Garlick* | Slp | S | On the point of Cape Henlopen, DE |
| | Nov | *Hannah* [Nor] | Bark | S | Near the pier at Lewes, DE |
| | Dec 11 | *Frank* | Slp | S | ½ mile SE of Cobb Island LSS, VA |
| | — | *Elizabeth A. Hooper* | Sch | S | ¾ mile W of Lewes LSS, DE |
| 1890 | Jan 27 | *Caroline Miller* | StS | S | Isaac Shoal, S of Smith Island, VA |
| | Jan 29 | *Pettiquamscott* | Sch | S | Isaac Shoal, 4 miles SW of Smith Island LSS |
| | Feb 8 | *Golden Rule* | Slp | F | Lynnhaven Roads, VA |
| | Feb 8 | *Wyandotte* | Slp | U | 2 miles N of Seatack LSS, VA |
| | Mar 15 | *Ida* | Slp | S | Cape Charles, VA |
| | Mar 15 | *Nellie C. Paine* | Sch | W | Delaware Bay |
| | Mar 18 | *Francis L. Godfrey* | Sch | C [37] | Off Fenwick Island |
| | Apr 1 | Unidentified [Nor] | Bark | S | 8 miles S of North Beach LSS, MD |

| Date | | Vessel | Type | Manner | Location |
|---|---|---|---|---|---|
| | Apr 19 | *Frank C. Pettis* | Sch | S | Fox Shoal (Isaac Shoal?), Chincoteague Inlet, VA |
| | June 7 | *Jamie Carlton* | Sch | U | Off Cape Charles, VA |
| | July 26 | *Charles Morand* | StS | C | Off the Delaware capes |
| | Aug 30 | Unidentified | U | S | 1 mile ESE of Metomkin Island LSS, VA |
| | Sept 27 [28] | *Oceanus* | Sch | F | 1 mile SSE of Cape Henry LSS, VA |
| | Sept 27 | *Hattie Perry* | Sch | S | Carter's Bar, VA |
| | Sept 28 (p) | *John Young* | Sch | A | Off the Delaware capes |
| | Sept 28 | *Cricket* | Brg | L | Five Fathom Bank |
| | Sept 28 | *Oceanus* | Sch | W | Off Delaware capes |
| | Nov 6 | *Josie Smith* | Slp | S | 1½ mile NE of Wachapreague LSS, VA |
| | Nov 18 | *Lehman Blew* | Sch | S | 2½ miles S of Popes Island LSS, MD |
| | Nov 20 (p) | *Jousted* (Rus) | Sch | F | 50 miles off Cape Henry, VA |
| | — | *W. W. Kerr* | PSch | S | Near the Lewes LSS, DE |
| 1891 | Jan 9 | *Phoebe* | Sch | S | 4 miles SW of Smith Island LSS, VA |
| | Jan 11 | *Alsenbon* | StS | W | Delaware Bay |
| | Jan 13 | *Sussex* | Sch | S | 1 mile S of Cobb Island LSS, VA |
| | Jan 27 [30] | *Minnie and Gussie* | Sch | C [38] | 12 miles SE of Fenwick Island |
| | Feb 4 | *June Bright* | Sch | S | Brandywine Shoal, Delaware Bay |
| | Feb 11 | Unidentified | U | F | 2 miles SE of Fenwick Island Light |
| | Feb 11 | Unidentified | U | F | Off Five Fathom Bank Lightship |
| | Feb 29 | *Hattie Perry* | Sch | S | Hen and Chickens Shoal, DE |
| | Mar 12 | *Principessa Margherita de Piemonte* | Bark | F | 1 mile SSE of Cape Henry LSS on the Hen and Chickens Shoal |
| | Mar 14–15 | *Mary C. Carroll* | Sch | S | On Dawson Shoal, off Wachapreague, VA |
| | Mar 20 | *Ada P. Gould* | Brigt | F | Winter Quarter Shoals, VA |
| | Mar 27 | *Dictator* [Nor] | Bark | S | 4 miles S of Cape Henry, VA, 2 miles N of Virginia Beach Hotel |
| | Mar 27 | *Hattie* | HBrig | S | 1½ miles SSW of Ocean City LSS, MD |
| | Mar 28 | *Charles C. Dame* | Sch | S | Near Plum Point, above Lewes, DE |
| | Apr 1 | *Admiral* | Bark | S | 3½ miles SSW of North Beach LSS, MD |
| | Apr 2 | Unidentified | Sch | B | Delmarva coast |
| | Apr 25 | *Lizzie D. Barker* | Sch | S | Near Smith Island, VA |
| | Apr 28 | *William B. Orr* | Sch | W | Delaware Bay |
| | Apr 29 | *William M. Bird* | Sch | S | 3 miles SSW of Popes Island LSS, VA |
| | May 24 (p) | *Vibilia* [BrCol] | Bark | S&B | On the Virginia coast |
| | May 27 | *Libby P. Hallock* | Sch | S | 7 miles NE of Smith Island LSS and 7 miles NE of Myrtle Shoal, VA |
| | June 19 | *George Henry* | Sch | S | 9 miles NNW of Lewes LSS, DE |
| | June 19 | *Spray* | Sch | U | Cobb Island, VA |
| | July 2 | *Syringa* | Bark | B | Delaware Bay |
| | July 28 | *Archer and Reeves* | Sch | S&F | On Brandywine Shoal, Delaware Bay |
| | Aug 26 | *E. S. Newins* | Sch | S | 3½ miles NE of Fisherman's Island (Parramore Island LSS?), VA |
| | Aug 30 | Unidentified | Boat | S | Folly Creek, opposite Metomkin Inlet, VA |
| | Aug | *Seth and Ishmael* | Sch | F | ½ mile N of North Beach LSS, MD |
| | Sept 27 | *John Young* | Sch | S | Carter's Creek, Cobb Island, VA |
| | Oct 10 | *William H. Bradley* | Sch | F | Off Virginia capes |
| | Oct 10 | USS *Despatch* | StS | S | 2 miles S of Sheep's Pen Hill, on Assateague Island |
| | Oct 12 | *Rattler* | StS | S | On the point of Cape Henlopen, DE |
| | Oct 13 (p) | *Wapella* | Sch | AS | Off Winter Quarter Shoals, VA |
| | Oct 14 | *Energy* | Brg | C | Off Virginia capes |
| | Oct 14 | *Harvey W. Anderson* | Sch | S | On Hog Island, VA |

| Date | | Vessel | Type | Manner | Location |
|---|---|---|---|---|---|
| | Oct 22 [23] | Red Wing | Sch | S | 3½ miles S of Indian River Inlet LSS, DE |
| | Nov 29 | John Hooper | Sch | S | Isaac Shoal, near Smith Island, VA |
| 1892 | Jan 6 | Stephen G. Hart | Sch | W | Off Delaware Breakwater |
| | Jan 7 | Ashburne | StS | S | 5½ miles S of Wachapreague Island, VA |
| | Jan 7 | Unidentified | StS | S | 4 miles S of Dawson Shoal, VA |
| | Jan 12 | Miranda | StS | S [R] | Ragged Point, VA, 4 miles S of Popes Island LSS |
| | Jan 19 | Sir William Armstrong | StS | S [R] | SE point of Carter's Shoal, VA |
| | Jan 20 | Mary Rogers | Sch | W | 2 miles NE of Lewes LSS, DE |
| | Feb 6 (p) | Unidentified | StS | F | 9 miles SE of Cape Henlopen, DE |
| | Feb 21 | Govino | StS | S | ½ mile NNE of Cape Henry LSS, VA |
| | Feb 22 | San Albano [Sp] | StS | S | 6 miles NE by E of Hog Island LSS, VA, 37° 26' 18" N, 75° 37' 12" W |
| | Feb 29 | William Phillips | Barkt | S | At Cape Henry, VA |
| | Mar 1 | Hannah M. Lollis | Sch | S | On bar 1 mile NE of Assateague Beach LSS |
| | Mar 2 | Tecumseh | Sch | F | Off Fenwick Island Shoal, DE |
| | Aug 1 | E. K. Wilson | Sch | Cap | Delaware Breakwater |
| | Aug 22 (p) | Thomas W. Waters | Sch | W | On Hog Island Shoal, VA |
| | Aug 27 (p) | Henry A. Tabor | CSch | W | Near Delaware Breakwater gapway |
| | Nov 5 | Annie S. Gaskill | Sch | Cap | Off the Delaware capes |
| | Nov 20 | Ella T. Little | Sch | S | Carter's Bar, VA |
| | Dec 19 | A. P. Nowell | Sch | S | Hog Island, VA |
| | Dec 20 | Magellan [BrCol] | Sch | F | On Ship Shoal Island, VA |
| | Dec 20 | Robert H. Parker | Sch | S | Cape Charles, VA, 1 mile SE of Smith Island |
| | Dec 24 | Mary E. H. G. Dow | Sch | S | Middle Ground, Chesapeake Bay, VA |
| | Dec 27 (p) | James Waples Ponder | Sch | AS | At the mouth of Chesapeake Bay |
| | — | Water Witch | Slp | S | 2½ miles NE of Smith Island LSS, VA |
| 1893 | Jan 1 | Edith Berwind | Sch | S | 6 miles S of Smith Island LSS, VA |
| | Jan 5 (p) | Minnie Smith | Sch | C [39] | 60 miles E of Cape Henry, VA |
| | Feb 19 | Grace Van Dusen | Sch | C [40] | Middle Ground, Chesapeake Bay, VA |
| | Feb 20 | Georgiana F. Geery | Brig | C? | Near Delaware Lightship |
| | Mar 4 | Ella M. Watts | Sch | S | On the point of Cape Henlopen, DE |
| | Mar 23 | Equator | Brg | F | Off Fenwick Island |
| | Mar 24 | L. B. Chandler | Sch | S | Outer bar of Hog Island, VA |
| | Mar 25 | Robert Morgan | Sch | C [41] | Between Winter Quarter Shoals and Fenwick Island |
| | Apr 20 | North Star | Sch | S | Near Little Island, VA |
| | Apr 27 | Helen [Ire] | StS | S | 2½ miles SE by S of False Cape LSS, VA |
| | May 4 | Emma W. Barton | Sch | F | Off Winter Quarter Light |
| | May 12 | Morien | Sch | C? | "At Brandywine" [Shoal?], Delaware Bay |
| | June 16 (p) | John Holland | Sch | C | 10 miles E of Cape Henry, VA |
| | July 31 | Rachael Seaman | Sch | C | Off the Delaware capes |
| | Aug 23 | Light Vessel No. 37 | LS | F | Five Fathom Bank Station, near Delaware Bay |
| | Aug 28 | Ida Potter | Sch | U | 2 miles NE by E of Cape Henlopen LSS, DE |
| | Aug 28 | William C. Bee | Sch | W | At Milford, DE |
| | Sept 15 | William T. Sherman | Slp | S | 4 miles N of Fenwick Island LSS |
| | Oct 4 | Colter C. Davidson | Sch | S | 2½ miles N of Seatack LSS, VA |
| | Oct 4 | William Applegarth | Sch | S | 200 yards E of Seatack LSS, VA |
| | Oct 9 | J. B. Denton | Slp | F | 4 miles E of Hog Island LSS, VA |
| | Oct 23 | Murciano | StS | S | 1½ miles S of Wallops Island LSS, VA |
| | Nov 4–5 | Jacob I. Housman | Sch | W | 1¼ miles NNE of Lewes LSS, in Delaware Breakwater Gap |
| | Dec 3 | Martha E. Bayard | Sch | W | 1½ miles N of Lewes LSS, DE |
| | Dec 4 | Prohibition | Slp | Cap | 1½ miles S of Metomkin Inlet LSS, VA |

| Date | | Vessel | Type | Manner | Location |
|------|---|--------|------|--------|----------|
| | Dec 6 | *Faust* | Bark | Cap | Hen and Chickens Shoal, DE |
| | — | *Rebecca* | Sch | S | 2 miles NNE of Lewes LSS, DE |
| | — | *Thomas Thomas* | Sch | S | Fox Shoals, off Wallops Island, VA |
| 1894 | Jan 7 | *Nettie* | Brigt | S | 1½ miles S of Little Island LSS, VA |
| | Jan 22 | *Clythia* [Nor] | Bark | S | 2 miles S of False Cape, VA |
| | Jan 24 | *Josie Smith* | Slp | S | ½ mile S of Wallops Beach LSS, VA |
| | Feb 9 | *John A. Griffin* | U | W | On ice breaker, Delaware Breakwater, 1½ miles NE of Lewes LSS |
| | Feb 10 (p) | *James E. Kelsey* | Sch | F | Off Fenwick Island |
| | Apr 9 | *Chester* | StS | F | 7 miles NE of Smith Island LSS, VA |
| | June 22 | *James McFadden* | Tug | F | Off Bombay Hook, Delaware Bay |
| | Oct 1 | *Allegheny* [Br] | StS | C | In Delaware River |
| | Oct 11 | *Mina Belle* | Sch | W | On Brandywine Shoal, Delaware Bay |
| | Oct 12 | *Sea Foam* | Sch | S | 3 miles from Cape Henlopen LSS, DE |
| | Oct 17 | *W. L. Willis* (*L. L. Willis*) | SchB | S | South end of Williams Shoal, VA |
| | Oct 31 | Unidentified | Sch | S | 3 miles SE of Wachapreague LSS, VA |
| | Nov 11 | *Sachem* | Slp | S | S end of Cedar Island, VA |
| | Dec 6 | *Odorilla* | Brigt | S | 4 miles N of Fenwick Island LSS |
| | Dec 27 | *Venus* | SchB | F | 37° 30' N, 75° 00' W |
| 1895 | Jan 27 | *James Ives* | Sch | W | Off Delaware capes |
| | Feb 2 | *Marion F. Sprague* | Sch | AS | 10 miles NE of Cape Charles, VA |
| | Feb 8 (p) | *Alma Cummings* | Sch | AS | 10 miles NE of Cape Charles, VA |
| | Feb 8 | *Georgia* | Slp | Ice | Bone Island, near Cobb Island, VA |
| | Feb 8 | *Sunbeam* | Sch | S | 2 miles SE of Assateague Beach LSS, VA |
| | Feb 8 | *Water Lilly* | Sch | AS | Fishing Point, 2½ miles S of Assateague Beach LSS, VA |
| | Feb 12 | *Elsie Marie* | StS | S | 6½ miles SW of Parramore Beach LSS, VA |
| | Mar 16 | *Siam* [Nor] | Bark | W | On Fenwick Island |
| | Mar 17 | *Zimri S. Wallingford* | Sch | S&B | 7 miles E of Metomkin Inlet LSS, VA |
| | Apr 2 | *Oakdene* [Br] | StS | S | 3 miles NE of Assateague Beach, VA 37° 54' 00" N, 75° 19' 42" W |
| | Apr 28 | *A. W. Howe* | Sch | S | At breakwater, 2 miles NNE of Lewes LSS, DE |
| | Apr 29 | *Henry Parker* | Sch | S | 4 miles SW of Smith Island on Isaac Shoal, VA |
| | May 14 | *Midnight* | SlpY | S | ½ mile E of Wachapreague LSS, VA |
| | May 16 | *Josephine* | Sch | W | At False Cape, 1½ miles SE of Little Island, VA |
| | Sept 14 | *Centennial* | Sch | S | 1½ miles ESE of Wachapreague LSS, VA |
| | Sept 21 | *Lottie K. Friend* | Sch | C [42] | Opposite Ship John Light, Delaware Bay |
| | Sept 29 | *Margaret* | StS | S | 4 miles NW of Cape Henry LSS, VA |
| | Oct 23 | *H. J. Bradshaw* | Sch | S | 4¼ miles NW of Cape Henry LSS, VA |
| | Oct 30 | *Carrie L. Godfrey* | Sch | W | Machipongo Shoal, at Little Machipongo Inlet |
| | Nov 8 | *William Hales* | Bark | F | 38° 00' N, 74° 19' W |
| | Dec 25 (p) | *Emma C. Cotton* | Sch | W | Near Cape Henry, VA |
| 1896 | Feb 5 | *Annie B. Cathrall* | Sch | W | ½ mile SE by E of False Cape LSS, VA |
| | Feb 9 | *Caroline Hall* | Sch | W | 4 to 5 miles SSE of Smith Island LSS, VA |
| | Feb 21(p) | *H. L. Straight* | Sch | AS | Fenwick Island, MD |
| | Mar 21(p) | *R. F. Hastings* | Sch | C [43] | 2½ miles ESE of Wachapreague LSS, VA |
| | Mar 21(p) | *Sunshine* | StS | F | At Government Dock, Hog Island, VA |
| | Oct 2 | *Maggie E. Davis* | Sch | S | At Pleasure House, Princess Anne Co., VA |
| | Oct 12 | *Henry A. Litchfield* | Bark | S | ½ mile N of Cape Henlopen LSS, DE |
| | Oct 11 | *Luther A. Roby* | Sch | F | 2½ miles SSE of Assateague Beach LSS |
| | Nov 29 | *City of Philadelphia* | Sch | S | 25 miles NE of Little Island LSS, VA |
| | Dec 3 (p) | *A. J. Bentley* | Sch | W | Ocean View, VA |
| | Dec 3 | *S. Walker Armington* | StY | S | 3 miles N of False Cape LSS, VA |

| Date | | Vessel | Type | Manner | Location |
|---|---|---|---|---|---|
| 1897 | Jan 15 | *Haxby* | StS | S | $^2/_{10}$ mile NE of Dam Neck Mills LSS, VA |
| | Jan 16 | *Staffa* [Eng] | StS | S | 2½ miles SE of False Cape LSS, VA |
| | Mar 4 | *Emma L. Shaw* | Brigt | W | Near Lewes, DE |
| | Mar 8–14 | *Ville de Nazaire* | StS | F | About 37° 48′ N, 74° 05′ W |
| | Mar 28 | *Mary* | Sch | F | At Hog Island, VA |
| | Apr 14 | *Sarah A. Staples* | SchB | F | 20 miles E of Cape Henry, VA |
| | Apr 20 | *James Ponder* | Sch | W | Carter's Bar, Hog Island, VA |
| | May 26 | *Emma B. Shaw* | CSch | L [R] | Reedy Island Dike, Delaware River |
| | Aug 2 | *A. D. Lamson* | Sch | C | 2 miles off Cape Henry, VA |
| | Sept 28 | *Ranger* | Y | S | ½ mile N of Cape Henlopen LSS, DE |
| | Oct 2 | *Elias Ross* | Sch | S | 2 miles N of Cape Henlopen LSS, DE |
| | Oct 3 | Unidentified | Sch | AS | 37° 40′ N, 71° 00′ W |
| | Oct 9 | *J. G. Conner* | Sch | S | Dawson Shoal, ESE of Wachapreague LSS, VA |
| | Oct 24 | *Dredge No. 1* | Drg | S | ½ mile W of Lewes, DE |
| | Oct 25 | *H. W. Laws* | Sch | S | Lewes, DE |
| | Oct 25 | *L. A. Rose* | Sch | W | Chincoteague Light, 1 mile SE of Assateague LSS, VA |
| | Oct 25 | *Lillie Falkenburg* | Sch | W | Lewes, DE |
| | Oct 25 | *Sarah Jane Vaughn* | Sch | S | 1⅛ miles W of Lewes LSS, DE |
| | Oct 25–26 | *Elizabeth S. Lee* | Sch | S | 2½ miles E of Lewes LSS, DE |
| | Oct 26 | *Francesco R.* | Bark | BrU | At Fourteen Foot Bank, Delaware Bay |
| | Oct 26–27 | *Emma B. Shaw* | Sch | W | At Reedy Island Light, Delaware Bay |
| | Nov 23 | *Straits of Magellan* | StS | S | 2 miles N of Little Island LSS, VA |
| | Dec 17 | *H. H. Wright* | Brg | W | On Cross Ledge, Delaware Bay |
| | Dec 24 | *Katie J. Hoyt* | Sch | S | Carter's Bar, 5 miles SE of Cobb Island LSS, VA |
| 1898 | Jan 9 | *Manson* | Brg | W | 20 miles E of Cape Henry, VA |
| | Apr 14 | *Sarah A. Staples* | Sch* | F | Turners Lump, 5 miles SE of Assateague LSS, VA |
| | May 8 | *Scow No. 7* | Sch | L | 1½ mile N of Fenwick Island LSS, DE |
| | May 18 | *Eugene Hall* | Sch | S | At Hog Island, VA |
| | May 28 (p) | *Vala* | SlpY | S | Little Inlet Shoals, near Smith Island, VA |
| | June 14 | *Shenandoah* | Sch | B | Off Thimble Shoal, Chesapeake Bay, VA |
| | Sept 21 | *Rebecca* | SchY | U | 4½ miles NNE of Lewes LSS |
| | Nov 1 (p) | *Croatan* | StS | B | Off Cape Charles, VA |
| | Nov 27 (p) | *William M. Wilson* | Sch | F | 4 miles S of Metomkin Inlet LSS, VA |
| | Nov 28 | *Harry B. Ritter* | Sch | AS | 37° 58′ N, 70° 11′ W |
| | — | *Jamie* | Sch | S | 2 miles NE of Wallops Island LSS, VA |
| | — | *Thomas G. Smith* | Tug | F | 15 miles S of Fenwick Island, MD |
| | — | *T. Harris Kirk* | Sch | S | 1½ miles S of North Beach LSS, MD |
| 1899 | Feb 8 | *George E. Dudley* | Sch | S | 6 miles S of Cobb Island, VA |
| | Feb 10 | *Annie M. Reynolds* | Sch | F | On Metomkin Point, 2½ miles ENE of Metomkin Inlet, VA |
| | Mar 5 | *Tamesi* | StS | S | South of Chincoteague Bar, 3 miles E of Wallops Beach LSS, VA |
| | Mar 7 | *William B. Steelman* | Sch | S | The "Stone Pile," 2 miles NNE of Lewes LSS, DE |
| | May 7 | *James Borden* | StS | F | 5 miles E of Hog Island Light, VA |
| | May 28 | *Caravan* | Brg | W | Middle Ground, off Cape Henry, VA |
| | Aug 16 | *Harold J. McCartny* | Sch | S | 3½ miles NNE of Lewes LSS, DE |
| | Aug 19 | *Augustus Palmer* | Sch | S&F | On the Horseshoe, near Thimble Shoal Light, Chesapeake Bay, VA |
| | Aug | *Lameta* | Sch | F | 4½ miles NNE of North Beach LSS, MD |
| | Sept 19 | *Annie* | Sch | S | 1¼ miles NW of Parramore Beach LSS, VA |
| | Oct 30 | *J. W. Somers* | Sch | S | Willoughby Spit, VA |
| | Oct 31 | *Bayard Barnes* | Sch | S | 200 yards S of Indian River Inlet LSS, DE |

| Date | | Vessel | Type | Manner | Location |
|------|---|--------|------|--------|----------|
| | Oct 31 | *Falmouth* | Sch | S | Ocean View Beach, VA |
| | Oct 31 | *Kate Darling* | Sch | W | 2½ miles N of Rehoboth Beach LSS, DE |
| | Dec 14 | *Rillie S. Derby* | Sch | S | 4½ miles SE of Hog Island LSS, VA |
| | — | *M. E. Bayard* | Sch | W | E end of icebreaker, Delaware Breakwater |
| | — | *Patriot* | Bark | S | 1¼ miles NNW of Lewes LSS, DE |
| 1900 | Jan 20 (p) | *Sutton* [Br] | Str | S | Fenwick Island Shoal, DE |
| | Feb 2 | *J. T. Ford* | Sch | S | 3 miles ESE of Wachapreague LSS, VA |
| | Feb 28 | *General Cogswell* | Sch | S | 1½ miles N of Cape Henlopen LSS, DE |
| | Mar 26 | *Vidar* | StS | S | ¾ mile SSW of Dam Neck Mills LSS, VA |
| | Apr 25 | *Cordelia R. Price* | Sch | S | 1 mile W of Cobb Island LSS, VA |
| | May 1 | *Isle of Kent* | StS | F | 2½ miles E of False Cape LSS, VA |
| | Sept 19 | *John Shay* | Sch | S | 1⅞ miles N of Cape Henlopen LSS, DE |
| | Oct 16 | *Carrie E. Pickering* | Sch | S | On the point of Cape Henlopen, DE |
| | Dec 1 | *S. B. Wheeler* | Sch | S | 4½ miles SE of Hog Island LSS, VA |
| | Dec 20 | *Volunteer* | Slp | S | Horseshoe Channel, off Parramore LSS, VA |
| | Dec 21 | *Jennie Hall* | Sch | S | ¼ mile NE of Dam Neck Mills, VA |
| | Dec 21 | *N. H. Skinner* | Sch | S | 2 miles N of Cape Henlopen LSS, DE |
| | Dec 24 | *Astoria* | Sch | S | Ship Shoal, VA |
| | Dec 24 | *Ocean King* | StS | S | Ship Shoal, VA |
| | Dec 24 | *Rondout* | Sch | S | 8 miles NE of Smith Island LSS, VA |
| | Dec 27 | *Kestrel* | Slp | S | Hog Island Shoal, VA |
| 1901 | Jan 19 | *Hercules* | Brg | U | ½ mile W of the point of Cape Henlopen, DE |
| | Feb 23 | *L. S. Levering* | Sch | F | On the point of Cape Henlopen, DE |
| | Mar 11 | *Mary Standish* | Sch | S | 1 mile W of Assateague Beach LSS, VA |
| | July 14 | *Malden* | Sch | S | ¼ mile SE of False Cape LSS, VA |
| | July 26 | *Monhegan* | Sch | S | 2 miles SSE of Assateague Beach LSS, VA |
| | Aug 2 | *Starlight* | Sch | S | 200 yards N of Rehoboth Beach LSS, DE |
| | Aug 25 | *Cape Henry* | Sch | F | E of Cape Henry Lighthouse, VA |
| | Sept 10 | *Rapidan* | StY | S | 2 miles N of Cape Henlopen LSS, DE |
| | Sept 13 (p) | *Lavinia Campbell* | Sch | C&S | Fourteen Foot Bank, Delaware Bay |
| | Sept 17 | *Edith G. Fowell* | Sch | W | 1 mile N of Cape Henry, VA |
| | Sept 19 | *John Shay* | Sch | S | 1⅞ miles N of Cape Henlopen LSS, DE |
| | Sept 27 (p) | *Brooklyn* | SchB | L | 27 miles off Fenwick Island, DE |
| | Oct 24 | *Lida Fowler* | Sch | C [44] | Off Fourteen Foot Bank, Delaware Bay |
| 1902 | Feb 2 (p) | *Navarino* | Sch | C | Delaware coast |
| | Feb 17 | *Anna Murray* | Sch | S | 2½ miles S of Indian River Inlet LSS, DE, 38° 35' 30" N, 75° 03' 24" W |
| | Feb 17 | *Juanita* | Brg | S | Off Delmarva coast |
| | Feb 17 | *Western Belle* | Brg | F | Off Delmarva coast |
| | Feb 19 (p) | *Charles D. Hall* | Sch | L | Fenwick Island, DE |
| | Feb 27 | *Annie T. Bailey* | Sch | S | Cape Henlopen, DE |
| | Feb 28 | *N. B. Morris* | Bark | S | 200 yards N of Cape Henlopen LSS, DE |
| | Sept 10 | *William Ellison* | Sch | S | Near Indian River Inlet, DE |
| | Nov 1 | *Express* | Sch | S | ½ mile NE of False Cape LSS, VA |
| | Nov 7 | *Addie* | Sch | F | 1¼ miles S and 5 miles E of Indian River Inlet, DE |
| | Nov 16 | *Onancock City* | Slp | S | 4½ miles SW of Smith Island LSS, VA |
| | Dec 12 | *Virginia Rulon* | Sch | F [R] | 1 mile S of Assateague Beach LSS, VA |
| | Dec 16 | *Lillian Russell* | Sch | S | 4 miles ESE of Hog Island LSS, VA |
| 1903 | Jan 10 | *Celeste* | Sch | S | 1¾ miles NNE of Green Run Inlet LSS, MD |
| | Jan 10 | *Juno* | StS | F | 2½ miles ESE of False Cape, VA |
| | Jan 30 | *William H. Smith* | Sch | F | Off the Delaware coast |
| | Feb 17 | *Rebecca* | Sch | S | 4 miles S of Hog Island LSS, VA |
| | Feb 19 (p) | *Sovereign of the Sea* | SchB | L | Off Delaware Breakwater |

| Date | | Vessel | Type | Manner | Location |
|---|---|---|---|---|---|
| | Mar 5 | *Saginal* | Slp | F | Near Winter Quarter Shoals, VA |
| | Mar 23 (p) | *Dreadnaught* | Sch | C | Off Delaware capes |
| | Mar 26 (p) | *William H. Davidson* | CSch | L | 2½ miles S of Indian River LSS, DE |
| | Apr 13 | *Daybreak* | StS | S | 2½ miles E of False Cape LSS, VA |
| | Apr | *Nettie R. Willing* | Sch | F | Off the Delaware coast |
| | Apr | *Princess Caroline* [Br] | Ship | S | Winter Quarter Shoals |
| | Mar 28 [29] | *Carrigan* | Sch | S | On the point of Cape Henlopen, DE |
| | May 1 (p) | *Fidelia* | SchB | S | 3 miles W of Hen and Chickens Lightship, DE |
| | May 5 | *Saginaw* | StS | C [45] | Between Winter Quarter LS and Fenwick Island |
| | Sept 16 | *Beatrice* | Sch | L | Several miles N of Chincoteague, VA |
| | Sept 16 | *Elmwood* | SchB | F | Old Bear Shoal, off Delaware Breakwater |
| | Sept 16 | *Gilberton* | SchB | F | Off Brown Shoal, off Delaware Breakwater |
| | Sept 16 | *Hattie A. Marsh* | Sch | S | Delaware capes |
| | Sept 16 | *Kalmia* | SchB | F | Old Bear Shoal, off Delaware Breakwater |
| | Sept 16 | *Sea Bird* | Sch | S | ¾ mile NNE of Lewes LSS, DE |
| | Sept 16 | *Spartan* | Tug | F | Brown Shoal, in Delaware Bay |
| | Oct 10 | *Georgia* | SchB | S | 37 miles N of Virginia Beach, VA |
| | Oct 10 | *Nellie W. Howlett* | Sch | S | 3 miles S of Dam Neck Mills, VA |
| | Oct 10 | *Ocean Belle* | SchB | S | 2½ miles N of Virginia Beach LSS, VA |
| | Oct 10 | *Oregon* | Slp | F | 4 miles NE of Smith Island LSS, VA |
| | Oct 11 | *Benjamin Russell* | Sch | F | 3 miles SSE of Cobb Island LSS, VA |
| | Oct 30 | *Blanche Hopkins* | Sch | C [46] | Near Lodge Light, Delaware Bay |
| | — | *Alaska* | Sch | F | Near the beach at Lewes, DE |
| 1904 | Jan 3 | *Joseph J. Pharo* | Sch | S | 8 miles S of Cobb Island, VA |
| | Feb 11 | *Henry B. Hyde* | Sch | S [R] | South of Cape Henry, VA |
| | Apr 9 | *Phantom* | StY | S | 1 mile S of Indian River Inlet LSS, DE |
| | June 13 (p) | *Ellida* [Ur] | Brg | F | 10 miles off Fenwick Island, DE |
| | Sept 15 | *E. C. Allen* | Sch | S | 1½ miles NNE of Lewes LSS, DE |
| | Oct 20 | *Annie T Rutland* | Slp | F | Fenwick Island |
| | Nov 11 | *Robert J. Poulson* | Sch | F | ½ mile SW of Hog Island, VA |
| | Dec 3 | *Santiago* | SchB | C [47] | Off Delaware Breakwater |
| | Dec 15 (p) | *John R. Halladay* | Sch | S | On the point of Cape Henlopen, DE |
| | — (ca.) | *Jenna Hughes* | SchB | F | Fenwick Island, DE |
| | — | *Nebraska* (ex-*Congress*) | StS. | U | Lynnbren Bay, MD (Lynnhaven Bay, VA?) |
| | — | *Rena A. Callow* | Sch | S | Isaac Shoal, VA |
| 1905 | Feb 3 | *D. M. Anthony* | Sch | S | 1½ miles N of False Capes LSS, VA |
| | Feb 8 | *San Ignacio de Loyola* | Barkt | S | 2 miles SE of Wachapreague, VA |
| | Feb 24 | *Bangor* | StS | S | ½ mile SE of Little Island LSS, VA |
| | Apr 8 | *M. R. Howlett* | Sch | S | 4 miles SE of Assateague Beach LSS, VA |
| | May 5 | *Emmett Arthur* | Slp | S | 6 miles SW of Wallops Beach LSS, VA |
| | July 18 | *Reliance* | GaS | B | Cape Charles, VA |
| | July 22 | *Minnivia Miles* | Sch | S | Diamond Marsh, VA |
| | Sept 4 | *Saxon* | Brg | S | 2¼ miles SSE of False Cape LSS, VA |
| | Dec 15 | *Bath* | Brg | F | Cape Charles, VA |
| | Dec 15 | *Pendleton Sisters* | Sch | S | 5½ miles NNE of Metomkin Inlet LSS, VA |
| | Dec 23 | *Fannie Reiche* | Sch | C [48] | Off Winter Quarter Light |
| | Dec 24 | *C. H. Moore* | Sch | S | 1 mile SSE of Little Island LSS, VA |
| 1906 | Jan 9 | *Fannie Palmer* | Sch | S | ¾ mile N of Little Island LSS, VA |
| | Feb 15 | *Ida D. Sturgis* | Sch | S | Near Indian River, DE |
| | Feb 27 | *Jesse W. Starr* | Sch | AS | 37° 33' N, 74° 36' W |
| | Feb 28 | *Number Eleven* | SchB | F | 10 miles ESE of Fenwick Island Lightship, DE |
| | Mar 5 | *John S. Deering* | Sch | AS | 37° 05' N, 71° 50' W |

| Date | | Vessel | Type | Manner | Location |
|---|---|---|---|---|---|
| | Mar 6 | *Stetson and Ellison* | Sch | F | Delaware Bay |
| | Mar 19 | *Oak* | Brg | S | Thimble Shoal, Chesapeake Bay, VA |
| | Mar 23 | *Asher F. Hudson* | Tug | S | 250 yards NE of Dam Neck Mills LSS, VA |
| | Mar 31 | *Antonio* (It) | Bark | S | ¹/₂ mile N of Cape Henry LSS, VA |
| | Mar 31 | *William H. Van Name* | Sch | C | Thimble Shoal, Chesapeake Bay, VA |
| | Apr 23 | *Norumbega* | Sch | C [49] | Fenwick Island |
| | May 7 | *Alice* | Sch | S | 1¹/₂ miles N of Wallops Island LSS, in Chincoteague Cove, VA |
| | Sept 25 | *Marion Grimes* | Sch | S | 4³/₄ miles SW of Assateague Beach LSS, VA |
| | Oct 20 | *George Farwell* | StS | S | ¹/₂ miles SE of Cape Henry LSS, VA |
| | Dec 6 | *Florence I. Lockwood* | Sch | S | 2¹/₂ miles E of Wallops Island LSS, VA |
| | Dec 8 | *Charles L. Mitchell* | Sch | AS | Off Cape Henry, VA |
| | Dec 12 | *Gen'l J. L. Selfridge* | Sch | S | Fisherman's Island, VA |
| | — | *Ida B. Gibson* | Sch | S | 3 miles SSW of North Beach LSS, MD |
| 1907 | Feb 4 | *Tena A. Cotton* | GaS | S | 4 miles S of Ocean City LSS, MD |
| | Mar 6 [5] | *John J. Ward* | Sch | S | Lewes, DE |
| | Mar 24 | *J. F. Whitcomb* | Sch | S | Assateague Beach, VA |
| | May 9 | *Horn Point* | Slp | F | East Lynnhaven Inlet, Chesapeake Bay, VA |
| | June 2 | *Pactolus* | SchB | F | Off Hog Island, VA |
| | Aug 12 | *Henry A. Litchfield* | SchB | B | Near Virginia Beach, VA |
| | Oct 30 | *Foam* | Sch | F | 100 miles E of Cape Henry, VA |
| | Nov 7 | *Wicomico* | Ship | S | 1 mile SSE of Assateague Beach LSS, VA |
| | Nov 24 | *Grace Collins* | Slp | F | Mispillion Creek, DE |
| 1908 | Jan 10 | *John E. Devlin* [*Sevlin*] | Sch | S | 5 miles NNE of Metomkin Inlet LSS, VA |
| | Jan 22 | *Baltimore* | Bark | F | Sailed from Hampton Roads, not heard from |
| | Jan 24 (p) | *William Bard* | SchB | F | Delaware Breakwater |
| | Jan 26 | *Mascot* | Brg | F | Thimble Shoal, Chesapeake Bay, VA |
| | Jan 27 | *George R. Vreeland* | Sch | F | Sailed from Hampton Roads, not heard from |
| | Jan 28 | *Helen G. Moseley* | Sch | AS | 20 miles E of Cape Henry, VA |
| | Feb 4 | *Emelie E. Birdsall* | Sch | C [50] | Winter Quarter Shoals, VA |
| | Feb 28 | *Number Eleven* | SchB | F | 10 miles SE of Fenwick Island Lightship, DE |
| | Apr 16 | *Glenaen* | StS | S | Carters Bar, Cobb Island, VA |
| | Apr 24 | *Katherine* | Brg | F | 20 miles W of Ship Shoal, VA |
| | Aug 24 | *Margaret H. Vane* | Sch | S | Cobb Island, VA |
| | Sept 3 | *Patrick McCabe* | Sch | C [51] | Winter Quarter Shoals, VA |
| | Oct 21 | *Dessoug* | Sch | F | 17 miles NE of Winter Quarter Shoals |
| | Oct 30 | *John M. Brown* | Sch | F | 37° 00' N, 71° 00' W |
| | Oct 31 | *Arleville H. Peary* | Sch | S | 3¹/₄ miles S of False Cape LSS, VA |
| | Nov 12 | *Florence Shay* | Sch | S | 3¹/₂ miles S of Little Island, VA |
| | Nov 14 | *Independent* | SchB | F | Off Hog Island, VA |
| | Nov 14 | *Marie F. Cummins* | Sch | S | 12 miles below Delaware Breakwater |
| | Dec 22 | *Jeanie Lippen* | Sch | S | Winter Quarter Shoals, VA |
| | — | *Lena* | StS | S | ³/₄ miles W of Lewes LSS, DE |
| 1909 | Jan 6 | *Anglo-African* [Eng] | StS | S | 4 miles S of Smith Island LSS, VA |
| | Jan 12 | *Adeline Townsend* | Sch | C [52] | Off Cape Henlopen, DE |
| | Jan 28 | *P. E. Wharton* | Sch | S | 2³/₄ miles S by W of North Beach LSS, MD |
| | Feb 10 | *Sarah W. Lawrence* | Sch | S | 38° 30' 13" N, 74° 43' 48" W |
| | Feb 21 | *P. Rasmussen, Jr.* | Sch | S | Smith Island Inlet, VA |
| | Sept 13 | *John Proctor* | Sch | S | 1³/₄ miles N of Cape Henlopen LSS, DE |
| | Nov 29 | *Gatherer* | SchB | F | Assateague, VA |
| | Dec 26 | *William B. Rambo* | Sch | F | Broadkiln Creek, DE |
| 1910 | Feb 4 | *Jennie N. Huddell* | Sch | S | Carter's Shoal, 2 miles SSE of Cobb Island LSS, VA |

| Date | | Vessel | Type | Manner | Location |
|---|---|---|---|---|---|
| | Feb 6 | *Carrie A. Norton* | Sch | S | 2 miles N of False Cape LSS, VA |
| | Feb 6 | USS *Nina* | Tug | F | Loran 27032.3, 42450.7 |
| | Feb 18 | *Norwood* [NS] | Ship | S | 10 miles SSE of Cobb Island, VA |
| | Mar 7 | *Manchuria* | StS | S | 3½ miles S of Little Island LSS, VA |
| | Apr 1 | *D. M. Margherita* | StS | S | 2½ miles E of False Cape LSS, VA |
| | June 3 | *Aerial* | Sch | F | Off Cape Henry, VA |
| | July 29 | *Eugene H. Cattrall* | Sch | F | Ship John Shoal, Delaware Bay |
| | Nov 14 | *Lucy E. Friend* | Sch | F | Fenwick Island |
| | Aug 17 | *Sunbury* | SchB | F | Fenwick Island Light, 5 miles E of Rehoboth LSS, DE |
| | Sept 1 | *Leif Eriksen* | Sch | C [53] | Fenwick Island Light |
| | Dec 3 | *Marie Thomas* | StS | B | Milton, DE |
| | — | *Earl P. Mason* | Sch | S | 4 miles NNE of Lewes LSS, DE |
| 1911 | Mar 30 | *Howard W. H. Taylor* | Sch | F | Delaware River |
| | Apr 21 | *O. D. Witherell* | Sch | S | 1½ miles N of Fenwick Island LSS, DE |
| | May 12 | *Merida* | StS | C [54] | 55 miles E of Cape Charles, VA |
| | July 29 | *Eugene H. Cattrall* | Sch | B | Ship John Shoal, Delaware Bay |
| | Sept 18 | *Stella Kaplan* | Sch | S | Tail of Horseshoe, Chesapeake Bay, VA |
| | Nov 24 | *Joseph G. Ray* | Sch | S | Tail of Horseshoe, Chesapeake Bay, VA |
| | Dec 17 | *Katherine D. Perry* | Sch | S | 5 miles SW of Smith Island LSS, VA |
| 1912 | Jan 5 | *James Thomas* | Sch | S | Delaware Bay |
| | Feb 27 | *Goldsboro* | StS | S | Brandywine Shoal, Delaware Bay |
| | Mar 5 | *Helen Thomas* | Sch | S | Cape Charles Shoal, VA |
| | Mar 5 | Unidentified | U | F | Off False Cape, VA, at 36° 35' N, 75° 18' W |
| | Mar 12 | *John H. Hall* | Sch | S | 4 miles S of Ocean City LSS, MD |
| | Mar 25 | *Gaston* | SchB | S | 3 miles SE of Cobb Island LSS, VA |
| | Mar 25 | *S. D. Carleton* | SchB | S | 3 miles SE of Cobb Island LSS, VA |
| | Mar 25 | Unidentified | U | W | Between Fenwick Island and Winter Quarter LS, DE |
| | Apr 10 [30] | *James Duffield* | Sch | S | 2 miles ENE of Lewes LSS, DE |
| | Oct 24 | *Crown* | Slp | AS | 36° 35' N, 75° 14' W |
| | Dec 3 | *Charmer* | SchB | S | On the Middle Ground, 3½ miles ENE of Cape Henry LSS, VA |
| 1913 | Jan 3 | *C. R. Bennett* | Sch | S | 1¼ miles NNE of Lewes LSS, DE |
| | Jan 3 | *Julia Luckenbach* | StS | C [55] | Near entrance of Chesapeake Bay |
| | Jan 30 | *Monroe* | StS | C [56] | Off Hog Island, VA, Loran 27049.1, 41805.7 |
| | Feb 2 | *City of Georgetown* | Sch | C [57] | Delaware capes, Loran 26979.6, 42621.0, 38° 46' 33.89" N, 74° 33' 37.57" W |
| | Mar 2 | *Laura Tompkins* | Sch | F | 2½ miles SSW of Cobb Island LSS, VA |
| | Mar 15 | *J. W. Padgett* | Skj | AS | Cape Charles, VA |
| | May 24 | *Lucia* | StS | F | 7 miles NE of Virginia Beach, VA |
| | Sept 28 | *T. Morris Perot* | Sch | C [58] | Fenwick Island, MD |
| | Oct 20 | *Hero* | Brg | F | At Brandywine Lighthouse, Delaware Bay |
| | Dec 24 | *Frieda* | StS | S | 3½ miles NE of False Cape LSS, VA |
| 1914 | Jan 4 | *Oklahoma* | Tkr | F | Loran 26972.4, 42277.2 |
| | Feb 14 | *Dom Pedro II* | SchB | S | Horseshoe Shoal, Chesapeake Bay, VA |
| | June 3 | *Warner Moore* | Sch | S | Cobb Island, VA |
| | July 9 | *Lizzie Godfrey* | Sch | S | Williams Shoal, Chincoteague Inlet, VA |
| | Sept 12 | *Dunlo* | SchB | F | Harbor of Refuge, DE |
| | Nov 15 | *Massasoit* | Sch | S | Off Smith Island, VA (also cited as 1915) |
| | Dec 4 | *Wm. Donnelly* | Sch | S | Virginia coast |
| | Jan 9 | *Frank E. Swain* | Sch | F | SE of Cape Henry, VA |
| 1915 | Jan 15 | *Alice Lord* | Sch | F | 37° 16' N, 71° 06' W |

| Date | | Vessel | Type | Manner | Location |
|---|---|---|---|---|---|
| | Jan 26 | *Washingtonian* | StS | C [59] | Fenwick Island LSS, 38° 27' 04" N, 74° 47' 02" W |
| | Jan 27 [26?] | *Elizabeth Palmer* | Sch | C [60] | 1 mile E of Fenwick Island Lightship, DE, Loran 27019.5, 42420.1 |
| | Apr 3 | *Edward Luckenbach* | StS | F | False Capes, VA |
| | Apr 3 | *Number Six* | SchB | S | On Hen and Chickens Shoal, DE |
| | Apr 3 | *Number Nine* | SchB | S | On Hen and Chickens Shoal, DE |
| | Apr 5 | *Bessie Brown* | Sch | S | Off Cobb Island LSS, VA |
| | Apr 5 | *William H. Macy* | SchB | S | Near Wash Wood LSS, VA |
| | May 27 | *Winthrop* | SchB | F | 15 miles from Assateague Lighthouse, VA |
| | June 3 | *Edwina H. Redmond* | Sch | F | SE of Cape Henry, VA |
| | June 4 | *Abbie S.* | Sch | S | Kitts Hammock Beach, DE |
| | Oct 1 | *Dora* | SchB | F | SE of Fenwick Island Lightship, DE |
| | Oct 5 | *Schuykill* | SchB | F | Chincoteague Shoal, VA |
| | Nov 19 | *Carrie Haley* | Sch | F | Delaware Bay |
| | Nov 19 | *F. A. Allen* | Sch | S | Reedy Island, Delaware Bay |
| | Dec 15 | *Lucy Neff* | StS | F | 20 miles E of Fenwick Island, DE |
| 1916 | Jan 14 | *Lightning* | StS | S | Lewes Dock, DE |
| | Feb 13 | *Albert H. Gheen* | Sch | S | Metompkin Inlet, VA |
| | Feb 13 | *N. H. Burrows* | Sch | S | Hog Island, VA |
| | Feb 19 | *J. Canton Hudson* | SchB | F | Off Hog Island, VA |
| | Feb 21 | *Shamokin* | SchB | F | Cape Henry, VA |
| | Feb 25 | *Trecarell* | StS | F | Blackfish Shoal, 37° 54' 02" N, 75° 16' 00" W |
| | Apr 7 | *Emma F. Angell* | Sch | C [61] | Off Virginia coast |
| 1917 | Feb 6 | *Tobyhanna* | SchB | S | Off Winter Quarter Lightship |
| | Feb 12 | *Lyman L. Law* | Sch | WL | 38° 32' N, 75° 58' W |
| | May 1 | *Progress* | Brg | C | Off Ship John Light, DE |
| | May 8 | *Joseph F. Clinton* | SchB | F | Off Hog Island, VA |
| | July 5 | *Edna B* | GaS | B | Claymont, DE |
| | Sept 23 | *Western Belle* | SchB | F | 22 miles E of Fenwick Island, DE |
| | Sept 24 | *Ella A. Call* | Sch | F | Off Reedy Island, Delaware Bay |
| | Oct 10 [11] | *New Orleans* | StS | F | 38° 41' N, 74° 51' W |
| | Dec 8 | *Andrew Hicks* | Bark | F | Off Cape Henry, VA |
| | Dec 8 | *Ruhama Shaw* | Brg | F | Off Black Fish Bank, VA |
| | Dec 9 | *Georgia* | SchB | F | Chincoteague, VA |
| | Dec 9 | *Lancaster* | SchB | F | Chincoteague, VA |
| | Dec 9 | *Lottie* | Brg | F | Off Black Fish Bank, VA |
| | Dec 9 | *Ruth* | Brg | F | Off Black Fish Bank, VA |
| 1918 | Feb 7 | *Dendron* | SchB | F | 13 miles NW of Hog Island Light, VA |
| | Feb 21 | USS *Annie E. Gallup* | MS | S | Harbor of Refuge, DE |
| | Feb 26 | *Cherokee* | Tug | F | 12½ miles off Fenwick Island Lightship, DE |
| | Mar 10 | *Hampshire* | Sch | F | Off Five Fathom Bank Lightship, DE, 38° 49' 11" N, 74° 31' 17" W |
| | Mar 30 | *American Team* | Sch | F | Off Winter Quarter Light, VA |
| | Apr 10 | *Merrimac* | SchB | S | Rehoboth, DE |
| | Apr 12 | *Florence O'Brien* | Brg | F | 2 miles off Stingray Point Light, Parramore Island, VA |
| | Apr 12 | *Hermod* | StP | F | 37° 55' N, 75° 03' W (also reported 1917) |
| | May 1 | *City of Athens* | StS | C [62] | 38° 51' 54" N, 74° 23' 03" W, Loran 26920.3, 42705.3 |
| | May 25 | *Hattie Dunn* | Sch | WL | East of Hog Island, VA, 37° 24' N, 75° 05' W |
| | May 25 | *Hauppauge* | Sch | WL | 38 miles off Black Fish Bank, VA |
| | June 2 | *Alice M. Guthrie* | GaS | C [63] | 3 miles E of Cape Henry, VA |

| Date | | Vessel | Type | Manner | Location |
|---|---|---|---|---|---|
| | June 2 | *Carolina* | StS | WL | 38° 56' N, 73° 03' W (also given as 38° 57' N, 73° 06' W) |
| | June 2 | *Samuel C. Mengel* | Sch | WL | 38° 58' N, 73° 35' W |
| | June 2 | *Texel* [Du] | StS | WL | 38° 58' N, 73° 13' W |
| | June 5 | *Harpathian* | Frt | | 38° 18' N, 74° 08' W, in 220 feet of water |
| | June 5 | *Vineland* [Nor] | StS | WL | Cape Henry, VA, Loran 26633.0, 41296.3 |
| | June 9 | *Pinar Del Rio* | StS | WL | Sandbridge Beach, VA, Loran 26590, 41216.9 |
| | June 14 | *Kringsja* [Nor] | Bark | WL | 38° 02' N, 71° 40' W |
| | June 14 | *Samon* [Nor] | Bark | WL | 37° 30' N, 72° 10' W |
| | June 16 | *Dwinsk* | StS | WL | Off Delaware capes |
| | June 24 | *Charles W. Alcon* | Sch | F | 50 miles SE of Hog Island Light, VA |
| | June 25 | *Mark Pendleton* | Sch | S | Cobb Island, VA |
| | June 26 | USS *Cherokee* | Tug | F | 12 miles off Fenwick Island, DE, Loran 26982.0, 42519.1 |
| | July 31 | USS *C. F. Sargent* | Brg | F | Hen and Chickens Shoal, DE |
| | July 31 | *Poseidon* [Du] | StS | C [64] | 5 miles NNE of Five Fathom Lightship, Loran 26980.0, 42620.4 |
| | Aug 4 | *O. B. Jennings* | Tkr | WL | 60 miles SE of Cape Henry, VA |
| | Aug 5 | *Madrugada* | GaS | WL | 37° 50' N, 74° 55' W |
| | Aug 17 | *Nordhav* [Nor] | Bark | WL | East of False Cape, VA, Loran 26838, 41155.8 |
| | Sept 3 | *Warren H. Potter* | Sch | S | Cape Charles, VA |
| | Oct 11 | *H. K. Mulford* | Slp | F | Egg Island Light, Delaware Bay |
| | Nov 9 | *Saetia* | StS | WL | Loran 26973.6, 42264.3 |
| | Dec 6 | *Bertha* | Brg | F | 2 miles below Hog Island gas buoy, VA |
| | Dec 22 | *Wm. H. Meekins* | Sch | S | Chincoteague Inlet, VA |
| | — | *Eidvold* | StS | F | Off Virginia coast |
| | — | *SC-187* | PGbt | WL | Approximately 12 miles off Wreck Island, VA |
| 1919 | Jan 4 | *Bayard Hopkins* | Sch | F | Sailed from Norfolk, VA, not heard from |
| | Jan 5 | *Piedmont* | StS | F | Off Cape Henry, VA |
| | Mar 30 | *Scully* | SchB | F | Entrance to Inner Harbor, Delaware Breakwater |
| | May 9 | *F. H. Odone* | Sch | F | Off Chincoteague, VA |
| | Apr 30 | *Hesper* | GaS | S | Delaware capes |
| | Aug 13 | *Ella A. Dempsey* | Brg | F | Off Wachapreague, VA |
| | Aug 18 | *Neosho* | SchB | F | Off Fenwick Island Lightship, DE |
| | Aug 31 | *Caroline* | GaS | F | Thimble Shoal Light, Chesapeake Bay, VA |
| | Nov 30 | *Mary and Alice* | Sch | S | Cape Charles Harbor, VA |
| 1920 | Feb 24 | *Tallac* | StS | S | 18 miles S of Cape Henry, VA |
| | Mar 7 | *Eva B. Douglas* | Sch | AS | 37° 52' N, 71° 23' W |
| | Apr 6 | *Powell* | StS | F | Cape Henry, VA, Loran 27013.5, 41269.7 |
| | Apr 17 | *H. P. Converse #5* | Ltr | F | Off Fenwick Island Lightship, DE |
| | May 27 | *Risoer* [Nor] | Sch | B&F | B at 38° 48' N, 73° 27' W; F 57 miles away |
| | June 21 [July 20] | *Winthrop* | Tug | F | 37° 24' N, 71° 30' W |
| | July 15 | *William C. May* | Sch | F | Cape Henry, VA |
| | Sept 1 | *S-5* | Sub | F | 38° 41' N, 74° 08' W |
| | Sept 24 | *Maid of the Mist* | GaS | F | Near Rehoboth Beach, DE |
| | Oct 1 | *Thomas P. Pollard* | Sch | F | Off Cape Henry, VA |
| | Oct 9 | *Esther Ann* (*Ester Ann*) | U | C [65] | 38° 15' 09" N, 75° 02' 01" W |
| | Dec 4 | *Betty Hearn* | GaS | B | Claymont, DE |
| 1921 | May 23 | *Emma Reis* | Sch | F | Mispillion River, DE |
| | June 20 | *U-117* [Ger] | Sub | AB | 60 miles SE of Cape Charles, VA |
| | June 22 | *U-140* [Ger] | Sub | NG | 50 miles E of Cape Charles, VA, Loran 26874.1, 41574.5 |

| Date | | Vessel | Type | Manner | Location |
|---|---|---|---|---|---|
| | June 22 | *U-148* [Ger] | Sub | NG | East of Cape Charles, VA |
| | June | *Maud* | GaS | F | Leipsic River, DE |
| | July 13 | *G-102* [Ger] | TB/D | AB | Loran 26823.4, 41640.4 |
| | July 15 | *S-132* [Ger] | TB/D | NG | Loran 26824.0, 41717.0 |
| | July 15 | *V-43* [Ger] | TB/D | NG | Loran 26818.0, 41718.0 |
| | July 18 | *Frankfurt* [Ger] | Cr | AB | Loran 26827.1, 41611.7 |
| | July 21 | *Ostfriesland* [Ger] | BB | AB | Loran 26825.0, 41589.0 |
| | Aug 7 | *Cecilia Cohen* | Sch | F | Off Cape Henry, VA |
| | Sept 19 | *Florence and Lillian* | Sch | F | SW of Chincoteague Lighthouse, VA |
| | Oct 25 | *Daisy May* | GaS | S | Virginia Beach, VA |
| | Nov 6 | *Singleton Palmer* | Sch | C [66] | 10 miles NNE of Fenwick Shoal Light, DE |
| 1922 | Jan | *A-2* (*Adder*) | Sub | NG | Off the Chesapeake capes |
| | Jan | *A-3* (*Grampus*) | Sub | NG | Off the Chesapeake capes |
| | Jan | *A-4* (*Moccasin*) | Sub | NG | Off the Chesapeake capes |
| | Jan | *A-5* (*Pike*) | Sub | NG | Off the Chesapeake capes |
| | Jan | *A-6* (*Porpoise*) | Sub | NG | Off the Chesapeake capes |
| | Jan | *A-7* (*Shark*) | Sub | NG | Off the Chesapeake capes |
| | Feb 8 | *Northern Pacific* | StS | B | Loran 26898.7, 42557.0 |
| | Feb 16 | *Norge* | GaS | B | Middle Ground Light, Chesapeake Bay, VA |
| | Mar 7 | *Balsa* | Sch | S | Smith Island, VA |
| | Mar 15 | *Lillie Ernestine* | Sch | S | Wachapreague Beach, VA |
| | May 27 | *Beechwood* | SchB | F | SW of Fenwick Island Lightship, DE |
| | May 27 | *Passaic* | SchB | F | 14 miles SSW of Fenwick Island Lightship, DE |
| | May 28 | *Elk Garden* | Sch | F | North of Hog Island, VA |
| | May 28 | *Larimer* | Sch | F | North of Hog Island, VA |
| | July 13 | *Amaganset* | StS | S | Off Cobb Island, VA |
| | July 14 | *Ella Flaherty* | GaS | B | South of Cape Henry, VA |
| | Aug 15 | *Bayview* | GaS | B | NW of Ledge Light, Delaware Bay |
| | Aug 31 | *U-111* [Ger] | Sub | NG | 37° 45' 15" N, 74° 07' 45" W |
| 1923 | Jan 3 | *Buttonwood* | StS | B | Lynnhaven Roads near Cape Henry, VA |
| | Feb 6 | *Frank M. Deering* | Sch | S | Near Cobb Island, VA |
| | Apr 11 | *Crew Leverick #5* | Brg | F | 14 miles SSW of Fenwick Island Lightship, DE |
| | Apr 14 | *Stroudsburg* | SchB | F | NW of Brown Shoal, Delaware Bay |
| | June 2 | *Glen Beulah* | Slp | C [67] | 10 miles SE of Cape Charles Lighthouse, VA |
| | July 25 | *Samuel H. Hartman* | StS | F | Delaware Bay |
| | Oct 5 | *Wm. J. Lemmond* | SchB | F | Lynnhaven Bay, VA |
| | Oct 24 | *Fort Pierce* | SchB | F | Off Assateague Light |
| | Nov 12 | *Marion O'Boyle* | Brg | F | 20 miles SSE of Fenwick Island Lightship, DE, 38° 37' 57" N, 74° 55' 34" W |
| | Nov 13 [14] | *City of Orleans* | SchB | F | 38° 18' N, 74° 00' W, in 220 feet of water |
| | Nov 16 | *Wade Hampton* | StS | F | Delaware Bay |
| 1924 | Jan 16 | *Francis O'Boyle* | Brg | S | Off Cape Henry, VA |
| | Mar 26 | *Mary L. Cooper* | Sch | F | Milton, DE |
| | May 3 | *Skipjack* | SchB | C [68] | Delaware Bay |
| | Sept 17 | *Corrotoman* | Brg | F | Brown Shoal, Delaware Bay |
| | Oct 10 | *Marion Chappell* | SchB | F | Fenwick Island Light, DE |
| | Oct 12 | *Jennie R. Foote* | Sch | B | Smith Island Light, VA |
| | Nov 17 | *Susan B.* | Sch | F | Winter Quarter Light, VA |
| | Nov 25 | USS *Washington* | BB | NG | Loran 26843.3, 41420.0 |
| 1925 | Jan 1 | *Mohawk* | StS | B | Fourteen Foot Bank, Delaware Bay, 39° 00' 08.50" N, 75° 12' 16.10" W |
| | Apr 21 | *Lincoln* | SchB | F | Chincoteague, VA |
| | Apr 25 | *Thomaston* | SchB | C [69] | Delaware Bay |

The U.S. Navy submarine A-4 *Moccasin* was sunk by naval gunfire as a target ship during fleet reduction operations in January 1922. (The Mariners' Museum, Newport News, VA)

| Date | | Vessel | Type | Manner | Location |
|---|---|---|---|---|---|
| | July 1 | *Alberta* | Sch | S | Toms Cove, VA |
| | Sept 20 | *Benjamin A. Van Brunt* | Sch | C [70] | 36° 56' N, 74° 46' W, Loran 26840.5 ,41418.3 |
| | Oct 10 | *Marion Chappell* | SchB | S | Delaware capes |
| | Oct 21 | *Isabella Parmenter* | Sch | F | Cape Henry, VA, Loran 26855.1, 41397.9 |
| | Nov 18 | *Lenape* | StS | B&S | Close to Coast Guard Station, Lewes, DE |
| | Dec 7 | *Edna M. McKnight* | Sch | F | Cape Henry, VA |
| | — | *Nellie A.* | LtB | C [71] | Delaware Bay |
| 1926 | Jan 24 | *Solvang* [Nor] | Frt | C [72] | Near Winter Quarter Lightship |
| | Oct 18 | *David R. Lake* | GaS | B | Reedy Island, Delaware Bay |
| 1927 | Feb 8 | *Marie C. Beazley* | SchB | B | 38° 34' 30" N, 74° 41' 30" W |
| | Feb 14 | *Northern 35* | SchB | F | 38° 44' 30" N, 74° 37' 50" W |
| | Mar 15 | *Estelle* | OlS | F | Thimble Shoal, Chesapeake Bay, VA |
| | Apr 14 | *604 Steel* | Brg | F | Cape Charles, VA |
| | Sept 29 | *Bear Ridge* | SchB | W | 38° 56' N, 74° 46' W |
| 1928 | Mar 13 | *J. Henry Edmons* (*Edmonds*) | GaS | S | Cape Henlopen, DE |
| | Apr 15 | *Emily* | O1S | F | Lynnhaven Bay, VA |
| | Sept 19 | *Tigress* | SlpY | S | Lewes, DE |
| | Sept 19 | *Lottie* | Brg | F | Lewes, DE |
| | Nov 12 | *Vestris* [Br] | U | F | Off Virginia capes |
| 1929 | — (p) | Unidentified | U | F | 38° 27' 26" N, 74° 56' 04" W |

| Date | | Vessel | Type | Manner | Location |
|---|---|---|---|---|---|
| | — (p) | Unidentified | U | F | 38° 27' 22" N, 74° 56' 24" W |
| | Mar 7 | Early Bird | Sch | S | Ship Shoal, Assateague, VA |
| | June 27 | Carpenas | Brg | S | Atlantic off Delmarva coast |
| 1930 | May 13 | Sarah Quinn | Sch | S | Cobb Island, VA |
| | Aug 23 | Emily A. Foote | OlS | F | Harbor of Refuge, Delaware Breakwater |
| | Sept 12 | Florence Marie II | GaS | S | 5.5 miles NE of Metomkin Inlet, VA |
| | Oct 27 | Rebecca C. Scott | Sch | C [73] | 36° 39' N, 74° 00' W |
| 1931 | Aug 9 | Pompano | OlS | F | Wachapreague, VA |
| | Oct 19 | Louise Virginia | GaS | B | Hog Island Light, VA |
| 1932 | Mar 6 | Deepwater | Brg | L | ESE of Parramore Bank Buoy, VA |
| | Aug 17 | Campelo Pardaus | GaY | F | Off Mahon River, DE |
| | Oct 21 | Katie Durm | GaS | B | Off Cape Henlopen, DE |
| | Nov 8 | Ripogenus | StS | C [74] | Off Cape Henry, VA |
| | Dec 2 | Appomattox | GaS | B | In lower Delaware Bay |
| 1933 | Feb 15 | Maud E. | GaS | F | Lewes, DE |
| | Feb 16 | Maurice R. Shaw | Brg | F | Winter Quarter Shoals, VA |
| | Mar 13 | Victor | OlS | B | Chesapeake Lightship, VA |
| | May 8 | Beauty of (St.) Joseph | OlS | B | Off Cape Henry, VA |
| | May 26 | Amscray | GaY | F | Delaware Bay |
| | June 14 | Smuggler | OlS | B | Willoughby Spit, Chesapeake Bay, VA |
| | July 2 | Shawara | GaS | F | Delaware Bay |
| | July 3 | S. G. Wilder | Brg | F | Fenwick Island, Loran 26971.7; 42265.4 |
| | July 4 | White Haven | Brg | F | 3–4 miles NW of Winter Quarter Lightship, VA |
| | July 3–4 | Brunswick | Brg | F | 3–4 miles NW of Winter Quarter Lightship, VA |
| | July 3–4 | Matagorda | Brg | F | 3–4 miles NW of Winter Quarter Lightship, VA |
| | Aug 23 | Annie May | GaS | F | Dewey Beach (also Bowers Beach), DE |
| | Nov 19 | Idasel | GaY | B | Delaware City, DE |
| | Dec 10 | Northern 29 | Brg | F | Loran 26885.1, 43134.1 |
| | Dec 12 | Carpender | SchB | F | 33° 22' 07" N, 74° 58' 08" W |
| 1934 | Feb [Jan 23, 1935] | T. J. Hooper | Tug | F | 18 miles off MD in 23 feet of water |
| | April | Barnstable | Brg | F | Winter Quarter, 37° 58' 00" N, 75° 08' 07 W |
| | Sept 3 | William B. Diggs | Brg | F | 38° 56' 29" N, 74° 41' 56" W |
| 1935 | — (p) | Unidentified | U | F | 38° 26' 30" N, 74° 46' 30" W |
| | Jan 23 | Steel Barge No. 2 | Brg | F | Off Blackfish Bank Buoy, VA |
| | Jan 24 | Pattie Morrisette | Brg | F | In 60 feet, 38° 37' 16" N, 74° 43' 00" W |
| | Jan 25 | Octorara | Brg | F | Delaware Bay, DE |
| | June 24 | Helmi II | GaS | B | Near Delaware Breakwater |
| | Sept 28 | Hanover No. 1 | SchB | F | 51 miles S of Fenwick Island Whistling Buoy, DE, 37° 33' 05" N, 77° 56' 00" W |
| | Nov 14 | Saratoga | Brg | F | 3 miles below Bowers, DE |
| | Nov 21 | John Leonard | OlS | S | Between New Inlet and Myrtle Inlet, VA |
| | Dec 5 | Therese White | GaY | F | 6 miles E of Cape Henry, VA |
| 1936 | Sept 18 | Long Island | StS | F | 1 mile SW of Red No. 6, inside Overfalls Bell Buoy, Delaware Bay |
| | Oct 18 | Maryland | StS | F | Thimble Shoal Light, Chesapeake Bay, VA |
| 1937 | Jan 10 | Director | OlS | B | E of Mahon River Light, Delaware Bay |
| | Feb 6 | Catonsville | Brg | F | 17 1/2 miles E by N, 3/4 mile N from Chesapeake Lightship, VA |
| | Feb 18 | Jonesport | Brg | F | 38° 17' 33" N, 75° W |
| | Feb 20 | Andrew McDonald | SchB | F | About 11 miles N of Parramore gas buoy, VA |
| | Apr 26 | Unidentified | Brg | S | 38° 17' 33" N, 75° 00' 00" W |
| | June 14 | Raiford | GaS | B | Off Ocean View, Chesapeake Bay, VA |

| Date | | Vessel | Type | Manner | Location |
|---|---|---|---|---|---|
| | Sept 22 | *R. H. Beckwith* | StS | F | 38° 53' 05" N, 74° 51' 12 W |
| | Oct 18 | *Maryland* | StS | F | Thimble Shoal Light, Chesapeake Bay, VA |
| 1938 | Mar 30 | *Olympia* | OlS | U | 45 miles E of Cape Henry, VA |
| | Oct 28 | *Talbot* | Brg | B | Delaware Breakwater |
| | Nov 20 | *Pacific* | Brg | S | 37° 18' 52" N, 75° 36' 30" W |
| | Dec 1 | *William D. Sanner* | OlS | C [75] | 2 miles NW of Cape Henry Lighthouse, VA |
| | — | *Gemini* | Tug | F | Several miles SSE of Fisherman's Island, VA |
| 1939 | Aug 12 | *Sunbeam* | GaS | B | 3 miles off Lewes, DE |
| | July 1 | *L. B. Shaw* | Brg | F | 38° 54' 54" N, 74° 13' 00" W |
| | Oct 3 | Westmoreland | Brg | F | Off Cape Henry Lighthouse, VA, 36° 56' 45.35" N, 75°57' 29.96" W |
| | — | *Gem* | GaS | B | Leipsic, DE |
| 1940 | Feb 7 | *Angie and Vence* | OlS | C [76] | 55 miles E of Chesapeake Lightship, VA |
| | Aug 31 | *Bright* | SchB | C | 38° 33' N, 76° 26' W |
| 1941 | Jan 19 | *Adventure* | OlY | F | 20–30 miles SW of Winter Quarter Lightship, VA |
| | Mar 18 | *T. J. Hooper* | StS | S | 38° 26' 06" N, 74° 23' 42" W, Loran 26875.1, 42428.1 |
| | Apr 2 | *The Major* | GaS | B | Off Fisherman's Island, VA |
| | July 28 | *P.R.R. No. 100* | Brg | F | Off the Whistling Buoy, off Delaware Bay |
| | Aug 23 | *White City* | GaS | B | Murder Kill River, DE |
| | Sept 10 | *Harry K. Fooks* | OlS | C [77] | 1,000 yards off Hen and Chickens Shoal, DE, 38° 42' 36" N, 74° 59' 48" W (also given as 38° 42' 40.57" N, 74° 59' 33.21" W) |
| | Nov 22 | *Effie M. Lewis* | OlS | F | Delaware Bay |
| | — | *P. J. Cooper* | Tug | F | SE of Chincoteague, VA |
| 1942 | Jan 25 | *Varanger* [Nor] | Tkr | WL | 39° 00' 30" N, 74° 05' 00" W, Loran 26825.5, 42803.7 |
| | Jan 27 | *Francis E. Powell* | Tkr | WL | 37° 27' 08" N, 75° 16' 07" W, also given 37° 45' N, 74° 53' W |
| | Jan 28 | *Lycoming* | Brg | F | Thimble Shoal Light, Chesapeake Bay, VA, |
| | Jan 30 | *Rochester* | StS | WL | 37° 10' N, 75° 38' W |
| | Jan 30 | *Tacoma Star* [Br] | Frt | WL | 37° 33' N, 69° 21' W |
| | Feb 2 | *W. L. Steed* | Tkr | WL | 38° 25' 08" N, 74° 46' 01" W |
| | Feb 2–3 [4] | *San Gil* [Pan] | Frt | WL | 38° 06' 06" N, 74° 37' 00" W, Loran 26906.1, 42180.7 |
| | Feb 4 | *India Arrow* | Frt | WL | 38° 33' 30" N, 73° 50' 06" W |
| | Feb 5 | *Amerikaland* [Swed] | Frt | WL | 36° 36' N, 74° 10' W |
| | Feb 5 | *China Arrow* | Tkr | WL | 38° 58' 48" N, 75° 09' 42" W |
| | Feb 8 | *Ocean Venture* [Br] | Frt | U | 37° 03' 35" N, 74° 55' 20" W |
| | Feb 15 | *Buarque* [Braz] | Frt | WL | 36° 35' N, 75° 20' W |
| | Feb 16 | *Azalea City* | Frt | WL | Off the coast of Virginia |
| | Feb 16 | *E. H. Blum* | TB | WL [R] | 36° 57' N, 75° 52' W |
| | Feb 18 | *Olinda* [Braz] | Frt | WL | Loran 26701.2, 42121.5 |
| | Feb 28 | USS *Jacob Jones* | DE | WL | 38° 37' 00" N, 74° 23' 12" W [stern], 38° 40' 11.73" N, 74° 28' 42.45" W [bridge], 38° 41' N, 74° 29' W [bow] |
| | Feb | *William L. Hooper* | Brg | F | Lewes, DE |
| | Mar 3 | *Otho* | Frt | WL | E of Smith Island, VA, Loran 26231.0, 41458.0 |
| | Mar 4 | *Gypsum Prince* | Frt | C [78] | Off Lewes, DE, Loran 27146.2, 42641.5 |
| | Mar 11 | *Hvoslef* [Nor] | Frt | WL | Loran 26931.6, 42450.1 |
| | Mar 13 | *Trepsca* [Youg] | Ore | WL | 37° 00' N, 73° 25' W |
| | Mar 15 | *San Demetrio* [Br] | Frt | WL | 37° 03' N, 73° 50' W |

| Date | | Vessel | Type | Manner | Location |
|---|---|---|---|---|---|
| | Mar 26 | *Equipoise* [Pan] | Frt | WL | 36° 36' N, 74° 45' W |
| | Mar 31 | *Alleghenny* (*Alleghany*) | Brg | WL | 37° 32' 02" N, 75° 26' 06" W |
| | | | | | (also given 37°32.12 N, 75° 24.42W) |
| | Mar 31 | *Barnegat* | Brg | WL | 37° 32' 01" N, 75° 15' 08" W |
| | Mar 31 | *Menominee* | Tug | WL | Off Parramore buoy, VA, 37° 32' N, 75° 26' W |
| | Mar 31 | *Tiger* | StS | WL | 36° 50' N, 75° 49' W |
| | Apr 2 | *David H. Atwater* | Frt | WL | 37° 37' N, 75° 10' W, Loran 27047.5, 27058.0 |
| | | | | | (also given as 27047.7, 42059.4) |
| | Apr 15 | *Robin Hood* | Frt | WL | 37° 10' N, 73° 58' W |
| | Apr 18 | *Victoria* [Arg] | Tkr | WL | 36° 41' N, 68° 48' W |
| | Apr 24 | *Empire Drum* [Br] | Frt | WL | 37° 00' N, 69° 15' W |
| | June 15 | *Robert C. Tuttle* | Tkr | WL | 36° 51' N, 75° 51' W |
| | June 17 | *Kingston Ceylonite* [Br] | Frt | WL | 36° 49' 39" N, 75° 52' 09" W |
| | June 17 | *Santore* | Frt | WL | 1½ miles NE of No. 2 Chesapeake Bay gas buoy, 36° 54' N, 75° 46' W |
| | June 24 | *John R. Williams* | StS | WL | 38° 45' 09.30" N, 74° 54' 23.5 1" W |
| | June 27 | *Moldanger* [Nor] | Frt | WL | 36° 50' N, 69° 22' W |
| | July 24 | *Chilore* | Frt | WL | 36° 27' 38" N, 76° 00' 39" W |
| | Sept 11 (21) | *Druid Hill* | Brg | F | Thimble Shoal, VA, 37° 07' N, 74° 14' W |
| | Nov 12 | *Rogist* | OlS | C [79] | Loran 27098.0, 41366.1 |
| | Dec 3 | *Calinarcher* | Y | W | On Delaware Breakwater |
| | — | *Brazil* | Frt | WL | Loran 27153.9, 41377.2 |
| | | | | | (also given as 2753.4, 41376.1) |
| 1943 | Jan 24 | *Edwin R. Smith* | Sch | S | 37° 49' N, 75° 22' W |
| | Mar 27 | *Lillian Luckenbach* | StS | C [80] | Loran 27032.1, 41372.9 |
| | Apr 7 | *Birch Lake* | Brg | U | Off Wreck Island, VA, 37° 15' 00" N, 75° 37' 34" W, Loran 27114.7, 41538.6 |
| | May 9 | *Juniata* | Brg | F | Off Virginia capes |
| | June 1 | *John Morgan* | StS | C [81] | Cape Henry, VA, Loran 27032.8, 41390.2, and 27033.7, 41391.4 and 27033.1, 41391 |
| | June 2 | *U-521* [Ger] | Sub | WL | 37° 43' N, 73° 16' W |
| | Sept 15 | *Betsy Richards* | Sch | S | North slope of Delaware Breakwater |
| | Sept 25 | *Perseverance* | OlS | F | Mouth of Lynnhaven River, VA |
| | Oct 15 | USS *Moonstone* | PY | C [82] | 38° 29' 03" N, 74° 32' 40" W, Loran 26927.4, 42470.8 |
| | Nov 21 | *Altair* | Frt | F | 37° 17' N, 74° 08' W |
| 1944 | — (p) | Unidentified | U | F | 38° 39' 36" N, 74° 26' 36" W |
| | Mar 9 | *Accomac* | GaS | S | Chincoteague, VA |
| | Apr 5 | *Spring Chicken* | OlS | F | 35 miles E of Cape Henry, VA |
| | June 1 | *Sapho* | GaS | B | Ocean City, MD |
| | June 16 | *Hannah A. Lennen* | StS | C [83] | Entrance to Delaware Bay, 38° 50' 31" N, 74° 05' W |
| | June 17 | *Tex* | GaS | B | In Delaware Bay off Lewes, DE |
| | Jan 6 | USS *St. Augustine* | PGbt | C [84] | 38° 04' N, 74° 06' W |
| | Aug 17 | *Reliance* | Sch | W | 38° 27' N, 75° 03' W |
| | Sept 14 | *Thomas Tracy* | Tkr | S | Rehoboth Beach, DE, 38° 42' N, 75° 04' W |
| | Sept 15 | *May D* [*May Dee*] | GaS | F | Ocean View, VA |
| | Dec 12 | Unidentified | U | F | 38° 36' 18" N, 74° 39' 36" W |
| | Dec 28 | *Marie Hooper* | Brg | F | 5¾ miles W by 5½ miles S of Hen and Chicken Lightship, DE |
| 1945 | — (p) | Unidentified | U | F | 38° 31' 30" N, 74° 31' 54" W |
| | Jan 31 | *Mildred Silva* | OlS | B | 25 miles ENE of Cape Henry, VA |

| Date | | Vessel | Type | Manner | Location |
|------|------|--------|------|--------|----------|
| | Apr 18 | *Swiftscout* | Frt | WL | 37° 30' N, 74° 45' W (also given 73° 03' W) |
| | Apr 30 | *U-548* [Ger] | Sub | WL | 36° 34' N, 74° 00' W |
| | Dec 15 | *Joseph E. Hooper* | SchB | F | 38° 28' 00" N, 74° 58' 08" W, Loran 27021.7, 42415.4 |
| 1946 | — (p) | *Martha* | GaS | S | Indian River Inlet, DE |
| | — (p) | *B. H. Minch* | GaS | F | Little Creek, DE |
| | Jan 1 | *Frank R. Digges* | Brg | F | Rogues Harbor, below C&D Canal, DE |
| | Mar 18 | *Southern Sword* | Brg | F | Loran 27080.3, 42516.3 |
| | July 20 | *B. F. Macomber* | OlS | F | 38° 48' 45.11" N, 75° 04' 25.20" N (also given 38° 48' 46.73" N, 75° 04' 04.11" W) |
| | July 20 | *Phillie Boy* | GaS | B | 1 mile S of Ben Davis Point, Delaware Bay |
| | — | *Barge 887* | Brg | F | Delmarva coast |
| 1947 | Jan 17 | *Balila* | OlS | B | 3½ miles E of Cape Henry, VA |
| | Feb 27 | *Catherine L. Brown* | OlS | F | SW ½ S of Chesapeake Lightship, 50 miles off Portsmouth, VA |
| | Apr 12 | *Gordon S. Cook* | Brg | F | 38° 05' 04" N, 74° 48' 06" W |
| | Apr 12 | *Seminole* | OlS | C [85] | 1¼ miles NE of Thimble Shoal Light, Chesapeake Bay, VA |
| | Sept 30 | *Lu Lu* | GaS | F | At the rock jetty of Indian River Inlet, DE |
| | Oct 12 | *Pearl B* | O1S | F | In Delaware Bay, between Cape Henlopen, DE, and Cape May, NJ |
| 1948 | May 3 | *Puds* | GaS | F | In Delaware Bay off Hog Shoal Buoy |
| 1949 | May 2 | *U.F 3* | GaS | F | Between False Egg Island and old Ledge Light, lower Delaware Bay |
| | June 20 | *Iris* | GaS | U | At Virginia Beach, VA |
| | Nov 6 | *Alice Ann* | OlS | F | In vicinity of False Cape, VA |
| | Nov 6 | *Irvirna* | GaS | B | Port Mahon, DE |
| 1950 | Mar 15 | *Rex* | GaS | B | At New Inlet, near Cobbs Channel, VA |
| | June 13 | *Peconic* | OlS | F | Off starboard edge of Cape Charles channel |
| | June 27 | *Harrison* | StS | B | Ben Davis Shoal, DE |
| | Sept 24 | *Teddy* | GaS | S | Willoughby Beach, Chesapeake Bay, VA |
| | Oct 3 | *E.E. Moore* | OlS | F | Off Myrtle Island, Cape Charles, VA |
| | Nov 29 | *Margaret B* | OlS | U | 38° 51' 54" N, 74° 23' 03" W |
| | Dec 7 | *Myrna Loy* | OlS | B | North of Cape Charles in Chesapeake Bay |
| 1951 | — | *Voyager II* | OlS | F | 30–35 miles SE of Winter Quarter Lightship, VA |
| 1952 | Feb 28 | *Belle Isle* | OlS | F | On beach near Cape Henry Lighthouse, VA |
| | Mar 22 | *Captain Swann* | OlS | Cap | In Chincoteague Inlet, VA |
| | May 25 | *Dorothy May* | GaS | S | ½ mile off Willoughby Beach, VA |
| | Sept 29 | *A. C. Dodge* | OlS | C [86] | Off Reedy Island, Delaware Bay |
| 1953 | Jan 6 | *Lula Scott* | Slp | A | Cape Charles, VA |
| | Mar 16 | *Caspian* | OlS | F | 48 miles due E of Assateague Island, VA |
| | Dec 1 | *Tommy* | GaS | B | Between Stingray Point and Grey Point, Parramore Island, VA |
| 1954 | Jan 22 | *Louise* | OlS | F | SE of Cherrystone Buoy near Cape Charles, VA |
| | Mar 12 | *Thelma II* | GaS | F | Off Chincoteague, VA |
| | Apr 12 | *Linda M. Stockwell* | GaS | F | Delaware Bay, 3 miles NNW of Brown Shoal buoy, off Mispillion River, DE |
| | Apr 20 | *Ablisi* | Brg | F | Off Calumet River, DE |
| | July 11 | *Chesapeake* | GaS | F | Off Fenwick Island, MD |
| | Oct 7 | *Jane* | GaS | F | At Kiptopeake, near Cape Charles, VA |
| 1956 | Jan | *Machipongo* | GaS | B | Point Farm, Quimby, VA |
| | Jan | *Edna E. Bateman* | GaS | B | In St. James Creek, near Leipsic, DE |
| | May 2 | *Charles Wright* | GaS | B | Port Mahon, Delaware River, DE |

View of the wreck of *Peconic,* built in 1879 and foundered on the edge of Cape Charles Channel, June 13, 1950 (The Mariners' Museum, Newport News, VA)

| Date | | Vessel | Type | Manner | Location |
|---|---|---|---|---|---|
| | Oct 15 | *Nelfred* | OlS | B | Near Five Fathom Bank, off Cape May, NJ |
| 1957 | Mar 20 | USS *Mission San Francisco* | Tkr | C [87] | New Castle, DE |
| | Nov 2 | *Mart Jean IV* | GaS | F | Vicinity of Cape Charles Lighthouse, VA |
| 1958 | Dec 30 | *African Queen* | Tkr | F | 9 miles off Ocean City, MD, Loran 27022.7, 42202.2 |
| 1959 | Jan 1 | *Lillie* | GaS | B | South Bay entrance, 4 miles SE of Cobb Island Coast Guard Station, VA |
| | Aug 7 | *Blanch* | GaS | F | Approximately 1 mile N of Kiptopeake, VA |
| | Aug 15 | *Minnie V* | OlS | W | Lynnhaven Bay, near Cape Henry, VA |
| | Sept 17 | *Rupert II* | GaS | F | At Bowers Beach, DE |
| | Oct 19 | *Phantom* | GaS | C [88] | In Cape Charles Harbor, VA |
| 1960 | Feb | *Northampton* | OlS | W | Little Creek, VA |
| | Apr 16 | *Ethel C* | Frt | F | Off Parramore Island, VA |
| | Apr 21 | *Nancy Owen [Nancy Give?]* | OlS | U | 60 miles ENE of Cape Henry, VA |
| 1961 | Apr 10 | *Powhattan* | OlS | C [89] | 43 miles SE of Cape May, NJ, in 32 fathoms |
| 1962 | Jan 15 | *Maine* | GaS | W | In Delaware Bay off Port Mahon, DE |
| | Jan 15 | *Aque* | GaS | W | Chincoteague, VA |
| | Mar 7 | *Maine* | GaS | W | Off Port Mahon, in Delaware Bay, DE |
| | Mar 7 | *Jean H* | GaS | Ice | At Oak Orchard, DE |

| Date | | Vessel | Type | Manner | Location |
|---|---|---|---|---|---|
| | Mar 7 | *Karma* | OlS | W | Chincoteague, VA |
| | Mar 7 | *Miss Nottingham* | GaS | W | At Rehoboth Beach, DE |
| | Mar 7 | *Priscilla* | GaS | W | Chincoteague, VA |
| | Mar 7 | *Sonya* | OlS | W | Vicinity of Winter Quarter Shoals, VA |
| | Mar 7 | *Susie P. Barnes* | GaS | W | Off Wallops Island, at Chincoteague, VA |
| 1963 | Jan 15 | *Iva May* | GaS | Ice | In Delaware Bay off Lewes, DE |
| | July 15 | *Tucaway* | OlS | B | Near Norfolk Ship Channel junction and Kiptopeake Ferry Channel, VA |
| | Aug 22 | *Linda L* | OlS | C [90] | Off Ocean City, MD |
| 1964 | Mar | *Pauline M. Boland* | OlS | F | About 42 miles SE of Assateague Island, VA |
| | June 7 | *Flo-Mel* | GaS | B | Rehoboth, DE |
| | Sept 18 | *Jane E. L.* | GaS | B | At Cedar Island, Accomack County, VA |
| | Dec 1 | *Liki Tiki* | OlS | F | About 40 miles E of Norfolk, VA |
| 1965 | Jan 15 | *Courier* | OlS | B | Approx. 80 miles off Cape Henry, VA |
| | Oct 7 | *Ruth Conway* | OlS | F | About 1 mile W of Thimble Shoal Light, Chesapeake Bay, VA |
| 1966 | June 17 | *Phil Mar* | OlS | F | 15 miles 60° off Chesapeake Light Station, VA |
| | — | *Osprey* | Tug | S | South end of Smith Island, VA |
| 1967 | —(p) | *Theresa I* | U | F | 3,900 yards and 20° from elbow of Cross Ledge Light, Delaware Bay |
| | Jan 16 | *Thomas E* | GaS | B | At Indian River Inlet, DE |
| | June 19 | *Eleanor A. Warner* | OlS | F | Off the Delaware coast |
| | Sept 7 | *Sea Chanty* | OlS | C [91] | Reedy Island, Delaware Bay |
| | Oct 2 | *Beachcomber II* | GaS | B | Off Cape Henry, VA |
| | Nov 4 | *Guavina* | Sub | NT | Delaware Bay 3 miles N of Harbor of Refuge Light |
| | Nov 28 | *Island Lady* | OlS | B | Off Cobb Island, VA |
| 1968 | Jan 30 | *Nancy Jane* | OlS | F | Off Chincoteague, VA |
| | Feb | *Til* | GaS | F | In Rehoboth Bay, Rehoboth, DE |
| | May 7 | *Clifford Jr.* | GaS | F | At Peppers Creek, Dagsboro, DE |
| | May 17 | *Walton Grace* | OlS | F | In Delaware Bay, 38° 12' N, 75° 15' W |
| | May 27 | *Resolute* | OlS | F | Off Bethany Beach, DE |
| | June 22 | *Fan Tail* | GaS | S | Off Buoy no. 104, Liston Range, S of Reedy Island, DE |
| | July 30 | *Swan* | OlS | S | About 400 yards W of Little Creek Inlet, VA |
| | Nov | *Hess Hausler* | Tkr | S [R] | Between Wreck and Cobb Island, VA |
| | — | *Gee Bee Gee* | Y | F | Virginia Avenue, Rehoboth Beach, DE |
| 1969 | Mar 16 | *San Jacinto* | U | F | 40 miles off the Virginia coast |
| | June 25 | *Easygo* | GaS | F | 25 miles off Norfolk, VA |
| | July 4 | *Judy B.* | GaS | B | Virginia Capes Marina, Virginia Beach, VA |
| | July 16 | *Manta* | Sub | NT | Off Norfolk, VA |
| | Aug 20 | *Leader* | OlS | F | 4 miles E of Cape Henry, VA |
| | Oct 21 | *Muriel Eileen* | OlS | F | 37° 48' 00" N, 75° 14' 08" W |
| | Dec 18 | *Florence* | GaS | B | In Pepper Creek, DE |
| 1970 | Feb 28 | *Neighbor* | OlS | F | Ocean City Inlet, Ocean City, MD |
| | May 27 | *P. Tee* | OlS | F | Hen and Chickens Shoal, 1/2 mile from Harbor of Refuge Light Station, DE |
| | July 30 | *Sea Fin* | GaS | F | Ocean City, MD |
| | Sept 4 | *Altair* | GaS | S | On Cobb Island, VA |
| | Sept 29 | *Venture* | OlS | F | 38° 08' 10" N, 75° 04' 24" W |
| 1971 | Aug 2 | *Anna M. Frome* | U | F | 39° 14' 48" N, 75° 29' 48" W |
| | Aug 10 | *Briarwood II* | GaS | B | Thimble Shoal Light, Chesapeake Bay, VA |
| | Sept 6 | *Turtle* | OlS | F | In Atlantic Ocean off Quimby Inlet, VA |

| Date | | Vessel | Type | Manner | Location |
|------|------|--------|------|--------|----------|
| | Nov 7 | *Dolfin* | GaS | F | In Atlantic Ocean off Virginia Beach, VA |
| 1972 | Feb 3 | *Nancy Jane* | OlS | F | 60 miles SE of Cape May, NJ |
| | Apr 19 | *Esther Joy* | OlS | B | Off Chincoteague, VA |
| | Sept 17 | *Wander* | GaS | B | Lynnhaven River, Lynnhaven Marina Dock, VA |
| | Oct | *Saltsea II* | OlS | F | Virginia Beach, VA |
| | Nov 8 | *Georgia B* | GaS | C [92] | Lewes, DE |
| | Nov 23 | *Morning Star* | GaS | F | 36° 49' 57" N, 75° 41' 24" W |
| | Dec 6 | *Eugenia* | OlS | C [93] | Off Metomkin Inlet, Parramore Beach, VA |
| | Dec 7 | *Mary Beth* | GaS | F | Near Chesapeake Bay Bridge-Tunnel, 12 miles from Cape Charles, VA |
| | — | *Mary L. Lewis* | FV | S | Between Wreck and Cobb Island, VA |
| 1973 | Mar 6 | *Matapike* | OlS | F | 37° 10' 02" N, 75° 49' 02" W |
| | Sept 29 | *Queen* | GaS | F | 38° 71' N, 74° 56' W |
| 1974 | (ca.) | *Effie K.* | GaS | F | At Chincoteague, VA |
| | Mar 15 | *Malolo* | OlS | F | 3 miles S of Sandbridge, Virginia Beach, VA |
| | Mar 28 | *Thomas F. Jubb* | OlS | F | In Chesapeake Bay, off Grand View, VA |
| | Oct 20 | *Colleen C.* | OlS | F | 36° 56' 03" N, 75° 48' 03" W |
| | Oct 21 | *Jeannette II* | OlS | B | Delaware City, DE |
| | — | *Gulf Hustler* | FV | F | Loran 27069.8, 41273.0 |
| | — | *Webster* | Tank | F | East of entrance to Chesapeake Bay |
| 1975 | Jan 22 | *Captain N. Rick (Capt'n Rick)* | OlS | F | Loran 27035.7, 41188.0 |
| | Mar 17 | *Doxie Girl (Dixie Girl?)* | Tug | F | Loran 27092.2, 41462.8, in 60 feet of water |
| | May 27 | *Casey and Brown* | OlS | F | 2½ miles NE of Indian River Inlet, DE |
| | July 3 | *Funhouse* | GaS | F | 39° 27' N, 75° 33' W, lower Delaware Bay |
| | Aug 13 | *Suntan* | GaS | B | Chesapeake Bay, 7 miles N of Little Creek Inlet, off Virginia Beach, VA |
| | Dec 21 | *Carolyn* | GaS | W | 2 miles 180° T from Sand Shoal Light, VA |
| | — | *George P. Garrison* | StS | W | Loran 27020.7, 41390.2 |
| | — | *Mona Island* | Frt | F | Loran 27096.0, 42744.0 |
| 1976 | June | *Little Harold* | OlS | F | Ocean City Inlet, ½ mile off Buoy No. 5, MD |
| | Aug 15 | *Goose* | GaS | B | At Dover, DE |
| | — | *James E. Haviland* | Frt | AR | Loran 27020.0, 41389.6 |
| 1977 | (p) | *Emma* | GaS | F | Indian River Inlet, DE |
| | — | *Edgar Clark* | Tug | AR | Loran 27018.9, 41386.2 |
| | June 25 | *Crosswinds* | OlS | F | In upper Delaware Bay |
| 1978 | Jan 26 | *Miss Maxine* | OlS | F | In Chincoteague Inlet, Chincoteague, VA |
| | Feb 27 | *Pari Passu* | OlS | F | In Atlantic Ocean off Chincoteague, VA |
| | Apr 17 | *Tern Sand* | GaS | B | In Chincoteague Inlet, VA, ¼ mile S of Black Fish Bank bell buoy |
| | Dec | USCG *Cuyahoga* | OlS | Sc | Loran 27022.4, 41369.6 |
| | Dec 10 | *Rendezvous* | OlS | F | Chincoteague, VA, Loran 26972.8, 41963.3 |
| | Dec 15 | *Captain William* | OlS | F | At Chincoteague Inlet, VA |
| 1979 | Jan 3 | *King Cobra* | Tug | F | Loran 27096.1, 42675.3 |
| | Feb 22 | *Triton VII* | OlS | S | Virginia capes, 36° 15.3' N, 75° 15.3' W |
| | — | *Coral Dawn* | U | F | Chincoteague, VA |
| | — | *Tiru* | Sub | NT | In Atlantic off Sand Shoal NE Channel, VA |
| 1980 | —(p) | *Asphalt Merchant* [Ger] | Tkr | F | Off coast of Virginia |
| | Feb 12 | *Marine Electric* | Frt | F | Loran (bow) 26942.7, 42038.5, (stern) 26943.2, 42037.5 |
| 1983 | Apr 12 | *Misty Blue* | OlS | F | Loran 26885.9, 42641.4 |
| | Jan 1 | *Atlantic Mist* | OlS | F | Loran 27030.1, 42039.8 |
| 1984 | Mar (p) | *Darlene* | FV | F | 39° 10' 36" N, 75° 08' 21" W |
| | May 28 | *Miss Lee* | FV | F | 39° 03' 18" N, 75° 20' 20" W |

| Date | | Vessel | Type | Manner | Location |
|---|---|---|---|---|---|
| | | *Bethlehem Drydock No. 5* | Dry | F | 38° 30' 39" N, 74° 31' 49" W |
| 1985 | — | *Ocean Quest* | FV | F | 38° 38' 48" N, 74° 48' 00" W |
| 1987 | Aug 9 | *Muff Diver* | FV | F | Loran 26785.4, 42251.1 |
| 1989 | June 7 | *USS Blenny* | Sub | BU-FR | Loran 27024.1, 42203.4 |
| 2004 | Feb 27 | *Bow Mariner* | Tkr | Exp | 55 miles E of Chincoteague, VA |
| Unk | | *Caryu* | U | F | Loran 26724.5, 42963.0 |
| Unk | | *Chris F* | U | F | Loran 26851.1, 41791.1 |
| Unk | | *Clark No. 2* | U | F | Loran 27020.2, 41387.4 |
| Unk | | *Dorothy* | U | F | Loran 27332.5, 41913.8 |
| Unk | | *E. L. Mayberry* | U | F | Loran 25982.0, 41474.0 |
| Unk | | *E. R. Smith* | Frt | F | Loran 27118.4, 41946.7 |
| Unk | | *Edna* | U | U | Loran 26926.0, 41769.5 |
| Unk | | *Eleanor Warren* | FV | U | 38° 54' 32" N, 74° 45' 28" W |
| Unk | | *Evening Star* | Tkr | U | 38° 51' 06" N, 74° 36' 06" W |
| Unk | | *F. W. Schepper II* | U | U | 38° 49' 00" N, 74° 55' 08" W |
| Unk | | *Hampshire* | U | F | 38° 49' 11" N, 74° 31' 17" W |
| Unk | | *Harold Weston* | S&B | U | Loran 26987.4, 41972.6 |
| Unk | | *Hendrik Lund* | U | U | Loran 26020.0, 41608.0 |
| Unk | | *Independence Day* | U | U | Loran 26935.6, 42498.4 |
| Unk | | *Irene Muriel* | FV | F | Loran 27031.9, 41977.3 |
| Unk | | *Inis Paradine* | U | F | Loran 26842.0, 41489.5 |
| Unk | | *J. R. Bergen* | U | U | Loran 26266.0, 41334.0 |
| Unk | | *Katie Lynn* | U | AR | Off coast of Maryland |
| Unk | | *Lawson* | U | F | Loran 26876.1, 41513.0 |
| Unk | | *Margaret Hanks* | FV | F | Loran 27048.3, 41188.9 |
| Unk | | *Morna Kite* | U | F | Loran 26456.0, 41113.0 |
| Unk | | *Muriel Arlene* | FV | F | Approximately 20 miles E of Virginia Beach, VA |
| Unk | | *Nancy* | U | F | Loran 26864.4, 41276.9 |
| Unk | | *Page* | Frt | F | Loran 27095.5, 41746.3 |
| Unk | | *Patty B.* | U | F | Loran 26908.7, 41988.6 |
| Unk | | *Paul Russell* | U | F | Loran 26967.3, 42106.4 |
| Unk | | *Pharoby Dragger* | U | F | Loran 27026.8, 42307.2 |
| Unk | | *Prince of Peace* | U | F | Loran 26866.1, 41281.5 |
| Unk | | *Queen* | U | F | Loran 27049.4, 41874.5 |
| Unk | | *Rhoda* | FV | F | Loran 26972.8, 41963.3 |
| Unk | | *"River Front Junction"* | U | F | Loran 27024.3, 41260.3 |
| Unk | | *Sergeant* | U | U | 38° 41' 38" N, 75° 00' 48" W |
| Unk | | *Salty Sea II* | U | F | Loran 27087.7, 41241.7 |
| Unk | | *"Texaco Tanker"* | Tkr | U | Loran 27232.1, 41487.8 |
| Unk | | *Torpedo* | U | U | Loran 26863.0, 41672.0 |
| Unk | | *Trepico* | Ship | F | Loran 27032.9, 41388.7 |
| Unk | | *"USS Bone"** | U | U | 37°45' 46.93" N, 75° 11' 50.86" W |
| Unk | | *Vestas* | Tug | F | 6 miles off Indian River inlet, DE |
| Unk | | *Vicki* | U | U | Loran 26880, 41409.6 |
| Unk | | *Walter Graze* | FV | F | 3,680 yards from elbow of Cross Ledge Light, Delaware Bay |
| Unk | | *Walter Hines Page* | StS | AR | Loran 27095.5, 41746.3 |
| Unk | | *Webster* | StS | AR | Loran 27020.6, 41390.1 |
| Unk | | Unidentified | Sch | F | Loran 27098.0, 42658.3 |
| Unk | | Unidentified | U | U | Loran 26825.5, 42803.7 |
| Unk | | Unidentified | U | U | 38° 51' 54" N, 74° 23' 06" W |
| Unk | | Unidentified | U | U | 38° 40' 06" N, 74° 27' 48" W |

* This identity (USS *Bone*) is undoubtedly colloquial as no U.S. Navy vessel was ever commissioned under this name.

# Collision Key

This numbered list gives the objects involved in collisions. The numbers correspond with the numbers in brackets under "Manner."

1. *Medora* (Ship)
2. *Freeman Rawdon* (StS)
3. *Hanover* (Sch)
4. *Keystone State* (StP)
5. *Keystone State* (StP)
6. *Roanoke* (StP)
7. *Elizabeth English* (Sch)
8. *Charles Miller* (Brig)
9. *Charles Miller* (Brig)
10. *General Meigs* (StP)
11. *Richard Vaux* (Ship)
12. *John Crystal* (Brig)
13. *Major Reybold* (StP)
14. *Two Marys* (Sch)
15. *Zodiac* (Str)
16. *Illinois* (Str)
17. *Ellen Tobrin* (Sch)
18. Unknown vessel (Sch)
19. *George Leary* (StS)
20. *Seminole*
21. *Mariposa* (Brig)
22. *Andion Townsend*
23. *Lady Octavia* (Bark)
24. With iron pier
25. With ice breaker
26. *Algiers* (StS)
27. *Alvah* (StS) (Br)
28. *Royal Arch* (Sch)
29. *City of Ontario* (Str)
30. *Industry* (Sch)
31. Unknown vessel

32. Unknown vessel
33. *Crystal Wave* (StS)
34. *Cleopatra* (StS)
35. *Manhattan* (StS)
36. *Agnes Manning* (Sch)
37. Derelict vessel
38. Unknown vessel
39. *Ionia* (Sch)
40. Submerged wreck
41. Unknown vessel (Tug)
42. *S. N. Lawrence* (Sch)
43. Wreck
44. Sunken wreck
45. *Hamilton* (StS)
46. *Maria Palmer* (Sch)
47. *Philadelphia* (StS)
48. *Martha E. Wallace* (Sch)
49. *Edith L. Allen* (Sch)
50. *Jefferson* (StS)
51. *Concord* (StS)
52. *Mohican* (Str)
53. *Chesapeake* (StS)
54. *Admiral Farragut* (StS)
55. *Indrakula* (StS)
56. *Nantucket* (StS)
57. *Prinz Oskar*
58. *Shawmut* (StS)
59. *Elizabeth Palmer* (Sch)
60. *Washingtonian* (StS)
61. *Chepston Castle* (StS) (Br)
62. *La Gloire* (Cr) (Fr)

63. *Arnold M. Bangs* (StS)
64. *Somerset* (Str)
65. *Dusquesne* (StS)
66. *Apache* (Str)
67. Unknown vessel (StS)
68. *J. E. O'Neill* (StS)
69. *London* (StS)
70. USS *Milwaukee*
71. Unknown vessel
72. *Vacuum* (StS)
73. *Atlas* (StS)
74. *Evansville* (StS)
75. *Leverband* (StS)
76. *Esso Annapolis* (StS)
77. *E. J. Dodds* (StS)
78. *Voco* (StS)
79. *SC-330* (SC)
80. *Cape Henlopen* (StS)
81. *Montana* (StS)
82. USS *Greer* (DD)
83. *Buena Vista* (Tkr)
84. *Camas Meadow* (Tkr)
85. *Elisha Lee* (StS)
86. *Michael* (Tkr)
87. *W. R. Rowe* (OlS)
88. *W. R. Rowe* (OlS)
89. *South African Pioneer* (StS)
90. Unknown vessel
91. Unknown object
92. With pier
93. Unknown vessel

## Abbreviations

AGI    Archivo General de Indias, Seville, Spain

CNO    Navy Department, Office of the Chief of Naval Operations, Division of Naval History, Washington, DC

*CRNC*    William L. Saunders et al., eds., *Colonial Records of North Carolina,* 10 vols. (Raleigh: P. M. Hale et al., 1886–1890)

*EJC*    Henry R. McIlwaine and Wilmer L. Hall, eds., *Executive Journals of the Council of Virginia, 1680–1754,* 6 vols. (Richmond: Virginia State Library, 1945)

*JCC*    Worthington C. Ford et al., *Journals of the Continental Congress, 1774–1789,* 34 vols. (Washington, DC: U.S. Government Printing Office, 1904–1937)

LC    Library of Congress, Washington, DC

*LDC*    Paul H. Smith, ed., *Letters of Delegates to Congress, 1774–1789,* 26 vols. (Washington, DC: Library of Congress, 1986–2000)

MDA    Maryland Archives, Annapolis

*NDAR*    William Bell Clark et al., eds., *Naval Documents of the American Revolution,* 11 vols. (Washington, DC: Naval Historical Center, 1964–2005)

NHC    Naval Historical Center, Washington, DC

*ORN*    Richard Rush et al., eds., *Official Records of the Union and Confederate Navies during the War of the Rebellion,* 1st and 2nd series, 30 vols. (Washington, DC: U.S. Government Printing Office, 1894–1922)

PCC    Papers of the Continental Congress, National Archives, Washington, DC

PRO    Public Record Office, London

UVL    University of Virginia Library, Charlottesville

## Introduction

1. Harry Franklin Covington, "The Discovery of Maryland, or Verrazzano's Visit to the Eastern Shore," *Maryland Historical Magazine* 10, no. 3 (September 1915): 217.

2. Jane Scott, *Between Ocean and Bay: A Natural History of Delmarva* (Centreville, MD: Tidewater Publishers, 1991), 157.

3. Francis Ross Holland Jr., *America's Lighthouses: An Illustrated History* (New York: Dover, 1972), 109–11, 122; John W. Beach, *Cape Henlopen Lighthouse and Delaware Breakwater* (Dover, DE: privately printed, 1970), 70–71.

4. Scott, *Between Ocean and Bay,* 158.

5. Maude Radford Warren, "The Island of Chincoteague," *Harper's Monthly,* July–December 1913, 781.

6. Ibid.; Brooks Miles Barnes and Barry R. Truitt, eds., *Seashore Chronicles: Three Centuries of the Virginia Barrier Islands* (Charlottesville: University Press of Virginia, 1997), 7.

7. *Archives of Maryland* (Baltimore: Maryland Historical Society, 1833–), 13:549–50; Scott, *Between Ocean and Bay,* 180.

8. Jay Abercrombie, *Walks and Rambles on Delmarva Peninsula: A Guide for Hikers and Naturalists* (Woodstock, VT: Backcountry Publications, 1985), 188–89; Scott, *Between Ocean and Bay,* 178, 180.

## Chapter 1. Indians with English Jackets

1. David Petersen De Vries, *Voyages from Holland to America,* ed. and trans. Henry C. Murphy (New York: James Lenox, 1853), 49–50.

2. Ibid., 50.

3. Ibid., 50–51. It is quite probable that De Vries meant 30 leagues, or 90 miles.

4. Ibid.

5. Samuel Purchas, *Hakluytus Posthumas, or Purchas His Pilgrims* (Glasgow: James MacLehose and Sons, 1906), 19:83, 91.

6. George Yeardley to Sir Henry Peyton, November 18, 1610, in Edward Wright Haile, ed., *Jamestown Narratives: Eyewitness Accounts of the Virginia Colony. The First Decade: 1607–1617* (Champlain, VA: Round House, 1998), 479.

7. Purchas, *Hakluytus Posthumas,* 19:91.

8. C. A. Weslager, *The English on the Delaware, 1610–1682* (New Brunswick, NJ: Rutgers University Press, 1967), 6–7.

9. Ibid., 33–34.

10. Purchas, *Hakluytus Posthumas,* 19:91.

11. Ibid.

12. E. B. O'Callaghan, ed., *Documents Relative to the Colonial History of the State of New York* (Albany: Weed, Parsons, and Co., 1853–1861), 12:201, 215.

13. Brookes Miles Barnes and Barry R. Truitt, *Seashore Chronicles: Three Centuries of the Virginia Barrier Islands* (Charlottesville: University of Virginia Press, 1997), 19–21.

14. *Archives of Maryland* (Baltimore: Maryland Historical Society, 1833–), 20:292.

15. "Sixteenth Century Virginia Hurricanes," www.hpc.ncep.noaa.gov/research/roth/va16hur.htm.

16. *Maryland Gazette,* February 18–25, 1728/29, reprinted in *The American Weekly Mercury,* March 13–20, 1728/29.

17. *Maryland Gazette,* January 14, 1745/46.

18. *Boston News Letter,* February 4, 1711/12.

19. *Boston News Letter,* February 11, 1711/12.

20. David Beers Quinn, ed., *The Roanoke Voyages, 1584–1590* (New York: Dover, 1991), 2:703 n. 1.

21. Deposition of James Lemount, October 30, 1691, in William P. Palmer, ed., *Calendar of Virginia State Papers and Other Manuscripts* (Richmond: Printed for the Commonwealth, 1875–93), 1:20, 30; Martha W. McCartney, "A Study of the Africans and African Americans on Jamestown Island and at Green Spring, 1619–1803," prepared by Colonial National Historical Park, National Park Service, U.S. Department of the Interior, Williamsburg, VA, 2003, 83.

22. *Boston News Letter,* October 27, 1712.

23. *The American Weekly Mercury,* August 15–22, 1723; *The Boston Gazette,* August 26–September 2, 1723.

24. *The Virginia Gazette,* April 7–14, 1738.

25. For a full account of Hudson's exploration of the Delaware and Hudson, see J. Franklin Jameson, ed., *Narratives of New Netherlands, 1609–1664* (New York: Barnes and Noble, 1949).

26. *The Virginia Gazette,* November 9, 1713. The vessel was most likely an armed merchantman or privateer as no Royal Navy vessel named *Carleton* was then in commission.

27. Donald G. Shomette, *Pirates on the Chesapeake* (Centreville, MD: Tidewater Publishers, 1985), 66–68, 101–13, 123–37; Virginia Cullen, *History of Lewes, Delaware* ([Lewes, DE]: Colonel David Hall Chapter, Daughters of the American Revolution, 1981), 8–9.

28. Shomette, *Pirates on the Chesapeake,* passim.

29. *The American Weekly Mercury,* June 11–18, 1724.

30. *Maryland Gazette,* January 15, 1749.

31. Ibid.

## Chapter 2. A Good Many Chests of Money

1. Pedro de Pumarejo to Don Francisco de Vares y Valdes, October 15, 1750, Legajo 5157, Sección de Contratación, AGI.

2. Ibid.; *CRNC,* 4:1300–1308; Account of the vessels that departed from Havana to Spain on August 10, 1750, their cargo and halting place, Legajo 5157, Sección de Contratación, AGI (hereafter cited as Account of the vessels); *New York Gazette,* September 17, 1750; *Maryland Gazette,* September 12, 1750; Governor Gabriel Johnston to Duke of Bedford containing "An Account of Five Ships of the Spanish Flota put on Shore on the Coast of North Carolina by the Great Storm August 18, 1750" (hereafter cited as Respaldizar's report), *CRNC,* 4:1304, 1305; A report given to the Honourable Thomas Lee, Esq., Proceedings from the Council of Virginia in Williamsburg, September 28, 1750 (hereafter Report to Lee, September 28, 1750), in Richard Cook and Daniel Koski-Karell, "An Account of the Spanish Shipwreck 'La Galga' and the Loss of the Treasure Fleet of 1750," [undesignated study], 1989 (copy in author's collection), 22. Various reports later reaching Virginia of the treasure aboard stated that the ship was carrying between 15,000 pesos and $300,000.

3. Pumarejo to Vares y Valdes, October 15, 1750; President Lee to the Commissioners for Trade and Plantations, August 30, 1750, in Cook and Koski-Karell, "La Galga," 40–41; President Lee to Secretary of State, August 30, 1750, S.R. 246, Colonial Office 5/1338, ff. 85–86, PRO; Report to Lee, September 28, 1750; *Maryland Gazette,* September 12, 1750. The *Maryland Gazette* claimed *Los Godos* carried forty guns, but President Lee's count is certainly far more reliable, although some guns tossed overboard may account for the difference.

4. Account of the vessels; Report to Lee, September 28, 1750; *EJC,* 5:334, 481; *Maryland Gazette,* September 12, 1750. It was reported that besides the 350 chests of dollars on board, *Los Godos* was also laden with a great quantity of cochineal, sugar, indigo, cocoa, and dye woods when she reached Norfolk. The *Maryland Gazette,* September 12, 1750, stated the ship carried 12 million pieces-of-eight onboard. Originally an English-built warship captured in the last conflict, *Guadeloupe* was somewhat atypical of the vessel types that made the annual round-robin tour between Old and New Spain. During the late war she had once narrowly missed capture by a British expedition that attacked an assembling fleet off Cuba. In late October 1749, she had sailed from Cadiz for Vera Cruz with European commercial goods, discharged her cargo, picked up another intended for Cuba, and at Havana loaded with sugar, logwood, and other merchandise intended for home. Lee to Secretary of State, August 30, 1750; *EJC,* 5:334–35.

5. Pumarejo to Vares y Valdes, October 15, 1750; *South Carolina Gazette,* October 29, 1750; *EJC,* 5:335; *Maryland Gazette,* September 5, 1750. A more accurate estimate of the

value of her treasure was provided to the Council of Virginia as 150,000 pesos. Account of the vessels; Report to Lee, September 28, 1750. A snow was a two-masted merchant vessel, rigged as a brig with square sales on both masts but with a small try-sail mast stepped abaft the mainmast.

6. Pumarejo to Vares y Valdes, October 15, 1750; Account of the vessels; Respaldizar's report; Report to Lee, September 28, 1750.

7. Pumarejo to Vares y Valdes, October 15, 1750; Account of the vessels; Respaldizar's report; Report to Lee, September 28, 1750; *South Carolina Gazette,* October 29, 1750.

8. Pumarejo to Vares y Valdes, October 15, 1750; Account of the vessels; Report to Lee, September 28, 1750; *Maryland Gazette,* September 12, 1750. The vessel is variously described as a schooner, a sloop, a brig, and a brigantine.

9. Registry of *La Galga,* Legajo 138, Sección de Contratación, AGI.

10. Pumarejo to Vares y Valdes, October 15, 1750; Registry of *La Galga,* Captain, D. Daniel Huoni, master, D. Thomas Velando, Legajo 2476, Sección de Contratación, AGI; *Maryland Gazette,* September 5, 1750; *Virginia Gazette,* September 5,1750. The official inventory included 480 pesos "*fuertes*"; 4,800 pesos in doubloons; 218 "*castellanos*", seven "*tomines*" and 8 grains of goldware; 30 marks of silverware; 119 "*castellanos*" of gold in three small chests; two pairs of "*hevillas*"[?] and one of Inquisition emblems; five marks, six ounces of silver in seven little silver boxes; one Ivaro de Asta[?] with gilded foot; and one leather bag and twelve ornate spoons (or scoops) of shell. The name Huoni may possibly be derived from the Gaelic Mahoney.

11. Registry of *La Galga,* Legajo 138; *Maryland Gazette,* September 5, 1750.

12. Peter Wood and the Editors of Time-Life Books, *The Spanish Main* (Alexandria, VA: Time-Life Books, 1979), 171.

13. The sailing order is conjectural and is based on the final disposition of the fleet following the storm of August 25–31. However, it was standard procedure for the most valuable vessels, such as *Los Godos, San Pedro,* and *Guadeloupe,* to have taken up position in the center of the fleet, proceeded, followed, and/or flanked by lesser ships.

14. *South Carolina Gazette,* October 29, 1750; Pumarejo to Vares y Valdes, October 15, 1750.

15. Pumarejo to Vares y Valdes, October 15, 1750.

16. *EJC,* 5:335.

17. Pumarejo to Vares y Valdes, October 15, 1750.

18. Ibid.

19. *South Carolina Gazette,* October 29, 1750.

20. David Stick, *Graveyard of the Atlantic* (Chapel Hill: University of North Carolina Press, 1952), 1. The Outer Banks are a series of undersea sandbars but differ from the Newfoundland Banks and Bahama Banks in that they are also above the surface. They were first shown on Theodore DeBry's engraving of John White's 1585 map as "Promontorium Tremendum" and on the Velasco map of 1611 as "Cape Feare." The Outer Banks were used by Spanish privateers in the 1740s as a hiding place. Bankers living in the vicinity were sometimes employed in whaling, sighting them from the higher hills and then going out in rowboats. Ibid., 2, 308.

21. Account of the vessels; Respaldizar's report; Report to Lee, September 28, 1750; *South Carolina Gazette,* October 29, 1750; Pumarejo to Vares y Valdes, October 15, 1750; *New York Gazette,* September 17, 1750; *CRNC,* 3:1300–1308.

22. *South Carolina Gazette,* October 29, 1750; Respaldizar's report; Account of the vessels.

23. Respaldizar's report; Account of the vessels; Report to Lee, September 28, 1750. The first report of *Soledad*'s loss was carried north by a merchant captain named Rivers who reached Philadelphia in but a few days, where it was soon being reported—out of all proportion to the truth—that the unfortunate register ship had been "cast away about 12

Leagues more to the South [of Ocracoke], and had on board a Million of Dollars, which was saved." *New York Gazette,* September 17, 1750; Pumarejo to Vares y Valdes, October 15, 1750.

24. *South Carolina Gazette,* October 29, 1750; Respaldizar's report; *New York Gazette,* September 17, 1750.

25. Harold T. Wilkins, *Pirate Treasure* (New York: E. P. Dutton, 1937), 57–58.

26. Ibid., 58.

27. Ibid., 58–59.

28. Ibid., 59; Respaldizar's report.

29. Wilkins, *Pirate Treasure,* 59–60.

30. Ibid.

31. Pumarejo to Vares y Valdes, October 15, 1750.

32. Ibid.

33. Ibid.

34. Ibid.; *EJC,* 5:333–36. The creek that was sighted was probably Currituck Inlet, which was closed off entirely some years later.

35. The president of Virginia, Thomas Lee, reported the vessel was heading for Porto Bello. *EJC,* 5:480; Pumarejo to Vares y Valdes, October 15, 1750; Report to Lee, September 28, 1750; *South Carolina Gazette,* October 29, 1750.

36. Pumarejo to Vares y Valdes, October 15, 1750; Account of the vessels; Report to Lee, September 28, 1750; *Maryland Gazette,* September 5, 1750. The only suggestion that part of the treasure might have been saved, and that the ship was lost, came in a report published in the *Maryland Gazette* stating that "the Brigantine [*sic*], having an board a good many Chests of Money, was drove on Machapungo Shoals, and lost, but the Crew and part of the Money saved." *Maryland Gazette,* September 12, 1750. Pumarejo reported only that the vessel was "grounded" (not lost) and that there was no news of the eight men aboard.

37. *New York Gazette,* September 10, 1750; *South Carolina Gazette,* October 29, 1750.

38. *New York Gazette,* September 10, 1750.

39. *Maryland Gazette,* September 5, 1750; *South Carolina Gazette,* October 29, 1750.

40. *Maryland Gazette,* September 5, 1750; *New York Gazette,* September 10, 1750. The initial Spanish report stated that everyone aboard except one soldier was saved, although Pumarejo's account correctly reported five men lost but incorrectly noted they were all sailors. Account of the vessels; Pumarejo to Vares y Valdes, October 15, 1750.

41. *Maryland Gazette,* September 5, 1750.

42. Although as many as 50 prisoners may have been aboard *La Galga,* it was reported in the *Maryland Gazette* that "By the Man of War's being lost, about 20 Englishmen, who had been made Prisoners by the Spaniards, and were on board her, have got their Liberty. One of the Men belonged to Capt. Walter Wrench, in a fine Ship from Virginia; who we hear, was seized at the Havanna, where Capt. Wrench now remains a Prisoner." *Maryland Gazette,* September 5, 1750.

43. *Archives of Maryland,* 28:481, 482, 493; *Maryland Gazette,* September 5, 1750.

44. *Archives of Maryland,* 28:482; *EJC,* 5:337; *Maryland Gazette,* September 5, 1750.

45. *Archives of Maryland,* 28:482.

46. Account of the vessels; Report to Lee, September 28, 1750; *New York Gazette,* September 10, 1750; *South Carolina Gazette,* October 29, 1750; *Maryland Gazette,* September 5, 1750. Maloney stated that the gale occurred on August 18 and 19, and she struck the shoals on August 24 and the island on August 26, which contravenes Pumarejo's sequence for the storm, which is obviously extracted from a daily log of the event. As Maloney had long been a prisoner and may have lost track of time, he is to be forgiven. If *La Galga* had been lost 14 leagues south of the Delaware Capes, the position would be about 24 miles north of the present Maryland-Virginia border and clearly in Maryland territorial jurisdiction.

47. *Archives of Maryland,* 28:82.

48. Ibid.

49. Ibid, 483, 486.

50. Ibid, 493.

51. Ibid, 493–94.

52. Ibid, 494.

53. Wilkins, *Pirate Treasure,* 60.

54. Ibid.

55. Ibid., 61; Respaldizar's report; Account of the vessels.

56. Wilkins, *Pirate Treasure,* 61; Respaldizar's report; Account of the vessels.

57. Wilkins, *Pirate Treasure,* 61; Respaldizar's report; Account of the vessels; *South Carolina Gazette,* October 29, 1750; *CRNC,* 3:1306–7; Frederick W. Ricord, ed., *Documents Relating to the Colonial History of the State of New Jersey* (Trenton: John L. Murphy, 1891), 4:278.

58. Wilkins, *Pirate Treasure,* 61–62; *South Carolina Gazette,* October 29, 1750; *CRNC,* 3:1307; Ricord, *Documents,* 4:278, 279.

59. Wilkins, *Pirate Treasure,* 62; *South Carolina Gazette,* October 29, 1750; *New York Gazette,* November 12, 1750; *CRNC,* 3:1307.

60. *CRNC,* 3:1307. The value of the treasure carried back to Spain aboard *Scorpion* was later reported by Johnston "to the Sum of 16275 1/2 heavy Dollars, as well for the Freight of the Ship at the Rate of 2 p cent." Ibid., 1310.

61. *New York Gazette,* September 10, 1750; *Maryland Gazette,* September 12, 1750; *EJC,* 5:333–36, 347; Pumarejo to Vares y Valdes, October 15, 1750.

62. *EJC,* 5: 333–36; Lee to the Lords of Trade, October 3, 1750, in Cook and Koski-Karell, "La Galga," 40; Lee to Commissioners of Trade and Plantations, August 30, 1750.

63. Pumarejo to Vares y Valdes, October 15, 1750. One might suggest that there is some irony in Pumarejo's attitude regarding the English, especially in light of Spanish seizures of English vessels and men on the high seas and their own cruel treatment of them.

64. Lee to Commissioners for Trade and Plantation, August 30, 1750; *EJC,* 5:335–36; Lee to Secretary of State, October 3, 1750, in Cook and Koski-Karell, "La Galga," 49.

65. Survey Report [of *Nuestra Señora de los Godos*]; 46; Lee to Secretary of State, November 6, 1750; Survey Reports [of *San Pedro*], all in Cook and Koski-Karell, "La Galga," 46, 51, 47.

66. Lee to Secretary of State, November 6, 1750; *EJC,* 5:346. The only conditions set forth by the Council of Virginia were that the Spanish be obliged to pay out of the proceeds of the public vendue for the transport to Spain of the passengers who had been aboard the fleet, and that the commanders of both *Los Godos* and *San Pedro* be permitted to leave only if they carried them onboard their European-bound charters. Overall, the Virginians were, given the recent state of affairs, quite moderate. *EJC,* 5:340.

67. *EJC,* 5:337; Lee to Secretary of State, October 3, 1750.

68. *New York Gazette,* November 12, 1750, reprinted in *Maryland Gazette,* November 23, 1750.

69. *Maryland Gazette,* December 15, 1750.

70. Ricord, *Documents,* 4:278–82; 7:599–600; *Boston News Letter,* December 20,1750; Wilkins, *Pirate Treasure,* 63–75.

71. Lee to Commissioner of Trade and Plantations, November 6, 1750, in Cook and Koski-Karell, "La Galga," 50.

72. *EJC,* 5:347.

73. *Virginia Gazette,* February 7, 1751; October 27, 1752.

Chapter 3. The *Roebuck*'s Horns

1. Lord Sandwich to Philip Stephens, June 29, 1775, Colonial Office, Public Record Office, London.

2. Lord Commissioners of the Admiralty to Vice Admiral Samuel Graves, July 6, 1775, *NDAR*, 1:1317.

3. J. J. Cooledge, *Ships of the Royal Navy: An Historical Index* (Devon, UK: David and Charles, 1969), 1:468.

4. Count de Guines to Count de Vergennes, July 7, 1775, *NDAR*, 1:1320.

5. Lords Commissioners of the British Admiralty to Vice Admiral Samuel Graves, August 25, 1775, *NDAR*, 2:690; Count de Guines to Count de Vergennes, September 1, 1775, *NDAR*, 2:700.

6. Stephens to Graves, September 6, 1775, *NDAR*, 2:705; Captain Andrew Snape Hamond to Admiral Samuel Graves, November 3, 1775, Letter Book, 1771–77, Hamond Papers, UVL; *NDAR*, 2:743.

7. Commodore Marriot Arbuthnot to Hamond, Halifax, November 3, 1775, Hamond Papers, Orders Received, 1775–76; Admiral Marion Arbuthnot to Graves, November 7, 1775, *NDAR*, 2:912; Arbuthnot to Hamond, November 8, 1775, General Orders, 1775–76, Hamond Papers.

8. Graves to Hamond, December 25, 1775, *NDAR*, 3:235

9. Henry Fisher to the Pennsylvania Committee of Safety, March 25, 1776, *Pennsylvania Archives,* 1st ser., Samuel Hazard et al., eds. (Philadelphia: J. Stevens and Co., 1852–56), 4:724–25.

10. Journal of HMS *Roebuck,* March 26–29, 1776, *NDAR,* 4:596–97; Narrative of Captain Andrew Snape Hamond (hereafter cited as Hamond narrative), [March 28, 1776], Hamond Papers; Fisher to Pennsylvania Committee of Safety, April 1, 1776, PCC (Pennsylvania State Papers), M247, RG 360, R 83.

11. Journal of HMS *Roebuck,* March 26–29, 1776, *NDAR,* 4:596–97; Hamond narrative, [March 28, 1776]; Fisher to Pennsylvania Committee of Safety, April 1, 1776. *Maria* had been captured on March 22, 1776. *NDAR,* 4:597 n. 2.

12. Hamond narrative [March 26, 1776]; *London Gazette,* May 10–13, 1777.

13. Journal of HMS *Roebuck,* March 26–27, 1776, *NDAR,* 4:529. At the time, *Roebuck* was anchored in "Old Hoar kill road in 5 fathoms, the light house SE 1/2 S 1 Mile." Henry Fisher, the Pennsylvania Committee of Safety observer at Cape Henlopen, reported that the sloops were stripped, scuttled, and set adrift, and their crews were sent ashore in their own small boats. Fisher to the Pennsylvania Committee of Safety, April 1, 1776.

14. Hamond narrative, March 30, 1776; Journal of HMS *Roebuck,* March 28, 1776, *NDAR,* 4:596; Howe's Prize List, March 31, 1777, *NDAR,* 4:597; Captain Andrew Snape Hamond to Captain Henry Bellew, April 8, 1777, Letters and Orders: *Roebuck,* 1775–78, Hamond Papers.

15. Journal of HMS *Roebuck,* March 28, 1776.

16. Captain Andrew Snape Hamond to Lieutenant John Orde, March 7, 1776, Hamond Orders issued, Hamond Papers.

17. Hamond narrative, March 28 and 29, 1776; Journal of HMS *Roebuck,* March 28, 1776.

18. Journal of HMS *Roebuck,* March 28 and 29, 1776, *NDAR,* 4:596; Howe's Prize List, March 31, 1777.

19. Fisher to the Pennsylvania Committee of Safety, April 1, 1776; Journal of HMS *Roebuck,* March 28 and 29, 1776, *NDAR,* 4:596–97; Hamond narrative, March 30, 1776. Hamond did his best to free Ball and on March 30 sent a flag of truce into Lewes to negotiate an exchange, but he found no satisfaction. During a subsequent engagement on May 7, Ha-

mond took the opportunity of an enforced lull in action to dispatch a flag of truce to Philadelphia in another effort to arrange an exchange for Lieutenant Ball and a safe conduct for Captain Bellew's wife, who was then in the city. The exchange was eventually agreed to, and Bellew's wife was permitted to travel to New England.

20. Fisher to the Pennsylvania Committee of Safety, April 1, 1776.

21. Journal of HMS *Roebuck*, April 29 and March 4, 1776, *NDAR*, 4:596 and 755; Howe's Prize List, March 31, 1777, *NDAR*, 4:597.

22. Journal of HMS *Roebuck*, 31 March 1776, *NDAR*, 4:597; Fisher to the Pennsylvania Committee of Safety, April 1, 1776.

23. Hamond narrative, April 6 and 7, 1776; *Pennsylvania Journal*, April 10, 1776; Journal of HMS *Roebuck*, April 5 and 6, 1776, *NDAR*, 4:755.

24. *London Chronicle*, June 8–11, 1776, *NDAR*, 4:686.

25. Journal of HMS *Roebuck*, April 6 and 7, 1776, *NDAR*, 4: 755–56.

26. Ibid.; Hamond narrative, April 7, 1776.

27. *Pennsylvania Evening Post*, April 13, 1776.

28. Ibid.

29. Ibid.

30. Hamond narrative, April 7, 1776.

31. Hamond to Captain Henry Bellew, April 8, 1776, Letters and Orders: *Roebuck, 1775–78*, Hamond Papers; Journal of HMS *Roebuck*, April 8, 1776, *NDAR*, 4:756.

32. General order from Vice Admiral Molyneux Shuldham to Captain Andrew Snape Hamond, April 11, 1776, Orders Received, 1775–76, Hamond Papers.

33. Ibid.

34. *Philadelphia Evening Post*, March 9, 1776; Hamond narrative, April 11, 1776; Journal of HMS *Roebuck*, April 14, 1776, *NDAR*, 4:821.

35. Journal of the Continental Schooner *Wasp*, April 13, 1776, *NDAR*, 4:802; Journal of HMS *Roebuck*, April 13, 1776, *NDAR*, 4:820–21.

36. Dixon and Hunter's *Virginia Gazette*, April 13, 1776.

37. *Pennsylvania Post*, April 20, 1776.

38. Hamond narrative, April 22, 1776; PCC (Ships Bonds Required for Letters of Marquis and Reprisal, 1776–1783), M247, RG 360, R 202; Journal of HMS *Roebuck*, April 22, 1776, *NDAR*, 4:1218; *Connecticut Courant*, May 6, 1776.

39. Hamond narrative, April 23, 1776; Disposition of His Majesty's Ships and Vessels in North America under the Command of Vice Admiral Shuldham, April 24, 1776, *NDAR*, 4:1225–27.

40. Hamond narrative, April 24, 1776; Hamond to Lord Dunmore, April 26, 1776, *NDAR*, 4:1268.

41. Shuldham to Captain Charles Hudson, April 27, 1776, *NDAR*, 4:1280.

42. Journal of HMS *Roebuck*, April 27, 1776, *NDAR*, 4:1297; Howe's Prize List, March 31, 1777, *NDAR*, 4:1297; *Connecticut Courant*, May 6, 1776.

43. Journal of HMS *Roebuck*, April 28, 1776, *NDAR*, 4:1297; Fisher to Pennsylvania Committee of Safety, April 28, 1776, *Pennsylvania Archives*, 1st ser., 4:737.

44. Fisher to Pennsylvania Committee of Safety, April 28, 1776.

45. Pennsylvania Committee of Safety to Captain Thomas Read, April 29, 1776, Committee of Safety, Navy Papers, Pennsylvania Archives; James S. Biddle, *Autobiography of Charles Biddle, 1745–1821* (Philadelphia: E. Claxton, 1883), 83–84; John Nixon to Commodore Andrew Caldwell, April 30, 1776, in *Pennsylvania Archives*, 1st ser., 4:738; *Connecticut Courant*, May 6, 1776; *Constitutional Gazette*, May 1, 1776.

46. Hamond narrative, April 30, 1776; Howe's Prize List, March 31, 1777, *NDAR*, 4: 1344; Fisher to the Pennsylvania Committee of Safety, May 1, 1776, *Pennsylvania Archives*, 1st ser., 4:740–41.

47. Hamond narrative, April 30, 1776; Howe's Prize List, March 31, 1777, *NDAR*, 4: 1344; Fisher to the Pennsylvania Committee of Safety, May 1, 1776, *Pennsylvania Archives*, 1st ser., 4:740–41; Journal of HMS *Roebuck*, April 30, 1776, *NDAR*, 4:1383.

48. Hamond narrative, April 30, 1776; Journal of HMS *Roebuck*, May 1, 1776, *NDAR*, 4:1383.

49. Journal of HMS *Liverpool*, April 30, 1776, *NDAR*, 4:1371.

50. Ibid., May 2, 1776, *NDAR*, 4:1383; Hamond to Captain George Montagu, May 4, 1776, Orders issued, Hamond Papers; Journal of HMS *Liverpool*, May 2 and 4, 1776, *NDAR*, 4:1409, 1446.

51. *New York Gazette*, May 6, 1776.

52. Hamond to Major General Henry Clinton, May 4, 1776, Letters and Orders, Hamond Papers. On May 6, while en route to Virginia, *Fowey* captured the sloop *Polly* (W. Gardner, master, Nathaniel Shaw Jr., owner, from Saltatuda to New York, with salt) and placed a petty officer and five men aboard as a prize crew. Journal of HMS *Fowey*, May 6, 1776, *NDAR*, 4:1449.

53. Hamond narrative, May 5, 1776; *Pennsylvania Evening Post*, June 20, 1776.

54. Fisher to the Pennsylvania Committee of Safety, May 5, 1776, *Pennsylvania Archives*, 1st ser., 4:743–44; *Pennsylvania Evening Post*, May 7, 1776.

55. Minutes of the Pennsylvania Committee of Safety, May 7, 1776, *NDAR*, 4:1443–45; Journal of HMS *Roebuck*, May 5 and 6, *NDAR*, 4:1446; Journal of HMS *Liverpool*, May 6, 1776, *NDAR*, 4:1447.

56. Journal of HMS *Roebuck*, May 7, *NDAR*, 4:1447; Hamond narrative, May 7, 1776; Caesar Rodney to Captain Thomas Rodney, May 8, 1776, Rodney Papers, Historical Society of Delaware; Biddle, *Autobiography*, 85.

57. *Pennsylvania Evening Post*, June 20, 1776; John W. Jackson, *The Pennsylvania Navy, 1775–1781: The Defense of the Delaware* (New Brunswick, NJ: Rutgers University Press, 1974), 44–45; Journal of HMS *Roebuck*, May 8, 1776, *NDAR*, 4:1470; *JCC*, 4:341, 345.

58. Journal of HMS *Roebuck*, May 8, 1776, *NDAR*, 4:1470; *Constitutional Gazette*, May 11, 1776; Jackson, *Pennsylvania Navy*, 46. Hamond believed *Betsey* had deserted to the enemy.

59. *Constitutional Gazette*, May 11, 1776; Journal of HMS *Liverpool*, May 8, 1776, *NDAR*, 4:1471.

60. Journal of HMS *Roebuck*, May 8 and 9, 1776, *NDAR*, 4:1470 and 5:18; Journal of HMS *Liverpool*, May 8, 1776, *NDAR*, 4:1471; *Pennsylvania Evening Post*, June 20, 1776.

61. Journal of HMS *Roebuck*, May 9, 1776, *NDAR*, 5:18.

62. Ibid.; Journal of HMS *Liverpool*, May 9, 1776, *NDAR*, 5:19

63. Journal of HMS *Roebuck*, May 9 and 10, 1776, in *NDAR*, 5:18, 37; Journal of HMS *Liverpool*, May 9, 1776, *NDAR*, 5:19; Jackson, *Pennsylvania Navy*, 51; *Pennsylvania Evening Post*, June 20, 1776.

64. Journal of HMS *Roebuck*, May 9, 1776, *NDAR*, 5:18; Jackson, *Pennsylvania Navy*, 51; *New York Packet*, May 16, 1776.

65. Captain Henry Dougherty to Robert Morris, May 11, 1776, *Pennsylvania Archives*, 1st ser., 4:754.

66. John Adams to Abigail Adams, May 12, 1776, Lyman H. Butterfield et al., eds., *The Adams Papers*, ser. 2: *Adams Family Correspondence* (Cambridge: The Belknap Press of Harvard University Press, 1963), 1:406; Journal of HMS *Liverpool*, May 13, 1776, *NDAR*, 5:78; Fisher to the Pennsylvania Committee of Safety, May 15, 1776; Hamond narrative, [May 15, 1776].

67. Hamond narrative, [May 15, 1776]; Journal of HMS *Roebuck*, May 16, 1776, *NDAR*, 5:129.

Chapter 4. A Column of Liquid Fire

1. Nicholas Brown to John Brown, December 11, 1775, Nicholas Brown Papers, John Carter Brown Library, Providence, RI.

2. Ibid.; Captain William Hull to Andrew Adams, December 18, 1775, Trumbull Papers, Yale University Library.

3. Brown to Brown, December 11, 1775.

4. Ibid.

5. George Washington to John Hancock, December 14, 1775, Washington Papers, LC; Richard de Bonvouloir to Count De Guines, December 28, 1775, *NDAR,* 3:285; Washington to Nicholas Cooke, December 14, 1775, Washington Papers; Nicholas Cooke to Rhode Island Delegates to the Continental Congress, December 17, 1775, Cooke Papers, Rhode Island Historical Society, Providence; Cooke to John Hancock, December 18, 1775, PCC (Rhode Island State Papers), 64, 356.

6. *JCC,* 3:465; Samuel Ward to Henry Ward, December 31, 1775, *Correspondence of Governor Samuel Ward, May 1775–March 1776,* Bernard Knollenberg, ed. (Providence: Rhode Island Historical Society, 1952), 157.

7. *JCC,* 2:253, 254.

8. Nathan Miller, *Sea of Glory: The Continental Navy Fights for Independence, 1775–1783* (New York: David McKay, 1974), 185.

9. Captain Hyde Parker Jr. to Lord Sandwich, January 6, 1776, Colonial Office, 5/123, 61b, PRO, *NDAR,* 3:654.

10. Gilbert Barkly to Sir Gray Cooper, January 10, 1776, *Pennsylvania Magazine of History and Biography* 85 (1877): 30.

11. Penet and Pliarne to Nicholas Brown, February 8, 1776, Nicholas Brown Papers; Emanuel Michael Pliarne to Recule de Basmarin and Raimbeaux, January 18, 1777, Board of War Letters, 1776–77, 152:26–27, Massachusetts Archives, Boston; *NDAR,* 7:989; Gilbert Barkly to Sir Grey Cooper, March 16, 1776, *Pennsylvania Magazine of History and Biography* 85 (1877): 31.

12. On learning of Penet and Pliarne's activities, the Count de Vergennes wrote the following from Versailles to one of the French king's agents: "M. de Paul claims that one of the two Frenchmen who appeared in Congress as the so-called deputies of our country is on his way back to France. I do not know who it is, probably some merchant's clerk who went and begged Congress for contracts, or some adventurer. We are not lacking men of his kind and we would not be sorry if they would go and live in some other country but France. I am curious to find out about the one whose return has been announced, as well as the purpose of his trip. You can imagine that if he showed himself in Philadelphia as an official representative, he will have no reason to be happy about this deceit of his." Vergennes's agents were eventually able to learn something of the two mysterious men. One Dr. Barbeau Dubourg wrote Vergennes on May 31, 1776, with the following information: Penet was born in Alsace, France, the son of an artillery storekeeper who, having many children, could provide but a mediocre education for them. He went to seek his fortune in America and, at his departure, did a stroke of business "not indeed of a dishonest man but of a not very scrupulous adventurer." He obtained "from M. de Monthieu 600 muskets on credit of a private venture" and their lender was many years without hearing from him. At last, when believed lost, he received half of his principal and interest combined. Count de Vergennes to M. Gamier, April 20, 1776, *NDAR,* 4:1057; Dr. Barbeau Dubourg to Count de Vergennes, Paris, May 31, 1776, *NDAR,* 6:398; Instructions of Nicholas and John Brown to Captain Samuel Avery, May 23, 1776, Nicholas Brown Papers.

13. Secret Committee Minutes of Proceedings, November 22, 1776, *LDC,* 5:528.

14. Secret Committee Minutes of Proceedings, October 18, 1776, *LDC,* 5:351–52; Barkly to Cooper, January 10, 1776. Morris not only was serving as an agent of the Secret

Committee but was also on the payroll of the French firm acting as its own agent. Conflict of interest does not seem to have been an issue.

15. Secret Committee Minutes of Proceedings, October 27, 1776, *LDC,* 5:413.

16. Captain Lambert Wickes to the Secret Committee of Correspondence, December 13, 1776, PCC (Letters addressed to Congress), M247, RG 360, R 90.

17. Thomas Morris to the American Commissioners in France, January 14, 1777, Silas Deane Papers, Connecticut Historical Society.

18. Lord Stormont to Lord Weymouth, February 19, 1777, *NDAR,* 8:595.

19. William Whipple to John Langdon, April 19, 1777, Force Transcripts, 333–35, William Whipple Papers, LC; William Whipple to John Langdon, April 19, 1777, *LDC,* 6:624.

20. Sir Andrew Snape Hamond Autobiography, 2:2–3, UVL.

21. Journal of HMS *Camilla,* April 11, 1777, *NDAR,* 8:321–22.

22. Ibid.; Hamond Autobiography, 2:2–3.

23. Fisher to Pennsylvania Navy Board, April 12, 1777, PCC (Letters addressed to Congress), 78, 9:79–80.

24. Hamond Autobiography, 2:2–3.

25. Fisher to Pennsylvania Navy Board, April 12, 1777. The ship carried several letters, including the February 6, 1777, letter of the Commissioners at Paris to the Secret Committee of Correspondence. The name of the ship has occasioned considerable confusion because it was referred to as both *Morris* and *Success.* That both references are to the same ship seems clear from a business letter Robert Morris wrote explaining the condition of "the muskets saved from the Ship *Success* (late the *Morris*) blown up at our Capes." Robert Morris to Daniel St. Thomas Jenifer, May 15, 1777, Red Book 4:1, MDA. See also Samuel Adams to James Warren, April 17, and Secret Committee to Caesar Rodney, April 25, 1777.

26. Journal of HMS *Camilla,* April 11, 1777.

27. Ibid.; Mann Page to John Page, April 15, 1777, *LDC,* 6:586.

28. Hamond Autobiography, 2:2–3; Narrative of Captain Andrew Snape Hamond, [April 11–12, 1777], Hamond Papers, UVL.

29. Fisher to Pennsylvania Navy Board, April 12, 1777, PCC (Letters addressed to Congress), 78, 9:79–80; John Adams to Abigail Adams, April 13, 1777, *LDC,* 6:574–75.

30. Red Book 3, MDA; Robert Morris to Caesar Rodney, April 15, 1777, William Buell Sprague Autograph Collection, Historical Society of Pennsylvania, Philadelphia.

31. Secret Committee [Robert Morris, Richard Henry Lee, William Whipple] to Caesar Rodney, April 25, 1777, *LDC,* 6: 653.

32. Robert Morris to Thomas Johnson, May 1, 1777, Red Book 3, MDA. Articles recovered from *Morris* (*Success*) included the following: 225 bayonets, 165 guns without locks, 154 guns with locks, a barrel of pins marked "111," one box of pins, 1 chest marked "AB", 1 barrel of gun locks, "12 Bales a 1.12 Marked . . . W," 2 bales of stockings marked "P.S. 300. 300 156," 3½ pieces of canvas, 1 small trunk marked "Geo. Ross," and 1 trunk belonging to Captain Anderson. The salvaged items recovered totaled seven wagonloads of goods in all. *Delaware Archives: Military and Naval Records* (Wilmington: Merchantile Printing Company, 1911–16), 3:1261.

33. William Whipple to John Langdon, April 19, 1777, *LDC,* 6:624.

## Chapter 5. Le Serpent

1. See John W. Jackson, *The Pennsylvania Navy, 1775–1781: The Defense of the Delaware* (New Brunswick, NJ: Rutgers University Press, 1974), 58–73, for a comprehensive account of the contest between the officer corps and the Committee of Safety.

2. *NDAR,* 6:6.

3. *JCC,* 4: 229–33.

4. Henry Steele Commager and Richard B. Morris, eds., *The Spirit of Seventy Six* (Indianapolis: Bobbs-Merrill, 1958), 924.

5. *NDAR,* 6:327, 366.

6. *London Chronicle,* March 20–22, 1777, *NDAR,* 8:701; *Pennsylvania Gazette,* March 26, 1777.

7. For HMS *Emerald* and *Phoenix* journals, see *NDAR,* vol. 8.

8. *Pennsylvania Journal,* March 19, 1777; *Pennsylvania Gazette,* March 26, 1777.

9. *Pennsylvania Journal,* March 19, 1777; *Pennsylvania Gazette,* March 26, 1777.

10. J. J. Cooledge, *Ships of the Royal Navy: An Historical Index* (Devon, UK: David and Charles, 1969), 1:359.

11. *NDAR,* 5:1372; 6:493, 595; 7:254, 285, 305; 8:1062–63.

12. *NDAR,* 7:1260; 8:80, 95–96, 409, 1059. *Mermaid* sailed in company with *Roebuck, Perseus, Pearl,* and *Camilla* on March 25, 1777. *NDAR,* 8:342.

13. *New York Gazette,* April 28, 1777; *NDAR,* 8:1059. Eight or ten guns salvaged from *Lyon* were used soon afterward to arm a small fortification called the Fox Burrows at a privateering base established on the Mullica River at Chestnut Neck, NJ. Arthur D. Pierce, *Smugglers Woods: Jaunts and Journeys in Colonial and Revolutionary New Jersey* (New Brunswick, NJ: Rutgers University Press, 1960), 45.

14. *NDAR,* 9:20, 33, 41, 52.

15. *NDAR,* 273, 750–51, 757–58.

16. *NDAR,* 10:528, 579, 966–67; *New York Gazette,* January 12, 1778.

17. Gardner W. Allen, *A Naval History of the American Revolution,* 2 vols. (1913; reprint, Williamstown, MA: Corner House, 1970), 1:227–28.

18. David J. Hepper, *British Warship Losses in the Age of Sail, 1650–1859* (East Sussex, UK: Jean Boudnot, 1994), 52; Pierre Ozanne, *L'Escadre françoise entrant dans la Delaware et chassant la fregate la* Mermaid, reproduced in Donald H. Cresswell, ed., *The American Revolution in Drawing and Prints* (Washington, DC: Library of Congress, 1975), 96.

19. *Archives of Maryland* (Baltimore: Maryland Historical Society, 1833–), 21:162, 172, 176, 178.

20. *NDAR,* 7:1237; 8:81; 10:810.

21. *NDAR,* 8:202, 429, 430, 461; *Pennsylvania Journal,* April 23 and June 18, 1777; *Pennsylvania Gazette,* April 30, 1777. The *London Chronicle,* May 24–27, 1777, states *Endeavour* carried forty slaves, not ninety.

22. *NDAR,* 8:699, 871; *Pennsylvania Journal,* May 14, 1777.

23. *NDAR,* 8:999; 9:545; 10:748.

24. *Maryland Gazette,* November 18, 1777; *NDAR,* 9:93, 899; 10:463, 732, 810.

25. *NDAR,* 10:373; Dixon and Hunter's *Virginia Gazette,* November 27, 1778; *Maryland Journal and Baltimore Advertiser,* December 1, 1778.

26. Hepper, *British Warship Losses,* 52; Cooledge, *Ships of the Royal Navy,* 1:539.

27. Hepper, *British Warship Losses,* 52; Dixon and Hunter's *Virginia Gazette,* November 27, 1778; *Maryland Journal and Baltimore Advertiser,* December 1, 1778.

28. Hepper, *British Warship Losses,* 52.

29. Ibid.; Dixon and Hunter's *Virginia Gazette,* November 27, 1778; *Maryland Journal and Baltimore Advertiser,* December 1, 1778.

30. Dixon and Hunter's *Virginia Gazette,* November 27, 1778; *Maryland Journal and Baltimore Advertiser,* December 1, 1778.

31. Dixon and Hunter's *Virginia Gazette,* March 26, 1779; *Maryland Journal and Baltimore Advertiser,* March 26, 1779.

## Chapter 6. The Infamous Tar

1. Barton Haxall Wise, *Memoir of General John Cropper of Accomack County, Virginia* (1892; reprint, Onancock: Eastern Shore of Virginia Historical Society, 1974), 11.

2. Ralph T. Whitelaw, *Virginia's Eastern Shore: A History of Northampton and Accomack Counties* (1951; reprint, Camden, ME: Picton Press, 1996), 1:1041.

3. Ibid.; Wise, *General John Cropper,* 11.

4. Wise, *General John Cropper,* 11.

5. *Pennsylvania Journal,* September 25, 1776; *Maryland Journal,* August 7, 1776; Robert Morris to James Martin, December 17, 1776, Bank of North America Papers, Historical Society of Pennsylvania, Philadelphia; *NDAR,* 7:505; Robert Morris to John Hancock, December 21, 1776, PCC (Letters and Reports from Robert Morris), M247, RG 360, R 148; B[enjamin] Harrison and R[ichard] H[enry] Lee to Captain Larkin Hammond, January 2, 1777, PCC (Letters Letter of the Committee for Foreign Affairs, 1776–1783), M247, RG 360, R 148.

6. Journal of the Virginia Council of Safety, August 19, 1776, *EJC,* 1:119.

7. Harrison and Lee to Hammond, January 2, 1777.

8. Samuel and Robert Purviance to Samuel Phillips Savage, May 31, 1777, Board of War Letters, 1776–1777, 152:229, Massachusetts Archives, Boston; *NDAR,* 8:1050.

9. Ibid.

10. Autobiography of Joshua Barney, Daughters of the American Revolution Library, Washington, DC. *Thomas* made for the Delaware, but was taken by HMS *Perseus,* Captain George Keith Elphinstone. Journal of HMS *Perseus, NDAR,* 7:939–40.

11. *Pennsylvania Gazette,* July 23, 1777; Howe's Prize List, October 24, 1777, *NDAR,* 10:286; Purdie's *Virginia Gazette,* July 18, 1777.

12. Zadock Purnell to Gov. Thomas Johnson, July 4 [*sic*], 1776, Red Book, 16:117, MDA.

13. Gov. Patrick Henry to Gov. Thomas Johnson, August 30, 1777, Revolutionary War Collection, MS 1814, Maryland Historical Society, Baltimore.

14. Wise, *General John Cropper,* 11.

15. Ibid., 12.

16. Ibid., 12, 20.

17. Ibid., 13.

18. Ibid.

19. Ibid.

20. Ibid.

21. Ibid., 13, 14.

22. Ibid., 14.

23. Ibid.

24. Ibid.

25. Ibid., 14, 15.

## Chapter 7. Now That Is What I Call Combat

1. J. J. Cooledge, *Ships of the Royal Navy: An Historical Index* (Devon, UK: David and Charles, 1969), 1:554.

2. N. A. M. Rodger, *The Wooden World: An Anatomy of the Georgian Navy* (Annapolis, MD: Naval Institute Press, 1986), 60–61.

3. *NDAR,* 6:447–52.

4. A. B. C. Whipple, *Fighting Sail* (Alexandria, VA: Time-Life Books, 1978), 22–23, 46.

5. *NDAR,* 4:502; 8:601–2, 768–69. See Cooledge, *Ships of the Royal Navy,* vol. 1, for ages of the British vessels.

6. Whipple, *Fighting Sail,* 50.

7. French Ensor Chadwick, ed., *The Graves Papers and Other Documents Relating to the Naval Operations of the Yorktown Campaign, July to October, 1781* (1916; reprint, New York: New York Times, 1968), 67.

8. Ibid., 165.

9. Commager and Morris, *The Spirit of Seventy-Six,* 1219.

10. Chadwick, *Graves Papers,* 165.

11. J. G. Shea, ed., *The Operations of the French Fleet under the Count de Grasse in 1781–2, as Described in Two Contemporaneous Journals* (New York: The Bradford Club, 1864), 69; Harold A. Larrabee, *Decision at the Chesapeake* (New York: Bramhill House, 1964), 197.

12. Larrabee, *Decision at the Chesapeake,* 202; Chadwick, *Graves Papers,* 72, 165.

13. Chadwick, *Graves Papers,* 72.

14. Larrabee, *Decision at the Chesapeake,* 203.

15. Commager and Morris, *The Spirit of 'Seventy-Six,* 1219.

16. Ibid., 203–4; Karl Gustaf Tomquist, *The Naval Campaigns of Count de Grasse during the American Revolution, 1781–1783,* trans. Amandus Johnson (Philadelphia: Swedish Colonial Society, 1942), 59–60.

17. Larrabee, *Decision at the Chesapeake,* 216; Tornquist, *Naval Campaigns,* 65–66.

18. Larrabee, *Decision at the Chesapeake,* 219; Chadwick, *Graves Papers,* 78.

19. Larrabee, *Decision at the Chesapeake,* 219–20; *Political Magazine and Parliamentary Journal* [London], 2 (1782): 154; Chadwick, *Graves Papers,* 169. Larrabee gives the date incorrectly if Graves's own logs are to be accepted.

20. *Political Magazine and Parliamentary Journal* 2 (1782): 154.

## Chapter 8. Plunder till They Could Plunder No More

1. Bob "Frogfoot" Weller, "The Treasure of Delaware Beach," www.treasureexpeditions.com/Delaware_Beach.htm.

2. *New York Times,* April 19, 1879; February 23, 1937.

3. *New York Times,* March 14, 1937; March 18, 1937.

4. "John Elliott, 1762–1843," Indian Hill Historical Society, www.indianhill.org/History/Pploo1.htm.

5. Ibid.

6. Ibid.; *Daily Universal Register,* November 22, 1785; November 24, 1785. The precise number of passengers is in dispute as the *Pennsylvania Packet* of September 12, 1785, states that *Faithful Steward* carried 240 passengers.

7. Joan Berseold, e-mail communication, January 18, 2004. One of Lee's sisters would one day have a poem written about her entitled "Pretty Polly Lee, the Irish Beauty."

8. "Descendants of Hugh Espey," http://freepages.genealogy.rootsweb.com/~espey/pafno1.htm.

9. *Meadville Courier,* August 30, 1831.

10. *Daily Universal Register,* November 22, 1785; November 24, 1785; *Pennsylvania Packet,* September 1, 1785; January 4, 1786. Some professional treasure hunters claim that the ship also carried to the United States 350,000 English copper pennies and half pennies dated 1775–83 to relieve the shortage of hard money in America. The claim has some support among numismatists. At the time few mints had been established so "paper money" was used. The Spanish "milled dollar" was sought after, but there were adequate supplies of English coinage already available for recirculation in the new nation. Copper coins were a source of profit to the minters in England. During the reigns of George II and III, copper coins were considered as "tokens" rather than legal tender. As a result, counterfeiting of the coins was not illegal and at the same time there was an incentive to mint them, considering

that a half penny contained only a farthing of copper. After Parliament passed a law against counterfeiting copper coins, however, copper coins were shipped to the "colonies," where the English penny had an inflated value of twelve per shilling. In September 1785, according to some modern treasure hunters, barrels of copper coins allegedly carried aboard *Faithful Steward* scattered on the beach when the ship wrecked. Other supporters of the story claim that a treasure in silver bullion, valued at $500,000, went down with the ship. I have yet to find any record to confirm any substantive treasure was ever aboard the ship, although the probability of the transport of limited quantities of copper coinage was indeed possible, even likely. Weller, "The Treasure of Delaware Beach"; Adrian L. Lonsdale and H.R. Kaplan, *A Guide to Sunken Ships in American Waters* (Arlington, VA: Compass, 1964), 43; John S. Potter Jr., *The Treasure Diver's Guide* (Garden City, NY: Doubleday, 1972), 485; John M. Kleeberg, "The Shipwreck of the Faithful Steward: A 'Missing Link' in the Epic of British and Irish Halfpence," in *Coinage of the Americas Conference, Proceedings no. 11,* ed. Philip L. Massur (New York: American Numismatic Society, 1996), 55–77.

11. *Daily Universal Register,* November 22, 1785.

12. *Meadville Courier,* August 30, 1831.

13. Ibid.; *Pennsylvania Packet,* September 12, 1785.

14. *Meadville Courier,* August 30, 1831; *Daily Universal Register,* November 24, 1785.

15. *Meadville Courier,* August 30, 1831.

16. The *Daily Universal Register* of November 24, 1785, published a letter from a survivor of the disaster stating that the vessel lay a hundred yards from shore, a position supported by John McIntire's recollections of the loss published in 1831. The *Pennsylvania Packet* of September 12, 1785, states the ship lay 150 yards from the shore. Later writers, such as Gary Gentile, for unknown reasons, incorrectly state the ship lay a mile from the shore. *Daily Universal Register,* November 24, 1785; *Meadville Courier,* August 30, 1831; Gary Gentile, *Shipwrecks of Delaware and Maryland* (Philadelphia: Gary Gentile Productions, 1990), 77.

17. *Daily Universal Register,* November 22, 1785.

18. *Meadville Courier,* August 30, 1831; *Pennsylvania Packet,* September 12, 1785.

19. *Pennsylvania Packet,* September 12, 1785.

20. *Meadville Courier,* August 30, 1831.

21. The *Delawarian,* in an 1874 article recollecting the events of the loss of *Faithful Steward,* reported that "a Miss Milby, afterwards mother of Nathaniel Wolfe, Esq., who was to become sheriff of this county," as a girl in her teens on her father's farm, close to the site of the wreck, had witnessed the disaster. As she was seventy-seven years of age in 1874, she clearly could not have been present at the event, which took place twelve years before her birth. Another purported witness was a Mrs. Marshall, widow of the respected pilot William Marshall, who was about seven years old at the time. The paper erroneously reported that there were 460 people aboard the ship and only sixty had been saved. *The Delawarian,* October 24, 1874.

22. *Pennsylvania Packet,* September 12, 1785; *Meadville Courier,* August 30, 1831.

23. *Meadville Courier,* August 30, 1831.

24. Ibid.

25. *Meadville Courier,* August 30, 1831; *Daily Universal Register,* November 24, 1785; *The Delawarian,* October 24, 1874.

26. *Meadville Courier,* August 30, 1831.

27. *Pennsylvania Packet,* September 12, 1785; Berseold, e-mail communication; *Daily Universal Register,* November 22, 1785. The known officers, crew, and passengers who survived the wreck of the *Faithful Steward* are as follows: Ships Crew—Capt. Connoly M'Causland; Mr. Standfield, 1st mate; Mr. Given [Gwyn], 2nd mate; Mr. [William] Lin [Linn], boatswain; John Brown, sailor; Wm. Dalrample [Dalrymple], sailor; Robert Kelly, sailor; Samuel Irwin, [sailor]; John Quigly, [sailor]; Pat[rick] Mourn, [sailor]; Edward

M'Caffry [Caifrey], [sailor]; Pelick Hudson, [sailor]; Owne Phillips, [sailor]; Cabin Passengers—Thomas Blair, John O'Neill [O'Neil], John York; Passengers—James Aspill, John Aspill, Thomas Baskin, James Beaty, John Brocket, Mary Burns, Matthew Caldwell, Gustavus Calhoun [Colhoun], Thomas Calhoun [Colhoun], Sarah Campbell, James Devin, Robert Dinmore [Dinsmore], James Doughherty, James Ellist [Ellit] (Elliott), Simon Ellist [Ellit] (Elliott), Robert Espey, John Espey, Jean Morehead Espey, Samuel Heburn, Arthur Higginbottom, Margaret Kincade, Robert Laurence, James Lee, Mary Lee, [—] Lee, [—] Lee, Mary (Espey?) Maginniss [Maginnis], James Marshall, John M'Calister [McCallister], Hugh M'Clean, Docor M'Dougle [McDougal], John M'Ilheney [McIlheney], Matthew [Mathew] M'Manes, John M'Mullen [McMullan], Charles M'Williams, James M'Intire junior, James M'Intire senior, Rebecca M'Intire, Neill M'Kinon, Sarah M'Kinon, Wm. M'Clintock, John M'Nab, Alexander Moore, Samuel Moore, Thomas Moore [More], George Munro, Thomas Ranolles [Ranolls], George Richford, John Scott, John Shaw, James Smyth [Smith], John Spires, James Stunkard [Stankard], Andrew Watt, James Watt, Samuel Wright. *The Pennsylvania Packet,* January 4, 1786, provided the first listing of survivors. This list was reprinted in the *Londonderry News,* February 21, 1786, with variants of the same names (indicated by brackets). The genealogy of the Espey family has added four Espeys. Robert, John, and Jean Morehead Espey are in this listing, as is a sister named Mary. Mary was probably one and the same as Mary Maginniss, but this bears further investigation. The presumed owners of the ship, John Maxwell Nesbitt, James Campbell, and William Allison, signed the listing published in the *Pennsylvania Packet.* Whether they were aboard or were merely the ship owner's representatives in Philadelphia is uncertain. *Pennsylvania Packet,* January 4, 1786; *Londonderry News,* February 21, 1786; "Descendants of Hugh Espey."

28. *Meadville Courier,* August 30, 1831; "Descendants of Hugh Espey."

29. "John Elliott."

30. Gentile, *Shipwrecks,* 78.

## Chapter 9. So Much for Attending Congress

1. *Biographical Directory of the United States Congress, 1774–1989* (Washington, DC: United States Government Printing Office, 1989), 704; Catherine Drinker Bowen, *Miracle at Philadelphia: The Story of the Constitutional Convention, May to September 1787* (Boston: Little, Brown, 1966), 293.

2. The following account comes from *Maryland Gazette,* December 16, 1790.

3. *Biographical Directory,* 293.

## Chapter 10. The Captain Was in a Hilarious Mood

1. J. F. Van Dulum to Paul E. Smith, March 26, 1964, and J. C. Van Ooesten to J. B. DeSwort, July 24, 1973, *De Braak* file, Zwaanendael Museum, Lewes, DE; David V. Beard, "HMS *de Braak:* A Treasure Debunked, a Treasure Revealed" (Masters' thesis, East Carolina University, 1989); Donald G. Shomette, *The Hunt for HMS* De Braak: *Legend and Legacy* (Durham, NC: Carolina Academic Press, 1993), 15–16.

2. *De Braak* plans, Registration 6346, box 65, Admiralty Draughts Collection, National Maritime Museum, London; Howard I. Chapelle and M. E. S. Laws, "HMS *De Braak:* The Stories of a 'Treasure Ship,'" *Smithsonian Journal of History,* spring 1967, 58; Beard, "HMS *de Braak,*" 81–82; Van Dulum to Smith, March 24, 1964.

3. Shomette, *Hunt for HMS* De Braak, 16.

4. Van Ooesten to DeSwort, July 24, 1973; Van Dulum to Smith, March 26, 1964.

5. Van Ooesten to DeSwort, July 24, 1973; Van Dulum to Smith, March 26, 1964;

George Le Favre, *The French Revolution from 1793 to 1799* (New York: Columbia University Press, 1964), 14.

6. Van Dulum to Smith, March 26, 1964.

7. The Batavian Republic was established in the Netherlands in 1795 by the invading armies of revolutionary France. The republic ended in 1806 when Napoleon I made his brother, Louis, king of Holland.

8. "The State of the Naval Forces of the Republic of Batavia, Vendemaire 12, Year 5 [October 3, 1796]," transcript, and "The General Register of the Naval Forces of the Netherlands, Subsequently, the Batavian Republic, from 1795 to 1811," transcript, both in *De Braak* file, Zwaanendael Museum.

9. Navy Board to Admiralty, September 30, 1795, Admiralty 2/374, PRO.

10. *The Times* (London), March 8, 1796.

11. Chapelle and Laws, "HMS *De de Braak*," 58; Spencer, Phybus, and Gambier to Lord Dundas, July 18, 1795, Admiralty 2/374, PRO.

12. Chapelle and Laws, "HMS *de Braak*," 58.

13. Ibid., 58–59.

14. Chief Surveyor of the Navy to the Navy Board, September 1, 1796, Admiralty 106/1935, PRO; Navy Board to Admiralty, September 8, 1796, Admiralty 106/1222, part 25, PRO.

15. *De Braak* plans, Registration 6346 and 6347; Beard, "HMS *de Braak*," 88–90.

16. *De Braak* plans, Registration 6347; Beard, "HMS *de Braak*," 88–90.

17. *De Braak* plans, Registration 6347; Beard, "HMS *de Braak*," 88–90. See William N. Boog Watson, "Alexander Brodie and His Firehearths for Ships," *The Mariners Mirror* 45, no. 4 (November, 1968): 409–11, for a comprehensive discussion of the development of the Brodie firehearths.

18. See William Falconer, *An Universal Dictionary of the Marine* (1780; reprint, Devon, UK: David and Charles, 1970), 261, and R. J. B. Knight, "The Introduction of Copper Sheathing into the Royal Navy, 1779–1786," *The Mariner's Mirror* 59, no. 3 (August 1973): 299–310, for definition, history, and importance of copper sheathing in Royal Navy warships.

19. Navy Board to Admiralty, October 11, 1797, PRO, Admiralty 106/2088; Chapelle and Laws, "HMS *De Braak*," 59.

20. Shomette, *Hunt for HMS* De Braak, 4–13.

21. Ibid., 13–15.

22. Chapelle and Laws, "HMS *De Braak*," 59.

23. Ibid.; Shomette, *Hunt for HMS* De Braak, 25.

24. Shomette, *Hunt for HMS* De Braak, 25.

25. Ibid., 25–26.

26. James Drew to Evan Nepean, September 13, 1797; September 27, 1797, PRO, Admiralty 1/1719.

27. *The Times* (London), December 16, 18, 1797.

28. *The Times* (London), December 19, 20, 21, 1797.

29. *The Times* (London), December 25, 1797.

30. Navy Board to Mr. Marsden, December 11, 1797, Admiralty 1/1719, PRO; Navy Board to Admiralty, December 16, 1797, Admiralty 106/2088, PRO.

31. Admiralty to Drew, December 24, 1797, Admiralty 2/135, PRO.

32. Admiralty to Drew, February 8, 1798, Admiralty 2/284, Part 201, PRO; Admiralty to Francis Pender. February 23, 1798, Admiralty 2/1099, PRO; Admiralty to George Vandeput, February 24, 1798, Admiralty 2/135, parts 99 and 100, PRO; J. J. Cooledge, *Ships of the Royal Navy: An Historical Index* (Devon, UK: David and Charles, 1969), 1:479.

33. Admiralty to Drew, February 8, 1798; Admiralty to Pender, February 23, 1798.

34. Admiralty to Drew, February 8, 1798.

35. Drew to Nepean, February 18, 1798, Admiralty 1/1720, PRO.

36. Ibid.; HMS *De Braak* Muster Book, Admiralty 36/12890, PRO; *De Braak* Pay Books, January 9, 1801, Admiralty 35/211, PRO. See James Dugan, *The Great Mutiny* (New York: G. P. Putnam's Sons, 1965), for the most complete account of the Great Mutiny and of the roles of the crews of HMS *Saturn* and *Ramilles* in the uprising.

37. HMS *De Braak* Muster Book; *De Braak* Pay Books.

38. Drew to Nepean, March 2, 1798, Admiralty 1/1720, PRO; Drew to Nepean, March 7, 1798, Admiralty 1/1720, PRO.

39. See Captain's Log, HMS *St. Albans,* May 26, 1797–September 16, 1798, Admiralty 51/1272, PRO, for particulars of the convoy's Atlantic voyage.

40. Pender to Admiralty, March 26, 1798, Admiralty 1/1720, PRO.

41. Captain's Log, HMS *St. Albans,* April 1–4, 1798.

42. Chapelle and Laws, "HMS *De Braak,*" 57, note that the payroll for the entire Halifax garrison was "far less than $30,000."

43. *Norfolk Herald,* August 29, 1798.

44. Ibid.

45. *The Daily Advertiser,* May 28, 1798; Beard, "HMS *de Braak,*" 15–16; Captain's log, HMS *St. Albans,* May 24, 1798; *Norfolk Herald,* May 29, 1798; Shomette, *Hunt for HMS* De Braak, 36–37, 357–58 n. 42.

46. *Claypool's American Daily Advertiser,* May 28,1798; *New York Times,* April 29, 1879; *The Sun,* July 25, 1887.

47. Shomette, *Hunt for HMS* De Braak, 37.

48. *The Sun,* July 25, 1887.

49. *Claypool's American Daily Advertiser,* May 28, 1798.

50. Ibid. Until the wreck of *De Braak* was excavated in 1984–86, what occurred on board at the moment of loss could only be surmised, although the 1887 recounting of the story mentions a report by Allen that when the brig careened, the guns shifted to the leeward on the deck and helped drag her down. *The Sun,* July 25, 1887.

51. Phineas Bond to Lord Grenville, May 28, 1798, Admiralty 1/5121/3, PRO; *Claypool's American Daily Advertiser,* May 28, 1798.

52. *The Sun,* June 25, 1887, indicates that fifteen Spanish prisoners had been transferred from the prize ship to *De Braak.* Several prisoners purportedly floated ashore and escaped.

53. See Shomette, *Hunt for HMS* De Braak, for the convoluted evolution of the *De Braak* treasure legend.

## Chapter 11. The Unfortunate Spaniards Waved Their Handkerchiefs

1. Captain Bob Payne, personal communication, September 13, 2004; *Chincoteague Beachcomber,* June 27, 1997.

2. *Gazette of the United States & Philadelphia,* November 8, 1802.

3. Ibid. The remainder of the account comes from Cesáreo Fernández Duro, *Naufragios de la Armada Española* (Madrid, 1867), 170–75.

4. Duro, *Naufragios,* 175; *Gazette of the United States & Philadelphia,* November 8, 1802.

5. Duro, *Naufragios,* 171–75.

## Chapter 12. Rothschilds among the Toilers of the Sea

1. Arthur Godfrey and Peter J. Lassey, *Shipwrecks of the Yorkshire Coast* (Clapham, UK: Dalesman, 1974), 9.

2. William H. Wroten Jr., *Assateague* (Cambridge, MD: Tidewater Publishers, 1972),

38; Nathaniel T. Kenney, "Chincoteague: Watermen's Island Home," *National Geographic Magazine,* June 1980, 812; Reginald V. Truitt and Millard G. Les Callette, *Worcester County: Maryland's Arcadia* (Snow Hill, MD: Worcester County Historical Society, 1977), 68.

3. Bella Bathurst, *The Wreckers* (Boston: Houghton Mifflin, 2005), 11.

4. Ibid., 12–13.

5. Ibid., 14–15.

6. David R. Owen and Michael C. Tolley, *Courts of Admiralty in Colonial America: The Maryland Experience, 1634–1776* (Durham, NC: Carolina Academic Press, in Association with the Maryland Historical Society, 1995), 12–13.

7. John Lawson, *A New Voyage to Carolina,* ed. Hugh Talmage Lefler (Chapel Hill: University of North Carolina Press, 1967), 157. Lawson was speaking of the Carolina coast, but his comments are applicable to the Atlantic seaboard from Georgia to New York.

8. *Archives of Maryland* (Baltimore: Maryland Historical Society, 1833–), 20:102–3.

9. Ibid., 100, 101, 105, 301.

10. Ibid., 102–3.

11. Ibid. In 1817 Lord Coke defined *flotsam* as when a vessel is sunk or otherwise perished and the goods float on the sea. *Jetsam* is when a ship is in danger of sinking and, to lighten the ship, the goods are cast into the sea, but the ship still perishes. *Lagan,* or *lingan,* is when goods are cast into the sea, and afterward the ship perishes, and the goods are so heavy that they sink to the bottom, but the mariners intending on having them again, tie to them a buoy or cork, or such other thing that will not sink, so that they may find them again. A *derelict* is a ship or cargo that has been abandoned by the owner with no hope of recovery or repossession. Bathurst, *The Wreckers,* 10.

12. *Archives of Maryland,* 20:103.

13. Ibid., 105.

14. Ibid., 241–42, 292.

15. Ibid., 292.

16. Ibid., 292, 302.

17. Ibid., 301.

18. Truitt and Les Callette, *Worcester County,* 68

19. Stephen M. Voynick, *The Mid-Atlantic Treasure Coast: Coin Beaches and Treasure Shipwrecks from Long Island to the Eastern Shore* (Wallingford, PA: Middle Atlantic Press, 1984), 34.

20. Truitt and Les Callette, *Worcester County,* 65; Wroten, *Assateague,* 39.

21. See Van R. Field, *Wrecks and Rescues on Long Island* (Center Moriches, NY: privately printed, 1997), for comparison with New York wreckers and wreckmasters.

22. Wroten, *Assateague,* 39–40.

23. *Maryland Gazette,* June 7, 1787. The reef of rocks may well have been a submerged wreck or mound of oyster shells, as there are no known submerged rocks or reefs that form hazards to navigation in Delmarva coastal waters, especially in the vicinity of Smith Island.

24. *Lloyd's List,* February 20, 1795.

25. Truitt and Les Callette, *Worcester County,* 69.

26. Ibid. Fassitt's home still stands and is now known as Bayside Farm.

27. Ibid., 69–70.

28. Ibid. 70.

29. "An Act for Appointing a Wreckmaster in Worcester County," *Archives of Maryland,* 100:63.

30. Ibid.

31. Ibid., 63–64.

32. Ibid., 64.

33. Ibid.

34. "A Supplement to the Act Entitled, 'An Act to Appoint a Wreckmaster for Worcester County,'" *Archives of Maryland*, 192:678.

35. "A Further Supplement to the Act Entitled, 'An Act for Appointing a Wreckmaster in Worcester County,'" *Archives of Maryland*, 192:714.

36. Constitutional Revision Study Documents of the Constitutional Convention Commission, *Archives of Maryland*, 138:1006.

37. Otho Scott and Hiram M'Cullough, eds., *The Maryland Code: Public General Laws and Public Land Laws* (Baltimore: John Murphy and Co., 1860), *Archives of Maryland*, 145:963–64. The Act was slightly revised again in 1888. For revised text, see *Archives of Maryland*, 138:2189–91.

38. George P. Bagley, ed., *The Annotated Code of the Public Civil Laws of Maryland* (Baltimore: King Bros., 1911), *Archives of Maryland*, 372:88; Horace E. Flack, ed., *Code Public Local Laws of Maryland* (Baltimore, 1930), *Archives of Maryland*, 377:5323–25; Truitt and Les Callette, *Worcester County*, 71.

39. *Baltimore Sun*, October 28, 1872; *Salisbury Advertiser*, November 9, 1872; *Delawarian*, November 30, 1872.

40. Kessler Burnett, "Oyster," *Chesapeake Life Magazine*, January/February 2000, http://www.chesapeakelifemag.com/tourismloyster.html.

41. Ibid.

42. Ibid.; Barnes and Truitt, *Seashore Chronicles*, 10.

43. Burnett, "Oyster."

44. Ibid.; Barnes and Truitt, *Seashore Chronicles*, 10. Burnett claims the award was for $10,000.

45. George and Suzanne Hurley, *Shipwrecks and Rescues along the Barrier Islands of Delaware, Maryland, and Virginia* (Norfolk: Donning Company, 1984), 20.

46. Ibid.

## Chapter 13. Assailed by Overwhelming Odds

1. Philip Van Dorn Stern, *The Confederate Navy* (New York: Bonanza Books, 1962), 27–28.

2. R. N. Scott et al., eds., *The War of the Rebellion: A Compilation of the Official Records of the Union and Confederate Armies* (Washington, DC: U.S. Government Printing Office, 1880–1901), 51:458.

3. *ORN*, 2nd ser., 1:129.

4. *Civil War Naval Chronology, 1861–1865* (Washington, DC: Naval History Division, Navy Department, 1971), 1:26.

5. *ORN*, 1st ser., 6:288.

6. Ibid., 6:288, 289. Lieutenant Hopkins would have commanded the expedition except he was sick in bed.

7. Ibid., 6:288.

8. Ibid.

9. Scott et al., *War of the Rebellion*, 1st ser., 51: part 2, 380.

10. *ORN*, 1st ser., 6:415.

11. Scott et al., *War of the Rebellion*, 1st ser., 33: part 1, 401–3.

12. William M. Lytle and Forrest R. Holdcamper, eds., *Merchant Steam Vessels of the United States, 1790–1868* (Staten Island, NY: Steamship Historical Society of America, 1975), 168; *ORN*, 2nd ser., 1:216. Lytle claims the ship was purchased in 1858.

13. *ORN*, 2nd ser., 1:216.

14. *Civil War Naval Chronology*, 2:38.

15. *ORN*, 1st ser., 9:67.

16. Ibid., 9:89.

17. Ibid., 9:90. *General Meigs* was an iron-hulled vessel of 329 tons, built in 1862 at Philadelphia, PA, where she was first home ported. She was sold to the U.S. Quartermaster's Department on April 30, 1863. On December 15, 1865, she was redocumented as *Lavaca* and foundered in 1877. Lytle and Holdcamper, *Merchant Steam Vessels,* 81.

18. *ORN,* 1st ser., 9:89–90.

19. Ibid., 90.

20. Ibid.

21. *ORN,* 2nd ser., 1:252

22. Ibid.

23. *Civil War Naval Chronology,* 6:228–29.

24. Stern, *The Confederate Navy,* 213.

25. *ORN,* 1st ser., 3:623, 645.

26. Ibid.

27. Ibid.

28. Ibid.

29. Ibid.

30. *ORN,* 1st ser., 3:623, 645; *Dictionary of Transports and Combatant Vessels Steam and Sail Employed by the Union Army, 1861–1868,* comp. Charles Dana Gibson and E. Kay Gibson (Camden, ME: Ensign Press, 1995), 124. *General Berry* was taken at 37°33′ N, 74°20′ W and then sunk thirty-five miles off the coast of Maryland.

31. *ORN,* 1st ser., 3:623, 645. Morris's reports and his log differ on the number of prisoners that were transferred to Howard, one saying sixty-two, and the other saying sixty-eight. The report and log also differ on where Zelinda was from, one saying Brunswick, Maine, and the other Eastport, Maine.

32. *ORN,* 1st ser., 3:623.

33. Ibid., 625, 646. Again Morris's report and log vary, with his report saying forty-three passengers and thirty-six crewmen, and his log reporting forty-two passengers and thirty-nine crewmen.

34. Ibid.

35. Ibid.

36. The pipes cut included the injection pipe of the engine; the bottom blowpipe of the boilers, the feed pipe of the donkey engine, the discharge pipe of same, a pipe for the watering journal, and a discharge pipe. All of the cuts were made above the waterline. Segments cut away ranged from three and a half to fifteen inches in length. Ibid., 622.

37. *ORN,* 1st ser., 3:625, 646. On opening the mailbags taken from *Electric Spark,* Morris discovered no dispatches but $12,000 worth of postage stamps. He threw all of the remaining mail overboard. In the Adams Express Company's chest he found: $1,305 U.S. dollars, $328 in New Orleans bank notes, $132.25 in New Orleans city notes, $219 in gold, one gold watch, one silver watch, and a diamond pin. All of the above were placed in the care of the *Florida*'s paymaster.

38. Ibid., 625, 626.

39. *ORN,* 2nd ser., 1:252; *Civil War Naval Chronology,* 6:229.

## Chapter 14. Unprecedented Disregard

1. *ORN,* 1st ser., 16:196, 530, 531–32, 544.

2. *Dictionary of American Naval Fighting Ships* (Washington, DC: Naval History Division, Navy Department, 1959–1981), 4:428; *ORN,* 1st ser., 4:150; 16:524. *Montgomery* was formally purchased for the navy on August 24, 1861. In 1877 she was described as fitted with iron and copper fastenings, her frame being strapped on with iron, and her keel

and part of the hull covered with yellow metal. She was then reported as brig-rigged and approximately 1,100 tons burthen, 198 feet in length, 29 feet breadth of beam, and with a draft of 16 feet. *New York Times,* January 9, 1877; *ORN,* 1st ser., 16:808.

3. *ORN,* 1st ser., 17:24. For Jouett's career, see *Dictionary of American Naval Fighting Ships,* 3:567.

4. *ORN,* 1st ser., 17:56–57, 71–72.

5. Ibid., 18:456.

6. Ibid., 104–6.

7. Ibid., 718; 34:130–31, 692.

8. Ibid., 18:500.

9. Ibid., 18:454, 500–501.

10. Ibid., 18:455–56, 501.

11. Ibid., 18:547.

12. Ibid., 19:108, 158.

13. Ibid., 19:238, 269.

14. Ibid., 19:269, 271, 274, 280.

15. Ibid., 19:279–80.

16. Ibid., 19:280.

17. Ibid., 19:269, 270, 271, 279–80.

18. Ibid., 279–80.

19. Ibid., 19:269, 270, 271, 281.

20. Ibid., 19:269, 270, 275.

21. Ibid., 19:274–75.

22. *ORN,* 2nd ser., 3:563.

23. *ORN,* 1st ser., 19:280–81.

24. Ibid., 1:505–6.

25. *ORN,* 2nd ser., 3:562; 1st ser., 19:278–279.

26. Ibid., 19:269, 270.

27. *ORN,* 1st ser., 19:271, 300.

28. Ibid., 19:268.

29. Ibid., 19:304, 309, 317, 725.

30. Ibid., 19:271–72.

31. Ibid., 19:275.

32. Ibid., 19:490.

33. Ibid., 19:273–74.

34. Ibid., 19:275, 276–77.

35. *ORN,* 2nd ser., 3:727.

36. Ibid., 3:726–28.

37. Ibid.

38. Ibid.

39. Ibid., 2:28, 29, 34, 60, 342, 385, 387; 10:151, 156–58, 220, 229, 227–38, 269, 287, 318, 350, 377, 385–86, 388–89, 390, 391, 396–98, 400–401, 485–87, 500, 544, 547–51, 554, 586, 713; 11:40, 66, 136–37, 141, 245–46, 384, 399, 426, 443, 445, 498, 562–63, 737; 12:5; 15:224.

40. Ibid., 12:90, 1555–56.

41. *New York Times,* January 9, 1877.

42. Ibid.

43. *New York Times,* January 9 and 12, 1877.

44. Ibid.

45. Ibid.

46. *New York Times,* January 9, 1877.

47. *New York Times,* January 12, 1877.

48. *New York Times,* January 9 and 12, 1877.

49. Ibid.

50. *New York Times,* January 9, 1877.

51. Ibid.

52. *New York Times,* January 9 and 12, 1877.

## Chapter 15. Suits of Ice

1. *Philadelphia Inquirer,* March 15 and 16, 1888.

2. Ibid.

3. *New York Times,* March 15, 1888; *Philadelphia Inquirer,* March 15, 1888.

4. *Philadelphia Inquirer,* March 15, 1888.

5. Ibid.; *New York Times,* March 15, 1888.

6. *Philadelphia Inquirer,* March 15, 1888; *New York Times,* March 15, 1888.

7. *Philadelphia Inquirer,* March 15, 1888; *New York Times,* March 15, 1888.

8. *Philadelphia Inquirer,* March 15, 1888.

9. *New York Times,* March 15, 1888; *Philadelphia Inquirer,* March 15 and 16, 1888.

10. *Philadelphia Inquirer,* March 15, 1888.

11. Ibid.

12. Ibid.; *New York Times,* March 15, 1888.

13. *Philadelphia Inquirer,* March 15, 1888.

14. *New York Times,* March 15, 1888.

15. *Philadelphia Inquirer,* March 15, 1888.

16. Ibid.

17. Ibid.

18. *Merchant Vessels of the United States, 1887* (Washington, DC: U.S. Government Printing Office, 1887). Crewmen included Henry Thompson, Charles Coffman, George Haywood, August Asphund, and Albert Johnson. *Philadelphia Inquirer,* March 16, 1888.

19. *New York Times,* March 15, 1888; *Philadelphia Inquirer,* March 15, March 16, 1888.

20. George and Suzanne Hurley, *Shipwrecks and Rescues along the Barrier Islands of Delaware, Maryland, and Virginia* (Norfolk: Donning Company, 1984), 129. See the *Annual Report of the Operations of the United States Life-Saving Service, 1888* (Washington, DC: US Government Printing Office, 1888) for detailed reports on the actions taken by the Lewes, Cape Henlopen, and Rehoboth Life Saving Stations during the storm.

21. Hurley and Hurley, *Shipwrecks and Rescues,* 130.

22. Ibid.; *Merchant Vessels of the United States, 1887; Philadelphia Inquirer,* March 16, 1888.

23. Hurley and Hurley, *Shipwrecks and Rescues,* 130.

24. Ibid.

25. Ibid.

26. Ibid.

27. Ibid.

28. Ibid.

29. Ibid., 129.

30. Delaware Bay Pilots Scrapbook, ca. 1882–89, 49, 51, RG 200, Small Manuscript Collection, Delaware State Archives. The barge *C. B. Hazeltine* was commanded by Captain William Van Kirk, owned by John Schreader, and bound from Philadelphia for Boston. The tug reported lost at the same time is not identified but may have been *Philadelphia.*

31. *Philadelphia Inquirer,* March 15 and 16, 1888.

32. *Philadelphia Inquirer,* March 15, 16, and 17, 1888.

33. *New York Times,* March 17, 1888.

34. *Philadelphia Inquirer,* March 15, 1888.

35. *Philadelphia Inquirer,* March 15 and 16, 1888; Delaware Bay Pilots Scrapbook, 83. The Philadelphia Maritime Exchange was organized in 1875 and incorporated in 1882. It included among its original founders railroad, insurance, and steamship companies, which had organized to provide an adequate headquarters at which marine intelligence of incoming and outgoing shipping could be gathered for the benefit of trade at the Port of Philadelphia. The exchange was not a strictly for-profit organization. Central to its operation was telegraphic communications between the exchange office on Delaware Breakwater and Philadelphia regarding the arrival and departure of shipping. Excerpted from *The Call,* February 4, 1888, in Delaware Bay Pilots Scrapbook, 38.

36. Delaware Bay Pilots Scrapbook, 81.

37. *New York Times,* March 15, 1888; *Philadelphia Inquirer,* March 15, 1888.

38. *Philadelphia Inquirer,* March 15, 1888.

39. Ibid.; *New York Times,* March 15, 1888; "The Disappearance of the Esk," *The Islands,* fall 1979, 1–2. *Esk's* bones would immediately disappear beneath the sands but reappeared in 1900. From time to time the hulk was reburied by the sea, cyclically uncovered, and reportedly moved about the beach only to be reburied. Frames from the wreck are still visible on occasions and have been picked over by souvenir hunters.

## Chapter 16. Chips of Wood on the Angry Waves

1. *Philadelphia Inquirer,* September 13, 1889.

2. *New York Times,* September 13, 1889.

3. *Philadelphia Inquirer,* September 11, 1889.

4. *Philadelphia Inquirer,* September 11 and 12, 1889; *New York Times,* September 13, 1889; George and Suzanne Hurley, *Shipwrecks and Rescues along the Barrier Islands of Delaware, Maryland, and Virginia* (Norfolk: Donning Company, 1984), 142.

5. *Philadelphia Inquirer,* September 11 and 12, 1889; *New York Times,* September 13, 1889.

6. *Philadelphia Inquirer,* September 11, 1889. The observer was undoubtedly lumping volunteers with the lifesaving crew, which numbered only seven men.

7. *Philadelphia Inquirer,* September 12, 1889; Hurley and Hurley, *Shipwrecks and Rescues,* 142.

8. *Philadelphia Inquirer,* September 12, 1889; *New York Times,* September 12, 1889.

9. *Philadelphia Inquirer,* September 13, 1889.

10. Ibid.

11. *Philadelphia Inquirer,* September 12 and 13, 1889.

12. *Philadelphia Inquirer,* September 13, 1889; *New York Times,* September 13, 1889.

13 *Philadelphia Inquirer,* September 13, 1889.

14. Ibid.

15. Ibid. What stranded boat the master of Babcock saw is uncertain, "but there is no doubt from her location that the vessel is one that has not hitherto been accounted for."

16. Ibid.; *New York Times,* September 13, 1889.

17. *Philadelphia Inquirer,* September 13, 1889; *New York Times,* September 14, 1889.

18. *Philadelphia Inquirer,* September 13, 1889; *New York Times,* September 14, 1889.

19. *Philadelphia Inquirer,* September 13, 1889; *New York Times,* September 14, 1889.

20. *Philadelphia Inquirer,* September 12, 1889. See the *Annual Report of the Operations of the United States Life-Saving Service, 1890* (Washington, DC: U.S. Government Printing Office, 1890) for detailed reports on the actions taken by the Lewes, Cape Henlopen, and Rehoboth Life Saving Stations during the storm.

21. *Philadelphia Inquirer,* September 12, 1889. *Bryan* had slipped her cable about 5:00 P.M.

22. *Consilda,* Captain Nelson, and *St. Cloud,* Captain Everson, both barges, left Philadelphia laden with coal. *St. Cloud* carried a crew of eight. The tug *C. W. Morse,* Captain Blair, was to have accompanied them as far as the Delaware Breakwater and having heard of the expected storm came to anchor on Brandywine Shoal on Saturday, September 6. The next day they were joined by the barge *Tonawanda,* Captain Clark, owned by John Schader of Philadelphia, and barge *Wallace,* owned by Bartlett and Shepherd of Philadelphia, and manned by a crew of eight. The four barges lay within hailing distance and rested in security until Tuesday at 4:00 P.M. when *Consilda,* having lost her rudder, put up a distress flag. *C. W. Morse* had remained within a short distance of the barges, and her behavior when the flag was raised was later severely criticized by Captain Nelson. Nelson informed the *Philadelphia Inquirer* that when *Consilda* raised the flag, *Morse* "made a pretense of saving us, but after running within a few feet of us she gave us the stern and went off towing one of the other barges, either the *Tonawanda* or *Wallace,* I don't know which, and there took off a woman, and we have never seen the tug since. Captain Blair must have seen our danger. A few minutes after they left we were compelled to take to a dory we had with us, and soon our boat was in pieces. In our little boat there were four men, Alban Maltson, James Wilson, W. W. Hickess and myself. We took refuge on a stranded schooner and we were taken from that." *St. Cloud* was still floating when *Consilda*'s men left, and the rescued crew reported they did not know if *St. Cloud*'s men were drowned. Late that afternoon, the men of *Tonawanda* were rescued by tugboat and taken ashore. They reported that the men of *St. Cloud* and *Tonawanda* had been drowned. On the morning of the 13th, however, it was reported in Philadelphia that the crews of *Wallace* and *St. Cloud* had been taken off the day before by *C. W. Morse* and carried to the city. Only one man was lost. *Philadelphia Inquirer,* September 13, 1889.

23. Ibid.; Hurley and Hurley, *Shipwrecks and Rescues,* 144.

24. *Philadelphia Inquirer,* September 13, 1889; Hurley and Hurley, *Shipwrecks and Rescues,* 142, 144.

25. *Philadelphia Inquirer,* September 12, 1889.

26. Hurley and Hurley, *Shipwrecks and Rescues,* 144, call the ship a brig. All news reports refer to her as a bark. *New York Times,* September 12 and 13, 1889; Delaware Bay Pilots Scrapbook, ca. 1882–89, 82, RG 200, Small Manuscript Collection, Delaware State Archives.

27. Hurley and Hurley, *Shipwrecks and Rescues,* 142, 144, 146.

28. Ibid., 145.

29. Ibid.

30. Ibid.

31. Ibid. *Byron M.* was home ported in Windsor, Nova Scotia, and sailed under a Captain Leecain. She had been en route from Santo Domingo with a cargo of sugar valued at $7,000. Delaware Bay Pilots Scrapbook, 86.

32. *New York Times,* September 12 and 13, 1889.

33. *New York Times,* September 13, 1889.

34. Hurley and Hurley, *Shipwrecks and Rescues,* 147–48, 150.

35. Ibid. 148; *New York Times,* September 12, 1889.

36. *Philadelphia Inquirer,* September 12, 1889; *New York Times,* September 13, 1889.

37. Hurley and Hurley, *Shipwrecks and Rescues,* 148.

38. Ibid., 148, 150.

39. Ibid.; *Philadelphia Inquirer,* September 13, 1889; *New York Times,* September 13, 1889.

40. Hurley and Hurley, *Shipwrecks and Rescues,* 150.

41. Ibid.

42. Ibid., 144; *New York Times,* September 13 and 14, 1889.

43. *Philadelphia Inquirer,* September 14, 1889.

44. Hurley and Hurley, *Shipwrecks and Rescues,* 151.

45. *Philadelphia Inquirer,* September 13, 1889; *New York Times,* September 13, 1889.

46. *Philadelphia Inquirer,* September 13, 1889.

47. *Philadelphia Inquirer,* September 14, 1889; Delaware Bay Pilots Scrapbook, 87.

48. *Philadelphia Inquirer,* September 14, 1889; Delaware Bay Pilots Scrapbook, 87; *New York Times,* September 13, 1889.

49. *Philadelphia Inquirer,* September 16, 1889.

50. *New York Times,* September 12 and 13, 1889.

51. *Philadelphia Inquirer,* September 12, 13, and 14, 1889; *New York Times,* September 12, 13, and 14, 1889.

52. *Philadelphia Inquirer,* September 13, 1889.

53. *New York Times,* September 16, 1889.

54. Virginia Cullen, *History of Lewes, Delaware* ([Lewes, DE]: Colonel David Hall Chapter, Daughters of the American Revolution, 1981), 55.

55. *Philadelphia Inquirer,* September 13, 1889.

Chapter 17. Poor Pussy

1. *Philadelphia Inquirer,* October 10, 1891.

2. *Washington Post,* October 11, 1891; *Baltimore Sun,* October 12, 1891; *The Illustrated American,* October 31, 1891. The tests would eventually be conducted on November 14, 1891, and would be hosted by Dashiell and witnessed by two senators, Secretary Tracy, the assistant secretary of the navy, Professor Alger of the U.S. Naval Academy, and two U.S. Army generals. The tests consisted of the firing of armor-piercing shells against the new 10-inch-thick nickel-steel plates, with Tracy giving the firing commands. Rodney Carlisle, *Powder and Propellants: Energetic Materials at Indian Head, Maryland, 1890–1990* (Annapolis, MD: U.S. Navy, 1990), 13.

3. *Washington Post,* October 11, 1891; *The Sun,* October 12, 1891; *The Illustrated American,* October 31, 1891. The report of Captain James T. Tracy, Keeper of the Assateague Beach Life Saving Station, gives the ship's tonnage in 1891 as 750. George and Suzanne Hurley, *Shipwrecks and Rescues along the Barrier Islands of Delaware, Maryland, and Virginia* (Norfolk: Donning Company, 1984), 81.

4. *The Illustrated American,* October 31, 1891, states the government paid $90,000 but that Smith owned her for three years, while the *Baltimore Sun* notes that she was sold for $98,000 but incorrectly gives the sale date as "about 1878."

5. "USS Despatch," www.navyhistory.com/MISC/Despatch2.html; *Washington Post,* October 11, 1891.

6. "USS Despatch"; *The Sun,* October 12, 1891.

7. "USS Despatch"; *The Sun,* October 12, 1891.

8. "USS Despatch"; *The Sun,* October 12, 1891. *Washington Post,* October 11, 1891, states the date the orders were received was October 17, while *The Sun,* October 12, 1891, states the date was October 19, 1880.

9. *Washington Post,* October 11, 1891; *The Sun,* October 12, 1891; *The Illustrated American,* October 31, 1891.

10. *Washington Post,* October 11, 1891; *Richmond Dispatch,* October 15, 1891.

11. *Washington Post,* October 11, 1891; *Richmond Dispatch,* October 15, 1891.

12. *Washington Post,* October 11, 1891; *Richmond Dispatch,* October 15, 1891.

13. *The Sun,* October 21, 1891; *The Illustrated American,* Friday, October 31, 1891; *Peninsula Enterprise,* November 17, 1891; *New York Herald,* October 12, 1891.

14. *The Washington Post,* October 11, 1891.

15. Ibid.

16. *The Illustrated American,* October 31, 1891; *The Washington Post,* October 11, 1891.

17. *The Illustrated American,* October 31, 1891; *The Washington Post,* October 11, 1891.

18. *The Illustrated American,* October 31, 1891; *The Washington Post,* October 11, 1891.

19. *The Washington Post,* October 11, 1891; *The Sun,* October 12, 1891; Hurley and Hurley, *Shipwrecks and Rescues,* 81.

20. *The Washington Post,* October 11, 1891; *The Sun,* October 12, 1891; *New York Herald,* October 12,1891; *Peninsula Enterprise,* November 17, 1891.

21. *The Sun,* October 12, 1891.

22. *Evening Star,* October 10, 1891; *The Philadelphia Inquirer,* October 11, 1891; *The Sun,* October 12, 1891; *New York Herald,* October 11, 1891; *Richmond Dispatch,* October 15, 1891.

23. *The Illustrated American,* October 31, 1891.

24. *Evening Star,* October 12, 1891; *The Sun,* October 12, 1891; *New York Herald,* October 12, 1891; *Richmond Dispatch,* October 15, 1891.

25. *Evening Star,* October 10, 1891; *The Washington Post,* October 11, 1891; *The Sun,* October 12, 1891; Hurley and Hurley, *Shipwrecks and Rescues,* 81.

26. *Evening Star,* October 13, 1891.

27. *The Sun,* October 12, 1891; *Peninsula Enterprise,* October 17, 1891.

28. *The Sun,* October 12, 1891; *Peninsula Enterprise,* October 17, 1891; *The Illustrated American,* October 31, 1891.

29. *The Illustrated American,* October 12, 1891; *The Sun,* October 12, 1891.

30. *Evening Star,* October 13, 1891.

31. Kirk Mariner, *True Tales of the Eastern Shore* (New Church, VA: Miona Publications, 2003), 157–58.

32. *New York Herald,* October 15, 1891; *Peninsula Enterprise,* October 24, 1891.

33. Mariner, *True Tales,* 158.

34. *The Illustrated American,* October 31, 1891;"USS Despatch"; *Accomac Times,* July 29, 1905.

## Chapter 18. Five-Poler

1. Paul C. Morris, *American Sailing Coasters of the North Atlantic* (Chardon, OH: Bloch and Osborn, 1973), 83.

2. Ibid.

3. Ibid., 84.

4. Ibid., 7.

5. Gary Gentile, *Shipwrecks of Delaware and Maryland* (Philadelphia: Gary Gentile Productions, 1990), 74; *New York Times,* January 27, 1915.

6. Morris, *American Sailing Coasters,* 84.

7. Gentile, *Shipwrecks,* 182; *New York Times,* January 27, 1915. Gentile states the ship was built by the Maryland Steel Company.

8. *Washington Post,* January 27, 1915; *New York Times,* January 27, 1915; *The Sun,* January 27, 1915. The *Washington Post* states *Washingtonian* passed through the Panama Canal on January 18, and the *New York Times* gives the passage date as January 19. The author accepts the *Times,* which had the opportunity to interview Captain Brodhead following the catastrophe, which the *Washington Post* did not.

9. *The Sun,* January 27, 1915; *New York Times,* January 27, 1915; *Washington Post,* January 27, 1915.

10. *Washington Post,* January 27, 1915; *New York Times,* January 27, 1915.

11. *Washington Post,* January 27, 1915; *New York Times,* January 27, 1915; *The Sun,* January 27, 1915.

12. *The Sun,* January 27, 1915; *New York Times,* January 27, 1915.

13. *The Washington Post,* January 27, 1915. I presume, though it is not corroborated by

any witnesses, that the ship went down bow first and turned turtle en route to the bottom since the ship remains lie upside down and the bow is broken and turned to one side, a common effect of bow-first impact on sinking ships.

14. *New York Times,* January 27, 1915. The collision was not *Elizabeth Palmer*'s first. On December 27, 1907, she collided with the 922-ton schooner *Estelle Phinney* off Barnegat, New Jersey, sinking the smaller vessel, which went down with the loss of one of her ten-man crew.

15. Ibid.; *The Sun,* January 27, 1915; *Washington Post,* January 27, 1915.

16. *The Sun,* January 27, 1915; *Washington Post,* January 27, 1915.

17. *The Sun,* January 27, 1915; *New York Times,* January 27, 1915. Not everyone kept quiet. Thomas Brannan, 26, of Baltimore, who had been an oiler for the line for a year, may have been the source of the only undocumented public comments regarding the accident. His father was Benjamin F. Brannan, chief engineer of the steamer *Virginia,* belonging to the Baltimore, Chesapeake, and Atlantic Railroad. Ten years earlier, an older brother, Howard Brannan, had been lost on the schooner *Lizzie Babcock* while en route to Cuba. Upon his arrival in New York, young Tom Brannan called his father by long-distance telephone to inform him that he had landed safely. *The Sun,* January 27, 1915.

18. *New York Times,* January 27, 1915.

## Chapter 19. The Rules of Engagement

1. Archibald D. Turnbull and Clifford L. Lord, *History of United States Naval Aviation* (New Haven: Yale University Press, 1949), 193–204; *New York Times,* January 30, 1921, and February 18, 1918.

2. Brian Johnson, *Fly Navy: The History of Naval Aviation* (New York: Morrow, 1981), 123–25; William F. Trimble, *Admiral William A. Moffett, Architect of Naval Aviation* (Washington, DC: Smithsonian Institution Press, 1994), 88–89; Clark G. Reynolds, *Admiral John Towers: The Struggle for Naval Air Supremacy* (Annapolis, MD: Naval Institute Press, 1991), 169–97; Burke Davis, *The Billy Mitchell Affair* (New York: Random House, 1961), 94, 112; *New York Times,* February 7 and 13. 1921.

3. Turnbull and Lord, *History of U.S. Naval Aviation,* 193–204; Davis, *Billy Mitchell Affair,* 94–112; William Mitchell, *Winged Defense: The Development and Possibilities of Modern Air Power—Economic and Military* (Port Washington, NY: Kennikat Press, 1925), 42–45; *New York Times,* January 29 and February 7, 1921.

4. Turnbull and Lord, *History of U.S. Naval Aviation,* 196–97; *New York Times,* February 7 and May 21, 1921.

5. Davis, *Billy Mitchell Affair,* 94–112; *New York Times,* June 30, 1921; Mitchell, *Winged Defense,* 56–76; Turnbull and Lord, *History of U.S. Naval Aviation,* 196–99; *New York Times,* June 22 and 23, 1921.

6. *New York Times,* July 14, 1921.

7. Ibid.

8. *New York Times,* July 15, 1921.

9. Ibid.

10. *New York Times,* July 14, 1921.

11. Ibid.

12. Ibid.

13. Ibid.

14. Ibid.

15. Ibid.

16. Ibid.

17. Mitchell, *Winged Defense,* 62; *New York Times,* July 14, 1921; Trimble, *Admiral William A. Moffett,* 87–89.

18. Mitchell, *Winged Defense*, 62; *New York Times,* July 14, 1921; Trimble, *Admiral William A. Moffett,* 87–89.

19. Mitchell, *Winged Defense*, 62; *New York Times,* July 14, 1921; Trimble, *Admiral William A. Moffett,* 87–89. Among the visitors were Representatives Sisson, Herrick, Davis, McClintock, Collins, Lineberger, and Hamilton Fish Jr., of New York. Foreign military observers included Air Commodore Charlton of the British embassy, the Japanese naval attaché Lt. Commander Hubino, the Argentine military attaché Colonel Vacarezza; Lt. Colonel Gudoni of Italy, and representatives of the Brazilian and Cuban navies.

20. Mitchell, *Winged Defense*, 62; *New York Times,* July 14, 1921; Trimble, *Admiral William A. Moffett,* 87–89.

21. Mitchell, *Winged Defense*, 62; *New York Times,* July 14, 1921; Trimble, *Admiral William A. Moffett,* 87–89.

22. Mitchell, *Winged Defense*, 62; *New York Times,* July 14, 1921; Trimble, *Admiral William A. Moffett,* 87–89.

23. *New York Times,* July 16, 1921.

24. Ibid.

25. Ibid.

26. Ibid.

27. Ibid.

28. Ibid.

29. Ibid.

30. Ibid.

31. *New York Times,* July 18, 1921.

32. *New York Times,* July 19, 1921.

33. *New York Times,* July 19 and 23, 1921. The Fourth Division was piloted by Lt. Commander J. H. Strong, Lt. Musk [Aircraft no. 3012], Lts. D. W. Carter and D. L. Richards [no. 3606], Lts. Walter Hinton and E. W. Nelson [no. 3695], and Lts. M. E. Reddy and J. H. Sheehan [no. 3693]. The second attack was conducted by three planes of the Fifth Division commanded by Lts. Price, Stump, and Williams. The Marine Corps aircraft were piloted by Lts. Vaini, Carlson, and Farham.

34. Mitchell, 66; David, 98–99; *New York Times,* July 19, 1921.

35. *New York Times,* July 19, 1921. The planes were piloted by Lts. Thomas, Keene, Runmill, and Garvey and carried one observer.

36. *New York Times,* July 19 and 20, 1921.

37. *New York Times,* July 19, 1921.

38. Ibid.

39. Ibid. Lawson's pilots included Captain Pascale and Lts. Post, Raley, Speck, Harris, Meyers, and Morris.

40. *New York Times,* July 19 and 21, 1921.

41. *New York Times,* July 19, 1921.

42. *New York Times,* July 19 and 29, 1921. During the day, a total of seventy-eight bombs had been dropped, not including dummy and range-finding bombs, scoring an even dozen hits. Fifty-seven bombs weighing between 250 and 300 pounds each had been used in the first phase, and twenty-one bombs weighing six hundred pounds had been dropped in phase two, seven of the latter actually being 520-pounders dropped by three navy bombers, and fourteen being 600-pounders dropped by Army Martins. Five hits were duds. A total of six were direct on deck of target, but the twelfth was not a direct hit, for it fell in water on starboard side and crushed the bow all the way under the ship and on port side.

Chapter 20. Billy and the Battleship

1. Burke Davis, *The Billy Mitchell Affair* (New York: Random House, 1961); *New York Times,* July 20, 1921.

2. *New York Times,* July 20 and 21, 1921.

3. *New York Times,* July 21, 1921.

4. Ibid.

5. *New York Times,* July 21 and 29, 1921.

6. Ibid.

7. *New York Times,* July 21, 1921.

8. Ibid.

9. Ibid.

10. Ibid.

11. Ibid.

12. Ibid.

13. *New York Times,* July 21 and 28, 1921.

14. *New York Times,* July 21 and 22, 1921.

15. *New York Times,* July 21, 1921.

16. Noble Lee Snaples Jr., "Institutionalizing Aircraft Procurement in the U.S. Navy, 1919–1925," Ph.D. diss., Texas A&M University, August 1999.

17. *New York Times,* July 21, 1921.

18. Davis, *Billy Mitchell Affair,* 102–3; Turnbull and Lord, *History of U.S. Naval Aviation,* 198–99.

19. *New York Times,* July 21, 1921.

20. Ibid.

21. Ibid.

22. Ibid.; Mitchell, *Winged Defense,* 71.

23. *New York Times,* July 21, 1921; Mitchell, *Winged Defense,* 12.

24. *New York Times,* July 21, 1921.

25. Ibid.

26. Ibid.

27. Ibid.

28. Ibid.

29. *New York Times,* July 22, 1921.

30. *New York Times,* July 21, 1921.

31. Ibid.

32. *New York Times,* July 22, 1921.

33. Davis, *Billy Mitchell Affair,* 108–12; Turnbull and Lord, *History of U.S. Naval Aviation,* 199–200; Trimble, *Admiral William A. Moffett,* 66, 88–89; *New York Times,* July 29, 1921.

34. *New York Times,* August 20, 1921.

35. *New York Times,* September 14, 1921. The board comprised Admiral R. E. Coontz, Chief of Naval Operations; Major General W. G. Haan, Assistant to the Chief of Staff; Rear Admiral C. S. Williams, Naval Operations; Brigadier General Henry Jervey, General Staff; and Captain W. C. Cole, Naval Operations.

36. Ibid.

37. Ibid.

## Chapter 21. Chopping the Bank Right Off

1. Mary Corddry, *City on the Sand: Ocean City, Maryland, and the People Who Built It* (Centreville, MD: Tidewater Publishers, 1991), 86. The fishing concerns included: Elliott Brothers Fish Company, Davis and Henry E. Davis Fish Companies, L. D. Lynch Fish Company, and Captain Charles Ludlam Fish. There were also the Quillen, Cropper Brothers, Atlantic, and Thomas and Mumford companies.

2. Ibid., 100.

3. Ibid., 100–101.

4. Reginald V. Truitt, *Some Devastating North Atlantic Hurricanes of the 20th Century*, revised ed. ([Washington, DC]: U.S. Department of Commerce, National Oceanic and Atmospheric Administration, U.S. Government Printing Office, 1977), 7.

5. Ibid.

6. Ibid., 2–4.

7. Ibid., 7; Corddry, *City on the Sand,* 97, 98.

8. *Baltimore Sun,* August 22, 1933; *Washington Post,* August 22, 1933; *Philadelphia Inquirer,* August 21, 22 and 24, 1933.

9. Corddry, *City on the Sand,* 98.

10. *Baltimore Sun,* August 22, 1933.

11. Ibid.; "The Great 1933 Storms," www.newpointcomfort.com/history/history_html/33_storms.html; *Washington Post,* August 22, 1933.

12. *Washington Post,* August 22, 1933.

13. Truitt, *Devastating Hurricanes,* 4, 6.

14. *Baltimore Sun,* August 24, 1933; "The Chesapeake/Potomac Hurricane of August 23, 1933," www.weatherbook.com/hurricane1933.html.

15. *Baltimore Sun,* August 24, 1933; "The Chesapeake/Potomac Hurricane"; *Washington Post,* August 24, 1933.

16. *G. A. Kohler* left for Cap-Haïtien May 17 and returned July 21. Since her return from that voyage, the ship had been painted and caulked at the plant of the Bethlehem Shipbuilding Corporation, and repairs to the masts were made at the yards of the Redman-Vane Company. She was built in Wilmington, Delaware, in 1919. C. C. Paul & Co. was her operator. The skipper's wife, who had accompanied her husband on most of his trips during the previous eighteen years, had been signed on as a member of the crew to avoid the formalities involved in the carrying of passengers. She had technically shipped as a "stewardess." Also aboard were two cats, Mickey and Billy, and Mrs. Hopkins's white Spitz dog, which had come to be regarded almost as members of the crew. Mickey had been at sea for thirteen years, while the dog, who was taken aboard only three years before, was the junior member of the outfit. Mrs. Hopkins didn't make the last trip completed by *G. A. Kohler,* as the cabin she usually occupied was taken by the Rev. George E. Zachary, rector of the Protestant Episcopal Church of the Reformation and of All Souls' Protestant Episcopal Church of Brooklyn. *Baltimore Sun,* September 22, 1933; *Washington Post,* August 24, 1933.

17. *Baltimore Sun,* August 24, 1933; *Philadelphia Inquirer,* August 24, 1933; *Washington Post,* August 24, 1933.

18. *Baltimore Sun,* August 24, 1933; *Philadelphia Inquirer,* August 24, 1933.

19. *Baltimore Sun,* August 24, 1933; *Philadelphia Inquirer,* August 24, 1933; *Washington Post,* August 24, 1933.

20. *Philadelphia Inquirer,* August 24, 1933; "The Great 1933 Storms."

21. *Washington Post,* August 24. 1933; *Baltimore Sun,* August 24, 1933; *Philadelphia Inquirer,* August 24, 1933.

22. *Baltimore Sun,* August 24, 1933.

23. Ibid.

24. *Washington Post,* August 26, 1933.

25. *Baltimore Sun,* August 24, 25, and 26, 1933; *Washington Post,* August 26, 1933; *Philadelphia Inquirer,* August 25, 1933. Some accounts indicate four persons were electrocuted.

26. *Washington Post,* August 24, 1933.

27. Ibid.; *Baltimore Sun,* August 24, 1933.

28. *Baltimore Sun,* September 24, 1933.

29. *Philadelphia Inquirer,* August 26, 1933; *Washington Post,* August 26, 1933; *Baltimore Sun,* August 26, 1933.

30. *Philadelphia Inquirer,* August 26, 1933.

31. *Baltimore Sun,* August 25 and 26, 1933.

32. *Baltimore Sun,* August 24, 1933; *Washington Post,* August 24, 1933.

33. *Philadelphia Inquirer,* August 24 and 26, 1933; *Baltimore Sun,* August 24, 25, and 26, 1933; *Washington Post,* August 24, 1933.

34. *Washington Post,* August 24, 25, and 26, 1933; http://www.weatherbook.com/hurricane1933.html.

35. *Philadelphia Inquirer,* August 24, 1933; *Baltimore Sun,* August 24, 1933.

36. *Baltimore Sun,* August 24 and 25, 1933; *Philadelphia Inquirer,* August 24, 1933.

37. *Baltimore Sun,* August 24, 1933; *Washington Post,* August 24, 1933.

38. *Baltimore Sun,* August 25 and 26, 1933.

39. *Philadelphia Inquirer,* August 24, 1933; *Baltimore Sun,* August 24, 1933.

40. *Washington Post,* August 24 and 25, 1933.

41. *Philadelphia Inquirer,* August 24, 1933; *Baltimore Sun,* August 24 and 25, 1933.

42. *Baltimore Sun,* August 24 and 25, 1933.

43. *Baltimore Sun,* August 24, 1933.

44. Ibid.; Corddry, *City on the Sand,* 96; *Philadelphia Inquirer,* August 26, 1933.

45. Corddry, *City on the Sand,* 97–98; *Baltimore Sun,* August 24 and 25, 1933; *Philadelphia Inquirer,* August 26, 1933.

46. *Philadelphia Inquirer,* August 24, 1933; *Washington Post,* August 24, 1933; *Baltimore Sun,* August 24, 1933.

47. *Philadelphia Inquirer,* August 24, 1933; *Baltimore Sun,* August 24, 1933.

48. *Baltimore Sun,* August 24, 1933.

49. *Philadelphia Inquirer,* August 26, 1933.

50. *Washington Post,* August 27, 1933.

51. *Philadelphia Inquirer,* August 26, 1933; *Washington Post,* August 26, 1933; *Baltimore Sun,* August 26, 1933.

52. *Philadelphia Inquirer,* August 26, 1933; *Washington Post,* August 26, 1933; *Baltimore Sun,* August 26, 1933.

53. *Philadelphia Inquirer,* August 26, 1933; *Washington Post,* August 26, 1933; *Baltimore Sun,* August 26, 1933.

54. *Baltimore Sun,* August 26, 1933.

55. *Washington Post,* August 26, 1933.

56. *Baltimore Sun,* August 25 and 26, 1933; *Philadelphia Inquirer,* August 26, 1933; *Washington Post,* August 26, 1933.

57. *Baltimore Sun,* August 24, 1933.

58. *Baltimore Sun,* August 25, 1933.

59. *Baltimore Sun,* August 26, 1933.

60. Ibid.

61. Truitt, *Devastating Hurricanes,* 3; *Washington Post,* August 25, 1933.

62. *Washington Post,* August 27, 1933.

63. *Washington Post,* August 25, 1933.

64. *Baltimore Sun,* August 25, 1933.

65. Ibid.

66. *Washington Post,* August 24, 1933; *Baltimore Sun,* August 24 and 25, 1933.

67. *Baltimore Sun,* August 25, 1933.

68. Ibid.

69. Ibid.

70. Corddry, *City on the Sand,* 86, 98, 99, 100; *Philadelphia Inquirer,* August 26, 1933; *Democratic Messenger,* August 24, 1933.

71. Corddry, *City on the Sand,* 100.

72. *Philadelphia Inquirer,* August 26, 1933; *Baltimore Sun,* August 26, 1933; Corddry, *City on the Sand,* 98.

## Chapter 22. *Unterseeboot*

1. Michael Gannon, *Operation Drumbeat* (New York: Harper Perennial, 1991), xv.

2. Ibid., xvi, xvii.

3. Alpheus J. Chewning, *The Approaching Storm: U-Boats off the Virginia Coast during World War II* (Lively, VA: Brandylane Publishers, 1994), 1.

4. Ibid.

5. Ibid., 1, 2.

6. Ibid., 4; Gannon, *Operation Drumbeat,* 214–19.

7. Gannon, *Operation Drumbeat,* 271; *New York Times,* January 26, 1942. Between January 18 and 25, *Allan Jackson, City of Atlanta, Malay, Venore,* and *West Ives* would be sunk off North Carolina by *U-66, U-123,* and *U-125.*

8. Chewning, *Approaching Storm,* 37. *Olney* had been attacked by *U-125,* which sank *St. Ives* off North Carolina the same day.

9. "Fifth Naval District Intelligence Office," Operational Archives, Naval Historical Center [hereafter NHC], 41–45; *New York Times,* January 28 and 29, 1942; Gannon, *Operation Drumbeat,* 272, Chewning, *Approaching Storm,* 39. The wreck is variously said to lie at 37°45'00" N, 74°53'00" W; 37°27'08" N, 75°16'07" W; 36°49'06" N, 75°23'00" W; and 37°27'00" N, 75°16'07" W. Adrian L. Lonsdale and H. R. Kaplan, *A Guide to Sunken Ships in American Waters* (Arlington, VA: Compass, 1964), 46, 49; Chewning, *Approaching Storm,* 39.

10. Chewning, *Approaching Storm,* 40; Gannon, *Operation Drumbeat,* 272.

11. David J. Seibold and Charles J. Adams, *Shipwrecks, Sea Stories, and Legends of the Delaware Coast* (Barnegat Light, NJ: Exeter House, 1989), 101.

12. Chewning, *Approaching Storm,* 41; Gannon, *Operation Drumbeat,* 273; Summary of Statements by Survivors: SS *Rochester,* February 3, 1942, CNO. Lonsdale and Kaplan, *Guide to Sunken Ships,* 45, state the ship was sunk at 38°10' N, 73°58' W, but Chewning, whose research is far better documented from both German and American sources, states the loss was at 37°10' N, 75°38'01" W.

13. Chewning, *Approaching Storm,* 44; Summary of Statements by Survivors: SS *Amerikaland,* March 31, 1942, CNO.

14. Chewning, *Approaching Storm,* 126.

15. Ibid., 43.

16. Statements by Survivors: SS *Amerikaland;* Chewning, *Approaching Storm,* 44.

17. Statements by Survivors: SS *Amerikaland;* Chewning, *Approaching Storm,* 44.

18. Statements by Survivors: SS *Amerikaland;* Chewning, *Approaching Storm,* 44.

19. Chewning, *Approaching Storm,* 152.

20. Ibid., 42.

21. Ibid., 42–43.

22. Seibold and Adams, *Shipwrecks, Sea Stories,* 102–4; Gentile, *Shipwrecks,* 167.

23. Lonsdale and Kaplan, *Sunken Ships,* 44; Gentile, *Shipwrecks,* 90; Seibold and Adams, *Shipwrecks, Sea Stories,* 110.

24. Gentile, *Shipwrecks,* 91; Seibold and Adams, *Shipwrecks, Sea Stories,* 110–11.

25. Gentile, *Shipwrecks,* 90–91.

26. Chewning, *Approaching Storm,* 45; Seibold and Adams, *Shipwrecks, Sea Stories,* 112.

27. Chewning, *Approaching Storm,* 45; Seibold and Adams, *Shipwrecks, Sea Stories,* 113. It was reported soon afterward that the submarine that had sunk *China Arrow* had been sighted and sunk further up the coast by aerial bombardment. The air crew that had reported it were awarded special commendations at Governors Island, New York, on February 16. In fact, however, no such success would be achieved for months. *U-103* would not be eliminated until an Allied bombing raid on the Nazi sub pens at Kiel, Germany, destroyed her on April 15, 1945. Chewning, *Approaching Storm,* 152.

## Chapter 23. Like a Knife Gutting a Fish

1. Alpheus J. Chewning, *The Approaching Storm: U-Boats off the Virginia Coast during World War II* (Lively, VA: Brandylane Publishers, 1994), 46, 47, 48, 49, 53, 54, 64, 66–67, 70, 71, 80, 85; Summary of Statements by Survivors: SS *Ocean Venture,* February 14, 1942, CNO; Summary of Statements by Survivors: SS *Buarque,* February 26, 1942, CNO; Summary Combat Intelligence Report: SS *Olinda,* March 3, 1942, CNO; David J. Seibold and Charles J. Adams, *Shipwrecks, Sea Stories, and Legends of the Delaware Coast* (Barnegat Light, NJ: Exeter House, 1989), 107–9; Gary Gentile, *Shipwrecks of Delaware and Maryland* (Philadelphia: Gary Gentile Productions, 1990), 86–87, 88; Summary of Statements by Survivors: SS *Trepaca,* March 6, 1942, CNO; Lonsdale and Kaplan, *Sunken Ships,* 45, 46, 48, 49; Summary of Statements by Survivors: SS *San Demetrio,* April 9, 1942, CNO; Summary of Statements by Survivors: SS *Equipoise,* April 10, 1942, CNO; Summary of Statements by Survivors: SS *Menominee,* April 11, 1942, CNO; Summary Combat Intelligence Report: SS *Menominee,* March 31, 1942, CNO; Summary of Statements by Survivors: SS *Tiger,* May 2, 1942, CNO; Summary of Statements by Survivors: SS *Victoria,* April 28, 1942, CNO; Summary of Statements by Survivors: SS *Empire Drum,* May 4, 1942, CNO.

2. Chewning, *Approaching Storm,* 5; Michael Gannon, *Operation Drumbeat* (New York: Harper Perennial, 1991), 381.

3. Chewning, *Approaching Storm,* 17; Gannon, *Operation Drumbeat,* 171.

4. Chewning, *Approaching Storm,* 18; Gannon, *Operation Drumbeat,* 176.

5. Chewning, *Approaching Storm,* 18.

6. Ibid., 19; Seibold and Adams, *Shipwrecks, Sea Stories,* 99–100.

7. Chewning, *Approaching Storm,* 19.

8. Gannon, *Operation Drumbeat,* 309–10.

9. Ibid.; War Diary, Commandant Fourth Naval District Eastern Sea Frontier, Chapter 7, February 1942, National Archives, Washington, DC; Gentile, *Shipwrecks,* 95–96.

10. Gannon, *Operation Drumbeat,* 309–10; Eastern Sea Frontier diary, February 1942; Gentile, *Shipwrecks,* 95–96.

11. Chewning, *Approaching Storm,* 20, 21.

12. Ibid., 100; Summary of Statements by Survivors: SS *Moldanger,* July 22, 1942, CNO.

13. Chewning, *Approaching Storm,* 95.

14. Ibid., 144; Summary of Statements by Survivors: SS *Robert C. Tuttle,* July 1, 1942, CNO.

15. Chewning, *Approaching Storm,* 96; Summary of Statements by Survivors: SS *Esso Augusta,* March 31, 1942, CNO.

16. Chewning, *Approaching Storm,* 21.

17. Ibid., 21, 137; Department of the Navy, Transcript of the United States Board of Inquiry Concerning Loss of H.M.T. *Kingston Ceylonite,* June 15, 1942, Records of the Office of the Chief of Naval Operations, RG 125, National Archives.

18. Chewning, *Approaching Storm,* 21, 146, 161; Summary of Statements by Survivors: SS *Santore,* July 1, 1942, CNO; Summary Combat Intelligence Report: *U-701,* July 7, 1942, CNO.

19. Gentile, *Shipwrecks,* 99–100.

20. Gannon, *Operation Drumbeat,* 388.

21. U.S. Hydrographic Office, *Wreck Information List* (Washington, DC: Government Printing Office, 1945), 41; Gentile, *Shipwrecks,* 116–22; Henry C. Keatts and George C. Farr, *Warships* (Houston: Pisces Books, 1990), 1:176–79.

22. Erik Hofman, *The Steam Yachts* (Tuckahoe, NY: John de Graf, 1970), 5, 17, 18, 23, 242–43, 245; Gentile, *Shipwrecks,* 174–78; USS *St. Augustine,* Log Book Number 5 (December 20, 1940–November 30, 1943), Records of the Bureau of Naval Personnel, RG 24, National Archives; Ship Historical Identification Card, USS *St. Augustine* (PG 54), Naval Historical Center, Washington, DC; Navy Department, "History of USS *St. Augustine* (PG 54)," report prepared for Office of the Chief of Naval Operations, Division of Naval History, Ship's History Section, restenciled April 10, 1959, NHC; Navy Department; "History of USS *St. Augustine* (PG 54)," report prepared for the Office of Public Information, Ships Section, stenciled June 14, 1946, NHC; OCR War News Summary, January 7, 1944, Records of the Office of the Chief of Naval Operations, RG 38, National Archives; War Diary, Commandant Fourth Naval District Eastern Sea Frontier, January 1, 1943–December 31, 1944, Records of the Office of the Chief of Naval Operations; *Dictionary of American Naval Fighting Ships* (Washington: Naval History Division, Navy Department, 1959–81), 4:236.

23. Chewning, *Approaching Storm,* 106.

24. Ibid., 107; *Dictionary of American Naval Fighting Ships,* 5:20.


## Chapter 24. A Long Shudder

1. *Washington Post,* December 31, 1958; *The Sun,* December 31, 1958.

2. *Washington Post,* December 31, 1958; *The Sun,* December 31, 1958.

3. *Washington Post,* December 31, 1958; *The Sun,* December 31, 1958.

4. *New York Times,* December 31, 1958; *Evening Star,* December 30, 1958; *The Sun,* December 31, 1958; *Washington Post,* December 31, 1958.

5. *Washington Post,* December 31, 1958; *The Sun,* December 31, 1958.

6. *Washington Post,* December 31, 1958; *The Sun,* December 31, 1958.

7. Gary Gentile, *Shipwrecks of Delaware and Maryland* (Philadelphia: Gary Gentile Productions, 1990), 10; *The Sun,* December 31, 1958; *Washington Post,* December 31, 1958.

8. *The Sun,* December 31, 1958; *Washington Post,* December 31, 1958; Gentile, *Shipwrecks,* 11.

9. Gentile, *Shipwrecks,* 11; *Evening Star,* December 30, 1958; *Washington Post,* December 31, 1958; *New York Times,* December 31, 1958.

10. *The Sun,* December 31, 1958.

11. *Washington Post,* December 31, 1958.

12. Gentile, *Shipwrecks,* 11; *The Sun,* December 31, 1958; *Washington Post,* December 31, 1958; *New York Times,* December 31, 1958.

13. *The Sun,* December 31, 1958.

14. Ibid.; *Washington Post,* December 31, 1958; Gentile, *Shipwrecks,* 11.

15. *The Sun,* December 31, 1958.

16. *Evening Star,* December 30,1958; *New York Times,* December 31, 1958; *Washington Post,* December 31, 1958; *The Sun,* December 31, 1958.

17. *Washington Post,* December 31, 1958; *The Sun,* December 31, 1958.

18. *Evening Star,* December 30, 1958; *Washington Post,* December 31, 1958; *New York Times,* December 31, 1958. *The Sun,* December 31, 1958, states the first rescued seamen were dropped off at 10:30 A.M.

19. *Washington Post,* December 31, 1958; *The Sun,* December 31, 1958.

20. *Washington Post,* December 31, 1958; *The Sun,* December 31, 1958.

21. *The Sun,* January 1, 1959; *Washington Post,* December 31, 1958; Gentile, *Shipwrecks,* 12.

22. Gentile, *Shipwrecks,* 13–14.

23. Ibid., 13.

24. See Jerry Korn, *The Raising of the Queen* (New York: Simon and Schuster, 1961), for a comprehensive account of the recovery of *African Queen* and the legal travails of Lloyd Deir and Beldon Little.

## Chapter 25. The Trouble with Treasure

1. Jeannette Eckman, ed., *Delaware: A Guide to the First State* (1938; reprint, New York: Hastings House, 1955), 106–7; *The Sun,* July 25, 1887; *Every Evening* (Wilmington, DE), August 9, 1888.

2. *The Sun,* July 25, 1887.

3. Ibid.; *Every Evening,* August 9, 1888; *New York Times,* April 29, 1879.

4. *The Sun,* July 25, 1887; *Every Evening,* August 9, 1888; *Philadelphia Inquirer,* July 23, 1888; "Record of the Work Done with Steamer *City of Long Branch* in Search of Treasures of H.B.M. Ship *Braak,*" Pancoast Expedition Collection, William L. Clements Library, University of Michigan, Ann Arbor; *New York Tribune,* June 26 and July 8, 1888; *Philadelphia Public Ledger,* August 11, 1888; "Ocean Wrecking Company," prospectus, Pancoast Expedition Collection.

5. John Thomas Scharf, *History of Delaware* (1888; reprint, Port Washington, NY: Kennikat Press, 1988), 2:1225.

6. "The Many Attempts to Raise the *De Braak*" (photocopy), *De Braak* file, Delaware State Museums, Dover; *Every Evening,* July 26, 1889; *New York Times,* December 7, 1889; September 25 and 30, November 2, 3, and 30, 1932; March 26, 1933; July 12, August 2, 1936; March 7, 1937; William S. Dutton, "The Shipwrecks They've Seen!" *Saturday Evening Post,* February 13, 1954, 76–78; *Philadelphia Inquirer,* September 4, 1936; August 1, 1965; June 23, 1968; *Wilmington Morning News,* September 5 and 26, 1936; July 18, 1956; June 10, August 3, 8, and 18, 1965; June 29, 1966; July 12, 1967; May 12, 1969; July 22, 1971; Eckman, *Delaware,* 197; *De Braak* chronology, Delaware State Museums; *Wilmington Evening Journal,* June 10, July 27, August 3 and 7, 1965; March 2, April 21, June 29, 1966; April 26, July 12, August 8, November 10, 1967; November 19, 1968; August 6, 7, and 21, November 1, 1969; February 12, May 23, September 2, 1970; *Delaware Coast Press* (Rehoboth), August 19, 1966; March 26, 1969; April 9, 1970; Donald G. Shomette, *The Hunt for HMS De Braak: Legend and Legacy* (Durham, NC: Carolina Academic Press, 1993), 202.

7. *Wilmington Evening Journal,* June 29, 1966; Howard I. Chapelle and M. E. S. Laws, "H.M.S. *De Braak:* The Stories of a 'Treasure Ship,' "*Smithsonian Journal of History,* spring 1967, 58; *Delaware Coast Press,* April 9, 1970.

8. John S. Potter Jr., *The Treasure Diver's Guide* (1971; reprint, Garden City, NY: Doubleday and Company, 1972), 483.

9. *The Whale,* October 8, 1980; *Delaware Coast Press,* October 15, 1980. See Voynick, *Mid-Atlantic Treasure Coast,* 119, for an account of the purported loss of *Three Brothers*

and the military payroll aboard, and Shomette, *Hunt for HMS* De Braak, 380 n. 28, for debunking of the story.

10. *The Whale,* October 8, 1980; *Delaware Coast Press,* October 15, 1980.

11. *The Whale,* October 15, 1980.

12. Ibid.

13. *The Whale,* October 22, 1980.

14. Ibid.

15. *The Whale,* October 15, 1980.

16. Paul Brodeur, "The Treasure of the *De Braak,*" *New Yorker,* April 16, 1988, 37.

17. J. Ashley Roach, "Salvage Law (Historic Wrecks)," *British Museum Encyclopedia of Underwater and Maritime Archaeology,* ed. James P. Delgado (London: British Museum Press, 1997), 353–54.

18. Ibid., 354.

19. *New York Times,* July 31, October 7, 1984; Brodeur, "Treasure of the *De Braak,*" 38–39; *The Whale,* July 31, 1984; *The Washington Post,* July 31, 1984.

20. Brodeur, "Treasure of the *De Braak,*" 37, 40, 46–47; Shomette, *Hunt for HMS* De Braak, 131.

21. Brodeur, "Treasure of the *De Braak,*" 47–48; L. John Davidson to Paul Brodeur, August 11, 1988, *De Braak* file, Delaware State Museums.

22. Brodeur, "Treasure of the *De Braak,*" 50; Daniel Griffith, "H.M.S. *De Braak:* The Legend Revealed," paper presented at the First Joint Archaeological Congress, Baltimore, MD, January 7, 1989 (tape recording); H. Henry Ward, David V. Beard, and Claudia F Melson, "Preliminary Report on the Archaeological Monitoring of the Salvage Activities on the H.M.S. *De Braak,*" [1985], University of Delaware Center for Archaeological Research, February 1986, 16–17; "Outline of Procedures for the Salvage of *De Braak* Hull and Artifacts, July 27, 1986," *De Braak* file, Delaware State Museums; David V. Beard, "*De Braak* Recovery Project: Summer-Fall Operations," report prepared for the Delaware Division of Historical and Cultural Affairs, April 1987, *De Braak* file, Delaware State Museums, 16–17.

23. Griffith, "The Legend Revealed"; Brodeur, "Treasure of the *De Braak,*" 33; *Morning News,* August 12, 1986; *New York Times,* August 13, 1986; Beard, "H.M.S. *De Braak:* A Treasure Debunked, A Treasure Revealed," 52, 56; Beard, "*De Braak* Recovery Project," 14–15; *News Journal* (Wilmington, DE), August 13, 1986.

24. *New York Times,* August 28, 1986; *Sunday News Journal* (Wilmington, DE), August 17, 1986; Griffith, "The Legend Revealed"; Brodeur, "Treasure of the *De Braak,*" 54; *News Journal,* August 14, 1986; Shomette, *Hunt for HMS* De Braak, 334.

25. J. Brian Cole to Kevin McCormick, June 7, 1989, *De Braak* file, Delaware State Museums; *Baltimore Sun,* July 13, 1989.

26. *Sub-Sal Inc. v. The DeBraak v. Edward H. Clark II and McK Ltd. and the Six Former Seamen,* 84-296-CMW (U.S. District Court for the District of Delaware, 1992), order, February 4, 1992, 5–7, *De Braak* File, Delaware State Museums.

27. *Society for Historical Archaeology Newsletter* 21, no. 2 (June 1988); Protection of Submerged Historic Property, *Annotated Code of Maryland,* Article 83-B, sections 5-601, 5-611.1, 5-620, 5-621, and 5-630, *Archives of Maryland,* 436:391–94, 396.

## Chapter 26. Treasure Redux

1. *Prince George's Star* (Washington, DC), November 7, 1980. See Donald G. Shomette, *The Hunt for HMS* De Braak: *Legend and Legacy* (Durham, NC: Carolina Academic Press, 1993), 375–76, for details on Donald Stewart's fabrications of historic records.

2. *Maryland Beachcomber* (Ocean City, MD), May 16, 1980; *Morning Sun* (Baltimore), August 26, 1980; *Prince George's Star,* November 7, 1980.

3. *Maryland Beachcomber,* May 16, 1980; *Baltimore Morning Sun,* August 26, 1980; *Prince George's Star,* November 7, 1980.

4. *Baltimore Sun,* January 30, 1984.

5. *Maryland Beachcomber,* May 16, 1980. No record in the U.S. Copyright Office of Stewart's purported copyright application for the 1750 treasure fleet story has to date been found by this author.

6. *Prince George's Star,* November 7, 1980. Ocean Pines realtors Richard K. and Robert J. Firth claimed to have raised between $60,000 and $80,000 from investors in Baltimore, Ocean City, and Washington. *Morning Sun,* August 26, 1980.

7. *Morning Sun,* August 26, 1980.

8. *Prince George's Star,* November 7, 1980.

9. *The Sun,* March 20, 1981; January 1, 1984. This author has been unable to discover any record of either a *Santa Clara* or *Royal George* being lost on the Delmarva coast. Later charges by one of Stewart's associates and investors claimed that *San Lorenzo de Escorial* was also invented, although a *San Lorenzo* has been noted as lost on Assateague in 1821 by Jay Abercrombie in his well-researched 1985 work *Walks and Rambles on Delmarva Peninsula: A Guide for Hikers and Naturalists,* 188–89, but without citing a source.

10. *The Sun,* January 30, 1984.

11. Ibid.

12. Ibid.

13. Ibid.; *Maritime Heritage Quarterly News,* summer 1984; John L. Amrhein Jr., "Discovery of an Historic Spanish Shipwreck on Chincoteague National Wildlife Refuge, Assateague Island, Virginia," [undesignated study], 1983 (copy in author's collection).

14. Richard Cook and Daniel Koski Karell, "An Account of the Spanish Shipwreck 'La Galga' and the Loss of the Treasure Fleet of 1750," [undesignated study], 1989 (copy in author's collection), 5, 6.

15. *The Sun,* August 31, 1989.

16. Ibid.

17. *The Sun,* November 2, 1997.

18. Ibid.; Maura Singleton, "Sea Hunt," *Virginia Business Magazine,* August 1999, www.gatewayva.com/biz/virginiabusiness/magazine/yr1999/aug99/itsup/cover.html.

19. *Virginian-Pilot* (Norfolk), March 26, 1997; *USA Today,* May 7, 1998; *The Sun,* November 2, 1997.

20. *The Sun,* November 2, 1997.

21. Ibid.

22. *Virginian-Pilot,* March 26, 1998; May 1, 2000.

23. *Virginian-Pilot,* March 26, 1998; May 1, 2000; *Washington Post,* March 10, 1998.

24. *Virginian-Pilot,* March 26, 1997; *The Sun,* November 2, 1997; Chincoteague Town Council Special Meeting, minutes, June 11, 1998.

25. *Washington Post,* March 14, 1998; *USA Today,* May 7, 1998, Minutes of Meeting, June 11, 1998; Singleton, "Sea Hunt."

26. *Washington Post,* March 26, 1998.

27. United Nations Convention on the Law of the Sea, UN doc. A/CONIF 62/122, reprinted in *International Legal Materials* 21 (1982): 1261–1354 (hereafter, UNCLOS), articles 2, 3, 95, and 96; 1958 High Seas Convention, articles 8–9; "Submarine Antiquities and the International Law of the Sea," *Netherlands Yearbook of International Law* 13 (1982): 3, 22 n. 74; "The Recovery of Sunken Warships in International Waters," in *Essays on the New Law of the Sea,* ed. Budislav Vukas (Zagreb, Yugoslavia: Sveučilišnanaklada Liber, 1985), 250–51; J. Ashley Roach, "Underwater Archaeology and the *Titanic:* The Legal Considerations," presented at the International Conference of Maritime Museums, Greenwich, England, September 1996.

28. UNCLOS, articles 33 and 303.

29. See "Treaty of Peace with Japan," September 8, 1951, V, article 14(a) 2(1), in *Cumulative Index to United States Treaties and Other International Agreements, 1950–1970: 1 UST, TIAS, nos. 2010–7034,* comp. Igor I. Kavass and Adolph Sprudzs (Buffalo, NY: W. S. Hein, 1973), 3: no. 3181, which states that each of the Allied Powers "shall have the right to seize, retain, liquidate or otherwise dispose of all property, rights and interests" of Japan "which on the first coming into force of the present Treaty were subject to its [the Allied Powers'] jurisdiction." The procedures for abandonment of sunken U.S. warships and aircraft located outside the territory of the United States are set forth in *U.S. Code* 10 (1988): 7305-6 and 7545, and its implementing regulation, *Code of Federal Regulations* 32 (1994): parts 172 and 736. See also Roach, "Underwater Archaeology and the *Titanic*," 7–8.

30. J. Ashley Roach, "France Concedes United States Has Title to CSS *Alabama*," *American Journal of International Law* 85 (1991): 381.

31. *Digest of U.S. Practice in International Law* (1980), 999 and 1006.

32. Roach, "Underwater Archaeology and the *Titanic*," 9. See Larry Murphy, "Shipwrecks as Data Base for Human Behavioral Studies," in *Shipwreck Anthropology,* ed. Richard A. Gould (Albuquerque: University of New Mexico Press, 1983), 65–89, for archaeological process.

33. *Virginian-Pilot,* March 26, 1998.

34. *USA Today,* May 7, 1998; *Virginian-Pilot,* March 25 and 26, 1998; May 1, 2000.

35. *USA Today,* May 7, 1998; *Virginian-Pilot,* March 25 and 26, 1998; May 1, 2000.

36. *Virginian-Pilot,* March 25 and 26, 1998.

37. Ibid.

38. Ibid.

39. *Virginian-Pilot,* March 26, 1998.

40. Singleton, "Sea Hunt"; Kristin M. Romey, "Spain's Day in Court," *Archaeology,* November 1999, 20.

41. Romey, "Spain's Day in Court," 20; *Virginian-Pilot,* May 1, 2000.

42. *Virginian-Pilot,* May 2, 2000.

43. *Washington Post,* July 22, 2000.

# SELECT BIBLIOGRAPHY

## Manuscript Collections

Admiralty Draughts Collection. National Maritime Museum, London.

Admiralty Records. Public Record Office, London.

Barney, Joshua. Manuscript autobiography. DAR Library, Washington, DC.

Brown, Nicholas, Papers. John Carter Brown Library, Providence, RI.

Colonial Office. Public Record Office, London.

Cooke Papers. Rhode Island Historical Society, Providence.

Deane, Silas, Papers. Connecticut Historical Society. Hartford, CT.

*De Braak* File. Delaware State Museums, Dover.

*De Braak* File. Zwaanendael Museum, Lewes, DE.

Delaware Bay Pilots Scrapbook, c. 1882–89. Small Manuscript Collection, RG 200. Delaware State Archives, Dover.

Fifth Naval District Intelligence Office Operational Archives. Navy Department, Office of the Chief of Naval Operations, Division of Naval History, Washington, DC.

Hamond Papers. University of Virginia Library, Charlottesville.

Hamond, Sir Andrew Snape. Autobiography. University of Virginia Library, Charlottesville.

Pancoast Expedition Collection. William L. Clements Library, University of Michigan, Ann Arbor.

Papers of the Continental Congress. National Archives, Washington, DC.

Records of the Bureau of Naval Personnel, RG 24. National Archives, Washington, DC.

Records of the Office of the Chief of Naval Operations, RG 38. National Archives, Washington, DC.

Records of the Office of the Judge Advocate General (Navy), RG 125. National Archives, Washington, DC.

Red Books. Maryland State Archives, Annapolis.

Revolutionary War Collection, MS 1814. Maryland Historical Society, Baltimore.

Sección de Contratación. Archivo General de Indias, Seville, Spain.

Trumbull Papers. Yale University Library, New Haven, CT.

Washington Papers. Library of Congress, Washington, DC.

Whipple, William, Papers, 1777–1789. Library of Congress, Washington, DC.

## Public and Published Documents

*Annual Report of the Operations of the United States Life-Saving Service.* Washington, DC: U.S. Government Printing Office, 1875–1914.

*Archives of Maryland.* Baltimore: Maryland Historical Society, 1833–.

Biddle, James S., ed. *Autobiography of Charles Biddle, Vice President of the Supreme Executive Council of Pennsylvania, 1745–1821*. Philadelphia: E. Claxton, 1883.

Butterfield, Lyman H., et al., eds. *The Adams Papers,* 2nd ser., 7 vols. Cambridge: The Belknap Press of Harvard University Press, 1963–2005.

Chadwick, French Ensor, ed., *The Graves Papers and Other Documents relating to the Naval Operations of the Yorktown Campaign, July to October, 1781*. New York: Printed for the Naval History Society by the Devinne Press, 1916.

Clark, William Bell, et al., eds. *Naval Documents of the American Revolution.* 11 vols. Washington, DC: Naval Historical Center, 1964–2005.

Commager, Henry Steele, and Richard B. Morris. *The Spirit of 'Seventy-Six.* Indianapolis: Bobbs-Merrill, 1958.

Cresswell, Donald H., ed. *The American Revolution in Drawing and Prints.* Washington, DC: Library of Congress, 1975.

*Delaware Archives: Military and Naval Records.* 5 vols. Wilmington: Mercantile Printing Company, 1911–16.

Ford, Worthington C., et al., eds. *Journals of the Continental Congress, 1774–1789.* 34 vols. Washington, DC: U.S. Government Printing Office, 1904–1937.

Gibson, Charles Dana, and E. Kay Gibson, eds. *Dictionary of Transports and Combatant Vessels Steam and Sail Employed by the Union Army, 1861–1868.* Camden, ME: Ensign Press, 1995.

Haile, Edward Wright, ed. *Jamestown Narratives: Eyewitness Accounts of the Virginia Colony. The First Decade: 1607–1617.* Champlain, VA: Round House, 1998.

Knollenberg, Bernard, ed. *Correspondence of Governor Samuel Ward, May 1775–March 1776.* Providence, RI: Rhode Island Historical Society, 1952.

Lawson, John. *A New Voyage to Carolina.* 1709. Reprint edited by Hugh Talmage Lefler. Chapel Hill: University of North Carolina Press, 1967.

Lytle, William M., and Forrest R. Holdcamper, eds. *Merchant Steam Vessels of the United States, 1790–1868.* Staten Island, NY: The Steamship Historical Society of America, 1975.

McIlwaine, Henry R., and Wilmer L. Hall, eds. *Executive Journals of the Council of Virginia, 1680–1754.* 6 vols. Richmond: Virginia State Library, 1945.

*Merchant Vessels of the United States.* Washington, DC: U.S. Government Printing Office, 1868–1980.

*Naval Records of the American Revolution, 1775–1788.* Washington, DC: U.S. Government Printing Office, 1906.

O'Callaghan, E. B., ed. *Documents Relative to the Colonial History of the State of New York.* 15 vols. Albany: Weed, Parsons and Co., 1853–57.

Palmer, William P., ed. *Calendar of Virginia State Papers and Other Manuscripts . . . Preserved in the Capitol at Richmond.* 11 vols. Richmond: Printed for the Commonwealth, 1875–93.

*Pennsylvania Archives,* 1st ser. Samuel Hazard et al., eds. 12 vols. Philadelphia: J. Stevens and Co., 1852–56.

———, 2nd ser. 19 vols. William Henry Egle and John B. Linn, eds. Harrisburg, 1874–90.

*Pennsylvania Magazine of History and Biography.* Philadelphia: The Historical Society of Pennsylvania, 1877–.

Protection of Submerged Historic Property. *Annotated Code of Maryland,* Article 83-B, sections 5-601, 5-611.1, 5-620, 5-621, and 5-630. *Archives of Maryland,* vol. 436. Annapolis: Department of Legislative Reference, 1990.

Purchas, Samuel. *Hakluytus Posthumus, or Purchas His Pilgrims.* 20 vols. Glasgow: James MacLehose and Sons, 1906.

Quinn, David Beers, ed. *The Roanoke Voyages, 1584–1590: Documents to Illustrate the Eng-*

*lish Voyages to North America under the Patent Granted to Walter Raleigh in 1584.* 2 vols. New York: Dover, 1991.

Ricord, Frederick W., ed. *Documents Relating to the Colonial History of the State of New Jersey.* Trenton: John L. Murphy, 1891.

Rush, Richard, et al., eds. *Official Records of the Union and Confederate Navies during the War of the Rebellion,* 1st and 2nd series. 30 vols. Washington, DC: U.S. Government Printing Office, 1894–1922.

Saunders, William L., et al., eds. *Colonial Records of North Carolina.* 10 vols. Raleigh: P. M. Hale et al., 1886–90.

Scott, R. N., et al., eds. *The War of the Rebellion: A Compilation of the Official Records of the Union and Confederate Armies.* 70 vols. Washington, DC: U.S. Government Printing Office, 1880–1901.

Shea, J[ohn] G[ilmary], ed. *The Operations of the French Fleet under the Count de Grasse in 1781–2, as Described in Two Contemporaneous Journals.* New York: Bradford Club, 1864.

Smith, Paul H., ed. *Letters of Delegates to Congress, 1774–1789.* 26 vols. Washington, DC: Library of Congress, 1986–2000.

Truitt, Reginald V. *Some Devastating North Atlantic Hurricanes of the 20th Century.* Revised ed. [Washington, DC]: U.S. Department of Commerce, National Oceanic and Atmospheric Administration, U.S. Government Printing Office.

Vries, David Petersen de. *Voyages from Holland to America.* Edited and translated by Henry C. Murphy. New York: James Lenox, 1853.

United Nations Convention on the Law of the Sea. UN doc. A/CONIF 62/122. Reprinted in *International Legal Materials* 21 (1982): 1261–1354.

*United States Coast Pilot: Atlantic Coast, Section C: Sandy Hook to Cape Henry including Delaware and Chesapeake Bays.* 4th edition. Washington, DC: U.S. Government Printing Office, 1937.

U.S. Hydrographic Office. *Wreck Information List.* Washington, DC: U.S. Government Printing Office, 1945.

## Books

Abercrombie, Jay. *Walks and Rambles on Delmarva Peninsula: A Guide for Hikers and Naturalists.* Woodstock, VT: Backcountry Publications, 1985.

Allen, Gardner W. *A Naval History of the American Revolution.* 1913. 2 vols. Reprint, Williamstown, MA: Corner House, 1970.

Barnes, Brooks Miles, and Barry R. Truitt, eds. *Seashore Chronicles: Three Centuries of the Virginia Barrier Islands.* Charlottesville: University of Virginia Press, 1997.

Bathurst, Bella. *The Wreckers.* Boston: Houghton Mifflin, 2005.

Beach, John W. *Cape Henlopen Lighthouse and Delaware Breakwater.* Dover, DE: privately printed, 1970.

*Biographical Directory of the United States Congress, 1774–1989.* Senate document no. 100-34. Washington, DC: U.S. Government Printing Office, 1989.

Botting, Douglas. *The U-Boats.* Alexandria, VA: Time-Life Books, 1979.

Bowen, Catherine Drinker. *Miracle at Philadelphia: The Story of the Constitutional Convention, May to September 1787.* Boston: Little, Brown, 1966.

Carlisle, Rodney. *Powder and Propellants: Energetic Materials at Indian Head, Maryland, 1890–1990.* Annapolis, MD: U.S. Navy, 1990.

Charles, Joan. *Mid-Atlantic Shipwreck Accounts to 1899.* Hampton, VA: privately printed, 1997.

———. *New Jersey, Delaware, Pennsylvania Shipwreck Accounts, 1705 to 1950.* Hampton, VA: privately printed, 2003.

Chewning, Alpheus J. *The Approaching Storm: U-Boats off the Virginia Coast during World War II*. Lively, VA: Brandylane Publishers, 1994.

*Civil War Naval Chronology, 1861–1865*. 6 vols. Washington, DC: Naval History Division, Navy Department, 1971.

Cooledge, J. J. *Ships of the Royal Navy: An Historical Index*. 2 vols. Devon, UK: David and Charles, 1969.

Corddry, Mary. *City on the Sand: Ocean City, Maryland, and the People Who Built It*. Centreville, MD: Tidewater Publishers, 1991.

Cullen, Virginia. *History of Lewes, Delaware*. [Lewes, DE]: Colonel David Hall Chapter, Daughters of the American Revolution, 1981.

Davis, Burke. *The Billy Mitchell Affair*. New York: Random House, 1961.

*Dictionary of American Naval Fighting Ships*. 8 vols. Washington, DC: Naval History Division, Navy Department, 1959–81.

Dugan, James. *The Great Mutiny*. New York: G. P. Putnam's Sons, 1965.

Eckman, Jeannette, ed. *Delaware: A Guide to the First State*. 1938. Reprint, New York: Hastings House, 1955.

Fernández Duro, Cesáreo. *Naufragios de la Armada Española*. Madrid, 1867.

Falconer, William. *An Universal Dictionary of the Marine*. 1780. Reprint, Devon, UK: David and Charles, 1970.

Field, Van R. *Wrecks and Rescues on Long Island*. Center Moriches, NY: privately printed, 1997.

Gannon, Michael. *Operation Drumbeat*. New York: Harper Perennial, 1991.

Gentile, Gary. *Shipwrecks of Delaware and Maryland*. Philadelphia: Gary Gentile Productions, 1990.

Godfrey, Arthur, and Peter J. Lassey. *Shipwrecks of the Yorkshire Coast*. Clapham, UK: Dalesman, 1974.

Hepper, David J. *British Warship Losses in the Age of Sail, 1650–1859*. East Sussex, UK: Jean Boudriot, 1994.

Hofman, Erik. *The Steam Yachts*. Tuckahoe, NY: John de Graf, 1970.

Holland, Francis Ross, Jr. *America's Lighthouses: An Illustrated History*. New York: Dover, 1972.

Hurley, George, and Suzanne Hurley. *Shipwrecks and Rescues along the Barrier Islands of Delaware, Maryland, and Virginia*. Norfolk, VA: Donning, 1984.

Jackson, John W. *The Pennsylvania Navy, 1775–1781: The Defense of the Delaware*. New Brunswick, NJ: Rutgers University Press, 1974.

Johnson, Brian. *Fly Navy: The History of Naval Aviation*. New York: Morrow, 1981.

Keatts, Henry C., and George C. Fan. *Warships*. 3 vols. Houston: Pisces Books, 1990.

Korn, Jerry. *The Raising of the Queen*. New York: Simon and Schuster, 1961.

Larrabee, Harold A. *Decision at the Chesapeake*. New York: Bramhill House, 1964.

Le Favre, George. *The French Revolution from 1793 to 1799*. New York: Columbia University Press, 1964.

Lonsdale, Adrian L., and H. R. Kaplan. *A Guide to Sunken Ships in American Waters*. Arlington, VA: Compass Publications, 1964.

Mariner, Kirk. *True Tales of the Eastern Shore*. New Church, VA: Miona Publications, 2003.

Marx, Robert F. *Shipwrecks of the Western Hemisphere, 1492–1825*. New York: World Publishing, 1971.

Miller, Nathan. *Sea of Glory: The Continental Navy Fights for Independence, 1775–1783*. New York: David McKay, 1974.

Mitchell, William. *Winged Defense: The Development and Possibilities of Modern Air Power—Economic and Military*. Port Washington, NY: Kennikat Press, 1925.

Morris, Paul C. *American Sailing Coasters of the North Atlantic.* Chardon, OH: Bloch and Osborn, 1973.

Owen, David R., and Michael C. Tolley. *Courts of Admiralty in Colonial America: The Maryland Experience, 1634–1776.* Durham, NC: Carolina Academic Press, in Association with the Maryland Historical Society, 1995.

Pierce, Arthur D. *Smugglers Woods: Jaunts and Journeys in Colonial and Revolutionary New Jersey.* New Brunswick, NJ: Rutgers University Press, 1960.

Potter, John S., Jr. *The Treasure Diver's Guide.* Garden City, NY: Doubleday, 1972.

Pouliot, Richard A., and Julie J. Pouliot, *Shipwrecks on the Virginia Coast and the Men of the Life-Saving Service.* Centreville, MD: Tidewater Publishers, 1986.

Reynolds, Clark G. *Admiral John Towers: The Struggle for Naval Air Supremacy.* Annapolis, MD: Naval Institute Press, 1991.

Rodger, N. A. M. *The Wooden World: An Anatomy of the Georgian Navy.* Annapolis, MD: Naval Institute Press, 1986.

Scharf, John Thomas. *History of Delaware.* 2 vols. 1888. Reprint, Port Washington, NY: Kennikat Press, 1988.

Scott, Jane. *Between Ocean and Bay: A Natural History of Delmarva.* Centreville, MD: Tidewater Publishers, 1991.

Seibold, David J., and Charles J. Adams. *Shipwrecks, Sea Stories, and Legends of the Delaware Coast.* Barnegat Light, NJ: Exeter House, 1989.

Shomette, Donald G. *Pirates on the Chesapeake.* Centreville, MD: Tidewater Publishers, 1985.

———. *Hunt for HMS* De Braak: *Legend and Legacy.* Durham, NC: Carolina Academic Press, 1993.

Stern, Philip Van Dorn. *The Confederate Navy.* New York, Bonanza Books, 1962.

Stick, David. *Graveyard of the Atlantic.* Chapel Hill: University of North Carolina Press, 1952.

Tornquist, Karl Gustaf. *The Naval Campaigns of Count de Grasse during the American Revolution, 1781–1783.* Translated by Amandus Johnson. Philadelphia, PA: Swedish Colonial Society, 1942.

Trimble, William F. *Admiral William A. Moffett, Architect of Naval Aviation.* Washington: Smithsonian Institution Press, 1994.

Truitt, Reginald V., and Millard G. Les Callette. *Worcester County: Maryland Arcadia.* Snow Hill, MD: Worcester County Historical Society, 1977.

Turnbull, Archibald D., and Clifford L. Lord. *History of United States Naval Aviation.* New Haven: Yale University Press, 1949.

Voynick, Stephen M. *The Mid-Atlantic Treasure Coast: Coin Beaches and Treasure Shipwrecks from Long Island to the Eastern Shore.* Wallingford, PA: Middle Atlantic Press, 1984.

Weslager, C. A. *The English on the Delaware, 1610–1682.* New Brunswick, NJ: Rutgers University Press, 1967.

Whipple, A. B. C. *Fighting Sail.* Alexandria, VA: Time-Life Books, 1978.

Whitelaw, Ralph T. *Virginia's Eastern Shore: A History of Northampton and Accomack Counties.* 1951. 2 vols. Reprint, Camden, ME: Picton Press, 1996.

Wilkins, Harold T. *Pirate Treasure.* New York: E. P. Dutton, 1937.

Wise, Barton Haxall. *Memoir of General John Cropper of Accomack County, Virginia.* 1892. Reprint, Onancock: Eastern Shore of Virginia Historical Society, 1974.

Wood, Peter, and the Editors of Time-Life Books. *The Spanish Main.* Alexandria, VA: Time-Life Books, 1979.

Wroten, William H., Jr. *Assateague.* Cambridge, MD: Tidewater Publishers, 1972.

## Articles and Papers

Brodeur, Paul. "The Treasure of the De Braak." *New Yorker,* April 16, 1988, 33–60.

Burnett, Kessler. "Oyster." *Chesapeake Life,* January–February 2000, www.chesapeake-lifemag.com/tourismloyster.html.

Chapelle, Howard I., and M. E. S. Laws. "HMS De Braak: The Stories of a 'Treasure Ship.'" *Smithsonian Journal of History,* spring 1967, 57–68.

Covington, Harry Franklin. "The Discovery of Maryland, or Verrazzano's Visit to the Eastern Shore." *Maryland Historical Magazine* 10, no. 3 (September 1915): 199–217.

"The Disappearance of the Esk." *The Islands,* fall 1979, 1–2.

Dutton, William S. "The Shipwrecks They've Seen!" *Saturday Evening Post,* February 13, 1954, 76–78.

Griffith, Daniel, "H.M.S. De Braak: The Legend Revealed." Presented at the First Joint Archaeological Congress, Baltimore, Maryland, January 7, 1989.

Kenney, Nathaniel T. "Chincoteague: Watermen's Island Home." *National Geographic Magazine,* June 1980, 810–29.

Kleeberg, John M. "The Shipwreck of the Faithful Steward: A 'Missing Link' in the Export of British and Irish Halfpence." *Coinage of the Americas Conference, Proceedings no. 11,* edited by Philip L. Massur. New York: American Numismatic Society, 1963.

Knight, R. J. B. "The Introduction of Copper Sheathing into the Royal Navy, 1779–1786." *The Mariner's Mirror,* August 1973, 299–310.

Murphy, Larry. "Shipwrecks as Data Base for Human Behavioral Studies." In *Shipwreck Anthropology,* edited by Richard A. Gould, 65–89. Albuquerque: University of New Mexico Press, 1983.

"The Recovery of Sunken Warships in International Waters." In *Essays on the New Law of the Sea,* edited by Budislav Vukas, 7–12. Zagreb, Yugoslavia: Sveučilišnanaklada Liber, 1985.

Roach, J. Ashley. "France Concedes United States Has Title to CSS Alabama." *American Journal of International Law* 85 (1991): 381.

——— "Salvage Law (Historic Wrecks)." In *British Museum Encyclopedia of Underwater and Maritime Archaeology,* edited by James P. Delgado. London: British Museum Press, 1997.

——— "Underwater Archaeology and the Titanic: The Legal Considerations." Presented at the International Conference of Maritime Museums, Greenwich, UK, September 1996.

Romey, Kristin M. "Spain's Day in Court." *Archaeology,* November 1999, 20.

"Submarine Antiquities and the International Law of the Sea." *Netherlands Yearbook of International Law* 13 (1982): 2–74.

Warren, Maude Radford. "The Island of Chincoteague." *Harper's Monthly,* July–December 1913, 775–85.

Watson, William N. Boog. "Alexander Brodie and His Firehearths for Ships." *The Mariner's Mirror,* November 1968, 409–11.

## Dissertations, Theses, Reports

Amrhein, John L., Jr. "Discovery of an Historic Spanish Shipwreck on Chincoteague National Wildlife Refuge, Assateague Island, Virginia." [Undesignated study], 1983. Copy in author's collection.

Beard, David V. "HMS De Braak: A Treasure Debunked, a Treasure Revealed." M.A. thesis, East Carolina University, 1989.

Cook, Richard, and Daniel Koski-Karell. "An Account of the Spanish Shipwreck 'La

Galga' and the Loss of the Treasure Fleet of 1750." [Undesignated study], 1989. Copy in author's collection.

McCartney, Martha W. "A Study of the Africans and African Americans on Jamestown Island and at Green Spring, 1619–1803." Study prepared by Colonial National Historical Park, National Park Service, U.S. Department of the Interior, Williamsburg, VA, 2003.

Snaples, Noble Lee, Jr. "Institutionalizing Aircraft Procurement in the U.S. Navy, 1919–1925." Ph.D. diss., Texas A&M University, 1999.

Ward, H. Henry, David V. Beard, and Claudia F. Melson. "Preliminary Report on the Archaeological Monitoring of the Salvage Activities on the H.M.S. De Braak, 1985." University of Delaware Center for Archaeological Research, February 1986.


## Newspapers and Periodicals

*Alexandria* (VA) *Gazette*
*American and Commercial Daily Advertiser* (Baltimore)
*American Beacon & Commercial Diary* (Norfolk, VA)
*American Beacon for the Country* (Norfolk, VA)
*American Beacon. Virginia & North Carolina Gazette* (Norfolk, VA)
*American Weekly Mercury* (Philadelphia)
*The Boston Gazette*
*Boston News Letter*
*Chincoteague* (VA) *Beachcomber*
*Claypool's American Daily Advertiser* (Philadelphia)
*Columbian Mirror and Alexandria Gazette* (Alexandria, VA)
*Connecticut Courant* (Hartford)
*Constitutional Gazette* (Philadelphia)
*The Daily Advertiser* (New York)
*Daily Journal* (Wilmington, DE)
*The Daily Press* (Newport News, VA)
*Daily Universal Register* (London)
*Delaware Coast Press* (Rehoboth)
*The Delawarian* (Dover)
*Democratic Messenger* (Snow Hill, MD)
*Evening Journal* (Wilmington, DE)
*Every Evening* (Wilmington, DE)
*Federal Gazette & Baltimore Daily Advertiser*
*Federal Republican & Commercial Gazette* (Baltimore)
*Evening Star* (Washington, DC)
*Gazette of the United States & Philadelphia*
*The Illustrated American*
*London Chronicle*
*London Gazette*
*Londonderry* (Ireland) *News*
*Lloyd's List* (London)
*Lloyd's Register-Wreck Returns* (London)
*Maritime Heritage Quarterly News* (New York)
*Maryland Beachcomber* (Ocean City)
*Maryland Gazette* (Annapolis)
*Maryland Journal and Baltimore Advertiser*
*Meadville* (PA) *Courier*
*The Monthly Nautical Magazine and Quarterly Review* (New York)

*Morning News* (Wilmington, DE)
*Morning Sun* (Baltimore)
*New Jersey Gazette* (Trenton)
*New York Daily Times*
*New-York Gazette*
*New York Herald*
*New York Journal and Weekly Register*
*New York Packet*
*New York Times*
*New York Tribune*
*News Journal* (Wilmington, DE)
*Norfolk & Portsmouth Herald*
*Norfolk Herald*
*Norfolk Weekly Journal & Country Intelligencer*
*Peninsula Enterprise* (Accomac Court House, VA)
*Pennsylvania Evening Post* (Philadelphia)
*Pennsylvania Gazette* (Philadelphia)
*Pennsylvania Packet* (Philadelphia)
*Pennsylvania Post* (Philadelphia)
*Pennsylvania Journal and Weekly Advertiser* (Philadelphia)
*Phenix Gazette* (Alexandria, VA)
*Philadelphia Inquirer*
*Political Magazine and Parliamentary Journal* (London)
*Prince George's Star* (Washington, DC)
*Public Ledger* (Norfolk, VA)
*Public Ledger* (Philadelphia)
*Richmond Dispatch*
*Royal Gazette* (New York)
*Salisbury* (MD) *Advertiser*
*Snow Hill* (MD) *Messenger*
*Society for Historical Archaeology Newsletter*
*South Carolina Gazette* (Charleston)
*Southern Argus* (Norfolk, VA)
*The Sun* (Baltimore)
*Sunday News Journal* (Wilmington, DE)
*The Times* (London)
*Turner's New York Shipping and Commercial List*
*USA Today* (New York)
*Virginia Gazette* [Dixon and Hunter] (Norfolk)
*Virginia Gazette* [Dixon and Nicholson] (Williamsburg)
*Virginia Gazette* [Purdie and Dixon] (Williamsburg)
*Virginia Gazette* [Rind] (Williamsburg)
*Virginia Journal and Alexandria Advertiser* (Alexandria)
*The Virginian-Pilot* (Norfolk)
*The Washington Post*
*The Whale* (Rehoboth, DE)
*Wilmington* (DE) *Daily Commercial*

MMAP, 308. *See also* Maryland Maritime Archaeology Program

Mobile, Alabama, 144, 147, 157

Mockhorn Island, VA, 3, 139

Moffett, Adm. William A., USN, 214, 236

Mohoba Bank, DE, 97. *See also* Mahogan's Bay

Moise, Maj. T. S., CSA, 158

Molviedo, Don Manuel, 19, 35

Montagu, Capt. George, RN, 52

Montgomery, Capt. James, PN, 66–67

Morris, Lt., 81

Morris, Lt. Charles M., CSN, 144–49

Morris, Robert, 64, 76, 78

Morris, Thomas, 61

Morris River, NJ, 182

Morro Castle, Havana, Cuba, 19, 153

Morse & Co., 180

Mosquito Coast, 18, 20

Mouswel, Capt. Thomas, 16

Mulligan, Lt., USN, 200

Murphy, Pedro, 6–7

Murray, Lt. Cdr. Alexander, USN, 139–41

Myrtle Island, VA, 5


Nags Head, NC, 244, 272

Nantes, France, 58, 61–62, 76

Nanticoke River, MD, 249

National Maritime Initiative, 315

National Park Service, 5, 311–15

Navigation Acts, 15

Neel, Lt., USN, 200

Nelson, Adm. Lord Horatio, 296

Nepean, Evan, 111, 113

Netherlands, 8, 49, 60, 105–7; States General, 11

New Bern, NC, 34–35

New Castle, DE, 53–54, 56, 253–54

New England, 10, 14, 34, 39, 41–42, 44, 57, 78, 123, 144, 149, 200, 206–7, 241, 243, 281

New Hampshire, 301, 310

New Jersey, 9, 11, 13, 35–36, 42, 67, 69, 72, 75, 127, 139, 163, 167, 181–82, 192, 200, 241, 243, 257, 263, 267, 269, 273–74, 277, 287, 289

New Netherlands, 8, 11–12

New Orleans, Louisiana, 147, 157

New Providence, Bahamas, 48, 52

New Spain, 18, 20

New York, 9, 17, 23, 29, 34, 38, 43–45, 47–49, 52, 62, 65–66, 74–75, 78, 83–84, 86, 92, 97, 106, 110–11, 114, 127, 148, 151, 153–54, 161, 164, 166

New York and Havana Line, 160

New York, Philadelphia, and Norfolk Railroad, 251

New York City, NY, 43, 48–49, 58, 64, 80–81, 85, 87, 92, 96, 117–18, 127, 135, 139, 144–45, 149–51, 155, 158, 163

New York (Brooklyn) Navy Yard, 142, 152, 158, 196, 203, 227, 280

New York Shipbuilding Corp., 274

*New York Times,* 172, 189, 192, 195, 222, 226, 237, 286

Newfoundland, 49, 85, 262

Newport, RI, 57, 197, 279

Newport News, VA, 139, 148–49, 246–48, 264

Nicholas & John Brown Co., 58, 61

Nicholson, Governor Francis, 12, 127–28

Norfolk, VA, 14, 31, 34–35, 37, 40–41, 52, 159, 175, 182, 196, 198, 203, 206, 209, 211, 229, 245–48, 254–55, 257–58, 265, 278, 289, 292–93, 316; City Fire Department, 248; Federal District Court, 293, 312; harbor, 43; Naval Air Station, 257

Norfolk–Portsmouth ferry, 246

North America, 2, 18, 36, 42, 48, 59, 62, 84, 86, 112, 263, 316

North Atlantic Blockading Squadron, 139, 142–43, 159

North Beach Life Saving Station, 137

North Carolina, 21, 23–24, 34, 38, 40, 44, 46, 138, 147, 159, 230, 244, 257, 263, 273, 279, 284, 289

Northampton County, VA, 4, 76, 130, 139, 249, 254

Norway, 262, 286, 291

Nova Scotia, 69, 118, 265, 281

Nyborg, Capt. Eric, 278


Ocean City, MD, 1, 5, 193, 241–44, 249, 251–52, 255–56, 258–60, 269, 288, 290–91, 305–6, 308; Baltimore Avenue, 252, 286; blimp base, 273; Boardwalk, 286, 309; Coast Guard Station, 290; Coast Guardsmen, 256; elementary school, 286; Life Saving Station, 137, 194; Talbot St., 309; Third Street, 286; 18th St., 309; 37th St., 309

Ocean Pines, MD, 305–6

Ocean Recovery Operations, Inc., 307

Ocean View, VA, 245, 247–48

Ocean Wrecking Co., 296

Ocracoke Bar, NC, 24–25, 36

Ocracoke Inlet, NC, 23, 25, 36

Ocracoke Island, NC, 24–26, 31, 34, 37, 46

Ogden, Chief Engineer, USN, 200

Ogle, Governor Samuel, 30–31

Old Dominion Line, 210, 257

Old Hore (Hoar) Kill Road, DE, 43, 51, 295, 297. *See also* Horekill Roads; Old Kiln Roads

Rogers, Midshipman, 78

Roosevelt, Col. Theodore, Jr., 229, 231, 236, 238

Roosevelt Inlet, DE, 8, 302, 318

Rose, Capt. Leon, 119, 310

Rose, Capt. Thomas, 49

Rossakatum Branch, DE, 254

Royal Co., 20

Royal Marines, 42, 69, 113

Royal Navy, 15, 41, 43, 46, 50, 53, 60, 68, 79–80, 83, 85, 87, 105, 108–11, 114–15, 118, 278, 295, 300, 319

Rules of Oleron, 125


St. Croix, West Indies, 50, 52

St. Eustatia, West Indies, 39, 47, 50–52, 68, 78

St. Georges Bank, 69

St. Lawrence River, 262, 281

St. Pierre [St. Peter], Martinique, 61, 71

Salem Cove, NJ, 181

Salmons, Theodore, USLSS, 163, 168, 170, 188–89, 191

San Antonio, Texas, 151, 239

Sanborn, Capt. Charles, 295

Sand Shoal Island, VA, 135. *See also* Cobb's Island, VA

Sandwich, Lord, 42, 60

Santo Domingo [St. Domingo], West Indies, 19, 27, 61

Sandy Hook, NJ, 1, 69, 72, 243, 257

Sandy Island, VA, 5

Sandy Point, MD, 131, 259

Sandy Point Inlet, MD, 241

Saxis Island, VA, 254

Scales, Rear Adm. A. H., USN, 220

Scarborough, Sheriff John, 29–31

Schug, Kapitanleutnant Walter, GN, 265

Schultz, Capt. Ragnar, 265–66

Scotland, 13, 113

SEA, Ltd., 305, 307. *See also* Sub-aqueous Exploration and Archaeology, Ltd.

Sea Hunt, Inc., 310, 312, 316–17

Seaborne Ventures, Inc., 296–97

Secret Committee of Correspondence, 59–62, 64, 76–77

Seivers, Capt., 16

Seven Foot Knoll, Chesapeake Bay, 243

Seven Years War, 68. *See also* French and Indian War

Shaler, Capt. Timothy, 68

Shaw, Cdr. T. Darrah, USN, 150

Shears Shoal, DE, 5, 15, 103

Ship Shoal Island, VA, 5

Shuldham, Vice Adm. Molyneux, RN, 48–52

Simpson, Maj. Southy, 80–82

Sinclair, Midshipman William B., CSN, 148

Sinepuxent, MD, 14, 67, 70, 76, 78–79, 125, 131

Sinepuxent Bay, MD, 241, 243, 255, 258–59; bridge across, 252

Sinepuxent Inlet, MD, 70

Sinepuxent Neck, MD, 243

Sinepuxent Point, MD, 241, 259

Singleton, Capt., 72

Skidmore, Capt., 115

Skimmer, Capt. John, 69

Slater, Capt. Thomas, 52

Slaughter Beach, DE, 192, 194, 253

Smith, Capt., 15

Smith, Capt. R. N., 153, 155–56

Smith, Lt. W. McK., RNR, 276

Smith Island, MD, 247, 250

Smith Island, VA, 4–5, 130, 136; Life Saving Station, 136; Lighthouse, 4

Smith Shoals, VA, 5

Snow Hill, MD, 29, 31, 243

Socony Mobile Oil Co., 287

Socony Vacuum Oil Co., 265, 268, 287, 291

Solomons Island, MD, 250

Somers Point, NJ, 163, 182

Somerset County, MD, 13, 128, 129

South America, 18–19, 106, 115, 142, 144, 268, 281, 308

South Bay, 8–9

South Carolina, 14, 41, 113, 138, 279; constitutional convention, 101; Courts of Equity, 104; legislature, 104

South River, 9–12. *See also* Delaware River

Southeast Archaeological Research, Inc., 318

Spain, 7, 10, 16, 18, 19–21, 28, 31, 37–38, 58, 85, 106, 111, 153, 155–59, 197, 305, 308–9, 312–18; government, 90; navy, 313–15, 317

Spanish Main, 18–19, 21

Sparrows Point, MD, 207, 265

Spaatz, Gen. Carl, USAF, 240

Spencer, Acting Ensign Thomas W., USN, 142

Standard Oil Company of New Jersey, 267, 277

Standefer, Dennis, 297–98

Stanton, William H., 157–58

Stewart, Donald, 304–7

Stiles, Capt. Richard, 69

Stone, Capt. William, CN, 44

Stone, Lt. S. G., CSN, 147

Strong, Lt. Cdr. J. H., USN, 222

Sub-aqueous Exploration and Archaeology, Ltd., 305. *See also* SEA, Ltd.

Sub-Sal, Inc., 299–302

Suffolk, VA, 40, 247

vessels *(continued)*